Food Law

Food Law

Third Edition

Barry Atwood LLB, Solicitor
Public law consultant and former Under-Secretary (Legal), Ministry of Agriculture, Fisheries and Food

Katharine Thompson
Senior Lecturer in Law, De Montfort University

Chris Willett
Professor of Consumer Law, De Montfort University

Tottel
publishing

Tottel Publishing
Maxwelton House
41–43 Boltro Road
Haywards Heath
West Sussex
RH16 1BJ

ISBN 9 781 847660 954
© Tottel Publishing Ltd 2009

British Library Cataloguing-in-Publication Data
A CIP Catalogue record for this book is available from the British Library.

Typeset by Columns Design Ltd, Reading
Printed in the UK by CPI William Clowes Beccles NR34 7TL

Preface to the third edition

The second edition of this book foretold of changes proposed in 2000 by the European Commission Food Safety White Paper to remedy weaknesses exposed by the BSE and other crises of the 1990s. This new edition attempts to summarise the torrent of food and feed legislation affecting England and Wales that continues to emanate from these proposals.

At the centre of the picture now are general Regulation (EC) 178/2002 and official controls Regulation (EC) 882/2004 which have launched the European Food Safety Authority, improved the mechanisms for managing emergencies, imposed new responsibilities on business and established a framework for future action and enforcement.

For both food and feed, comprehensive rules are now in place for prevention, control and eradication of transmissible spongiform encephalopathies. There have been major initiatives in respect of genetically modified food and feed, organic products and pesticide residues. And vital hygiene measures have been enacted which, for feed, have imposed new obligations on business operators and, for food, have consolidated and amended existing provisions and are enforced domestically by discrete Regulations emulating the Food Safety Act 1990.

For food, the legislation on contaminants and flavourings has been further developed, the standards Directives have been simplified and significant new measures have been enacted as regards vitamins and minerals, nutrition claims and food supplements. Plans for consolidation and amendment of the food labelling and additive rules are well advanced. The regulation of animal nutrition has also been strengthened particularly in respect of additives and undesirable substances in feed.

Meanwhile, the law in related fields has been far from static. Revision of the marketing standards for agricultural products is nearing completion, prescribed quantity rules are being relaxed, new Community consumer protection legislation has substantially replaced the Trade Descriptions Act 1968 and there have been important developments with regard to prosecutions and evidence.

Finally, changes in the machinery of Government must not be overlooked. The Department of Environment, Food and Rural Affairs has supplanted the Ministry of Agriculture, Fisheries and Food; Welsh Ministers now exercise most functions in Wales; the Wine Standards Board has merged with the Food Standards Agency; the Pesticides Safety Directorate has been transferred to the Health and Safety Executive.

This is truly a dynamic area. Merely keeping pace with the flow of new material has at times seemed like running up a down escalator. We hope we have nevertheless succeeded in covering the essentials of the current provisions in this densely regulated area.

Preface

Our thanks are due to colleagues and others for their advice, the editorial staff of Tottel for their help and to our families for their patient support. In particular, we should like to thank Harriet Gray, Tom McDonnell, David Templeton, Alex Rae and Pauline Robertson.

The food and feed law of England and Wales is stated as at 30 September 2008, although it has been possible to take account of some subsequent developments. Readers should note that the traditional UK term 'feeding stuffs' does not appear uniformly throughout this edition. We have often felt constrained to use the form 'feedingstuffs' regularly used in EC feed legislation

BTA, KT and CW
January 2009

Preface to the second edition

Since the first edition of this book there have been significant developments in food law. Radical measures have been required not only to combat dangers from bovine spongiform encephalopathy, E coli 157 and chemical contamination of food and feed, but also to tighten controls on genetically modified organisms and other technological innovations. Most fundamental of the consequent changes have been those wrought by the establishment of the United Kingdom Food Standards Agency and the plans for parallel provision in the European Community. Major initiatives have also been implemented to modernise rules on labelling, hygiene, additives and contaminants and to raise the quality of agricultural products, while reducing unnecessary restrictions in the harmonised rules for specific processed foodstuffs.

Nor have relevant developments been restricted to food law alone. Practitioners must additionally have regard to the reordering of the United Kingdom constitutional arrangements by the Government of Wales Act 1998 and other devolution legislation, the amplification of enforcement requirements by provisions such as the Criminal Procedure and Investigation Act 1996, and the extension of civil law remedies by amendments to the sale of goods and product liability legislation.

Substantial revision of the first edition has thus been necessary to explain the current rules, including now those on feeding stuffs. An attempt has been made to place them clearly in their Community and English law framework. There has also been some reordering and amalgamation of material, in particular to give more prominence to the food safety requirements, to reflect the modern structure of hygiene law and to gather together all regulations on the chemical safety of food. Nevertheless, the aim has always been to honour Tony Painter's objective of providing a concise guide to a big and complex subject. Until recently he edited *Butterworths Law of Food and Drugs* and to him (and indeed to his predecessor the late John O'Keefe) I owe a particular debt. In preparing the second edition of this book, as throughout most of my professional life, I have relied greatly on that comprehensive work.

I am certainly glad to have this opportunity to acknowledge the generous help I have received from many busy people. My thanks are particularly due to Roland Rowell who made time to read and give informed and practical comment on the draft text; to my new colleagues at Butterworths, as well as to many former ones in the Civil Service, for so quickly responding to my importunate demands for information; to Margaret and Emrys Powell for access to the Internet; and to my wife Jenny, without whose patient support and encouragement this second edition would never have been completed.

Preface

Errors and shortcomings in this edition are my responsibility. The law of England and Wales is stated as at 31 January 2000, although it has been possible to take account of some subsequent amendments.

Barry Atwood
Croydon
January 2000

Preface to the first edition

As a consultant on food law, and editor of *Butterworths Law of Food and Drugs* and *O'Keefe's Law of Weights and Measures*, it has been apparent to me for some time that there is a need for a concise book on food law drawing attention to new developments, discussing matters of particular difficulty and identifying all the legislation applying to food. Quite independently, my colleagues in Butterworth Law Publishers Ltd had come to the same conclusion and this book is our attempt to fulfil that need.

It has proved to be a daunting task, for the ever widening and constantly changing scope of food law has made it difficult to decide what to include and what to omit. Another difficulty has been that there will be further important developments during the next year or two as the EC Single Market is established.

My approach has been to draw an outline portrait of food law and then to concentrate on important and long-established provisions which have been re-enacted in the Food Safety Act 1990, to explain the new provisions of that Act, and to clarify the role and influence of EC law. I have been influenced in my choice of topics by my experience as a consultant which suggests the issues which continue to give rise to difficulties of interpretation and implementation.

Another problem facing the author of a book on food law is that so much of it is new. The Food Safety Act 1990 is, of course, the most portentous source of new law and many EC developments also break entirely new ground. With only a limited period of operation, and without the benefit of judicial interpretation, I have felt it necessary to be cautious in offering opinions on new law, and I have tried to make my summaries of it as accurate as possible. However, the fact remains that this is a small book dealing with a huge subject and I have been obliged to seek a balance between essential principles and detail.

Food law is a fascinating subject. It has an infinite capacity to surprise; it poses the most intractable of problems; it attempts to control an ever changing and highly technological industry; and it can be most rewarding. If this modest book stimulates an interest in the subject I will be well satisfied.

Finally, I freely and gratefully acknowledge the help I have received and the collective wisdom I have enjoyed from trading standards and environmental health officers, from lawyers I have worked with over the years, from my friends in science and technology and from my colleagues in Butterworth Law Publishers Ltd.

AA Painter
Aldwick, West Sussex
January 1992

Contents

Contents

Abbreviations

A&HA 1964	Agriculture and Horticulture Act 1964
AAMGG	Additives and Authenticity Methodology Working Group
AA 1970	Agriculture Act 1970
ACAF	Advisory Committee on Animal Feeding Stuffs
ACCE	Advisory Committee on Consumer Engagement
ACMSF	Advisory Committee on Microbiological Safety of Food
ACNFP	Advisory Committee on Novel Foods and Processes
ACOS	Advisory Committee on Organic Standards
ACP	Advisory Committee on Pesticides
ACRE	Advisory Committee on Releases to the Environment
AHA 1981	Animal Health Act 1981
ASA	Advertising Standards Association
ATP	Agreement on the International Carriage of Perishable Foodstuffs
BSE	Bovine Spongiform Encephalopathy
C&EMA 1979	Customs and Excise Management Act 1979
CA 1985	Companies Act 1985
CAP	Common Agricultural Policy
CCPs	Critical Control Points
CGCSC	Consultative Group on Campylobacter and Salmonella in Chickens
CJA 1988	Criminal Justice Act 1988
CJA 1991	Criminal Justice Act 1991
CJA 2003	Criminal Justice Act 2003
CJD	Creutzfeld-Jakob Disease
COC	Committee on Carcinogenicity of Chemicals in Food, Consumer Products and the Environment
COM	Committee on Mutagenicity of Chemicals in Food, Consumer Products and the Environment
COT	Committee on Toxicity of Chemicals in Food, Consumer Products and the Environment
CP&IA 1996	Criminal Procedure and Investigation Act 1996
CPA 1987	Consumer Protection Act 1987
CPS	Crown Prosecution Service
D&COA 1994	Deregulation and Contracting Out Act 1994
DEFRA	Department for Environment, Food and Rural Affairs
DH	Department of Health
DTI	Department of Trade and Industry
EC	European Community Treaty
ECA 1972	European Communities Act 1972

ECJ	European Court of Justice
EEA	European Economic Area
EFSA	European Food Safety Authority
EFTA	European Free Trade Area
EPA 1990	Environmental Protection Act 1990
F&EPA 1985	Food and Environment Protection Act 1985
FA 1984	Food Act 1984
FAO	Food and Agriculture Organisation
FSA 1990	Food Safety Act 1990
FSA 1999	Food Standards Act 1999
GACS	General Advisory Committee on Science
CGCSC	Consultative Group on Campylobacter and Salmonella in Chickens
GHP	good hygiene practices
GMO	Genetically Modified Organism
GMP	good manufacturing practices
GWA 1998	Government of Wales Act 1998
GWA 2006	Government of Wales Act 2006
H&SWA 1974	Health and Safety at Work etc Act 1974
HACCP	Hazard Analysis and Critical Control Point
HPA	Health Protection Agency
IA 1978	Interpretation Act 1978
LACORS	Local Authorities Co-ordinators of Regulatory Services
LACOTS	Local Authorities Co-ordinating Body on Food and Trading Standards
LBRO	Local Better Regulation Office
LGA 1992	Local Government Act 1992
MA 1968	Medicines Act 1968
MAFF	Ministry of Agriculture, Fisheries and Food
MCA 1980	Magistrates' Courts Act 1980
MHPF	Meat Hygiene Policy Forum
MHS	Meat Hygiene Service
MRLs	Maximum residue levels
MSM	Mechanically separated meat
NSSG	Nutrition Strategy Steering Group
NWML	National Weights and Measures Laboratory
OIE	World Organisation for Animal Health
OVS	Official veterinary surgeon
PA 1974	Prices Act 1974
PACE	Police and Criminal Evidence Act 1984
PARNUTS	Food intended for particular nutritional uses
PDO	Protected designation of origin
PGI	Protected geographical indication
PHLS	Public health laboratory service
PRC	Pesticide Residues Committee
PSD	Pesticides Safety Directorate
QUID	Quantitative ingredient declaration
RASFF	Rapid Alert System for Food
RSA 1993	Radioactive Substances Act 1993
S&SGA 1994	Sale and Supply of Goods Act 1994
SA 1998	Scotland Act 1998
SACN	Scientific Advisory Committee on Nutrition
SEAC	Spongiform Encephalopathy Advisory Committee
SGA 1979	Sale of Goods Act 1979

SPS Agreement	World Trade Organisation Agreement on the Application of Sanitary and Phytosanitary Measures
SSRC	Social Sciences Research Committee
TBT Agreement	World Trade Organisation Agreement on Technical Barriers to Trade
TDA 1968	Trade Descriptions Act 1968
TEU	Treaty on European Union
TNE	Tolerance negative error
TRIPS Agreement	World Trade Organisation Agreement on Trade-Related Aspects of Intellectual Property Rights
TSE	Transmissible Spongiform Encephalopathies
TSG	Traditional Speciality Guaranteed
TSO	Trading Standards Officer
UKROFS	United Kingdom Register of Organic Food Standards
vCJD	Variant Creutzfeldt-Jakob Disease
VPC	Veterinary Products Committee
VRC	Veterinary Residues Committee
W&MA 1985	Weights and Measures Act 1985
WHO	World Health Organisation
WTO	World Trade Organisation
WPFCM	Working Party on Materials and Articles in Contact with Food and Drinks

Table of Cases

Decisions of the European Court of Justice are listed numerically after the main table.

Decisions of the European Court of Justice, the Court of First Instance and the EFTA Court are listed below numerically. These decisions are also included in the preceding alphabetical table.

Chronological Table of Statutes

Chronological Table of Statutory Instruments

1

Table of European Communities Legislation

Chapter 1

The development of modern food law

1.1 THE ORIGINS OF FOOD LAW

1.1.1 Although from the Middle Ages onwards rules in respect of particular foodstuffs were from time to time enacted by central government, it was not until the nineteenth century that general legislation as now understood was put into place. Two statutes of the same year established a food safety and consumer protection framework still recognisable in current British law. The Sale of Food and Drugs Act 1875 laid the foundations of modern provisions controlling the composition of food. Added to an existing ban on injurious ingredients[1] was the key prohibition on selling food not of the nature, substance and quality demanded by the purchaser[2] together with the important supplemental procedures relating to sampling, analysis and legal proceedings[3]. The main protection against chemical contamination of food was thus established. Basic control on biological (bacterial) contamination began with the Public Health Act 1875 which provided an offence of selling unfit food, as well as powers for its inspection, seizure and condemnation[4].

It is beyond the scope of this book to describe the origins of other food safety and consumer controls that it considers[5]. However, it might usefully be noted that quantity marking powers were removed from food legislation by the 1963 predecessor of the Weights and Measures Act 1985 (W&MA 1985), that price marking rules are essentially a modern development and that the late nineteenth century source of current feeding stuffs legislation is briefly mentioned in para **17.1.1** below.

1   See now Food Safety Act 1990 (FSA 1990), s 7.
2   See now FSA 1990, s 14.
3   See now FSA 1990, Pt III and the Food Safety (Sampling and Qualifications) Regulations 1990.
4   See now FSA 1990, ss 8 and 9, Regulation (EC) 178/2002, Art 14 and the General Food Regulations 2004.
5   See in particular ch 16 (quantity and price marking requirements) and ch 17 (feeding stuffs).

1.1.2 Modern British food law developed on the bases described, supplemented in particular by statutory powers[1], which enabled ministers to make a multiplicity of regulations on the composition, labelling and hygiene of food. These have been both 'vertical' (applying to specific foods) and 'horizontal' (dealing generally with matters such as labelling, additives and contaminants).

1   See now FSA 1990, s 16.

1.1.3   When in 1973 the United Kingdom acceded to the European Economic Community (the EEC)[1], ministers' subordinate legislative powers were extended by the European Communities Act 1972[2] so that provisions implementing Community food Directives and Regulations[3] could be readily integrated into the existing national structure. Since then, despite an unjustified reputation as the odd-man-out in Europe, the United Kingdom has loyally complied[4] with its obligation to harmonise national food legislation with Community law[5] and today most new food law in this country derives from that source.

1   At that time, the United Kingdom also acceded to the European Coal and Steel Community (ECSC), for which the Treaty expired on 23 July 2002, and to the European Atomic Energy Community (Euratom) .
2   See now FSA 1990, s 17.
3   See further section **1.5** below.
4   See, for example, the UK response to Decision 2006/694/EC described in para **7.4.7**. See also the Commission's Internal Market Scoreboard.
5   See, in particular Art 10 EC and Regulation (EC) 178/2002, Art 17(2).

1.1.4   A word should be said here about European legislative terminology. In 1993 the Maastricht Treaty on European Union (TEU) added to the existing Community system two further pillars – on Common Foreign and Security Policy and on Cooperation in the fields of Justice and Home Affairs – under the overarching umbrella of the 'European Union' that it created. In the process it redesignated the EEC as the 'European Community'[1]. At the time of writing, the 1957 Treaty of Rome, as thus amended[2], remains in existence and European food law continues to be made under its powers and to be properly described as 'Community law'[3]. However, the story moved on again with the signing of the European Reform Treaty at Lisbon on 13 December 2007. If ratified by all Member States, this will amend the European Community Treaty on 1 January 2009 so that its title will become the 'Treaty on the Functioning of the European Union' and, within it, the words 'Community' and 'European Community' will be replaced by 'Union' and the words 'European Communities' will generally be replaced by 'European Union'[4].

1   See TEU, Art G(A)(1).
2   And also, in particular, by the 1987 Single European Act, the 1997 Treaty of Amsterdam and the 2001 Treaty of Nice.
3   See, for example, general food Regulation (EC) 178/2002.
4   European Reform Treaty Art 2(1) and (2)(a).

1.1.5   The structure of British food law was further reinforced by the FSA 1990, which augmented the core food safety provisions[1], strengthened controls in respect of food businesses[2], food premises[3] and emergencies[4] and added powers to regulate food sources, novel foods, genetically modified food sources and food contact materials[5]. The FSA 1990 extends to England, Wales and Scotland. Northern Ireland has its own parallel legislation.

1   See FSA 1990, ss 7–9.
2   See FSA 1990, ss 10–12.
3   See FSA 1990, s 19.
4   See FSA 1990, ss 12–13.
5   See FSA 1990, ss 16–18.

1.1.6   In 1997 the James Report[1] recognised the FSA 1990 as a good tool for ensuring food safety, but identified significant weaknesses in the organisation responsible for applying it. In consequence, the Food Standards Agency was established by the Food Standards Act 1999 (FSA 1999) as the central UK food department and ministerial responsibility was concentrated in the Secretary of State for Health and the devolved authorities in Scotland, Wales and Northern

Ireland. Meanwhile, the 1998 devolution legislation conferred on Scotland and Wales power to make their own food regulations [2].

1 'Food Standards Agency: An interim proposal by Professor Philip James: 30 April 1997'.
2 See ch 2.

1.1.7   Until recently Community law had required little ostensible change to the bases of British food law in the FSA 1990. For example, although specific provision was included in s 15 in order to adapt it to what is now Art 2 of the general food labelling Directive 2000/13/EC, the food safety requirements of the Act were evidently regarded as wide enough as they stood to implement Article 2 of the food contaminants framework Regulation (EEC) 315/93. In fact, most Community food law had been quite suitable for detailed implementation by regulations under the FSA 1990 or, where appropriate, under the W&MA 1985, the Consumer Protection Act 1987 Part II, the Food and Environment Protection Act 1985 Part III, or the European Communities Act 1972[1].

It appeared that extensive amendment of the FSA 1990 might at last be needed when, as a result of the food crises of the 1990s, the Commission published its White Paper on Food Safety[2] containing proposals for the establishment of a legal framework covering the entire food chain 'from farm to fork'. In the event, this was not required. Notwithstanding that the 1990 Act's food safety requirements, consultation provisions and 'food' definition were superseded when the core element of the White Paper was given effect by general food Regulation (EC) 178/2002[3], it has otherwise proved to be compatible with Community law. The provisions of the 1990 Act have, moreover, been mirrored by domestic Regulations providing for the execution and enforcement of instruments that gave effect to other key White Paper proposals, such as the official controls Regulation (EC) 882/2004 and hygiene Regulations (EC) 852/2004, 853/2004 and 854/2004[4].

But, while the FSA 1990 remains the primary domestic source, food law in the United Kingdom has been significantly advanced by Community legislation implementing the White Paper. Thus, not only does Regulation (EC) 178/2002 apply to both food and feed, it also imposes on traders important new general obligations regarding import, export, safety, traceability and withdrawal of products[5].

1 Read, in particular, with the European Communities (Designation) (No 4) Order 2003.
2 COM (1999) 719 final, published on 12 January 2000.
3 See in particular paras **3.2.20–3.3.30**, **4.1.4** and **4.3.1**.
4 See ch 18 on the Official Feed and Food Controls (England) Regulations 2007 and chs 6, 13 and 14 on the Food Hygiene (England) Regulations 2006.
5 See paras **3.2.12-3.2.54**.

1.1.8   In recent years there has been a tendency in food legislation to return to reliance on general controls. For example, on the one hand, the general food safety provisions were strengthened by the FSA 1990 and then by food Regulation (EC) 178/2002 while, on the other, sundry specific rules were removed or simplified by the Food (Miscellaneous Revocations and Amendments) Regulations 1995. Furthermore, in 2005 it was judged possible to revoke bespoke national provisions respectively requiring the licensing of butchers' shops[1] and prohibiting meat from cattle aged over 30 months[2] and to rely instead on the general EC safeguards relevant to the specific dangers in question. Through its 2006/2007 Simplification Plan[3], the Food Standards Agency certainly continues to pursue the objective of making food regulations simpler and easier to observe, yet the amount of detailed provision in the current body of law remains formidable.

1   See the Food Hygiene (England) Regulations 2005 and the Food Safety (General Food Hygiene) (Amendment) (England) Regulations 2005 revoking the provisions made by the Food Safety (General Food Hygiene) (Butchers' Shops) (Amendment) Regulations 2000.
2   See the Bovine Products (Restriction on Placing on the Market) (England) Regulations 2005 revoking the Fresh Meat (Beef Controls) (No 2) Regulations 1996.
3   See para **2.3.2** below.

1.1.9   The legislation for England and Wales is listed in Appendices A and B respectively. References throughout this book to English subordinate legislation, Food Law Codes of Practice or Food Law Practice Guidance are, in respect of Wales, to be read as references to the Welsh equivalents.

1.2   THE NATURE OF COMMUNITY LAW

1.2.1   The rest of this chapter explains relevant aspects of Community, European Economic Area and international law so far as, within the compass of this book, it is possible to do so. For a full understanding of these topics, readers are referred to the many learned works that deal specifically with them.

Central to this consideration, is the European Community Treaty that is the core element of a special order of international law characterised by two essential and complementary features. First, the subjects of Community law are not only Member States but also individual citizens who may, if a Community provision has 'direct effect' (that is, essentially if it is unconditional and sufficiently precise) and has not been properly implemented, rely on it before a national court[1]. Secondly, in case of conflict with Member States' national law, Community law is supreme[2].

It must also be borne in mind that, even where Community provisions do not have 'direct effect', the Community principle of consistent interpretation requires national legislation, whether subsequent or precedent, to be interpreted so as to give effect to them[3].

1   Case 26/62 *NV Algemene Transport en Expeditie Onderneming Van Gend en Loos v Nederlandse Administratie der Belastingen* [1963] ECR 1; case 126/82 *D J Smit* [1983] ECR 73, [1983] 3 CMLR 106, ECJ. See also on direct effect, para **1.5.2** below.
2   Case 6/64 *Costa v ENEL* [1964] ECR 585.
3   See case 14/83 *Von Colson and Kamann v Land Nordrhein-Westfalen* [1984] ECR 1891; and case C-106/89 *Marleasing SA v La Commercial Internacional de Alimentation SA* [1990] ECR I-4135.

1.3   FOOD REGULATION AND THE FREE MOVEMENT OF GOODS

1.3.1   As might be expected, food is subject to the fundamental Community law principle of free movement of goods that aims at the abolition of all state commercial and tariff barriers to intra-Community trade[1]. For national food legislation the most significant aspect of this principle has been the prohibition imposed by Art 28 EC on measures having effect equivalent to quantitative restrictions on imports from other Member States[2]. Until the celebrated *Cassis de Dijon* judgment by the European Court of Justice (ECJ) in 1979[3], it was assumed that this prohibition was confined to measures that discriminated against such imports. The judgment made clear that the prohibition extends to any measure applying to imports and home products alike, if it restricts imports of products lawfully produced and marketed in another Member State. The measure will only escape this prohibition if it is shown to be necessary in order to satisfy a compelling public interest requirement (a 'mandatory requirement') such as the protection of public health, the fairness of commercial transactions or the defence of the consumer[4]. To be justified on one of these grounds, the measure must be proportionate to its objective[5]. For example, in an important 1987 judgment the ECJ took the view that it was unnecessary for consumer protection and therefore illegal to impose a national beer standard on imports: compulsory labelling with the nature of the product would be sufficient for the purpose[6]. And further instances continue to come before the Court. It has recently decided that the free movement of pre-baked frozen bakery products that are reheated at sales outlets was unreasonably hindered by the application to them of the full national requirements prescribed for the manufacture and marketing of traditional bread[7].

1   Articles 23–31 (ex-Arts 9–37) EC. The provisions of the EC Treaty were renumbered by the Amsterdam Treaty. The Community law principle of freedom to provide services set out in Arts 49–55 (ex-59–66) EC may also sometimes be relevant: see case C-393/05 *Commission v Austria* [2007] ECR I-10195, [2008] 1 CMLR 42; and case 404/05 *Commission v Germany* [2007] I-10239, [2008] 1 CMLR 43.
2   See, for example, the quality label for national products declared illegal in case C-325/00 *Commission v Germany* [2002] ECR I-9977.
3   Case 120/78 *Rewe-Zentral AG v Bundesmonopolverwaltung für Branntwein* [1979] ECR 649, [1979] 3 CMLR 494, ECJ.
4   See further joined cases C-267/91 and C-268/91 *Keck and Mithouard* [1993] ECR I-6097, paras 15–17.
5   Case 261/81 *Walter Rau Lebensmittelwerke v De Smedt* [1982] ECR 3961 (margarine packaging).
6   Case 178/84 *EC Commission v Germany* [1987] ECR 1227.
7   Joined cases C-158/04 and 159/04 *Alfa Vita Vaissilopoulos* [2006] ECR I-8135.

1.3.2   Since 1979 the *Cassis de Dijon* doctrine (of which the extended interpretation of Art 28 EC and the public interest derogation from it are sometimes respectively called the 'mutual recognition principle' and the 'rule of reason') has been well established by application in numerous ECJ cases. The Member States' obligation is moreover not only confined to acceptance, in the normal way, of adequately labelled products that have been lawfully manufactured and marketed in the Community: they must likewise normally accept third country products that have been put in free circulation there[1]. As interpreted in these judgments, Art 28 EC has significantly limited the scope for a Member State to enact its own national food compositional standards. Unless a national standard can be justified in the way described in para **1.3.1** or under the narrowly interpreted derogation in Art 30 EC[2], the State must either exempt Community imports from the standard or forego it altogether[3].

The pressure exerted by the *Cassis de Dijon* doctrine was an added stimulus to deregulation in the United Kingdom and sundry national food standards were revoked by instruments such as the Food (Miscellaneous Revocations) Regulations 1991 and the Food (Miscellaneous Revocations and Amendments) Regulations 1995.

However, as we shall see in ch 10, others survive albeit in simplified forms. In these cases it has been necessary, by a 'mutual recognition clause'[4], to exempt products from other Member States where either they are lawfully produced and marketed or, in the case of third country imports, they are in free circulation. Examples of such exemptions are in reg 3(2) of the Bread and Flour

Regulations 1998 and reg 3(3) of the Meat Products (England) Regulations 2003, which contain food standards of wholly national inspiration.

Less obvious instances are to be found in instruments that, although mainly concerned with the implementation of Community law, include national standards for margarine vitamin content[5], fruit curds and mincemeat[6] and sundry specific food descriptions that might otherwise be misleading[7]. These mutual recognition exemptions also take account of Art 8 of the European Economic Area Agreement that, as explained in para **1.8.1** below, provides for free movement between contracting States of goods originating in those States.

A mutual recognition clause is not required where a Member State has opted for legislation that subjects to prior authorisation the marketing of a foodstuff containing specified substances. However, such legislation will fall foul of Community law if two conditions are not fulfilled. Traders must be able to apply for inclusion of substances in the national permitted list by means of an accessible procedure resulting in a prompt decision that is open to appeal; and inclusion of a substance may be refused only if it poses a genuine risk to public health[8].

1 See case 41/76 *Criel (née Donckerwolke)* [1976] ECR 1921. As to 'free circulation', see Art 23.2 EC.
2 In particular Art 30 EC permits 'restrictions on imports, exports or goods in transit justified on the grounds of ... the protection of health and life of humans ...' provided that such 'prohibitions or restrictions shall not ... constitute a means of arbitrary discrimination or a disguised restriction on trade between Member States'. See, for example, case C-95/01 *Greenham and Abel* [2005] All ER (EC) 903; [2004] ECR I-1333 as to prohibition of imported food containing added vitamins and minerals; and case C-434/04 *Ahokainen and Leppik*, [2007] 1 CMLR 11, [2006] ECR I-9171 as to import licensing of spirits.
3 The application of a national rule contrary to Articles 28 and 30 EC is prohibited only in respect of imported, not of national products: see case C-448/98 *Criminal Proceedings against Jean-Pierre Guimont* [2000] ECR I-10663 para 21.
4 See case C-184/96 *EC Commission v France* [1998] ECR 1–6197.
5 See the Spreadable Fats (Marketing Standards) and Milk and Milk Products (Protection of Designations)(England) Regulations 2008, regs 3 and 4.
6 See the Jam and Similar Products (England) Regulations 2003, regs 3(3) and 4 and Sch 1.
7 See the Food Labelling Regulations 1996, regs 3(1) and 42 and Sch 8. See also *Hackney London Borough Council v Cedar Trading Ltd* (1999) 163 JP 749.
8 See case C-24/00 *EC Commission v France* [2004] 3 CMLR 25, [2004] ECR I-1277 paras 24–28.

1.3.3   As a result of the *Cassis de Dijon* case, the Commission reviewed its policy on the harmonisation of foodstuffs legislation[1]. In 1985 it presented a Communication[2] to the Council and the European Parliament proposing that Community food legislation should henceforth be limited to the harmonisation of national rules justifiable in terms of the mandatory requirements identified by the Court. To ensure free movement of foodstuffs, reliance would otherwise be placed on the *Cassis de Dijon* doctrine with reinforcement of the labelling rules to guarantee consumer information and fair trading. In addition, the Commission encouraged the food industry to develop quality policies based on the use of voluntary instruments, such as codes of practice.

By another Communication of 1989[3], the Commission reiterated its view, in the light of the *Cassis de Dijon* doctrine, as to the rules applicable in the absence of Community provisions and as to the measures that must continue to be subject to Community legislation: it also confirmed its intention to bring forward proposals for labelling to identify specific quality products. This was supplemented in 1991 by a controversial interpretative Communication[4] giving the Commission's opinion about the conditions under which Member States of destination might impose on a product a name different from that under which it is marketed in the producing Member State[5].

Yet difficulties continue to be encountered in application of mutual recognition. That food products remained the goods most affected by free movement infringements, was in particular revealed by a further Communication proposing ways of improving mutual recognition in the single market that was published in 1999 by the Commission[6] and supported by the Council[7]. Within this framework, the Commission issued two biennial reports on application of the mutual recognition principle[8] and a practical guide in the form of another interpretative Communication[9] which summarises the rights afforded to economic operators bringing products from other Member States. Regulation (EC) 764/2008, referred to in para **1.4.1** below, has now been enacted to replace Decision 3052/95/EC and strengthen those rights by requiring producers to be given express justification for decisions hindering entry of their products lawfully on sale elsewhere in the Community.

Brief mention should also be made of two further Community initiatives aimed at the speedy removal of obstructions to the free movement of goods. The first of these is the Rapid Intervention Mechanism established under Regulation (EC) 2679/98 to enable the Commission to require the Member State to correct serious and abrupt breaches such as have been caused by farmers obstructing agricultural imports from other Member States[10]. Secondly, there is the SOLVIT network of Member States' centres established in 2002, which help find informal solutions to complaints by consumers and businesses about the misapplication of internal market law by public authorities[11].

The Community approach to quality promotion is further explained in para **10.5.1** below.

1   Communication concerning the consequences of the *Cassis de Dijon* judgment (OJ C256, 3.10.1980 p.2).
2   Communication (COM (85) 603 final) on the completion of the internal market in the foodstuffs sector.
3   Communication (89/C271/03) on the free movement of foodstuffs within the Community.
4   Interpretative Communication (91/C270/02) on the names under which foodstuffs are sold.
5   See further para **9.2.5** (iii) below.
6   Communication (COM (1999) 299 final on mutual recognition in the context of the follow-up to the Action Plan for the Single Market.
7   Council Resolution of 28 October 1999 (OJ C141, 19.5.2000 p.5).
8   SEC (1999) 1106 and COM (2002) 419 final.
9   On facilitating the access of products to the markets of other Member States: the practical application of mutual recognition ((OJ C256, 4.11.2003 p.2).
10 See case C-265/95 *Commission v France* [1997] ECR I-6959. See also case C-112/00 *Schmidberger* [2003] ECR I-5659.
11 See Commission Communication COM (2001) 202 final of 27 November 2001 on Effective Problem Solving in the Internal market ('SOLVIT) and Commission Recommendation 2001/893/EC on principles for using 'SOLVIT'.

1.4   COMMUNITY NOTIFICATION PROCEDURES

1.4.1   Two specific Community measures – Directive 98/34/EC and Decision 3025/95/EC – have required Member States to give notice of actions that may hinder the free movement of goods.

Directive 98/34/EC aims to prevent the creation of new barriers to trade by requiring prior notification to the Commission of any draft technical regulation proposed by a Member State[1]. Failure to fulfil the obligation to notify or to postpone adoption of the regulation renders it unenforceable against individuals before a national court insofar as it hinders the use or marketing of non-compliant products[2].

By contrast, Decision 3052/95/EC was concerned with the practical operation of national technical regulations[3]. Generally speaking, if a Member State took action that impeded or prohibited marketing of any product lawfully produced or marketed in another Member State, it has been obliged to notify the Commission that in turn informed the other Member States. In practice the application of national rules have continued to hamper free movement of goods so, as from 13 May 2009, Decision 3052/95/EC is replaced by Regulation (EC) 764/2008 which generally requires a Member State to justify any such action to the producer concerned and to advise him of his potential remedies. The Regulation also enhances dialogue between competent authorities by establishing 'product contact points' in each Member State.

Additionally for food, specific Community notification procedures apply to proposed national legislative initiatives in respect of labelling[4], contaminants[5], hygiene[6], nutrition and health claims[7] and rapid action[8].

1   By way of example, see the Tryptophan in Food (England) Regulations 2005.
2   Case C-194/94 *CIA Security International SA v Signalson SA* [1996] ECR I-2201, [1996] All ER (EC) 557; case C-226/97 *Lemmens* ECR I-3711; and case C-443/98 *Unilever* [2000] ECR I-7535.
3   See joined cases C-388/00 and C-429/00 *Radiosistemi Srl v Prefetto di Genova* [2002] ECR I-5845.
4   Directive 2000/13/EC, Art 19. By way of example, see Decision 2008/35/EC.
5   Regulation (EEC) 315/93, Art 5(3)(b).
6   Regulation (EC) 852/2004, Art 13(5); Regulation (EC) 853/2004, Art 10(5); and Regulation (EC) 854/2004, Art 17(5).
7   Regulation 1924/2006, Art 23.
8   Regulation (EC) 178/2002, Art 50(3). See further, para **7.3.5** below.

1.5   COMMUNITY FOOD LEGISLATION

1.5.1   The European Union impacts most conspicuously on national food law through its substantial body of vertical and horizontal EC legislation that Member States must implement in response to the general duty of loyal cooperation in Art10 (ex-Art 5) EC. A list of the principal Community food and feeding stuffs measures is set out in Appendix C.

Three kinds of binding Community secondary legislative act are prescribed by Art 249 (ex-Art 189) EC. They are the Regulation, the Directive and the Decision. The Article also specifies Recommendations and Opinions that are non-binding but – like certain other Community acts not mentioned in Art 249 EC – may nonetheless have legal effects. The respective features of these various acts are briefly considered below.

In relation to food and feeding stuffs, acts are made mainly under three Treaty powers, that is to say, Art 37 (ex-Art 43) EC where the subject falls within the common agricultural policy[1]; Art 95 (ex-Art 100a) EC in relation to internal market matters[2]; and Art 152(4)(b) (ex-Art 129(4)(b) authorising 'by way of derogation from Art 37, measures in the veterinary and phytosanitary fields that have as their direct objective the protection of public health' [3]. The legislative basis and the recitals set out at the beginning of each Regulation, Directive and Decision are no mere technicalities. They constitute the underlying reasoning that the Council or Commission is obliged by Art 253 EC to give. They are, moreover, vital to the interpretation of an act, for which purpose the ECJ looks to its context and objectives.

As briefly explained in paras **1.6.3** and **1.6.4** below, different legislative procedures apply in respect of Arts 95 and 152 on the one hand and Art 37 on the other.

For completeness, it should also be mentioned that Decision 768/2008/EC now sets out the common framework of general principles and reference provisions for the drawing up of Community legislation harmonising the conditions for marketing of products[4]. However, as recital (5) of the Decision notes, 'the specificities of sectoral needs may provide grounds for recourse to other regulatory solutions'. In particular, this is said to be the case where there are specific, comprehensive legal systems already in place in a sector, such as in the fields of feed and food; common market organisations for agricultural products; plant health and plant protection; and medicinal products for human and veterinary use. It is by no means clear, therefore, that Decision 768/2008 will have much, if any, application to legislation that is the subject of this book.

1   See, in particular, single common market organisation Regulation (EC) 1234/2007, Title II, Chapter I, Section I and Annexes XIa-XVI.
2   See, for example, labelling Directive 2000/13/EC; and nutrition and health claims Regulation (EC) 1924/2006.
3   See, for example, TSE Regulation (EC) 999/2001; and food of animal origin hygiene Regulation (EC) 853/2004.
4   See further para **10.5.1** below.

The Regulation

1.5.2   The chief characteristic of a Community Regulation is that it is part of national law without specific incorporation: in the words of Article 249 (ex-Article 189) EC, a Regulation is 'directly applicable'[1]. Provisions of a Regulation may also be 'directly effective' and confer rights on individuals[2]. In the United Kingdom the European Communities Act 1972, s 2(1) gives effect both to the direct applicability of Community Regulations, and to the rights conferred on individuals by directly effective Community provisions.

Originally, Community food legislation was seldom couched in the form of a Regulation except when made as part of the common agricultural policy[3], including the provisions as to fishery and aquaculture products[4]. However, particularly since the Commission's food law Green Paper[5], legislation for approximation of food law has increasingly been made by Regulation for provisions that leave little margin of discretion to Member States in their implementation[6].

1   Even in civil proceedings between individuals, see case C-253/00 *Muñoz v Frumar* [2002] I-ECR 7289; [2003] Ch 328; [2003] All ER (EC) 56.
2   As to 'direct effect' generally, see para **1.2.1**.
3   See, for example, Regulations 509/2006 (traditional specialities guaranteed), 510/2006 (geographical indications and designations of origin, 834/2007 (organic production) and 1234/2007 (single common market organisation).
4   See Regulations 2136/89 (preserved sardines), 1536/92 (preserved tuna and bonito) and 2406/96 (specified fishery products).
5   Commission Green Paper COM (97) 176 on 'the General Principles of Food Law in the European Union', Pt III.3.
6   See, for example, Regulations 2065/2003 (smoke flavourings), 1935/2004 (materials and articles) and 1924/2006 (nutrition and health claims).

1.5.3   Although Community food Regulations are directly applicable, most of their provisions are intended to impose obligations on citizens and need to be supplemented by national law imposing penalties for non-observance and providing for enforcement. This supplementation is achieved in a variety of ways. Thus, fruit and vegetable marketing standards are enforced by special provision adapting the agricultural grading legislation in the Agriculture and Horticulture Act 1964, Part III[1]. Sometimes, as in the case of the EC poultrymeat marketing standards Regulations, reliance for enforcing sanctions has temporarily been placed on the general offences in the FSA 1990 and Food Labelling Regulations 1996. For the majority of Regulations however, provision for enforcement is made without delay by bespoke subordinate legislation.

1   See the European Communities Act 1972, s 4(1) and Sch 4C and the Grading of Horticultural Produce (Amendment) Regulations 1973 upheld in *DEFRA v ASDA* [2003] UKHL 71, [2004] 1 WLR 105. See also SIs 2003/1846 and 2004/2604.

The Directive

1.5.4   The Directive was initially the form most frequently employed by the Community for harmonising national food law. From the Member States' point of view it is more flexible than the Regulation since, although binding on national authorities as to the result to be achieved, it leaves to them the choice of form and methods.

Although Directives under Art 37 (ex-Art 43) EC have been made as part of the common agricultural policy, they have mainly been used for the approximation of national laws. Indeed, until the Single European Act added Art 95 (ex-Art 100a) to the EC Treaty, the Directive was the only kind of measure that could – under Art 94 (ex-Art 100) – be taken for this latter purpose. Although, as explained in para **1.5.2**, the Regulation is often now the chosen vehicle for Community food law, Directives have continued in recent years to be used for enacting important rules on general labelling and advertising, particular foodstuffs, food supplements and additives.

1.5.5   A time limit is normally laid down in a Directive within which it must be implemented by Member States. Provisions of Directives will often be directly effective[1]. Those that create rights and obligations for individuals must be incorporated into national law with the precision and clarity necessary in order to satisfy fully the requirement of legal certainty[2]. In Great Britain, provisions of food and feeding stuffs Directives are customarily transposed into national law by subordinate legislation under the FSA 1990, Agriculture Act 1970, or other statutes cited in para **1.1.7**.

1   See, for example, case 8/81 *Becker v Finanzamt Münster-Innenstadt* [1982] ECR 53; case C-319/97 *Kortas* [1999] ECR I-3143; and case C-201/02 *R (on the application of Wells) v Secretary of State for Transport, Local Government and the Regions* [2004] ECR I-723; [2005] All ER (EC) 323. As to 'direct effect' generally, see para **1.2.1**.
2   Case C-131/88 *Commission v Germany* [1991] ECR I-825.

The Decision

1.5.6   A Decision is binding in its entirety on those to whom it is addressed. Decisions addressed to Member States may, like Directives, be directly effective and require implementation[1]. They are used for matters such as the imposition of import conditions, the authorisation of novel foods and the speedy enactment of emergency measures.

1   Case 9/70 *Franz Grad v Traunstein* [1970] ECR 825. As to 'direct effect' generally, see para **1.2.1** above.

The Recommendation, the Opinion and other acts

1.5.7   Article 249 EC provides specifically that 'recommendations and opinions shall have no binding force'. However, national courts may have to take into consideration a recommendation that is capable of clarifying the interpretation of national or Community law[1]. Moreover, although the ECJ has regularly denied that the Commission can give an authoritative opinion on the interpretation of Community law[2], a veterinary expert's opinion as to whether imported meat is unfit for human consumption was held to represent an important factor to be taken into account by national authorities or courts before which proceedings may be brought[3]. Likewise, an opinion delivered by the European Food Safety Authority may constitute evidence that a national court should take into account[4].

Community acts not covered by the EC Treaty may sometimes have legally binding force[5], although they cannot thereby circumvent its implied and express legislative requirements[6]. They may also be useful aids to interpretation[7], as well as exercising an indirect influence on Member States' law. In implementation of its Communications, described in para **1.3.3** above, following the *Cassis de Dijon* judgment, the Commission confined harmonisation to national rules that were justifiable on the public interest grounds identified by the ECJ and took action in the Court against those that in its view were not[8].

1   Case 322/88 *Grimaldi v Fonds des Maladies Professionelles* [1989] ECR 4407; and case C-207/01 *Altair Chimica Spa v ENEL Distribuzione Spa* [2003] ECR I-8875.
2   See, for example, case 133/79 *Sucrimex and Westzuker v Commission* [1980] ECR 1299; and case T-234/04 *Netherlands v Commission* [2007] ECR II-4589.
3   Case 332/88 *Alimenta v Doux* [1990] ECR I-2077.
4   Joined cases C-211/03 and C-316 to C-318/03 *HLH Warenvertriebs GmbH and Orthica BV v Germany* [2005] I-5141. See further paras **3.3.9–3.3.11**.
5   Case 22/70 *Commission v Council* [1971] ECR 263; case C-313/90 *CIRFS v Commission* [1993] ECR I-1125.
6   Case C-325/91 *France v Commission* [1993] ECR I-3283; case C-57/95 *France v Commission* [1997] ECR I-1627.
7   Joined cases 98 and 99/75 *Carstens Keramik v Oberfinanzdirektion* [1976] ECR 241; and case C-486/06 BVBA *Van Landeghem v Belgische Staat* [2007] ECR I-10661.
8   Under Art 226 EC, see para **1.7.2**.

1.6   THE MAKING OF COMMUNITY SECONDARY LEGISLATION

1.6.1   Community legislative procedures are complex and it will suffice to highlight the main features of the co-decision and the consultation procedures that are currently relevant in respect of food and feeding stuffs. If the Reform Treaty signed on 13 December 2007 is ratified, the co-decision procedure will replace the consultation procedure for common agricultural policy legislation and will alone be relevant. It is also proposed that the Reform Treaty will repeal the co-operation procedure that is now specified in Art 252 (ex-Art 189c) EC and that formerly applied to Art 95 (ex-Art 100a) EC. For a fuller description of the legislative processes, the reader should consult a specialist work on the subject.

1.6.2   The Council, the European Parliament and the Commission are all involved in EC law-making. The process is initiated by proposals for draft legislation formulated by the Commission through working groups made up of nominees from national governments.

11

The co-decision procedure

1.6.3   For food or feed legislation made under Art 95[1] (ex-Art 100a) EC or Art 152(4)(b) EC the legislative procedure is that specified in Art 251 (ex-Art 189b) EC. It is commonly known as the co-decision procedure because it aims at legislation adopted jointly by the Parliament and the Council. A Conciliation Committee of the two institutions is convened if agreement is not otherwise reached.

1   See case C-66/04 *United Kingdom v European Parliament and Council* [2005] ECR I-10553.

The consultation procedure

1.6.4   Unless and until the 2007 Reform Treaty is ratified and the co-decision procedure replaces it for the purpose, the consultation procedure applies for food or feed legislation made as part of the common agricultural policy under Art 37 (ex-Art 43) EC. Dating back to the Treaty of Rome, this confers on the Council the power to make the legislation. The European Parliament is entitled only to be consulted before the decision is taken.

The Commission's implementing powers

1.6.5   No matter under which Treaty Article it is enacted, food or feed legislation made by the Council with or without the European Parliament usually confers on the Commission powers for its implementation. The exercise of these powers is governed by requirements, imposed by the Council under Art 202 EC third indent, whereby each proposed implementing measure is normally submitted to a committee of officials from the Member States. The procedures that respectively apply to the different categories of committee are currently prescribed by 'Comitology' Decision 1999/468/EC.

Leaving aside special provision in relation to the taking of safeguard measures, the Decision as enacted in 1999 prescribed three basic procedures for the exercise of implementing powers by the Commission. In ascending order of the restrictions placed on Commission freedom of action, they were the advisory procedure, the management procedure and the regulatory procedure of which, by virtue of Art 2[1], the last two normally apply to food and feed rules. For 'management measures, such as those relating to the application of the common agricultural and common fisheries policies' which include CAP marketing standards rules[2], the management procedure is to be used whereby the Commission's decision may be overruled by the Council – acting by qualified majority[3] – unless it follows the committee's opinion – also delivered by qualified majority. For 'measures of general scope designed to apply essential provisions of basic instruments, including measures concerning the protection of the health and safety of humans, animals or plants' and in consequence most food and feed legislation, the regulatory procedure applies requiring a favourable opinion from a qualified majority of the committee before the Commission can take a decision[4].

Subsequent legislative developments have rationalised the committees concerned with Commission food and feed measures. Although particular committees assist the Commission with specialist topics[5], most of its food and feed legislation is referred to the Standing Committee on the Food Chain and Animal Health established by Regulation (EC) 178/2002[6]. Moreover, the Management Committee for the Common Organisation of Agricultural Markets set up under single common market organisation Regulation (EC)

1234/2007 Art 195 henceforth will evidently consider all Commission implementation proposals in respect of marketing standards for agricultural products.

Recently Comitology Decision 1999/468/EC itself has been amended. Decision 2006/512/EC has now added to it the 'regulatory procedure with scrutiny'. This is to apply 'where a basic instrument' adopted in accordance with the co-decision procedure[7], 'provides for the adoption of measures of general scope designed to amend non-essential elements of that instrument, *inter alia* by deleting some of those elements or by supplementing the instrument by the addition of new non-essential elements'[8]. The complex procedure allows the Council and the European Parliament to scrutinise the proposal prior to adoption. Where the proposal accords with the opinion of the committee, they may oppose it on specified fundamental grounds. Where the proposal does not so accord, the Council may oppose or envisage adopting it. In the latter case, the Parliament may nonetheless oppose it on fundamental grounds.

A recent example of legislation in which the regulatory procedure with scrutiny has been applied in respect of Commission power to amend lists of permitted substances and to make provision of similar importance is to be found in Regulation (EC) 108/2008 amending Regulation (EC) 1925/2006 on the addition of vitamins and minerals and of certain other substances to food[9].

1   The criteria laid down in Art 2 are not binding but where the Community legislature departs from them in the choice of a committee procedure, it must give reasons for its choice: see case C-378/00 *Commission v European Parliament and Council* [2003] ECR I-937, paras 48 and 55.
2   See, in particular, single common market organisation Regulation (EC) 1234/2007, Title II, Chapter I, Section I and Annexes XIa-XVI.
3   The vote weighting and numbers for adoption of measures by qualified majority are specified in Art 205(2) EC.
4   As to the distinction between management and regulatory measures, see further case C-122/04 *Commission v European Parliament and Council* [2006] ECR I-2001.
5   See, for example, the Standing Committees on Traditional Specialities Guaranteed and on Protected Geographical Indications and Protected Designations of Origin under Regulations (EC) 509/2006 and 510/2006 respectively.
6   See para **3.4.2** below.
7   See para **1.6.3** above.
8   See Decision 1999/468/EC, Art 2(2), as amended.
9   See also the proposal in COM(2006)423 for a Regulation establishing a common authorisation procedure for food additives, food enzymes and food flavourings.

1.7   ENFORCEMENT OF COMMUNITY LAW

1.7.1   ECJ judgments to enforce Community law against Member States and Community institutions may be obtained both through direct actions and through proceedings begun in national courts. The following paragraphs briefly explain how cases come before the Court under Arts 226, 227 and 228 EC (infraction proceedings), Arts 230 and 232 EC (proceedings for annulment and failure to act) and Art 234 EC (preliminary rulings). This section again concentrates on and takes its examples from Community law concerning free movement of food and the public interests that may impede it. No attempt is made to deal with proceedings under Art 235 EC (non-contractual liability). The reader should consult a specialist work for a full description of ECJ remedies.

As regards Arts 230 and 232 EC, it should be noted that, subject to a right of appeal to the ECJ on points of law, the Court of First Instance (CFI) has jurisdiction in actions brought by natural or legal persons against acts or failures to act by Community institutions; and in actions brought by Member States against the Commission[1]. To this extent, references to the ECJ in paras **1.7.4** and **1.7.5** include the CFI.

1 Article 225 EC. See, for example, case T-215/00 *La Conqueste v Commission* [2001] ECR II-181; and case C-151/01P *La Conqueste v Commission* [2002] I-1179 (Canard à foie gras du Sud-Ouest).

Infraction proceedings

1.7.2   The EC Treaty enables the Commission under Art 226 (ex-Art 169) EC, or another Member State under Art 227 (ex-Art 170) EC, to bring infraction proceedings against a Member State for failure to fulfil a Community law obligation. Proceedings by Member States are rare[1], but the Commission has proved itself to be both diligent and generally successful in pursuing infractions. Art 226 proceedings in relation to food seem to have been provoked less by Member States' failure to implement Community rules than by their obstruction of the free movement of goods, as described in para **1.3.1** above. Under what is now Art 226, notable ECJ decisions striking down national import restrictions have related to UHT milk[2], poultrymeat[3], wine vinegar[4], beer[5], bearnaise sauce[6] and, more recently, chocolate[7] and regionally labelled products[8].

1 Case C-388/95 *Belgium v Spain* [2000] ECR I-3123 is a recent example in which the ECJ upheld the Spanish requirement that 'Rioja' be bottled in the region of production.
2 Case 124/81 *Commission v United Kingdom* [1983] ECR 203.
3 Case 40/82 *Commission v United Kingdom* [1984] ECR 283.
4 Case 193/80 *Commission v Italy* [1981] ECR 3019.
5 Case 178/84 *Commission v Germany* [1987] ECR 1227.
6 Case C-51/94 *Commission v Germany* [1995] ECR I-3599.
7 Case C-12/00 *Commission v Spain* [2003] ECR I-459 and case C-14/00 *Commission v Italy* [2003] ECR I-513.
8 Case C-6/02 *Commission v France* [2003] ECR I-2389.

1.7.3   In the event of an adverse infraction ruling by the European Court, Art 228 (ex-Art 171) EC has always required the defaulting State to take the necessary steps to comply with the judgment[1] and, since the Maastricht Treaty, has laid it open to the possibility of a lump sum or penalty payment imposed by the ECJ[2].

1 See, for example, Case 281/83 *Commission v Italy* [1985] ECR 3397 (wine vinegar).
2 See, for example, case C-387/97 *Commission v Greece* [2000] ECR I-5047; case C-278/01 *Commission v Spain* [2003] ECR I-14141; case C-304/02 *Commission v France* [2005] ECR I-6263; and case C-177/04 *Commission v France* [2006] I-ECR 2461.

Proceedings for annulment and failure to act

1.7.4 Under Art 230 (ex-Art 173) EC, proceedings may be brought in the ECJ for the annulment of acts of the European Parliament and Council jointly, of the Council, of the Commission and – where they are intended to produce legal effects vis-à-vis third parties – of the European Parliament. The 'acts' in question are mainly Regulations, Directives and Decisions. Recommendations and Opinions are expressly excluded but other acts not specified in the Treaty may be challenged if they produce legal effects[1].

Actions may be brought by Member States, the European Parliament, the Council and the Commission on four specified grounds, that is to say, lack of competence; infringement of an essential procedural requirement; infringement of the Treaty or any rule of law relating to its application; or misuse of powers. Natural or legal persons may also institute proceedings for annulment of Decisions addressed to them and of regulatory acts that, although addressed to others, are of direct and individual concern to them.

In a notable recent Art 230 case, the Court dismissed actions for annulment of Commission Regulation (EC) 1829/2002 which registered 'feta' as a protected designation of origin for goat's cheese from a large part of Greece thus finally (and questionably) denying it as a generic name to producers in other Member States[2].

1   See, for example, case 22/70 *Commission v Council* [1971] ECR 263, para 42. See further para **1.5.7** above.
2   See joined cases C-465/02 and C-466/02 *Germany and Denmark v Commission* [2005] ECR I-9115. See further para **10.5.2** below.

1.7.5   Under Art 232 (ex-Art 175) EC, proceedings may also be brought in the ECJ by a Member State, the European Parliament, the Council or the Commission against the European Parliament, the Council or the Commission, where the institution, having been called on the act, fails to do so in breach of Community law. Such an action may also be brought by natural or legal persons, against a Community institution that has failed to address to them any act other than a Recommendation or Opinion. Natural or legal persons must additionally demonstrate an interest in taking action and prove that the failure to act concerns them directly and individually.

Preliminary rulings

1.7.6   A national court or tribunal may under Art 234 (ex-Art 177) EC refer Community law questions to the ECJ for interpretation and must do so where there is no judicial remedy against its decision under national law. The ECJ provides answers to enable the national court to determine the case before it. Natural and legal persons thus have a means to challenge the legality under Community law of national or Community measures.

1.7.7   In relation to national legislation, proceedings in national courts have provided individuals with a way of enforcing Community law that has direct effect, ever since the ECJ expounded that principle in 1963[1]. Through Art 234 references, successful challenges have been mounted against the defective implementation by Member States of various Community provisions related to food. Particular examples have concerned the use of preservatives and antioxidants[2] and the labelling of deep frozen yoghurt[3] and artificial sweeteners[4]. However, as with Art 226 actions by the Commission, the most significant ECJ decisions resulting from Art 234 references have related to Member States' national laws that hindered free trade. Among the many examples of foods that have formed the subject of such proceedings are the low alcohol blackcurrant liqueur '*Cassis de Dijon*' (in the leading case noted in para **1.3.1** above), wine vinegar[5], pasta products[6] and Emmenthal cheese without rind[7].

Sometimes a Member State's dubious import restriction has been attacked in the ECJ through a 'pincer movement' which involves both an Article 226 action by the Commission and an Article 234 reference resulting from proceedings by disgruntled traders in the national court. For example, an Italian minimum fat standard for cheese imposed on imports from other Member States was declared illegal by the ECJ on 11 October 1990 not only in infraction proceedings by the Commission, but also in a reference from the Pretore di Milano[8].

1 See para **1.2.1** text and n 1.
2 Case 88/79 *Ministére Public v Grunert* [1980] ECR 1827.
3 Case 298/87 *Smanor* [1988] ECR 4489.
4 Case C-241/89 *SARPP v Chambre Syndical des Raffineurs et Conditionneurs de Sucre de France* [1990] ECR I-4695.
5 Case 788/79 *Gilli and Andres* [1980] ECR 2071.
6 Case 407/85 *Drei Glocken* [1988] ECR 4233.
7 Case C-448/98 *Jean-Pierre Guimont* [2000] ECR I-10663.
8 See respectively case C-210/89 *Commission v Italy* [1990] ECR I-3697 and case C-196/89 *Italy v Nespoli and Crippa* [1990] ECR I-3647.

1.7.8   Since 1991 the scope for individuals to take action in national courts has been extended by the ECJ's decision that compensation can in principle be obtained from a Member State for damage caused by breach of Community law irrespective of whether the provision in question is directly effective[1]. Compensation may, for example, be awarded for obstructing the free movement of goods[2] and for failure to implement a Directive[3]. The conditions for reparation are: (i) that the rule of law infringed must have been intended to confer rights on individuals; (ii) that the breach must be sufficiently serious; and (iii) that there must be a direct causal link between the breach of the obligation resting on the State and the damage sustained by the injured parties. In principle, a Member State can be rendered liable for damages even by a breach of Community law resulting from the decision of a national court of last instance although, for condition (ii) to be fulfilled in such a case, the breach would have to be manifest and very serious indeed [4].

This Community law-based remedy is additional to an English law action for misfeasance in a public office that would lie where, in an exceptional case, the breach of Community law was found to be a deliberate abuse of power. Such an action was brought by French turkey importers to reclaim damages suffered as a result of a UK poultrymeat import ban[5]. As indicated in para **1.7.2** above, the ban had been declared illegal in case 40/82.

1 Joined cases C-6 and 9/90 *Francovich v Italy* [1991] ECR I-5357. As to 'direct effect' generally, see para **1.2.1**. As to civil proceedings against competitors, see para **21.1.1** below.
2 See, for example, joined cases C-46/93 and C-48/93 *Brasserie du Pêcheur and Factortame* [1996] ECR I-1029; and case C-5/94 *R v Ministry of Agriculture, Fisheries and Food, ex p Hedley Lomas* [1996] ECR I-2553.
3 See, for example, joined cases C-178/94, C179/94 and C-188/94 to C-190/94 *Dillenkofer v Germany* [1996] ECR I-4845.
4 Case C-224/01 *Köbler v Austria* [2003] ECR I-10239.
5 *Bourgoin SA v Minister of Agriculture, Fisheries and Food* [1986] QB 716.

1.7.9   The legality of Community measures is often considered by the ECJ under Art 234. Not only must they be *intra vires*. They must also in particular, like national measures, respect the free movement of goods principle[1] unless they can be justified on public interest grounds. Recent Art 234 cases in which Community legislation restricting free movement has nevertheless been upheld by the ECJ have related to Regulations (EC) 2081/92 and 1107/96, as regards the protected designations of origin 'Grana Padano'[2] and Prosciutto di Parma'[3] (see further para **10.5.2**), and to food supplements Directive 2002/46/EC[4] (see further para **11.8.1**).

1 See, for example, joined cases 80/77 and 81/77 *Société Les Commissionaires Réunis SARL v Receveur des douanes; SARL Les fils de Henri Ramel v Receveur des douanes* [1978] ECR 927, para 35.
2 Case C-469/00 *Ravil v Bellon* [2003] ECR I-5053.

3   Case C-108/01 *Consorzio del Prosciutto di Parma v Asda Stores Ltd* [2003] ECR I-5121.
4   Joined cases C-154/04 and C-155/04 *Alliance for Natural Health* [2005] ECR I-6451.

1.8   THE EUROPEAN ECONOMIC AREA (EEA) AND THE EUROPEAN FREE TRADE ASSOCIATION (EFTA)

1.8.1   The EEA Agreement is a treaty between the Member States of the European Union[1] and the three EFTA states, Norway, Iceland and Liechtenstein. It is basically implemented in the United Kingdom by the European Economic Area Act 1993.

The EEA Agreement is of concern to food and feed law because, as between contracting States, it provides for the application of the EC Treaty and secondary legislation rules on the free movement of goods. By contrast with Community law, however, the freedom of trade established by Art 8(1) of the Agreement is generally limited to products originating in the contracting States: by virtue of Art 8(2), it does not extend to products from third countries unless otherwise specified. Moreover, the EEA Agreement did not adopt the common agricultural policy.

The products covered by the EEA Agreement are mainly specified in Art 8(3). Agricultural products (including prepared foodstuffs) are not generally caught, but some are specified in Protocol 3 to the Agreement and substantial groups of products are brought in through EEA adoption of Community harmonising provisions by Art 17 and Annex I chapter I (veterinary issues) and chapter II (feedingstuffs), and by Art 23 and Annex II chapter XII (foodstuffs)[2].

Within its limits, the EEA closely shadows the European Community. The Agreement adopted pertinent rulings of the European Court[3] thus, for example, applying the *Cassis de Dijon* doctrine described in section **1.3** above and limiting the scope for national import restrictions on food originating in the EEA contracting States[4].

EFTA countries are consulted on relevant proposals for Community legislation and, when this has been enacted, the EEA Joint Committee implements parallel EEA rules[5]. For example, the EEA Agreement has recently been amended to apply Regulations (EC) 852/2004 (food hygiene), 853/2004 (hygiene of food of animal origin), 854/2004 (official controls on products of animal origin), 882/2004 (official feed and food controls) and, subject to adaptations, 178/2002 (general food). The adoption of this package of food law measures has in particular formalised EEA-EFTA participation in the European Food Safety Authority and in the Rapid Alert System for Food and Feed[6].

The EFTA Surveillance Authority and EFTA Court have functions akin to those of the European Commission and the European Court, and provision is made for coordination and reconciliation of differences by the EEA Joint Committee[7]. That the ECJ and EFTA Court take careful account of each other's rulings may be seen from their respective judgments concerning national prohibitions on food fortified with vitamins and minerals[8]. Moreover, the ECJ is competent to interpret the EEA Agreement as an act of a Community institution within the meaning of Art 234 EC[9].

1   By EEA Agreement Art 128, a country becoming a Member of the EU shall also apply for membership of the EEA. On 25 July 2007 an instrument was signed to enlarge the EEA to include Bulgaria and Romania and thus embrace all 27 current EU Member States. At the time of writing, the instrument is in course of ratification by national parliaments.

2   Thus, unlike beer, wine is not caught by Art 11 EEA prohibiting, between the Contracting
      Parties, quantitative restrictions on imports and all measures having equivalent effect. See, for
      example, case E-9/00 *EFTA Surveillance Authority v Norway* [2002] EFTA Court Report 72,
      para 30.
3   Article 6 EEA.
4   See case E-1/94 *Restamark* [1994–1995] EFTA Court Report 15, para 51.
5   Article 102 EEA.
6   See paras **3.3.1** and **7.3.4** respectively.
7   Part VII Chapter 3 EEA.
8   See case E-3/00 *EFTA Surveillance Authority v Norway* [2000–2001] EFTA Court Report 73;
      and case C-192/01 *Commission v Denmark* [2003] ECR I-9693.
9   See, for example, case C-286/02 *Bellio F.lli Srl v Prefettura di Treviso* [2004] ECR I-3465.

1.9   THE INTERNATIONAL DIMENSION

The European Union and international organisations

1.9.1   Together with its Member States, the European Union joined the
World Trade Organisation (WTO) when it was established in 1995 as the global
international body to deal with the regulation of trade between nations[1]. Since
then, WTO rules have been invoked on a number of occasions to support
demands by third countries for changes to European Community food law. In
particular, there have been high profile disputes with the USA and others over
hormones in meat and retaliatory measures[2], protection of geographical
indications[3] and biotechnical products[4].

WTO rules of special relevance to food and feed are to be found in the
agreement on Sanitary and Phytosanitary Measures (SPS) that covers safety,
the agreement on Technical Barriers to Trade (TBT) that embraces consumer
protection, and the agreement on Trade-Related Aspects of Intellectual
Property Rights (TRIPS) that includes the protection of geographical
indications. Also of importance is the Understanding on Rules and Procedures
Governing the Settlement of Disputes that, as its name suggests, provides a
forum for resolving disagreements between signatories.

The endorsement by the SPS and TBT Agreements of international standards
for the purpose of protecting health and consumer interests has enhanced the
role of the Codex Alimentarius Commission, the World Organisation for
Animal Health (OIE)[5]and other international organisations that prescribe them.

1   Decision 94/800/EC.
2   See as yet unresolved disputes WT/DS 26, 48, 320 and 321.
3   See disputes WT/DS 174 and 290 resolved by the making of Regulation (EC) 510/2006. See
      also COM(2005) 698 final/2.
4   See disputes WT/DS 291, 292 and 293 in which, on 29 September 2006, a disputes panel ruled
      against Community approval and marketing practices in respect of genetically modified
      products. The Commission decided not to appeal the ruling and is currently seeking to arrange
      Community compliance with it.
5   Until May 2003 the Organisation was known as the International Office of Epizootics and has
      retained its historic acronym.

The Codex Alimentarius Commission

1.9.2   The Codex Alimentarius Commission was jointly set up in 1962 by the
FAO and WHO to protect the health of consumers, to ensure fair practices in the
food trade and to draw up international food standards. It now has a
membership of 177 countries, including the European Union that, at the end of
2003, joined its Member States as a member of the Codex[1].

The Codex Alimentarius Commission is supported by a series of committees that have developed a significant number of vertical and horizontal food standards. Although not binding on member countries, a considerable influence has in practice been exercised over national and Community law[2] and this may reasonably be expected to increase now that the WTO SPS and TBT Agreements have effectively made Codex standards the basis for evaluating food measures[3].

1   Decision 2003/822/EC.
2   As in sundry European Court judgments. See, for example, case 178/84 *Commission v Germany* [1987] ECR 1227 para 44 (additives in beer); case 298/87 *Smanor* [1988] ECR 4489 para 22 (deep-frozen yoghurt); case C-448/98 *Criminal Proceedings against Jean-Pierre Guimont* [2000] ECR I-10663 para 32 (Emmenthal cheese without rind); and case C-236/01 *Monsanto Agricolta Italia SpA v Presidenza del Consiglio dei Ministri* [2003] ECR I-8105 para 79 (safety assessment of food from genetically modified maize).
3   See para **1.9.1**.

1.10   SOURCES OF INFORMATION

1.10.1   For busy practitioners, the problem often is to be able to check quickly the latest developments on a particular aspect of food law. A list of useful addresses, websites and contact numbers is to be found in Appendix D.

Chapter 2

Central and local government control of food

2.1 FOOD STANDARDS ACT 1999 AND DEVOLUTION

2.1.1   Responsibility for administration of food law was essentially determined when modern legislation began to be enacted in the second half of the nineteenth century[1]. Prior to the Food Standards Act 1999 (FSA 1999) and the 1998 devolution changes, central government responsibilities for policy and legislation were primarily borne by the Minister of Agriculture, Fisheries and Food, who took the lead on food composition and chemical safety, and by the Secretary of State for Health, who led on hygiene and biological safety except in respect of the hygiene of meat, milk, eggs and egg products that were perceived to fit most readily with the minister's agricultural responsibilities. The Scottish and Welsh Secretaries also shared responsibility under the Food Safety Act 1990 (FSA 1990). The bulk of enforcement work was in the hands of county councils and district councils where the division between the composition and the hygiene of food was reflected in the respective responsibilities of their trading standards officers and environmental health officers.

By the late 1990s a decade of food problems, and above all the BSE/CJD crisis, had eroded public confidence in this structure. Three main weaknesses in it were identified by the James Report of 30 April 1997[2]. They were:

(1)   the conflict between the functions of the Minister of Agriculture, Fisheries and Food under the food legislation and his promotional responsibilities for the agricultural, fishing and food industries;

(2)   the fragmentation and lack of coordination between the different bodies involved in food policy and in the monitoring and control of food safety; and

(3)   the uneven enforcement of food law.

As a solution, the Report proposed a Food Standards Agency, which was fully established on 1 April 2000 by the FSA 1999[3]. This chapter explains the FSA 1999 and devolution legislation as it relates to food and feeding stuffs. In summary, the Agency is responsible for the development of United Kingdom food policy to the Secretary of State for Health and devolved authorities, who took over food functions from the Minister of Agriculture, Fisheries and Food. The Agency is a non-ministerial government department with the important power to make public the advice it has given to the Secretary of State and others. It is able to survey the full range of activities connected with the production and supply of food and feeding stuffs, to sponsor necessary regulations and to set standards for, and monitor the performance of, local authority food law enforcement. A number of other public bodies inevitably remain involved in food matters and enforcement (notably the Department in the charge of the Secretary of State for Environment, Food and Rural Affairs who succeeded to the central agricultural functions when the Ministry of Agriculture, Fisheries and Food was wound up[4]), but with the establishment of the Agency there now exists a central department dedicated to and capable of safeguarding public health and protecting consumer interests in relation to food and feeding stuffs.

1   See para **1.1.1**.
2   see para **1.1.6**.
3   Food Standards Act 1999 (Commencement No 1) Order 2000; and Food Standards Act 1999 (Commencement No 2) Order 2000. See also the Food Standards Act 1999 (Transitional and Consequential Provisions and Savings) (England and Wales) Regulations 2000.
4   See the Ministry of Agriculture, Fisheries and Food (Dissolution) Order 2002 and paras **2.2.4–2.2.7** below.

2.1.2   The establishment of the Scottish Parliament and the National Assembly for Wales has also had significant effects on central government food and feeding stuffs control.

Since Scotland has a jurisdiction separate from that in England and Wales, the law there falls outside the scope of this book. It should, however, be observed that among the subjects devolved to Scottish Ministers by and under the Scotland Act 1998 (SA 1998) are food, food contact materials, feeding stuffs and agricultural and horticultural produce[1]. On the other hand, consumer protection, product standards, safety and liability and weights and measures are generally reserved matters[2] and outside legislative and devolved competence[3].

In Wales, food and feeding stuffs and other agricultural functions, including the power to make secondary legislation, were devolved to the National Assembly by the National Assembly for Wales (Transfer of Functions) Order 1999 and subsequent Orders[4] made under the Government of Wales Act 1998 (GWA 1998)[5]. The long list of functions thus transferred included, in particular and subject to minor exceptions, not only those under the FSA 1990, but also those under the AA 1970, the Food and Environment Protection Act 1985 Part I and the Agriculture and Horticulture Act 1964[6], as well as under various statutory instruments. So that the 1999 Order took account of changes made in other legislation by the Food Standards Act 1999, those changes were treated as having preceded the devolution provisions[7].

These constitutional arrangements were significantly revised by the Government of Wales Act 2006, as amended (GWA 2006), in particular so as to separate the executive and legislative branches of the Assembly. The functions for Wales, including those described above, have been largely transferred from the Assembly to the Welsh Ministers[8]. Although the Assembly has thus lost to the Welsh executive the power to make statutory instruments, it continues to scrutinise them and, under Part 3 of and Sch 5 to the GWA 2006, has gained a power to make 'Assembly Measures' in respect of matters specified in the Schedule, as amended from time to time by Order in Council approved by each House of Parliament, or by Act of Parliament. Among the 'Fields' to which such a matter must relate and which are initially specified in the Act are 'food' (Field 8) and 'agriculture, fisheries, forestry and rural development' (Field 1). Competence to make Assembly Measures is circumscribed by the restrictions in Sch 5, Part 2 as read with the exceptions in Part 3. In particular, a Measure cannot change functions of Ministers of the Crown or, generally speaking, the provisions of an Act of Parliament.

Part 4 of and Schs 6 and 7 to the GWA 2006 admit the future possibility of primary legislation by the Assembly ('Assembly Acts') in respect of specified subjects, including 'food' and 'agriculture, fisheries, forestry and rural development'. However, the pre-condition for this is a favourable referendum, the holding of which is itself subject, in particular, to approval by each House of Parliament and by two thirds of the Assembly.

Transferred subordinate legislative powers continue to be exercisable by the Whitehall Minister for the purpose of implementing Community obligations or dealing with matters arising out of or related to them[9], although s 59 of the GWA 2006 enables the Welsh Ministers, like Ministers of the Crown, to be designated to exercise the power conferred by s 2(2) of the European Communities Act 1972 (ECA 1972) to make subordinate legislation to implement Community law[10].

1 SA 1998, ss 29 and 53 and Sch 5, s C8; and the Scotland Act 1998 (Transfer of Functions to the Scottish Ministers etc) Orders 2005 and 2006.
2 SA 1998, s 30 and Sch 5, ss C7, C8 and C9. There seem to be some anomalies: for example, trade descriptions and misleading and comparative advertising specifically in relation to feeding stuffs are evidently reserved matters.
3 SA 1998, ss 29 and 54.
4 See the National Assembly for Wales (Transfer of Functions) Orders 2000 and 2004.
5 GWA 1998, s 22.
6 As to the relevance of these provisions in the present context, see below section **17.2**; para **7.4.12**; and paras **10.4.16** and **10.4.17**.
7 See FSA 1999, s 40(3). For kindred provision in relation to the SA 1998, see FSA 1999, ss 18(2) and 40(2).
8 GWA 2006, s 162 and Sch 11, para 30.
9 GWA 1998, s 22(5) and Sch 3, Pt II, para 5 re-enacted by the GWA 2006. s 58 and Sch 3, para 5, as read in conjunction with s 162 and Sch 11, para 26(1). For the kindred power in relation to Scotland, see SA 1998, s 57.
10 See SIs 2005/1971 and 2766 as regards food and agriculture respectively. (It should be noted that important amendments have now been made to the ECA 1972 by the Legislative and Regulatory Reform Act 2006, s 27.)

2.1.3   The Food Standards Agency thus reports to the Secretary of State for Health and his counterparts in the devolved administrations, but operates at arm's length from them in developing policy and in carrying out its other other functions. In consequence, there is a rather complex network of central government responsibilities, the main elements of which are described in sections **2.2** and **2.3** below. To facilitate 'joined up government', the reciprocal administrative relationships that the Agency has with the Department of Health, the Department for Environment, Food and Rural Affairs and other relevant government Departments are recorded in published 'administrative concordats' which set out the respective Departmental responsibilities.

2.2   MINISTERIAL RESPONSIBILITIES

The Secretary of State for Health and the Food Safety Act 1990

2.2.1   If the complexities of devolution[1] are discounted, ministerial responsibility under the FSA 1990 was simplified by the FSA 1999. The functions formerly exercised by the Minister of Agriculture, Fisheries and Food were essentially passed to the Secretary of State[2] who will normally, but not always[3], be the Secretary of State for Health as minister responsible for Food Standards Agency interests.

The power to make regulations under the FSA 1990 is exercised, not by the Agency, but by the Secretary of State – or in Wales and Scotland, by the devolved authorities. Although the protection of public health is paramount, political judgments on legislation must take account of economic and other factors beyond the Agency's remit. However, as indicated in para **2.3.3**(a) below, the Agency is the primary source of policy advice on food safety and standards and, in particular, drafts necessary subordinate legislation. Moreover, the Government cannot brush aside Agency recommendations. Using the power explained in para **2.3.7**(d) below, the Agency publishes its advice to ministers who in consequence would have to justify publicly any decision to reject it.

1   See para **2.1.2** above.
2   See FSA 1999, s 26(1)(b) and also ss 18 and 40(1) together with Schs 3 and 5.
3   See, for example, paras **2.2.5** and **2.2.7** below.

The Secretary of State for Health and feeding stuffs

2.2.2   Despite the Agency's extensive functions in respect to animal feeding stuffs[1], responsibility for making regulations on the composition and labelling in Great Britain under Part IV of the AA 1970 remains with ministers. For Wales and Scotland the responsibility is devolved[2], while in England – by virtue of reg 14 of the Food Standards Act 1999 (Transitional and Consequential Provisions and Savings) (England and Wales) Regulations 2000 and art 2 of the Ministry of Agriculture, Fisheries and Food (Dissolution) Order 2002 – it now rests with the Secretary of State, that is, again in practice the Secretary of State for Health. Although continued application of reg 14 is dependent on the non-exercise of the power in FSA 1999, s 30 to make provision for feeding stuffs, it now seems unlikely, for the reasons explained in para **2.3.9**(e) below, that the s 30 power will ever be invoked.

In any event, ministerial powers were to some degree strengthened by the FSA 1999 in relation to the control of feeding stuffs because, as mentioned in para **4.1.4** below, Sch 5, para 23 extended the regulatory powers of the FSA 1990 to cover the production of food sources.

For feeding stuffs of a veterinary nature mentioned in para **2.2.5**, the Secretary of State for Environment, Food and Rural Affairs has lead responsibility.

1   See in particular para **2.3.4** below.
2   See the National Assembly for Wales (Transfer of Functions) Order 1999, Sch 1 and the Government of Wales Act 2006, s 162 and Sch 11, para 30. See also the SA 1998, ss 29 and 53 and Sch 5, s C8 and the Scotland Act 1998 (Transfer of Functions to the Scottish Ministers etc.) Order 2006.

The Secretary of State for Health and other primary legislation

2.2.3   The FSA 1999 transferred to the Secretary of State for Health other functions concerning food. Paragraph 4 of Sch 5 to the 1999 Act amended the Trade Descriptions Act 1968 (TDA 1968) so that orders under the latter Act concerning food or feeding stuffs are now made jointly by the Health Secretary with the Board of Trade[1].

More important, however, are functions in respect of making emergency orders under Part I of the Food and Environment Protection Act 1985 (F&EPA 1985)[2]. In relation to England, they are now conferred on the Secretary of State[3]. In addition to being able to make emergency orders[4], the Secretary of State has power, shared with the Food Standards Agency, to consent to the doing of things that would otherwise contravene an emergency order and to give directions in relation to an emergency order[5], as well as power to confer authority on investigation and enforcement officers[6].

In relation to Wales, the functions under the 1985 Act, Part I, are now transferred to Welsh Ministers but those under s 1(1) and s 3(1) and (2) are exercisable concurrently with the Secretary of State[7].

1 TDA 1968, s 38(2A).
2 As to emergency orders under the F&EPA 1985, Pt I, see further paras **7.4.12–7.4.13** below.
3 See F&EPA 1985, s 1(2), as amended by SI 1999/1756, and FSA 1999, s 26(1)(a) and Sch 5, para 6. By virtue of these provisions, a further amendment made by SI 2000/2040 and the definition of 'Scottish zone' in the Scotland Act 1998, s 126(1), the Scottish Ministers act in relation to Scotland and the sea within British fishery limits adjacent to Scotland.
4 F&EPA 1985, s 1.
5 F&EPA 1985, s 2.
6 F&EPA 1985, s 3.
7 See the National Assembly for Wales (Transfer of Functions) Order 1999, SI 1996/672, art 2(a) and (b) and Sch 1 and the Government of Wales Act 2006, s 162 and Sch 11, para 30.

The Secretary of State for Environment, Food and Rural Affairs and food-borne zoonoses and transmissible spongiform encephalopathies

2.2.4   The development of a strategy for reduction of zoonoses throughout the foodchain is an important aspect of the Agency's function of protecting public health from risks that may arise in connection with the consumption of food. However, in view of the veterinary expertise of his department and his responsibilities in particular under the Animal Health Act 1981 (AHA 1981), the Secretary of State for Environment, Food and Rural Affairs, with the devolved authorities[1], retains responsibility for aspects of the strategy on farm up to the point of slaughter[2]. In consequence that Secretary of State has made the subordinate legislation to implement Directive 2003/99/EC (on the monitoring of zoonoses and zoonotic agents)[3] and Regulation (EC) 2160/2003 (on the control of salmonella and other specified food-borne zoonotic agents)[4].

As noted in the Concordat with the Department for Environment, Food and Rural Affairs (DEFRA), the Agency leads on the hygiene legislation of milk and milk production[5], including on farm incidents putting milk or milk products at risk of tuberculosis contamination, while DEFRA's Animal Health executive agency is responsible for the control of TB infection in cattle.

The Concordat also emphasises the continuing need for a close working relationship between the two Departments as regards Bovine Spongiform Encephalopathy (BSE) and other Transmissible Spongiform Encephalopathies (TSEs). The Agency is in particular the competent authority for the purposes of the provisions related to specified risk material, mechanically separated meat and slaughtering techniques under the regulations made by the Secretary of State for Environment, Food and Rural Affairs to enforce Regulation (EC) 999/2001 laying down rules for the prevention, control and eradication of certain TSEs[6].

The arrangements for sharing information on food-borne zoonoses are explained in para **2.3.9**(c).

1 See the National Assembly for Wales (Transfer of Functions) Order 1999, Sch 1 and the Government of Wales Act 2006, s 162 and Sch 11, para 30. See also the SA 1998, ss 29 and 53.
2 See AHA 1981, s 29 and SI 1988/2264, as amended, and SI 1989/285.

3   See the Zoonoses (Monitoring)(England) Regulations 2007.
4   See, for example, the Poultry Breeding Flocks and Hatcheries (England) Order 2007.
5   DEFRA's Animal Health dairy hygiene inspectors undertake the necessary enforcement inspections on behalf of the Agency.
6   See the Transmissible Spongiform Encephalopathies (England) Regulations 2008 and section **14.6** below.

The Secretary of State for Environment, Food and Rural Affairs and veterinary residues, zootechnical products and medicated feeding stuffs

2.2.5   Through his executive agency, the Veterinary Medicines Directorate, the Secretary of State for Environment, Food and Rural Affairs takes the lead responsibility in the control of veterinary products[1], zootechnical products and medicated feeding stuffs[2] which are not devolved matters[3]. On general policy in relation to the regulation of veterinary products, he is required to consult the Agency[4] which also, by agreement, nominates to the Veterinary Products Committee[5] a member with the expertise to advise on food safety concerns.

Veterinary residues in food[6] are essentially controlled under the FSA 1990. Responsibility in England now falls to the Secretary of State for Environment, Food and Rural Affairs[7] and, in Wales and Scotland, is respectively devolved as explained in para **2.1.2** above.

1   See the European Communities (Designation) (No 2) Order 1999, the Ministry of Agriculture, Fisheries and Food (Dissolution) Order 2002, art 2 and the Veterinary Medicines Regulations 2007.
2   See section **17.6** below.
3   See the National Assembly for Wales (Transfer of Functions) Order 1999 and the Government of Wales Act 2006, s 162 and Sch 11, para 30. See also the SA 1998, Sch 5, section J4 and the Scotland Act 1998 (Transfer of Functions to the Scottish Ministers etc.) Order 2006.
4   See para **2.3.9**(d) below.
5   See para **2.4.13** below.
6   As to veterinary residues, see section **12.8** below.
7   See the Transfer of Functions (Agriculture and Food) Order 1999, art 2(6); the Food Standards Act 1999 (Transitional and Consequential Provisions and Savings) (England and Wales) Regulations 2000, reg 13(1)(d); and the Ministry of Agriculture, Fisheries and Food (Dissolution) Order 2002, art 2.

The Secretary of State for Environment, Food and Rural Affairs and pesticide residues

2.2.6   Primary responsibility for pesticides and pesticide residues[1] lies with the Secretary of State for Environment, Food and Rural Affairs acting through the Pesticides Safety Directorate (PSD). Formerly an executive agency of DEFRA, the PSD was transferred to the Health and Safety Executive on 1 April 2008 following DEFRA's review of its regulatory agencies in accordance with the 2005 Hampton Review of regulators[2]. DEFRA ministers retain overall strategic policy responsibility for pesticides and the PSD retains its distinct identity within HSE. Governance arrangements are being put in place to ensure that all departmental and cross-departmental interests are fully represented.

Regulations on pesticide residues in food and feeding stuffs used to be made under Part III of the F&EPA 1985 in England by the Secretary of State[3] and in Wales jointly by him and Welsh Ministers[4], the function in Scotland having been wholly devolved[5]. Since amendment of the 1985 Act by the FSA 1999, the Food Standards Agency is consulted about regulations and about the general approach to the giving, revocation or suspension of approvals and the imposition of conditions on approvals[6].

F&EPA 1985 seems to have proved increasingly inadequate for the purpose of implementing European Community common agricultural policy pesticide residue legislation, so regulations for this purpose have most recently been made exclusively under s 2(2) of the ECA 1972 for England and Wales together[7].

1 As to pesticide residues, see section **12.7** below.
2 See further para **2.3.2** below.
3 See in particular F&EPA 1985, ss 16(2)(k) and 24; and the Ministry of Agriculture, Fisheries and Food (Dissolution) Order 2002, art 2.
4 See the National Assembly for Wales (Transfer of Functions) Order 1999, Sch 1 and the Government of Wales Act 2006, s 162 and Sch 11, para 30.
5 See the Scotland Act 1998, ss 29 and 53 and Sch 5 section C8.
6 See section **2.3.7**(c)(i) below.
7 See now the Pesticides (Maximum Residue Levels) (England and Wales) Regulations 2008.

The Secretary of State for Environment, Food and Rural Affairs and CAP food standards

2.2.7   Yet another class of legislation for which distinct responsibilities should be noted is comprised of those European Community Regulations that, as part of the common agricultural policy (CAP), prescribe marketing standards or quality marks[1]. Given the framework in which it is made, the Secretary of State for Environment, Food and Rural Affairs plays the central role in implementing this legislation[2]. Since agriculture is a devolved matter[3], he acts in conjunction with authorities in Scotland and Wales and Northern Ireland but, as noted in para **2.1.2** above, retains power to make regulations under the ECA 1972, s 2(2) in respect of the whole of Great Britain[4].

Although the Food Standards Agency has a manifest interest in CAP food standards legislation by virtue of its consumer protection objective[5], it takes direct responsibility only for the milk and milk product designations protected by Art 114(1) of and Annex XII to Regulation (EC) 1234/2007 and the spreadable fat standards specified by Art 115 of and Annex XV to that Regulation[6].

Section 17(2) and other bespoke subordinate legislative powers of the FSA 1990 remain available to the Secretary of State for Environment, Food and Rural Affairs as to the Health Secretary for the purpose of implementing CAP marketing standards Regulations.

1 See respectively sections **10.4** and **10.5** below. Most CAP marketing standards are now prescribed by Regulation (EC) 1234/2007, Title II, Chapter I, Section I and Annexes XIa-XVI.
2 See the European Communities (Designation) Order 1972 and the Ministry of Agriculture, Fisheries and Food (Dissolution) Order 2002, art 2.
3 See SA 1998, ss 29 and 53 and Sch 5, s C8; and National Assembly for Wales (Transfer of Functions) Order 1999, Sch 1 and the Government of Wales Act 2006, s 162 and Sch 11, para 30.
4 See, for example, the Olive Oil (Marketing Standards) Regulations 2003.
5 FSA 1999, s 1(2).
6 See para **10.4.4** below.

2.3   THE FOOD STANDARDS AGENCY

Constitution of the Agency

2.3.1   The Food Standards Agency is a Crown department established by the FSA 1999 for the purposes of carrying out the specific functions conferred by or under the Act[1]. The way in which these functions are carried out is limited by subsequent requirements, particularly those in ss 22 and 23 which relate to the Agency's general objectives[2].

The Agency's main objective in carrying out its functions is to protect public health from risks that may arise in connection with the consumption of food (including risks caused by the way in which it is produced or supplied) and otherwise to protect the interests of consumers in relation to food[3]. Consonant with the scope of the FSA 1990 – and indeed with Community law[4] – the Agency is thus concerned with protecting the public not only from unhealthy food, but also from fraudulent food trading.

The Agency consists of a chairman and deputy chairman and not less than eight or more than 12 other members of whom:

- one member is appointed by the National Assembly of Wales[5];
- two members are appointed by the Scottish Ministers[6];
- one member is appointed by the Department of Health and Social Services for Northern Ireland[7]; and
- the others are appointed by the Secretary of State (in practice, the Secretary of State for Health)[8].

Defined as 'the appropriate authorities' by s 36(1) of the FSA 1999, these authorities also jointly appoint the chairman and deputy chairman and must consult before appointing other members of the Agency[9].

Particular considerations are specified that the authorities are required to take into account before making appointments[10]. They must have regard to the desirability of securing that a variety of skills and experience is available among the Agency's members (including experience in matters related to food safety or other interests of consumers in relation to food). They must also consider whether prospective appointees have financial or other interests that are likely to prejudice the exercise of their duties. Such interests will not automatically disqualify a person from appointment as a member. Under para 9 of Sch 1, the Agency is obliged to establish a register of private interests and, although not specifically required by the Act, the Board's Standing Orders provide for exclusion of any member having such an interest in a matter under discussion.

The Agency is a body corporate, detailed provision being made by FSA 1999, s 2(4) and Sch 1 for tenure, remuneration and parliamentary disqualification of members, for the appointment of staff, for proceedings and execution of documents, and for delegation of powers. Paragraph 12(2) of Sch 1 preserves the rule in *Carltona Ltd v Works Comr*[11] whereby officials of central government may exercise the powers of their minister or Agency without formal delegation of authority.

Provision is also made for appointment of a chief executive and Directors for Wales, Scotland and Northern Ireland, who are responsible for securing that the Agency is run efficiently and effectively within their own respective remits[12].

Besides its headquarters in London, the Agency has Scottish, Welsh and Northern Irish Executives established in Edinburgh, Cardiff and Belfast to develop and implement, within the overall framework set by the Agency, policies on food issues that are specific to their own countries. They provide support to their Parliaments, Assemblies and Ministers on the Agency's local activities, and prepare legislation, modified to meet local needs, as required to implement the Agency's policies. The Agency is accountable to the relevant devolved legislatures for its activities within and for their geographical areas.

The other main element of the Agency is its Meat Hygiene Service (MHS). As explained at para **14.3.3** below, the MHS's principal function is inspection and enforcement of legislation in approved British fresh meat premises[13]. In July 2007, the Agency endorsed the key recommendations of the MHS Review of the Delivery of Official Controls in Approved Meat Premises with the object of aligning it more closely with regulation of other foods by adopting a more risk and evidence-based approach.

The Agency's annual report is laid before Parliament, the National Assembly of Wales, the Scottish Parliament and the Northern Ireland Assembly in accordance with FSA 1999, s 4 and Food Advisory Committees, set up under s 5 and Sch 2, advise the Agency on food safety and standards matters related to Wales, Scotland and Northern Ireland respectively. Under these provisions, the Secretary of State may, after consulting the Agency, establish a committee for England or any English region, while the Agency was given power, which as can be seen from section **2.4** below has been vigorously exercised, to take over pre-existing non-statutory advisory committees and, after consultation, to abolish committees and to set up new ones.

Financial provision for the Agency is made by the FSA 1999, s 39 and Sch 4, as amended by the Government of Wales Act 2006 (Consequential Modifications and Transitional Provisions) Order 2006.

1   FSA 1999, s 1(1) and (3).
2   See para **2.3.8**(a) and (b) below.
3   FSA 1999, s 1(2).
4   See para **3.2.5** below regarding Regulation (EC) 178/2002 Art 5.
5   See para **2.1.2** above regarding the GWA 2006.
6   'Scottish Ministers' is a collective term for the members of the Scottish executive of the devolved administration. See SA 1998, s 44(2).
7   Renamed the Department of Health, Social Services and Public Safety by the Departments (Northern Ireland) Order 1999. Powers are now vested in the NI Executive – see the Northern Ireland Acts 1998 and 2000 and the Northern Ireland Act 2000 (Restoration of Devolved Government) Order 2007.
8   FSA 1999, s 2(1).
9   FSA 1999, s 2(2).
10   FSA 1999, s 2(3).
11   [1943] 2 All ER 560.
12   FSA 1999, s 3.
13   In Northern Ireland, the function is undertaken for the Agency by the Department of Agriculture and Rural Affairs' Veterinary Public Health Unit.

2.3.2   Within this constitutional structure, the Agency has developed its approach in updated Strategic Plans setting out what it wishes to achieve over the ensuing period, together with annual Corporate Plans showing the short-term goals and milestones against which it measures and reports its progress. The current Strategic Plan runs to 2010 and articulates the Agency's core values as Putting the consumer first; Openness and independence; and Science and evidence-based.

'Putting the consumer first' and 'independence' are, as explained above, integral to the Agency, which also quickly established a reputation for 'openness'. In particular, the provision in its published Code of Practice for open Board meetings initially set it apart from most other organisations. An independent review of its openness commissioned by the Agency concluded that it had performed well but that there were weaknesses that should be addressed if trust and goodwill was not to be eroded[1].

'Science and evidence-based' decision making has likewise from the outset been vital to the Agency's operation, but extra efforts have recently been made to improve performance. It now publicises, via the Chief Scientist's blog, how the latest scientific evidence underpins its consumer advice and policies; and it has improved its scientific governance by making the Chief Scientist the head of the profession for the Agency's staff who are scientists, by separating his role from that of the Chief Executive and by arranging that the chairs of scientific advisory committees sit in on the Open Board meetings[2]. Additionally, the Agency has established a new General Advisory Committee on Science that will provide independent advice on the Agency's governance and use of science[3].

The current Strategic Plan also maintains the Agency's key aims of Food Safety, Eating for Health and Choice, together with the supporting strategies for their delivery. Of these aims, 'Food Safety' and 'Choice' at base pursue the traditional regulatory objectives of protecting the consumer's health and pocket: particular strategic targets are respectively 'delivering proportionate BSE and TSE controls based on the latest scientific knowledge' and 'to protect consumers from food fraud and illegal practices'. For the former purpose, in pursuit of its aim of reducing foodborne illness by 20% and on the lines of pilot local 'scores on the doors' schemes, the Agency has consulted on a UK wide system to notify consumers of how well particular food businesses are complying with food hygiene regulations. For the latter purpose, the Agency is following up the recommendations of the Food Fraud Task Force that it established to help tackle trade in illegal food. The Task Force focussed on the meat sector where there have been serious abuses[4]. The aim is to apply the lessons learnt to the rest of the food industry[5]. To assist in the investigation of major meat frauds, the Agency sought and has been authorised to acquire specified communications data under the Regulation of Investigatory Powers Act 2000[6]. The Agency has also established a national Food Fraud Database that assembles information from local authorities and recently made possible the seizure of a large quantity of counterfeit vodka[7].

The Agency's third key aim – 'Eating for Health'– is related to each of the other two. It overlaps with 'Choice' in regulating nutrition labelling and health claims[8]. But, in providing scientifically based information to reduce diet-related diseases by helping the consumer maintain a healthier diet, it also, like 'Food Safety', aspires to protect public health.

On nutrition, the Agency works closely with the Department of Health that remains responsible for public health policy in which nutritional status is only one of a number of risk factors. In 2006 they together established a Nutrition Strategy Steering Group, under the chairmanship of the Minister of State for Public Health or the Agency chair, for the purpose of encouraging industry, government departments, agencies and non-government organisations to deliver key strategic dietary health objectives, including those in the Government's White Paper on *Choosing Health*[9]. The Agency has been prominent in implementation of the major White Paper initiatives to change the way in which food is promoted to children[10] and to provide 'at a glance' nutritional information on levels of fat, saturated fat, salt and sugar by front of pack signpost labelling [11].

It is apparent from what is said above that a range of actions is available to the Agency in pursuing its objectives. For the purposes of deciding whether it should intervene on a particular issue and of keeping in mind the different options that it has for intervention, in 2006 the Agency published the framework that it will use for regulatory decision making. Among other things, the framework takes account of the published statement of the Agency's Approach to Risk. In pursuance of the 2005 Better Regulation Task Force report[12], the Agency has also published a 2006/2007 Simplification Plan setting out its initiatives to facilitate compliance with food regulations. Complementary to this and following the Hampton Review[13], the Agency is undertaking the 'Changes to Local Authority Enforcement (CLAE) project' in which it is reviewing the current enforcement policy, monitoring, audit arrangements and Framework Agreement so as to establish revised arrangements that will provide local authorities with 'a suite of flexible interventions for improving business compliance'. In implementation of a specific Hampton Review recommendation, the Agency was also expanded on 1 July 2006 to incorporate the work of the Wine Standards Board.

In making the changes described above the Agency was guided by the 2005 Dean Review that it commissioned to assess its performance since inception[14]. Besides the recommendations for closer working with the Department of Health on nutrition and for giving a higher profile to the scientific foundation of the Agency's decisions, mention should be made of the Review's concerns about the taking of consumers' views. The Agency is now implementing a three pronged approach to obtaining consumer input to policy development that will aim to engage with individual consumers, with consumer stakeholders and with 'hard to reach/hard to hear' groups. It is also establishing an Advisory Committee on Consumer Engagement to monitor and advise on the Agency's performance in this regard and a Social Sciences Research Committee to provide independent expert advice on its use of social science[15].

1   Dr JA Bailey Review of *Openness in the Food Standards Agency* (February 2007).
2   See FSA News December 2006/January 2007.
3   See further para **2.4.2** below.
4   See South Yorkshire unfit poultry meat case (Meat Hygiene Enforcement Report January 2001); Denby Poultry Products case (FSA News September 2003); and the Fermanagh Resident Magistrate's decision of 21 August 2006 in *Food Standards Agency Northern Ireland v George McCabe and Eurofreeze (Ireland) Ltd*.
5   See, for example, 'Shoppers deceived in free-range egg scandal' *The Times*, 16 November 2006.
6   See the Regulation of Investigatory Powers (Communications Data) Order 2003, art 3 and Sch 2, Part III.
7   See FSA News October 2008 p. 5.
8   See ch 11.
9   The White Paper on improving public health in England *Choosing Health: Making Healthy Choices Easier* was published by the Department of Health in November 2004 (Cm 6374).
10 See, for example, FSA Press Notice 2004/0499 'Food Standards Agency agrees action on promotion of foods to children'; and the FSA chair's letter of 21 December 2006 to the Chairman of Ofcom on TV Advertising to children. See further para **9.3.2** below.
11 See FSA Press Notice 2006/0636 'Food Standards Agency Board agrees principles for front of pack signposting labelling'.
12 The Better Regulation Task Force Report to the Prime Minister *Regulation – Less is More. Reducing Burdens, Improving Outcomes*. March 2005.
13 Review for HM Treasury on *Reducing administrative burdens: effective inspection and enforcement*: Philip Hampton: March 2005.
14 *2005 Review of the Food Standards Agency*: Rt. Hon. Baroness Brenda Dean of Thornton-le-Fylde: February 2005.
15 See the Consumer Engagement model set out for the Board in FSA 06/10/04 of 12 October 2006.

General functions of the Agency in relation to food

2.3.3   The general functions in relation to food summarised below are conferred on the Agency by ss 6–8 of the FSA 1999.

(a) Development of food policy and provision of advice etc to public authorities

The Agency has the function of (i) developing policy on food safety and standards and (ii) providing advice, information and assistance to public authorities. Within government it is under a duty to provide such advice, information and assistance on request, unless it is not reasonably practicable for it to do so (for example, because the costs of providing any particular item of information would be disproportionate). Such advice, information and assistance, for example, include detailed recommendations to ministers on the need for primary legislation or proposing subordinate legislation to improve food safety and standards. It also represents the UK at working level in relevant European Community and other international fora.

As a UK body, it is the primary source of policy advice in relation to food safety and standards to the Government as a whole, and to the devolved authorities. It also advises other departments on matters for which it is responsible, such as the Department for Business, Enterprise and Regulatory Reform about relevant consumer protection matters.

(b) Provision of advice, information and assistance to other persons

The Agency also has the function of providing advice, information and assistance in respect of matters connected with food safety or other interests of consumers in relation to food to the general public and to anyone other than public authorities. The general public must be kept adequately informed about matters that the Agency considers significantly affect their capacity to make informed decisions about food. The power allows for information to be given to particular sections of the public including groups representative of food industry sectors, such as its *Safer food, better business* hygiene initiative for small catering and retail businesses. Under the power, the Agency has undertaken a whole range of other public information activities ranging from its campaigns to reduce salt consumption and to provide consumers, by signpost labelling, with 'at a glance' details of the nutritional content of food, to the issue of food alerts, as described in section **7.3** below, and the publication of factsheets for those with food allergies, food intolerance and coeliac disease.

(c) Acquisition and review of information

To furnish it with sufficient information for the taking of decisions and performance of its tasks, the Agency has the function of obtaining, compiling and keeping under review information about matters connected with food safety and standards. This function includes monitoring scientific developments and undertaking or commissioning research. As described in its Science Strategy 2005–2010, the Agency's research is organised into the following seven themes derived from and supporting its objectives: food safety (microbiological risks); food safety (TSEs); food safety (chemical and radiological risks); eating for health; choice; underpinning delivery; and FSA Scotland's research programme. Additionally, the Agency collects data by analytical and other surveys in order to monitor the safety, authenticity and nutritional quality of food and to inform international discussions on statutory limits for contaminants in food.

An annual Consumer Attitudes Survey is also mounted for the purpose of ascertaining views on issues such as hygiene, safety, shopping, diet and nutrition and identifying areas that will require future attention.

General functions of the Agency in relation to feeding stuffs

2.3.4   Section 9 of the FSA 1999 provides for the Agency to have the same general functions in relation to matters connected with the safety of animal feeding stuffs and other interests of users of animal feeding stuffs, as are summarised in para **2.3.3** above in relation to matters connected with food safety and other interests of consumers in relation to food. It thus has oversight in respect of medicated feeding stuffs notwithstanding that direct responsibility for them lies with the Secretary of State for Environment, Food and Rural Affairs's Veterinary Medicines Directorate[1].

1   See para **2.2.5** above.

Observations by the Agency with a view to acquiring information

2.3.5   For the purposes of its functions, noted at para **2.3.3**(c) read with **2.3.4** above, of obtaining and keeping under review information relevant to its work, ss 10 and 11 of the FSA 1999 confer powers enabling the Agency to carry out observations. The Agency is authorised to carry out observations with a view to acquiring information about any aspect of the production or supply of food or food sources, or any aspect of the production, supply or use of animal feeding stuffs. The information may in particular concern (a) food premises, food businesses or commercial operations being carried out with respect to food, food sources or contact materials[1], (b) agricultural premises, agricultural businesses or agricultural activities[2] and (c) premises, businesses or operations involved in the production, supply or use of animal feeding stuffs.

Supplementary powers are provided by s 11 that enable the Agency to authorise its staff or agents to enter premises, take samples and inspect records, including health records of food industry workers.

The term 'observations' describes the gathering of general information on food safety and standards through surveillance programmes or other appropriate means. It does not relate to the investigation of particular alleged offences. For these, enforcement authorities use powers in the FSA 1990, the Official Feed and Food Controls (England) Regulations 2007 and other enforcement provisions[3].

1   By FSA 1999, s 36(4), the expressions 'food', 'food source', 'contact material', 'food premises', 'food business' and 'commercial operation', have the same meanings as in FSA 1990 (ss 1 and 53(2)), that statute now having adopted the definition of 'food' in Regulation (EC) 178/2002. See further ch 4.
2   As to 'agricultural activity', 'agricultural business' and 'agricultural premises', see FSA 1999, s 10(3).
3   See further ch 18.

Monitoring by the Agency of enforcement action

2.3.6   The Agency's function of monitoring performance of enforcement authorities[1] in enforcing relevant legislation is conferred by s 12 of the FSA 1999 as supplemented by ss 13–16.

A major weakness in previous arrangements identified by the James Report was the uneven enforcement of food law (see section **2.1** above). Accordingly, the Agency has the function of monitoring and setting standards for the performance of enforcement authorities in enforcing the provisions in and under:

(a)   the FSA 1990;

(b)   the Food Safety (Northern Ireland) Order 1991; and

(c)   Part IV of the AA 1970 relating to matters connected with animal feeding stuffs.

The Agency's monitoring function is extended by the Food Standards Act 1999 (Transitional and Consequential Provisions and Savings) (England and Wales) Regulations 2000, reg 11 so as additionally to cover a specified list of Regulations made under the ECA 1972.

Each annual report of the Agency[2] must give an account of its own performance as an enforcement authority in respect not only of meat and dairy hygiene legislation [3], but also now of wine standards[4].

The Agency may make a report to any other enforcement authority as to their performance including guidance as to improvement. Further, it may direct the authority to arrange for publication of the report and to notify the Agency of action they have taken or propose to take in response.

For the purpose of monitoring enforcement action, the Agency may require specified information from enforcement authorities, their officers and employees and from persons subject to duties enforceable by authorities. Provision is made for powers of entry, sampling, inspection and copying of records and the requiring of assistance. These powers apply to enforcement authority premises, laboratories at which enforcement authority work has been carried out and premises in respect of which the authority powers are or have been exercisable.

Paragraph **2.3.7**(b) below notes how the FSA 1990 has been amended to confer other enforcement powers on the Agency. It may be specified as an enforcement authority for regulations or orders; it may be directed to discharge an enforcement authority's duty; and it may take over the conduct of proceedings either with the consent of the person who instituted them or when directed to do so by the Secretary of State. It may also require the submission of reports and returns by food authorities and be empowered by order to discharge any duty of a defaulting food authority.

The mechanism by which the Agency has exercised its power under FSA 1999, s 12 is the Framework Agreement on Local Authority Enforcement. This requires publicly available local service plans, specifies an agreed enforcement standard, emphasises inspection outcomes and local authority performance, and applies an audit scheme aimed at securing improvements and sharing good practice. Operation of the Agreement is overseen by the Framework Sub-Group of the Enforcement Liaison Group. As noted in para **2.3.2** above, the Agreement is being re-evaluated as part of Agency's major review of enforcement policy in the 'Changes to Local Authority Enforcement (CLAE) project'.

Also to be noted here is the complementary function of monitoring the performance of enforcement authorities that the Agency has under reg 7, as supplemented by regs 8–11, of the Official Feed and Food Controls (England) Regulations 2007 which execute and enforce official controls Regulation (EC) 882/2004[5]. These provisions concern enforcement authority performance in enforcing relevant feed law and relevant food law in respect of which the Agency is designated as a competent authority, other than 'relevant legislation' defined in the FSA 1999, s 15[6].

1 'Enforcement authority' is defined in FSA 1999, s 15(2).
2 See para **2.3.1** above.
3 See para **14.3.3** below.
4 See paras **2.3.2** and **10.4.8**.
5 See section **18.3** below.
6 Official Feed and Food Controls (England) Regulations 2007, reg 10(1). As to publication of information obtained, see para **2.3.7**(d) below.

Other functions of the Agency

2.3.7   Sundry further functions were conferred on the Agency by the FSA 1999. Thus, para 4 of Sch 5 amends the TDA 1968 to require that the Agency be consulted by the Board of Trade before the making of any order of the kind described in para **2.2.3** above[1]. However, the main block of other functions is conferred on the Agency by ss 17–21 of and Sch 3 to the FSA 1999. These functions are summarised below.

(a) Delegation of powers to make emergency orders

The Secretary of State (or appropriate devolved authority) may delegate to the Agency the power to make emergency orders under s 1(1) of the F&EPA 1985 and s 13(1) of the FSA 1990[2]. In practice, the Agency will probably be authorised to act only when the Secretary of State, appropriate devolved authority or authorised member of their respective staffs is unavailable.

(b) Functions of the Agency under the Food Safety Act 1990

The FSA 1999, s 18 and Sch 3, Part I specify the functions conferred on the Agency by the FSA 1990, as amended.

Section 18(2) provides that any amendment made by Sch 3 which extends to Scotland is to be taken as a pre-commencement enactment for the purposes of the SA 1998. Although much of the legislation in question has been devolved, the provisions of the SA 1998 and orders made under it did not generally amend the texts of Acts of Parliament to show what has been done. In consequence when the FSA 1999 amended an Act that has been subject to Scottish devolution, it did not attempt to alter the text to reflect the post devolution responsibilities. Instead the amendments were deemed to pre-date the SA 1998 which automatically made the transfer to the relevant Scottish authority and attracted the powers to make further provision.

As to enforcement, the Agency may be directed to discharge the duties of enforcement authorities under s 6(3) of the FSA 1990[3], may be specified as an enforcement authority for regulations or orders and may take over the conduct of proceedings either with the consent of the person who instituted them or when directed to do so by the Secretary of State.

The Agency also has power, shared with the Secretary of State, to grant consent to the doing of anything prohibited by an emergency control order and give directions to prevent commercial operations with respect to food, food sources or food contact materials to which an emergency control order applies[4].

As to codes of practice under s 40[5], the Agency may, after consulting the Secretary of State, give directions to food authorities as to steps to be taken in order to comply with codes and enforce those directions. It may also undertake consultation with representative organisations regarding proposals for such codes of practice.

Moreover, the Agency may require the submission of reports and returns by a food authority (under s 41)[6], may be empowered by order to discharge any duty of a food authority (under s 42)[7] and may undertake consultation with representative organisations regarding proposals for regulations or orders under the FSA 1990 (under s 48)[8].

(Provision parallel to Sch 3, Part I is made by Part II in respect of the Food Safety (Northern Ireland) Order 1991.)

(c) Functions of the Agency under other Acts besides the Food Safety Act 1990

The FSA 1999, s 18 and Sch 3, Part III specifies functions conferred on the Agency by the provisions of other Acts, as amended. Those provisions that are still extant are summarised below. As explained at (b) above, amendments that extend to Scotland are taken as pre-commencement enactments for the purposes of the SA 1998.

(i) Food and Environmental Protection Act 1985

In relation to emergency orders under Part I of the Food and Environmental Protection Act 1985 (F&EPA 1985)[9], the Agency has the power to give consents and directions and to recover expenses.

In relation to the control of pesticides under Part III[10], the Secretary of State must consult the Agency on regulations and as to the general approach to the giving, revocation or suspension of approvals and the imposition of conditions on approvals. The Advisory Committee on Pesticides[11] must also include one member on the nomination of the Agency.

The Agency also has certain functions in respect of deposits in the sea under Part II of the F&EPA 1985.

(ii) Environmental Protection Act 1990 (EPA 1990)

Functions were conferred on the Agency by amendment to the provisions relating to control of genetically modified organisms ('GMOs') in Part VI of the EPA 1990. The Secretary of State for the Environment, Food and Rural Affairs (together with the devolved authorities)[12] now has lead responsibility for these provisions but the Agency is responsible for the safety of GM food and feeding stuffs. It is the UK competent authority for the purposes of Chapters II and III of GM food and feed Regulation (EC) 1829/2003[13]. In considering applications for consent to release GMOs, the Government is advised by an independent statutory committee, the Advisory Committee on Releases to the Environment (ACRE).

To reflect the Agency's responsibilities for food safety and consumer protection, Part VI was amended so that:

- as regards matters with which it is concerned, the Agency acts jointly with the Secretary of State in requiring persons to apply for authorisation to release, market, import or acquire GMOs or in prohibiting persons from doing any of these things;

- the Agency may be appointed by regulations, jointly with the Secretary of State, to grant exemptions from risk and notification requirements or from the requirement for consent to release, market, import or acquire GMOs;

- the Agency must be consulted before regulations are made (other than those on fees and charges) or consents are granted or varied.

(iii) Radioactive Substances Act 1993 (RSA 1993)

The Agency has the right to be consulted on the grant or variation of authorisations to dispose of radioactive waste in the case of nuclear sites. As to the ending of the functions of the Minister of Agriculture, Fisheries and Food under the RSA 1993, see para **2.3.9**(a) below.

(d) Publication by the Agency of information and advice

Section 19 of the FSA 1999 empowers the Agency to publish advice given by it in accordance with its general functions of developing food policy and providing advice etc to public authorities (paras **2.3.3**(a) and **2.3.4** above) and providing advice, information and assistance to other persons (paras **2.3.3**(b) and **2.3.4** above) or information obtained by it as a result of its observations or enforcement monitoring (paras **2.3.5** and **2.3.6** above).

The Agency's power to publish the advice it gives to ministers is important to its influence and independence. There would obviously be strong moral pressure on ministers to produce convincing reasons were they to contemplate rejecting Agency advice. The power also underpins the Agency's core commitment, mentioned in para **2.3.2** above, to operating in an open and transparent way.

There are certain express limitations on publication. The power cannot be exercised where publication is prohibited by an enactment[14], is incompatible with any Community obligation or would constitute contempt of court. Before deciding to exercise the power, the Agency is required to consider whether publication of the advice or information in question is outweighed by any considerations of confidentiality attaching to it. Subject to these limitations, the Agency may also disclose information to other public authorities, which could, for example, assist them in carrying out their enforcement responsibilities.

It should also be noted that s 19 applies in relation to information obtained through monitoring performance of enforcement authorities under reg 7 of the Official Feed and Food Controls (England) Regulations 2007 as if it were information obtained through FSA 1999, s 12 discussed in para **2.3.6** above.

(e) Power to issue guidance on control of food-borne diseases

Supplementing its general function of giving advice, information and assistance, the Agency has the specific function of issuing general guidance to local authorities and other public authorities (for example, health authorities) on matters connected with the management of outbreaks of 'food-borne disease'. This expression refers to diseases of humans that are capable of being caused by the consumption of infected or otherwise contaminated food. It includes, for example, salmonella, E-coli 0157 and campylobacter. Paragraph

7.2.5 below explains the advice given in the Food Law Code of Practice on food hazards associated with outbreaks of food-borne illness. More specifically, extensive *Guidance on the investigation and control of outbreaks of foodborne disease in Scotland* has been produced by the Agency and the Scottish Executive Health Department.

(f) Supplementary powers

The Agency also has power to do anything that is calculated to facilitate, or is conducive or incidental to, the exercise of its functions. In particular it may carry on educational or training activities, give financial or other support to activities carried on by others, acquire and dispose of property and, in England and Wales and in Northern Ireland, institute criminal proceedings. It may charge for facilities and services it provides.

1   TDA 1968, s 38(2B).
2   See paras **7.4.12-13** and **7.4.8–11** below.
3   See para **2.5.2** below.
4   See para **7.4.12** below. The Agency also has power shared with the Secretary of State, to recover certain expenses incurred in respect of emergency control orders — see FSA 1990, s 13(7) as amended by FSA 1999, Sch 5, para 11(4).
5   See para **2.5.3** below.
6   See para **2.5.3** below.
7   See para **2.5.4** below.
8   See para **4.1.4** below.
9   As to emergency orders under the F&EPA 1985, Pt I, see section **7.4.12** below.
10 As to the control of pesticides, see para **2.2.6** above and section **12.7** below.
11 As to the Advisory Committee on Pesticides, see para **2.4.12** below.
12 See, in particular, the Secretaries of State for Transport, Local Government and the Regions and for Environment, Food and Rural Affairs Order 2001 and the Ministry of Agriculture, Fisheries and Food (Dissolution) Order 2002; the National Assembly for Wales (Transfer of Functions) Orders 1999 and 2000; and the SA 1998, s 53.
13 See further sections **10.3** and **17.9** below.
14 However, see para **2.3.8**(d) below as to the power to relax or lift statutory prohibitions.

General provisions relating to the functions of the Agency

2.3.8   Sections 22–25 of the FSA 1999 make the following general provisions relating to the functions of the Agency.

(a) Statement of general objectives and practices

The Agency is required to prepare and publish (with the approval of the appropriate authorities) a statement of the general objectives it intends to pursue, and general practices it intends to adopt, in carrying out its functions. The statement must remain within the scope of the Agency's main objective set out in s 1(2)[1]. The statement must specifically include objectives (i) securing consultation with interested parties, (ii) promoting links with government departments, local authorities, other public authorities and devolved authorities[2] to ensure that the Agency is consulted on food safety and standards matters, (iii) securing that its decisions and their bases are recorded and available so that the public can make informed judgments, and (iv) notified to the Agency by the appropriate authorities acting jointly. The Agency must publish the objectives after approval by the appropriate authorities, who may (subject to consultation with the Agency) modify them.

In 2000 the Statement of General Objectives and Practices was laid before Parliament and the devolved assemblies and approved by health ministers in

England, Northern Ireland, Scotland and Wales. In particular, it states the Agency's core values as putting the consumer first, openness and independence. By way of working practices, the Agency further undertook that it will be accountable, be open and consultative, be consistent and proportionate and adopt best practices.

(b) Consideration of objectives, risks, costs and benefits etc

In carrying out its functions, the Agency must have due regard for its statement of objectives and practices. It must also take account of the nature and size of the risks relevant to a decision; the likely costs and benefits associated with the action under consideration; and relevant advice or information from an advisory committee[3]. This duty does not apply where it would be unreasonable or impractical for it to do so (e g in relation to decisions on appointments) and does not affect the Agency's obligation to discharge other duties (e g those over which it has no discretion).

(c) Directions relating to breach of duty or to international obligations

The Secretary of State (or devolved authorities[4]) may give the Agency directions if it appears there has been a serious failure by the Agency to pay due regard to its statement of objectives and practices or to take into consideration specified risks, costs and benefits, advice and information (subparas (a) and (b) above), or to perform any other duty.

The Secretary of State (or devolved authorities[5]) may also give the Agency directions for the implementation of UK obligations under the Community Treaties[6] or any international agreement of the United Kingdom. Ministers bear ultimate responsibility for the performance of international obligations but resort to this power is hardly likely to be frequent since, as indicated at para **2.3.3** (a) above, the Agency represents the United Kingdom at working level in the relevant international discussions and thus well informed of most relevant obligations.

The authority giving directions must first have consulted the Agency and other authorities and, if the Agency fails to comply, may give effect to them by exercising the Agency's powers. In the event of non-compliance by the Agency, the Secretary of State[7] may also (with the agreement of the other appropriate authorities) remove all the members of the Agency from office and make other arrangements for carrying out the functions until new appointments are made. Resort to these powers is most unlikely to be needed. Informal methods might generally be expected to secure necessary action.

(d) Power to modify enactments about disclosure of information

Power is conferred on the Secretary of State enabling him by order to remove or relax any statutory prohibition in so far as this appears to prevent disclosure to the Agency of information that would facilitate the carrying out of its functions, or to prevent the Agency from exercising its function of publishing information described in para **2.3.7**(d) above.

1   See para **2.3.1**.
2   That is the Welsh Assembly Government, the Scottish Administration and Northern Ireland Department, see FSA 1999, s 22(2)(b)(ii) as amended by the Government of Wales Act 2006 (Consequential Modifications and Transitional Provisions) Order 2007, art 3 and Sch 1, para 66.
3   See paras **2.3.1** and **2.4.1**.
4   As to Scotland, see FSA 1999, s 24 as amended by the Scotland Act 1998 (Transfer of Functions to the Scottish Ministers etc.) Order 2005.
5   See note 4.
6   See Interpretation Act 1978, Sch 1 and ECA 1972, s 1.
7   See note 4.

Miscellaneous provisions

2.3.9   Sections 26–35 of the FSA 1999 enact certain miscellaneous provisions that are summarised below.

(a)   Statutory functions ceasing to be exercisable by the Minister of Agriculture, Fisheries and Food

In pursuance of the policy of removing the conflict with the promotional responsibilities of the Minister of Agriculture, Fisheries and Food for the agricultural, fishing and food industries, his functions under the FSA 1990[1], Part I of the F&EPA 1985[2] and the RSA 1993[3] were removed by the FSA 1999 and detailed provision for transfer of his responsibilities to the Secretary of State, the devolved authorities and the Agency was made by Schs 3 and 5. The Ministry of Agriculture, Fisheries and Food (Dissolution) Order 2002 dissolved the Ministry, transferring its functions in general to the Secretary of State and its property, rights and liabilities in general to the Secretary of State for Environment, Food and Rural Affairs.

(b)   Notification of tests for food-borne disease

The Secretary of State and the devolved authorities are empowered by s 27 to make regulations requiring the notification of information about tests on samples taken from individuals (whether living or dead) for the presence of (i) organisms of a description specified in the regulations or (ii) any substances produced by or in response to the presence of organisms of a description so specified. The organisms specified must be capable of causing disease in humans and commonly transmitted to humans through the consumption of food. As to civil sanctions for breach of the regulations, see the Regulatory Enforcement and Sanctions Act 2008 described in para **18.3.3** below.

For the present, reporting remains voluntary. Other sources of data are available on human food-borne disease besides diagnostic laboratory reports to the Health Protection Agency Centre for Infections (or, in Wales, the National Public Health Service Communicable Diseases Centre). Moreover, routine tests are available only for some food-borne pathogens and the system records only those cases in which a sample has been tested and a pathogen identified.

(c) Arrangements for sharing information about food-borne zoonoses

The Agency and the ministers and devolved authorities with responsibility for any matter connected with food-borne zoonoses are required to make arrangements for sharing information about food-borne zoonoses and may make arrangements for coordinating their activities. 'Food-borne zoonosis' is defined[4] as any disease of, or organism carried by, animals that constitutes a risk to the health of humans through the consumption of, or contact with, food.

The Concordat between DEFRA and the Agency notes that, in addition to informal contacts between officials, the UK Surveillance Group on Diseases and Infections of Animals, the Agency-DEFRA Foodborne Pathogens Liaison Group and the UK Zoonoses Group provide formal and regular opportunities for sharing information and co-ordinating activities in respect of food-borne zoonoses.

(d) Consultation on veterinary products

The Agency's position was further strengthened in relation to the protection of food from chemical contamination by veterinary residues. Ministers responsible for the regulation of veterinary products (principally the Secretary of State for Environment, Food and Rural Affairs through his executive agency, the Veterinary Medicines Directorate) must consult the Agency on the general policy in relation to this subject[5].

(e) Animal feeding stuffs

Given the effect that feeding stuffs can have on food safety, the Agency was assigned responsibility for them by the FSA 1999[6]. The relevant national legislation for control of their chemical composition and biological safety in and under Part IV of the AA 1970 and the AHA 1981[7] was also perceived to be due for updating and improvement in the light of modern practices and hazards. Section 30 of the FSA 1999[8], therefore, conferred power, now exercisable by the Secretary of State alone, to make provision by order in England and Wales[9] for the regulation of feed based on the FSA 1990. The provisions of the order need not be confined to protecting human health, but may be made with a view to protecting animal health or any other purpose that appears to ministers to be appropriate.

It is doubtful whether the s 30 power will ever be exercised. It has evidently been overtaken by major European Community developments. General food Regulation (EC) 178/2002 has made its own fundamental directly applicable provision for assimilating the feed rules with those prescribed for food[10] and it might be questioned how far, in any case, provisions analogous to those of the FSA 1990 would now be adequate for the purpose of implementing current EC feeding stuffs legislation[11].

(f) Miscellaneous devolution provisions

Further miscellaneous provisions are made by ss 32–35 of the FSA 1999 consequent upon devolution.

A 'Henry VIII' section[12] provides powers, by Order in Council subject to prior consultation with the Agency, to modify the Act to deal with changes that might be required in the light of the unprecedented experience of operating a UK body (the Agency) in a devolved area (essentially, food safety and standards).

Power to act by Order in Council is also provided to deal with the consequences of any legislation by the Scottish Parliament or Northern Ireland Assembly withdrawing functions from the Agency.

The Agency has a duty to take account of activities of the Food Safety Promotion Board for which provision was made as an all-Ireland implementation body following the Belfast Agreement between the United Kingdom and the Republic of Ireland.

Detailed provisions are also made concerning devolution in Scotland.

1 Food functions noted in paras **2.2.5** and **2.2.7** above were in particular retained by the Minister of Agriculture, Fisheries and Food and then passed to to the Secretary of State for Environment, Food and Rural Affairs.
2 See para **2.3.7**(c)(i) above and para **7.4.12** below.
3 See para **2.3.7**(c)(iii) above.
4 FSA 1999, s 28(5).
5 FSA 1999, s 29, as amended by the Ministry of Agriculture, Fisheries and Food (Dissolution) Order 2002 and the Veterinary Medicines Regulations 2007. As to veterinary medicines, see further para **2.2.5** above and section **12.8** below.
6 See in particular paras **2.2.2** and **2.3.4** above.
7 As to the current rules, see ch 17.
8 As amended by the Ministry of Agriculture, Fisheries and Food (Dissolution) Order 2002 and the Feeding Stuffs (Safety Requirements for Food-Producing Animals) Regulations 2004.
9 The Scottish ministers act in relation to Scotland.
10 See ch 3.
11 See, for example, feeding stuffs hygiene Regulation (EC) 183/2005.
12 FSA 1999, s 32, as amended by the Government of Wales Act 2006 (Consequential Modifications and Transitional Provisions) Order 2007.

2.4 ADVISORY COMMITTEES

2.4.1   For many years it was the practice of ministers to appoint non-statutory committees of eminent independent specialists to provide advice on food safety and standards matters and inform their decisions under the FSA 1990 and related legislation. By the FSA 1999, the Food Standards Agency was expressly authorised to establish advisory committees (including joint committees with other public authorities)[1] and, in exercise of its powers, is required to take into account relevant advice and information that they give[2].

Annex 3 to the Agency Chief Scientist's First Annual Report on Science[3] identifies the 10 committees specified in paras **2.4.2** to **2.4.11** as advising the Agency. Of these independent science committees, the four described in paras **2.4.2** to **2.4.5** are its own, while responsibility for the remaining six is shared with other interested Government departments. The Agency is also concerned with the various other committees summarised below.

First, there are the independent pesticides and veterinary products committees described in paras **2.4.12** and **2.4.15**. The Advisory Committee on Pesticides (ACP) and the Veterinary Products Committee (VPC) advise ministers on these groups of chemicals and are singular in being statutory committees established under distinct legislation. They are the respective responsibilities of the HSE Pesticides Safety Directorate and the DEFRA Veterinary Medicines Directorate but, given their relevance to food safety, the Agency, in each case, nominates an independent member with special interest in that subject and provides an assessor and adviser.[4] Additionally, specific advice is needed on pesticide and veterinary residues and for the purpose of overseeing the annual residues surveillance programmes. In 2000 ministers replaced bodies that formerly undertook these functions with the fully independent Pesticide Residues Committee (PRC) and Veterinary Residues Committee (VRC). The Agency nominates a member having specific responsibility for food safety to each Committee and provides specialist advisers.[5]

Further scientific, hygiene and nutritional aspects of food are dealt with by the committees and working groups described in paras **2.4.16-2.4.22**. All but one of these are chaired by Agency officials who also have a major interest in the Department of Health's Food and Drink Advertising and Promotion Forum.

Enforcement liaison committees[6] are not considered in this section, but a summary of Agency advisory committees would certainly be incomplete without reference to those which assist communication with important stakeholders. The Meat Hygiene Policy Forum (MHPF) provides consumers, enforcers, retailers and the meat industry with the opportunity to discuss meat hygiene issues with Agency officials responsible for policy development and implementation. The Industry Stakeholder Forum aims to provide an informal communication channel for stakeholders in the food sector and to give them an opportunity to discuss current and emerging issues with the Agency. And the new Advisory Committee on Consumer Engagement (ACCE) reports on the effectiveness of the Agency's engagement with consumers and makes recommendations for strengthening the way it engages with them[7].

1   FSA 1999, s 5 and Sch 2; and see para **2.3.1**.
2   FSA 1999, s 23; and see para **2.3.8**(b).
3   Document FSA 07//05/05 of May 2007.
4   As to the Pesticides Safety Directorate, see para **2.2.6**.
5   See in particular MAFF Press Release 80/00 of 14 March 2000.
6   For example, the Enforcement Liaison Group and the Animal Feed Law Enforcement Liaison Group.
7   See para **2.3.2**.

The principal scientific committees

2.4.2   General Advisory Committee on Science (GACS)

The GACS is a new committee that provides independent advice on the Agency's governance and use of science. Its work includes horizon scanning, developing good practice and informing science priorities. In addition to the Chairman and six new members, the GACS is composed of the chairs of the nine other scientific committees advising the Agency.

2.4.3   Social Sciences Research Committee (SSRC)

The SSRC is another new committee established to strengthen the Agency's capacity for social science research and to provide it with advice about the acquisition and use of social science evidence.

2.4.4   Advisory Committee on the Microbiological Safety of Food (ACMSF)

The ACMSF provides advice on microbiological issues regarding food. It assesses the risk to humans from micro-organisms that occur in food. For example, it has recently been concerned with the risk of infant botulism from chilled and frozen baby food.

2.4.5   Advisory Committee on Novel Foods and Processes (ACNFP)

The ACNFP advises the Agency on novel foods (including genetically modified foods) and novel processes, including food irradiation. It carries out safety assessments of novel foods and processes submitted for approval under Novel Foods Regulation (EC) 258/97[1]. Since April 2004, foods produced using genetically modified organisms have been subject to risk assessments by the European Food Safety Authority (EFSA) under Regulation (EC) 1829/2003[2], but the ACNFP continues to contribute to these assessments and also to advise the Agency on other issues relating to genetically modified foods.

1   See para **10.3.2** below.
2   See para **10.3.3** below.

2.4.6   Advisory Committee on Animal Feedingstuffs (ACAF)

The ACAF advises on the safety and use of animal feeds and feeding practices, including those that are the subject of EC legislative proposals. Its advice extends widely to cover matters such as animal feed ingredients, including genetically modified organisms, and labelling and information for animal feed purchasers. The Committee's remit is not confined to the consideration of animal health implications: its terms of reference lay specific emphasis on protecting human health.

2.4.7   Spongiform Encephalopathy Advisory Committee (SEAC)

The SEAC advises on transmissible spongiform encephalopathies (TSEs) such as BSE, CJD and scrapie. It provides independent scientific advice and risk assessments on food safety, public health and animal health issues relating to TSEs. The terms of reference in particular include responsibility for advising on the introduction or the reduction, phasing out or withdrawal of control measures to protect human and animal health from TSEs.

2.4.8   Scientific Advisory Committee on Nutrition (SACN)

The SACN is concerned with the scientific aspects of nutrition and health with specific reference to the nutrient content of individual foods and the diet as a whole, including the definition of a balanced diet.

Among specific matters on which the Committee is expected to advise are the nutrition of infants, the elderly and other vulnerable groups, and public health issues, such as cardiovascular disease, in which nutritional status is one of the risks involved.

2.4.9   Committee on Toxicity of Chemicals in Food, Consumer Products and the Environment (COT)

The COT advises Government Departments and Agencies on the toxicity of chemicals in food, consumer products and the environment, including possible chemical causes of ill health in humans. As regards food, it assesses the risk to human health from chemicals that may enter the human food chain either deliberately or inadvertently. Its evaluations may include assessment of carcinogenicity or mutagenicity provided respectively by the COC and the COM described in paras **2.4.10** and **2.4.11**. The COT also advises on general principles and new scientific discoveries in relation chemical toxicity. However,

44

dossiers for new food additives are not as a rule submitted to the COT, but to the EFSA for EC authorisation under Directive 89/107/EEC[1].

1   But see the proposal 2006/0145 (COD) of 28 September 2006 for a Regulation on food additives. See further paras **3.3.9–11** and ch 12 below.

2.4.10   Committee on Carcinogenicity of Chemicals in Food, Consumer Products and the Environment (COC)

The COC advises Government Departments and Agencies on the potential carcinogenicity of chemicals in food, consumer products and the environment, including the possible chemical causes of cancer in humans. Although as with the COT, dossiers for new food additives are generally not presented to the COC, its opinion is sought if there is particular UK concern about their carcinogenicity. The Committee also advises on carcinogenic risks in connection with new scientific discoveries and general science issues. The COC opinions frequently include advice on mutagenicity from the COM described in para **2.4.11**.

2.4.11   Committee on Mutagenicity of Chemicals in Food, Consumer Products and the Environment (COM)

The COM advises on the potential mutagenicity of a wide range of chemicals. It assesses the mutagenic risk to man of substances used or proposed for use in foods, household goods, pharmaceuticals and by industry and those that occur as environmental pollutants. Advice from the COM is often sought by other scientific committees, especially the COT and the COC described above and the Advisory Committee on Pesticides (see para **2.4.12**). The Committee also advises on important general principles and new scientific discoveries in connection with mutagenic risks, and on testing methods and strategies for assessing mutagenicity.

The pesticides and veterinary products committees

2.4.12   Advisory Committee on Pesticides (ACP)

The ACP advises ministers on regulations for the control of pesticides, on approvals of pesticides to be given, revoked or suspended, and on conditions to which approvals are to be made subject[1]. Similar advisory functions are undertaken for central Government in respect of active substances and authorisation of plant protection products under plant protection products Directive 91/414/EEC[2] which is harmonising arrangements for authorisation of plant protection products within the Community.

1   See in particular F&EPA 1985, s 16(7) and (9) and the Control of Pesticides (Advisory Committee on Pesticides) Order 1985.
2   OJ L 230, 19.8.91, p 1; and see the Plant Protection Products Regulations 2005, as amended.

2.4.13   Veterinary Products Committee (VPC)

The VPC advises ministers on veterinary medicinal products and specified feed additives. It hears representations on decisions relating to the granting, refusal, variation, suspension or revocation of marketing authorisation for veterinary products and, for the purpose of advising ministers, promotes the collection of information relating to suspected adverse reactions. Since 2005, the Medicines Act 1968 under which the VPC was originally established no longer applies to veterinary medicines and the Committee now continues in existence under the Veterinary Medicines Regulations 2008.

2.4.14 Pesticide Residues Committee (PRC)

The PRC advises ministers, the Pesticides Safety Directorate and the Agency on the planning of nationwide surveillance programmes for pesticide residues in UK food, on evaluation of the results and on procedures for sampling, sample processing and new methods of analysis. Although these residues have been monitored since the 1950s, it was not until 2000 that this independent Committee was established for the purpose.

2.4.15 Veterinary Residues Committee (VRC)

The VRC advises ministers, the Veterinary Medicines Directorate and the Agency on residues of veterinary medicines and similar substances in samples collected under the Directorate's surveillance programmes, as well as on the observance of withdrawal periods for these products. The terms of reference also require it to advise on the scope and operation of the Directorate's EC surveillance programmes and to formulate and advise on annual non-statutory programmes and on Agency surveys. The fully independent VRC replaced its predecessor, the Advisory Group on Veterinary Residues, in January 2001.

Other scientific, hygiene and nutrition committees

2.4.16 Working Party on Materials and Articles in Contact with Food or Drink (WPFCM)

The Working Party on Materials and Articles in Contact with Food or Drink (WPFCM) advises the Agency on research needed to ensure that consumers are protected from chemical migration into food from packaging and other materials in contact with it.

2.4.17 Working Party on Food Additives

This Working Party provides guidance and information to the Agency on food additives and flavourings with specific reference to the cost-effectiveness and relevance of research and surveillance, assessing new methods of analysis, identifying current and emerging issues and keeping under review the intake of additives in the United Kingdom.

2.4.18 Additives and Authenticity Methodology Working Group (AAMWG)

The AAMGG advises the Agency on measures to prevent misdescription and adulteration of food with specific reference to identifying current and emerging issues, assessing methods of analysis, understanding consumer concerns, advising on and monitoring the food authenticity research programme and encouraging the application of techniques to ensure product authenticity.

2.4.19   Foodborne Disease Strategy Consultative Group

This Group assists the Agency develop and implement strategies for the reduction of foodborne illness – a continuing primary objective of the Agency.

2.4.20   Consultative Group on Campylobacter and Salmonella in Chickens (CGCSC)

The CGCSC assists the Agency to develop and implement strategies for the reduction of campylobacter and salmonella in chickens.

2.4.21   Nutrition Strategy Steering Group (NSSG)

As indicated in para **2.3.2**, this high level Group was established to encourage industry, government departments, agencies and non-government organisations to deliver key strategic dietary health objectives through a range of voluntary nutritional initiatives. Foremost amongst these are the reformulation of food, front of pack signpost labelling with nutritional information, control of food promotion to children and the Healthy Living Social Marketing Campaign, which seeks to reduce obesity through increased physical activity and a balanced diet.

2.4.22   Food and Drink Advertising and Promotion Forum

This Forum, chaired for the Department of Health by the Deputy Chief Medical Officer, was established as part of a series of commitments in the Government's White Paper *Choosing Health*[1] and the Agency's Action Plan on food promotions and children's diets.

1   See para **2.3.2** above.

2.5   FOOD AUTHORITIES

Definition

2.5.1   In implementation of the James Report and subsequent White Paper, the FSA 1999 makes provision, summarised in paras **2.3.6** and **2.3.7** above, for firmer co-ordination and oversight to reinforce the effectiveness of food law enforcement. However, the work continues to be undertaken primarily by local authorities.

In the FSA 1990, the responsible local authorities are designated 'food authorities'. By s 5(1) of that Act, in England they are the London boroughs, the district councils, the non-metropolitan county councils, the Common Council of the City of London, the appropriate Treasurer of the Inner Temple or of the Middle Temple and, as respects the Isles of Scilly, the Council of the Isles of Scilly[1]. By s 5(1A) of the FSA 1990 food authorities in Wales are the county councils and the county borough councils[2].

By s 5(3), where functions under the FSA 1990 are assigned by order, in England and Wales, to a port health authority[3] or joint board for a united district[4] or, in England, to a single authority for former metropolitan counties[5], that authority is deemed to be the food authority in relation to those functions. Section 5 makes parallel provision for Scotland.

1   FSA 1990, s 40(1) and Sch 5, para 9.
2   Local Government (Wales) Act 1994, s 22(3) and Sch 9, para 16.
3   Public Health (Control of Disease) Act 1984, ss 2 and 7.
4   Public Health Act 1936, s 6.
5   Local Government Act 1985, Sch 8, para 15(6).

Enforcement responsibilities under the 1990 Act

2.5.2   By s 6(1) of the FSA 1990, the authority that is to enforce and execute any provision in or under the Act is 'the enforcement authority' with powers to institute proceedings[1] and, through its authorised officers[2], to sample[3], enter and inspect[4].

By s 6(2), every food authority is required to enforce and execute the Act's provisions within their area except where that duty is expressly or by necessary implication imposed on some other authority[5]. Yet the local authority structure in England makes responsibility for food law enforcement somewhat complex.

With the abolition of the Greater London Council and the six metropolitan county councils by the Local Government Act 1985, the London borough and metropolitan district councils became single tier or 'unitary' authorities and, since the Local Government Act 1992, more such authorities have progressively been created, most recently under mechanism provided by the Local Government and Public Involvement in Health Act 2007.

Generally however, as contemplated by the definition described in para **2.5.1**, two tiers of local authority continue to be 'food authorities' in most English areas. This is so where there are both non-metropolitan county and district councils, as well as with the Inner and Middle Temples in the City of London. In such areas the authorities potentially have concurrent enforcement authority functions by virtue of s 6(2). A local authority may arrange for another local authority to discharge functions on its behalf[6], but, in the absence of such an arrangement, the possibility still exists for confusion over which authority is to act in any particular case. To avoid this, provision of two kinds has been made.

First, the Food Safety (Enforcement Authority) (England and Wales) Order 1990[7] provides in relation to such areas, on the one hand, that the functions in respect of emergency prohibition notices and orders[8] shall be exercised only by the district councils (or, within the Temples, by the appropriate Treasurer) and, on the other hand, that the provisions as to false presentation and description of food[9] shall be enforced solely by the county councils (or, within the Temples, by the Common Council of the City of London).

Secondly, advice is provided by ch 1.1 of the Food Law Code of Practice and Practice Guidance[10]. This recommends lead food officers of district and county council food authorities to ensure that effective day-to-day liaison arrangements between their respective authorities are in place, and re-states and develops the traditional division of functions. District councils should investigate and take enforcement action in cases relating to the microbiological quality of food, contamination by micro-organisms and their toxins and contamination by foreign matter. County councils should investigate and take enforcement action in relation to chemical contamination, composition, adulteration and labelling (including cases in which the public analyst has identified a clear risk to health in a submitted sample). Nevertheless, district councils may act, in cases of chemical contamination, where there is an imminent risk to public health, where assigned a role in a Food Alert issued by the Agency[11] and, in labelling cases, where food is sold after the 'use by' date, or where a 'best before' or 'use by' date has been removed[12], as well as in relation to the identification marking requirements of the EC hygiene Regulations[13]. Moreover, county councils should be informed within 28 days by authorities receiving initial registration information under Art 6(2) of Regulation (EC) 852/2004, or approving establishments under Regulation (EC) 853/2004[14]. Finally, although the Quick-Frozen Foodstuffs Regulations 1990[15] concern quality rather than safety so that the county council has primary responsibility, district councils, who enforce other temperature controls, should enforce relevant parts of the Regulations including the verification of temperatures in stores and vehicles and at the point of sale. No doubt wisely, the Practice Guidance points out that, in areas where there are two tiers of food authority, the division of enforcement responsibility between district and county council may not be readily apparent to consumers. The food authorities are therefore enjoined to provide an enforcement service that is, so far as consumers are concerned, as seamless, effective and accessible as possible.

In relation to a particular case or cases the Secretary of State has power to direct that an enforcement duty imposed on food authorities by s 6(2) shall be discharged by the Secretary of State, or the Food Standards Agency[16].

The enforcement authorities for Regulations under the Act are specified by those Regulations[17]. Food authorities are for the most part so specified, as well as playing a major role in enforcing important food Regulations made under the ECA 1972, s 2(2) [18].

The Secretary of State may take over proceedings instituted by some other person[19] or may direct the Food Standards Agency to do so[20]. Unless so directed, the Agency may take over proceedings only with the consent of the person who instituted them[21].

1   FSA 1990, s 6(5).
2   See para **2.6.1**.
3   FSA 1990, s 29.
4   FSA 1990, s 32.
5   As to food authority liaison, LACORS and the Home Authority principle, see para **18.3.2** below.
6   Local Government Act 1972, s 101.
7   Made under FSA 1990, s 5(4).
8   FSA 1990, s 12.
9   FSA 1990, s 15.
10   As to Codes of Practice, see para **2.5.3**.
11   See paras **7.3.2** and **7.3.3**.
12   See para **9.2.15** below.
13   See para **14.4.1** below.
14   See paras **13.2.1** and **14.4.1** below.
15   See section **15.4** below.
16   FSA 1990, s 6(3), as amended by FSA 1999, Sch 5, para 10(2) and by the Ministry of Agriculture, Fisheries and Food (Dissolution) Order 2002, art 5(2) and Sch 2; and FSA 1999, Sch 3, para 2(a).
17   FSA 1990, s 6(4) as amended by FSA 1999, Sch 5, para 10(3) and by the Ministry of Agriculture, Fisheries and Food (Dissolution) Order 2002, art 5(2) and Sch 2; and and FSA 1999, Sch 3, para 2(b).
18   See in particular the Food Hygiene (England) Regulations 2006, reg 5 and the Official Feed and Food Controls (England) Regulations 2007, reg 3 and Sch 5, and reg 24.
19   FSA 1990, s 6(5A).
20   FSA 1990, s 6(5B) and FSA 1999, Sch 3, para 2(c).
21   FSA 1990, s 6(5C) and FSA 1999, Sch 3, para 2(c).

Statutory codes of practice and food authority returns

2.5.3   The Secretary of State is empowered to issue Codes of Practice for the guidance of food authorities as regards the execution and enforcement of the Act and of regulations and orders made under it[1]. Food authorities are required to have regard to the relevant provisions of any such Code and must comply with any direction that is given to them by the Food Standards Agency to take any specified steps to comply with a code[2]. Any such direction is specifically enforceable in England and Wales, on the Agency's application for judicial review, by the order known as *mandamus* commanding the authority to perform its public duty[3]. Before exercising its power to give or enforce a direction, the Agency must consult the Secretary of State.

By reg 24 of the Food Hygiene (England) Regulations 2006 and reg 6 of the Official Feed and Food Controls (England) Regulations 2007, the Secretary of State and the Agency have been given very similar powers to issue Codes and directions for guidance of food authorities as regards the Community Hygiene Regulations and the official controls Regulation (EC) 882/2004[4]. Parallel legislation has been made for Wales[5].

Under these three powers, comprehensive Codes of Practice have been issued for England and for Wales respectively, complemented in each case by non-statutory Practice Guidance issued by the Agency on the approach to enforcement and on the law where its intention might be unclear. The Codes have recently been amended to bring UK enforcement practice into line with official controls Regulation (EC) 882/2004 by replacing inspections with a range of interventions tailored to the rating of individual food establishments. All food establishments have also been moved into the risk-based inspection regime.

The Agency may additionally require reports and returns from food authorities[6] in order to monitor their activities. Prior to the enactment of FSA 1999, s 13 (see para **2.3.6** above), this was the only power available to assemble returns of enforcement information required by the Commission under Directive 89/397/EEC, the forerunner of official controls Regulation (EC) 882/2004[7].

1   FSA 1990, s 40 (1).
2   FSA 1990, s 40(1A) and (2) and FSA 1999, Sch 3, para 4(1)(a).
3   FSA 1990, s 40(3) and FSA 1999, Sch 3, para 4(1)(b).
4   See, on the Hygiene Regulations, chs 13 and 14 and, on the Official Controls Regulations, ch 18.
5   The Food Hygiene (Wales) Regulations 2006, reg 24; and the Official Feed and Food Controls (Wales) Regulations 2007, reg 6.
6   FSA 1990, s 41 and FSA 1999, Sch 3, para 5.
7   See ch 18.

Default of food authorities

2.5.4   As noted in para **2.5.2**, s 6 of the FSA 1990 enables central government to take over enforcement duties imposed on food authorities by the FSA 1990 or proceedings instituted by persons other than the Secretary of State. These powers apply whether or not a food authority is in default. Where a local authority fails to fulfil a public function or acts illegally, judicial review may well lie. Additionally however, the FSA 1990 makes express provision for any case in which the Secretary of State is satisfied that a food authority has failed to discharge a duty imposed by or under the FSA 1990 and that the authority's failure affects the general interests of consumers of food. In such a case he may by order empower another food authority, the Food Standards

Agency or a person (whether or not an officer of his) to discharge the duty in place of the authority in default. He may, but is not obliged to, cause a local inquiry to be held where he believes a food authority is in default[1].

Given the Food Standards Agency's responsibility for monitoring enforcement performance[2], it would be surprising if the Secretary of State did not, in the normal way, follow its advice when deciding under s 6 or 42 of the FSA 1990 to remove functions from an enforcement authority.

1   FSA 1990, s 42, as amended by the Deregulation and Contracting Out Act 1994, s 76 and Sch 16 and FSA 1999, s 40 and Sch 5; and FSA 1999, Sch 3, para 6.
2   See para **2.3.6** above.

2.6   AUTHORISED OFFICERS

2.6.1   The statutory duties of enforcement under the FSA 1990 are generally carried out by 'authorised officers'[1]. An authorised officer 'in relation to a food authority' means, in essence, any person, whether or not an officer of the authority, who is authorised by them in writing, either generally or specially, to act in matters arising under the Act[2]. In much the same terms, 'authorised officer' is now also defined 'in relation to an enforcement authority'[3], which may be specified, for the purposes of subordinate legislation, from a list including not only food authorities, but also the Secretary of State, the Food Standards Agency or, in regulations, the Commissioners of Customs and Excise[4]. It should also be noted that provisions of the Act itself often apply to 'an authorised officer of an enforcement authority'[5]. In the case of two-tier authorities, most authorised officers of district councils are environmental health officers and most authorised officers of county councils, trading standards officers. Veterinarians and other appropriately qualified officers are employed by the Meat Hygiene Service to carry out official EC controls on meat in slaughterhouses, game handling establishments and cutting premises[6].

Officers performing duties under food Regulations made under the ECA 1972, s 2(2), such as the Food Hygiene (England) Regulations 2006 and the Official Feed and Food Controls (England) Regulations 2007, require separate written authorisation to deal with those matters[7].

1   As to 'proper officers' and others authorised to authenticate documents, see FSA 1990, s 49.
2   FSA 1990, s 5(6).
3   FSA 1990, s 6(6) as amended by the Deregulation and Contracting Out Act 1994, s 76 and Sch 16.
4   FSA 1990, s 6(4), as amended by the FSA 1999, s 40(1) and Sch 5 and the Ministry of Agriculture, Fisheries and Food (Dissolution) Order 2002.
5   See FSA 1990, ss 10, 12, 29, 30 and 32.
6   See paras **14.3.2** and **14.3.3** below.
7   See Food Law Code of Practice para 1.2.2.

2.6.2   The qualifications and experience required of Food Authority authorised officers are set out in ch 1.2 of the Food Law Codes of Practice and Practice Guidance for England and for Wales in implementation of the qualification and training provisions of official controls Regulation (EC) 882/2004[1]. In particular, the specific qualifications and experience required to carry out food hygiene and food standards inspections are explained, food authorities being warned to ensure that contracted or temporary staff meet the requirements and to accept relevant non-UK qualifications and experience for EEA nationals.

As to qualifications for food analysts and food examiners, see section **2.8**.

The Authorised Officers (Meat Inspection) Regulations 1987, which continue in force under FSA 1990, s 5(6), prescribe the qualifications required to undertake work that in 1995 essentially passed to the Meat Hygiene Service (ie inspections in respect of meat) [2].

1   See ch 18.
2   See para **14.3.3** below.

2.6.3   By s 44 of the FSA 1990, an officer of a food authority is not personally liable for anything done by him for the purpose of the execution or purported execution of the Act and within the scope of his employment, if he acted in the honest belief that his duty under the Act required or entitled him to do it. Further, if an action is brought against an officer of a food authority in respect of an act done by him in the execution or purported execution of the Act but outside the scope of his employment, his food authority may indemnify him in whole or in part against any damages or costs that he may be ordered to pay if they are satisfied that he acted in the honest belief that the act complained of was within the scope of his employment.

It is questionable whether s 44 protection extends to those, such as consultants and freelance staff, who are not 'officers of the authority' but engaged on the authority of ss 5(6) and 6(6) for the enforcement of provisions in and under the FSA 1990.

2.7   PUBLIC ANALYSTS

2.7.1   The public analyst has been the key figure in the enforcement of law relating to the composition of food since the beginnings of the modern legislation in the second half of the nineteenth century. While acting as principal scientific adviser to the food authority on this subject, the public analyst holds a public office with a certain independence of status[1]. Over the years the expert evidence of public analysts has been influential in helping courts establish the standards of food demanded by purchasers under what is now s 14 of the FSA 1990[2] and important for the purposes of determining whether chemically contaminated food is unfit for human consumption for the purposes of s 9 of the Act. For certain additive and contaminant Regulations, the public analyst's certificate that food does not comply has been prescribed as evidence that the food may be treated as unfit and seized and destroyed on the order of a justice of the peace[3].

Food authorities are required to appoint one or more public analysts[4] who must be qualified in accordance with regulations under s 27(2) of the FSA 1990[5]. The authority must pay to the public analyst such remuneration as may be agreed and may also appoint a deputy public analyst.

For the purposes of the provisions protecting officers acting in good faith described at para **2.6.3**, the public analyst is deemed to be an officer of the food authority whether or not his is a whole-time appointment[6].

1   See FSA 1990, ss 27–31.
2   *Bowker v Woodroffe* [1927] All ER Rep 415. As to s 14, see further section **8.2** below.
3   See, for example, the Flavourings in Food Regulations 1992, as amended, reg 6.
4   FSA 1990, s 27, as amended in particular by the Local Government (Wales) Act 1994, s 22(3) and Sch 9, para 16(2); and the Local Government Changes for England Regulations 1994, reg 24. 'Food authority' here does not include the council of a non-metropolitan district in England (except where the county functions have been transferred to that council pursuant to structural change) or the appropriate Treasurers of the Temples.
5   Food Safety (Sampling and Qualifications) Regulations 1990, as amended, reg 3.
6   FSA 1990, s 44(4).

2.7.2   Some public analysts are employed by a food authority and work from laboratories provided by that authority. Others are independent. They may be appointed by more than one food authority and engage in commercial consultancy work. However, a person is prohibited by the Act from acting as a public analyst for an area if he is engaged directly or indirectly in any food business in that area[1] and a director, owner or employee of a food business, or partner in a food business, is prohibited by regulations from acting as a public analyst for the area in which that business is situated[2]. Breach of these prohibitions might be expected to invalidate the public analyst's appointment and render inadmissible any evidence he gave.

1   FSA 1990, s 27(2).
2   Food Safety (Sampling and Qualifications) Regulations 1990, as amended, reg 5(1).

2.7.3   Public analysts thus continue to be responsible for the analyses necessary in enforcement of the legislation relating to food standards, labelling, claims, additives and contaminants. Much of this now is EC inspired and public analysts' establishments must themselves comply with prescribed European standards in order to be designated as official laboratories under official controls Regulation (EC) 882/2004[1].

1   See para **18.2.4** below.

2.7.4   The 1998 Turner Report on the Review of Public Analyst Arrangements in England and Wales endorsed retention of the requirement that food authorities appoint public analysts and recommended continuing professional development as part of their qualifications. Nevertheless, concern is still being expressed[1], by local authorities and others, about the underfunding and perceived decline of this vital enforcement service.

1   See, for example, the minutes of the Enforcement Liaison Group meeting of 8 June 2007.

2.8   FOOD ANALYSTS AND FOOD EXAMINERS

2.8.1   The FSA 1990 introduced the concepts of 'food analyst' and 'food examiner'. In the Act, 'analysis' includes microbiological assay and any technique for establishing the composition of food[1] and 'food analyst' is defined[2] as a public analyst or other person having the requisite qualifications to carry out analyses for the purposes of the Act. 'Examination' means microbiological examination[3] and 'food examiner' is defined[4] as a person who possesses the requisite qualifications to carry out examinations for the purposes of the Act (see further para **2.8.4** below).

1   FSA 1990, s 53(1).
2   FSA 1990, s 30(9).
3   FSA 1990, s 28(2).
4   FSA 1990, s 30(9).

2.8.2   Although samples for analysis must be submitted to the public analyst for the area in question[1], the work may actually be carried out on his or her behalf by a food analyst who, by definition, must have the prescribed qualifications (see further para **2.8.4** below). The 1998 Turner Report on the Review of Public Analyst Arrangements in England and Wales recommended continuing professional development as part of the qualification for food analysts.

1   FSA 1990, s 30(1)(a) and (2)(a).

2.8.3   Unlike public analysts, food examiners are not appointed by food authorities for their areas, nor do they hold statutory office. Samples for examination must, however, be submitted to a food examiner[1] who, by definition, must have the prescribed qualifications (see further para **2.8.4** below). To this extent the food examiner, in carrying out the statutory function of microbiological examination of food, corresponds with the public analyst undertaking its chemical analysis. In exercise of their power in s 28(1) of the FSA 1990, a few food authorities provide facilities for examinations for the purposes of the Act and certain private companies also offer the service, but, for the most part, food examination laboratories are either owned by the Health Protection Agency (HPA), or are NHS facilities directly managed by the HPA, or undertaking work on its behalf. Like those of public analysts, food examiners' laboratories must comply with prescribed European standards in order to be designated as official laboratories under official controls Regulation (EC) 882/2004[2].

1   FSA 1990, s 30(1)(b) and (2)(b).
2   See para **18.2.4** below.

2.8.4   The qualifications for food analysts and food examiners are prescribed by regs 3 and 4 respectively of the Food Safety (Sampling and Qualifications) Regulations 1990, as amended. Evidently with the object of avoiding conflicts of interest[1], reg 5 prohibits a director, owner or employee of a food business, or partner in a food business from analysing or examining any sample that he knows was taken from that business.

Certificates of analysis and examination given by food analysts and food examiners have evidential status[2].

1   FSA 1990, s 31(1)(g).
2   See para **18.4.7** below.

2.9   THE GOVERNMENT CHEMIST

2.9.1   Recourse to the Government Chemist as a referee analyst in the event of dispute has been part of food standards law since 1875 and the mechanism, in modern form, appears in and under the FSA 1990. An authorised officer who has retained part of a sample is required to submit it to the Government Chemist, or such other food analyst as the Government Chemist may direct, for analysis if he and the owner agree or if a court so orders[1].

Although the laboratory of the Government Chemist is now in private hands, it is subject to contractual constraints so that the Government Chemist can fulfil the regulatory role imposed on that office which remains an independent appointment.

1   FSA 1990, s 31(2)(h) and Food Safety (Sampling and Qualifications) Regulations 1990, as amended, reg 7. See further para **18.4.8** below.

Chapter 3

General principles and requirements of Community food law

3.1 INTRODUCTION

3.1.1 The Commission's Food Safety White Paper of January 2000[1] proposed a comprehensive legal framework covering the food chain 'from farm to fork', including animal feed production. This framework has been established by general food Regulation (EC) 178/2002 considered in this chapter.

1   COM (1999) 719 final, published on 12 January 2000. See further para **1.1.7**above.

3.1.2 The aim and scope of Regulation (EC) 178/2002 is described by Art 1. It provides the basis for the assurance of a high level of protection of human health and consumers' interest in relation to food, taking account in particular of the diversity in the supply of food including traditional products, whilst ensuring the effective functioning of the internal market. It establishes common principles and responsibilities, the means to provide a strong science base, efficient organisational arrangements and procedures to underpin decision-making in matters of food and feed safety.

For these purposes, the Regulation 'lays down the general principles governing food and feed in general, and food and feed safety in particular, at Community and national level', establishes the European Food Safety Authority and lays down procedures for matters with a direct impact on food and feed safety.

It applies to all stages of production, processing and distribution of food and feed, although not to primary production for private domestic use or to the domestic preparation, handling or storage of food for private domestic consumption.

3.1.3 Despite its wide application, Regulation (EC) 178/2002 claims, in accordance with the principle of proportionality as set out in Art 5 EC, to remain within the boundaries of what is necessary to achieve the objectives pursued[1].

1   Regulation (EC) 178/2002, recital (66).

3.1.4 Described below in sections **3.2**, **3.3** and **3.4** respectively are Chapter II of Regulation (EC) 178/2002 on General Food Law, Chapter III on the European Food Safety Authority and Chapter V on Procedures and Final Provisions. In the process, key definitions from Chapter I are identified. Chapter IV concerns the Rapid Alert System, Crisis Management and Emergencies and is explained in ch 7 of this book, together with related national provisions.

Some assistance in the interpretation of the provisions of Chapter II is available from guidance issued by the Commission on 20 January 2005 concerning Arts 11, 12 and 17–20, and by the Food Standards Agency on 20 July 2007 concerning Arts 14, 16, 18 and 19. By contrast with the Commission guidance, the Agency guidance notes admit greater discretion to food businesses over retention of traceability records; allow for production of traceability records within 'a short timescale'; and generally concentrate on the requirements of the legislation and providing succinct advice on good practice. The Agency believe that their notes are more appropriate for business in the United Kingdom and has agreed this approach with the Commission.

3.2   GENERAL FOOD LAW

Scope

3.2.1   The provisions on general food law are established by Chapter II of Regulation (EC) 178/2002 which, in order to ensure the safety of food, relates to all stages of production, processing and distribution of food, and also of feed produced for, or fed to food producing animals[1]. The definitions employed significantly expand the scope of the Chapter. Thus, 'food law' is defined[2] as meaning 'the laws, regulations and administrative provisions governing food in general, and food safety in particular, whether at Community or national level; it covers any stage of production, processing and distribution of food, and also of feed produced for, or fed to food-producing animals'. The term 'stages of production, processing and distribution' is defined[3] as meaning 'any stage, including import, from and including the primary production of a food, up to and including its storage, transport, sale or supply to the final consumer and, where relevant, the importation, production, manufacture, storage, transport, distribution, sale and supply of feed'. It is used not only in Art 1 and the definition of 'food law', but also in Arts 4, 14, 17 and 18, as well as the definitions of 'food business' and 'traceability' (see further below).

1   Regulation (EC) 4.1 and recitals (12) and (13).
2   Regulation (EC) 178/2002, Art 3(1).
3   Regulation (EC) 178/2002, Art 3(16).

3.2.2   The definitions of 'food' and 'feed' are fundamental to Regulation (EC) 178/2002 and beyond[1]. Article 2 provides that:

'For the purposes of this Regulation, "food" (or "foodstuff") means any substance or product, whether processed, partially processed or unprocessed, intended to be, or reasonably expected to be ingested by humans.

"Food" includes drink, chewing gum and any substance, including water, intentionally incorporated into the food during its manufacture, preparation or treatment. It includes water after the point of compliance as defined in Article 6 of Directive 98/83/EC and without prejudice to the requirements of Directives 80/778/EEC and 98/83/EC.

"Food" shall not include:

(a)   feed;
(b)   live animals unless they are prepared for placing on the market for human consumption;
(c)   plants prior to harvesting;

(d)   medicinal products within the meaning of Council Directives 65/65/EEC and 92/73/EEC[2];

(e)   cosmetics within the meaning of Council Directive 76/768/EEC;

(f)   tobacco and tobacco products within the meaning of Council Directive 89/622/EEC;

(g)   narcotic or psychotropic substances within the meaning of the United Nations Single Convention on Narcotic Drugs, 1961, and the United Nations Convention on Psychotropic Substances, 1971;

(h)   residues and contaminants.'

1   The definition is now applied in the Food Safety Act 1990: see para **4.3.1** below.
2   Now to be read as a reference to Directive 2001/83 by which Directives 65/65 and 92/73 were repealed.

3.2.3   The following matters should be noted about the exclusions listed in the third paragraph of this definition:

(1)   as to exclusion (a), Art 3(4) defines 'feed' (or feedingstuff') for the purposes of Regulation (EC) 178/2002 as meaning 'any substance or product, including additives, whether processed, partially processed or unprocessed, intended to be used for oral feeding to animals';

(2)   as to exclusion (b), oysters and other shellfish prepared for placing on the market for human consumption are caught by the definition;

(3)   as to exclusion (d), the European Court has interpreted the definition in relation to commodities that could equally be classified as foodstuffs or medicinal products. It held that the provisions of Community law specific to medicinal products alone apply and that, as Community law stands, import into a Member State is permitted only upon acquisition of a marketing authorisation issued in accordance with Directive 2001/83, even when the product is lawfully marketed as a foodstuff in another Member State' [1]. In the United Kingdom, it is the Medicines and Healthcare Products Regulatory Agency, on behalf of the Licensing Authority, which regulates medicinal products for human use[2] and decides in borderline cases whether a product is a 'medicinal product'.

1   Joined cases C-211/03, C-299/03 and C-316/03 to C-318/03 *HLH Warenvertriebs GmbH and Orthica BV v Germany* [2005] ECR I–5141 concerning certain bacterial cultures, vitamin C and bioflavins. Contrast case C-319/05 *Commission v Germany* [2007] ECR I-9811, [2008] 1 CMLR 36 where it was held that a garlic capsule is not a medicinal product.
2   Under the Medicines for Human Use (Marketing Authorisations Etc) Regulations 1994, as amended, and the Medicines Act 1968.

3.2.4   The general principles of food law laid down in Arts 5–8 of Regulation (EC) 178/2002 and those regarding transparency in Arts 9 and 10 are described in paras **3.2.5–3.2.11** below. Together, they form a general 'horizontal' framework for future measures. Existing food law principles and procedures are to be adapted to comply with these provisions and in the mean time must be implemented taking account of the principles that they lay down.[1]

1   Regulation (EC) 178/2002, Art 4(2), (3) and (4).

General principles of food law

General objectives

3.2.5   Article 5 of Regulation (EC) 178/2002 lays down the general objectives of food law.

The protection of human life and health, or the protection of consumers' interests, including fair practices in food trade, or both must be pursued to a high standard. Food law must also, where appropriate, take account of the protection of animal health and welfare, plant health and the environment. Moreover, it must aim to achieve the free movement in the Community of food and feed manufactured or marketed according to the general principles and requirements in Chapter II. Finally, existing or imminent international standards must be taken into account in the development or adaptation of food law, except (a) where they would be an ineffective or inappropriate means for the fulfilment of the legitimate objectives of food law, (b) where there is a scientific justification, or (c) where they would result in a different level of protection from the one determined as appropriate for the Community. Section **1.9** above explains the Codex Alimentarius and other international fora in which food standards are agreed.

Risk analysis

3.2.6　Article 3(9) and (10) respectively of Regulation (EC) 178/2002 provides that:

' "risk" means a function of the probability of an adverse health effect and the severity of that effect, consequential to a hazard' and

' "risk analysis" means a process consisting of three interconnecting components: risk assessment, risk management and risk communication'[1].

These components of risk analysis are themselves defined thus, together with the term 'hazard', in Art 3(11), (12), (13) and (14):

' "risk assessment" means a scientifically based process consisting of four steps: hazard identification, hazard characterisation, exposure assessment and risk characterisation';

' "risk management" means the process, distinct from risk assessment, of weighing policy alternatives in consultation with interested parties, considering risk assessment and other legitimate factors, and, if need be, selecting appropriate prevention and control options';

' "risk communication" means the interactive exchange of information and opinions throughout the risk analysis process as regards hazards and risks, risk-related factors and risk perceptions, among risk assessors, risk managers, consumers, feed and food businesses, the academic community and other interested parties, including the explanation of risk assessment findings and the basis of risk management decisions'; and

' "hazard" means a biological, chemical or physical agent in, or condition of, food or feed with the potential to cause an adverse health effect'.

1　See also Regulation (EC) 178/2002 recital (17).

3.2.7　In order to achieve the objective of a high level of protection of human life and health, Art 6 of Regulation (EC) 178/2002 requires food law to be based on risk analysis except where this is not appropriate to the circumstances or nature of the measure. Risk assessment must be based on available scientific evidence and undertaken in an independent, objective and transparent manner. In order to achieve the general objectives of food law described in para **3.2.5** above, risk management is required to take into account not only the results of risk assessment, but also in particular, (a) the opinions of the European Food Safety Authority (see para **3.3.2** below), (b) other factors legitimate to the matter under consideration and (c) where appropriate, the precautionary principle (see para **3.2.8** below). Recital (19) puts this another way. Scientific risk assessment alone cannot always provide all the information on which a risk management decision should be based. Other relevant factors should then be taken into account including societal, economic, traditional, ethical and environmental factors as well as the feasibility of controls[1]. Particular examples of 'other factors legitimate to the matter under consideration' are detection methods and feasibility of controls for the purpose of avoiding risks from misuse of veterinary medicines[2]. The new risk analysis framework also plays a significant part in the procedures set up by Regulation (EC) 1829/2003 for authorisation of genetically modified food and feed. New products may be authorised for placing on the Community market only after a scientific evaluation by the European Food Safety Authority of any risks for human and animal health and, as the case may be, for the environment. Armed with this evaluation, the Community makes a risk management decision in cooperation with the Member States.

Further, risk analysis is employed by the Food Standards Agency as part of the UK's operational contingency plan explained in section **7.5** below. Its application in that context is to be found in their Incident Task Force's guidance document *Principles for preventing and responding to food incidents: April 2008* referred to in para **7.5.4**.

1   See also Commission Communication COM(2000)1 final of 2 February 2000 on the precautionary principle.
2   See recital (9) to Regulation (EC) 1873/2003 amending Regulation (EC) 2377/90 on maximum residue limits of veterinary medicinal products in foodstuffs of animal origin.

Precautionary principle

3.2.8   As noted in Art 6, an important feature of the risk management decision is the precautionary principle. This is to be applied when scientific uncertainty precludes a full assessment of the risk and when decision-makers consider that the chosen level of health protection may be in jeopardy. 'In specific circumstances where, following an assessment of available information, the possibility of harmful effects on health is identified but scientific uncertainty persists,' Art 7 of Regulation (EC) 178/2002 authorises the adoption of 'provisional risk management measures necessary to ensure the high level of health protection chosen in the Community', until further scientific information enables a more comprehensive risk assessment to be made. Such measures must be proportionate and no more restrictive of trade than is required to achieve the high Community level of health protection, regard being had to technical and economic feasibility and other legitimate factors. They must also be reviewed within a reasonable period of time. Article 7 measures are understood not to be confined to instruments with legal effects, but to include such decisions on fund research programmes and informing the public of possible ill effects from a product.[1] Nor will exercise of the power be subject only to the specified principle of proportionality that precludes the imposition of greater restrictions than necessary to achieve the objective. Other general principles of Community law, such as non-discrimination, will apply as they do in relation to the exercise of all Community powers.[2]

1   See Commission Communication COM(2000)1 final of 2 February 2000 on the precautionary principle.

2   With regard to proportionality and other general principles applied to a measure taking account
    of the precautionary principle, see joined cases C-154/04 and C-155/04 *R* (*on the application of
    Alliance for Health*), *Nutri-Link Ltd v Secretary of State for Health* [2005] ECR I-6451.

Protection of consumers' interests

3.2.9   Being in essence a response to BSE and the other food crises of the
1990s, Regulation (EC) 178/2002 concentrates above all on food safety.
However, a comprehensive basic food law needs also to protect consumer
finances and choice. Article 8 enlarges on this second principal objective
established by Arts 1 and 5. Food law is required to aim at the protection of the
interests of consumers and provide a basis for them to make informed choices in
relation to the foods they consume. It must also aim at the prevention of:

(a)   fraudulent or deceptive practices;
(b)   the adulteration of food; and
(c)   any other practices that may mislead the consumer.

Article 8 is evidently intended to embrace such classic consumer protection
measures as restriction of names to food of dependable quality, on the one hand,
and compulsory ingredient labelling, on the other.

Principles of transparency

Public consultation

3.2.10   Except where precluded by urgency, there must be open and
transparent public consultation, directly and through representative bodies,
during the preparation, evaluation and revision of food law.[1] This obligation
and that relating to 'Public Information' that follows are intended to maintain
the confidence of consumers and international trading partners.[2] The major, but
not exclusive, channel of relevant Commission consultation is the Advisory
Group on the Food Chain and Animal and Plant Health set up by Decision
2004/613. The Group is consulted on food and feed safety, food and feed
labelling and presentation, human nutrition, in relation to food legislation,
animal health and welfare and matters relating to crop protection, plant
protection products and their residues, and conditions for the marketing of seed
and propagating material, including biodiversity, and including matters
pertaining to industrial property. The Advisory Group is made up of
representatives of not more than 45 European trade, industry, consumer and
welfare bodies aimed at protecting interests in these fields.

1   Regulation (EC) 178/2002, Art 9.
2   Regulation (EC) 178/2002, recital (22).

Public information

3.2.11   Where there are reasonable grounds for suspecting that food or feed
may present a risk for human or animal health, public authorities are required to
take steps, appropriate to the nature, seriousness and extent of that risk, to
inform the general public of the nature of the risk to health, identifying to the
fullest extent possible the food or feed, or type of food or feed, the risk that it
may present, and the measures that are taken or to be taken to prevent, reduce or
eliminate it. This obligation is without prejudice to applicable Community and
national law on access to documents[1].

1   Regulation (EC) 178/2002, Art 10.

General obligations of food trade

Food and feed imported into the Community

3.2.12   By Art 11 of Regulation (EC) 178/2002, food and feed imported into the Community for placing on the market within the Community must comply with the relevant requirements of food law, with conditions recognised by the Community as at least equivalent, or with requirements contained in any specific agreement between the Community and the exporting country.

In elaboration of Art 11, specific import requirements are prescribed by particular EC instruments. Thus, official feed and food controls Regulation (EC) 882/2004 Title VI Chapter II makes provision for import conditions. For food generally, Regulation (EC) 852/2004 Art 10 requires compliance with the food business operators' hygiene obligations[1]; to which are added, for products of animal origin, by Regulation (EC) 853/2004, Art 6, obligations to health mark, as well as to meet particular import conditions and, by Regulation (EC) 854/2004, Art 10, bespoke import procedures. Similarly, for feed, hygiene Regulation (EC) 183/2005, Art 23 lays down import conditions, while additives Regulation (EC) 1831/2003 imposes on imports requirements at least equivalent to those for Community products[2].

Although Community law – such as Art 18 on traceability addressed in paras **3.2.40–3.2.43** below – does not have extra-territorial effect and the requirements of food law bite on third country products only at the point of import, bilateral legal arrangements are sometimes made, for example in the veterinary sector, with regard to certification of the origin of third countries goods.

1   In Regulation (EC) 852/2004, Art 3–6.
2   See, in particular, recital (5) to Regulation (EC) 1831/2003.

3.2.13   'Placing on the market' is an important control threshold not only for Art 11 but also for Arts 12, 14, 15, 18, 19 and 20 of Chapter II and the definition of 'food', as well as in Arts 50 (Rapid Alert System) and 53 (Emergencies) considered in ch 7 below. The concept is defined by Art 3(8) as meaning 'the holding of food or feed for the purpose of sale, including offering for sale or any other form of transfer, whether free of charge or not, and the sale, distribution, and other forms of transfer themselves'.

3.2.14   In implementation of Art 11, as read with Art 10 of Regulation (EC) 852/2004 on the hygiene of foodstuffs, reg 27 of the Official Feed and Food Controls (England) Regulations 2007 prohibits the introduction from third countries (albeit via specified Community territory[1]) of feed and food products of non-animal origin that do not comply:

(a)   in the case of feed, with the feed safety requirements (see para **3.2.31–3.3.35** below);

(b)   in the case of food, with the food safety requirements (see paras **3.2.20–3.3.30** below) or the hygiene requirements of Arts 3–6 of Regulation (EC) 852/2004.

An offence and penalties are prescribed for reg 27 by reg 39.

Pending the making of a specific statutory instrument for the purpose, reg 27 is also relied on for the enforcement of Regulation (EC) 733/2008 on the conditions governing import of agricultural products originating in third countries following the accident at the Chernobyl nuclear power station[2].

As regards medicated feedingstuffs and specified feed additives, the Veterinary Medicines Regulations 2008[3] specify an offence and penalties for contravention of Art 11 of Regulation (EC) 178/2002 and designate the enforcement authority.

1   Subject to minor exceptions, the territories of Austria, Belgium, Bulgaria, Cyprus, the Czech Republic, Denmark, Estonia, Finland, France, Germany, Greece, Hungary, Ireland, Italy, Latvia, Lithuania, Luxembourg, Malta, the Netherlands, Poland, Portugal, Romania, the Slovak Republic, Slovenia, Spain, Sweden and the United Kingdom .
2   See further para **7.4.13** below.
3   See reg 14 and Sch 5, para 2, and reg 43.

Food and feed exported from the Community

3.2.15   In making provision for food and feed exported or re-exported from the Community for placing on the market of a third country, Regulation (EC) 178/2002 aims to take into account the level of protection established by the importing country. By Art 12(1), such food and feed must, unless otherwise requested by the authorities of the importing country or established by the laws, regulations, standards, codes of practice and other legal and administrative procedures as may be in force there, 'comply with the relevant requirements of food law[1].

In other circumstances, except in the case where foods are injurious to health or feeds are unsafe, food and feed can only be exported or re-exported if the competent authorities of the country of destination have expressly agreed, after having been fully informed of the reasons for which and the circumstances in which the food or feed concerned could not be placed on the market in the Community'. The meaning of the words 'in other circumstances' which introduce the second part of Art 12(1) is not wholly clear. At first sight and when read with recital (24), they might appear to mean 'if the food or feed exported etc does not comply with Community law or the requirements set by the importing country'. Commission guidance, however, reads them as meaning 'if there is no relevant Community food law and the third country has not set any specific requirements applicable to imports'. Either way, even where there is agreement with an importing country, food injurious to health and unsafe feed is not to be exported or re-exported.

1   See para **3.2.1** above.

3.2.16   Specific Regulations enlarge upon this basic principle. The official controls prescribed for feed and food must, by Regulation (EC) 882/2004, Art 3(4), be applied, with the same care, to exports outside the Community. By Regulation (EC) 1946/2003, Art 10(3), no genetically modified organism that may be subject to transboundary movements for direct use as food or feed or for processing may be exported, unless it is authorised within the Community or the competent authority of a third country has expressly agreed to the import as required under Art 12 of Regulation (EC) 178/2002. As regards the hygiene of exported or re-exported food, Regulation (EC) 852/2004, Art 11 provides that the relevant requirements of Regulation (EC) 178/2002, Art 12 include the food business operators' hygiene obligations[1].

Feed hygiene Regulation (EC) 183/2005, Art 25 requires that feed, including feed for animals not kept for food production, which is produced in the Community for placing on the market in third countries, must satisfy the provisions of Regulation (EC) 178/2002, Art 12.

1   In Regulation (EC) 852/2004 Arts 3–6.

3.2.17 Where the provisions of a bilateral agreement concluded between the Community or one of its Member States and a third country are applicable, Art 12(2) requires that food and feed exported from the Community or that Member State to that third country shall comply with the said provisions.

3.2.18 In implementation of Art 12 of Regulation (EC) 178/2002, provision is made for offences, penalties and enforcement:

(a)   in so far as it relates to food, by regs 4, 5, and 6 of the General Food Regulations 2004, as amended by the Official Feed and Food Control (England) Regulations 2005;

(b)   in so far as it relates to feed, by regs 15 and 16 of the Feed (Hygiene and Enforcement) (England) Regulations 2005; and

(c)   in so far as it relates to medicated feedingstuffs and specified feed additives, by reg 14, together with Sch 5, para 2, and reg 43 of the Veterinary Medicines Regulations 2008.

Additionally as explained in para **4.7.2** below, reg 6A(a) of the General Food Regulations 2004, as amended by the Official Feed and Food Control (England) Regulations 2005, provides a defence, in proceedings for offences against food law, for items intended for export to non-Member States, which could lawfully be exported there under Art 12.

International standards

3.2.19 Regulation (EC) 178/2002 also establishes the principles for the Community contribution to developing international standards and trade agreements. Article 13 provides that, without prejudice to their rights and obligations, the Community and the Member States shall:

(a)   contribute to the development of international technical standards for food and feed and sanitary and phytosanitary standards;

(b)   promote the coordination of work on food and feed standards undertaken by international governmental and nongovernmental organisations;

(c)   contribute, where relevant and appropriate, to the development of agreements on recognition of the equivalence of specific food and feed-related measures;

(d)   give particular attention to the special development, financial and trade needs of developing countries, with a view to ensuring that international standards do not create unnecessary obstacles to exports from developing countries;

(e)   promote consistency between international technical standards and food law while ensuring that the high level of protection adopted in the Community is not reduced.

As indicated in para **3.2.5**, the Codex Alimentarius and other international fora for establishment of food standards are explained in section **1.9** above.

General requirements of food law

Food safety requirements

3.2.20 A crucial element of the Community's general food law established by Regulation (EC) 178/2002 is Art 14. This supersedes diverse national provisions prohibiting unsafe food[1], including those in s 8 of the Food Safety Act 1990.

1 Regulation (EC) 178/2002 recitals (26) and (27).

3.2.21 The basic requirement in Art 14(1) that 'food shall not be placed on the market if it is unsafe' is to be construed in the light of the criteria in paras (2), (3), (4) and (5). These provide as follows:

'2. Food shall be deemed to be unsafe if it is considered to be:

(a)   injurious to health;
(b)   unfit for human consumption.

3. In determining whether any food is unsafe, regard shall be had:

(a)   to the normal conditions of use of the food by the consumer and at each stage of production, processing and distribution, and
(b)   to the information provided to the consumer, including information on the label, or other information generally available to the consumer concerning the avoidance of specific adverse health effects from a particular food or category of foods.

4. In determining whether any food is injurious to health, regard shall be had:

(a)   not only to the probable immediate and/or short-term and/or long-term effects of that food on the health of a person consuming it, but also on subsequent generations;
(b)   to the probable cumulative toxic effects;
(c)   to the particular health sensitivities of a specific category of consumers where the food is intended for that category of consumers.

5. In determining whether any food is unfit for human consumption, regard shall be had to whether the food is unacceptable for human consumption according to its intended use, for reasons of contamination, whether by extraneous matter or otherwise, or through putrefaction, deterioration or decay.'

3.2.22 These paragraphs are similar in approach and terminology to s 8 of the Food Safety Act 1990, which Art 14 has replaced. As recalled in ch 5 below, food 'injurious to health' and 'unfit for human consumption' have been important elements of our national food law since the nineteenth century and were in 1990 drawn together by s 8 in the concept of 'food safety requirements'. However, as the FSA Guidance points out, their meaning in Regulation (EC) 178/2002 is not necessarily the same. Under the 1990 Act, 'food injurious to health' was certainly limited to cases in which it had been so rendered by specified operations, while the courts did not always find it easy to state what 'food unfit for human consumption' comprised. In 1961 when upholding a conviction for sale of a pork pie bearing mould of the penicillin type, Parker LCJ said that the phrase meant more than unsuitable. A stale loaf would be unsuitable but not unfit. The phrase had to be looked at in a broad sense. When an article of food was admittedly going mouldy, it was prima facie unfit for human consumption whether or not there was evidence as to whether there would be any injury to health if it were eaten. It was a matter of degree in every case[1].

1   *David Greig Ltd v Goldfinch* (1961) 105 Sol Jo 367, LGR 304, DC. Applied in *Guild v Gateway Foodmarkets Ltd* 1991 SLT 578. See also *Kyle v Laird* 1951 JC 65.

3.2.23   It remains to be seen how Art 14(1)–(5) will be interpreted by the European Court. As was the case under s 8, 'unfit for human consumption' extends to food that is not detrimental to health albeit contaminated by extraneous matter or mould or otherwise. It is thus a concept more extensive than food 'injurious to health'. Generally, Art 14 should prove somewhat wider in scope than its predecessor. 'Injurious to health' is not restricted to food subjected to specified operations, and unfit food is described by Art 14(5) in terms of unacceptability for human consumption. The amplification by that paragraph also obviates the need for separate provision like s 8(2)(c) which was added in 1990 to overcome difficulties in establishing the unfitness of food containing clean foreign bodies[1].

Paragraphs 19–22 of the FSA Guidance give advice on the two concepts. In particular, once a hazard is identified that might make food injurious to health, a risk assessment should be carried out that addresses both what harm might be caused and how likely it is to occur.

The provisions of Art 14(3), (4) and (5) are considered further below.

1   Eg metal in a cream bun (*J Miller Ltd v Battersea Borough Council* [1956] 1 QB 43, [1955] 3 All ER 279); and string in a loaf (*Turner & Son Ltd v Owen* [1956] 1 QB 48, [1955] 3 All ER 565).

3.2.24   For the purposes of determining whether food is unsafe, Art 14(3) requires account to be taken of its normal conditions of use and the information provided to the consumer. The FSA Guidance offers cooking as an example of a normal condition of use.

Although not hitherto generally articulated in legislation[1], the Art 14(3) criteria are not unfamiliar to English law. For example, in 1983 the Court of Appeal held that 'unfitness for human consumption' should be judged in the context of the specific use intended. Although the contaminated dates there in question were unsuitable for direct consumption, they might have been rendered wholesome by processing into brown sauce as the importer had proposed[2]. And in Community law, Art 4 of contaminants Regulation (EC) 466/2001 (now replaced by Regulation (EC) 1881/2006) had already allowed for a higher level of aflatoxins in groundnuts, nuts and dried fruit that are to be subjected to sorting or treatment to reduce contamination before human consumption or use as an ingredient in foodstuffs.

1   But see the reference to 'ordinary quantities' in s 7(2) of the Food Safety Act 1990 before amendment by the General Food Regulations 2004.
2   *R v Archer, ex p Barrow, Lane & Ballard Ltd* (1983) 147 JPR 503.

3.2.25   The criteria specified in Art 14(4) for food 'injurious to health' are also not wholly new to domestic food law. Prior to implementation of Regulation (EC) 178/2002, s 7(2) of the Food Safety Act 1990 already contained specific provision requiring regard to be had to probable cumulative effect. Nor, as to the obligation in Art 14(4)(c) to have regard for the particular health sensitivities of any specific category of consumer for which the food is intended, can it necessarily be assumed, in the absence of relevant consumer information specified in Art 14(3)(b), that food that would harm the sensitive category will be deemed safe because it is intended for consumers generally. When considering the alleged unfitness of food under the previous legislation, the English courts had long required the effect on children and invalids to be taken into account[1]. On the other hand, as the FSA Guidance points out, there is no prohibition on selling peanuts (when properly labelled) even though some people are allergic to them and food intended for consumers requiring a gluten-free diet could certainly be considered to be injurious to health if it were found to contain gluten.

1   See *Cullen v McNair* (1908) 6 LGR 753, 72 JP 280; and *Haigh v Aerated Bread Co Ltd* [1916] 1 KB 878.

3.2.26   Although, as indicated above, the criteria that have to be taken into account under Art 14(5) in determining whether any food is unfit for human consumption, appear to cover much the same ground as those that were in practice applied by English courts in respect of the former Food Safety Act 1990, s 8(2)(b) and (c), it is manifestly helpful to have them expressly set out in the legislation in terms of unacceptability.

3.2.27   The food safety requirements of Art 14 are amplified by the presumptions in paras (6)–(9) considered below.

3.2.28   Article 14(6) provides that where any food that is unsafe is part of a batch, lot or consignment of food of the same class or description, it shall be presumed that all the food in that batch, lot or consignment is also unsafe, unless following a detailed assessment there is no evidence that the rest of the batch, lot or consignment is unsafe. The paragraph supersedes and seems to derive directly from former s 8(3) of the Food Safety Act 1990. As with the Food Safety Act version, the onus on the food owner of rebutting the presumption is a heavy one. The presumption in some form certainly needed to survive the replacement of s 8. It is vital to s 9 of the Food Safety Act 1990 if the seizure powers which that confers are not to be restricted to samples of suspect food (see section **5.4** below).

3.2.29   Article 14(7) and (9) respectively provide that food that complies with specific Community food safety provisions or, in their absence, the Member State's national food law[1] is, to that extent, deemed to be safe. In the light of para (7), the European Court has construed Regulation (EC) 178/2002 as an additional set of rules in relation to food supplements Directive 2002/46, the application of which is precluded to the extent to which a Community rule, such as that Directive, contains specific provisions for certain categories of foodstuffs[2]. But the presumption of safety is not irrebuttable. Notwithstanding conformity of food with specific rules, Art 14(8) enables competent authorities to restrict its marketing or require its withdrawal where there are reasons to suspect that it is unsafe.

Conversely, where food is found to be in breach of specific legislation governing its safety, it can be presumed to be either injurious to health or unfit for human consumption and thus unsafe for the purposes of Art 14. By way of example, the FSA Guidance cites a breach of a particular legal limit within legislation on contaminants in food that would mean it was likely that the food was injurious to health in the light of Art 14(4) or unfit for human consumption in the light of Art 14(5). In such a case – the Guidance advises – an assessment should still be carried out considering the factors in Arts 14(3)–(5) in the light of the legislation on contaminants in food. If this shows that the food is neither injurious to health nor unfit for human consumption it would not be regarded as unsafe for the purposes of Art 14. However, it would still be a breach of and subject to prosecution under the legislation on contaminants in food.

1   Without prejudice to the free movement of goods and other rules of the EC Treaty.
2   Joined cases C-211/03, C-299/03 and C-316/03 to C-318/03 *HLH Warenvertriebs GmbH and Orthica BV v Germany* [2005] ECR I-5141.

3.2.30   Regulations 3, 4, 5 and 6 of the General Food Regulations 2004, as amended by the Official Feed and Food Controls (England) Regulations 2005, provide for the enforcement of Art 14 by creating an offence and penalty for para (1) (food safety requirements), specifying the competent authorities for Art 14(8) (imposing restrictions and withdrawing food from the market) and generally assigning enforcement responsibility. They also consequentially amended the Food Safety Act 1990 and Regulations that referred to the repealed s 8(3) (see above).

There have already been high profile prosecutions that exemplify the importance of Art 14. In July 2007 Cadbury Schweppes pleaded guilty to placing on the market chocolate products that were unsafe in that they were injurious to health and unfit for human consumption due to the presence of Salmonella organisms. They were subsequently fined £1m by the Birmingham Crown Court for this and two other offences[1] relating to a salmonella outbreak caused by a defective drainage pipe and roof vent in their chocolate manufacturing plant.

The following month a Bridgend butcher, William John Tudor, pleaded guilty to seven offences, six of which involved placing unsafe food on the market contrary to Art 14[2], and was subsequently sentenced to 12 months' imprisonment. The offences related to the supply to local schools of meat contaminated with E-coli 0157 as a result of which one boy died and 157 others, mainly children, became ill. A public inquiry under the chairmanship of Professor Hugh Pennington set up by the Welsh Assembly is currently looking into the causes of the outbreak and will make recommendations for the future.

1   The other offences involved failure immediately to inform the competent authorities as required by Regulation (EC) 178/2002, Art 19(3) and failure to meet the HACCP requirements of hygiene Regulation (EC) 852/2004, Art 5. (As to these requirements, see paras **3.2.47** and **13.6.1.**)
2   The seventh concerned failure to keep food premises clean contrary to the now revoked Food Safety (General Hygiene) Regulations 1995.

Feed safety requirements

3.2.31   As in the case of food, Regulation (EC) 178/2002 establishes general requirements to prohibit unsafe feed and ensure that the internal market functions effectively[1].

1   Regulation (EC) 178/2002 recitals (26) and (27). As to the definition of 'feed', see para **3.2.3** above.

3.2.32   The basic requirement in Art 15(1) that 'feed shall not be placed on the market or fed to any food-producing animal if it is unsafe' must be read in the light of the criteria in para (2). This provides that:

'2. Feed shall be deemed to be unsafe for its intended use if it is considered to:

–   have an adverse effect on human or animal health;
–   make the food derived from food-producing animals unsafe for human consumption[1].'

1   As to 'unsafe for human consumption', see Regulation (EC) 178/2002, Art 14(2) described in para **3.2.21** above.

3.2.33 Although concise, these provisions significantly extend the pre-existing obligations under s 73 (deleterious ingredients in feeding stuff) and s 73A (unwholesome or dangerous material in feeding stuff) of the Agriculture Act 1970, which are effectively disapplied in so far as they may duplicate Art15[1]. Not only is unsafe feed generally to be excluded from the market, but the feeding of it to food-producing animals is also banned, thus bringing livestock farmers very much into the frame. As with food, the intended use of feed has to be taken into account in assessing its safety. But, as might be expected in the context of general food Regulation (EC) 178/2002, the criteria by which the safety of feed is to be judged under Art 15(2) give priority to its effect on derived food and human health.

1   See ss 73(5) and 73A(5) of the Agriculture Act 1970 as amended by the Feeding Stuffs (Safety Requirements for Feed for Food-Producing Animals) Regulations 2004, reg 11.

3.2.34 The feed safety requirements of Art 15 are augmented by essentially the same supporting provisions as are prescribed in Art 14 for food. Thus, a batch, lot or consignment is presumed not to satisfy the requirements on the basis of a non-compliant part (para (3)); and feed complying with specific Community or national safety provisions are deemed safe (paras (4) and (6)), although competent authorities are not thereby precluded from restricting or withdrawing suspect feed from the market (para (5)).

3.2.35 In implementation of Art 15 of Regulation (EC) 178/2002, provision is made for offences, penalties and enforcement:

(a)   in so far as it relates to feed, by regs 15 and 16 of the Feed (Hygiene and Enforcement) (England) Regulations 2005; and

(b)   in so far as it relates to medicated feeding stuffs and specified feed additives, by reg 14, together with Sch 5, para 2, and regn 43 of the Veterinary Medicines Regulations 2008.

Presentation

3.2.36 In further pursuit of the objective of protecting consumer finances and choice established by Arts 1, 5 and 8 of Regulation (EC) 178/2002, Art 16 requires that the labelling, advertising and presentation of food or feed, including their shape, appearance or packaging, the packaging materials used, the manner in which they are arranged and the setting in which they are displayed, and the information that is made available about them through whatever medium, shall not mislead consumers. The Article is expressed to be without prejudice to more specific provisions of food law, thus in particular preserving Art 2 of food labelling Directive 2000/13 as implemented by s 15 of the Food Safety Act 1990 described in section **8.3** below. The FSA Guidance notes that Art 16 also covers cases where a consumer is misled as to the nature, substance or quality of the food by the setting in which food is displayed. By way of example, it refers to a cake containing synthetic cream displayed in a chill cabinet in such a way as to give the impression that it contained fresh dairy cream.

A general prohibition on misleading feed labelling is for the first time provided by Art 16. Specific feed labelling rules are mentioned in ch 17.

3.2.37 In implementation of Art 16 of Regulation (EC) 178/2002, offences, penalties and enforcement provisions are prescribed:

(a)   in so far as it relates to food, by regs 4, 5 and 6 of the General Food

Regulations 2004, as amended by the Official Feed and Food Control (England) Regulations 2005;

(b)   in so far as it relates to feed, by regs 15 and 16 of the Feed (Hygiene and Enforcement) (England) Regulations 2005; and

(c)   in so far as it relates to medicated feedingstuffs and specified feed additives, by reg 14, together with Sch 5 para 2, and reg 43 of the Veterinary Medicines Regulations 2008.

Responsibilities

3.2.38 Article 17 of Regulation (EC) 178/2002 realises the aim of the Commission's 2000 Food Safety White Paper to define the roles of the food chain stakeholders in respect of food and feed safety. The primary responsibility lies with food and feed business operators who are best placed to devise safe systems for supplying food and feed and ensuring that the food and feed they supply is safe[1]. They cannot expect to rely on promptings from enforcement authorities. Paragraph (1) requires them, at all stages of production, processing and distribution within the businesses under their control, to ensure that foods or feeds satisfy the requirements of food law that are relevant to their activities and to verify that such requirements are met. Read with the following definitions in Art 3, it is apparent that Art 17(1) applies to each link of the chain including primary production and supply to the final consumer[2]:

'2. "food business" means any undertaking, whether for profit or not and whether public or private, carrying out any of the activities related to any stage of production, processing and distribution of food.'

'3. "food business operator" means the natural or legal persons responsible for ensuring that the requirements of food law are met within the food business under their control.'

'5. "feed business" means any undertaking whether for profit or not and whether public or private, carrying out any operation of production, manufacture, processing, storage, transport or distribution of feed including any producer producing, processing or storing feed for feeding to animals on his own holding.'

6. "feed business operator" means the natural or legal persons responsible for ensuring that the requirements of food law are met within the feed business under their control.'

The provision is a novel in concept to our national food law because, as the Commission's guidance advises,:

'Though the requirement laid down in Article 17(1) is directly applicable ..., the liability of food business operators should flow in practice from the breach of a specific food law requirement (and from the rules for civil or criminal liability which can be found in the national legal order of each Member State). The liability proceedings will not be based on Article 17 but on a legal basis to be found in the national order and in the specific infringed legislation.'[3]

So no offence or penalty is prescribed for Art 17(1). A food business operator who markets unsafe food contrary to Art 14(1) will be guilty of an offence under regulation 4(a) of the General Food Regulations 2004 and may well have laid himself open to civil action as described in ch 21.

1   Regulation (EC) 178/2002 recitals (30) and (31).
2   See case C-315/05 *Lidl Italia v Comune di Arcole* (*VR*) [2006] ECR I-11181.
3   In the Guidance 'food business operator' and 'food law' respectively include 'feed business operator' and 'feed law'.

3.2.39 Article 17(2) specifies the distinct responsibilities of the Member States. They are required to enforce food law, and monitor and verify that the relevant requirements are fulfilled by food and feed business operators at all stages of production, processing and distribution. For that purpose, they must maintain a system of official controls and other activities as appropriate to the circumstances, including public communication on food and feed safety and risk, food and feed safety surveillance and other monitoring activities covering all stages of production, processing and distribution. Finally, they are obliged to lay down rules for effective, proportionate and dissuasive measures and penalties applicable to infringements of food and feed law.

Traceability

3.2.40 The food scares of the 1990s made very clear that a comprehensive system was needed so that food, feed, food producing animals and ingredients could be traced throughout the marketing chain for the purposes of providing enforcement officers and consumers with reliable information and of enabling unsafe products to be identified and withdrawn[1]. Article 18(1) of Regulation (EC) 178/2002 provides that the traceability of food, feed, food-producing animals, and any other substance intended to be, or expected to be, incorporated into a food or feed shall be established at all stages of production, processing and distribution. 'Traceability' is defined by Art 3(15) as 'the ability to trace and follow a food, feed, food-producing animal or substance intended to be, or expected to be incorporated into a food or feed, through all stages of production, processing and distribution'.

1   Regulation (EC) 178/2002 recital (28). See also recital (29).

3.2.41 In development of this framework, Art 18(2) and (3) imposes on food and feed business operators the following new obligations:

'2. Food and feed business operators shall be able to identify any person from whom they have been supplied with a food, a feed, a food-producing animal, or any substance intended to be, or expected to be, incorporated into a food or feed. To this end, such operators shall have in place systems and procedures which allow for this information to be made available to the competent authorities on demand.

3. Food and feed business operators shall have in place systems and procedures to identify the other businesses to which their products have been supplied. This information shall be made available to the competent authorities on demand.'

Given the wide definitions of 'food business' and 'feed business'[1], the duty of traders under Art 18 to be able to inform competent authorities of the provenance and destination of products evidently extends to persons such as primary producers, importers, brokers, transporters and storage operators involved in distribution, and caterers except in relation to supplies to final consumers. However, Art 18 is not understood as applying in relation to products such as seeds for sowing, veterinary medicines, plant protection products or fertilisers, which are not 'intended to be, or expected to be, incorporated into a food or feed'. Article 18 does not say how the food or feed operator's obligation is to be discharged, but – in respect of food – the Food Standards Agency Guidance suggests the following reading:

> 'Taken at face value, the only information Article 18 requires food business operators to provide is the name of businesses who supply them and to whom they supply their products, ie one step back – one step forward. However, EC law should be interpreted according to its purpose, and account has to be taken of the relevant recitals (7, 28 and 29) and role of Article 18 in supporting the notification requirements of Articles 19 and 20. It follows that, as a minimum, traceability records should also include the address of the customer or supplier, nature and quantity of products, and the date of the transaction and delivery. It is expected that the provision and retention of this type of information is already standard practice in basic accounting. It can also be helpful to record the batch number or durability indication (where applicable).'

The FSA Guidance also in particular points out that the format is not prescribed, that the records must be available on demand and that it is for businesses to decide how long they should keep their records, bearing in mind the nature of the food, its product life, and the circumstances under which they might be required to produce records, should a notice under 19, or assistance to enforcement authorities, be subsequently required,

1   See para **3.2.38** above.

3.2.42   Article 18 is completed by the requirement (in para (4)) that food or feed that is or is likely to be placed on the market be adequately labelled or identified and a Commission power (in paragraph (5)) to adopt provisions for the purpose of applying the traceability requirements to specific sectors.

3.2.43   In respect of Art 18(2) and (3) of Regulation (EC) 178/2002, provision is made for competent authorities, offences, penalties and enforcement:

(a)   in so far as it relates to food, by regs 3, 4, 5 and 6 of the General Food Regulations 2004, as amended by the Official Feed and Food Control (England) Regulations 2005;

(b)   in so far as it relates to feed, by regs 15 and 16 of the Feed (Hygiene and Enforcement) (England) Regulations 2005; and

(c)   in so far as it relates to medicated feedingstuffs and specified feed additives, by reg 14, together with Sch 5, para 2, and reg 43 of the Veterinary Medicines Regulations 2008.

Responsibilities for food: food business operators

3.2.44   Article 19 of Regulation (EC) 178/2002 specifies the obligations of food business operators to withdraw and recall unsafe food and to inform competent authorities and consumers. Readers are recommended to consult the Guidance issued by the Commission and by the Food Standards Agency. The provisions of the Article are explained below.

'If a food business operator considers or has reason to believe that a food which it has imported, produced, processed, manufactured or distributed is not in compliance with the food safety requirements' Article 19(1) requires that 'it shall immediately initiate procedures to withdraw[1] the food in question from the market where the food has left the immediate control of that initial food business operator and inform the competent authorities thereof. Where the product may have reached the consumer, the operator shall effectively and accurately inform the consumers of the reason for its withdrawal, and if necessary, recall from consumers products already supplied to them when other measures are not sufficient to achieve a high level of health protection.'

1 General Product Safety Directive 2001/95 defines withdrawal as 'any measure aimed at preventing the distribution, display or offer of a product dangerous to the consumer'.

3.2.45   The following points may be noted about this:

(1)   Article 19(1) catches food that breaches the food safety requirements of Art 14. In the normal way, this will include food that fails to comply with specific Community or national provisions governing food safety within the meaning of Art 14(7) and (9). Not only will that not be deemed to be safe, but it is also unlikely, for example, to be suitable for 'normal conditions of use' within the meaning of Art 14(3).

(2)   Article 19(1) catches all food business operators who have imported, produced, processed, manufactured or distributed unsafe food, including retailers who supply food to final consumers.

(3)   The obligations apply only once the food is on the market and has left the immediate control of the initial food business operator. Article 19(1) is thus concerned with circumstances in which withdrawal depends on cooperation from other operators, not where the operator is able to remedy the situation itself.

(4)   The obligation under Art 19(1) to inform the competent authorities is a consequence of the obligation to withdraw. It should be contrasted with the obligation under Art 19(3) explained in para **3.2.47** below, where an operator at any stage in the food distribution chain considers that food that it has placed on the market may be injurious to health.

(5)   If in addition the product may have reached consumers, the operator must also inform them about the withdrawal and, if necessary, recall the product.

(6)   The decision whether to withdraw/recall should be made objectively. Food business operators should consider whether the food is likely to injure the health of consumers or whether it is otherwise unfit for human consumption.

(7)   The obligation to inform competent authorities must be distinguished from the Rapid Alert System for Food and Feed now established by Art 50 (see paras **7.3.4–7.3.6** below) which involves only the Commission, Member States and the European Food Safety Authority.

3.2.46   Article 19(2) provides that:

'A food business operator responsible for retail or distribution activities which do not affect the packaging, labelling, safety or integrity of the food shall, within the limits of its respective activities, initiate procedures to withdraw from the market products not in compliance with the food-safety requirements and shall participate in contributing to the safety of the food by passing on relevant information necessary to trace a food, cooperating in the action taken by producers, processors, manufacturers and/or the competent authorities.'

The aim here is to ensure that retailers and others further down the food supply chain play their part in withdrawal of unsafe food. 'Retail' is defined by Art 3(7) as meaning 'the handling and/or processing of food and its storage at the point of sale or delivery to the final consumer, and includes distribution terminals, catering operations, factory canteens, institutional catering, restaurants and other similar food service operations, shops, supermarket distribution centres and wholesale outlets'.

3.2.47   Article 19(3) provides that:

'A food business operator shall immediately inform the competent authorities if it considers or has reason to believe that a food which it has placed on the market may be injurious to human health. Operators shall inform the competent authorities of the action taken to prevent risks to the final consumer and shall not prevent or discourage any person from cooperating, in accordance with national law and legal practice, with the competent authorities, where this may prevent, reduce or eliminate a risk arising from a food.'

The aim of this paragraph is to ensure that competent authorities are informed of potential risks to health and are not obstructed in acting for their removal. Unlike Art 19(1), it applies even before the food has left the food business operator's 'immediate control'. An operator would be required to notify the authorities immediately if it forms the view that food in its possession for sale is injurious to human health.

3.2.48   Article 19(4) requires food business operators to collaborate with the competent authorities on action taken to avoid or reduce risks posed by a food that they supply or have supplied. For example, if in doubt about whether they have complied with Art 19 obligations, food business operators should contact the competent authorities.

3.2.49   Article 19 of Regulation (EC) 178/2002 is implemented by regs 3, 4, 5 and 6 of the General Food Regulations 2004, as amended by the Official Feed and Food Control (England) Regulations 2005 which make provision for competent authorities, an offence, penalties and enforcement.

The very substantial fine in the Cadbury Schweppes prosecution described in para **3.2.30** was in part imposed for failure on the part of the operator immediately to inform the competent authorities, as required by Regulation (EC) 178/2002, Art 19(3), that salmonella infected chocolate had been placed on the market. This sent an important message to food business operators as to the new duties that Regulation (EC) 178/2002 has imposed on them. They now manifestly have the primary legal responsibility for food safety. They can no longer deal covertly with unsafe food but must actively co-operate with competent authorities to avoid or reduce risks. As will be seen from paras **3.2.50–3.2.53** below, parallel responsibilities have been imposed on feed business operators.

Responsibilities for feed: feed business operators

3.2.50   Article 20 of Regulation (EC) 178/2002 specifies the obligations of feed business operators to withdraw and recall unsafe feed and to inform competent authorities and feed users. Although Art 20 is very similar, as regards feed, to Art 19, as regards food, it is somewhat more severe extending even to the destruction of unsafe products. The differences from Art 19 are explained below. Once again, further guidance is to be found in the Notes issued by the Commission and by the Food Standards Agency.

3.2.51   Article 20(1) provides that:

'If a feed business operator considers or has reason to believe that a feed which it has imported, produced, processed, manufactured or distributed does not satisfy the feed safety requirements, it shall immediately initiate procedures to withdraw the feed in question from the market and inform the competent authorities thereof. In these circumstances or, in the case of Article 15(3), where the batch, lot or consignment does not satisfy the feed safety requirement, that feed shall be destroyed, unless the competent authority is satisfied otherwise. The operator shall effectively and accurately inform users of the feed of the reason for its withdrawal, and if necessary, recall from them products already supplied when other measures are not sufficient to achieve a high level of health protection.'

These obligations engage where the feed safety requirements are not satisfied and so depend on Art 15, as those of Art 19 depend on Art 14. The other points noted in para **3.2.45** in respect of Art 19(1) also apply, with the necessary changes, in respect of Art 20(1) except that:

(a)   feed business operators must withdraw and notify unsafe feed that has been placed on the market even though it is still under their immediate control; and

(b)   the unsafe feed (and any related batch, lot or consignment that is presumed under Art 15(3) to be unsafe) must be not only withdrawn, but also destroyed unless the competent authority is satisfied otherwise.

3.2.52   Article 20(2), (3) and (4) specify further responsibilities for feed business operators that are very similar to those for food business operators in Art 19(2), (3) and (4). Although the para (2) duties of feed business operators responsible for retail or distribution activities are in the same terms, the para (3) duties, to inform and prevent obstruction of competent authorities over potential health risks, necessarily extend to all feed that may not satisfy the feed safety requirements, not just to products injurious to health. Moreover, the para (4) duty to collaborate with competent authorities bears only on action to avoid – not to reduce – the risks posed.

3.2.53   In respect of Art 20 of Regulation (EC) 178/2002, provision is made for competent authorities, offences, penalties and enforcement:

(a)   in so far as it relates to feed, by regs 15 and 16 of the Feed (Hygiene and Enforcement) (England) Regulations 2005; and

(b)   in so far as it relates to medicated feedingstuffs and specified feed additives, by reg 14, together with Sch 5, para 2, and reg 43 of the Veterinary Medicines Regulations 2008.

Liability

3.2.54   The General Food Law provisions of Regulation (EC) 178/2002 Chapter II are without prejudice to the civil liability of producers of defective products prescribed by Directive 85/374[1] which is described below in section **21.4**.

1   Regulation (EC) 178/2002, Art 21.

3.3   EUROPEAN FOOD SAFETY AUTHORITY

3.3.1   In response to the need perceived by the Commission's 2000 Food Safety White Paper, the European Food Safety Authority now provides independent scientific advice on matters related to food and feed safety, including nutrition, animal health and welfare and plant protection. Its two main duties are risk assessment and risk communication. The taking of risk management measures and their enforcement are not within the Authority's sphere but remain the responsibility of the European Commission, Council, Parliament and the Member States. Chapter III of Regulation (EC) 178/2002 deals successively with the mission and tasks of the Authority; its organisation; its operation; its independence, transparency, confidentiality and communication; its financial provisions; and its general provisions. These legislative provisions are explained below in this section while para **3.4.4** describes the obligation of the Authority under Art 61 of Regulation (EC) 178/2002 periodically to commission an independent external evaluation of its achievements.

Mission and tasks

Mission of the Authority

3.3.2   Established by Art 22 of Regulation (EC) 178/2002[1], the European Food Safety Authority provides scientific advice and scientific and technical support for the Community's legislation and policies in all fields that have a direct or indirect impact on food and feed safety. It also provides an independent source of information on all matters within these fields and risk communication in order to improve consumer confidence. It is required to contribute to a high level of protection of human life and health in the operation of the food and feed supply chains within the internal market, taking account of the related issues of animal health and welfare, plant health and the environment. It collects and analyses data so that risks that have a direct or indirect impact on food and feed safety can be characterised and monitored. Its mission also includes the provision of:

(a)   scientific advice and scientific and technical support on human nutrition in relation to Community legislation and, at the request of the Commission, assistance concerning communication on nutritional issues within the framework of the Community health programme;

(b)   scientific opinions on other matters relating to animal health and welfare and plant health;

(c)   scientific opinions on products other than food and feed relating to genetically modified organisms as defined by Directive 2001/18, but without prejudice to the procedures established by that Directive.

More generally, the Authority must provide opinions as the scientific basis for the drafting and adoption of Community measures in the fields within its mission; and serve as a point of reference by virtue of its independence, the scientific and technical quality of its opinions and the information it disseminates, the transparency of its procedures and methods of operation, and its diligence in performing assigned tasks. Finally, the Authority is required to cooperate with the competent bodies in the Member States carrying out similar tasks, and with the Commission and Member States to promote the effective coherence between risk assessment, risk management and risk communication functions. Conversely, the Member States are obliged to cooperate with the Authority to ensure that it accomplishes its mission.

1   See also Regulation (EC) 178/2002 recitals (32)–(40).

Tasks of the Authority

3.3.3   As regards the fields within its mission, Art 23 of Regulation (EC) 178/2002 allots the Authority the following tasks that are enlarged upon by the Articles of the Operation section of Chapter III of the Regulation respectively specified in brackets and explained further below:

(a)   to provide the Community institutions and the Member States with the best possible scientific opinions (Art 29);

(b)   to promote and coordinate the development of uniform risk assessment methods;

(c)   to provide scientific and technical support to the Commission (Art 31);

(d)   to commission scientific studies necessary for the accomplishment of its mission (Art 32);

(e)   to search for, collect, collate, analyse and summarise scientific and technical data (Art 33);

(f)   to undertake action to identify and characterise emerging risks (Art 34);

(g)   to establish a system of networks of organisations and be responsible for their operation (Art 36);

(h)   to provide scientific and technical assistance, when so requested by the Commission, in the crisis management procedures implemented by the Commission with regard to the safety of food and feed[1];

(i)   to provide scientific and technical assistance, when so requested by the Commission, with a view to improving cooperation between the Community, applicant countries, international organisations and third countries[2];

(j)   to ensure that the public and interested parties receive rapid, reliable, objective and comprehensible information[3];

(k)   to express independently its own conclusions and orientations[4];

(l)   to undertake any other task assigned to it by the Commission.

1   See Regulation (EC) 178/2002, Art 55 described at para **7.5.2**ff.
2   See for example Regulation (EC) 178/2002, Arts 13 and 49 respectively described at paras **3.2.19** and **3.3.17**.
3   See further Regulation (EC) 178/2002, Art 40 described at para **3.3.15** below.
4   See further Regulation (EC) 178/2002, Art 37 described at para **3.3.15** below.

Organisation

Management Board

3.3.4   The Authority's Management Board is composed of 14 members appointed by the Council[1] in consultation with the European Parliament from a list drawn up by the Commission and includes a Commission representative. Four of the members must have a background in organisations representing consumers and other interests in the food chain. Although a member's term of office is four years, which may be renewed once, the first mandate for half of the members was six years. The Board elects one of its members as its Chair for a renewable two-year period. The Executive Director takes part in the meetings of the Management Board and the Chair of the Scientific Committee may be invited to attend, in each case, without voting rights.[2]

1   Council Decision of 15 July 2002 OJ C 179, 27/07/2002 p.9.
2   Regulation (EC) 178/2002, Art 25, as amended by Regulation (EC) 1642/2003.

3.3.5   Every year the Management Board adopts:

(a)   the Authority's programme of work for the coming year and revisable multi-annual programme;

(b)   the general report on the Authority's activities for the previous year;

(c)   the draft statement of estimates and establishment plan for submission to the Budgetary Authority comprised of the European Parliament and Council;

(d)   the Authority's budget that, subject to any necessary adjustment, becomes final after adoption of the European Union's general budget[1].

More generally, the Board is charged with ensuring that the Authority's mission and tasks are carried out according to law and that its work programmes are consistent with the Community's legislative and policy priorities in the area of food safety.[2]

1   See further para **3.3.16** below.
2   Regulation (EC) 178/2002, Arts 25 and 43, as amended by Regulation (EC) 1642/2003.

Executive Director

3.3.6   The Executive Director represents the Authority and is responsible in particular for day-to-day administration, preparation of the draft estimates, execution of the resulting budget, preparation of draft work programmes in consultation with the Commission, implementation of programmes and decisions adopted by the Management Board, liaison with the European Parliament and publication of the Authority's annual report to Community bodies and generally. The Executive Director is answerable to and appointed by the Management Board, on the basis of a list of candidates proposed by the Commission, for a period of five years that may be renewed.[1]

1   Regulation (EC) 178/2002, Art 26.

Advisory Forum

3.3.7   Each Member State has a place on the Authority's Advisory Forum for a representative of its national food safety agency. A consultative body, the Forum advises on the performance of the Executive Director's duties, particularly in drawing up the Authority's work programme and in prioritising requests for scientific opinions.

It also constitutes a mechanism for exchanging information on potential risks and pooling knowledge, in particular ensuring cooperation to avoid duplication of scientific studies, to resolve diverging scientific opinions, to promote European networking and to deal with identified emerging risks. The Advisory Forum is chaired by the Executive Director and meets at least four times a year.[1]

1   Regulation (EC) 178/2002, Art 27.

Scientific Committee and Scientific Panels

3.3.8   The Authority's Scientific Committee and permanent Scientific Panels have replaced the former Commission scientific committees that advised on food, animal health and welfare and plant health[1]. They are composed of scientific experts appointed for three years by the Management Board on a proposal from the Executive Director. They provide the risk assessments and other scientific opinions of the Authority and can, where necessary, organise public hearings. The Scientific Committee is comprised of the Chairs of the Scientific Panels and six independent scientific experts who do not belong to any of the Panels. It is responsible for general coordination and provides opinions on subjects that span the competence of several Scientific Panels or (with the help of external working groups that it sets up) are outside the competence of any of the Panels. The current Scientific Panels deal with (a) food additives and nutrient sources added to food; (b) additives and products or substances used in animal feed; (c) plant protection products and their residues; (d) genetically modified organisms; (e) dietetic products, nutrition and allergies; (f) biological hazards; (g) contaminants in the food chain; (h) animal health and welfare; (i) plant health; and (j) food contact materials, enzymes, flavourings and processing aids.[2]

1   See Regulation (EC) 178/2002 recital (45), reg 62(1) and Commission Decision 2008/721.
2   Regulation (EC) 178/2002 recitals (45) and (46) and Art 28, as amended by Regulations 575/2006 and 202/2008.

Operation

Scientific opinions

3.3.9   Article 29 of Regulation (EC) 178/2002[1] specifies the cases in which the Authority gives scientific opinions on matters within its mission. They are, where the Commission so requests; where Community legislation makes provision for the Authority to be consulted; where the Authority acts on its own initiative; where the European Parliament so requests; and where a Member State so requests. Provision for the information to accompany requests and the time limits for and refusals of opinions is made by Art 29 and implementing Regulation (EC) 1304/2003, which has established a Register of requested and own-initiative opinions.

1   See also Regulation (EC) 178/2002 recital (47).

3.3.10   The primary purpose of the Authority's scientific opinions is to inform Community risk management decisions. Although in cases of uncommon urgency the Commission may act before seeking advice[1], the Authority's opinion is the normal precursor for measures in which the safety of food or feed is in issue[2]. Indeed, those Community sectoral framework instruments that subject substances, products or processes to a system of prior authorisation or inclusion on a positive list[3] now customarily lay down procedures whereby the Authority's scientific evaluation of them is to be delivered before the relevant measure is submitted by the Commission for the opinion of the Standing Committee on the Food Chain and Animal Health as described in para **3.4.2** below. Such provision has, for example, been made in respect of food supplements (Directive 2002/46)[4], genetically modified food and feed (Regulation (EC) 1829/2003), smoke flavourings (Regulation (EC) 2065/2003), food contact materials and articles (Regulation (EC) 1935/2004), additives for animal nutrition (Regulation (EC) 1831/2003), plant protection products (Regulations (EC) 1490/2002 and 2229/2004) and pesticide residues (Regulation (EC) 396/2005). Moreover, the Community – evidently mindful that some at least of these opinions are acts capable of producing direct legal effects – has gone on to provide in some cases[5] for their administrative review by the Commission on its own initiative, in response to a request from a Member State or from any person directly and individually concerned. The legality of the Commission's resulting decision will itself be liable to judicial review by the European Court under Art 230 EC.

1   See, for example, Decision 2004/374 (jelly mini-cups containing specified additives).
2   See, for example, GMO Decisions 2004/643, 2005/608, 2005/635 and 2006/47.
3   Where only the listed items are permitted. A negative list approach permits all but the stated items.
4   As to the legality of the procedure, see joined cases C-154/04 and C-155/04 *R* (*on the application of Alliance for Health*), *Nutri-Link Ltd v Secretary of State for Health* [2005] ECR I-6451.
5   See Regulations 1829/2003 (genetically modified food and feed), 1831/2003 (additives in animal nutrition), 1935/2004 (food contact materials and articles) and 396/2005 (maximum pesticide residue levels).

3.3.11   For the purposes of exercising its right to request the Authority to issue scientific opinions, each Member State is required to inform the Authority of the government authority or authorities permitted to make the request[1]. The European Court has confirmed that, as Community rules stand, national courts may not refer questions on the classification of products to the European Food Safety Authority. However, if the Authority were to give an opinion corresponding to the subject-matter of a dispute pending before a national court, that court would have to ascribe to it the same value as it does to expert reports. The opinion would thus be capable of constituting evidence that the court would have to take into consideration[2].

1   Regulation (EC) 1304/2003, Art 9.
2   Joined cases C-211/03, C-299/03 and C-316/03 to C-318/03 *HLH Warenvertriebs GmbH and Orthica BV v Germany* [2005] ECR I-5141.

Diverging scientific opinions

3.3.12   The Authority is required to cooperate in resolving or clarifying substantive divergences over scientific issues with the Community or Member State body in question[1].

1   Regulation (EC) 178/2002, Art 30 and recital (47).

Scientific and technical assistance

3.3.13   The Authority may also, under Art 31 of Regulation (EC) 178/2002, be requested by the Commission to provide scientific or technical assistance in any field within its mission. This concerns scientific or technical work that involves the application of well-established scientific or technical principles and does not require the expertise of the Scientific Committee or a Scientific Panel. In particular the tasks include assistance to the Commission in the establishment or evaluation of technical criteria or in the development of technical guidelines. The Authority also provides scientific support when requested by the Commission in relation to crisis management under Arts 55–57 of Regulation (EC) 178/2002[1]. Further, the Authority assists the Commission with detailed implementing rules in relation to smoke flavourings (Regulation (EC) 2065/2003), specific hygiene provisions for food of animal origin (Regulation (EC) 853/2004), official controls on products of animal origin (Regulation (EC) 854/2004), genetically modified food and feed (Regulation (EC) 1829/2003), additives for animal nutrition (Regulation (EC) 1831/2003) and feed hygiene (Regulation (EC) 183/2005).

1   See para **7.5.2** below.

Scientific studies, data collection, emerging risks, rapid alerts and networking

3.3.14 Articles 32–36 of Regulation (EC) 178/2002 set out the remaining functions of the Authority[1]. By Art 32 it is required to commission *scientific studies* while avoiding duplication with Community or national research programmes. In collaboration with others working in the same field, under Art 33 it *collects, collates, analyses and summarises relevant scientific and technical data* in particular relating to risks from the consumption of food, biological risks, contaminants and residues. Under Art 34 it is to set up monitoring procedures for systematically seeking, collecting, collating and analysing information and data with a view to the *identification of emerging risks* and, when it suspects an emerging serious risk, to request information from Member States, other Community agencies and the Commission. To enable the Authority to monitor health and nutritional food risks, Art 35 provides that it shall receive messages forwarded via the enhanced *rapid alert system* established by Art 50[2]. Lastly, under Art 36 and implementing Regulation (EC) 2230/2004, the Authority promotes the *networking of organisations operating in the fields within its mission*, in particular to facilitate scientific cooperation by coordination of activities, development and implementation of joint projects and exchange of information, expertise and best practices. The Advisory Forum described in para **3.3.7** above contributes to this networking.

Designated Member State organisations listed by the Management Board are to be entrusted with certain tasks with a view to assisting the Authority with its general mission. They must in particular include those competent to assess genetically modified food and feed under Regulation (EC) 1829/2003. Evaluation of active substances in plant protection products is another example of scientific work distributed among Member States[3].

1   See also Regulation (EC) 178/2002 recitals (48)–(52).
2   See para **7.3.4**ff below.
3   See Regulations (EC) 1490/2002 and 2229/2004.

Independence, transparency, confidentiality and communication

3.3.15 Articles 37–42 of Regulation (EC) 178/2002 contain provisions vital to the maintenance of public confidence in the Authority. Consonant with the Authority's status as a functionally separate European Community agency, are the specific obligations to *act independently* that are imposed by Art 37 on the Management Board, the members of the Advisory Forum, the Executive Director and the members of the Scientific Committee and Scientific Panels. Every year they must make declarations of commitment and of interests potentially prejudicial to their independence. Additionally, at each meeting they, and any external expert participants, must declare such interests in respect of agenda items. The Authority is further required by Art 38 to carry out its activities with a high level of *transparency*. Thus, Management Board meetings must normally be held in public and among the items that must be published are the agendas, minutes and opinions of the Scientific Committee and the Scientific Panels, the results of its scientific studies, the annual report of its activities and the declarations of interest made annually and in relation to individual agenda items. The openness demanded by Art 38 is, however, subject to Art 39 which, except where disclosure is necessary to protect public health, imposes a duty of *confidentiality* in respect of information for which confidential treatment has been requested and justified. The provisions of Art 40 on *communications from the Authority* confirm its independent character. Although the Commission remains responsible for communicating its risk management decisions, the Authority has autonomous power to communicate and provide the public and interested parties with rapid, objective, reliable and easily accessible information, in particular with regard to the results of its own work. Providing food and feed safety advice – or 'risk communication' – is a vital part of this responsibility, in discharge of which the Authority acts in close collaboration with the Commission and Member States in particular via the Communications Working Group of the Advisory Forum. The Authority also cooperates with Member States and others over public information campaigns[1]. Complementary to the provisions of Arts 38 and 40 on the publication of information are those on *access to documents* in Art 41, as amended by Regulation (EC) 1642/2003. Regulation (EC) 1049/2001, regarding access to European Parliament, Council and Commission documents, is applied to documents held by the Authority and provision made, in the event of refusal, for a complaint to the European Ombudsman or an action before the European Court[2]. Last but not least of the Authority's responsibilities for actively engaging with the public is that enacted by Art 42. Under this provision the Authority is developing effective contacts with the *representatives of consumers, producers and other interested parties* in particular by the regular exchange of views with stakeholders through an annual 'colloque' and a 'Stakeholder Consultative Platform'.

1   See also Regulation (EC) 178/2002 recitals (53)–(55).
2   Under Arts 195 and 230 EC respectively.

Financial provisions

3.3.16   Provisions governing the Authority finances are laid down in Arts 43–45[1] of Regulation (EC) 178/2002, as supplemented by a Financial Regulation and implementing rules adopted by the Management Board on the basis of the EU framework Financial Regulation (EC, Euratom) 1605/2002[2]. Article 43 makes provision for *adoption of the Authority's budget*, its revenue being primarily derived from the Community. By 31 March each year the draft must be presented by the Management Board to the Commission and becomes final following adoption of the European Union's general budget by the European Parliament and Council. Under Art 44, *implementation of the Authority's budget* is the Executive Director's responsibility. On a recommendation from the Council, the European Parliament is responsible for giving a discharge to the Executive Director in respect of the implementation of the budget for year N before 30 April of year N + 2. Article 45, read with recital (57), also requires the Commission to report on the possibility of financing from *fees received by the Authority* for services it provides such as the processing of authorisation dossiers presented by industry[3].

1   As amended by Regulation (EC) 1642/2003.
2   And implementing Regulations (EC, Euratom) 2342/2002 and 2343/2002.
3   See Commission Staff Working Paper published in 2006 and the summary, published in August 2007, of the generally adverse comments received.

General provisions

3.3.17   Articles 47–49 of Regulation (EC) 178/2002 prescribe general provisions appropriate to a Community agency. The Authority has both *legal* *personality and privileges and immunities*[1] considered necessary for the performance by the Communities of their tasks and functions. The *liability* of the Authority is analogous to that of the European Community in general. Its contractual liability is governed by the law of the contract in question and the European Court has jurisdiction not only in cases of non-contractual liability, but also over arbitration clauses in Authority contracts[2]. The Authority's *staff* is subject to the rules applicable to other European Community officials. The Authority is also open to the *participation of third countries* that have concluded agreements with the European Community obliging them to apply Community legislation in the field covered by Regulation (EC) 178/2002.

1   Conferred by the Protocol on the privileges and immunities of the European Communities.
2   See Arts 288 and 238EC.

3.4   PROCEDURES AND FINAL PROVISIONS

3.4.1   Regulation (EC) 178/2002 is concluded by Chapter V of which Arts 58–60 concern Committee and Mediation procedures and Arts 61–65 comprise the final provisions.

Committee and mediation procedures

Standing Committee on the Food Chain and Animal Health

3.4.2   Made up of representatives of Member States and chaired by a Commission official, the Standing Committee on the Food Chain and Animal Health fulfils the important function of sanctioning delegated legislation made by the Commission. The Committee was established by Art 58 of Regulation (EC) 178/2002 to ensure a more effective and comprehensive approach to the food chain[1]. It thus not only replaced the former Standing Veterinary Committee, Standing Committee for Foodstuffs and Standing Committee for Feedingstuffs: it has also taken over from the Standing Committee on Plant Health functions relating to plant protection products and the setting of maximum residue levels[2]. In order to cover these subjects, the Committee is divided into the following eight sections: General Food Law; Biological Safety of the Food Chain; Toxicological Safety of the Food Chain; Controls and Import Conditions; Animal Nutrition; Genetically Modified Food and Feed and Environmental Risk; Animal Health and Animal Welfare; and Phytopharmaceuticals. The Commission may generally adopt implementing measures only if it obtains a favourable opinion from the Committee, given by qualified majority of the Member States (see further para **1.6.5** above). However, in emergencies, it is authorised by Art 53(2) to act provisionally and submit its measure to the Committee within 10 working days for confirmation, amendment, revocation or extension[3]. Besides carrying out the functions assigned to it by Regulation (EC) 178/2002 and many other relevant Community provisions, the Committee may, by Art 59, also examine any other issue falling under those provisions, either at the initiative of the Chairman or at the written request of one of its members.

1   Regulation (EC) 178/2002 recital (62).
2   See Regulation (EC) 178/2002 recital (62) and Art 62(2). Decisions 68/361/EEC, 69/414/EEC and 70/372/EEC were consequentially repealed by Regulation (EC) 178/2002, Art 62(4).
3   See para **7.4.2** below.

Mediation procedure

3.4.3   Article 60 of Regulation (EC) 178/2002 institutes a mediation procedure for cases in which a Member State is of the opinion that a food safety measure taken by another Member State is either incompatible with the Regulation or is likely to affect the functioning of the internal market. In such cases, the Commission – to which the matter is to be referred – and the two Member States are to make every effort to resolve the problem. An opinion from the European Food Safety Authority on any relevant scientific issue may be sought by the Commission if agreement cannot be reached.

Final provisions

3.4.4   Of the Final Provisions of Regulation (EC) 178/2002, only Art 61 calls for comment. This requires the European Food Safety Authority to commission an independent external evaluation of its achievements before 1 January 2005 and every six years thereafter. Following publication in January 2006 of the first report, the Management Board recommended that the Authority should focus its efforts on six priority fields, that is: (1) developing active networking and stronger co-operation with Member States; (2) strengthening the Authority's relationship with its institutional partners (EU and international) and stakeholders; (3) enhancing the Authority's organisation; (4) enhancing the impact and effectiveness of the Authority's communications; (5) developing the Authority's role in nutrition; and (6) defining the Authority's medium- and long-term vision.

Chapter 4

Food Safety Act 1990: extent, subordinate legislative powers, interpretation and presumptions

4.1 THE ACT

4.1.1   The preceding chapters have shown how the Food Safety Act 1990 (FSA 1990) has been modified by two important legislative initiatives to secure the safety of food. First, the Food Standards Act 1999 (FSA 1999) placed central government responsibility essentially in the hands of the Food Standards Agency and the Secretary of State for Health, subject to the devolution of functions effected by the Scotland Act 1998 (SA 1998) and under the Government of Wales Act 1998 (GWA 1998) and the Government of Wales Act 2006 (GWA 2006). Secondly, the Food Safety Act 1990 (Amendment) Regulations 2004 and the General Food Regulations 2004 made amendments to harmonise the provisions of the Act with general food Regulation (EC) 178/2002. Indeed, that Regulation is now the basic food law within the United Kingdom and throughout the European Union but, in Great Britain, the FSA 1990 remains the principal domestic food control measure.

Extent

4.1.2   Although this book is concerned with food law applying in England and Wales, the position elsewhere in the United Kingdom needs to be understood. In this field, legislative competence has been conferred on the Scottish Parliament by the SA 1998, s 29 and relevant functions have been transferred to the Scottish Executive by the SA 1998, s 53 and by the Scotland Act 1998 (Transfer of Functions to the Scottish Ministers etc.) Order 2005[1]. The Scottish Ministers thus generally exercise the subordinate legislative powers of the FSA 1990 which, for the present, still applies to Scotland[2]. With the exception of the power in respect of oil and gas installations referred to below, the substantive provisions of the FSA 1990 have never applied to Northern Ireland that has its own parallel legislation[3]. In practice, the food law rules of the various parts of the United Kingdom are unlikely to diverge very much because they are mostly made in implementation of common Community obligations.

Power to make special provision for the Isles of Scilly has now been removed from the FSA 1990, which applies there as it does to the rest of England[4].

Her Majesty may, by Order in Council, direct that any of the provisions of the Act shall apply to any of the Channel Islands with such exceptions and modifications as may be specified[5]. For the purposes of the FSA 1990, territorial waters of the United Kingdom adjacent to any part of Great Britain are treated as situated in that part[6]. There is also power, for the purposes of the FSA 1990 and subordinate legislation, to provide, by Order in Council, for oil and gas installations and safety zones to be treated as if they were situated in a specified part of the United Kingdom[7]. Note also that the Offshore Installations and Pipeline Works (Management and Administration) Regulations 1995, regs 17 and 18 require drinking water to be readily available on installations and that provisions on them are fit for human consumption, palatable and of good quality.

1   So far as they were not already devolved , functions in respect of all substances considered food under Regulation (EC) 178/2002 were transferred by the Scotland Act 1998 (Transfer of Functions to the Scottish Ministers etc) Order 2005.
2   See SA 1998, s 53, but also s 57(1) invoked, in respect of Scotland, by the Secretary of State for Health in making the Food Safety (Ships and Aircraft) (England and Scotland) Order 2003.
3   Food Safety (Northern Ireland) Order 1991, SI 1991/762 (NI 7).
4   FSA 1999, Sch 5, paras 9 and 22.
5   FSA 1990, s 57(2).
6   FSA 1990, s 58(1).
7   FSA 1990, s 58(2)–(4), as amended, and Petroleum Act 1998, s 11.

Enforcement of provisions in and under the Food Safety Act 1990

4.1.3   Chapters 18, 19 and 20 below describe the important provisions of the 1990 Act on food inspections, sampling, analysis and examination, on prosecutions of – the generally strict liability – offences and on the statutory defences that reduce their severity.

Regulations and orders

4.1.4   Since general food Regulation (EC) 178/2002 significantly extended food control, in particular to embrace feeding stuffs, the subordinate legislative powers in the FSA 1990 have not always proved extensive enough to cover the implementation of important Community food instruments. In such cases, the powers in s 2(2) of the European Communities Act 1972 (ECA 1972) have been used instead[1]. However, not only do s 2(2) regulations made for this purpose customarily apply or adapt provisions of the 1990 Act, but also many Directives and Regulations continue to be implemented directly under the wide-ranging powers to make regulations and orders that it confers on the Secretary of State for Health and devolved authorities[2].

FSA 1990 regulations and orders are made by statutory instrument subject to annulment in pursuance of a resolution of either House of Parliament[3] and, before making most of them, the Secretary of State is required to consult organisations representative of interests likely to be substantially affected[4]. Consultation undertaken by the Food Standards Agency may be treated as effective for this purpose[5], there being in any event an obligation to have regard to relevant advice given by the Agency[6]. While these requirements still subsist, the obligation to consult under the Act has now in practice largely been superseded by public consultation under Art 9 of general food Regulation (EC) 178/2002[7].

The powers in previous legislation to regulate food composition, labelling and hygiene and to provide for enforcement of Community obligations were extended in what are now FSA 1990, s 16, Sch 1 and s 17 to enable provision also to be made for food sources, contact materials and microbiological standards. Subordinate legislative capacity was further strengthened by powers to make emergency control orders (s 13) and to regulate novel foods and food sources, genetically modified foods and food sources, to prohibit imports of specified food classes (s 18) and to apply regulations to commercial operations (s 26), as well as to enable food premises to be registered or licensed (s 19) and enforcement authorities to make charges (s 45)[8]. Additionally, substances and activities relating to farm production of food sources may be regulated under a power inserted by the FSA 1999[9].

It may be helpful to mention here specific powers that are the respective sources of two familiar provisions in regulations. First, s 48(1)(a) is the authority for applying specified provisions of the FSA 1990 for the purposes of regulations[10]. Secondly, s 26(1)(b) is the authority for the provision, traditionally included in regulations banning additives, contaminants and other substances, for food certified by a public analyst as non-compliant to be treated as failing to comply with the food safety requirements[11] and so liable to condemnation under s 9 of the Act[12]. Recently, in certain regulations of this kind that execute and enforce Community Regulations under the FSA 1990, bespoke provisions have been included for the purposes of relating to s 9[13].

Regulations under Part 2 of the Food Safety Act 1990 are expected in due course to incorporate the civil sanctions provided for in the Regulatory Enforcement and Sanctions Act 2008 described in para **18.3.3** below.

1   See, for example, the Official Feed and Food Controls (England) Regulations 2007 providing for the execution and enforcement of Regulation (EC) 882/2004 on official controls performed to ensure the verification of compliance with feed and food law, animal health and animal welfare rules.
2   See, for example, the Food Supplements (England) Regulations 2007 implementing Directive 2002/46/EC on the approximation of the laws of the Member States relating to food supplements; and the Contaminants in Food (England) Regulations 2007 which make provision for the execution and enforcement of Regulation (EC) 1881/2006 setting maximum levels for contaminants in foodstuffs.
3   FSA 1990, s 48(2) and (3).
4   FSA 1990, s 48(4). Regulations under s 17(2) or 18(1)(c) and orders not made under Pt I are exempt from this requirement.
5   FSA 1990, s 48(4B).
6   FSA 1990, s 48(4A).
7   See para **3.2.10** above and FSA 1990, s 48 (4C) inserted by the Food Safety Act 1990 (Amendment) Regulations 2004, reg 5.
8   See further section **4.4** below as to food sources and contact materials, and section **4.5** as to commercial operations.
9   FSA 1990, Sch 1, para 6A.
10 See, for example, the Addition of Vitamins, Minerals and Other Substances (England) Regulations 2007, reg 5.
11 See, for example, the Tryptophan in Food (England) Regulations 2005, reg 9.
12 As to condemnation of food, see section **5.4** and in particular para **5.4.9** below.
13 See, for example, the Smoke Flavourings (England) Regulations 2005, reg 4; the Contaminants in Food (England) Regulations 2007, reg 5(2); and – see para **5.4.9** – the Food Hygiene (England) Regulations 2006, reg 27.

4.1.5   Regulations and orders made under earlier legislation were continued in force as if made under equivalent provisions of the FSA 1990[1]. Modifications were made to that subordinate legislation to adapt it to the provisions of the FSA 1990[2]. Regulations made under the ECA 1972 that referred to the previous food legislation were also adapted to the provisions of the FSA 1990[3].

1   FSA 1990, s 59(3) and Sch 4, para (2).
2   Food Safety Act 1990 (Consequential Modifications) (England and Wales) Order 1990.
3   Food Safety Act 1990 (Consequential Modifications) (No 2) (Great Britain) Order 1990.

Application to the Crown etc

4.1.6   Generally speaking, provisions in and under the FSA 1990 apply to food supplied in military bases, HM prisons and most other Crown premises and to people in the public service of the Crown. By s 54, the provisions of the Act and regulations and orders made under it bind the Crown, subject to specified limitations. First, the Crown cannot thereby be rendered criminally liable: instead, any Crown act or omission that constitutes a contravention may, on the application of an enforcement authority, be declared unlawful by the High Court. Secondly, the powers of entry conferred by s 32 of the Act are not exercisable in relation to any Crown premises for which the Secretary of State has, in the interests of national security, issued a certificate in compliance with s 54(4). Thirdly, Her Majesty is not in any way affected in her private capacity.[1] Although exemptions of this kind do not appear in EC food hygiene Regulations or the provisions made for their execution and enforcement under the ECA 1972 by the Food Hygiene (England) Regulations 2006[2], enforcement authorities are recommended by the Food Standards Agency Food Law Codes of Practice and Practice Guidance[3] to adopt the same approach to their enforcement in Crown premises as they do in respect of the FSA 1990.

As for other public bodies, police premises are vested in the respective police authorities and subject to food legislation, while the National Health Service (Amendment) Act 1986[4] applies it to NHS premises, Crown immunities having been removed from health service bodies by s 60 of the National Health Service and Community Care Act 1990.

Guidance on enforcement of food law in the premises of the kinds specified in this paragraph is given by chs 1.6 of the Food Law Codes of Practice and Practice Guidance for England and for Wales.

1   Similar provision is made by s 38 of the FSA 1999 to apply that Act to the Crown.
2   See chs 13 and 14 below.
3   See below.
4   As amended by FSA 1990, s 59(1) and Sch 3, para 36(1).

4.2   CONSTRUCTION OF SUBORDINATE LEGISLATION

4.2.1   Expressions used in regulations and orders made under the FSA 1990 have the meaning that they bear in the Act unless the contrary intention appears[1]. Definitions in regulations and orders apply only to the regulations or order in which they appear, in the absence of express provision to the contrary. It is a common misunderstanding to assume that definitions in, for example, food labelling regulations apply to regulations concerning particular classes of food and vice versa. They do not unless, of course, the regulations themselves so provide.

1   Interpretation Act 1978, s 11.

4.3   FOOD FOR HUMAN CONSUMPTION

4.3.1   In the FSA 1990 'food' now has the same meaning as it has in general food Regulation (EC) 178/2002. This substitution for the original definition in s 1 was made by the Food Safety Act 1990 (Amendment) Regulations 2004, not least so as to facilitate future implementation of European Community food law under the Act.

It will be recalled that the new definition, which was enacted by Art 2 of Regulation (EC) 178/2002, is set out in para **3.2.2** above with comments in para **3.2.3**. It covers much the same ground as the original definition in the Act so that, for example, water after supply to premises[1], chewing gum and live shellfish for human consumption are still included. The main difference from the original definition is that medicinal products within the meaning of medicines Directive 2001/83/EC are excluded even when unlicensed. Yet matters remain unclear because some products satisfy the conditions for classification not only as a medicinal product but also as a foodstuff and, in the current state of Community law, there is no harmonised classification method. It is the competent national authority of each Member State – in the United Kingdom, the Medicine and Healthcare Products Regulatory Agency – which is empowered to decide on a case-by-case basis how such a product is to be classified. Notwithstanding that an imported product is lawfully marketed as a foodstuff in the exporting Member State, the national authority, acting within the law, may determine that it is a medicinal product[2].

1   See further FSA 1990, s 55, as amended by SI 2005/2035.
2   See joined cases C-211/03, C-299/03 and C-316/03 to C-318/03 *HLH Warenvertriebs GmbH and Orthica v Germany* [2005] I-5141, briefly considered in para **3.2.3** above.

4.3.2   'Human consumption' appears in the FSA 1990 as a concept separate from 'food'[1]. It is defined[2] as including use in the preparation of food for human consumption, thus encompassing food ingredients, and is supported by three important presumptions specified in s 3 for the purposes of the Act. In summary, the presumptions are that:

(a)   any food commonly used for human consumption if sold or offered, exposed or kept for sale, shall be presumed, until the contrary is proved, to have been sold or, as the case may be, to have been or to be intended for sale for human consumption;

(b)   any food or article or substance commonly used for human consumption or in the manufacture of food for human consumption which is found on premises used for the preparation, storage or sale of that food shall, until the contrary is proved, be presumed to be intended for sale or for manufacturing food for sale for human consumption; and

(c)   any article or substance capable of being used in the composition or preparation of any food commonly used for human consumption which is found on premises on which that food is prepared shall, until the contrary is proved, be presumed to be intended for such use.

1   See FSA 1990, ss 7(1), 9(1), 14(2), 15(5), 16(5) and 17(3).
2   FSA 1990, s 53(1).

4.3.3   These presumptions place on the defendant the burden of proving, as the case may be, that the food, article or substance in question was not intended for sale or for manufacturing food for sale for human consumption, or that the article or substance in question was not intended for use in the composition or preparation of food commonly used for human consumption. The standard of proof is less than is generally required of the prosecution[1]: the defendant has simply to 'prove' his case[2], but positive evidence is required[3]. It would therefore, for example, be prudent for a manufacturer clearly to identify any food at the factory that has been rejected for human consumption. The same is no doubt also true of food that is not yet ready for sale for human consumption, or food that is awaiting acceptance and introduction to the manufacturing process, even though in these cases the presumptions may be easier to rebut.

In consequence of the House of Lords' judgment in *R v Lambert*[4], it is apparent that the legality of these presumptions, like others that place a burden of proof on the defendant in criminal proceedings, must now be considered under Art 6(2) of the European Convention on Human Rights that provides that 'everyone charged with a criminal offence shall be presumed innocent until proved guilty according to law'. As indicated in para **20.3.4** below, in order to be compatible with the Convention such presumptions must if possible be read as imposing only an evidential burden. If sufficient evidence is adduced by the defendant to raise the issue, it will be for the prosecution to show beyond reasonable doubt, that the defence is nevertheless not made out.

1　See para **19.3.2** below.
2　*Cant v Harley & Sons Ltd* [1938] 2 All ER 768.
3　*Hooper v Petrou* (1973) 71 LGR 347, [1973] Crim LR 198.
4　[2001] 3 All ER 577.

4.4　FOOD SOURCES AND CONTACT MATERIAL

4.4.1　In response to the sophistication of modern food production and the requirements of Community obligations, the scope of powers for regulating food was further broadened by applying them additionally to food sources and contact material. 'Food source' is defined as any growing crop or live animal, bird or fish from which food is intended to be derived (whether by harvesting, slaughtering, milking, collecting eggs or otherwise): 'contact material' is defined as any article or substance which is intended to come into contact with food[1].

1　FSA 1990, s 1(3). As to regulations on contact materials, see further section **12.6** below. As to an example of provision in respect of food sources, see the now revoked Food (Animals and Animal Products from Belgium) (Emergency Control) Order 1999, SI 1999/1542.

4.5　COMMERCIAL OPERATIONS

4.5.1　For the reasons given in section **4.4** above, the thresholds at which the requirements of regulations can be imposed were also increased and systematised by the FSA 1990. Where specified contraventions have occurred, s 26(1)(a) enables provision to be made for prohibiting or regulating the carrying out of any 'commercial operation'. This term is very widely defined by the Act[1]: in relation to any food or contact material, it means, any of the following, namely:

(a)　selling, possessing for sale and offering, exposing or advertising for sale;
(b)　consigning, delivering or serving by way of sale;
(c)　preparing for sale or presenting, labelling or wrapping for the purpose of sale;
(d)　storing or transporting for the purpose of sale;
(e)　importing and exporting;

and, in relation to a food source, means deriving food from it for the purpose of sale or for purposes connected with sale.

1　FSA 1990, s 1(3).

4.6 SALE

4.6.1   The point of sale, however, is the threshold at which British food controls have traditionally been imposed and it remains the principal one employed in and under the FSA 1990. Most of the prohibitions and restrictions thus imposed on sale are couched so as to bear also on offer, exposure and having in possession for sale. The general meaning of 'sale'[1] is extended by the FSA 1990 to include the supply of food, otherwise than on sale, in the course of a business, and any other thing that is done with respect to food and is specified in an order made by the Secretary of State for Health[2]. The Act also applies to food which is offered as a prize or reward or is given away in similar specified circumstances[3].

1   See summary in section **21.2** below.
2   FSA 1990, s 2(1). See *Swain v Old Kentucky Restaurants* (1973) 138 JP 84. As to 'business', see para **4.8.1** below.
3   FSA 1990, s 2(2).

4.6.2   Exposure for sale means exposure to view in a context where sales are carried out or anticipated[1]. Margarine has been held to be exposed for sale even though wrapped in paper and so not visible to the purchaser[2].

Offer for sale should not be confused with an invitation to do business. The mere display of food in a self-service store does not constitute an 'offer for sale': it is merely an invitation to the customer to offer to buy[3].

1   *McNair v Terroni* [1915] 1 KB 526; *Keating v Horwood* (1926) 90 JP 141.
2   *Wheat v Brown* [1892] 1 QB 418.
3   *Pharmaceutical Society of Great Britain v Boots Cash Chemists (Southern) Ltd* [1952] 2 QB 795, [1952] 2 All ER 456.

4.6.3   With the further strengthening of food law enforcement at all stages of production, processing and distribution[1], 'possession for sale' continues to be of importance to s 9 (on inspection and seizure of suspected food)[2] and otherwise in and under the FSA 1990.

'Possession' in the context of the Act is understood to mean actual possession by the defendant or his agent and should be given a popular and not a narrow construction[3]. Physical possession of food by an agent does not divest the owner of possession[4]; but food left for collection by a buyer at a place determined in the contract of sale may not be in the possession of the vendor[5].

1   See official controls Regulation (EC) 882/2004 and para **18.2.2** below.
2   See section **5.4** below.
3   *Webb v Baker* [1916] 2 KB 753, 80 JP 449.
4   *Towers & Co Ltd v Gray* [1961] 2 QB 351, [1961] 2 All ER 68; *City Fur Manufacturing Co Ltd v Fureenbond (Brokers) London Ltd* [1937] 1 All ER 799; *R v Sleep* (1861) 25 JP 532, CCR.
5   *Oliver v Goodger* [1944] 2 All ER 481.

4.6.4   The European Community food law equivalent of the extended concept of sale has itself been introduced into the FSA 1990. As explained in para **5.4.2** below, the inspection power in s 9 has been broadened[1] to apply to food intended for human consumption that is placed on the market within the meaning of general food Regulation (EC) 178/2002. The similarity of 'placing on the market' – explained in para **3.2.13** above – to the FSA 1990 concept has also made it possible to continue to implement Community instruments by applying suitably adapted provisions of the FSA 1990[2].

1   By the General Food Regulations 2004, reg 11(a).
2   See, for example, the General Food Regulations 2004, reg 7 in particular as it applies FSA 1990, ss 3 and 21.

4.7 IMPORT AND EXPORT

4.7.1 Import and export are obvious thresholds for the imposition of food rules, but the European Community free movement of goods principle customarily requires that controls at these points be confined to third country trade[1]. In the FSA 1990, however, the terms still relate to all goods entering and leaving the United Kingdom. By s 53(1) of the FSA 1990, 'exportation' and 'importation' have the same meanings in the Act as they have for the purposes of the Customs and Excise Management Act 1979 (C&EMA 1979) and 'export' and 'import' must be construed accordingly.

In fact there are no definitions of these terms in the C&EMA 1979. However, 'importer' is defined by s 1(1), in relation to any goods at any time between their importation and the time when they are delivered out of charge, as including any owner or other person for the time being possessed of or beneficially interested in the goods and, in relation to goods imported by means of a pipe-line, as including the owner of the pipe-line, while Part IV provides for reporting inwards and otherwise for the control of importation of goods from places outside the United Kingdom. Likewise, 'exporter' is defined, in relation to goods for exportation or for use as stores, as including the shipper of the goods and any person performing in relation to an aircraft functions corresponding to those of a shipper, and Part V provides for entry outwards and otherwise for the control of exportation of goods for a destination outside the United Kingdom[2].

The European Community legislation imposing conditions for import of products of animal origin for human consumption is implemented by regulations under s 2(2) of the ECA 1972[3].

1   See, for example, general food Regulation (EC) 178/2002, Arts 11 and 12 noted in paras **3.2.12–3.2.18** above.
2   Generally, goods removed to the United Kingdom from the Isle of Man are deemed not to be imported into the United Kingdom and goods removed to the Isle of Man from the United Kingdom are deemed not to be exported from the United Kingdom: see Isle of Man Act 1979, ss 8 and 9.
3   See ch 14 below.

Defence for exports

4.7.2 Regulation (EC) 6A of the General Food Regulations 2004, as amended by reg 41(5) of the Official Feed and Food Controls (England) Regulations 2005, provides for circumstances in which the relevant legislation of a country to which food is being exported is different from that in England[1]. In proceedings for an offence of contravening or failing to comply with food law, a defence is available if the accused proves that the item in respect of which the offence is alleged to have been committed was intended for export[2]. The further matters that the accused must establish depend on the intended destination of the food. They are :

(a)   in the case of export to a country that is not a Member State, that the item could lawfully be exported there under Art 12 of Regulation (EC) 178/2002[3]; and

(b)   in the case of export to a Member State, that (i) the legislation applicable to that item in that Member State is compatible with the applicable provisions of food law (except in so far as it relates to feed produced or fed to food producing animals) at Community level, and (ii) the item complies with that legislation.

Thus limb (a), by reference to Art 12 of Regulation (EC) 178/2002, provides a defence where the food, unless injurious to health, complies with Community law or the requirements of the importing third country, while limb (b) acknowledges that the underlying Community obligations must be respected: the defence will be unavailable if the importing Member State has failed to implement them.

The defence for exports must evidently be established on the balance of probabilities[4] and, for the purpose if necessary of discharging the onus that it imposes, the prudent food exporter should no doubt seek help from the overseas buyer in making advance preparations. Written evidence of the relevant foreign legislation will usually be needed so as to ensure that the product complies with it and, where appropriate, that the foreign legislation complies with the substantive Community obligation in question.

1   In respect of Wales, see reg 41(5) of the Official Feed and Food Controls (Wales) Regulations 2005.
2   For the meaning of 'food law', see para **3.2.1** above.
3   See paras **3.2.15–18** above.
4   See *Cant v Harley & Sons Ltd* [1938] 2 All ER 768 and para **4.3.3** above.

4.8   FOOD BUSINESS AND PREMISES

4.8.1   The terms 'food business' and 'premises' in the FSA 1990 are of somewhat less significance since the enactment of general food Regulation (EC) 178/2002 and of the EC hygiene Regulations enforced by the Food Hygiene (England) Regulations 2006 and described in chs 13 and 14. For those purposes, 'food business' and 'food business operator' as defined in Art 3 of Regulation (EC) 178/2002[1] now stand instead of 'food business' and 'proprietor of a food business'[2], while the Food Hygiene (England) Regulations 2006 adopts its own, wider definition of 'premises'[3].

Nevertheless, the terms remain important to the Act in respect of the licensing of food premises[4] and, so far as the relevant provisions have not been superseded by those of the Food Hygiene (England) Regulations 2006, the control of unhygienic food businesses[5]. Additionally, 'premises' is a key term in ss 3 (presumptions that food is intended for human consumption), 29 (procurement of samples) and 32 (powers of entry).

The relevant definitions are in s 1(3) of the FSA 1990. A 'food business' is defined as meaning 'any business in the course of which commercial operations with respect to food or food sources are carried out'[6] and a 'business' as including 'the undertaking of a canteen, club, school, hospital or institution, whether carried on for profit or not, and any undertaking or activity carried on by a public or local authority'.

'Food premises' means 'any premises used for the purposes of a food business', while 'premises' includes 'any place, any vehicle, stall or moveable structure, and for such purposes as may be specified in an order made by the Secretary of State, any ship or aircraft of a description so specified'. Under this power, the Food Safety (Ships and Aircraft) (England and Scotland) Order 2003, as amended, specifies as premises:

(a)   any home-going ship[7] for the purposes of applying the FSA 1990 and regulations and orders made under it; and
(b)   any other ship or any aircraft (other than an exempt ship or aircraft[8]) for the purposes of:

      (i) ascertaining whether the cargo contravenes regulations made under FSA 1990 Part II and

      (ii) of applying ss 11 and 12 of the Act

and references to 'premises' in ss 2, 3, 29, 32 and 50 include any such ship or aircraft in relation to any specified purposes.[9]

1   See para **3.2.38** above.
2   See para **6.1.2** and also paras **6.2.3**, **6.3.5** and **6.4.4** below.
3   That is, "premises" includes any establishment, any place, vehicle, stall or moveable structure and any ship or aircraft'.
4   See FSA 1990, s 19(1)(b) and the Food (Control of Irradiation) Regulations 1990.
5   See FSA 1990, ss 10, 11 and 12 explained in ch 6.
6   See *Salford City Council v Abbeyfield (Worsley) Society Ltd* [1993] COD 384.
7   That is 'a ship which is engaged exclusively in (a) plying in internal waters, or (b) excursions which last not more than one day, start and end in Great Britain and do not involve calling at any place outside Great Britain'.
8   That is, 'any sovereign immune ship or aircraft or any ship of a State other than the United Kingdom which is exercising the right of innocent passage through that part of the United Kingdom territorial sea adjacent to England or Scotland'.
9   For Wales, see the Food Safety (Ships and Aircraft) (Wales) Order 2003, as amended.

Chapter 5

Food safety: rendering food injurious to health and inspection and seizure of suspected food

5.1 INTRODUCTION

5.1.1   This chapter considers ss 7–9 of the Food Safety Act 1990 (FSA 1990), that is, its primary provisions dealing with food safety. It will be recalled from ch 1 that they derived from two sources. The first of these was the provision against rendering food injurious to health, still recognisable in s 7, which – together with what is now s 14 described in ch 8 – constituted the controls on the chemical composition of food prescribed by the Sale of Food and Drugs Act 1875. The second source was the prohibition on selling unfit food and the powers for its inspection, seizure and condemnation that formed the core of ss 8 and 9 and was introduced by the Public Heath Act 1875 to provide basic safeguards against biological (bacterial) contamination of food[1]. Although the two strands were eventually brought together in a single statute[2], they ostensibly remained separate until the FSA 1990. This acknowledged and extended an integration that had in practice taken place over the years. In particular, it classified the prohibition on rendering food injurious to health under a 'food safety' heading together with the biological controls. This modification was no mere formal change. The prohibition on selling food rendered injurious to health was incorporated with the prohibition on sale of unfit food in a new wider concept of 'food safety requirements' established by s 8. All food failing to comply with these requirements was moreover subjected to the s 9 powers to inspect and seize suspect food. Yet, the new provisions did not long remain unchanged. As an important part of the plan to guarantee a high level of food safety in the European Union, Art 14 of general food Regulation (EC) 178/2002 has now replaced s 8 with similar food safety requirements banning the marketing of unsafe food [3].

1   See para **1.1.1** above.
2   By the Food and Drugs Act 1938.
3   See paras **3.2.20–3.2.30**.

5.1.2   Before the detail of amended ss 7–9 of FSA 1990 is considered, mention should be made of the general safety requirement enacted by the General Product Safety Regulations 2005 whereby, in implementation of Directive 2001/95/EC, producers are forbidden to place unsafe products on the market[1]. Although food and feed products are within the scope of this legislation, it applies only to the extent that there is no provision with the same objective in rules of Community law other than the Directive[2]. Where such provision exists, its rules will apply. Given the extent of the safety provisions prescribed by general food Regulation (EC) 178/2002[3], as well as by more specific Community food and feed legislation, the situation will be rare indeed in which application of the General Product Safety Regulations 2005 will not in practice be excluded. This is true even of the obligations imposed by the Directive on producers, distributors and Member States and the mechanisms for exchange of information and rapid intervention that it establishes[4]. For all of these aspects, Regulation (EC) 178/2002, supplemented by more specific Community rules, makes bespoke provision. It remains to be seen whether there are any residual circumstances in which Regulation (EC) 178/2002 falls short and General Product Safety Regulations 2005 will apply to food or feed. One possible area is the control of certain products that can cause choking in children. On this ground, the Community used its emergency powers under Regulation (EC) 178/2002 to ban jelly sweets containing the thickening agent konjac (E425) [5]. But if, for example, the European Court were to conclude that the Regulation does not extend to danger arising from the size of a sweet such as an 'extra large' gob stopper comprised of safe ingredients, the General Product Safety Regulations 2005 would be there as a fail-safe.

1   General Product Safety Regulations 2005, reg 5.
2   General Product Safety Regulations 2005, reg 3.
3   See in particular ch 3 and paras **7.3.4–7.3.6, 7.4.2–7.4.7** and **7.5.1–7.5.6**.
4   Directive 2001/95/EC recital (13). For non-food and feed products posing a serious threat, RAPEX is the equivalent of the Rapid Alert System for Food and Feed (RASFF) described in paras **7.3.4–7.3.6**.
5   See para **7.4.5**.

5.2   RENDERING FOOD INJURIOUS TO HEALTH

5.2.1   Although having its roots in the Adulteration of Food and Drink Act 1860, it was not until the Sale of Food and Drugs Act 1875 that the prohibition on rendering food injurious to health by adulteration becomes recognisably like s 7 of the FSA 1990. The provision makes it an offence for any person to render food injurious to health by means of (a) the addition of any article or substance to food, (b) the use of any article or substance as an ingredient in the preparation of food, (c) the abstraction of any constituent from food, or (d) the subjection of food to any other process or treatment, in each case, with intent that it shall be sold for human consumption[1]. In requiring proof of intent, s 7 is exceptional. In the 1990 Act, offences are generally of strict liability[2].

1   FSA 1990, s 7(1).
2   See para **20.1.1** below.

5.2.2   To secure a conviction under s 7 of the FSA 1990, it is necessary to establish that the food was in fact injurious to health[1]. In determining this, a court is required to have regard to the matters specified in sub-paras (a)-(c) of Art 14(4) of general food Regulation (EC) 178/2002[2]. Set out and assessed in paras **3.2.21** and **3.2.25** respectively, these criteria form part of the European Community's new food safety requirements and replace those previously specified in s 7(2). As explained in ch 3, the new provisions extend beyond their predecessors so that regard must now be had not only to the cumulative effect on the individual, but also specifically to the effects on future generations and to the health sensitivities of consumer categories for whom the food is intended. In reconciling s 7 with Regulation (EC) 178/2002, the General Food Regulations 2004 also revoked sub-s (3), which provided that 'injury', in relation to health, included any impairment, whether permanent or temporary. However, given that 'injurious to health' must now be read in the light of the Community Regulation's aim of assuring a high level of protection of human health[3], it would be unwise to conclude that the reach of s 7 has thereby been restricted.

1   *Hull v Horsnell* (1904) 68 JP 591.
2   FSA 1990, s 7(2), as amended by the General Food Regulations 2004.
3   See paras **3.1.2** and **3.3.2** above.

5.2.3   Positive action by way of addition to, subtraction from or treatment of food is necessary for an offence to have been committed. Unlike Art 14 of Regulation (EC) 178/2002[1], s 7 does not apply to food that has become injurious to health by reason of decomposition or adventitious contamination. Moreover, illegal residues of pesticides and veterinary medicines are evidently not caught by this provision, because the substances in question are added not to 'food', but to 'food sources'. In food, such residues are properly to be regarded as contaminants, rather than additives[2].

1   See paras **3.2.21** and **3.3.23**.
2   See ch 12.

5.2.4   The term 'abstract' has given rise to difficulties in the past. A failure to correct the natural tendency of a constituent of a fluid to rise to the top or sink to the bottom of a container may amount to abstraction[1] as, presumably, would the failure to prevent the escape of an evanescent constituent. However, reducing the proportion of a constituent by dilution is not abstraction[2].

1   *Penrice v Brander* 1921 JC 63; *Bridges v Griffin* [1925] 2 KB 233.
2   *Dearden v Whiteley* (1916) 85 LJ KB 1420.

5.2.5   There is a lack of modern judicial authority on the s 7 prohibition since deliberate adulteration of food by producers with injurious substances is comparatively rare today. Deliberate contamination by food terrorists and the illegal use of food additives are practices covered by more specific offences[1]. However, as is shown by recent cases of methanol contaminated vodka, adulteration by producers has by no means been entirely eradicated and s 7 remains as a threat to any who contemplate committing this grave form of dishonest practice.

1   See respectively Public Order Act 1986, s 38 and the various regulations considered in section **12.2** below.

5.3 THE FOOD SAFETY REQUIREMENTS

5.3.1   As indicated above[1], the core of s 8 of the FSA 1990 has been superseded by Art 14 of general food Regulation (EC) 178/2002. It was consequently amended by the General Food Regulations 2004. Subsection (1) has been revoked because its prohibition on the sale of food that failed to comply with the food safety requirements has been replaced by Art 14(1)[2]. Likewise, sub-s (2), which defined food failing to comply with those requirements, and sub-s (3), whereby, until the contrary was proved, consignments were presumed to have failed to comply when a part had so failed, have been replaced by Art 14(2)–(5)[3] and Art 14(6)[4] respectively. In substitution for them, a new s 8(2) provides that food fails to comply with food safety requirements if it is unsafe within the meaning of Art 14 of Regulation (EC) 178/2002 and that references to food safety requirements or food complying with such requirements shall be construed accordingly. This substituted interpretation provision harmonises with Regulation (EC) 178/2002 the powers in Part II of the FSA 1990 for inspection and seizure of suspected food[5] and for the making of subordinate legislation[6].

1   See paras **1.1.7** and **5.1.1** above.
2   See paras **3.2.20–3.2.22** above.
3   See paras **3.2.23–3.2.26** above.
4   See para **3.2.28** above.
5   See section **5.4** below.
6   See para **4.1.4** above.

Meat from knackers' yards

5.3.2   The sole surviving portion of FSA 1990, s 8 as originally enacted is the presumption, in sub-s (4), that any product or part of a product derived wholly or partly from an animal that has been slaughtered in a knackers' yard, or of which the carcase has been brought into a knackers' yard, is unfit for human consumption. A knackers' yard is defined as 'any premises used in connection with the business of slaughtering, flaying or cutting up animals the flesh of which is not intended for human consumption'[1]. The presumption now applies only for the purposes of construing the subordinate legislative power, in para 3(1) of Sch 1 to FSA 1990, to regulate the treatment and disposal of unfit and similar food. The principle of consistent interpretation[2] will require that the expression 'unfit for human consumption' must now be read in accordance with Regulation (EC) 178/2002[3].

1   FSA 1990, s 53(1).
2   See para **1.2.1** above.
3   See paras **3.2.20–2.2.25** above.

5.4   INSPECTION, DETENTION AND SEIZURE OF SUSPECTED FOOD

5.4.1   Section 9 of FSA 1990 re-enacted and considerably extended the provisions of its predecessors as to the power of authorised officers to seize and detain suspect food and, on the order of a justice of the peace, have it destroyed or disposed of to prevent it being used for human consumption[1]. The powers have since been adapted by the General Food Regulations 2004 so that they now relate to the food safety requirements of general food Regulation (EC) 178/2002[2].

Chapter 3.4 of the Food Law Code of Practice and Practice Guidance for England give guidance on the seizure and detention powers under s 9, including on the powers as applied to the Food Hygiene (England) Regulations 2006[3]. The reader will wish to consult the full texts of the Code and Guidance, although particular aspects are referred to below. As elsewhere in this book, references to these texts must, where appropriate, be read as references to their Welsh equivalents.

1   FSA 1990, s 9(1), (2) and (3).
2   See paras **3.2.20–3.2.30**.
3   See para **5.4.9** below.

The powers

5.4.2   An authorised officer of a food authority may at all reasonable times inspect any food intended for human consumption which (a) has been sold or is offered or exposed for sale; (b) is in the possession of, or has been deposited with or consigned to, any person for the purpose of sale or preparation for sale; or (c) is otherwise placed on the market within the meaning of Regulation (EC)

178/2002[1]. Where it appears to the officer on such an inspection that the food fails to comply with the food safety requirements or, otherwise than on such an inspection[2], that food is likely to cause food poisoning or any disease communicable to human beings, he has two options. First, he may give notice to the person in charge of the food that, until the notice is withdrawn, the food or any specified portion of it is not to be used for human consumption and either is not to be removed or is not to be removed except to some place specified in the notice. Alternatively, the officer may seize the food and remove it in order to have it dealt with by a justice of the peace.

It is an offence knowingly to contravene the requirements of a Detention of Food Notice, the form of which is prescribed by Regulations[3]. The inclusion of the word 'knowingly' in this offence requires proof by the prosecution of criminal intention; that is, that the defendant knew of the existence of the notice and its contents[4]. Since the notice must be given to the person in charge of the food, it is submitted that proof of service of the notice in accordance with the FSA 1990[5] should normally be sufficient in the case of an inspection since the recipient would find it difficult to claim ignorance of its contents.

Ordinarily, 'reasonable times' for inspection will be when premises are open for business purposes[6]. However, in the case of a serious danger to public health, it may be reasonable to inspect at other times.

Chapter 3.4.4 of the Food Law Code of Practice (England) recommends discussion with the owner or person in charge of the food and, if appropriate, with the manufacturer before a decision to detain food, unless the circumstances require immediate action. That chapter of the Code also stresses the importance of securing the detained food, even to the extent where necessary of removing it to another food authority's area, and of prompt action, especially in the case of highly perishable food[7].

1   As to the advantages of (c), see para **4.6.4** above.
2   See Food Law Practice Guidance (England), ch 3.4.8.
3   The Detention of Food Notice prescribed by the Detention of Food (Prescribed Forms) Regulations 1990.
4   See further para **20.1.1** below.
5   FSA 1990, s 50.
6   *Small v Bickley* (1875) 40 JP 119.
7   See also Food Law Code of Practice (England), ch 3.4.5 and Food Law Practice Guidance (England), chs 3.4.5 and 3.4.6.

Termination of notice

5.4.3   Where an authorised officer has issued a Detention of Food Notice he must, as soon as is reasonably practicable and in any event within 21 days, determine whether or not he is satisfied that the food complies with the food safety requirements. If he is so satisfied he must forthwith withdraw the notice[1]. If he is not so satisfied, he must seize the food and remove it to be dealt with by a justice of the peace[2].

In respect of withdrawal of a Detention of Food Notice, the Food Law Code of Practice (England) recommends in particular that the authorised officer should consider whether, after treatment or processing, the food might satisfy the food safety requirements (ch 3.4.5) and that, notwithstanding the 21 days allowed for a decision, a withdrawal notice should be served as soon as possible to prevent possible deterioration of the food (ch 3.4.7).

1   See the Withdrawal of Detention of Food Notice prescribed by the Detention of Food (Prescribed Forms) Regulations 1990.
2   FSA 1990, s 9(4).

Batches, lots and consignments of food

5.4.4   Of crucial importance to the operation in modern conditions of the s 9 powers to detain and to seize food, is the presumption, laid down by Art 14(6) of general food Regulation (EC) 178/2002 and described in parag **3.2.28** above, that where any food that is unsafe is part of a batch, lot or consignment of food of the same class or description, it shall be presumed that all the food in that batch, lot or consignment is also unsafe, unless following a detailed assessment there is no evidence that the rest of the batch, lot or consignment is unsafe.

Chapter 3.4.8 of the Food Law Code of Practice (England) points out that if a quantity of different types or batches is being detained, the authorised officer should issue a separate Detention of Food Notice in respect of each type or batch. It also recommends that, when considering whether to seize or detain a batch, lot or consignment, the authorised officer should take into account the evidence available, the nature of the contamination, the nature and condition of any container holding the food, the risk to health and the quantity of food involved in relation to any sampling that has been undertaken[1].

1   See also Food Law Practice Guidance (England), ch 3.4.9.

Referral to a justice of the peace

5.4.5   Where the authorised officer exercises his powers to seize the food, he must inform the person in charge of the food of his intention to refer it to a justice of the peace[1]. A person who, under s 7 of the FSA 1990 (rendering food injurious to health) or reg 4(a) of the General Food Regulations 2004 (marketing unsafe food contrary to Art 14(1) of Regulation (EC) 178/2002), might be liable to prosecution in respect of the food concerned, must be given an opportunity to attend before the justice of the peace to give evidence and to call witnesses[2].

If it appears to the justice of the peace, on the basis of such evidence as he considers appropriate in the circumstances, that the food fails to comply with the food safety requirement, he must condemn the food and order it to be destroyed or to be so disposed of as to prevent it from being used for human consumption; and any expenses reasonably incurred in connection with the destruction or disposal must be defrayed by the owner of the food[3]. Having decided that there is a contravention of the food safety requirements, the justice has no discretion and is obliged to condemn the food[4].

Referral to a justice of the peace should normally be within two days of seizure and in the case of perishable food such referral should be as soon as possible[5].

Although, in condemning food, a justice is acting in administrative capacity[6], the powers must be exercised in accordance with natural justice that would be denied by a refusal to allow evidence to be tested by crossexamination[7]. The justice is moreover liable, under s 111 of the Magistrates' Courts Act 1980, to state a case for the opinion of the High Court on a question of law at the instance of any party aggrieved by the justice's decision[8].

As to the limitation of the s 9 powers of a justice of the peace by orders under s 13 of the FSA 1990, see para **7.4.11** below.

1 See the Food Condemnation Warning Notice prescribed by the Detention of Food (Prescribed Forms) Regulations 1990; and Food Law Practice Guidance (England), ch 3.4.7.
2 FSA 1990, s 9(5), as amended by the General Food Regulations 2004.
3 FSA 1990, s 9(6).
4 *R* (*on the application of the Food Standards Agency*) *v Brent Justices and Kelman's Kosher Products* (2004) 168 JP 241. See also, under the equivalent Northern Ireland provision (the Food Safety (Northern Ireland) Order 1991, art 8, the Fermanagh Resident Magistrate's decision of 21 August 2006 in *Food Standards Agency Northern Ireland v George McCabe and Eurofreeze* (*Ireland*) *Ltd*.
5 Food Law Code of Practice (England), ch 3.4.5.
6 *R v Cornwall Quarter Sessions, ex p Kerley* [1956] 2 All ER 872, [1956] 1 WLR 906.
7 *Errington v Wilson* 1995 SC 550, 1995 SLT 1193.
8 *R* (*on the application of the Food Standards Agency*) *v Brent Justices and Kelman's Kosher Products* (2004) 168 JP 241; *Jeffery v Evans* [1964] 1 WLR 505.

Compensation

5.4.6   If a Detention of Food Notice is withdrawn, or if a justice of the peace refuses to condemn the food, the food authority must compensate the owner of the food for any depreciation in its value resulting from the action taken by the authorised officer[1]. Any dispute as to the amount of compensation must be settled by arbitration[2]. As to the exclusion of compensation in particular circumstances by orders under s 13 of the FSA 1990, see para **7.4.11** below.

1 FSA 1990, s 9(7).
2 See Arbitration Act 1996, s 94.

Prosecution

5.4.7   Action by an authorised officer under the above provisions does not preclude a subsequent prosecution by the food authority in respect of the failure of the food safety requirements or the food having been rendered injurious to health.

Destruction or disposal of food

5.4.8   The food authority is responsible for ensuring destruction of food that has been seized or voluntarily surrendered[1], and arrangements should be made for the food to be supervised until it can be dealt with in the appropriate manner. If possible, and if there is likely to be some delay before destruction, the food should be disfigured so as to prevent any possibility of it being returned to the food chain.

The food authority should ensure the total destruction of the food by incineration or some other appropriate method or, if total destruction is not possible, such a degree of disfigurement that the food could never re-enter the food chain (e g by flattening tin cans for disposal in a suitably licensed land-fill site), having regard to the requirements of relevant waste disposal legislation[2].

1 As to voluntary procedures, see Food Law Code of Practice (England), ch 3.4.9 and Food Law Practice Guidance (England), ch 3.4.10.
2 Food Law Code of Practice (England), ch 3.4.10.

Section 9 and Regulations

5.4.9   Under the power in FSA 1990, s 26(1)(b) described in para **4.1.4** above, certain Food Safety Act Regulations, predominantly concerned with the chemical safety of foods and of which examples are listed in Food Law Practice

Guidance (England), ch 3.4.4, provide for food certified by the public analyst as non-compliant to be treated, for the purposes of s 9, as failing to comply with the food safety requirements. A similar approach has now been applied to the main Regulations relating to the biological safety of food by the Food Hygiene (England) Regulations 2006, made under the European Communities Act 1972 to enforce Regulation (EC) 852/2004 and other EC food hygiene Regulations. In this case, however, the certification is not independent of the enforcement authority. Regulation 27 provides that where an authorised officer of an enforcement authority certifies that food has not been produced, processed or distributed in compliance with the Hygiene Regulations, it shall be treated for the purposes of FSA 1990, s 9 as failing to comply with the food safety requirements. By reg 23, s 9 is modified for the purposes of the 2006 Regulations so that it applies in relation to an authorised officer of an enforcement authority as it applies in relation to an authorised officer of a food authority.[1]

1   See further para **6.5.6**; and, generally on the Food Hygiene (England) Regulations 2006, chs 13 and 14 below.

Wider implications

5.4.10   The provisions discussed above are intended and suitable for dealing with individual batches, lots or consignments of dangerous food discovered and dealt with within the area of a food authority. For cases with wider implications, the FSA 1990 provided powers for the making of the emergency prohibition notices and orders[1] and the emergency control orders[2] described in chs 6 and 7 respectively. As will be seen there, the domestic powers have now been considerably supplemented by European Community legislation.

1   FSA 1990, s 12.
2   FSA 1990, s 13.

Chapter 6

Food safety: unhygienic food businesses

6.1 INTRODUCTION

6.1.1   The general prohibitions on unsafe food discussed in chs 3[1] and 5 are supplemented by stringent powers to act in respect of defective food businesses[2].

Food businesses must not only, as explained in chs 13–15, generally be registered (or, in some cases, approved or licensed): those that are unhygienic are also liable to the imposition of administrative restrictions by enforcement authorities and magistrates' courts. The modern powers under which these restrictions are imposed were established by ss 10–12 of the Food Safety Act 1990 (FSA 1990) and recall certain provisions of the Health and Safety at Work etc Act 1974 (H&SWA 1974)[3]. These powers have now in practice been largely superseded by similar but augmented provisions in regs 6–9 of the Food Hygiene (England) Regulations 2006 made to execute and enforce Regulation (EC) 852/2004 and other European Community hygiene Regulations specified in para **6.2.3** below and described in chs 13 and 14. Considered together in this chapter are the powers in the FSA 1990 and the 2006 Regulations to impose improvement notices and hygiene improvement notices (section **6.2**), prohibition orders and hygiene prohibition orders (section **6.3**), and emergency prohibition notices and orders and hygiene emergency prohibition notices and orders (section **6.4**), as well as the wholly original powers, taken by the 2006 Regulations, to impose remedial action notices and detention notices (section **6.5**). It should be noted that, notwithstanding the apparent subjective form of the powers under which they are made, all of these notices and orders must be objectively justifiable[4].

The Food Law Code of Practice and Practice Guidance for England give guidance on Hygiene Improvement Notices/Improvement Notices (see the respective chs 3.2), on Prohibition Procedures (see the respective chs 3.3) and on Remedial Action Notices/Detention Notices (ch 3.5 of the Food Law Code). Specific points are mentioned in this chapter, but resort is to the full texts or their Welsh equivalents is recommended for a proper appreciation of the Food Standards Agency advice. As elsewhere in this book, references are to the Code and Practice Guidance for England. Where appropriate, these are to be read as references to the equivalent passages in the texts for Wales.

---

1   See paras 3.2.20–3.2.30.
2   As to action that may also be taken against persons, see para 6.3.3.
3   See H&SWA 1974, ss 21–24.
4   For example, as to the decision maker's reasonable grounds for belief, see *Nakkuda Ali v Jayaratne* [1951] AC 66; and as to the decision maker's satisfaction as to specified

circumstances, see *Secretary of State for Education and Science v Tameside Metropolitan Borough Council* [1977] AC 1014, [1976] 3 All ER 665.

6.1.2   Each 'proprietor of a food business' is subject to the obligations imposed by ss 10–12 of the FSA 1990, 'proprietor' being defined, in relation to a food business, as meaning 'the person by whom the business is carried on'[1]. Case law now affords some assistance with the interpretation of these words. Although ownership is not essential to bring a person within their ambit, they do involve an entrepreneurial role, namely the taking of risk with a view to profit. Employees do not fall within the definition, although franchisees may, depending on the circumstances of the case[2]. Normally, 'proprietor' equates to 'owner', but the definition has a wider meaning than that. It is not necessary for a 'proprietor' to be in daily charge of the business or even to visit the premises in order to be legally responsible. It is for the magistrate to determine if the defendant is the person, or one of the people, by whom the business is carried on[3]. It is not necessary for the proprietor to carry out any of the 'commercial operations'[4] referred to in the definition of 'food business', nor to be the owner of the business or involved in its day-to-day running, provided it can be said on the evidence that the person in question was carrying on the business. It follows that there may be more than one proprietor: a restrictive interpretation would make it difficult to identify the proprietor in the case of a complicated corporate structure, which is not in keeping with a statute intended to protect the public[5].

1   By FSA 1990, s 53(1). As to 'food business' and 'business', see para **4.8.1** above.
2   *Curri v Westminster City Council* [2000] EHLR 16; [2000] CLY 2678.
3   *Ahmed v Nicholls sub nom Ahmed v Leicester City Council* [2000] EHLR 182, [2000] CLY 967.
4   As to 'commercial operation', see para **4.5.1** above.
5   *Greene King plc v Harlow District Council* [2003] EWHC 2852, [2004] 1 WLR 2338, [2004] CLY 1580.

6.2   IMPROVEMENT NOTICES AND HYGIENE IMPROVEMENT NOTICES

The power to issue an improvement notice

6.2.1   Section 10 of the Food Safety Act 1990 (FSA 1990) introduced new provisions as to the issue of improvement notices by authorised officers. An 'improvement notice' may be served on the proprietor of a food business[1] by an enforcement authority's authorised officer who has reasonable grounds for believing that the proprietor is failing to comply with any hygiene regulations, or any regulations controlling the processing or treatment of food[2].

The notice must (a) state the officer's grounds for believing that the proprietor is failing to comply with the regulations; (b) specify the matters which constitute the proprietor's failure so to comply; (c) specify the steps which, in the officer's opinion, the proprietor must take in order to secure compliance; and (d) require the proprietor to take those measures, or measures which are at least equivalent to them, within such period (not less than 14 days) as may be specified in the notice. These are four separate requirements each of which must be observed to constitute a valid notice[3].

Failure to comply with an improvement notice is an offence[4] in respect of a prosecution for which the summons alleges a single offence and is not bad for duplicity notwithstanding that the notice requires more than one measure to be taken[5]. It has also been held that the evidence of an environmental health officer was admissible notwithstanding that she was not an expert witness. She gave evidence of what she saw in the food business kitchens and indicated that there was a risk of contamination. In context the evidence was fairly put to the jury. There had been no obligation to quantify the risk of contamination in terms of indicating a chance that someone would be harmed[6].

1 See para **6.1.2** above.
2 FSA 1990, s 10(1).
3 *Bexley London Borough Council v Gardiner Merchant* [1993] COD 383.
4 FSA 1990, s 10(2).
5 *Sabz Ali Khan v Rhondda Borough Council* (1995) unreported.
6 *R v Tang* [1995] Crim LR 813.

Regulations to which ss 10 and 11 apply

6.2.2   The regulations to which s 10 (and also s 11[1]) apply are defined, although not listed, in the legislation. The test for inclusion is whether the regulations are made under Part II of the FSA 1990 and make provision for requiring, prohibiting or regulating the use of any process or treatment in the preparation of food; or for securing the observance of hygienic conditions and practices in connection with the carrying out of commercial operations with respect to food or food sources[2]. Most of such regulations have now been revoked[3] and replaced by European Community food hygiene measures that are executed and enforced by the Food Hygiene (England) Regulations 2006[4], specified in para **6.2.3** below and considered in chs 13 and 14. Yet domestic regulations still remain that are caught by s 10(3). As to provision for requiring, prohibiting or regulating the use of any process or treatment in the preparation of food, the Food (Control of Irradiation) Regulations 1990[5] evidently invoke FSA 1990, s 16(1)(c), as read with Sch 1, para 4(b), while, in respect of securing the observance of hygienic conditions and practices in connection with the carrying out of commercial operations with respect to food or food sources, we should note the Ungraded Eggs (Hygiene) Regulations 1990[6] made under s 13 of the Food Act 1984 and now having effect as if made under the FSA 1990, s 16(1)(d)[7]. Even in the era of comprehensive European Community food hygiene legislation, FSA 1990 ss 10 and 11 continue to retain at least a theoretical place in the armoury of provisions for the control of food businesses.

1 See section **6.3** below.
2 FSA 1990, s 10(3).
3 See Food Hygiene (England) Regulations 2005, reg 33 and Sch 7.
4 See Food Hygiene (England) Regulations 2006, Sch 1.
5 See para**15.2.2** below.
6 See para **14.5.11** below.
7 See FSA 1990, s 59(3) and Sch 4, para 2.

The power to issue a hygiene improvement notice

6.2.3   As indicated in the introduction to this chapter, s 10 of FSA 1990 has in practice been largely superseded by reg 6 of the Food Hygiene (England) Regulations 2006, which enables authorised officers to issue hygiene improvement notices. With one major exception, reg 6 is in the same terms as those of s 10 described in para **6.2.1** above. By contrast with s 10, a notice under reg 6 may be served when the officer 'has reasonable grounds for believing that a food business operator is failing to comply with the Hygiene Regulations'. There are two points about this. First, 'food business operator' replaces 'proprietor of a food business' because that is the relevant expression defined by Art 3(3) of general food Regulation (EC) 178/2002[1]. Second and more important, reg 6 contains no equivalent of s 10(3). The regulations to which it applies are defined not by their purpose, but by interpretation of reg 2(1) as 'these Regulations and the Community Regulations'. 'Community Regulations' themselves are defined as meaning 'Regulation (EC) 852/2004, Regulation (EC) 853/2004, Regulation (EC) 854/2004, Regulation (EC) 2073/2005 and 2075/2005' – that is, the principal Community hygiene Regulations described in chs 13 and 14.

1   See Food Hygiene (England) Regulations 2006, reg 2(3) and para **3.2.38** above.

The use of improvement notices and hygiene improvement notices

6.2.4   In general, improvement notices and hygiene improvement notices might be seen as dealing with situations where there have been breaches of the relevant regulations, which are not sufficiently serious to justify emergency action (see section **6.4** below) but too immediate in their impact to await a prosecution.

The Food Law Practice Guidance emphasises that the primary objective of enforcement should always be to achieve compliance in the most effective way possible. The practice of giving advice, and communicating by letter about enforcement issues, are well established approaches to enforcement that are understood by food businesses. Such procedures are therefore encouraged whenever they are likely to secure compliance with the requirements of food law within a time that is reasonable in the circumstances. Conversely, the service of a hygiene improvement notice or improvement notice does not preclude action such as prosecution for matters that are subject of the notice. Such a course of action may be particularly appropriate where conditions are serious or deteriorating.

The Food Law Code of Practice states that the use of hygiene improvement notices may be appropriate in any of the following circumstances, or a combination thereof:

- where formal action is proportionate to the risk to public health;
- where there is a record of non-compliance with breaches of food hygiene or food processing regulations;
- where the authorised officer has reason to believe that an informal approach will not be successful.

The Code advises that the hygiene improvement notice procedure would not be appropriate in the following circumstances:

- where the contravention might be a continuing one, for example, personal cleanliness of staff, and a notice would only secure an improvement at one point in time;
- in transient situations, and it is considered that swift enforcement action is needed, for example, a one day festival or sporting event. A hygiene emergency prohibition notice[1] would be the only formal remedy that would have immediate effect;
- where there is a breach of a recommendation of good hygiene practice an improvement notice cannot be issued if there is no failure to comply with an appropriate regulation.

Given the reach of reg 6 of the Food Hygiene (England) Regulations 2006 and the restrictions in s 10(3) of the FSA 1990, the Code does not envisage the need for food authorities to issue improvement notices under s 10. Although the domestic Regulations identified in para **6.2.2** above are not referred to, it should be noted that, under the Food (Control of Irradiation) Regulations 1990, it is the Food Standards Agency that is responsible for enforcement in respect of irradiation licence holders. The Agency itself therefore probably has the main scope today for issuing improvement notices. Under those Regulations and the Ungraded Eggs (Hygiene) Regulations 1990, Food Authorities bear little, if any, responsibility for enforcing classic food hygiene requirements relating to the construction, condition and use of premises.

1   See section **6.4** below.

Formalities

6.2.5   The forms to be used for improvement notices and for hygiene improvement notices are to be found respectively in the Food Safety (Improvement and Prohibition – Prescribed Forms) Regulations 1991[1] and in Annex 7.1/2 to the Food Law Code. In each case the notice should contain all necessary information, with references as to the regulations that are allegedly contravened; as to the matters that do not comply; and how such compliance can be achieved, so that the recipient knows exactly what must be done and why[2]. The notice should make clear that measures at least equivalent to those specified may be taken by the food business proprietor or food business operator who should be recommended to discuss any such alternative solution with the enforcement officer before embarking on it.

The notice should clearly state the period (not being less than 14 days) within which the required remedial measures must be taken. The period must be realistic, justifiable and have regard to the extent and complexity of the measure required. It should take account of the following factors:

• the risk to public health;
• the nature of the problem;
• the availability of solutions.

Before issuing a notice, the officer should, where possible, agree the period with the food business proprietor or food business operator, or a person authorised to act on the proprietor's or operator's behalf. Where a series of contraventions is identified, it may be most appropriate to issue more than one notice each with its own compliance period.

Service of improvement notices and hygiene improvement notices should conform with the requirements respectively of s 50 of the FSA 1990 and reg 28 of the Food Hygiene (England) Regulations 2006, taking account of the provision that each includes for those cases in which it is not possible to identify the person who should primarily be served.

Although there is no provision in the FSA 1990 or Food Hygiene (England) Regulations 2006 for extension of time, it may be unreasonable not to allow this if the food business proprietor or food business operator has genuine difficulty in complying. Where the officer considers a request for an extension to be reasonable, the notice should be withdrawn and a new one issued specifying the revised compliance period.

Further advice on improvement notices and hygiene improvement notices is contained in chapter 3.2 of the Food Law Guidance and in guidance issued by LACORS, the Local Authorities Co-ordinators of Regulatory Services.

1   See Form 1.
2   The notice must be objectively justifiable. See para **6.1.1** above.

Appeals

6.2.6   A person who is aggrieved by a decision of an authorised officer to serve an improvement notice or a hygiene improvement notice may appeal to a magistrates' court[1] and, if that appeal is dismissed, to the Crown Court[2]. The effect of an appeal is to stop time running on the notice[3].

On an appeal against an improvement notice, the court may either cancel or affirm the notice and, if it affirms it, may do so either in its original form or with such modifications as the court may in the circumstances think fit[4]. However, the power of modification cannot be used to remedy a failure to comply with all four separate requirements for an improvement notice specified by s 10(1)[5] or so as to rewrite the regulations in question[6].

1   FSA 1990, s 37(1)(a); and Food Hygiene (England) Regulations 2006, reg 20(1)(a).
2   FSA 1990, s 38(a); and Food Hygiene (England) Regulations 2006, reg 21(a).
3   FSA 1990, s 39(2) and (3); and Food Hygiene (England) Regulations 2006, reg 22(2) and(3).
4   FSA 1990, s 39(1) and Food Hygiene (England) Regulations 2006, reg 22(1).
5   *Bexley London Borough Council v Gardiner Merchant* [1993] COD 383.
6   See *Salford City Council v Abbeyfield (Worsley) Society Ltd* [1993] COD 384.

Enforcement authority liability

6.2.7   Unlike s 12 in relation to emergency prohibition notices[1], s 10 does not provide compensation for the proprietor where the enforcement authority fails to obtain confirmation of an improvement notice by a magistrates' court. However, where an authorised officer negligently required the owner of food premises to undertake works that were unnecessary to secure compliance with the FSA 1990 and regulations made thereunder and the owner, in reliance on the officer's oral requirements, closure threat and close supervision, incurred substantial and unnecessary expenditure in executing the works, the local food authority was under a common law duty of care to the owner and liable in damages for the economic loss sustained[2]. On the other hand, no duty of care or liability was owed to a business by a health and safety inspector in giving advice that led to the issue of an improvement and prohibition notices under the H&SWA 1974[3]. It was held to be implicit in the H&SWA 1974 that such notices might cause economic loss and the Act itself provided remedies against errors or excesses on the part of inspectors and enforcing authorities. There is no reason to doubt that these authorities are of equal relevance to the interpretation of reg 6 of the Food Hygiene (England) Regulations 2006.

1   See para **6.4.7**.
2   *Welton v North Cornwall District Council* [1997] 1 WLR 570.
3   *Harris v Evans* [1998] 3 All ER 522, [1998] 1 WLR 1285.

6.3   PROHIBITION ORDERS AND HYGIENE PROHIBITION ORDERS

6.3.1   Section 11 of the FSA 1990 provides for two classes of administrative action by magistrates' courts, both of which are within the concept of a 'prohibition order'. First, courts have a duty, consequent on the conviction of the proprietor of a food business[1] for a contravention of hygiene or processing regulations made under Part II of the Act, to impose prohibitions on processes, treatment, premises and equipment used for the purposes of the business. Secondly, courts are empowered to ban proprietors or managers convicted of a contravention of hygiene regulations from participating in the management of food businesses. Before 1990, it was not possible to prevent a person, the closure of whose business had been ordered, from perpetuating dangerous practices in another business.

As explained in para **6.2.2** above, the number of Regulations caught by s 11 has been greatly reduced since the implementation of the new European Community food hygiene measures by the Food Hygiene (England) Regulations 2006. But, for the enforcement and execution of those measures, the s 11 administrative sanctions have been adopted by reg 7 of the 2006 Regulations in the modified form of the 'hygiene prohibition order'. The respective provisions of s 11 and reg 7 concerning prohibition orders and hygiene prohibition orders are considered in more detail below.

Guidance on s 11 and reg 7 orders and on voluntary closures[2] is included in chs 3.3 (prohibition procedures) of the Food Law Code of Practice and the Practice Guidance. For a proper understanding of the Food Standards Agency's views, recourse to the complete chapters is advocated.

1   See para **6.1.2** above.
2   See Food Law Code of Practice ch 3.3.2.4.

Mandatory prohibition orders on processes, treatment, premises or equipment

6.3.2   The first class of prohibition order applies where a food business proprietor is convicted of an offence under domestic regulations securing hygiene or controlling the processing or treatment of food[1] and the court by or before which he is so convicted is satisfied that the 'health risk condition' is fulfilled with respect to that business. In such a case, the court is required to impose the 'appropriate prohibition'[2].

The health risk condition is fulfilled if any of the following involves risk of injury to health[3]:

(a)   the use for the purposes of the business of any process or treatment;
(b)   the construction of any premises used for the purposes of the business, or the use for those purposes of any equipment; and
(c)   the state or condition of any premises or equipment used for the purposes of the business[4].

The appropriate prohibition is:

•   in a case within (a), a prohibition on the use of the process or treatment for the purposes of the business;
•   in a case within (b), a prohibition on the use of the premises or equipment for the purposes of the business or any other food business of the same class or description;
•   in a case within (c), a prohibition on the use of the premises or equipment for the purposes of any food business[5].

The imposition of prohibition orders in relation to the use of processes or treatment, or to the construction of premises or equipment or to their condition is thus mandatory in the prescribed circumstances. It will be noted that each appropriate prohibition is broadly tailored to the related category of health risk. The use of a risky process or treatment (category (a)) (e g one that fails to achieve the correct cooking temperature or pH level) is forbidden simply to the food business in question, but for risky premises or equipment more extensive prohibitions are laid down. If the risk relates to construction (category (b)) (e g flooding caused by drainage defects), the premises are, or the equipment is, regarded as unsuitable for all food businesses of the kind in question; and if the risk relates to condition (category (c)) (e g vermin infestation), the premises are, or the equipment is, regarded as unsuitable for any food business at all.

For further examples of circumstances in which the health risk condition may be fulfilled, see para **6.3.6** below.

1 See para **6.2.2** above.
2 FSA 1990, s 11(1).
3 'Injury' includes any impairment, whether permanent or temporary: see FSA 1990, s 11(2A).
4 FSA 1990, s 11(2).
5 FSA 1990, s 11(3).

Discretionary prohibition orders on persons

6.3.3   The second class of prohibition order differs from the first: it is discretionary and is in the nature of a penalty, since it relates to persons rather than processes, treatment, premises or equipment. It applies where a food business proprietor or a manager of a food business is convicted of an offence under those of the regulations described in para **6.2.2**, which are for securing the observance of hygienic conditions and practices in connection with the carrying out of commercial operations with respect to food or food sources. If the court by or before which the proprietor or a manager is so convicted thinks it proper to do so in all the circumstances of the case, it may by an order prohibit him from participating in the management of any food business, or any food business of a class or description specified in the order[1].

1 FSA 1990, s 11(4) and (10). Such an order was made against William John Tudor after his conviction, described in para **3.2.30** above, of offences of placing unsafe food on the market and failing to keep food premises clean.

Managers

6.3.4   For the purposes of the power described in para **6.3.3** above, a manager in relation to a food business means any person who is entrusted by the proprietor with the day-to-day running of the business, or any part of the business[1]. Before a manager can be the subject of a prohibition order he must himself have been convicted of a relevant offence. A manager by whose act or default an offence by the proprietor is alleged to have been committed[2] cannot, on the conviction of the proprietor, be the subject of a prohibition order. It is, of course, open to a prosecuting food authority, knowing that the proprietor will plead a defence of act or default of his manager, to bring proceedings against that manager in addition to or instead of the proprietor, thus enabling the court, if it thinks fit, to issue a prohibition order against the manager.

1 FSA 1990, s 11(11).
2 FSA 1990, s 20; see para **20.2.1** below.

Hygiene prohibition orders

6.3.5   Regulation 7 of the Food Hygiene (England) Regulations 2006 provides for hygiene prohibition orders. It derives directly from FSA 1990, s 11 described in paras **6.3.1–6.3.4** and, like reg 6, closely follows its 1990 Act model, subject to necessary modifications. The wording of s 11 is again generally followed and in one place achieves the same result by different means. It will be observed that, consequent on the repeal of the FSA 1990, s 7(3), FSA 1990, s 11(2A) and Food Hygiene (England) Regulations 2006, reg 9(2), both extend the meaning of 'injury' to include 'any impairment, whether permanent or temporary'. The primary difference between the two provisions is that reg 7 relates not to 'the proprietor of a food business ... convicted of an offence under any regulations to which this section applies', but to 'a food business operator ... convicted of an offence under these Regulations'. As explained in para **6.2.3**, 'food business operator' is now the relevant Community law expression, and there is also no reg 6 equivalent of s 10(3) defining the regulations to which ss 10 and 11 apply. Like s 11, reg 7 essentially applies to particular substantive hygiene requirements that, in its case, are contained in provisions of Community Regulations 852/2004, 853/2004, 2073/2005 and 2075/2005 specified and described in Sch 2[1], or are set out in domestic legislation derogating from Regulations (EC) 852/2004[2] or 853/2004[3]. Indeed, the scope of reg 7 is even wider than this. Additionally, it embraces offences under the procedural provisions in regs 6, 7, 8, 9 and 15 of the Food Hygiene (England) Regulations 2006.

The other substantive difference between the two provisions can be seen from a comparison of s 11(10) and (11) with reg 7(10). The latter reads 'Where the commission of a food business operator leads to the conviction of another person pursuant to reg 10, para (4) shall apply in relation to that other person as it applies in relation to the food business operator and any reference in para (5) or (8) to the food business operator shall be construed accordingly.' It would appear that, for the purposes of hygiene prohibition orders, the change aims at remedying, as regards prohibition orders, the limitation in s 11(10) and (11) identified in para **6.3.4** above. A manager who, by virtue of the by-pass procedure in reg 10, is convicted of an offence committed by the food business operator under the Food Hygiene (England) Regulations 2006, may be subjected by the court to a hygiene prohibition order under reg 7(4). It should be noted that reg 7(10) catches not only the food business operators' employees, but also their suppliers, agents and manufacturers and importers[4], although whether a court would be prepared to exercise its discretion to impose a reg 7(4) ban on any such other person can at this stage be no more than a matter of conjecture.

1   See Food Hygiene (England) Regulations 2006, regs 17(1) and 2(1), definition of 'specified Community provision'.
2   See Food Hygiene (England) Regulations 2006, Sch 3 (bulk transport by sea of liquid oils and fats and raw sugar) implementing Directives 96/3 and 98/28 saved by Regulation (EC) 852/2004 reg 17(3); and Food Hygiene (England) Regulations 2006, Sch 4 (temperature control requirements) authorised by Regulation (EC) 852/2004, Art 13.
3   See Food Hygiene (England) Regulations 2006, Sch 5 (direct supply of small quantities of farm slaughtered poultry and lagomorph meat) excluded from Regulation (EC) 853/2004 by Art 1(3)(d); and Food Hygiene (England) Regulations 2006, Sch 6 (sale of raw milk for direct consumption) authorised by Regulation (EC) 853/2004, Art 10(8).
4   See para **20.2.1** below.

Health risk condition

6.3.6   For illustrative purposes, ch 3.3.2 of the Food Law Code of Practice includes the following examples of circumstances in which the health risk condition may be fulfilled:

Where prohibition of premises may be appropriate

- infestation by rats, mice, cockroaches, birds or other vermin, serious enough to result in the actual contamination of food or a significant risk of contamination;
- very poor structural condition and poor equipment and/or poor maintenance or routine cleaning and/or serious accumulations of refuse, filth or other extraneous matter resulting in the actual contamination of food or a significant risk of food contamination;
- drainage defects or flooding of the establishment, serious enough to result in the actual contamination of food or a significant risk of food contamination;
- premises or practices that seriously contravene food law and have been or are implicated in an outbreak of food poisoning;
- any combination of the above, or the cumulative effect of contraventions that, taken together, represent the fulfilment of the health risk condition.

Where prohibition of a equipment may be appropriate

- use of defective equipment, e g a pasteuriser incapable of achieving the required pasteurisation temperature;
- use of equipment for the processing of high-risk foods that has been inadequately cleaned or disinfected or which is grossly contaminated and can no longer be properly cleaned.

Where prohibition of a process may be appropriate

- serious risk of cross contamination;
- failure to achieve sufficiently high processing temperatures;
- operation outside critical control criteria, for example, incorrect pH of a product that may allow *Clostridium botulinum* to multiply;
- the use of a process for a product for which it is inappropriate.

The Code of Practice cites these examples in relation to the Food Hygiene (England) Regulations 2006, but, as suggested in para **6.2.2** above, there seems no reason why some at least of them might not be appropriate, for instance, in relation to the proprietor of a food business convicted of an offence under the Food (Control of Irradiation) Regulations 1990.

Action before and at the hearing

6.3.7   Advice relevant to court proceedings at which a hygiene prohibition order or prohibition order may be at issue is contained in the Food Law Practice Guidance. This includes chapters on evidence required (3.3.12), continuing contraventions (3.3.13), when prohibition of a person may be appropriate (3.3.14), agreeing procedures with the court (3.3.15), action to be taken prior to the hearing (3.3.16) and information to be given to the court (3.3.17). The full guidance is too extensive to be reproduced here. The reader will wish to consult the actual text. In essence, however, careful preparation prior to a prosecution is recommended so that, where a defect in question has not been removed or, having been removed, has re-occurred, the court's attention may, in appropriate cases, be drawn to the need to consider a hygiene prohibition order or prohibition order, including, if necessary, an order prohibiting a person from food business management[1].

Consistent with natural justice, the enforcement authority should inform the food business operator or proprietor of the intention to draw the attention of the court to the provisions relating to prohibition and should make available the evidence prior to the hearing.

1   See paras **6.3.2–6.3.5** above.

Service of prohibition orders and hygiene prohibition orders

6.3.8   As soon as practicable after the making of a prohibition order or hygiene prohibition order, the enforcement authority must serve a copy of the order on the proprietor of the business or food business operator (and/or the manager or other person), and, in the case of a prohibition of the use of a process or treatment, or the premises or equipment, affix a copy of the order in a conspicuous position on such premises used for the purposes of the business as they consider appropriate[1]. The order must be served in accordance with the FSA 1990, s 50 or the Food Hygiene (England) Regulations 2006, reg 28, advice on service being given by chs 3.3.10 and 3.3.11 of the Food Law Practice Guidance[2]. Any person who knowingly[3] contravenes an order is guilty of an offence[4].

Neither the FSA 1990 nor the 2006 Regulations make specific reference to unauthorised removal or defacement of orders but ch 3.3.19 of Food Law Practice Guidance gives advice on the relevant legislation. Section 1 of the Criminal Damage Act 1971 makes it an offence for any person to destroy or damage property belonging to another without reasonable cause. Moreover, a court making an order may, under s 63 of the Magistrates' Act 1980, make ancillary provision such as requiring that it be not defaced or removed from the premises. If the enforcement authority obtains such ancillary provision from the court, defacement or removal would constitute an offence.

1   See FSA 1990, s 11(5) and (10) and Food Hygiene (England) Regulations 2006, reg 7(5) and (10). See also the Food Law Practice Guidance, ch 3.3.18.
2   As to notification of other Food Authorities that an order has been made against a person, see Food Law Code of Practice, chs 3.3.2.5 and 3.3.4.
3   As to 'knowingly' contravening the order, see para **20.1.1** below.
4   See further Food Law Practice Guidance, ch 3.3.21.

Appeals

6.3.9   Any person who is aggrieved by a decision of a magistrates' court to make a prohibition order or hygiene prohibition order may appeal to the Crown Court[1].

1   FSA 1990, s 38(b); and Food Hygiene (England) Regulations 2006, reg 21(b).

Termination of prohibition orders and hygiene prohibition orders

6.3.10   A prohibition order or hygiene prohibition order ceases to have effect, (a) in the case of a prohibition of the use of a process or treatment, or the premises or equipment, on the issue by an enforcement authority of a certificate to the effect that they are satisfied that the proprietor or food business operator has taken sufficient measures to secure that the health risk condition is no longer fulfilled with respect to the business, and, (b) in a case of a prohibition on the proprietor of the business, food business operator, manager or other person, on the giving by the court of a direction to that effect[1].

The certificate[2] must be issued within three days of the enforcement authority being satisfied as mentioned above. On an application by the proprietor or food business operator for such a certificate, the authority must determine, as soon as it is reasonably practical and in any event within 14 days, whether or not they are so satisfied. If they determine that they are not so satisfied, they must give notice[3] to the proprietor or food business operator of the reasons for that determination[4].

Any person aggrieved by an enforcement authority decision to refuse to issue a certificate may appeal to a magistrates' court and, if that appeal is dismissed, to the Crown Court[5].

A direction that a prohibition on the proprietor of the business, food business operator, manager or other person shall cease to have effect[6] is to be given by the court if, on application by the person in question, the court thinks it proper to do so, having regard to all the circumstances, including in particular the conduct of the person in question since the making of the order. However, no such application can be entertained if made within six months after the making of the prohibition order or hygiene prohibition order, or within three months after the making by the person in question of a previous application for such a direction[7].

Further advice on lifting prohibition orders and hygiene prohibition orders and on appeals against the refusal of a Food Authority to issue a certificate that the health risk condition no longer exists is to be found in chs 3.3.20 and 3.3.22 of the Food Law Practice Guidance[8].

1   FSA 1990, s 11(6); Food Hygiene (England) Regulations 2006, reg 7(6).
2   Under FSA 1990, s 11(6)(a); Food Hygiene (England) Regulations 2006, reg 7(6)(a). See Food Safety (Improvement and Prohibition—Prescribed Forms) Regulations 1991, Form 4; Annex 7.13/14 to the Food Law Code of Practice.
3   See Food Safety (Improvement and Prohibition—Prescribed Forms) Regulations 1991, Form 5; Annex 7.15/16 to the Food Law Code of Practice.
4   FSA 1990, s 11(7); Food Hygiene (England) Regulations 2006, reg 7(7).
5   FSA 1990, ss 37(1)(b) and 38(a); Food Hygiene (England) Regulations 2006, regs 20(1)(b) and 21(a).
6   Under FSA 1990, s 11(6)(b); Food Hygiene (England) Regulations 2006, reg 7(6)(b).
7   FSA 1990, s 11(8) and (10); Food Hygiene (England) Regulations 2006, reg 7(8) and (10).
8   See also the Food Law Code of Practice chs 3.3.2.3, 3.3.2.6 and 3.3.3.5.

6.4   EMERGENCY PROHIBITION NOTICES AND ORDERS AND HYGIENE EMERGENCY PROHIBITION NOTICES AND ORDERS

6.4.1   Section 12 of the FSA 1990 introduced further powers to enable urgent action to be taken with respect to food businesses in emergency situations. Where an authorised officer is satisfied that there is an imminent health risk (ie that the 'health risk condition' is fulfilled), he may act administratively to impose 'the appropriate prohibition' by serving an emergency prohibition notice. Within three days of service, this notice must be confirmed by an emergency prohibition order from a magistrates' court if the appropriate prohibition on the food business is not to lapse.

For the purposes of emergency prohibition notices and orders, the health risk condition and the appropriate prohibition are as explained in para **6.3.2** above, except that, in the health risk condition, the risk of injury to health must be 'imminent'[1]. This term is manifestly intended to identify the urgent nature of the risk addressed by s 12. The legislation contains no definition but is evidently not restricted to risks that are immediate. For 'imminent' the *Oxford English Dictionary* gives:

> 'impending threateningly, hanging over one's head; ready to befall or overtake one; close at hand in its incidence; coming on shortly.'

To complete the set of bespoke provisions to enforce and execute the Community hygiene Regulations, reg 8 of the Food Hygiene (England) Regulations 2006 gives power to make hygiene emergency prohibition notices and orders albeit in virtually identical terms to those of s 12. The two powers are explained and compared below.

The guidance on prohibition procedures in chs 3.3 of the Food Law Code of Practice and Practice Guidance includes advice and recommendations on emergency prohibition notices and orders, hygiene emergency prohibition notices and orders and related voluntary action. Amongst other things, the Practice Guidance advises on service of notices and orders (chs 3.3.10 and 11), affixing notices and orders to the premises (ch 3.3.18), unauthorised removal or defacement of notices or orders (ch 3.3.19) and breach of notices and orders (ch 3.3.21). Some other points from the Code and Practice Guidance are noted below, but a reading of the full texts is desirable.

1   FSA 1990, s 12(4). 'Injury' includes any impairment, whether permanent or temporary: see FSA 1990, s 11(2A).

Emergency prohibition notices[1]

6.4.2   If an authorised officer is satisfied that the health risk condition is fulfilled with respect to a food business, he may by an emergency prohibition notice[2] served[3] on the proprietor of the business[4], impose the appropriate prohibition.

As soon as practicable after the service of an emergency prohibition notice, the enforcement authority must affix a copy of the notice in a conspicuous position on such premises used for the purpose of the business as they consider appropriate[5]; and any person who knowingly contravenes the notice is guilty of an offence[6].

An emergency prohibition notice ceases to have effect if no application is made to a court for an emergency prohibition order within a period of three days beginning with the service of the notice; or, if such an application is so made, on the determination or abandonment of the application[7].

1   FSA 1990, s 12(1).
2   See Food Safety (Improvement and Prohibition – Prescribed Forms) Regulations 1991, Form 2.
3   As to service of documents, see FSA 1990, s 50.
4   See para **6.1.2** above.
5   As to unauthorised removal or defacement of notices, see para **6.3.8** above.
6   FSA 1990, s 12(5). As to 'knowingly' contravening the notice, see para **20.1.1** below.
7   FSA 1990, s 12(7). See further Food Law Practice Guidance, ch 3.3.3.2.

Emergency prohibition orders[1]

6.4.3   If a magistrates' court, on the application of an authorised officer, is satisfied that the health risk condition is fulfilled with respect to any food business, it is required by an emergency prohibition order to impose the appropriate prohibition. But an officer is precluded from making an application unless, at least one day before the application, notice[2] of intention to apply has been served[3] on the proprietor of the business[4].

As soon as practicable after the making of an emergency prohibition order, the enforcement authority must serve[5] a copy of the order on the proprietor of the business and affix a copy of the order in a conspicuous position on such premises used for the purposes of that business as they consider appropriate; and any person who knowingly contravenes the order is guilty of an offence[6].

Any person who is aggrieved by a decision of a magistrates' court to make an emergency prohibition order may appeal to the Crown Court[7].

1   FSA 1990, s 12(2).
2   See Food Safety (Improvement and Prohibition – Prescribed Forms) Regulations 1991, Form 3.
3   As to service of documents, see FSA 1990, s 50.
4   FSA 1990, s 12(3).
5   See n 3.
6   FSA 1990, s 12(6). As to 'knowingly' contravening the order, see para **20.1.1** below.
7   FSA 1990, s 38(b).

Hygiene emergency prohibition notices and orders

6.4.4   In making separate provision for hygiene emergency prohibition notices and orders, reg 8 of the Food Hygiene (England) Regulations 2006 essentially follows the text used by s 12 of the FSA 1990 to provide for emergency prohibition notices and orders[1]. The only real divergence from s 12 is the substitution throughout reg 8 of the Community expression 'food business operator' for the FSA 1990 concept of the 'proprietor' of the business[2]. By contrast with the provisions considered in sections **6.2** and **6.3** of this chapter, the power and duties respectively conferred by s 12 and reg 8 do not depend on the perceived commission or the actual conviction of an offence under separately defined Regulations. When acting under reg 8, as under s 12, the enforcement authority and the court have simply to be satisfied that, in any of the aspects specified by s 11(2) or reg 7(2), the food business involves an imminent risk of injury to health. In consequence, reg 8 is practically the same as s 12.

What is more, the adjectival provisions of the Food Hygiene (England) Regulations 2006 supporting reg 8 are again derived from and in the same terms as the provisions of the FSA 1990 specified in paras **6.4.2** and **6.4.3**. Of this kind are regs 21(b) and 28 which respectively make provision for appeal to the Crown Court against the decision of a magistrates' court to make a hygiene emergency prohibition order and prescribe the rules for service of hygiene emergency prohibition notices and orders.

The forms of hygiene emergency prohibition notice and of notice of intention to apply for a hygiene emergency prohibition order are respectively to be found at Annex 7.3/4 and 5/6 to the Food Law Code of Practice. Advice on hygiene emergency prohibition procedures is given by the Food Law Practice Guidance chs 3.3.2.2, 3.3.5 and 3.3.7.2.

1   Compare Food Hygiene (England) Regulations 2006, reg 8(1)–(7) with FSA 1990, s 12(1)–(7) considered in paras **6.4.1–6.4.3** above.
2   See paras **6.2.3** and **6.3.5** above.

The use of emergency prohibition notices and orders and hygiene prohibition notices and orders

6.4.5 The Food Law Code of Practice advises on circumstances where, in cases of imminent risk of injury to health, the use of reg 8 of the Food Hygiene (England) Regulations 2006 and of s 12 of the FSA 1990 may respectively be appropriate. For reg 8, they are exemplified by the extensive list of hygiene defects in premises, equipment or processes set out in ch 3.3.2 and reported in para **6.3.6** above. There appears to be no reason in principle why s 12 should not equally be used in these cases. It also is aimed at hygiene control of businesses and, as noted in para **6.4.4**, covers the same ground as reg 8. However, ch 3.3.3.2 of the Code of Practice[1] (albeit not prescriptively or exhaustively and for illustrative purposes only) merely cites the following examples of circumstances in which an authorised officer may consider the use of s 12 powers:

- A process or treatment that introduces a teratogenic chemical (one that damages a developing foetus in the womb) into food, which may cause injury to the developing foetus, but the damage will not be apparent until the baby is born.
- A process or treatment that introduces a genotoxic chemical (one that damages genes or chromosomes) into food the effects of which may not manifest themselves until abnormal offspring or a malignant tumour occurs at some time in the future.

Presumably on the basis that the Food Hygiene (England) Regulations 2006 enforce the Community Hygiene Regulations and that reg 8 should take precedence in matters of hygiene control, enforcement authorities are thus encouraged to confine use of the s 12 powers to those rare cases in which a defective process or treatment is resulting in the presence in food of a highly deleterious chemical.

1 See also Food Law Practice Guidance, ch 3.3.6.

Termination of emergency prohibition notices and orders and hygiene prohibition notices and orders

6.4.6 An emergency prohibition notice or order or hygiene prohibition notice or order ceases to have effect on the issue by the enforcement authority of a certificate[1] to the effect that they are satisfied that the proprietor has taken sufficient measures to secure that the health risk condition is no longer fulfilled with respect to the business[2].

The certificate must be issued within three days of the authority being so satisfied. If an application for a certificate is made by the proprietor of the business the authority must determine as soon as is reasonably practicable, and in any event within 14 days, whether or not they are so satisfied and, if they determine that they are not so satisfied, give notice[3] to the proprietor of the reasons for that determination[4]. Advice on lifting the notice or order is given generally by the Food Law Practice Guidance, ch 3.3.20 and specifically in respect of hygiene emergency prohibition notices and orders by the Food Law Code of Practice, ch 3.3.2.3.

Any person aggrieved by an enforcement authority decision to refuse to issue a certificate may appeal to a magistrates' court and, if that appeal is dismissed, to the Crown Court[5].

1   See Food Safety (Improvement and Prohibition – Prescribed Forms) Regulations 1991, Form 4; Annex 7.13/14 to the Food Law Code of Practice.
2   FSA 1990, s 12(8); Food Hygiene (England) Regulations 2006, reg 8(8).
3   See Food Safety (Improvement and Prohibition – Prescribed Forms) Regulations 1991, Form 5; Annex 7.15/16 to the Food Law Code of Practice.
4   FSA 1990, s 12(9); Food Hygiene (England) Regulations 2006, reg 8(9).
5   FSA 1990, s 37(1)(b) and 38(a) ; Food Hygiene (England) Regulations 2006, regs 20(1)(b) and 21(a).

Compensation

6.4.7   Paragraph **6.2.7** above commented on enforcement authority liability in respect of improvement notices and hygiene improvement notices. Where an emergency prohibition notice or hygiene emergency prohibition notice has been served on the proprietor of a business or food business operator, the enforcement authority must compensate him in respect of any loss suffered by reason of his complying with the notice unless an application for an emergency prohibition order or hygiene emergency prohibition notice is made within three days beginning with the service of the notice and the court declares itself satisfied, on the hearing of the application, that the health risk condition was fulfilled with respect to the food business at the time when the notice was served[1].

It has been held that an 'application' within the meaning of s 12(10) is the process whereby an application is made to the court and not the hearing of the application[2]. Any dispute as to compensation under s 12(10) or reg 8(10) must be determined by arbitration[3].

1   FSA 1990, s 12(10); Food Hygiene (England) Regulations 2006, reg 8(10). See also Food Law Practice Guidance, ch 3.3.23.
2   *Farrand v Tse* (1992) Times, 10 December.
3   As to statutory arbitrations, see Arbitration Act 1996, ss 94–98.

6.5   REMEDIAL ACTION NOTICES AND DETENTION NOTICES

6.5.1   The remedial action notices and detention notices prescribed by reg 9 of the Food Hygiene (England) Regulations 2006 and described below in this section are novel provisions that, unlike those made by regs 6, 7 and 8 and described above, are unprecedented in the FSA 1990. In common with those provisions, however, reg 9 implements the action that Art 54 of European Community official control Regulation (EC) 882/2004[1] requires of the competent authorities of Member States when non-compliance is identified. In particular, this action includes the 'monitoring and, if necessary, ordering the recall, withdrawal and/or destruction' of food and 'any other measure the competent authority deems appropriate'.

As explained below, remedial action notices and detention notices are currently applied only in respect of premises approved under Art 4(2) of Regulation (EC) 853/2004[2], that is, establishments producing specified products of animal origin for human consumption that understandably require particularly close hygiene controls. But when consulting on what became the Food Hygiene (England) Regulations 2006, the Food Standards Agency contemplated extending the use of these notices to all food businesses and will be considering the issue further in the light of experience[3].

Chapter 3.5 of the Food Law Code of Practice gives guidance on remedial action notices and detention notices. Attention is drawn below to specific points from this.

1   See further ch 18 below.
2   See section **14.5** below.
3   See Regulatory Impact Assessment for the Food Hygiene (England) Regulations 2006.

Remedial action notices

6.5.2   As indicated in para **6.5.1**, remedial action notices are used to deal with contraventions of the 'Hygiene Regulations' – defined in the Food Hygiene (England) Regulations 2006 and described in para **6.2.3** above – which relate to establishments subject to approval under Regulation (EC) 853/2004. Where it appears to an authorised officer of an enforcement authority that, in respect of such an establishment, (a) any requirement of the Hygiene Regulations is being breached, or (b) inspection under the Hygiene Regulations is being hampered, he may, by remedial action notice in writing served on the relevant food business operator or his duly authorised representative:

- prohibit the use of any equipment or any part of the establishment specified in the notice;
- impose conditions upon or prohibit the carrying out of any process; or
- require the rate of operation to be reduced to such extent as is specified in the notice, or to be stopped completely[1].

A remedial action notice must be served as soon as practicable, state why it is being served[2] and, if it is served under (a) above, specify the breach and the action needed to remedy it[3]. As soon as an authorised officer of the enforcement authority in question is satisfied that such action has been taken, he must withdraw the notice by a further notice in writing served on the food business operator or his duly authorised representative[4].

Regulation 28 of the Food Hygiene (England) Regulations 2006 sets out the rules for service of remedial action notices and notices for withdrawal. Model forms for these notices are given at Annex 7.7/8 and 11/12 respectively to the Food Law Code of Practice.

Failure to comply with a remedial action notice is an offence[5].

1   Food Hygiene (England) Regulations 2006, reg 9(1).
2   Food Hygiene (England) Regulations 2006, reg 9(2).
3   Food Hygiene (England) Regulations 2006, reg 9(3).
4   Food Hygiene (England) Regulations 2006, reg 9(4).
5   Food Hygiene (England) Regulations 2006, reg 9(7).

Detention notices

6.5.3   At an establishment subject to approval under Regulation (EC) 853/2004, an authorised officer of an enforcement authority may also require the detention of any animal or food for the purpose of examination, including the taking of samples. This is achieved by the service of a detention notice in writing on the relevant food business operator or his duly authorised representative[1].

The notice must be withdrawn, by a further notice in writing served on the food business operator or his duly authorised representative, as soon as an authorised officer of the enforcement authority is satisfied that the animal or food need no longer be detained[2].

The rules for service of detention notices and notices for withdrawal are prescribed by reg 28 of the Food Hygiene (England) Regulations 2006. Model forms for these notices for use in respect of food (although not apparently animals) are given at Annex 7.9/10 and 11/12 respectively to the Food Law Code of Practice.

Failure to comply with a detention notice is an offence[3].

1   Food Hygiene (England) Regulations 2006, reg 9(5).
2   Food Hygiene (England) Regulations 2006, reg 9(6).
3   Food Hygiene (England) Regulations 2006, reg 9(7).

Use of remedial action notices and detention notices

6.5.4 As regards contraventions of the specified Hygiene Regulations in establishments subject to approval under Regulation (EC) 853/2004, reg 9 of the Food Hygiene (England) Regulations 2006 provides enforcement authorities with significant new powers.

The remedial action notice affords them an administrative procedure for cases that require speedier action than a hygiene improvement notice[1] but are not serious enough to warrant seeking the backing of the court by issue of a hygiene emergency prohibition notice[2].

The detention notice enables animals and food of animal origin to be detained for examination and sampling where, for example, there is reason to believe that food from the establishment may be unsafe.

Guidance on the issue of notices is given by ch 3.5.3 of the Food Law Code of Practice. In particular, this points out that 'Such action should be proportionate to the risk to public health and where immediate action is required to ensure food safety. A Remedial Action Notice may be used if a continuing offence requires urgent action owing to a risk to food safety or where corrective measures have been ignored by the food business operator and there is a risk to public health.' It further recommends that 'If an Authorised Officer considers it necessary to serve a Remedial Action Notice owing to the conditions or practices found on the inspection of an establishment subject to approval under Regulation (EC) 853/2004, the officer should also consider whether food at the establishment should be detained for the purposes of examination by means of a Detention Notice under Regulation 9'.

1   See section **6.2** above.
2   See section **6.4** above.

6.5.5 Express restrictions on the power to serve remedial action notices are comparatively few. Unlike hygiene prohibition orders and emergency hygiene prohibition notices and orders, remedial action that they may require does not have to be imposed or endorsed by order of a court. Nor is there consequentially any provision for compensation such as is to be found in reg 8(10) of the Food Hygiene (England) Regulations 2006 for losses from unsustained hygiene emergency prohibition notices, although it would be unwise for an enforcement authority to discount the possibility of liability for negligent exercise of its power to serve remedial action notices[1].

Also lacking is any specific mechanism for the food business operator to apply for withdrawal such as is provided in respect of hygiene emergency prohibition notices[2]. However, a person aggrieved by a decision to serve a remedial action notice may appeal to the magistrates' court and, if that appeal is dismissed, to the Crown Court[3]. On appeal the court may cancel or affirm the notice and, if it affirms it, may do so either in its original form or with such modifications as it thinks fit[4].

1   See para **6.2.7** above.
2   See Food Hygiene (England) Regulations 2006, reg 8(8) described in para **6.4.6**.
3   Food Hygiene (England) Regulations 2006, regs 20(1)(c) and 21(a).
4   Food Hygiene (England) Regulations 2006, reg 22(1). See also para **6.2.6** n 6.

6.5.6   Conditions for exercise of the power to issue detention notices are also markedly absent from the legislation. Even the purpose of reg 9(5) examinations is unspecified, although this is evidently to check whether the requirement of the Hygiene Regulations[1] have been breached[2], authorised officers of enforcement authorities having the further power to certify non-compliant food so that it may be seized and removed to be dealt with by a justice of the peace under s 9(3)(b) of the FSA 1990[3].

By contrast with the power to detain food under s 9(3)(a) of the FSA 1990, no objective time limit is specified for detention notices, nor is any provision made to compensate for losses incurred by food business operators[4]. Once again, any remedy would have to be sought via civil proceedings.

A comparison with the express terms of s 9(3)(a) of the FSA 1990 also suggests that detention of the animal or food in question at some place other than the establishment at which they were found is not contemplated by reg 9(5).

1   See para **6.2.3** above
2   See Food Hygiene (England) Regulation (EC) 2006, reg 9(1)(a).
3   Food Hygiene (England) Regulations 2006, reg 27. See further para **5.4.9** above.
4   See FSA 1990, s 9(4) and (7) and paras **5.4.2**, **5.4.3** and **5.4.6** above.

Chapter 7

Hazards, warning systems, emergencies and crisis management

7.1 INTRODUCTION

7.1.1 This chapter explains (a) the guidance for enforcement authorities on handling food and feed incidents and hazards; (b) the UK and European Community systems for warning of safety problems; (c) the European Community and national powers to legislate on specific emergencies; and (d) the European Community and national plans for management of crises.

7.2 INCIDENTS AND HAZARDS

7.2.1 Action recommended by the Food Law Code of Practice ch 1.7 to be taken by enforcement authorities in respect of food incidents and hazards is summarised in this section. Action in respect of feed incidents and hazards recommended by the Feed Law Code of Practice ch 1.6 is essentially the same. Significant differences are identified below[1].

1   It will be recalled that references to the Food Law Code are, in respect of Wales, to be read as references to the Welsh Code. The Feed Law Code applies to Great Britain.

7.2.2 A food incident 'is defined as any event where, based on the information available, there are concerns about actual or suspected threats to the safety or quality of food that could require intervention to protect consumers' interests'[1].

A feed incident occurs when a feed authority or the Food Standards Agency 'becomes aware that the feed or its labelling fails or appears to fail to meet feed law requirements. A feed incident can be a relatively minor matter or a major feed hazard'.

A food hazard 'is a food incident involving a biological, chemical or physical agent in, or condition of, food with potential to cause an adverse effect on the health or safety of consumers[2]. In the case of a feed hazard, there must by contrast be a potential to cause 'an adverse effect on the health or safety of animals or the public'.

1   See further the *Incident Response Protocol* and *Principles for preventing and responding to food incidents* described in paras **7.5.4–7.5.6** below.
2   Compare the definition of 'hazard' in Regulation (EC) 178/2002 (see para **3.2.6**).

7.2.3 Food authorities are required to 'categorise food hazards according to the following criteria:

- a localised food hazard – one in which food is not distributed beyond the boundaries of the Food Authority and is not deemed to be a serious localised food hazard;
- a serious localised food hazard – one in which food is not distributed beyond the boundaries of the food authority but which involves E-coli 0157, other VTEC, C botulinum, Salmonella typhii, Salmonella paratyphi or that the food authority considers significant because of, for example, the vulnerability of the population likely to be affected, the numbers involved or any deaths associated with the incident;
- a non-localised food hazard – one in which food is distributed beyond the boundaries of the food authority'.

A serious localised feed hazard is defined as involving, not the diseases specified in respect of food, but 'injury or sickness to animals'.

Deliberate contamination and malicious tampering

7.2.4   Chapter 1.7.5 of the Food Law Code and ch 1.6.2.5 of the Feed Law Code advise that malicious tampering incidents – where deliberate contamination is thought to be due to terrorist activity[1] or with a view to blackmail[2] or extortion[3] – should immediately be notified to the Agency and, where required, handed over to the police, with whom pre-existing arrangements have been made. It should also be noted that cases of deliberate contamination less serious than 'malicious tampering' may yet constitute offences related to contamination or interference with goods contrary to the Public Order Act 1986, s 38[4] and require police involvement.

1   See in particular the Terrorism Act 2000, as amended.
2   See the Theft Act 1968, s 21.
3   The Scots law offence of obtaining goods by threat of future violence or some other kind of threat.
4   As to contamination of supermarket food with pins, needles and nails, see *R v Cruickshank (Gary Edmund)*, sub nom *R v Cruikshank (Gary Edmund)* [2001] EWCA Crim 98; [2001] 2 Cr App. R (S) 57, CA (Crim Div), per Pill LJ.

Food hazards associated with outbreaks of food-borne illness

7.2.5   Under Public Health (Control of Disease) Act 1984, s 11 medical practitioners are required to notify the local authority of food poisoning cases. In the event of a food hazard associated with an outbreak of food-borne illness, the Food Law Code para 1.7.6 recommends the food authority to consider with its Consultant in Communicable Disease Control or Consultant in Public Health Medicine (Communicable Disease/Environmental Health) the activation of its Outbreak Control Plan for communicable diseases. Serious localised outbreaks should immediately be notified to the appropriate contacts at the Health Protection Agency Centre for Infections[1] (formerly the HPA Communicable Disease Surveillance Centre) in England, the National Public Health Service (Communicable Disease Surveillance Centre) in Wales and the Food Standards Agency.

Food authorities should also arrange with their public analyst and food examiner to be notified immediately if a food hazard is identified during the analysis or examination of a food sample.

Applying only to food, the Agency advice described in this paragraph is not reproduced in the Feed Law Code of Practice.

1   The HPA was established by the Health Protection Agency Act 2004.

Action by the food or feed authority in the case of hazards

7.2.6   Once a food/feed hazard has been identified, the food/feed authority are advised by the Food and Feed Law Codes (chs 1.7.7 and 1.6.2.6 respectively) to carry out an assessment immediately to determine the likely scale, extent and severity of the risk to public health or safety of the hazard, involving other agencies as appropriate. These other agencies may include home, originating and neighbouring authorities, medical specialists and microbiologists, as well as food examiners and public analysts or, in the case of feed, agricultural analysts.

Food/feed authorities should have procedures in place to call the appropriate agencies together at short notice, to implement urgent control measures whenever they are required and to identify a lead authority if necessary.

The assessment should include the following:

- the nature of the hazard;
- the toxicity of the contaminant, the allergenicity of an undeclared ingredient/constituent, or the virulence and pathogenicity of the organism;
- the type of injury that might be caused by a physical contaminant;
- the population likely to be affected and its vulnerability;
- the likely quantity and distribution of the food/feed in the food/feed chain up to the point of consumption;
- the ability and willingness of the producer or distributor to implement an effective withdrawal of the product;
- the ability to identify accurately the affected batch(es) or lot(s);
- the accuracy and extent of records held by the producer or distributor or, in the case of feed, end-buyers;
- the likely effectiveness of any trade withdrawal at all stages of the food/feed chain;
- the stage(s) at which the fault is likely to have occurred (for example in processing, packaging, handling, storage or distribution) and its likely significance to the problem;
- whether other products produced in the same establishment may have been affected;
- whether the food/feed has been imported;
- whether any of the food/feed has been exported;
- whether there are wider implications for others in the same industry or for establishments using similar processes in other food/feed industries;
- the possibility that the complaint or problem has been caused by a malicious act (see para **7.2.4** above).

When a food/feed authority becomes aware of a food/feed hazard it should take action to protect public health and safety (and, in the case of feed, animal health and safety) at the earliest opportunity, including detaining or seizing the food concerned if it is located within the food/feed authority's area (see section **5.4** above).

Food/feed authorities should also consider the use of other powers, which may be appropriate and relevant to the circumstances involved, under:

-   in the case of food, the Food Hygiene (England) Regulations 2006 or the Food Safety Act 1990 (FSA 1990)[1]; and
-   in the case of feed, the Feed (Hygiene and Enforcement) (England) Regulations 2005[2].

Localised food/feed hazards should be dealt with locally by the food/feed authority, in conjunction with other relevant agencies and need not be reported to the Agency.

Serious localised food/feed hazards and non-localised food/feed hazards should be notified by the food/feed authority to the Agency and other relevant agencies at the earliest opportunity and by the quickest available means and confirmed in writing using a copy of the prescribed incident report form.

However, where a food/feed authority becomes aware that a food/feed business operator in their area has withdrawn food/feed from the market in accordance with Art 19 or 20 of Regulation (EC) 178/2002[3] due to non-compliance with the food/feed safety requirements of that Regulation, the food/feed authority should check that the Agency is also aware. Responsibility for action at local level remains with the food/feed authority unless the Agency notifies it otherwise.

1   See ch 6.
2   See section **18.6**.
3   See paras **3.2.44 –3.2.53** above.

Localised hazards – media relations

7.2.7   The Food and Feed Law Codes (chs 1.7.7.1 and 1.6.2.7 respectively) also advise on the issue of local press statements to alert the public in the event of a localised food/feed hazard. The relevant food/feed business should be consulted before the identity of a named business or branded food/feed is discussed with or released to the media. Such media releases should be sent to the Agency without delay. The food/feed authority should notify the Agency immediately if the food/feed business operator raises objections to the release of such information.

Action by the food or feed authority – incidents

7.2.8   According to the Food and Feed Law Codes (chs 1.7.8 and 1.6.2.8 respectively) food/feed incidents that are contraventions of food/feed law, but not food/feed hazards should normally be resolved by the food/feed authority and the food/feed business operator, through the home or originating authority if appropriate.

Feed incidents and the Rapid Alert System for Food and Feed

7.2.9   Where a feed incident is discovered at a port of entry and the feed is to be rejected, Feed Law Code ch 1.6.2.9 gives specific guidance on initiation of the Rapid Alert System for Food and Feed described at paras **7.3.4–7.3.6** below. In such cases, an RASFF form must be completed and forwarded with the appropriate documentation (shipping note, health certificates, importer details etc) to the Agency's Incident Branch.

Practice guidance on food incidents and hazards

7.2.10   Chapter 1.7 of the Food Law Practice Guidance (England) adds the following further advice in respect of incidents and hazards identified by food authorities. The Welsh Guidance is in the same terms. The Feed Law Code of Practice is not supplemented by a Practice Guidance document.

Information received locally that may indicate a wider problem

7.2.11   Food authorities are responsible for investigating and dealing with food that fails to comply with the food safety requirements in their areas. They may identify potential problems in a number of ways such as:

*   following microbiological examination or chemical analysis of samples submitted to a food examiner or public analyst;
*   as a result of complaints from members of the public, either directly or through a third party, for example, the police, citizens' advice bureaux, etc;
*   through notification from a manufacturing company, trade association, wholesaler, retailer, importer or caterer;
*   information from enforcement agencies in other countries;
*   as a result of a notification from a GP of one or more cases of communicable disease, including foodborne illness, or from the Consultant in Communicable Disease Control, or the Health Protection Agency Communicable Disease Surveillance Centre.

These illustrations are not intended to be comprehensive. Following consultation with the food examiner and/or public analyst, samples of relevant foods or ingredients and appropriate samples (vomit, stool) from any persons affected should be obtained where possible and sent for examination/analysis. These items can be critically important in identifying the cause of the illness and may even save lives.

Consumer complaints

7.2.12   Chapter 1.7.3 of the Food Law Practice Guidance also deals with food complaints from consumers. It gives advice on the notification of complaints to defendants, the involvement of other food authorities and the investigation of complaint samples. Apparently derived from the old Code of Practice No 2 on Legal Matters, this guidance is not in fact specific to food incidents and hazards but of general relevance to the enforcement topics considered in ch 18 below.

7.3   WARNING SYSTEMS

7.3.1   The United Kingdom and the European Community have both established warning systems to give notification of problems with the safety of food or feed.

UK food alerts

7.3.2   The UK alerts system is the means established by the Food Standards Agency to inform local authorities and consumers[1] about specific problems with food and, where appropriate, about the corrective action to be taken. More specifically, 'a food alert is a communication from the Agency to a food authority concerning a food hazard or other food incident'[2]. The system has now been extended to apply *mutatis mutandis* to feed problems and any corrective action required.[3]

1   Alerts are published on the Agency website and it is possible to register to receive automatic notification of them.
2   See Food Law Code of Practice, ch 2.2. As to food incidents and hazards, see para **7.2.2**.
3   See Feed Law Code of Practice, ch 2.2.

7.3.3   Until October 2004 what was then called the 'Food Hazard Warning System' included four notification categories, that is, A – for immediate action by the food authority; B – for action by the food authority specified in the notification; C – for action as deemed necessary by the food authority; and D – for information only. The current system is simpler and more flexible. Communications under it are issued, as appropriate, in the form of 'Food Alerts: for Action' (which replaced the category A, B and C notifications) or 'Food Alerts: for Information' (which replaced the category D notifications) and any action required on the part of the food authority is now specifically stated in the food alert. Often put out in conjunction with a product recall by the manufacturer, retailer or distributor, food alerts cover a whole range of problems. For example, those issued during 2006 related to topics such as extraneous matter; chemical, biological and toxin contamination; illegal health marking; products from unapproved premises or untested animals; packaging defects; unauthorised food irradiation; incorrect allergen information, date coding and other labelling errors; and undesirable flavours and odours.

EC Rapid Alert System

7.3.4   The Community Rapid Alert System for Food and Feed (RASFF) is a channel for the quick exchange of information between Member States about measures taken to ensure food and feed safety. The informal network of contacts in the Commission and Member States developed since 1979 to deal with problems relating to food was placed on a legislative basis and extended to animal feed by Arts 50–52 of Regulation (EC) 178/2002. Since then the number of annual notifications by Member States has progressively increased.

7.3.5   The RASFF system established by Art 50 of Regulation (EC) 178/2002 provides for the notification of direct or indirect risks to human health deriving from food or feed. The network involves the Member States, the European Food Safety Authority (the Authority) and the Commission that, rather than the Authority and contrary to what was proposed by the 2000 White Paper on Food Safety[1], is responsible for managing the network. By agreement with the Community, participation in the rapid alert system is also open to applicant countries, third countries and international organisations, the EFTA–EEA states now taking part by virtue of EEA adoption[2], with adaptations, of Regulation (EC) 178/2002.

Under the system, the Commission must immediately be notified by network members of serious risks and must circulate the information around the network. The Authority may supplement notifications with any scientific or technical information, which will facilitate rapid, appropriate risk management action by the participant States. In particular, they must notify the Commission of:

(a)   measures aimed at restricting the placing on the market or forcing withdrawal or recall of food or feed requiring rapid action;

(b)   recommendations or agreements with professional operators aimed at preventing, limiting or imposing conditions on the placing on the market or the eventual use of food or feed requiring rapid action;

(c)   rejections of batches, containers or cargoes of food or feed by competent authorities at EEA border posts.

Articles 51 and 52 of Regulation (EC) 178/2002 respectively provide powers to make measures for implementing Art 50 and, subject to the public's right in general to information in accordance with Art 10[3], confidentiality rules for the rapid alert system.

1   See para 53 of COM(1999) 719 final.
2   See para **1.8.1** above.
3   See para **3.2.11** above.

7.3.6   The information circulated under RASFF is classified under the following headings:

(a)   *Alert notifications*, which are sent when the food or feed presenting the risk is on the market and immediate action is required;

(b)   *Information notifications*, which concern a food or feed for which a risk has been identified, but for which other members of the network do not have to take immediate action because the product has not reached their markets;

(c)   *News notifications*, which have not been communicated by a Member State as an 'Alert' or 'Information' notification but that concern information considered to be of interest to Member States.

In 2006 significant notifications related to matters such as contamination by mycotoxins, dioxins, polycyclic aromatic hydrocarbons and mercury in fishery products, veterinary residues and migration from food contact materials, as well as illegal food supplements, genetically modified rice, dyes in spices and other additives in food and feed.

7.4   EMERGENCIES

7.4.1   Risks from food or feed are sometimes serious enough to call for emergency measures of general application. This section explains the Community powers in Arts 53 and 54 of general food Regulation (EC) 178/2002, Art 9 of Directive 89/662/EEC (veterinary checks in intra-Community trade) and Art 22 of Directive 97/78/EC (veterinary checks on products from third countries), and the national powers used for their implementation in the Products of Animal Origin (Import and Export) Regulations 1996, reg 35, the Products of Animal Origin (Third Country Imports) (England) Regulations 2006, reg 61, the Official Feed and Food Control (England) Regulations 2007, reg 33 and the European Communities Act 1972 (ECA 1972), s 2(2). It also describes the Community and domestic purposes to which the further enabling powers in FSA 1990, s 13 and the Food and the Environment Protection Act 1985, s 1 have been put.

EC emergency measures

7.4.2   The Commission's 2000 White Paper on Food Safety noted the absence of a comprehensive power to make emergency measures. Despite other means at its disposal, the Commission could not enact safeguard measures for feed or for processed food of non-animal origin from one of the Member States.

Article 53 of general food Regulation (EC) 178/2002 has now filled the gap. Where it is evident that food or feed originating in the Community or imported from a third country is likely to constitute a serious risk to human health, animal health or the environment, and 'that such risk cannot be contained satisfactorily by means of measures taken by the Member State(s) concerned', the Commission is authorised – via the Standing Committee on the Food Chain and Animal Health regulatory procedure[1] – to suspend marketing or use of the food or feed and to adopt other appropriate interim measures. Pending such Community action, Art 54 of Regulation (EC) 178/2002 permits a Member State, which has officially informed the Commission of the need to take emergency measures, to adopt interim protective measures.

1   See further para **3.4.2** above.

7.4.3   Of the previous emergency legislative powers, Art 10 of former hygiene Directive 93/43/EEC to act in respect of food from third countries has not been retained, but, for the purposes of emergency measures relating to products of animal origin, the Commission still regularly uses the veterinary checks powers in Art 9 of Directive 89/662/EEC (for intra-Community trade) and Art 22 of Directive 97/78/EC (for third country imports). This is so, for example, in relation to measures on avian influenza[1], while, in respect of fishery products from third countries, the Commission sometimes invokes Directive 97/78/EC, sometimes Regulation (EC) 178/2002, and sometimes both[2].

1   See, for example, Decisions 2006/415/EC and 2005/692/EC as regards intra-Community trade and third country importation respectively.
2   For example, see Decisions 2004/225/EC, 2007/642/EC and 2006/236/EC respectively.

Domestic implementation of EC emergency measures

7.4.4   Whatever the precise legal bases of Commission Decisions on products of animal origin, the domestic practice is to give them effect by Declarations made under the related veterinary checks implementing legislation, that is, for products from other Member States, reg 35 of the Products of Animal Origin (Import and Export) Regulations 1996, and, for products from third countries, reg 61 of the Products of Animal Origin (Third Country Imports) (England) Regulations 2006. Recent emergency Decisions have concerned products from third countries. Current Decisions are listed below with the Declarations that have implemented them:

• Decision 2002/249/EC (chloramphenicol in shrimps from Myanmar), by Declaration POAO REG 59/002;
• Decision 2002/251/EC (nitrofurans in poultrymeat and shrimps from Thailand), by Declaration POAO REGS 2003 59/001;
• Decision 2004/225/EC (bivalve molluscs, echinoderms, tunicates and marine gastropods and live fish and shellfish carried in water from Albania), by Declaration POAO REG 59/009;
• Decision 2002/805/EC (chloramphenicol in milk powder and milk replacer for animal nutrition from Ukraine), by Declaration IAH DEC 2004/02;
• Decision 2002/994/EC (chloramphenicol in products of animal origin from China), as amended, by Declarations (POAO REG 59/10) and (POAO REG 59/12);
• Decision 2006/27/EC (unauthorised products in horse meat from Mexico), by Declaration POAO REG 59/013;
• Decision 2006/236/EC (heavy metals and histamine in fishery products from Indonesia), by Declaration POAO REG 59/014;

- Decision 2006/698/EC (histamine in fishery products from Brazil), as amended, by Declaration POAO REG 61/016;
- Decision 2007/82/EC (fishery products from Guinea), by Declaration POAO REG 61/017;
- Decision 2007/642/EC (fishery products from Albania), by Declaration POAO REG 61/018;
- Decision 2008/352/EC (pentachlorophenol and dioxins in guar gum from India), by Declaration POAO REG 61/019;[1]
- Decisions 2002/994/EC, as amended, and 2008/463/EC (harmful residues in animal products from China), by Declaration POAO REG 61/020;[2]
- Regulation (EC) 601/2008 (special conditions on fishery products imported from Gabon and intended for human consumption), by Declaration POAO REG 61/021;
- Decision 2008/630/EC (emergency measures applicable to crustaceans imported from Bangladesh for human consumption), by Declaration POAO REG 61/022;
- Decisions 2002/994/EC, as amended, and 2008/463/EC (harmful residues in animal products from China), by Declaration POAO REG 61/023;
- Decision 2008/660/EC (special conditions imposed on fishery products imported from Indonesia for human consumption), by Declaration POAO REG 61/024;
- Decision 2008/798/EC (special conditions governing import of products containing milk or milk products from China), by Declaration POAO REG 61/026[3].

1   For Wales, POAO 2008/W/001.
2   For Wales, POAO 2008/W/004.
3   For Wales, POAO/W/2008/008 (see also POAO/W/2008/007).

7.4.5   For products of non-animal origin, there was until recently no such mechanism and the Community emergency measures made under Regulation (EC) 178/2002 were implemented by Emergency Control Regulations under the ECA 1972, s 2(2) on the lines of Emergency Control Orders under the FSA 1990 described in para **7.4.8** below. Thus, Decision 2002/247/EC, suspending the marketing and import of jelly confectionery containing E425 konjac, is transposed by the Food (Jelly Confectionery) (Emergency Control) (England) Regulations 2002 and Decision 2005/402/EC, prohibiting imports of products containing specified Sudan dyes, is transposed by the Food (Chilli, Chilli Products, Curcuma and Palm Oil) (Emergency Control) (England) Regulations 2005.

7.4.6   However, in the implementation of official controls Regulation (EC) 882/2004 by the Official Feed and Food Controls (England) Regulations 2007, a power similar to those for products of animal origin is included for products of non-animal origin coming from third countries. Under reg 33, Declarations may be issued suspending, or imposing conditions on, the introduction into England of third country food or feed of non-animal origin not included in the scope of Directive 97/78/EC, which is known to be or reasonably suspected of being likely to constitute a serious risk to animal or public health. Decisions implemented thus are listed below together with the relevant Declarations:

- Decision 2006/504/EC (aflatoxins in products from Brazil, China, Egypt, Iran, Turkey and the USA), as amended, implemented by Declaration OFFC/ 2007/E/003[1];

- Decision 2008/352/EC (pentachlorophenol and dioxins in guar gum from India), implemented by Declaration OFFC/2008/E/001;

- Decision 2008/433/EC (mineral oil in sunflower oil from the Ukraine), implemented by OFFC/2008/E/003;

- Decision 2008/798/EC (special conditions governing import of products containing milk or milk products from China), implemented by Declaration OFFC/2008/E/005.

The parallel Declarations for Wales are OFFC/W/003/2007, OFFC/2008/W/ 001, OFFC/2008/W/003 and OFFC/2008/W/005[2] made under Official Feed and Food Controls (Wales) Regulations 2007.

1   When certain Commission Decisions were repealed and replaced by Decision 2006/504/EC, the Regulations that had implemented them were revoked by the Food (Emergency Control) (Revocation) Regulations 2006 and its Welsh equivalent.
2   See also OFFC/2008/W/004.

7.4.7   There remain those cases in which Community emergency measures continue to be implemented by regulations under the ECA 1972, s 2(2) because the Declaration making powers are perceived to be inadequate for the purpose. Recent examples are:

- the Food (Suspension of the Use of E 128 Red 2G as Food Colour) (England) Regulations 2007, which provides for the execution and enforcement of Regulation (EC) 884/2007 suspending the use of this colouring matter on the basis of advice from the European Food Safety Authority that it may be carcinogenic;

- the Rice Products from the United States of America (Restriction on First Placing on the Market) (England) Regulations 2008, which implements Decision 2006/601/EC, as amended, prohibiting the marketing of specified US rice products, contaminated with unauthorised genetically modified LLRice601. In judicial review proceedings concerning the handling of this emergency, it was held that the Food Standards Agency would have been well-advised to issue a food alert and publicise the contamination, but that the product carried no risk of disease or illness and the claim that the Agency had failed properly to implement the Decision should be rejected[1]. The Agency has reviewed the incident and intends to publish its report;

- the Specified Products from China (Restriction on First Placing on the Market) (England) Regulations 2008, which implements Decision 2008/289/EC prohibiting the marketing of specified Chinese products, contaminated with genetically modified Bt63 rice.

In the main Community emergency measures and the related domestic instruments are relatively short lived. Thus, Decision 2005/317/EC and the Feed Corn Gluten Feed and Brewers Grains) (Emergency Control) Regulations 2005 prohibiting US produce containing genetically modified Bt10 maize were revoked in 2007[2] once the Commission was satisfied that contaminated exportation had ceased. Moreover, the prohibition, imposed by Decision 2006/694/EC and the Curd Cheese (Restriction on Placing on the Market) (England) Regulations 2006, on the marketing of curd cheese from a Lancashire processing establishment was removed[3] after five months following proper disposal of products containing excess antibiotic residues.

1   *R (Friends of the Earth) v Food Standards Agency* [2007] EWHC 558 (Admin).
2   By Decision 2007/157/EC and the Feed (Corn Gluten Feed and Brewers Grains) (Emergency Control) (England) Regulations 2007.
3   By Decision 2007/148/EC and the Curd Cheese (Restriction on Placing on the Market) (England) (Revocation) Regulations 2007.

Emergency control orders under the Food Safety Act 1990

7.4.8   Where there is imminent risk of injury[1] to health, the FSA 1990, s 13 confers power on the Secretary of State to make emergency control orders prohibiting the carrying out of commercial operations with respect to food, food sources or contact materials of any class or description[2]. It is an offence knowingly to contravene an emergency control order[3]. The Secretary of State or Food Standards Agency may consent conditionally or unconditionally to anything thus prohibited, give directions for the purpose of preventing the carrying out of the commercial operations and recover expenses incurred in acting against persons failing to comply[4].

Except where appropriate in relation to Community obligations, the Welsh Ministers act in Wales and the Scottish Ministers in Scotland[5].

1   'Injury' includes any impairment, whether permanent or temporary: FSA 1990, s 11(2A).
2   FSA 1990, s 13(1), as supplemented by s 48(1).
3   FSA 1990, s 13(2). As to 'knowingly' contravening the order, see para **20.1.1** below.
4   FSA 1990, s 13(3)–(7).
5   See para **2.1.2** above.

7.4.9   Before the emergency powers in general food Regulation (EC) 178/2002 were established, the FSA 1990, s 13 was mainly used to implement Community Decisions enacted to deal with serious health threats[1]. However, its value for this purpose was limited, in particular, by the fact that it does not extend to feed for which separate Regulations thus had to be made under the ECA 1972, s 2(2)[2]. In consequence, where Regulations are needed to implement a Community emergency measure, the 1972 Act powers are, as noted above, now customarily used.

1   See, for example, the Food (Star Anise from Third Countries) (Emergency Control) (England) Regulations 2002 implementing Decision 2002/75/EC made under Directive 93/43/EEC, Art 10, all of which legislation has now been revoked.
2   See, for example, the now revoked Food (Animal Products from Belgium) (Emergency Control) (England and Wales) Order 1999 and Animal Feedingstuffs from Belgium (Control) (England and Wales) (No 4) Regulations 1999, which together implemented Decision 1999/788/EC (on dioxin contamination of porcine and poultry products).

7.4.10   Even for purely domestic purposes, the specialist s 13 powers have been used sparingly and on a short term basis. As might be expected of an emergency power, s 13 order prohibitions have soon been lifted[1], or replaced with normal Regulations under the FSA 1990, s 16[2].

1   See the Food (Cheese) (Emergency Control) (Amendment No 2) Order 1998.
2   For example, the Fresh Meat Beef (Emergency Control) Order 1996 was revoked by SI 1996/1742 and replaced by the Fresh Meat (Beef Controls) Regulations 1996.

7.4.11   In *R v Secretary of State for Health, ex p Eastside Cheese* [1999] 3 CMLR 123 the proportionality of a s 13 emergency control order was considered. As a result of a case of E-coli 0157 poisoning, an order was made in 1998 prohibiting the carrying out of any commercial operation in relation to cheese originating from a particular Somerset farm[1]. A major wholesale customer of the farm sought a declaration that the order was disproportionate[2] and invalid on the ground that the draconian powers of s 13 should be exercised only if the powers of food authorities under the FSA 1990, s 9[3] (which would have afforded him the possibility of compensation) were considered inadequate. Reversing the judgment of the Queen's Bench Division, the Court of Appeal held that if s 9 powers are considered to be equally effective, then it is those powers that should be exercised. However, on the particular facts, the s 13 order was a proportionate response to a perceived imminent threat to the health and life of the public. In reaching this conclusion, the Court confirmed that, under s 13, provision may be made that restricts justices of the peace to considering under s 9 whether food is caught by a particular order, thus excluding compensation for any food so caught even where it is not actually unfit for human consumption. The judgment also established that particular firms may be exempted from s 13 orders provided that unfair discrimination is avoided.

1   Food (Cheese) (Emergency Control) Order 1998 as amended by SI 1998/1284 and, so as to disapply the prohibition in respect of cheese manufactured on or after 11 July 1998, by SI 1998/1673.
2   As to the proportionality test applied by Community law to national measures, see further para **1.3.1** above.
3   As to the FSA 1990, s 9, see section **5.4** above.

Emergency orders under the Food and Environment Protection Act 1985

7.4.12   Power to control contaminated things from which food is derived is provided by Part I of the Food and Environment Protection Act 1985 (F&EPA 1985), as amended. The Secretary of State may make an emergency order if in his opinion:

(a)   there exist or may exist circumstances which are likely to create a hazard[1] to human health through human consumption of food; and
(b)   in consequence, food which:
     (i) is, or may be in the future, in an area of the United Kingdom, and/or of sea within British fishery limits, or
     (ii) is or may be in the future derived from anything in such an area,

is or may become, unsuitable for human consumption.

The order designates the area in question and imposes 'emergency prohibitions' from a range of activities specified in Sch 1.

Although it refers to 'food'[2] and not to 'food sources', the scope of the power is otherwise extended by s 1(3) which provides that food derived from any creature is to be treated for the purposes of the Act as also derived from any feeding stuff that that creature has eaten, and from anything from which any such feeding stuff was derived.

It is an offence to contravene an emergency prohibition order or to cause or permit any other person to do so[3].

When an emergency order has been made, the Secretary of State or the Food Standards Agency may consent to the doing of anything prohibited by it, give directions to prevent the consumption of unsuitable food, and recover expenses incurred in acting in respect of failures to comply[4].

Paragraph **2.2.3** above explains the devolution of responsibilities for orders as regards Wales and Scotland although, as noted in para **2.1.2**, the Secretary of State retains power to act in respect of Community obligations.

1   'Hazard' is defined in Regulation (EC) 178/2002 (see para **3.2.6** above) but not in the F&EPA 1985.
2   By F&EPA 1985, s 24, 'food' has the same meaning as in the FSA 1990. See paras **3.2.2** and **4.3.1**.
3   F&EPA 1985, s 1(6) and (7).
4   F&EPA 1985, s 2.

7.4.13 Emergency orders under the 1985 Act have been used in a variety of different circumstances to prevent produce (including feeding stuffs) from leaving clearly identified contaminated areas of the United Kingdom. They have been in force since 1986[1] to prevent human consumption of food derived from sheep in areas still contaminated by radiation from the nuclear reactor at Chernobyl in the former Soviet Union[2]. In those cases and generally with the examples given below, orders are progressively revoked as the hazard recedes and only exceptionally do they subsist as long as the Chernobyl accident controls.

Prior to its amendment by the FSA 1990[3], the F&EPA 1985, s 1 was confined to circumstances in which there had been an 'escape' of hazardous substances. The removal of this limitation rendered the power additionally suitable for prohibiting the taking of shellfish that have consumed toxic algae[4], an especial problem in Scottish waters[5]. In this context it should be noted that maximum toxin levels are prescribed for live bivalve molluscs by Section VII of Annex III to Regulation (EC) 853/2004 laying down specific hygiene rules for food of animal origin.

Emergency orders have also been made in respect of contaminated feeding stuffs[6] and cattle[7], dioxin and heavy metal contamination on particular farms[8] and pollution of the sea by oil and chemicals[9] and by nuclear fuel[10].

1   See now the Food Protection (Emergency Prohibitions) (Radioactivity in Sheep) (Wales) Order 1991, as amended; the Food Protection (Emergency Prohibitions) (Radioactivity in Sheep) (England) Order 1991, as amended; and the Food Protection (Emergency Prohibitions) (Radioactivity in Sheep) Order 1991, as amended.
2   The European Community has fixed permitted levels of radioactivity in foodstuffs and feeding stuffs. See in particular, Regulation (Euratom) 3954/87, Regulation (EEC) 2219/89 (exports), Regulation (EEC) 733/2008 (third country imports) and Recommendation 2003/274 (information about wild food products).
3   FSA 1990, s 51 (1) and (2).
4   See for example, the Food Protection (Emergency Prohibitions) (Scallops) (Irish Sea) Order 2004, amended by SI 2004/2123 and revoked by SI 2004/2686.
5   See for example, the Food Protection (Emergency Prohibitions) (Amnesic Shellfish Poisoning) (West Coast) (No 18) (Scotland) Order 2005 [SSI 2005/626] revoked by SSI 2006/169; the Food Protection (Emergency Prohibitions) (Paralytic Shellfish Poisoning) (Orkney) (No 2) (Scotland) Order 2005 [SSI 2005/548] revoked by SSI 2006/38; and the Food Protection (Emergency Prohibitions) (Diarrhetic Shellfish Poisoning) (East Coast) (No 3) (Scotland) Order 2004 [SSI 2004/436] revoked by SSI 2004/502.
6   See for example, the Food Protection (Emergency Prohibitions) (Contamination of Feeding Stuff) (England) (No 3) Order 1989.
7   See for example, the Food Protection (Emergency Prohibitions) (Lead in Cattle) (England) Order 1991; and the Food Protection (Emergency Prohibitions) (Poisonous Substances in Cattle) (Wales) Order 1991.
8   See for example, the Food Protection (Emergency Prohibitions) (Dioxins) (England) (No 2) Order 1992 and the Food Protection (Emergency Prohibitions) (Lead in Ducks and Geese) (England) Order 1992.
9   See for example, the Food Protection (Emergency Prohibitions) (Oil and Chemical Pollution of Fish and Plants) Order 1996; and the Food Protection (Emergency Prohibitions) (Oil and Chemical Pollution of Salmon and Migratory Trout) Order 1996.
10 Food Protection (Emergency Prohibitions) (Dounreay Nuclear Establishment) Order 1997.

7.5   CRISIS MANAGEMENT

7.5.1 The final section of this chapter describes the provisions on crisis management prescribed for the Commission by Articles 55–57 of Regulation (EC) 178/2002; for the Member States by Art 13 of Regulation (EC) 882/2004; and for the United Kingdom, in particular, by the Food Standards Agency's Incidents Response Protocol.

Commission's crisis management procedures

7.5.2   In response to recent food crises, more rapid procedures for crisis management have been provided for the Commission. Under Art 55 of Regulation (EC) 178/2002, the Commission, in close cooperation with the European Food Safety Authority and the Member States, has made Decision 2004/478/EC drawing up a general plan for crisis management in the field of the safety of food and feed. In particular, the plan specifies the actual or potential crisis situations involving direct or indirect risks to human health that are not likely to be prevented, eliminated or reduced to an acceptable level by provisions in place or cannot adequately be managed solely by way of the application of Arts 53 and 54[1]. Decision 2004/478/EC also specifies the practical procedures necessary to manage a crisis including those relating to the establishment of a crisis unit as required by Art 56 of Regulation (EC) 178/2002. By Art 57 of that Regulation, the crisis unit is responsible for collecting and evaluating all relevant information and identifying the options available to prevent, eliminate or reduce to an acceptable level the risk to human health as effectively and rapidly as possible. It may request assistance and must keep the public informed of the risks involved and the measures taken.

1   See para **7.4.2** above.

Member States' crisis management contingency plans

7.5.3   For implementation of the Commission's general plan for crisis management, Art 13 of official control Regulation (EC) 882/2004 requires Member States to draw up operational contingency plans setting out measures to be implemented without delay when feed or food is found to pose a serious risk to humans or animals either directly or through the environment. The contingency plans must specify the administrative authorities to be engaged; their powers and responsibilities; and channels and procedures for sharing information between the relevant parties.

Food Standards Authority's Incident Response Protocol

7.5.4   A key element of the UK's operational contingency plan, to be applied if and when the Commission has to activate its crisis management plan under Art 55 of Regulation (EC) 178/2002, is the Incident Response Protocol created by the Food Standards Agency[1]. In fact, the Protocol is of general relevance, outlining the procedures to be followed by Agency staff during food and feed incidents and emergencies whether or not of Community significance, and includes provision for those cases in which the Agency acts in support when another government Department or unit has lead responsibility. To ensure a rapid and co-ordinated response during incidents and emergencies, the Agency has also established close links (by service level agreement, memorandum of understanding or otherwise) with various other departments and agencies such as DEFRA, the Environment Agency, the Veterinary Laboratories Agency, the Rural Payments Agency and the Scottish Agricultural College. Moreover, the Agency has, through its Food Incidents Task Force, produced a guidance document to aid food businesses and others to prevent and deal efficiently with food incidents if they occur[2].

1   See para 4.46ff of the Single Integrated National Control Plan for the United Kingdom January 2007 to March 2011. As to the National Control Plan, see further para **18.2.6**.
2   *Principles for preventing and responding to food incidents*: April 2008. See also the FSA Annual Report of Incidents 2007.

7.5.5 The Incident Response Protocol is risk-based and can take account of incidents of varying size and complexity. It sets out the staff roles and responsibilities (including in particular those of the Agency's Incident Branch), the procedures for notification of incidents and the arrangements for their closure and review.

7.5.6 The definition of an incident, for the purposes of the Incident Response Protocol, is the same as that for the purposes of the Food Law Code of Practice[1], that is, 'any event where, based on the information available, there are concerns about actual or suspected threats to the safety or quality of food that could require intervention to protect consumers' interests.' Incidents fall broadly into two categories:

- Incidents involving contamination of food or animal feed in the processing, distribution, retail and catering chains. These incidents may result in action to withdraw the food from sale and, in certain circumstances, to recall, alerting the public not to consume potentially contaminated food.
- Environmental pollution incidents, e g fires, chemical/oil spills, radiation leaks, which may involve voluntary or statutory action (such as orders made under the Food and Environment Protection Act 1985).

An 'emergency' under the Protocol is to be distinguished from that term as respectively used in Art 53 of Regulation (EC) 178/2002, the FSA 1990, s 13 and the F&EPA 1985, s 1[2]. Apparently drawing its inspiration from the Civil Contingencies Act 2004, the Protocol definition extends beyond human welfare and the environment to serious threats to political, administrative or economic stability and the security of the United Kingdom.

1   See para **7.2.2** above.
2   See paras **7.4.2**, **7.4.8** and **7.4.12** above.

Chapter 8

Consumer protection: general offences

8.1 INTRODUCTION

8.1.1   This chapter describes ss 14 and 15 of the Food Safety Act 1990 (FSA 1990) in the light of the substantial body of case law that has accumulated since these primary domestic provisions for the protection of food consumers from deception were originally enacted.

As explained in paras **1.1.1** and **5.1.1**, the prohibition on selling food not of the nature, substance or quality demanded by the purchaser now in s 14 has been one of the principal controls on the chemical composition of food since 1875. Although classified in the FSA 1990 under a 'consumer protection' heading, it should not be assumed that s 14 extends only to selling that threatens the pockets of purchasers. As explained below, it most certainly also continues to apply to the selling of food that threatens their health.

Itself also originating from before the second world war, the prohibition on the false description of food in s 15 of the FSA 1990 not only implements Art 2(1) of the European Community food labelling Directive 2000/13/EC but, together with Art 2(1), must now also be viewed in the context of the over-arching prohibition on misleading labelling, advertising and presentation of food and feed established by Art 16 of general food Regulation (EC) 178/2002[1].

Chapter 9 and para **11.3.2** below explain how the rest of labelling Directive 2003/13/EC is implemented.

It should be noted that ss 14 and 15 overlap with the Consumer Protection from Unfair Trading Regulations 2008, which have recently been made in implementation of commercial practices Directive 2005/29/EC and have substantially repealed the Trade Descriptions Act 1968. These Regulations generally prohibit unfair business-to-consumer commercial practices that (a) contravene the requirements of professional diligence and (b) materially distort the economic behaviour of the average consumer with regard to the product[2]. They also expressly prohibit any such practices that are misleading actions or omissions, that are aggressive or that are specified in Sch 1[3]. Unlike contraventions of these express prohibitions and of FSA 1990, ss 14 and 15, contraventions of the general prohibition are not strict liability in nature but require the trader 'knowingly or recklessly' to have engaged in the unfair commercial practice in order for an offence to have been committed[4].

---

1   See paras **3.2.36** and **3.3.37** above.
2   See Consumer Protection from Unfair Trading Regulations 2008, reg 3. 'Professional diligence' means 'the standard of special skill and care which a trader may reasonably be expected to exercise towards consumers which is commensurate with either (a) honest market

practice in the trader's field of activity, or (b) the general principle of good faith in the trader's field of activity'.
3   See ibid, regs 3–7 and Sch 1.
4   See ibid, reg 8 and, as to strict liability offences and those that require criminal intent, see para **20.1.1**.

8.2   FOOD NOT OF THE NATURE OR SUBSTANCE OR QUALITY DEMANDED

8.2.1   As indicated above, what is now s 14 of the FSA 1990 has been the principal protection for the consumer from unsatisfactory food since 1875. It is an offence for a person to sell to the purchaser's prejudice any food that is not of the nature or substance or quality demanded by the purchaser[1]. The section is thus responsive to a bespoke stipulation by the purchaser, but where, as in the normal way, there is none and where there is no statutory standard for the food, the court must decide from the evidence what was demanded. This is considered further in para **8.2.11**.

The section has proved remarkably flexible and has been used more than any other provision in current or former food law. It is by no means limited to the context, in which it was enacted, of ensuring that the composition of food is as described. Prior to 1990, where unfitness for human consumption in contravention of what became s 8 could not clearly be established, the predecessors of s 14 were used for cases of chemical contamination, for cases of bacterial contamination by mould or micro-organisms and their toxins and for cases of contamination by extraneous matter (i e foreign bodies)[2].

However, s 14 is not without limitation. By its very nature it is unavailable in respect of food in possession or offered or exposed for sale. There must be a sale to constitute an offence. This was perceived as a significant shortcoming particularly in relation to contamination cases and, on the enactment of FSA 1990, the opportunity was taken to fill the gap via the new concept of 'food safety requirements'[3]. This has itself now been superseded by the European Community version established by Art 14 of Regulation (EC) 178/2002, which covers similar ground to the national provisions that it replaced[4].

1   FSA 1990, s 14.
2   See further paras **8.2.5–8.2.8**.
3   See further para **5.1.1**.
4   See paras **5.3.1** and **3.2.20–3.2.30** and the definition of 'placing on the market' described in para **3.2.13**.

Sell

8.2.2   For the commission of an offence contrary to s 14 of the FSA 1990 there must have been a sale for human consumption[1], taking into account the extended meaning of 'sale'[2] — see para **4.6.1** above. In self-service stores a sale does not take place until the cash is accepted at the check-out[3]. This is of importance to authorised officers of enforcement authorities in purchasing samples for analysis or examination[4] and undertaking the subsequent procedures prescribed for these purposes[5].

It should also be noted that more than one person can be answerable for selling food in contravention of s 14. An owner of food, as well as his employee or agent who actually effects the transaction, will normally be vicariously liable for a prohibited sale[6]. Thus, a brewery was liable for the sale of under-strength

alcoholic beverages from a public house, notwithstanding that their employee
was the licensee authorised under the Licensing Act 1964[7].

1   *Thompson v Ball* (1948) 92 Sol Jo 272.
2   FSA 1990, s 2.
3   *Pharmaceutical Society of Great Britain v Boots Cash Chemists (Southern) Ltd* [1952] 2 QB
    795, [1952] 2 All ER 456.
4   See para **18.4.2** below.
5   See paras **18.4.3** and **18.4.4** respectively below.
6   See, for example, *Pearks, Gunston and Tee Ltd v Ward* [1902] 2 KB 1, 66 JP 774.
7   *Nottingham City Council v Wolverhampton and Dudley Breweries plc* [2003] EWHC 2847,
    [2004] QB 1274, [2004] 2 WLR 820.

Prejudice of the purchaser

8.2.3   For an offence to arise under this section the purchaser must have been
prejudiced[1]. The word 'prejudice' does not imply actual damage to the
purchaser. As early as 1879, it was decided[2] that the prejudice contemplated by
the legislation is paying for one thing but getting something inferior. Without
the words 'to the prejudice of the purchaser', an offence would be committed if
the purchaser received a product superior to what had been demanded.
Moreover, had the section been construed as meaning that the purchaser must
suffer pecuniary prejudice, much of the beneficial effect of the legislation
would have been nullified. Enforcement officers making test purchases use not
their own, but public money. On this point, later that same year an amending
provision (now to be found in s 14(2) of the FSA 1990) expressly excluded the
defence that a purchaser buying for analysis or examination is not prejudiced.

1   *TW Lawrence & Sons Ltd v Burleigh* (1981) 146 JP 134.
2   *Hoyle v Hitchman* (1879) 4 QBD 233.

8.2.4   The predecessors to the current Act contained provision for notices by
which the true nature, substance and quality of the food in question could be
declared thus avoiding prejudice to the purchaser and liability under the section.
There was much judicial consideration of the sufficiency or otherwise of
notices given to purchasers[1]. Although the FSA 1990 dropped specific
provision of this kind in favour of a general due diligence defence[2], it evidently
remains the case that a person cannot be prejudiced if given positive
information as to the true nature, substance and quality of the food. However,
such information, no matter how accurate, is no defence where a compositional
standard has been laid down by law for the food. Thus, a purchaser would be
prejudiced by the sale to him of pork sausages containing only 32% of meat or
cured meat notwithstanding a notice to that effect, because such products are
required by regulations[3] to contain not less than 42%. In such a case there
would be an offence of 'quality' under this section and one of deficiency of meat
content under the Regulations.

1   See, for example, *Sandys v Small* (1878) 3 QBD 449; and *Goldup v John Manson Ltd* [1982]
    QB 161, [1981] 3 All ER 257.
2   See section **20.3** below.
3   Meat Products (England) Regulations 2003. See further para **10.6.3**.

Nature, substance, quality

8.2.5   These terms are alternatives[1]: for the purposes of proceedings only
one of them must be selected, otherwise the information will be bad for
duplicity[2]. However, it is important to bear in mind, when considering what is
said of them below, that they are by no means mutually exclusive categories and

where a case falls within more than one, it is open to the prosecutor to choose whichever is considered the most appropriate[3]. See, for example, paras **8.2.7** and **8.2.8** below on the substance and quality of mouldy food.

1   Until the Food and Drugs (Adulteration) Act 1928, the provision read 'nature, substance *and* quality', but the Sale of Food and Drugs Amendment Act 1879 had already made clear that it was no defence to prove that food defective in nature, substance *or* quality was not defective in all three respects.
2   Criminal Procedure Rules 2005, r 7.3. *Bastin v Davies* [1950] 2 KB 579, [1950] 1 All ER 1095. See further para **19.3.7** below.
3   *Preston v Greenclose Ltd* (1975) 139 JP Jo 245; *Shearer v Rowe* (1985) 149 JP 698.

Nature

8.2.6   This term is evidently appropriate where a different sort of food is sold from that demanded by the purchaser. Thus, fruit or fish not of the variety or species requested would not be of the 'nature' demanded. It has, for example, been held to cover savin sold for saffron[1], reformed white fish sold as scampi[2], minced beef containing quantities of pork and lamb meat[3] and, in one startling case, caustic soda mistakenly sold as lemonade[4].

It should also be noted that where the food sold is of a different sort from that described there might also be contraventions of reg 5(a) of the Food Labelling Regulations 1996, s 15 of the FSA 1990 or Art 16 of Regulation (EC) 178/2002, as well as of reg 3 of the Consumer Protection from Unfair Trading Regulations 2008[5].

1   *Knight v Bowers* (1885) 14 QBD 845.
2   *Preston v Greenclose Ltd* (1975) 139 JP Jo 245.
3   *Shearer v Rowe* (1985) 149 JP 698.
4   *Meah v Roberts* [1978] 1 All ER 97, [1977] 1 WLR 1187.
5   See para **8.1.1** above.

Substance

8.2.7   This term is usually applied to circumstances in which the composition of the food is incompatible with what was demanded, as in cases where the food contains improper ingredients or adulterants. Until the 1990 Act, it would also have been the most obvious head for dealing with foreign bodies[1] and contaminants[2] in food, but first the former s 8(2)(c) of the Act and now Art 14(5) of Regulation (EC) 178/2002, referred to in para **3.2.23** above, have successively afforded a more specific basis.

Even though a foreign body is not of the substance demanded, an offence may not necessarily be committed. A distinction was drawn in two milk cases. There was a good defence where the foreign body was a sterile and harmless milk cap[3], but a conviction where it was a dangerous sliver of glass[4]. In a more recent case, however, a bottle of milk containing a green straw was held not to be of the quality demanded[5].

Mould has also been regarded as contamination of food and a matter affecting its substance[6].

1   *Smedleys Ltd v Breed* [1974] AC 839, [1974] 2 All ER 21 (caterpillar in a tin of peas).
2   *Hall v Owen-Jones and Jones (t/a Central Dairies)* [1967] 1 WLR 1362 (excess penicillin in milk).
3   *Edwards v Llaethdy Meirion Ltd* [1957] Crim LR 402.
4   *Southworth v Whitewell Dairies Ltd* (1958) 122 JP 322.
5   *Barber v Co-operative Wholesale Society Ltd* (1983) 147 JP 296.
6   See further para **8.2.8** below.

Quality

8.2.8   In *Anness v Grivell* [1915] 3 KB 685, it was held that 'quality' means 'commercial quality' and not merely description. The appellant sold as 'a very good mixture of butter and margarine' food containing 80% margarine, 15.5% water, salt etc and only 4.5% butter. The magistrates considered that such a small quantity of butter prevented the mixture being of the quality claimed for it. Because at that time the legislation prohibited sale of margarine containing more than 10% butter fat, the Divisional Court felt compelled to hold that no offence had been committed, but intimated that their decision might well have been otherwise had it not been for the limit on butter content. As indicated in para **8.2.1**, where there is neither statutory standard for the food nor special demand by the purchaser, the courts must decide what quality of food an ordinary purchaser would expect to receive. Other instances of food quality that have been considered by the courts have concerned deficient extract of meat and malt wine[1], alleged sugar deficiency in orange citric flavoured cordial[2], excess fat in minced beef[3] and excess sugar in diet cola[4].

Additionally, action under the quality head has been taken against mouldy, bad and decomposed food[5].

1   *Bowker v Woodroffe* [1928] 1 KB 217, [1927] All ER Rep 415.
2   *Collins Arden Products Ltd v Barking Corpn* [1943] KB 419, [1943] 2 All ER 249.
3   *TW Lawrence & Sons Ltd v Burleigh* (1981) 146 JP 134.
4   *McDonald's Hamburgers Ltd v Windle* (1986) 151 JP 333.
5   *Watford Corpn v Maypole Ltd* [1970] 1 QB 573, [1970] 1 All ER 554; *Swain v Old Kentucky Restaurants* (1973) 138 JP 84; *Tesco Stores Ltd v Roberts* [1974] 3 All ER 74, [1974] 1 WLR 1253. As to mouldy food, see also paras **3.2.23** and **8.2.7**.

The food demanded

8.2.9   As indicated in para **8.2.1** above, the nature, substance and quality of the food for the purposes of s 14 is defined in terms of the purchaser's demand.

8.2.10   Where there is a statutory standard, as indicated in para **8.2.4**, the purchaser will be deemed to have demanded a food of that standard. The logic of this proposition is that if a buyer demands a food for which there is a statutory standard but receives an inferior product, he is prejudiced and the offence is committed.

A purchaser who insisted on a product inferior to the statutory standard would evidently be guilty of a secondary party offence such as procuring the illegal sale.

8.2.11   Paragraphs **8.2.1** and **8.2.8** above have already noted that where there is no statutory standard the justices must determine the nature, substance and quality of the food demanded by the purchaser as a question of fact on the basis of the evidence[1]. There may have been an express contract term[2], but for the most part what was demanded must be ascertained from the surrounding circumstances of the case. In many cases, it has been concluded that the purchaser demanded food that corresponds in nature, substance or quality with that normally sold in the trade[3]. In some cases, the quality of the food impliedly demanded may depend on whether different qualities were available at different prices[4]. The public analyst's opinion about the normal standard for the food has always been an important contribution to the magistrates' deliberations. It cannot be substituted for the standard demanded by the purchaser[5], but has often been accepted as that standard where the defence has elected to call no evidence of its own on the point[6].

Non-statutory recommendations, such as those of the now defunct Food Advisory Committee[7], have afforded influential evidence of what purchasers normally demand[8]. But with the lifting of the Second World War emergency controls, the Government became justifiably wary of responding to requests to put out codes of practice and similar guidance containing specific recommendations about food composition. For the Government to have defined the citizen's obligations under s 14 by this backdoor method would potentially have obfuscated criminal liability and sidestepped the safeguards of parliamentary scrutiny and publicity attendant on standards set by the authorised process of regulations under s 16 or 17 of the Act. This inhibition on Government action was removed by s 7 of the Food Standards Act 1999, which enables the Food Standards Agency to give advice, information and assistance to persons other than public authorities[9]. Although standards published under this power are non-authoritative[10] and other opinions as to the definition of the food in question are not thereby excluded, the power is of particular use in enabling guidance to be provided pending issue of a more thoroughly considered standard in an industry code of practice[11] or legislation.

An important modern group of industry food and feed standards is to be found in the food assurance schemes[12] that have been developed since the enactment of the FSA 1990, not least in response to the need of retailers to be able to establish the 'due diligence' defence described in ch 20. Particularly well-known examples are the Assured Food Standards' 'Red Tractor' schemes and the British Egg Industry Council code of practice for 'Lion Quality' eggs.

1   *Roberts v Leeming* (1905) 69 JP 417 (margarine); *Wilson and McPhee v Wilson* (1903) 68 JP 175 (brandy); *Preston v Jackson* (1928) 73 Sol Jo 712 (vinegar); *Hunt v Richardson* [1916] 2 KB 446 (milk).
2   *Hunt v Richardson* [1916] 2 KB 446.
3   See, for example, *Sandys v Rhodes* (1903) 67 JP 352 (variety of tapioca sold as sago); *Webb v Jackson Wyness Ltd* [1948] 2 All ER 1054 (non-brewed vinegar); *Hughes v Traynor* [1916] 2 IR 275 (maize meal with husk and germ removed sold as white meal).
4   *Morton v Green* (1881) 8 R (Ct of Sess) 36, 18 Sc LR 570; *Goldup v John Manson Ltd* [1982] QB 161, [1981] 3 All ER 257.
5   *Goldup v John Manson Ltd* [1982] QB 161, [1981] 3 All ER 257.
6   *Bowker v Woodroffe* [1928] 1 KB 217, [1927] All ER Rep 415; *Broughton v Whittaker* [1944] 2 All ER 544, [1944] KB 269; *Webb v Jackson Wyness Ltd* [1948] 2 All ER 1054; *Mills (AJ) & Co Ltd v Williams* [1964] Crim L R 533, DC.
7   The Food Advisory Committee was a non-statutory committee of scientists set up by Ministers in 1983 to continue to advise them on the composition of food in succession to the Food Standards Committee and the Food Additives and Contaminants Committee. On the establishment of the Food Standards Agency in 2000, it became an advisory committee under FSA 1999, s 5(4) with revised terms of reference. It was closed down on 31 December 2001.
8   *Mills (AJ) & Co Ltd v Williams* [1964] Crim L R 533, DC.
9   See para **2.3.3**(b) above.
10   See, for example, the 2006 Food Standards Agency Guidance described in para **11.6.3** below on the use of the terms 'vegetarian' and 'vegan' in food labelling.
11   See, for example, the 2005 Code of Practice on Basmati Rice establish by the UK rice industry and the British Retail Consortium in consultation with LACORS and the Association of Public Analysts, which replaced the 2003 Food Standards Agency Guidance on the subject.
12   See further para **11.6.4** below and the FSA *Food Assurance Schemes Guidance Notes* (2003) and the reviews by Ruth Kirk-Wilson that, in 2002, preceded them and, in 2008, assessed their uptake by UK scheme operators.

The future

8.2.12   The withdrawal of the Government and the European Community in recent years from the wholesale fixing of food standards[1] could result in increased recourse to s 14. In any event, this venerable provision continues to stand as a primary protection for the consumer against the sale of unsatisfactory food.

1   See in particular section **1.3** above and paras **10.1.1** and **10.6.1** below.

8.3   FALSE OR MISLEADING LABELS AND ADVERTISEMENTS

8.3.1   The general prohibition on misleading labelling enacted by Art 2(1) of Directive 2000/13/EC is implemented in Great Britain by the FSA 1990, s 15(1)[1]. Under this provision it is an offence to give with any food sold, or to display with any food offered or exposed for sale, or in possession for sale, a label, whether or not attached to or printed on the wrapper or container, which (a) falsely describes the food or (b) is likely to mislead as to the nature or substance or quality of the food. The comprehensiveness of the prohibition imposed by s 15(1) is confirmed by Art 2(1)(a) of the Directive that governs its interpretation[2]. Thus, labelling must not mislead to a material degree as to the characteristics of the foodstuff and, in particular, as to its nature, identity, properties, composition, quantity, durability, origin or provenance, method of manufacture or production[3]. Additionally, misleading food claims are prohibited[4].

1   See also para **8.1.1** above in respect of misleading actions and omissions that are unfair consumer practices prohibited by the Consumer Protection from Unfair Trading Regulations 2008, regs 3, 5 and 6. As to the implementation of Article 2(1)(b) by the Food Labelling Regulations 1996, Sch 6, Pt I, para 2, see para **11.3.2** below.
2   See para **1.2.1** above. See also case C-366/98 *Geoffrey v Casino France* [2000] ECR I-6579 para 17.
3   Directive 2000/13/EC, Art 2(1)(a)(i).
4   Directive 2000/13/EC, Art 2(1)(a)(ii) and (iii) As to food claims, see further para **11.1.1** below.

8.3.2   Article 2(1) of Directive 2000/13/EC, as applied to advertising by Art 2(3)(b), is implemented by the FSA 1990, s 15(2). This provides that it is an offence to publish, or to be a party to the publication of, an advertisement that falsely describes any food or that is likely to mislead as to the nature or substance or quality of any food.

A label or advertisement

8.3.3   These offences are basic to the prevention of false or misleading labels and advertisements and are very wide in their application. 'Labelling' is defined by Art 1(3)(a) of Directive 2000/13/EC as 'any words, particulars, trade marks, brand name, pictorial matter or symbol relating to a foodstuff and placed on any packaging, document, notice, label, ring or collar accompanying or referring to such foodstuff'. That definition is not reproduced in the Act but the use of the words 'whether or not attached to or printed on the wrapper or container' suggests that information given visually by words or illustrations could give rise to an offence. A label would not include a verbal statement but the definition of 'advertisement' in the Act[1] includes any notice, circular, label, wrapper, invoice or other document, and any public announcement made orally or by any means of producing or transmitting light or sound. It should also be borne in mind that oral communications can also be unfair commercial practices prohibited by the Consumer Protection from Unfair Trading Regulations 2008[2]. For all practical purposes it may be assumed that any false or misleading statement as to food for human consumption, however given, is an offence.

1   FSA 1990, s 53(1).
2   See para **8.1.1** above. So far as provisions in and under the Trade Descriptions Act 1968 still
     subsist, see also s 4(2) of that Act.

Falsely describes the food[1]

8.3.4   Prosecuting authorities have not employed this offence as frequently
as the alternative 'likely to mislead ...' because the term 'false' is stronger and
more difficult to prove. It is necessary to prove that a label or advertisement is
explicitly false, that is, wholly untrue. However, a court is not precluded from
finding that a label or advertisement is false or misleading even if it contains an
accurate statement of the composition of the food[2].

The numerous occasions on which the concept of falseness of food labels has
been considered by the courts in civil litigation or with regard to offences
against the trade descriptions law should be treated with some caution bearing
in mind that the burden of proof of falseness in civil proceedings is different
from that in criminal law and that 'a false trade description' not only includes a
misleading statement[3] but also, since the Consumer Protection from Unfair
Trading Regulations 2008, is a concept of very limited application[4]. As regards
civil law, para **21.1.1** below gives examples of cases in which the public has
been held to have been deceived into believing that one producer's food is in
fact that of another (that is, where the tort of passing off has been committed).
Examples of false trade descriptions have been:

(a)   the use of the word 'port' for a product not from Portugal[5];
(b)   the labelling as 'Fine British Tarragona Wine', a mixture of British and
       Tarragona wine that was nothing like Tarragona wine[6];
(c)   the description of a solution of acetic acid and caramel as 'vinegar'[7].

Under a forerunner of s 15 of the FSA 1990, a fruit juice was held not to have
been falsely described as 'natural' even though it had been reconstituted in part
from concentrated juice and had been pasteurised[8].

1   FSA 1990, s 15(1)(a).
2   FSA 1990, s 15(4).
3   Trade Descriptions Act 1968, s 3(2).
4   See para **8.1.1** above.
5   *Sandeman v Gold* [1924] 1 KB 107.
6   *Holmes v Pipers Ltd* [1914] 1 KB 57.
7   *Kat v Diment* [1951] 1 KB 34, [1950] 2 All ER 657.
8   *Amos v Britvic Ltd* (1984) 149 JP 13.

Likely to mislead[1]

8.3.5   Although representations may be literally true but practically false
because of what is omitted[2], it would no doubt in general be prudent for a
prosecutor under s 15 of the FSA 1990 to employ a charge of 'likely to mislead'
unless there is a misstatement of fact that is sufficiently clear to sustain the
allegation of the 'falseness' of the description in question.

As indicated above, a label or advertisement may be misleading even where it
contains a factually correct statement of the composition of the food.
Notwithstanding that a label bears an accurate list of ingredients in compliance
with labelling requirements[3], it may be misleading by virtue of the product
name, instructions for use, background illustrations, processes or treatments. A
label that stated 'fully prepared, sliced, selected tinned apples (unsweetened)'

was held to be misleading because the fruit had lost about 25% of its original solids through the addition of water[4].

Attempts to prevent supposed misuses of traditional food names and terms have not proved an unqualified success. A label that stated '2 Chicken Breast Steaks – Flaked and formed chicken in a crispy crumb' was held by the Crown Court on appeal not be to be misleading, even though the product was not comprised of solid muscle meat[5]. Similarly, in proceedings under the Trade Descriptions Act 1968 and the Food Labelling Regulations, a product labelled 'Pura Vegetable Lard' with a subsidiary statement '100% vegetable oils' was held not to be misleading despite the fact that lard is a product wholly of pig fat[6]. On the other hand, labels stating 'Elmlea Single' and 'Elmlea Whipping', with the additional words 'the real alternative to cream', were held by the Crown Court on appeal to be misleading when used on products made from vegetable oil and packed in cartons resembling those usually used for cream[7]. The information given on the labels was factually correct but the average customer was likely to be misled.

The description 'naturally pure' for a strawberry jam that contains pectin and lawful residues of lead, cadmium and pesticides would not be regarded as misleading contrary to FSA 1990, s 15(1)(b). It was held by the European Court not to be precluded by Directive 79/112/EEC, Art 2(1)(a), the predecessor of Directive 2000/13/EC, Art 2(1)(a)[8].

In deciding whether a food label was false or misleading under the Trade Descriptions Act 1968, it had to be read as a whole, together with the list of ingredients required by the Food Labelling Regulations 1996. No offence was held to have been committed as regards 'Blackcurrant juice burst' and 'Cranberry juice burst' of which the ingredients lists showed a fruit content of 13% and 25% respectively, notwithstanding that the labels indicated that the drinks were 100% fruit juice[9].

1   FSA 1990, s 15(1)(b).
2   *R v Lord Kylsant* [1932] 1 KB 442; *R v Bishirgian* [1936] 1 All ER 586; *Curtis v Chemical Cleaning and Dyeing Co Ltd* [1951] 1 KB 805, [1951] 1 All ER 631, CA. Compare now misleading omissions under the Consumer Protection from Unfair Trading Regulations 2008, reg 6 (see para **8.1.1** above).
3   Food Labelling Regulations 1996, regs 5(b) and 12–18.
4   *Arlidge v Blue Cap Foods (Kent) Ltd* (1965) 63 LGR 167.
5   *GW Padley (Poultry) Ltd v Elkington* (1986) unreported.
6   *Wolkind and Northcott v Pura Foods Ltd* (1987) 151 JP 492.
7   *Burleigh v Van Den Berghs & Jurgens Ltd* [1987] BTLC 337.
8   Case C-465/98 *Verein gegen Unwesen in Handel und Gewerbe Köln v Darbo* [2000] ECR I-2297.
9   *Lewin v Purity Soft Drinks Ltd* (2005) 169 JP 84.

8.4   PRESENTATION

8.4.1   The Community prohibition on misleading presentation of foodstuffs imposed by Art 2(1) and 2(3)(a) of General Labelling Directive 2000/13/EC was a novel one to British law when imposed by its predecessor[1]. In implementation of these provisions the FSA 1990, s 15(3) makes it unlawful to sell, offer or expose for sale, or have in possession for the purpose of sale, any food the presentation of which is likely to mislead as to the nature or substance or quality of the food.

1   Directive 79/112/EEC, Art 2(1) and 2(3)(a).

Definition of presentation

8.4.2   Presentation is defined[1] as including the shape, appearance and packaging of the food, the way in which the food is arranged when it is exposed for sale and the setting in which the food is displayed with a view to sale[2], but does not include any form of labelling or advertising. Truthful labelling may mitigate or negate any misleading presentation.

1   FSA 1990, s 53(1).
2   In the English texts, the scope of 'presentation' as expressed in general food Regulation (EC) 178/2002, Art 16 (see para **3.2.36** above) is in much the same terms as in the labelling Directive 2000/13/EC, Art 2(3)(a) implemented by FSA 1990, s 15(3).

Examples of food presentation

8.4.3   Prosecutions for misleading presentation have included cases on fatty mince displayed under red lighting to give a misleading impression as to its fat content; meat containing novel protein displayed together with whole meat; analogue dairy products being displayed with genuine milk-based products; and artificially-flavoured fruit products being packed in fruit-shaped containers.

Chapter 9

Food labelling and advertising

9.1 INTRODUCTION

9.1.1   Rules for the protection of consumers through the control of labelling and advertising of food either restrict or require what is displayed. Labelling restrictions and requirements have long been employed in British food law, which thus needed only adaptation in order to comply with the same two-pronged approach adopted by Community law.

9.1.2   The basic Community provision restricting what may appear on food labels is Art 2(1) of the general labelling Directive 2000/13/EC as amended. Labelling and methods used are prohibited if they could mislead the purchaser to a material degree. This restriction is applied by Art 2(3)(a) and (b) of the Directive respectively to presentation and to advertising of foodstuffs[1].

1   For the British implementing law, see sections **8.3** and **8.4** above.

9.1.3   The basic Community provision requiring what is to appear on food labels is Art 3 of the general labelling Directive 2000/13/EC, as amended. In particular the name and the list of ingredients are compulsory in the labelling of foodstuffs[1]. These provisions assumed a special importance after the landmark European Court *Cassis de Dijon* judgment[2]. Since then, national measures have been permitted to restrict import of products lawfully marketed in other Member States only if they aim to protect an important public interest and are proportionate to that objective. For consumer protection and the defence of fair trading, the European Court has regarded compulsory labelling in compliance with the labelling Directive as adequate. It should be noted that the Commission intends to consolidate and update labelling legislation in the areas of general food and nutrition labelling, repealing and replacing the existing directives with a Regulation, with the intention of simplifying and clarifying the exisiting law. [3]

1   For the British implementing law, see section **9.2** below.
2   See section **1.3** above.
3   Proposal for a Regulation of the European Parliament and of the Council on the provision of food information to consumers, COM (2008) 40 final.

9.2 FOOD LABELLING REQUIREMENTS

9.2.1   The principal Community food labelling requirements are prescribed by the general food labelling Directive 2000/13/EC[1], as amended and implemented in Great Britain by the Food Labelling Regulations 1996, as amended.[2] The major part of this section is devoted to these implementing provisions. Paragraph **9.2.23** summarises provisions implementing additional labelling required by Directive 87/250 (alcoholic strength), Directive 2008/5 (packaging gases, sweeteners, polyols and glycyrrhizinic acid), Directive 2002/67 (caffeine)[3] and Regulation 608/2004 (food with added phytosterols and phytostanols). Paragraphs **9.2.24** and **9.2.25** respectively describe the separate but complementary EC provisions on beef and fish labelling. Paragraph **9.2.27** summarises the Food (Lot Marking) Regulations 1996 that implement Directive 89/396/EEC (on indications or marks the lot to which a foodstuff belongs).

1   This Directive is a codified version of Directive 79/112/EC.
2   The FSA has carried out research and public consultations into clear food labelling. As a result it has revised its *Food Labelling Clear Food Labelling Guidance*, 2008 to provide best practice advice that encourages greater clarity, whilst recognising that flexibility is important.
3   As to quinine and caffeine, see also para **9.2.9** below.

The Food Labelling Regulations 1996 generally

9.2.2   The Food Labelling Regulations 1996 are arranged into the following five parts:

- Part I (Preliminary)
- Part II (Food to be delivered as such to the ultimate consumer or to caterers)
- Part III (Claims, nutrition labelling and misleading descriptions)
- Part IV (Offences and legal proceedings)
- Part V (Revocations, amendments and transitional provisions).

The provisions of Part II are considered in this section together with the separate legislation on food with added phytosterols and phytostanols, beef and fish names and lot marking, while the provisions of Part III are explained in section **10.7** (on misleading descriptions), section **11.3** (on claims) and sections **11.4** and **11.5** (on nutrition labelling).

These substantive requirements are supported by the provisions of Parts I and IV. Besides containing essential definitions, Part I sets out the general exemptions. These include a mutual recognition clause[1] the general effect of which is to permit the import of food coming from a Member State and complying with the rules laid down by that State[2], as well as of food to which the EEA Agreement applies brought into Great Britain from an EEA State in which it was lawfully produced and sold[3]. Except in so far as they relate to advertising, the Regulations also do not apply to food that is not intended for sale for human consumption[4].

1   Food Labelling Regulations 1996, reg 3(1). See *Hackney London Borough Council v Cedar Trading Ltd* (1999) 163 JP 749.
2   As to mutual recognition and mutual recognition clauses, see para **1.3.2** above.
3   As to the EEA Agreement and EEA States, see para **1.8.1** above.
4   Food Labelling Regulations 1996, reg 3(3)(a).

The Food Labelling Regulations 1996, Part II

9.2.3   As indicated above, Part II of the Food Labelling Regulations 1996 generally implements food labelling Directive 2000/13/EC and applies to food that is ready for delivery to the ultimate consumer or to a catering establishment. However, for some foods specific labelling provision is made. As a result, except for the provisions relating to packaging gases and foods containing sweeteners, added sugar and sweeteners, aspartame or more than

10% added polyols[1], Part II does not apply to the following products so far as their labelling is controlled by other Regulations:

(a)   hen eggs;
(b)   spreadable fats;
(c)   wine and grape musts;
(d)   sparkling wines and aerated sparkling wines;
(e)   liqueur wines, semi-sparkling wines and aerated semi-sparkling wines;
(f)   spirit drinks;
(g)   fresh fruit and vegetables;
(h)   preserved sardines;
(i)   preserved tuna and bonito;
(j)   additives sold as such[2].

Part II also does not apply to certain alcoholic drinks bottled before 1 January 1993, to food prepared on domestic premises for sale for the benefit of the person preparing it by a society registered under the Industrial and Provident Societies Act 1965 and to food prepared otherwise than in the course of a business[3].

1   See para **9.2.23** below.
2   Food Labelling Regulations 1996, reg 4(2). For the additive labelling rules, see para **12.2.2** below.
3   Food Labelling Regulations 1996, reg 4(3).

General labelling requirement

9.2.4   Subject to the provisions of Part II of the Food Labelling Regulations 1996, all non-exempted food must be marked or labelled with[1]:

(a)   the name of the food;
(b)   a list of ingredients; and (added in 1998 to implement Directive 97/4/EC) the quantities of certain ingredients or categories of ingredients;
(c)   the appropriate durability indication;
(d)   any special storage conditions or conditions of use;
(e)   the name or business name and an address or registered office of the manufacturer or packer, or of a seller established within the European Community[2];
(f)   particulars of the place of origin or provenance of the food if failure to give such particulars might mislead a purchaser to a material degree as to the true origin of the food; and
(g)   instructions for use if it would be difficult to make appropriate use of the food in the absence of such instructions.

These requirements are considered in detail below.

1   Food Labelling Regulations 1996, reg 5.
2   The words 'established within the Community' refer only to the seller. See case C-83/96 *Provincia Autonoma di Trento v Dega di Depretto Gino Snc* [1998] All ER (EC) 252.

Food names

9.2.5   A food must be labelled or marked with (i) a name prescribed by law or, if there is none, (ii) a customary name, or (iii) a name that indicates the true nature of the food. These categories are explained below.

(i) Names prescribed by law[1]

Where there is a name prescribed by law that name must be used as the name of the food. Such a name may be qualified by other words that make it more precise unless such qualification is prohibited.

Foods for which names have been prescribed by Sch 1 to the 1996 Regulations are melons (the species must be given), potatoes (the variety must be given) and vitamins. As will be seen from ch 10, many other names are prescribed by legislation on specific products. Names are prescribed in implementation of Community Directives for sugar products, cocoa and chocolate products, coffee products, honey, fruit juices and fruit nectars, condensed milk and dried milk, jam and similar products, natural mineral waters and caseins and caseinates. Names are also prescribed by Community common agricultural policy Regulations for drinking milk, spreadable fats, poultrymeat, still wine, sparkling wine, aromatised wine, spirit drinks and olive oil.

The difference between prescribed and reserved names is explained in para **10.1.2** below. Even where the law does not prescribe but only reserves a name, it will in practice be very difficult to devise an alternative designation for the product that would satisfy the requirements as to 'true nature' etc discussed at (iii) below.

(ii) Customary names[2]

Where there is no name prescribed by law a customary name may be used. A customary name is one that has come to be accepted in the United Kingdom or in the area where the food is sold. Examples are 'fish fingers', 'Bakewell tart', 'Cornish Pasty', 'Welsh Rarebit', 'Lancashire Hot Pot' and so on. Some food names of foreign origin have become common in the United Kingdom over the years and may qualify as customary names. Examples are 'muesli', 'lasagne', 'macaroni' and 'petit fours'.

Whether a food name is customary in a given area is a question of fact. Some food manufacturers are tempted to apply geographical words to a common product or to search out old-fashioned and seldom used names that have a marketing appeal in the belief that they will qualify as customary names. And a name that is customary in a particular area (eg 'clutie dumpling') may not be understood on its own when sold outside that area. In such cases it will be wise to add an accompanying description satisfying the requirements as to indication of true nature discussed below. In time such a name or a fancy name (eg 'Mississippi Mud Pie') may possibly become acceptable as a customary name without the necessity of an accompanying description.

A trade mark, brand name or fancy name may not be used as a substitute for the name of the food[3].

(iii) Indication of the true nature of the food[4]

If there is no name prescribed by law and if there is no customary name or if the customary name is not used, the name used for the food must be sufficiently precise to inform the purchaser of the true nature of the food and to enable the food to be distinguished from products with which it could be confused[5] and, if necessary, must include a description of its use.

'True nature' means a clear and accurate description of the characteristics of the food but it does not require a detailed description including all the main ingredients. The name should be easy to understand and should not be confused by superfluous adjectives.

As indicated above, a trade mark, brand name or fancy name may not be used as a substitute for a name satisfying the requirements of this regulation. However, it is acceptable to print a trade mark, brand name or fancy name in large type followed by a name that meets these requirements, provided always that the provisions as to intelligibility in reg 38 are met[6].

Following the judgments of the European Court of Justice in the *Smanor*[7] and *Deserbais*[8] cases, the Commission published an interpretive Communication[9] on the conditions under which a name different from that used in the producing Member State may be required to avoid confusing consumers in the importing Member State. The Commission offered opinions as to the use of the names 'vinegar', 'caviar' and 'yoghurt'. Only the courts can give an authoritative interpretation of the law and the opinion on 'yoghurt' was particularly controversial since the Commission expressed the questionable view that an importing Member State was legitimately entitled to refuse to allow this description to be used where the product has undergone treatment and no longer contains live bacteria.

1 Food Labelling Regulations 1996, reg 6. See also FSA Guidance notes on the 1996 Regulations.
2 Food Labelling Regulations 1996, reg 7. See also FSA Guidance notes on the 1996 Regulations of which this passage takes account.
3 Food Labelling Regulations 1996, reg 10. See *Hackney London Borough Council v Cedar Trading Ltd* (1999) 163 JP 749; Times, 30 April.
4 Food Labelling Regulations 1996, reg 8.
5 As to the requirement that the name should enable the food to be distinguished from products with which it could be confused, see, in relation to the use of textured vegetable protein in meat products, *Bird's Eye Wall's Ltd v Shropshire County Council* (1994) 158 JP 961. See also *Wolkind and Northcott v Pura Foods Ltd* (1987) 151 JP 492.
6 See para **9.2.26** below.
7 Case 298/87 *Smanor* [1988] ECR 4489.
8 Case 286/86 *Ministère Public v Déserbais* [1988] ECR 4907.
9 Commission interpretative Communication (91/C 270/02) on the names under which foodstuffs are sold. See also para **1.3.3** above.

Physical condition or treatment[1]

9.2.6   Where a food is powdered or is in any other physical condition or if it has been dried, freeze dried, frozen, concentrated, smoked or subjected to any other treatment, and the omission of an indication of such condition or treatment would be misleading to a purchaser, then the name of the food must be accompanied by such an indication. The following particular requirements apply[2]:

(a)   Where meat has been treated with proteolytic enzymes or is derived from an animal that has been so treated, it must include or be accompanied by the word 'tenderised'.

(b)   Where food has been irradiated, it must include or be accompanied by the word 'irradiated' or the words 'treated with ionising radiation'.

Apart from these two special cases, whether or not a condition or treatment must be disclosed is a matter of common sense. It must not be assumed that a purchaser has special culinary skills that would render the statement unnecessary. The test is whether the ordinary consumer would be misled by its omission. Food Standards Agency guidance notes on the 1996 Regulations contain recommendations in relation to milk treatment, thawed meat and offal, fish products incorporating minced fish, sliced or diced vegetables and roasted, smoked and filleted foods. The guidance refers to the Advisory Committee on the Microbiological Safety of Food recommendations relating to the provision of information on cheeses made from raw milk from cows and other species.

1   Food Labelling Regulations 1996, reg 11.
2   Food Labelling Regulations 1996, Sch 2.

List of ingredients[1]

9.2.7   Food must normally[2] be labelled with a list of ingredients that is headed by the word 'ingredients' and sets out all the ingredients in descending order by weight as determined at the time of use in the preparation of the food.

The order of ingredients in the list is determined at the 'mixing bowl' stage of production and not as they may be when a sample is taken of the finished product. It is sometimes the case that the order of ingredients determined by analysis of the finished product is different from that of the recipe because of chemical changes and the leaching of ingredients. Provided the manufacturer can prove that the ingredients were introduced to the product in accordance with the recipe, subsequent changes in the order may be disregarded. Enforcement officers have the power to examine recipes to verify the correctness of lists of ingredients.

If an ingredient is used in the making of the food in a concentrated or dehydrated form and is reconstituted during the preparation of the food, its position in the list of ingredients may be that based on the weight before concentration or dehydration. Where the food itself is in concentrated or dehydrated form and is intended to be re-constituted before use by the addition of water, the ingredients may be listed according to their weight when reconstituted provided the list of ingredients is accompanied by the words 'ingredients of the reconstituted product' or 'ingredients of the ready to use product' or by similar words[3].

Further provision regarding the order of the ingredients list is made for food containing mixed fruit, vegetables or mushrooms, food containing mixed spices or herbs, ingredients constituting less than 2% of the finished product and ingredients which:

(a)   are similar or mutually substitutable;

(b)   are likely to be used in the preparation of a food without altering its nature or its perceived value;

(c)   are not additives, allergenic ingredients or ingredients originating from a specified allergenic ingredient; and

(d)   constitute less than 2% of the finished product.[4]

Added water must appear in the list of ingredients in its correct position unless it has been used in the preparation of the food solely for the re-constitution or partial reconstitution of an ingredient used in concentrated or dehydrated form, or it is used as a medium not normally consumed, or it does not exceed 5% of the finished product[5].

1   Food Labelling Regulations 1996, regs 5(a), 12 and 13.
2   Food Labelling Regulations 1996, reg 18.
3   Food Labelling Regulations 1996, regs 13(2)–(4) and 16.
4   Food Labelling Regulations 1996, reg 13(5)–(8).
5   Food Labelling Regulations 1996, reg 16. See case C-383/97 *Staatsanwaltschaft Osnabrück v Arnoldus van der Laan* [1999] ECR I-731.

The names of ingredients[1]

9.2.8   The name used for an ingredient in the list of ingredients must be a name which could be lawfully used if the ingredient was being sold as a food in its own right including appropriate indication of physical condition or treatment (see para **9.2.6** above) that it has undergone where omission of such indication could mislead. Listed names of ingredients that have been irradiated must include or be accompanied by the word 'irradiated' or the words 'treated with ionising radiation'.

In most cases the name used for an ingredient must be a specific name satisfying the requirements discussed in para **9.2.5** above. However, certain generic names may be used as prescribed in the regulations[2] subject to certain conditions. They are:

Part 1 General

Column 1	Column 2	Column 3
Generic name	*Ingredients*	*Conditions of use of the generic name*
Cheese	Any type of cheese or mixture of cheese	The labelling of the food of which the cheese is an ingredient must not refer to a specific type of cheese
Cocoa butter	Press, expeller or refined cocoa butter	
Crumbs *or* rusks, *as is appropriate*	Any type of crumbled, baked cereal product	
Dextrose	Anhydrous dextrose or dextrose monohydrate	
Fat	Any refined fat	The generic name must be accompanied by either- (a) the description 'animal' or 'vegetable', as is appropriate, or (b) the indication of the specific animal origin or the specific vegetable origin of the fat, as is appropriate. In the case of a hydrogenated fat, the generic name must also be accompanied by the description 'hydrogenated'.
Fish	Any species of fish	The labelling of the food of which the fish is an ingredient must not refer to a specific species of fish
Flour	Any mixture of flour derived from two or more cereal species	The generic name shall be followed by a list of the cereals from which the flour is derived in descending order of weight

Glucose syrup	Glucose syrup or anhydrous glucose syrup	The generic name may not be used where the glucose syrup contains fructose in proportions greater than 5% on a dry matter basis
Gum base	Any type of gum preparation used in the preparation of chewing gum	
Herb, herbs *or* mixed herbs	Any herb or parts of a herb or combination of two or more herbs or parts of herbs	The proportion of herb or herbs in the food of which it or they are an ingredient must not exceed 2 per cent by weight of the food
'Meat' and the name of the animal species from which it comes, *or* a word which describes the meat by reference to the animal species from which it comes	Any skeletal muscles, including the diaphragm and the masseters, of a mammalian or bird species recognised as fit for human consumption with any naturally included or adherent tissue, but excluding: (a) the heart, (b) the tongue, (c) the muscles of the head (other than the masseters), (d) the muscles of the carpus, (e) the tarsus; (f) the tail; and (g) the product obtained by removing the meat from flesh-bearing bones after boning or from the carcases of farmed birds (including birds that are not considered as domestic animals, but not including ratites) using mechanical means resulting in the loss or modification of the muscle fibre structure.	The total fat and connective tissue content must not exceed the limits specified in Part II of this Schedule and the meat must constitute an ingredient of another food. If such a limit is exceeded, but the ingredient falls within the description in column 2 of this entry, any reference to meat content must be adjusted downwards accordingly and the list of ingredients must also mention the presence of fat or connective tissue, as appropriate

Milk proteins	Any caseins, caseinates or whey proteins, or any mixture of these	
Oil	Any refined oil, other than olive oil	The generic name must be accompanied by either-(a)the description 'animal' or 'vegetable' as appropriate, or (b)an indication of the specific animal origin or the specific vegetable origin of the oil, as is appropriate. In the case of a hydrogenated oil, the generic name must also be accompanied by the description 'hydrogenated'.
Spice, spices *or* mixed spices	Any spice or any combination of two or more spices	The proportion of spice or spices in the food of which it or they are an ingredient must not exceed 2% by weight of the food
Starch	Any unmodified starch or any starch which has been modified either by physical means or by enzymes	In the case of a starch which may contain gluten, the generic name must be accompanied by an indication of the specific vegetable origin of the starch
Sugar	Any type of sucrose	
Wine	Any type of wine defined in Council Regulation (EEC) 822/87	

Part II Maximum fat and connective tissue contents for ingredients for which the generic name meat or equivalent as referred to in Part I is used

Species	*Fat (%)*	*Connective tissue (%)[3]*
Mammals (other than rabbits and porcines) and mixtures of species with mammals predominating	25	25
Porcines	30	25
Birds and rabbits	15	10

The FSA's guidance notes on the 1996 Regulations advise that combinations of generic terms are acceptable if their intention is made clear to the consumer (e g vegetable and animal oils, vegetable oils and fats, or vegetable and animal oils in varying proportions).

1   Food Labelling Regulations 1996, reg 14 and Sch 3. This provision is subject to reg 34B and Sch AAI on allergenic ingredients, as to which see para **9.2.23** below.
2   Food Labelling Regulations 1996, Sch 3.

3 The connective tissue content is calculated on the basis of the ratio between collagen content and meat protein content. The collagen content means the hydroxyproline content multiplied by a factor of 8.

Designation of flavourings in the list of ingredients[1]

9.2.9   Special rules have been enacted for ingredient listing of flavourings. They must be designated by the word 'flavouring(s)' or a more specific description. In the case of quinine or caffeine, where used as a flavouring, they must be specifically identified by name immediately after the word 'flavouring'. The use of the word 'natural' and any word of substantially the same meaning are restricted to specified flavouring ingredients in which the flavouring component consists exclusively of specified flavouring substances and/or flavouring preparations[2]. If the name of a flavouring ingredient refers to the vegetable or animal nature or origin of the incorporated material, the word 'natural' and any word of substantially the same meaning are restricted to such ingredients in which the flavouring component has been isolated by physical, enzymatic or microbiological processes, or by a process normally used in preparing food for human consumption, solely or almost solely from that vegetable or animal source[3].

1   Food Labelling Regulations 1996, reg 14(5)–(8).
2   As to 'flavouring substances' and 'flavouring preparations', see para **12.3.4** below.
3   As to 'physical process' and 'process normally used in preparing food for human consumption', see Food Labelling Regulations 1996, reg 14(8).

Identification of additives[1]

9.2.10   Additives must be declared in the list of ingredients in the same way as any other ingredient, but, subject to the allergenic ingredients rules in reg 34B[2], any additive serving the function of any of the following categories must be identified by the category name (or by the category name of the principal function) followed by its specific name and/or serial number (if any):

Acid[3]	Flour treatment agent
Acidity regulator	Gelling agent
Anti-caking agent	Glazing agent
Anti-foaming agent	Humectant
Antioxidant	Modified starch[4]
Bulking agent	Preservative
Colour	Propellant gas
Emulsifier	Raising agent
Emulsifying Salts	Stabiliser
Firming agent	Sweetener
Flavour enhancer	Thickener

Any additive that is required to be named in the list of ingredients and is neither a flavouring nor serves a function of one of these categories must be declared in the list of ingredients by its specific name.

For a discussion of the regulations on additives see ch 12.

1   Food Labelling Regulations 1996, reg 14(9), (10), (11) and Sch 4.
2   See para **9.2.23** below.

3   In the case of an additive that is added to or used in food to serve the function of an acid and those whose specific name includes the word 'acid', it is not necessary to use the category name.
4   Neither the specific name nor the serial number need be indicated. In the case of modified starch that may contain gluten, the category name must be accompanied by an indication of the specific vegetable origin of the starch.

Compound ingredients[1]

9.2.11   Food ingredients that themselves consist of two or more ingredients are known as compound ingredients. Mayonnaise, custard and seasoning mixes are given as examples by the FSA's guidance notes. The names of ingredients of compound ingredients must appear in ingredients lists either instead of or in addition to the name of the compound ingredient. If the name of the compound ingredient is given, the names of its ingredients must follow that name immediately in such a way as to make it clear that they are ingredients of the compound ingredient. Subject to the allergenic ingredients rules in reg 34B[2], it is not necessary to give the names of the ingredients of a compound ingredient:

(a)   where the compound ingredient would not be required to be marked or labelled with a list of ingredients if it were itself being sold prepacked as a food (see reg 18 of the 1996 Regulations);

(b)   where the compound ingredient is identified in the list of ingredients by a generic name (see para **9.2.8**);

(c)   in the case of specified compound ingredients constituting less than 2% of the finished product, although additives in and irradiated constituents of those ingredients must be identified as prescribed.

1   Food Labelling Regulations 1996, reg 15.
2   See para **9.2.23** below.

Ingredients that need not be named[1]

9.2.12   Subject to the allergenic ingredients rules in reg 34B[2], ingredients need not be named in the list of ingredients in the following circumstances:

(a)   where the constituents of an ingredient have become separated during a manufacturing process and are later re-introduced in their original proportions;

(b)   where an additive is used in an ingredient but serves no significant technological function in the finished product[3];

(c)   where an additive is used solely as a processing aid;

(d)   any substance other than water which is used as a solvent or carrier for an additive and is used in an amount no greater than that which is strictly necessary for the purpose;

(e)   any substance which is not an additive but which is used in the same way and for the same purpose as a processing acid.

1   Food Labelling Regulations 1996, reg 17.
2   See para **9.2.23** below.
3   As to an ingredient that serves no technological function in the finished product, see case C-144/93 *Pfanni Werke Otto Eckart KG v Landeshaupstadt München* [1994] ECR I-4605.

Foods that need not bear a list of ingredients[1]

9.2.13   Subject to the allergenic ingredients rules in reg 34B[2], the following foods are not required to bear a list of ingredients:

(a)   fresh fruit and vegetables, including potatoes, which have not been peeled or cut into pieces;

(b)   carbonated water, to which no ingredient other than carbon dioxide has been added, and whose name indicates that it has been carbonated;

(c)   vinegar that is derived by fermentation exclusively from a single basic product and to which no other ingredient has been added;[3]

(d)   cheese, butter, fermented milk and fermented cream to which no ingredient has been added other than lactic products, enzymes and micro-organism cultures essential to manufacture or, in the case of cheese other than fresh curd cheese and processed cheese, such amount of salt as is needed for its manufacture;[3]

(e)   flour, to which no substances have been added other than those that are required to be added;

(f)   any drink with an alcoholic strength by volume of more than 1.2%[4]

(g)   any food consisting of a single ingredient, where:

(i) the name of the food is identical with the name of the ingredients; or

(ii) the name of the food enables the nature of the food to be clearly identified.

If a list of ingredients is given in respect of any exempted food it must be a complete list in accordance with the Food Labelling Regulations.

1   Food Labelling Regulations 1996, reg 18.
2   See para **9.2.23** below.
3   In these cases only other added ingredients need be listed but the list must be headed by the words 'added ingredients'.
4   From time to time there have been proposals to introduce ingredient listing of alcoholic drinks.

Indication of quantities of certain ingredients or categories of ingredients[1]

9.2.14   Quantitative ingredient declarations for foodstuffs (QUID) must be indicated where:

(a)   that ingredient or category of ingredients appears in the name of the food or is usually associated with that name by the consumer;

(b)   that ingredient or category of ingredients is emphasised on the labelling in words, pictures or graphics; or

(c)   that ingredient or category of ingredients is essential to characterise a food and to distinguish it from products with which it might be confused because of its name or appearance[2].

The FSA Guidance Notes on QUID confirm that, subject to some exemptions, the requirement to give QUID declarations in principle apply to all food, including drink, with more than one ingredient. They offer illustrations of how the rules apply. Thus, under the first part of (a) above, the QUID declaration would be required for the underlined ingredients in the example 'ham and mushroom pizza' ('ingredient included in the name of the food'); but only in respect of the total vegetable content of 'vegetable pasty' (the 'category of ingredient in the name of the food'). It is thought that the last part of (a) is likely to apply where products are described using customary names[3] without additional descriptive words. For the purposes of deciding in such cases that ingredient or category of ingredients is usually associated by the consumer with the product's name, it might prove helpful to consider what the appropriate descriptive name of the product might be. For example, 'Lancashire hot pot' is mutton and potatoes with onions, carrots and gravy and would, it is suggested, need a QUID declaration for the mutton content.

A requirement to make a declaration under (b) above (ingredients or categories of ingredients emphasised on the labelling in words, pictures or graphics) is said to be likely to be triggered when a particular ingredient is given emphasis on the label otherwise than in the name of the food (e g 'made with butter') and when pictorial representation is used to emphasise selectively one or a few of the ingredients.

A requirement to make a declaration under (c) above (ingredients or categories of ingredients essential to characterise a food and to distinguish it from products with which it might be confused because of its name or appearance) is said to be designed to cover products whose composition can differ markedly from one Member State to another but that are usually marketed under the same name[4]. The range of foods affected is likely to be very narrow: the only agreed examples at EU level are mayonnaise and marzipan. In respect of products made in the United Kingdom, QUID declarations under this provision are unlikely to be necessary for home market sales, but may be required for marketing in some other Member States.

QUID declarations are not required in respect of an ingredient or category of ingredients:

(i) the drained net weight of which is indicated in accordance with Art 8(4) of Directive 2000/13/EC;

(ii) the quantities of which are already required to be given on the labelling by the Community provisions such as fruit juice Directive 2001/112/EC, jam Directive 2001/113/EC and the spreadable fats standards in Regulation (EC) 1234/2007, Art 115 and Annex XV;

(iii) which is used in small quantities for the purposes of flavouring;

(iv) which, though it appears in the name of the food, is not such as to govern the choice of the consumer because the variation in quantity is not essential to characterise the food or does not distinguish it from similar foods;

(v) for which the quantity is stipulated precisely by specific Community provisions without providing for the indication thereof on the labelling; or

(vi) covered by the provisions for food containing mixed fruit, vegetables or mushrooms and mixed spices or herbs described in para **9.2.7** above.

The FSA guidance comments on each of these exemptions. Some of the salient points are as follows. As to (i) above, Art 8(4) of Directive 2000/13/EC requires foods presented in a liquid medium (i e vinegar, fruit and vegetable juices or aquaeous solutions of salts, food acids, sugars or other sweetening substances) to declare on the label the drained net weight as well as the net weight. As a result of the discussions at both EU and UK level the exemption at (iv) above is understood at least to cover alcoholic drinks (such as malt whisky/whiskey and wheat beer); liqueurs and fruit-based spirits that include an ingredient in their name; rye bread and other breads (including rolls and flour confectionery), and single cereal breakfast cereals, which include mention a seed or cereal ingredient in their name (e g 'sesame seed bun'; 'corn flakes'; 'puffed rice'); products that mention several minor ingredients in their name (e g 'chicken platter, including potatoes, peas and carrots', where the exemption would apply to the vegetable ingredients); dried pasta that mentions more than one type of wheat on its label; products, such as pickles and sauces, which are highly processed and in which it is only the spices and/or flavourings that are likely to distinguish one product from another; products such as cake, bread, and dessert mixes, that are essentially mixtures of flour, oil/fat, sugar/salt and flavouring/ seasonings; seasonings that are generally named using a combination of characterising ingredients and end-usage description, for example 'chicken seasoning – a blend of salt, paprika, parsley and other spices'. As to (v) above, there appears to be no EC provision that stipulates precise quantities of ingredients without providing for indication on the labelling.

A QUID declaration is not required in the case of indications of sweeteners(s) and sugar(s) as required by Directive 2008/5/EC[5] or particulars of vitamins and minerals indicated in nutrition labelling[6].

The QUID indication of quantity of an ingredient or a category of ingredients must, subject to some derogations, be expressed as a percentage determined as at the time of use of the ingredient or category in the preparation of the food. The indication must appear in or next to the food name, or in the list of ingredients in connection with the ingredient or category in question.

1   Food Labelling Regulations 1996, reg 19.
2   Directive 2000/13/EC, Art 7 makes provision for QUID labelling to be required in further cases prescribed by the Commission through the Standing Committee on the Food Chain and Animal Health procedure (see para **3.4.2**).
3   See para **9.2.5**(ii) above.
4   See further para **9.2.5**(iii) above.
5   See para **9.2.23** below.
6   See sections **11.4** and **11.5** below.

Appropriate durability indication

9.2.15   Two kinds of food date marking are encapsulated in the term 'appropriate durability indication'. This term is defined by the Food Labelling Regulations 1996 as follows:

(a)   in the case of a food other than one specified in sub-para (b) of this definition, an indication of minimum durability; and

(b)   in the case of a food that, from the microbiological point of view, is highly perishable and in consequence likely after a short period to constitute an immediate danger to health, a 'use by' date[1].

The 'use by' date is thus for highly perishable foods that could become a food safety risk, such as some meat products or ready-prepared products, while most food that can safely be kept longer carries an indication of minimum durability (or 'best before' date) indicating the period for which it can reasonably be expected to retain its optimum condition and will not be stale.

The difference between the two kinds of food date marking is reflected in the remedies for contravention of the rules. It is an offence for any person other than the manufacturer, packer or seller originally responsible for marking the food to alter either kind of appropriate durability indication[2], but only in the case of 'use by' dates is it an offence to sell the food after the date shown[3]. Although not an offence in the case of 'best before' dates, if the food is not of the substance or quality demanded (see section **8.2**) or if it fails the food safety requirement (see paras **3.2.20- 3.2.30** and **5.3.1**), the fact that the date had expired could be damaging to the defendant. It might also be significant in any civil proceedings that may be brought by an aggrieved purchaser (see ch 21).

There is no national requirement, such as has been upheld by the European Court[4], that, where the period of minimum durability has expired, the fact must be indicated separately, clearly and in a generally intelligible manner. However, additional forms of date marking, such as 'display until', are sometimes used by retailers as instructions to shop staff .

The detailed rules for the two kinds of compulsory food date marking are summarised in paras **9.2.16** and **9.2.17** respectively. Foods that need not bear an appropriate durability indication are noted in para **9.2.18**.

1   Food Labelling Regulations 1996, reg 2(1).
2   Food Labelling Regulations 1996, reg 44(1)(e).
3   Food Labelling Regulations 1996, reg 44(1)(d). See *Lincolnshire County Council v Safeway Stores plc* (1999) unreported.
4   Case C-229/02 *Müller* [2003] ECR I-2587.

Form of indication of minimum durability[1]

9.2.16   Subject to what is said below, the minimum durability of a food must be indicated by the words 'best before' followed by the date up to and including which the food can reasonably be expected to retain its specific properties if properly stored, and by any storage conditions which need to be observed if the food is to retain its specific properties until that date.

The date in the indication of minimum durability must be expressed in terms of a day, month and year (in that order), except that, in the case of a food that can reasonably be expected to retain its specific properties:

(a)   for three months or less, the date may be expressed in terms of a day and month only (e g 'Best before 15 October');

(b)   for more than three months but not more than 18 months, the date may be expressed in terms of a month and year only (e g 'Best before end October 2008');

(c)   for more than 18 months, the date may be expressed either in terms of a month and year only or in terms of a year, but only if the formula 'best before end' is used (e g 'Best before end December 2008' or 'Best before end 2008').

The date and any storage conditions may appear on the labelling separately from the words 'best before' or 'best before end' if followed by a reference to the place where they appear (e g 'best before end – see top of can').

1   Food Labelling Regulations 1996, reg 20.

Form of indication of 'use by' date[1]

9.2.17   Subject to what is said below, a 'use by' date must be indicated by the words 'use by ...' followed by the date up to and including which the food, if properly stored, is recommended for use, and any storage conditions that need to be observed.

The 'use by date' must be expressed in terms either of a day and month (in that order) or of a day, a month and a year (in that order). The date and any storage conditions may appear separately from the words 'use by' provided that those words are followed by a reference to the place where they appear (e g 'see lid').

The decision as to whether a particular food requires a 'use by' date is one for the manufacturer or packer who originally marks it. However, the EC food labelling directive requires a 'use by' date to be used on those prepacked foods 'which, from the microbiological view, are highly perishable and are therefore likely after a short period to constitute an immediate danger to human health'. The FSA's guidance notes on use by dates suggest that in particular those foods that at ambient or chill temperatures are likely to support the growth of pathogenic micro-organisms or the formation of toxins and foods intended for consumption either without cooking or after treatment are unlikely to be sufficient to destroy food poisoning organisms that may be present should apply a 'use by' date attached.

1   Food Labelling Regulations 1996, reg 21.

Foods that need not bear an appropriate durability indication[1]

9.2.18   The following foods need not be labelled or marked with an indication of minimum durability or a 'use by' date:

(a)   fresh fruit and vegetables (including potatoes but not including sprouting seeds, legume sprouts and similar products) which have not been peeled or cut into pieces;

(b)   wine, liqueur wine, sparkling wine, aromatised wine and any similar drink obtained from fruit other than grapes;

(c)   any drink made from grapes or grape musts and coming within codes 2206 00 39, 2206 00 59 and 2206 00 89 of the Combined Nomenclature[2];

(d)   any drink with an alcoholic strength by volume of 10% or more;

(e)   any soft drink, fruit juice or fruit nectar or alcoholic drink, sold in a container containing more than five litres and intended for supply to catering establishments;

(f)   any flour confectionery and bread which, given the nature of its content, is normally consumed within 24 hours of its preparation;

(g)   vinegar;

(h)   cooking and table salt;

(i)   solid sugar and products consisting almost solely of flavoured or coloured sugars;

(j)   chewing gum and similar products;

(k)   edible ices in individual portions.

1   Food Labelling Regulations 1996, reg 22.
2   Regulation (EEC) 2658/87, as amended.

Special storage conditions and conditions of and instructions for use

9.2.19   The requirement to label with special storage conditions and conditions of use[1] must be distinguished from the storage condition required as part of the date mark to ensure that the consumer knows how to store the food if it is to last as long as the date indicates while unopened[2]. According to the FSA's Guidance Notes, special storage conditions and conditions of use should be given:

•   if the consumer needs to observe certain practices once the packaging of a food has been opened (eg 'once opened keep refrigerated and consume within 3 days');

•   if various options are available (eg 'suitable for home freezing');

•   if foods are not appropriate or suitable for use in certain circumstances (eg 'not suitable for frying or shake well before use').

Instructions for use[3] must be given if it would be difficult to make appropriate use of the food without them and must be sufficiently detailed to enable appropriate preparation or use to be made of the food.

1   Food Labelling Regulations 1996, reg 5(d).
2   See paras **9.2.15** and **9.2.16** above.
3   Food Labelling Regulations 1996, reg 5(g).

Origin or provenance of the food[1]

9.2.20   Origin marking is required if the consumer might be misled to a material degree as to the true place of origin of the food. The text of reg 5(f) is derived from general labelling Directive 2000/13/EC, Art 3(1)(8). The following comments on reg 5(f) draw on the FSA's guidance notes.[2]

It should be recalled that there is other legislation of relevance to origin marking in Art 2 of general labelling Directive 2001/13/EC, the FSA 1990, ss 14 and 15[3], the protected names Regulations (EC) 510/2006 and 509/2006 [4] and Art 16 of Regulation (EC) 178/2002[5].

As to 'the place of origin', s 36 of the TDA 1968 is considered to be a reasonable working guide for the purposes of the Food Labelling Regulations 1996. This provides, for the purposes of the TDA 1968, that goods are deemed to have been manufactured or produced in the country in which they last underwent a treatment or process resulting in a substantial change. Interpretation of this is a matter for the courts. By way of example, it is suggested that whilst the transformation of pork into bacon, ham or pies may be regarded as a treatment or process resulting in a substantial change, this is less likely to be the case with the simple slicing, cutting and/or packing of meat.

The true place of origin should always be given if the label as a whole would otherwise imply that the food comes from, or has been made in, a different place or area. Consumers are, however, unlikely to expect products such as Chelsea buns, Madras curry or Frankfurters to come from those areas in the absence of other material on the label suggesting that they do.

A specific place of origin on the label will clearly lead consumers to attribute a particular place of origin to a food. The use of country or place names in the name of the food, its trade name, brand name, or fancy name may also do so, as may other written or illustrative material appearing on the label (including maps, flags or famous landmarks). Care must be taken to ensure that health marks applied to meet the requirements of Community hygiene legislation[6] do not by reason of their size, prominence or position, contribute to a misleading impression of the origin of the food.

Place of origin indications should be provided when consumers may otherwise incorrectly attribute a particular place of origin to a food because of the way it has been labelled, described or presented. To avoid possible contravention of the FSA 1990 or Art 16 of Regulation (EC) 178/2002, care should be taken to avoid misleading consumers when giving place of origin information particularly where the labelling or presentation of the food might lead consumers to assume incorrectly that the source of the ingredients and the country of final processing are the same. If the place of origin of the food is not the same as place of origin of its ingredients it may be necessary to provide information on the origin of the ingredients. For example:

- bacon or ham made in Britain using Danish pork should not be described as 'British bacon' or 'British ham' but could be described as '[imported] [Danish] pork [cured] [baked] [roasted] in Britain';
- pork sausages made in Britain using pork from countries outside the UK should not be described as 'British pork sausages' but could be described as 'made in Britain from [imported] [country of origin] pork [from more than one country]';
- butter churned in England from milk brought in from outside the UK (eg Belgium) should not be labelled as 'English' or 'produced in England' but could be labelled as 'produced in England from [imported] [Belgian] milk'.

It may be better to use terms like 'bottled', 'packed', 'sliced and packed' or 'processed' instead of rather broader terms like 'produced'.

While reg 5(f) of the Food Labelling Regulations 1996 does not generally apply to non-prepacked foods, care should be taken to ensure that display material does not convey messages about places of origin that may conflict with the FSA 1990 or Regulation (EC) 178/2002.

1 Food Labelling Regulations 1996, reg 5(f).
2 At the time of writing the FSA had issued a draft revised Country of Origin Labelling Guidance. This will bring the guidance in line with more recent legislative developments and it is intended that the reformatted document will be more accessible to small and medium enterprises.
3 See ch 8.
4 See paras **10.5.2** and **10.5.3** below.
5 See paras **3.2.36** and **37** above.
6 See ch 14 below.

Indication of irradiation[1]

9.2.21 Food that has been irradiated or that contains irradiated ingredients must, subject to certain exemptions, be marked 'irradiated' or 'treated with ionising irradiation'. Non-prepacked food, food prepacked for direct sale, certain flour confectionery and fancy confectionery products need not be so marked if they are not exposed for sale.

1 Food Labelling Regulations 1996, regs 11(2), 14(2) and 25.

Omission of particulars from non-prepacked and other foods[1]

9.2.22 Although it must be remembered that all food that contains, consists of or is produced from genetically modified organisms must comply with specific labelling requirements[2], certain foods are exempt from labelling with most of the statutory information described in this chapter including in some cases, the additional declarations explained in para **9.2.23** below.

These foods are principally:

(a) food that is not prepacked (eg food sold loose from a delicatessen);
(b) food that is prepacked for direct sale (ie broadly, food packed by a retailer or dairy farmer for sale from his premises);
(c) specified flour confectionery;
(d) specified fancy confectionery products.

They are required only to bear:

(i) (except for non-irradiated white bread and flour confectionery) the name of the food; together with, in the case of milk, particulars of the place of origin[3] as well as, for raw milk, the name and address of the producer or packer; and, in the case of specified meat products, the quantity of the meat ingredients;

(ii) in the case of specified flour confectionery, information concerning allergenic ingredients and glycyrrhizinic acid or its ammonium salt;

(iii) a specified indication in respect of additives used to serve the function of an antioxidant, colour, flavouring, flavour enhancer, preservative or sweetener;

(iv) a specified indication in respect of irradiated ingredients.

Subject to provision for particular cases, prepacked foods in reusable indelibly marked glass bottles or in packaging of specified maximum dimensions, which are not caught by the above provisions or those below relating to catering establishments, need not be labelled with:

• the general labelling particulars specified in para **9.2.4** above except the name of the food and, where required, the appropriate durability indication; or

• indications of the use of packaging gas, sweeteners and glycyrrhizinic acid as described in para **9.2.23** below.

Exemptions are also provided for foods sold as an accompaniment to another food or service.

Labelling requirements for foods sold at catering establishments, which are not prepacked or are prepacked for direct sale, are confined to limited provisions in respect of high caffeine content drinks, milk prepacked for direct sale and irradiated food.

Seasonal selection packs do not need to be labelled if the individual items that they contain are correctly labelled.

1 Food Labelling Regulations 1996, regs 23, 24, 25, 26, 27, and 28. For the definitions of 'prepacked', 'prepacked for direct sale', 'flour confectionery', 'fancy confectionery product', 'catering establishment' and 'seasonal selection pack', see Food Labelling Regulations 1996, reg 2.

2 See paras **10.3.3** and **10.3.4**.

3 See para **9.2.20**.

Additional labelling requirements for certain categories of food[1]

9.2.23 Additional labelling requirements are imposed by Part II of the Food Labelling Regulations 1996 for certain categories of food.[2]

Vending machines must show on the front of the machine the name of the food sold (unless easily and clearly visible through the outside), together, for non-prepacked products, with abbreviated nutrition labelling information and, in appropriate cases, with reheating instructions. These requirements do not apply to natural mineral water, except water that has been artificially carbonated[3].

Prepacked alcoholic drinks with an alcoholic strength by volume of more than 1.2%, other than Community-controlled wine, must be marked or labelled with an indication of the alcoholic strength by volume in the form of a figure to not more than one decimal place in one of the following forms, eg:

'10.5% vol', or 'alcohol 10.5% vol' or 'alc 10.5% vol'.

Positive and negative tolerances for the indication are prescribed[4]. The alcoholic strength must be determined at 20°C.

A health warning in prescribed form must appear on the containers of raw milk, other than from buffaloes, and in catering establishments where the product is sold non-prepacked.

The container of any product consisting of skimmed milk together with non-milk fat, which is capable of being used as a substitute for milk and that is neither an infant formula or follow-on formula[5] nor a product specially for infants or young children for medical purposes, must bear a warning about its unsuitability as food for babies.

Next, two regulations impose requirements in implementation of Directive 2008/5. First, a food the durability of which has been extended by a packaging authorised pursuant to Council Directive 89/107/EEC (concerning food additives for use in foodstuffs for human consumption) must be labelled 'packaged in a protective atmosphere'.

Secondly, a food containing any of the following ingredients must bear the indication specified in relation to it:

- authorised sweetener – 'with sweetener(s)'[6];
- added sugar and authorised sweetener – 'with sugar(s) and sweetener(s)' [6];
- aspartame – 'contains a source of phenylalanine';
- more than 10% added polyols – 'excessive consumption may produce laxative effects'.

Three further regulations have recently imposed additional labelling requirements. Drinks with a high caffeine content must be clearly marked or labelled 'High caffeine content' unless the drink is based on coffee, tea or coffee or tea extract where the name of the food includes the term 'coffee' or 'tea'.[7]

The presence of named allergenic ingredients must be declared on the labels of pre-packed foods, including alcoholic drinks, whenever they are deliberately added to food. The list of allergenic ingredients is contained in Sch AA1 of the 1996 Regulations[8], which includes a number of cereals, nuts and seeds.

Finally, confectionery and drinks containing glycyrrhizinic acid (which occurs naturally in the liquorice plant) or its ammonium salt in certain quantities must be labelled with the indication 'contains liquorice', coupled in specified cases with the warning 'people suffering from hypertension should avoid excessive consumption'.[9]

In parallel with the Food Labelling Regulations 1996, the Food with Added Phytosterols or Phytostanols (Labelling) (England) Regulations 2004[10] implement rules on the labelling of foods and food ingredients with added phytosterols, phytosterol esters, phytostanols and/or phytostanol esters. The label must contain the statement 'with added plant sterols/plant stanols'; the amount of the added phytosterols, phytosterol esters, phytostanols or phytostanol esters must be stated on the list of ingredients. There must also be statements conveying that the product is intended exclusively for people who want to lower their blood cholesterol and that the consumption of more than 3g per day of added plant sterols/plant stanols should be avoided; that if a person is on cholesterol lowering medication the product should only be consumed under medical supervision; and that the product may not be nutritionally suitable for pregnant and breastfeeding women and for children under the age of five.

1 Food Labelling Regulations 1996, regs 29, 30, 32, 33, 34, 34A, 34B and 34C.
2 Other regulations (e g on lot marking, spreadable fat, meat products and fish products) also contain specific labelling requirements.
3 Food Labelling Regulations 1996, reg 3(4).
4 Food Labelling Regulations 1996, reg 30 and Sch 5 implementing Directive 87/250.
5 See para **11.6.2** below.
6 These indications must accompany the name of the food.
7 Food Labelling Regulations 1996, reg 34A implementing Directive 2002/67.
8 Food Labelling Regulations 1996, reg 34B.
9 Food Labelling Regulations 1996, reg 34C implementing Directive 2008/5.
10 SI 2004/3344, enforcing Commission Regulation (EC) 608/2004.

Labelling of beef and beef products

9.2.24 In an effort to remedy the fall in consumer confidence and destabilisation of the beef market caused by the BSE crisis a number of measures were taken at a European level. Council Regulation 820/97/EC was enacted to establish a system for the identification and registration of bovine animals and make provision for the labelling of beef and beef products. This was replaced by Regulation (EC) 1760/2000/EC, as amended, which remains in force. Title II of Regulation (EC) 1760/2000/EC establishes a system for the labelling of beef and beef products, detailed rules being laid down by Regulation (EC) 1825/2000[1]. Fresh and frozen beef at all stages of the production chain from slaughterhouse to retailer must be labelled with a reference number or code linking meat on sale to the original animal or group of animals from which the meat was derived; the country of birth and the country of rearing; the country of slaughter with plant approval number; and the country of cutting with plant approval number. In addition, further claims about origin, production methods or characteristics of beef may be made, subject to approval under the voluntary Beef Labelling Scheme. The Scheme, which controls voluntary labelling at all levels of the supply chain, requires operators to establish a traceability system and to employ a Government recognised independent third party to verify the information on the label. These compulsory and voluntary labelling requirements are currently enforced under the Beef Labelling (Enforcement) (England) Regulations 2000.

Regulation (EC) 1234/2007, as amended, now also requires the compulsory labelling of meat of bovine animals aged 12 months or less. The sales descriptions under which it must be sold[2] in the United Kingdom are 'veal', for meat from animals aged eight months or less, and 'beef', for meat from animals aged over eight months but not more than 12 months. Additionally, the label must show the age of the animal at slaughter and may also bear voluntary information approved in accordance with Regulation (EC) 1760/2000. Regulation (EC) 566/2008 lays down detailed rules on the manner of labelling, recording of information and official checks in respect of such meat. As a result of these recent legislative changes the Beef Labelling (Enforcement) (England) Regulations 2000 are to be repealed and replaced by the Beef and Veal Labelling (England) Regulations 2008.[3]

1 Regulation (EC) 1141/97 remains applicable for meat derived from animals slaughtered before 1 September 2000.
2 See para **9.2.5** above.
3 At the time of writing these Regulations were at the draft stage.

Labelling of fish[1]

9.2.25   The Fish Labelling (England) Regulations 2003 provide for the enforcement of EC Regulations 104/2000 and 2065/2001.[2] Where fish is offered for retail sale to the final consumer it must comply with the labelling requirements. Fish covered are all raw wet fish, headed, de-tailed and gutted fish, fish fillets, fish steaks, smoked fish, dried fish, salted fish and shellfish in some circumstances. At the point of retail sale, fish must be named using the accepted commercial designation. The commercial designations are listed in the Schedule to the 2003 Regulations, but alternatives accepted in other Member States may also be used and provisional designations may additionally be authorised by the Food Standards Agency. The consumer must also be informed about the manner in which the fish was 'harvested' ie caught at sea or in freshwater, or produced by aquaculture. Information concerning the catch area must also be indicated.

Small quantities of fish that have been sold directly to the consumer by a fisherman or aquaculture producers are exempt.[3]

1   See below at paras **10.4.12–10.4.15** for the marketing standards for fishery and aquaculture products, specified fishery products, preserved sardines and preserved tuna and bonito.
2   The FSA has issued Guidance Notes.
3   Small quantity is taken to mean a sale not exceeding €20.

Manner of marking or labelling[1]

9.2.26   All the information required to be marked or labelled on food must generally appear on the packaging; on a label attached to the packaging; on a label that is clearly visible through the packaging; or, where the sale is otherwise than to the ultimate consumer, in relevant trade documents.

For non-prepacked and similar food, fancy confectionery products and certain food sold at catering establishments in each case when sold to the ultimate consumer, the required particulars shall be on a label attached to the food or on a readily discernible menu, notice, ticket or label at the place where the food is chosen. Special provision is made for the manner of marking and labelling of irradiated food.

In the case of bottled milk, the required particulars, except the raw milk health warning, may appear on the bottle cap.

All information required by the Regulations must be easy to understand[2], clearly legible and indelible.

Subject to exceptions for small packages and indelibly marked glass bottles, the name of the food, the appropriate durability indication, the alcoholic strength indication, the warnings in respect of raw milk and of skimmed milk with non-milk fat, and the indication of net quantity, as required, must appear in the same field of vision.

The term 'same field of vision' is undefined, but might reasonably be expected to mean simultaneously visible under normal conditions of purchase.

1   Food Labelling Regulations 1996, regs 35, 36, 37, 38 and 39.
2   See *Hackney London Borough Council v Cedar Trading Ltd* (1999) 163 JP 749. As to language easily understood by consumers in a State or region and the use of other measures such as designs, symbols or pictograms, see also case C-85/94 *Groupement des producteurs, importeurs et agents généraux d'eaux minérales étrangères, VZW (Piageme) and Others v Peeters NV* [1995] ECR I-2955; case C-385/96 *Herman Josef Goerres* [1998] ECR I-4431; and case C-366/98 *Yannick Geffroy v Casino France* [2000] ECR I-6579; [2001] All ER (EC) 222.

Lot marking

9.2.27   Council Directive 89/396/EEC (on indications or marks identifying the lot to which a foodstuff belongs), as amended, aims at the establishment of a framework for a common 'lot' or 'batch' identification system throughout the European Community in order to facilitate the tracing and identification of products along the food chain where, for example, a product constitutes a health risk to consumers. The Directive is implemented in Great Britain by the Food (Lot Marking) Regulations 1996.

Subject to exceptions noted below, the Regulations prohibit the sale of food that forms part of a lot unless it is accompanied by a lot marking indication. A 'lot' is defined as a batch of sales units of food produced, manufactured or packaged under similar conditions. A 'lot marking indication' is defined as an indication that allows identification of the lot to which the sales unit belongs.

FSA Guidance Notes point out that the requirements are very flexible. They leave the producer, manufacturer or first seller established within the Community to determine the appropriate size of a lot and the form the lot marking indication should take. However, the Regulations require it to be preceded by the letter 'L' except in cases where it is clearly distinguishable from other indications on the label. It must appear on the prepackaging or on a label attached to the prepackaging or, if the food is not prepacked, on the container or on an accompanying commercial document. The indication must also be easily visible, clearly legible and indelible.

These requirements do not apply to:

- sales of agricultural products (ie the products of the soil, of stockfarming and of fisheries)[1] which are either sold or delivered to temporary storage, preparation or packing stations or to producers' organisations; or which are collected for immediate use in an operational preparation or processing system;
- sales to the ultimate consumer of food that is not prepacked, is packed at the request of the purchaser or is prepacked for immediate sale;
- sales units of food of specified maximum dimensions;
- prepacked sales units of food intended as a minor accompaniment to another food or service;
- sales units of individual portions of edible ice supplied to the seller in bulk packaging bearing the lot marking indication;
- sales units marked or labelled before 1 July 1992 or, in the case of indelibly marked glass bottles for reuse, before 1 July 1997;
- sales units of food bearing an indication of minimum durability or 'use by' date.

1   The FSA Guidance Notes advise that the term 'agricultural products' used in this context does not include products of first stage processing.

9.3 CONTROL OF MISLEADING AND COMPARATIVE ADVERTISING

9.3.1   In addition to the prohibition on misleading food advertising imposed by Art 2 of Directive 2000/13/EC but in no way affecting it, the Community has made provision, by Directive 2006/114/EC, in respect of misleading and comparative advertising.[1] Directive 2006/114/EC is implemented by the Business Protection from Misleading Marketing Regulations 2008, which prohibit misleading business-to-business advertising and set out the conditions under which comparative advertisements are permitted.

In the United Kingdom a number of organisations have a role to play in dealing with misleading advertisements. The Office of Fair Trading (OFT) has the main role in the formal enforcement of the Regulations and it can go to court to secure compliance. Under the Communications Act 2003 Ofcom is the independent regulator of television, radio, telecommunications and wireless communications in the United Kingdom. Ofcom sets the standards for television advertising and it is formally the regulator but in practice the main body concerned with the advertising of food is the Advertising Standards Association (ASA), an independent self-regulatory body.[2] Misleading business-to-consumer advertising is prohibited by the Consumer Protection from Unfair Trading Regulations 2008 that were made in implementation of commercial practices Directive 2005/29/EC as briefly explained in para **8.1.1** above.

The ASA's job is to ensure that advertisements are honest and decent. It adjudicates on the non-broadcast British Code of Advertising, Sales Promotion and Direct Marketing. In the context of broadcasting the ASA exercises powers contracted out to it by Ofcom and it oversees the broadcast advertising codes. With regard to broadcast advertising the ASA only deals with complaint handling up to the point where a statutory sanction might be appropriate, when the case would be referred to Ofcom.

9.3.2 Due to concerns about childhood obesity levels and poor diet, the Department of Health and the Food Standards Agency identified television advertising as an area where action should be considered and in December 2003 Ofcom was asked to consider proposals for strengthening the rules on television advertising of food aimed at children. Following research and consultation it was decided there should be some restrictions imposed on the advertising of food and drinks aimed at children that have a high fat, sugar or salt content. As a result the TV advertising code was changed in 2007 to incorporate restrictions on the content and timing of food and drink advertisements aimed at children. Foods that have a high fat, salt or sugar content cannot be advertised in or around programmes specifically made for children or which are of a particular appeal to children. In addition, the content rules for all food and drink advertising to children, irrespective of when the advert is scheduled, have been reconsidered.[3] In July 2008 Ofcom will begin a review of the impact of the broadcasting restrictions and it is possible that the rules will be tightened further.

1 This Directive replaced and codified the changes in the misleading and comparative advertising Directive 84/450/EEC, as amended.
2 Ofcom has contracted out its functions in this respect to the ASA under the Contracting Out (Functions relating to Broadcast Advertising) and Specification of Relevant Functions Order 2004, SI 2004/1975.
3 Television Advertising of Food and Drink Products to Children, Final Statement, Ofcom, February 2007.

Chapter 10

Food standards and descriptions

10.1 FOOD STANDARDS

Introduction

10.1.1   Section **8.2** above explained how magistrates' courts have used s 14 of the Food Safety Act 1990 (FSA 1990) and its predecessors since 1875 to establish (in the absence of bespoke or legislative requirements) what standard of food a purchaser must be deemed to have demanded of the seller. In fact one of the main ways of protecting the public from unhealthy or fraudulent food is by imposing specific standards with which it must comply. During the twentieth century, subordinate legislation was increasingly used by the Government to do this. The highpoint was probably reached in the years after the Second World War. Since then, Community free trade law[1] and the UK deregulation initiative has caused a movement away from this method of food control towards greater use of compulsory labelling with information about the product sold in the way described in section **9.2** above. However, food standards are still much employed in the areas noted in para **10.1.3** below.

1   See section **1.3** and para **9.1.3** above.

What are food standards?

10.1.2   Before considering the food standards imposed in various sectors of control, it is important to clarify what is meant here by the expression. Essentially it is used to cover any provision that, with regard to the composition of a specified food, prescribes a quantity or quality level or imposes a total ban. It includes such provisions when they are part of some wider emergency prohibition[1] and notwithstanding that they may also prescribe a microbiological standard[2]. Paragraph **10.1.3** explains the specific sectors in which food standards are imposed. However, the expression is not intended to include:

(a)   provisions of a general nature like ss 7, 14 and 15 of the FSA 1990;
(b)   provisions that require food to be labelled without setting a standard for it (see sections **9.2** and **11.5**);
(c)   preparation[3] and, except as mentioned in para **10.1.3**, hygiene requirements in respect of specific foods (see chs 13, 14 and 15); and
(d)   quantity and price marking provisions (see ch 16).

Within the limits explained, this chapter is certainly intended to embrace food standards imposed by different methods. Provisions establishing them appear in a bewildering variety of guises, but there are really only the three types described below.

(1)   Reserved name or description

This is the basic and least onerous method of imposing a standard. The use of a name or designation is reserved to food of the prescribed standard. For example, by reg 4 of the Jam and Similar Products Regulations 2003 descriptions such as 'jam' and similar products like 'marmalade', 'lemon cheese' and 'mincemeat' specified in Sch 1 are reserved to products that meet the respective compositional standards prescribed for those descriptions. The provision imposes no obligation to use the reserved name, but if it is used, the food to which it is applied must comply with the standard. Put another way, there is a commercial sanction against selling sub-standard food: you cannot call it by the name that the consumer expects. Setting standards by reserving names is a widely used device.

Decisions of the European Court on the Community free trade rules have often concerned the lawfulness of national food standards[4] and many of these have related to reserved names[5].

Some British provisions protect a 'word' or 'description'[6] rather than a 'name'. Nonetheless, these too are setting food standards: the use of the term is forbidden unless the standard is observed.

All such provisions reserving names and descriptions under the FSA 1990 are evidently caught by s 2(5)(a) of the Trade Descriptions Act 1968 so that the terms they protect are deemed not to be trade descriptions.

(2)   Prescribed name

Less frequently, the use of a specified name is made compulsory on the sale of food of a defined standard. These are the names 'prescribed by law' referred to in relation to food labelling in para **9.2.5**(i). In the example above concerning jam etc, reg 5 of the Jam and Similar Products Regulations 2003 requires use of the name by prescribing it for the food. In fact a requirement to use a prescribed name can work to set a standard only if that name is also reserved to food that meets the standard. Without this, there is nothing to prevent the use of the name on non-compliant food. National provisions declared by the European Court of Justice to be contrary to Community free movement rules include examples of prescribed name requirements[7].

(3)   Prohibited product

The last and most severe way of prescribing a standard is the total prohibition on the marketing of food that fails to comply. For a time after the Second World War this form was used in the United Kingdom to prevent misleading labelling. Since then, more sensibly and in line with Community philosophy, total prohibition on sale has been confined to cases where health is at risk. Given their oppressive character, it is not surprising that various national standards of this kind have been held by the European Court to be contrary to the free movement of goods principle[8].

As indicated above, the term 'composition' is often applied to any three categories in the sense that they all set standards for food. However, in the terminology of the powers in s 16 of the FSA 1990, only category (3) provisions directly regulate the 'composition' of food (see s 16(1)(a)). Strictly speaking, categories (1) and (2) regulate the 'labelling' of food defined according to its composition (see s 16(1)(e)).

1   See orders under Pt I of the Food and Environment Protection Act 1985 considered in para **7.4.12** above.
2   See, for example, the Natural Mineral Water, Spring Water and Bottled Drinking Water (England) Regulations 2007 considered in para **10.2.10** below.
3   As to food preparation, see FSA 1990, s 53(1) and section **15.2** below.
4   See section **1.3** above.
5   See for example case 281/83 *EC Commission v Italy* [1985] ECR 3397 (vinegar); case 178/84 *EC Commission v Germany* [1987] ECR 1227 (beer); case 286/86 *Minister Public v Déserbais* [1988] ECR 4907 (cheese).
6   See in particular section **10.7** below.
7   See for example case 27/80 *Fietje* [1980] ECR 3839 (liqueur); case 407/85 *Drei Glocken* [1988] ECR 4233 (pasta made from durum wheat).
8   See for example case 193/80 *EC Commission v Italy* [1981] ECR 3019 (vinegar); case 407/85 *Drei Glocken* [1988] ECR 4233 (dry pasta); Case C17/93 *Van der Veldt* [1994] ECR I-3537, [1991] CMLR 621 (bread).

Specific food standards and descriptions

10.1.3   As indicated above, specific standards are imposed in England and Wales to control various food sectors. The most obvious ones are explained in the rest of this chapter. Others of equal importance but applied for special purposes are dealt with elsewhere in the book. Thus, ch 11 on food claims and nutrition (apart from the sections on prescribed nutrition labelling, requirements for nutrition labelling given voluntarily and non-statutory guidance on claims) offers further examples. Still more are to be found in ch 12 (additives, flavourings, contaminants, contact materials, residues and other substances), section **7.4** (emergencies) and, in ch 14, the provisions prohibiting the marketing of products potentially affected by transmissible spongiform encephalopathies.

For completeness, mention should be made of the Agricultural Produce (Grading and Marking) Acts 1928 and 1931 which provide for the prescription and use of grade designations and marks for agricultural produce. The legislation has fallen into disuse because the voluntary trade quality schemes that it supported have evidently not been operated since the Second World War. Special provision in respect of preserved eggs also still subsists in the 1928 Act and the Eggs (Marketing and Storage) Regulations 1965, although cold and chemical storage of eggs seems no longer to be practised.

Considered in turn below are the following areas in which control is imposed by food standards:

(a)   Community internal market instruments;
(b)   novel food and genetically modified food;
(c)   Community common agricultural policy regulations;
(d)   Community regulations on quality marks or labels;
(e)   national regulations on specific foods;
(f)   Regulations to prevent misleading descriptions.

10.2   COMMUNITY INTERNAL MARKET INSTRUMENTS

10.2.1   The *Cassis de Dijon* judgment[1] significantly reduced the scope for national food standards restricting Community imports. In consequence, from 1985 the Commission decided[2] to concentrate its harmonisation policy on more informative labelling and on the public interest areas that potentially remained within Member States' competence.

Before that, the Commission's harmonisation programme had, in particular, involved the enactment of a series of vertical Directives laying down detailed specifications for particular foodstuffs, commonly known as 'recipe laws'. Most of these directives have been simplified and replaced but recipe law continue to exist and the domestic implementing regulations are summarised below, along with those on bottled waters. In considering more modern provisions implementing specific Community food standards, it is important not to overlook the special set of provisions implementing Community Directives on foods for particular nutritional purposes. These have been grouped in ch 11 with other nutrition-oriented provisions. Mention should also be made of the anomalous quick-frozen foodstuffs Directive 89/108/EEC, implementation of which is explained in section **15.4** below.

1   See paras **1.3.1** and **1.3.2** above.
2   See para **1.3.3** above.

10.2.2   The main group of foods for which standards are prescribed by Community internal market instruments are considered below.

Sugar products

10.2.3   The Specified Sugar Products (England) Regulations 2003,[1] as amended, implement Directive 2001/111/EC.

The Regulations reserve descriptions to specified sugar products and require the use of those descriptions and specified declarations. They also require sugar solution, invert sugar solution and invert sugar syrup to be labelled with the dry matter and invert sugar content of the product. Methods of analysis are prescribed for the specified sugar product definitions.

1   The FSA has produced Guidance Notes, 'The Specified Sugar Products Regulations 2003'.

Cocoa and chocolate products

10.2.4   The definition of chocolate under European law has long been a difficult issue because of the differences between Member States over the minimum cocoa content and the use of vegetable fat in place of cocoa butter. British chocolate has traditionally been made with vegetable fat and many Member States objected to this being marketed as 'chocolate'.[1] In the United Kingdom milk chocolate has also traditionally been made with more milk and less chocolate than in most of the rest of Europe. Had one of the early drafts of the original directive been passed, British dairy milk chocolate would have been re-named 'cocoa flavoured candy.' In the end a grudging compromise position was found. In the current cocoa and chocolate products Directive 2000/36/EC, other Member States agreed that milk chocolate made in the United Kingdom and Ireland would be traded freely in their countries under the label 'family milk chocolate'.[2]

The Cocoa and Chocolate Products (England) Regulations 2003, as amended, implement the 2000 Directive.[3] The Regulations prescribe definitions and reserve descriptions for designated cocoa and chocolate products and require the use of those descriptions and specified declarations as to vegetable fat, milk solids and cocoa solids content.

1   See case C-12/00 *Commission v Spain* [2003] ECR I-459 and case C-14/00 *Commission v Italy* [2003] ECR I-513.
2   An account of the 'chocolate debate' can be found in C MacMaoláin *EU Food Law* (Hart, 2007) 7–10.
3   The FSA has produced Guidance Notes, 'The Cocoa and Chocolate Products (England) Regulations 2003, revised 2006'.

Coffee and chicory

10.2.5   The Coffee Extracts and Chicory Extracts (England) Regulations 2000 as amended, implement Directive 1999/4/EC, as amended.

The Regulations reserve descriptions for coffee extracts and chicory extracts and require the use of those descriptions and specified declarations as to decaffeination and other matters. Other names, such as invented or trade names, are not precluded from being used alongside the product names.[1]

1   See case C-239/02 Douwe Egberts v Westrom Pharma and Souranis [2004] ECR I-7007.

Honey

10.2.6   The Honey (England) Regulations 2003, as amended, implement Directive 2001/110/EC.[1] The Regulations reserve descriptions to specified honey products. A food may only be considered a 'specified honey product' if, in addition to meeting the relevant prescribed specification, it has not had any other ingredient added to it. This is to ensure the purity of honey. Specified honey products must be labelled with reserved descriptions, with information about the country or countries of origin and, in the case of baker's honey, with the words 'intended for cooking only'. Bulk containers of filtered honey and baker's honey must also be labelled with the product's reserved description.

1   The FSA has issued Guidance Notes, 'The Honey (England) Regulations 2003, revised 2007'.

Fruit juices and fruit nectars

10.2.7   The Fruit Juices and Fruit Nectars (England) Regulations 2003, as amended, implement Directive 2001/112/EC, as amended.[1]

The Regulations require a clear distinction to be made between juice obtained directly from fruit and that obtained by the reconstitution of concentrated juice. This is achieved by the use of reserved descriptions. The Regulations prescribe the raw materials, treatment processes and additional ingredients to be used in the preparation of designated products. Designated products are required to be labelled with their reserved descriptions and, in specified cases, with declarations as to sweetening, the addition of pulp, the use of concentrates and other matters.

1   The FSA has issued Guidance Notes, 'The Fruit Juices and Fruit Nectars (England) Regulations 2003, revised 2007'.

Condensed milk and dried milk

10.2.8   The Condensed Milk and Dried Milk (England) Regulations 2003, as amended, implement Directive 2001/114/EC, as amended.[1]

The Regulations cover partly and totally dehydrated milk, as defined. Most of the products need to be labelled with the percentage of milk fat expressed by weight in relation to the finished product and the percentage of fat-free dried milk extract. They reserve descriptions and require their use in relation to specified condensed milk and dried milk products.

1   The FSA has issued Guidance Notes, 'The Condensed Milk and Dried Milk (England) Regulations (as amended) Version 2, 2008'.

Jam and similar products

10.2.9   The Jam and Similar Products (England) Regulations 2003, as amended, implement Directive 2001/113/EC, as amended.[1] They also extend to some related products not covered by the Directive, namely fruit curds and mincemeat.

The Regulations reserve descriptions to jam and similar products complying with compositional standards. Specified products must also be labelled with their reserved descriptions and with their residual sulphur dioxide content, fruit types and fruit and sugar content.

The Regulations do not apply to jams etc intended for use in the manufacture of bakery products, pastries and biscuits. The FSA Guidance explains that these products were specifically excluded because they normally require the addition of additives and flavourings to enable them to withstand the processing conditions. The Guidance concludes that labelling the jam filling of a jam tart as 'jam' should not be considered a breach of the Regulations even if it fails to meet the compositional standard that they set.

1   The FSA has issued Guidance Notes, The Jam and Similar Products (England) Regulations 2003, revised 2005.

Natural mineral water, spring water and bottled drinking water

10.2.10   Provision for the approximation of Member States' laws relating to the exploitation and marketing of natural mineral waters was made by Directive 80/777/EEC. This Directive has, in particular, been amended by Directive 96/70/EC so as to extend to spring waters some of the requirements that apply to natural mineral waters, such as bottling at source, certain microbiological criteria and restrictions on the treatment of water. The amendment also permits the treatment of natural mineral water and spring water with ozone-enriched air in prescribed circumstances. At the time of writing there are proposals to recast the Directive.[1]

The standards for other bottled drinking water are prescribed by Directive 98/83/EC on the quality of water for human consumption, as to which see further below. The provisions are now implemented by the Natural Mineral Water, Spring Water and Bottled Drinking Water (England) Regulations 2007. The Regulations with regard to natural mineral water:

(a)   prescribe the conditions for recognition of natural mineral waters[2];
(b)   prohibit the sale, as natural mineral water, of water that is not natural mineral water;
(c)   set out the exploitation requirements for natural mineral water springs;
(d)   regulate the treatment of natural mineral waters;
(e)   prohibit the bottling and sale of natural mineral water that fails to comply with specified colony count requirements or contains any organoleptic defect;

(f)   prohibit the bottling and sale of natural mineral water in other than a specified type of container;

(g)   prescribe labelling requirements for natural mineral water.

With regard to spring water, the Regulations prohibit the labelling of water as such, or sale of water so labelled, unless specified conditions concerning exploitation and bottling are met. The Regulations also prohibit the bottling or sale of bottled drinking water that fails to satisfy specified requirements and prohibit the use of specified labelling.

The FSA has provided guidance to the Regulations.

1   COM (2007) 0858 final.
2   Member States are precluded from making recognition of natural mineral water dependent on the water-possessing properties favourable to health: see case C-17/96 *Badische Erfrischungs-Getränke GmbH & Co KG v Land Baden Württemburg* [1998] 1 CMLR 341.

Caseins and caseinates

10.2.11 The Caseins and Caseinates Regulations 1985, as amended, implement Directive 83/417/EEC as amended.

The Regulations reserve descriptions for defined casein products and require the use of those descriptions and other specified indications. The use of any casein or caseinate in casein products is forbidden unless it has been subjected to heat treatment at least equivalent to pasteurisation.

10.3   NOVEL FOOD AND GENETICALLY MODIFIED FOOD

Introduction

10.3.1   The nutritional and safety aspects of novel food have been actively monitored in the United Kingdom since 1980[1], but no statutory evaluation system was put in place until the enactment of Regulation (EC) 258/97. As explained in para **10.3.2** below, this was applied to foods and food ingredients that had no significant history of consumption within the European Community before 15 May 1997 when the legislation came fully into effect. Scientific developments by that time had imported the need for protection not only against risks to public health, but also, in the case of novel foods and novel food ingredients containing or consisting of genetically modified organisms (GMOs), against risks to the environment. Provision was therefore made in Regulation (EC) 258/97 both for the assessment of these products as food, and for an environmental risk assessment in accordance with the rules on the deliberate release into the environment of GMOs. At the time these rules were in Directive 90/220/EEC, which has subsequently been repealed and replaced by Directive 2001/18/EC.

The Regulation (EC) 258/97 procedures proved in practice to lack clarity and transparency, particularly in respect of novel food containing or derived from GMOs. Moreover, the labelling provisions were perceived to need strengthening. The Commission's 2000 White Paper on Food Safety[2] therefore promised amending legislation. As explained in paras **10.3.3–10.3.4**, Regulation (EC) 1829/2003 on genetically modified food and feed has now been made. For novel foods and novel food ingredients that contain or consist of GMOs, this has replaced the authorisation procedure in Regulation 258/97.

Additionally, as the title implies, it provides the authorisation procedure for feed and feed ingredients consisting of or containing GMOs[3] that, until then, had been subject to the Directive 2001/18 procedures. As further explained by para **10.3.2**, the Commission published a proposal[4] in January 2008 which will complete the modernisation process by replacing and simplifying novel food Regulation 258/97. In future, the safety assessment is to be carried out in accordance with the new Regulation establishing a common authorisation procedure for food additives, food enzymes and flavourings[5].

1   The 1974 Food Standards Committee Report on Novel Protein Foods first recommended monitoring, The work is now undertaken by the Advisory Committee on Novel Foods and Processes, see para **2.4.5** above.
2   COM (1999) 719 final.
3   See further para **17.9.1** below.
4   COM (2007) 872 final.
5   See para **12.2.1** below.

Novel foods and novel food ingredients

10.3.2   Regulation (EC) 258/97 concerning novel foods and novel food ingredients is supplemented by the Novel Foods and Novel Food Ingredients Regulations 1997, as amended. The Novel Foods and Novel Food Ingredients (Fees) Regulations 1997 prescribes fees to be paid for the processing of requests to assess novel foods and novel food ingredients.

Before they may be placed on the market, novel foods and novel food ingredients must be subjected to a safety assessment procedure. This applies to foods and ingredients that have not hitherto been used for human consumption to a significant degree within the Community and that fall under the following categories:

(a)   foods and food ingredients with a new or intentionally modified primary molecular structure (e g a fat replacer);
(b)   foods and food ingredients consisting of or isolated from microorganisms, fungi or algae (e g a new non-genetically modified organism used as a yoghurt starter culture);
(c)   foods and food ingredients consisting of or isolated from plants and food ingredients isolated from animals, except for foods and food ingredients obtained by traditional propagating or breeding practices and having a history of safe food use (a new plant oil);
(d)   foods and food ingredients to which have been applied a production process not currently used, where that process gives rise to significant changes in the composition or structure of the foods or food ingredients that affect their nutritional value, metabolism or level of undesirable substances.

Provided the safety level of Regulation (EC) 258/97 is met, it does not apply to food additives[1], flavourings[2] or extraction solvents[3].

Foods and food ingredients falling within the scope of the Regulation must not:

•   present a danger for the consumer;
•   mislead the consumer;
•   differ from foods and food ingredients that they are intended to replace to such an extent that their normal consumption would be nutritionally disadvantageous for the consumer.

Subject to certain exceptions, for the purpose of placing such a food or food ingredient on the market, a request containing all necessary information[4] and copied to the Commission must be submitted to the competent authority in the Member State in which the product is to be marketed for the first time. Novel food assessments are carried out by the Advisory Committee on Novel Foods and Processes (ACNFP)[5] on behalf of the relevant food assessment bodies that are, for England, the Food Standards Agency and, for Wales, the Welsh Ministers.[6] It also appraises assessments carried out by other Member States.

The competent authority has three months to carry out the initial safety assessment after which the Commission and other Member States have 60 days in which to comment. If the initial assessment was favourable and there are no objections, the product may be marketed. If the Member State's initial assessment decided that an additional assessment is required or if objections are raised, an 'authorisation decision' must be taken. The application must be referred to the EC Standing Committee on the Food Chain and Animal Health (consulting the European Food Safety Authority as necessary) under a regulatory committee procedure. If the Commission does not follow the Standing Committee's opinion or if no opinion is given, the matter must be referred to the Council acting by qualified majority. If the Council has not acted within three months, the Commission may adopt its proposal[7].

A less rigorous procedure is prescribed for novel foods and food ingredients that are recognised as substantially equivalent to existing foods or ingredients as regards their composition, nutritional value, metabolism, intended use and level of undesirable substances. Where this is true of a food or ingredient referred to in (b) and (c) above, an applicant, who supplies prescribed evidence of the substantial equivalence, may notify the Commission when first marketing the product.

In every case, additional labelling requirements must be complied with to ensure that the final consumer is informed of any characteristic or food property that renders the novel food or ingredient no longer equivalent to an existing food or ingredient; or of the presence in the food or ingredient of material that is not present in an existing equivalent foodstuff and which may have implications for the health of certain sections of the population or gives rise to ethical concerns. Provision is made for temporary restriction or suspension of trade in and use of a food or ingredient where, as a result of new information or a reassessment of existing information, a Member State has grounds for considering that the use of the food or ingredient endangers human health or the environment.

At the time of writing there is a proposal for a new EC Regulation on novel foods, intended to repeal and replace the current legislation.[8] This is deemed necessary in order to reflect the fact that genetically modified food no longer falls under the scope of the legislation and 'to create a more favourable legislative environment for innovation in the food industry'. The proposal includes a centralised authorisation procedure and an updated definition of novel food.

1   See Directive 89/107/EEC and para **12.2.1** below.
2   See Directive 88/388/EEC and para **12.3.1** below.
3   See Directive 88/344/EEC and para **12.4.6** below.
4   Commission Recommendation 97/618/EC concerning the scientific aspects and the presentation of information necessary to support applications for placing on the market of novel foods and novel food ingredients and the preparation of initial assessment reports was published at OJ L, 253 16.9.97 p 1.
5   See para **2.4.5**.
6   See para **2.1.2**.
7   See para **1.6.5**.
8   COM (2007) 872 final.

Genetically modified food

10.3.3 The basic legislation now controlling genetically modified food is to be found in two important EC instruments – Regulations (EC) 1829/2003 and 1830/2003. The FSA and DEFRA have jointly issued Guidance notes on these Regulations.

Regulation (EC) 1829/2003 – on genetically modified food and feed – has introduced a safety assessment system for GMOs, centralised via the European Food Safety Authority, and has extended the labelling requirements imposed by previous Regulations[1] so as to include a wider range of products. Detailed rules for its implementation are provided by Regulation (EC) 641/2004[2] and Regulation (EC) 1981/2006[3].

The provisions on genetically modified feed are explained in para **17.9.1** below. Genetically modified food is regulated by Title II of Regulation (EC) 1829/2003 which applies to GMOs for food use, food containing or consisting of GMOs and food produced from or containing ingredients produced from GMOs.

GM food must not –

- have adverse effects on human health, animal health or the environment;
- mislead the consumer;
- differ from the food that it is intended to replace to such an extent that its normal consumption would be nutritionally disadvantageous for the consumer.

Marketing of a GMO for food use or of GM food is prohibited unless authorised in accordance with the Regulation. This makes extensive provision for the grant, supervision, modification, suspension, revocation and renewal of authorisations.

The labelling rules laid down for GM food by Regulation (EC) 1829/2003 Title II Section 2 are described in para **10.3.4** below.

Provision for the enforcement and execution of specified provisions of Regulation (EC) 1829/2003 relating to food are made by the Genetically Modified Food (England) Regulations 2004.

The second EC instrument – Regulation (EC) 1830/2003 – is an elaboration of provisions, formerly in Directive 2001/18, that required Member States to ensure the traceability and labelling of authorised GMOs throughout the marketing chain.

At the first stage of placing on the market of a product (such as soya) consisting of or containing GMOs, the recipient must be informed in writing both that it contains or consists of GMOs and of the unique identifier of the product assigned in accordance with the Regulation. This information must be passed on at subsequent marketing stages.[4] An alternative traceability procedure is provided for GMO products that are to be used only and directly for food, feed or processing.[5]

When products (such as soya lecithin) for food or feed produced from GMOs are placed on the market, the information to be transmitted in writing is:

- an indication of each of the food ingredients that is produced from GMOs[6]; and

- in the case of products for which no list of ingredients exists, an indication that the product is produced from GMOs.[7]

The labelling requirements laid down by Regulation (EC) 1830/2003 are described in para **10.3.4** below.

Regulation (EC) 1830/2003 is enforced by the Genetically Modified Organisms (Traceability and Labelling) (England) Regulations 2004.

1   Regulations (EC) 1139/98, 49/2000 and 50/2000 repealed by Regulation (EC) 1929/2003.
2   As regards the application for the authorisation of new genetically modified food and feed, the notification of existing products and adventitious or technically unavoidable presence of genetically modified material that has benefited from a favourable risk evaluation.
3   As regards the Community reference laboratory for genetically modified organisms.
4   Regulation (EC) 1830/2003, Art 4(1) and (2).
5   Regulation (EC) 1830/2003, Art 4(3).
6   In the case of feed, the requirement is for an indication of each of the feed materials or additives that is produced from GMOs.
7   Regulation (EC) 1830/2003, Art 5(1).

Labelling of genetically modified food

10.3.4   Foods that are to be delivered as such to the final consumer or mass caterers and that contain or consist of GMOs or are produced from or contain ingredients produced from GMOs must be appropriately labelled:[1]

(a)   where a food contains more than one ingredient, the following indication must be given: 'genetically modified' or 'produced from genetically modified (name of ingredient);[2]

(b)   where a food is designated by the name of a category, the following must appear in the list of ingredients: 'contains genetically modified (name of organism)', or 'contains (name of ingredient) produced from genetically modified (name of organism)';[3]

(c)   if there is normally no list of ingredients given on a specific product, the following must appear clearly on the labelling: 'genetically modified' or 'produced from genetically modified (name of organism)';[4] and

(d)   if the food is offered for sale to the final consumer as non-pre-packaged food, or as pre-packaged food in small containers of which the largest surface has an area of less than 10 cm², the information required must be permanently and visibly displayed either on the food display or immediately next to it, or in the packaging material, in a font sufficiently large to be easily identified and read.[5]

In the case of (a) and (b) the information can be given in the list of ingredients or as a footnote to the list of ingredients, providing the font size is the same size as that of the ingredient list.[6]

In addition, where a food is different from its conventional counterpart as regards its composition, nutritional values or effects, or there are particular indications in relation to the intended use of the food, or the food has implications for the health of certain sectors of the population, or the food could give rise to ethical or religious concerns, then the label needs to mention any characteristic or property, as specified in the authorisation.[7]

Finally, there are the labelling requirements of Regulation (EC) 1830/2003. In respect of products consisting of or containing GMOs, operators are required to ensure that:

(i)   for pre-packaged products consisting of, or containing GMOs, the words 'This product contains genetically modified organisms' or 'This product contains genetically modified [name of organism(s)]' appear on a label;

(ii)   for non-pre-packaged products offered to the final consumer, the words 'This product contains genetically modified organisms' or 'This product contains genetically modified [name of organism(s)]' appear on, or in connection with, the display of the product.[8]

1   Labelling is not required where the presence of the authorised GMO is less than 0.9% of the food ingredients considered individually or of a food consisting of a single ingredient, provided that the presence is adventitious or technically unavoidable.
2   Regulation (EC) 1829/2003, Art 13(1)(a).
3   Regulation (EC) 1829/2003, Art 13(1)(b).
4   Regulation (EC) 1829/2003, Art 13(1)(c).
5   Regulation (EC) 1829/2003, Art 13(1)(e).
6   Regulation (EC) 1829/2003, Art 13(1)(d).
7   Regulation (EC) 1829/2003, Art 13(2).
8   Regulation (EC) 1830/2003, Art 4(6).

10.4   COMMUNITY COMMON AGRICULTURAL POLICY REGULATIONS

Introduction

10.4.1   Marketing standards have been a feature of common market organisations from the early days of the common agricultural policy. They have been used to define agricultural products eligible for support and to facilitate sales. They are in practice enacted by Regulation and so have required national legislation only to provide enforcement mechanisms and penalties. Since the products in question are mostly also foodstuffs, British legislation for this purpose has often been made in whole or in part under the Food Safety Act 1990. Even where the Community objectives in question have extended beyond what the 1990 Act comprehends, the concepts and enforcement methods of the Act have, in Regulations under the European Communities Act 1972, been applied to the food standards aspects.

10.4.2   The European Commission proposed establishing a single Common Market Organisation for all agricultural products, to replace 21 separate Regulations. This was achieved by Council Regulation (EC) 1234/2007 (Single CMO Regulation), which establishes a system common to all products concerned. The marketing standards rules considered in relation to particular foods below are based on Regulation (EC) 1234/2007 Title II Chapter I Section I and Annexes XIa – XVI, except for those for spirits and fish, as well as for the moment wine, which are separately regulated.

Drinking milk

10.4.3   Council Regulation (EC) 1234/2007 now sets out the common organisation of the market in milk and milk products rules for drinking milk, and is supplemented by the Drinking Milk (England) Regulations 2008.

Only milk complying with the requirements laid down for drinking milk may be delivered or sold without processing to the final consumer. The sales descriptions given below must be used for those products.

The following products are considered as drinking milk:

(a)   raw milk: milk that has not been heated above 40°C or subjected to treatment having equivalent effect;

(b)   whole milk: heat-treated milk that, with respect to fat content, meets one of the following requirements:

   •   standardised whole milk: milk with a fat content of at least 3.5% (m/m);

   •   non-standardised whole milk: milk with a fat content that has not been altered since the milking stage either by the addition or removal of milk fats or by mixture with milk the natural fat content of which has been altered. However, the fat content may not be less that 3.5% (m/m);

(c)   semi-skimmed milk: heat-treated milk whose fat content has been reduced to at least 1.5% (m/m) and at most 1.80% (m/m);

(d)   skimmed milk: heat-treated milk whose fat content has been reduced to not more than 0.50% (m/m).

Modification of milk is authorised in particular to meet the fat content standards and to provide for enrichment with milk proteins, mineral salts or vitamins.

Spreadable fat and milk and milk product designations

10.4.4   Council Regulation (EC) 1234/2007 repealed and replaced Council Regulation (EC) 2991/94 (laying down standards for spreadable fats) and Council Regulation (EC) 1898/87 (on the protection of designations used in the marketing of milk and milk products). As a result the domestic implementing legislation had to be updated and the Spreadable Fats (Marketing Standards) and Milk and Milk Products (Protection of Designations) (England) Regulations 2008 were introduced. The essence of the legislation remains the same. Detailed rules are laid down in Regulation (EC) 445/2007.

10.4.5 The original Regulation (EEC) 1898/87 on milk caused such difficulty when enacted that the Ministry of Agriculture, Fisheries and Food produced a guidance note on its interpretation. This recalls that the Regulation was introduced largely to meet concerns about the marketing of so-called 'imitation products' ie those non-dairy or partly non-dairy products (for example fat spreads and 'imitation' cream and cheese) that can, by trading on the dairy image, mislead the consumer and thus compete unfairly with dairy products. Regulation (EC) 1234/2007 continues to reserve to dairy products the term 'milk' and the designations 'whey', 'cream', 'butter', 'buttermilk', 'butteroil', 'caseins', 'anhydrous milkfat', 'cheese', 'yoghurt', 'kephir', 'koumiss', 'viili/fil', 'smetana' and 'fil' and generally prohibits any label, commercial document, publicity material, advertising or presentation that claims, implies or suggests that a non-dairy product is a dairy product.

Regulation (EC) 1234/2007 sets standards for spreadable fats with a fat content of at least 10% but less than 90% by weight intended for human consumption. The Regulation:

   •   restricts supply to the ultimate consumer to specified milk fats, fats and fats composed of plant and/or animal to products complying with prescribed requirements;

   •   specifies, in relation to those products, the sales descriptions 'butter', 'three-quarter fat butter', 'half-fat butter', 'dairy spread X %', 'margarine', 'three-quarter fat margarine', 'half-fat margarine', 'fat

185

spreads X %', 'blend', 'three-quarter fat blend', 'half-fat blend' and 'blended spread X %'; and

- reserves those descriptions for those products.

Exempt from these provisions are concentrated products (butter, margarine, blends) with a fat content of 90% or more. Exemptions are also provided for designations of products the exact nature of which is clear from traditional usage and/or when the designations are clearly used to describe a characteristic quality of the product. Further provision is made for the use of the designation 'butter' in respect of composite products of which the essential part is butter.[1]

In addition to the rules laid down in general labelling Directive 2000/13/EC, requirements are specified as to the labelling and presentation of spreadable fats. In particular, the sales description, the total percentage fat content by weight, the vegetable, milk or other animal fat content and the percentage salt content must be indicated. Terms that suggest fat content for the specified products other than those prescribed are prohibited, but derogations are provided for the terms 'reduced-fat', 'low-fat' and 'light'.

As well as providing for the enforcement of these Community standards, the national Marketing Standards Regulations lay down compulsory vitamin content requirements for margarine sold by retail.

1 See Regulation (EC) 445/2007.

Eggs

10.4.6 Council Regulation (EC) 1234/2007 and Commission Regulation (EC) 589/2008 now govern the marketing standards for eggs. The domestic enforcement legislation is the Eggs and Chicks (England) Regulations 2008, which also allows for some permitted derogations.[1]

Marketing of hen eggs by way of business within the Community is prohibited unless they satisfy the marketing standards set by Council Regulation (EC) 1234/2007 and Commission Regulation (EC) 589/2008.

The quality grades for eggs are:

- Class A (or 'fresh')
- Class B.

The quality standards for Grade A eggs relate to the condition of the shell and cuticle; the air space; the clarity and consistency of the white; the visibility on candling of the yolk; clear, translucent white; imperceptible development of germ; and freedom from foreign matter and smell. Grade B eggs are those that do not meet the requirements for Grade A eggs and can only be delivered to the food or non-food industry.Additionally, weight grades are laid down for Class A eggs. They are:

- XL – very large: 73 g and more;
- L – large: from 63 g up to 73 g;
- M – medium: from 53 g up to 63 g;
- S – small: under 53 g.

Comprehensive provision is made in respect of the marking of eggs.[2] In labelling of the packs, the following information is mandatory:

- the packing centre code;
- the quality grading. Grade A eggs must be identified either by the words'Class A' or the letter 'A' whether alone or in combination with the word 'fresh';

- the weight grading;
- the date of minimum durability ('best-before date') followed by appropriate storage recommendations for grade A eggs, and the packing date for grade B;
- 'washed eggs' if the eggs have been washed;
- an indication advising consumers to keep eggs chilled after purchase.[3]

Additionally, packs containing grade A eggs must be labelled with the farming method. However, the only terms that may be used for this purpose are :

- for conventional farming, 'Free range eggs'; Barn eggs' and 'Eggs from caged hens' and then only if the eggs comply with conditions respectively specified in relation to each of those terms;
- for organic production, the terms permitted by the legislation on organic production and labelling of organic products explained in para **10.5.4** below.

This labelling may be complemented by the indication 'enriched cages' where the laying hens have been kept in accordance with Directive 1999/74/EC on minimum standards for the protection of laying hens.

The words 'extra' or 'extra fresh' may also be used in relation to packs containing class A eggs. They must be printed on a band or label that must be removed not later than the ninth day after laying.

Further requirements are prescribed for indications of how laying hens are fed and information to be displayed with loose eggs.

The importation of eggs from third countries is strictly controlled by Regulation (EC) 1234/2007.

The element of discretion left to Member States in organising supervision of the Community Regulations has the effect of authorising them to entrust exclusively to appointed agencies the taking of necessary implementing measures and services. In respect of such measures and services Member States may require payment provided that it is not in excess of the real costs involved.[4]

Member States can exempt from the requirements of Regulation (EC) 1234/2007 eggs sold directly to the consumer for his own use, by the producer on his own farm, in a local public market with the exception of auction markets, or by door-to-door selling.

1   Defra has produced Guidance on legislation covering the marketing of eggs, 2007.
2   See Regulation (EC) 1234/2007, Annex XIV, Part A, Point III; Regulation (EC) 589/2008, Arts 8–11 and 30(2); and the Eggs and Chicks (England) Regulations 2008, reg 9.
3   As a special storage condition, see paras **9.2.4**(d) and **9.2.19** above.
4   See case 31/78 *Bussone v Italian Ministry for Agriculture and Forestry* [1978] ECR 2429, [1979] 3 CMLR 18, ECJ.

Poultrymeat

10.4.7   Marketing standards for poultrymeat are laid down by Regulation (EC) 1234/2007 and by Commission Regulation (EC) 543/2008, which sets out detailed rules.

Marketing standards are prescribed for certain types and presentations of poultrymeat of the following species: domestic fowl, ducks, geese, turkeys and guinea fowl. The marketing of poultrymeat by way of business within the Community is prohibited unless these standards are satisfied.

The poultry carcases, the poultry cuts and foie gras to which the Regulations apply are defined and the names under which carcases and poultry cuts must be sold are prescribed. Products other than those defined may be marketed in the Community only under names that do not mislead the consumer to a material degree through confusion with the prescribed names or with indications of the type of farming referred to below.

Poultry carcases and poultry cuts must be graded Class 'A' or Class 'B', in respect of each of which minimum requirements are specified as to conformation and appearance.

Poultry carcases must be presented for marketing as partially eviscerated ('effilé', 'roped'), with giblets or without giblets. Poultrymeat also must be marketed in one of the respectively defined conditions of 'fresh', 'frozen'[1] or 'quick-frozen'[2], provision being made for the optional classification of the prepackaged frozen and quick-frozen products according to specified weight categories.

In addition to the general rules for the labelling of foodstuffs, poultrymeat must, subject to exceptions in the case of poultrymeat cut and boned at the place of sale, comply with specifically prescribed requirements. While the national rules described in para **9.2.22** above alone apply to non-prepacked poultrymeat, the following additional particulars must appear on the prepackaged product :

- the poultrymeat class;
- for retail sales of fresh poultrymeat, the total price and the price per weight unit;
- the condition in which the poultrymeat is marketed and the recommended storage temperature;
- the registered number of the slaughterhouse or cutting plant;
- for third country imports, the country of origin.

For fresh poultrymeat, a 'use by' date must be applied.

An indication of 'air chilling', 'air-spray chilling' or 'immersion chilling', as defined, may appear on the labelling as the method used for chilling poultry carcases.

Indications (sometimes referred to as special marketing terms) of the type of farming, other than organic or biological farming, are limited to the terms 'Fed with … % …'; 'Extensive indoor' ('Barn reared'); 'Free range'; 'Traditional free range' and 'Free range – total freedom' which are respectively restricted to products complying with specified criteria.[3]

Regulation 543/2008 also prescribes the percentages of technically unavoidable water content that must not be exceeded in frozen and quick frozen chickens marketed within the Community.

1   As to fresh and frozen poultrymeat, see also para **15.3.3** below.
2   As to quick-frozen poultrymeat, see also section **15.4** below.
3   See case C-203/04 *Stolle v Heidegold v Geflügelspezialitäten* [2005] ECR I-7239.

Wine

10.4.8   In accordance with Commission proposals published in 2007[1], Title III of the recently enacted Council Regulation (EC) 479/2008 on the common organisation of the market in wine is making major changes to the European Community wine standards rules. Those on oenological practices, which relate to the composition of wine, are, in particular, made more responsive to agreed international methods[2]. Those on labelling are amended in two important ways. First, consistent with the rules for other foods set out in Regulation (EC) 510/006 described in para **10.5.2** below, provision is made for the central registration and protection of names as designations of origin or geographical indications[3]. Secondly, save as otherwise provided by the Regulation, the EC labelling requirements for food described in ch 9 will apply to wine[4].

Until 1 August 2009, however, the previous rules subsist. These were established by former Council Regulation (EC) 1493/1999. Title V Chapter I and Annexes IV and V, together with the detailed provisions in Regulation (EC) 423/2008, prescribe the authorised oenological practices and processes, including the limits on sulphur dioxide and other additives that are permitted in wine. The offer or delivery of non-compliant products for direct human consumption is generally prohibited.

Comprehensive rules on the description, designation, presentation of products and the protection of particular indications, terms and expressions are laid down by Title V Chapter II of and Annexes VII and VIII to Regulation (EC) 1493/999, together with the detailed provisions in Regulation (EC) 753/2002. The legislation is specifically aimed at protecting legitimate consumer and producer interests, as well as advancing the smooth operation of the internal market and quality production. Marketing within the Community or export of products whose description or presentation does not conform with the prescribed rules is forbidden.

A common set of rules is also provided by Title VI of and Annex VI to Regulation (EC) 1493/1999 for the production of categories of quality wine produced in specified regions ('psr'). They are 'quality liqueur wines psr', 'quality sparkling wines psr', 'quality semi-sparkling wines psr' and other quality wines psr. Wines that no longer meet the requirements may be downgraded. Member States must notify the Commission of the quality wines psr that they have recognised[5]. Under the scheme operated in the UK, 'English Vineyards' and 'Welsh Vineyards' are specified regions for the production of quality still wines. A parallel scheme allows for still wine produced in England or Wales that meets conditions prescribed in accordance with Regulation (EC) 753/2002 to be identified by the relevant authorised county or district name and the designation 'Regional Wine'.

Provision for enforcement of the Community Regulations is currently made by the Common Agricultural Policy (Wine) (England and Northern Ireland) Regulations 2001[6], although, on 13 June 2008, DEFRA put out proposals for Wine Regulations 2008 to enforce the first phase of the new EC regime in England. Parallel Regulations are planned for Wales.

The Department for Environment, Food and Rural Affairs (DEFRA) coordinates UK enforcement and liaises with the European Commission; HM Revenue and Customs checks documentation for third country wine imports; and the Food Standards Authority and local authorities are responsible for enforcement at the wholesale and retail stages respectively[7].

Further information is available from the Food Standards Agency website in the form of leaflets on the legal requirements for different wines, supplemented by a series of practical guidance notes mainly for producers and local authorities.

For British legislation on the use of the word 'wine' in composite names for foods or drinks that are not wine, see para **10.7.18.**

1   Towards a sustainable wine sector COM(2006) 319 final.
2   See Regulation 479/2008, Title III, chapter II.

3   See Regulation 479/2008, Title III, chapter IV.
4   See Regulation 479/2008, Title III, chapter VI.
5   See List of quality wines produced in specified regions Commission Notice OJ C 106, 10.5.2007 p 1.
6   See *Hurley v Martinez & Co Ltd* (1990) 154 JP 821.
7   For the similar enforcement arrangements in Wales, see the Common Agricultural Policy (Wine) (Wales) Regulations 2001.

Aromatised wines, aromatised wine-based drinks and aromatised wine product cocktails

10.4.9   Council Regulation (EEC) 1601/91, as amended, lays down general rules on the definition, description and presentation of aromatised wines (such as 'vermouth'), aromatised wine-based drinks (such as 'sangria' and 'glühwein') and aromatised wine product cocktails.

The use of the descriptions specified in the Regulation is restricted to the products defined in it. The descriptions are prescribed for these products and other requirements laid down in addition to the general labelling rules[1]. Authorised additives are determined according to the general rules under Directive 89/107/EEC described in ch 12. The authorised oenological processes and practices are those prescribed by the former common market organisation Regulation (EEC) 822/87, replaced successively by Regulation (EC) 1493/1999 and Regulation (EC) 479/2008 described in the previous paragraph.

1   See para **9.2.4** above.

Spirit drinks

10.4.10   Regulation (EC) 110/2008 has replaced Regulation (EEC) 1576/89 to make provision for the definition, description, presentation, labelling and the protection of geographical indications of spirit drinks. Definitions are laid down for 46 named categories of spirit drinks of which numbers 1 to 14 (including rum, whisky/whiskey[1] and brandy) are obtained from specified raw materials and numbers 15 to 46 (including vodka and gin) are obtained from any agricultural raw material listed in Annex I to the EC Treaty. Ethyl alcohol used in the production of spirit drinks must be of agricultural origin. Further general rules are prescribed as to the addition of alcohol, colouring, sweetening and flavouring substances.

The provisions of the Regulation go beyond the horizontal rules established by general labelling Directive 2000/13/EC described in ch 9. The names (sales denominations) assigned to the respective categories must be borne by spirit drinks that meet their specifications and may not be used to describe any other drink. A product that complies with the definition of spirit drink but not the requirements of any of the 46 categories must be labelled 'spirit drink' [2].

Sales denominations may also be supplemented by geographical indications that are classified by product category and identify drinks as originating in a specific country, region or territory. An indication that is not a generic and is supported by a technical file attesting the spirit drink's compliance with conditions as to its provenance, characteristics and manufacture may be registered and listed in the Regulation. Registered indications are protected from becoming generics and from misuse by others. Registration may, however, be cancelled where compliance with the technical specification is no longer assured.

Commission Regulation (EEC) 1014/90, which provided detailed implementing rules for repealed Regulation (EEC) 1576/89, is itself due for replacement.

DEFRA has issued proposals for Spirit Drinks Regulations 2008 to enforce the Community legislation and revoke the Spirits Drinks Regulations 1990.

As to British legislation on Scotch whisky, see para **10.6.4**.

1 See *Scotch Whisky Association v Glen Kella Distillers* [1997] 16 LS Gaz R 29; *Matthew Gloag and Son Ltd and Another v Welsh Distillers Ltd and Others* (1998) Times, 27 February [1998] 2 CMLR 203.

2 Case C-136/96 *Scotch Whisky Association v Compagnie Financière Européenne de Prises de Participation (COFEPP)* [1998] ECR I-4571.

Olive oil

10.4.11 Article 118 of Regulation (EC) 1234/2007 makes compulsory, for the purpose of marketing, the use of descriptions and definitions of olive oil and olive-pomace oil specified in Annex XVI to that Regulation. It prohibits the retail sale of oil other than extra virgin olive oil, virgin olive oil, olive oil and olive-pomace oil. For the marketing of those products at the retail stage, Regulation (EC) 1019/2002 prescribes requirements as to packaging and additional labelling to inform consumers about the type of oil or blend offered[1]. It also lays down conditions for the use of specified further indications and restricts designations of origin to extra virgin and virgin olive oil.

Commission Regulation (EEC) 2568/91 lays down the characteristics of olive oil and olive residue oil for the purpose of differentiating between the various types and specifies methods of analysis.

These provisions are supplemented in Great Britain by the Olive Oil (Marketing Standards) Regulations 2003, as amended.

1 See case C-489/04 *Jehle and Weinhaus Kiderlen v Land Baden-Württemberg* [2006] ECR I-7509.

Fishery and aquaculture products

10.4.12 Regulation (EC) 104/2000 on the common organisation of the market in fishery and aquaculture products is also of concern to food law. Title I Chapter I includes power to determine marketing standards for these products in particular covering classification by quality, size or weight, packing, presentation and labelling.

When standards have been adopted, products to which they apply may not be displayed for sale, offered for sale or sold or otherwise marketed unless they conform to these standards, subject to special rules that may be adopted for trade with third countries. The standards that have been adopted are briefly considered in paras **10.4.13–10.4.15** below according to the different types of products.

Title I Chapter II of Regulation (EC) 104/2000 concerns consumer information. Without prejudice to the provisions of general labelling Directive 2000/13, specified fish, crustaceans and molluscs offered for retail sale to the final consumer must be labelled with the commercial name, production method and place where caught. For these purposes, Member States are required to draw up and publish a list of commercial fish designations accepted within its territory. As explained in para **9.2.25** above, this has been achieved by the Fish Labelling (England) Regulations 2003.

Specified fishery products

10.4.13 For specified saltwater fish, crustaceans (shrimps, edible crabs and Norway lobsters), cephalopods (cuttlefish), scallops and whelks, common marketing standards have been laid down by Council Regulation (EC) 2406/96, as amended, and as augmented by Commission Regulation (EEC) 3703/85 (laying down detailed rules for applying common marketing standards for certain fresh or chilled fish) and by Commission Regulation (EEC) 3863/91 (determining a minimum marketing size for crabs applicable in certain UK coastal areas).

Fishery products admitted as fit for human consumption must be classified by lot in defined freshness categories. These are E in the case of live Norway lobsters; Extra, A or B in the case of fish, selachii, cephalopods and other Norway lobsters; and Extra or A in the case of shrimps. Crabs, scallops and whelks are not subject to specific freshness standards. Products must also be sized by weight or by number per kilogram.

Products imported from third countries must comply with requirements as to packaging and labelling, while products landed from third country vessels are subject to the same provisions as Community catches.

Fishery products may be marketed only if they comply with Regulation (EC) 2406/96, for the purpose of which 'marketing' means the first offer for sale and/or the first sale on Community territory, for human consumption. The Sea Fish (Marketing Standards) Regulations 1986 provide for enforcement of these Community marketing standards by authorised officers of fishery ministers. References in the 1986 Regulations to Regulations (EC) 103/76 and 104/76 must now be read as referring to Regulation (EC) 2406/96 (see Art 15).

Preserved sardines

10.4.14 For preserved sardines and sardine type products, common marketing standards have been laid down by Council Regulation (EEC) 2136/89, which is supplemented in England and Wales by the Preserved Sardines (Marketing Standards) Regulations 1990, as amended. Requirements are prescribed as to the presentation, covering media, quality after sterilisation, trade descriptions and labelling. Marketing is restricted to compliant products.

Preserved tuna and bonito

10.4.15 For preserved tuna and bonito, common marketing standards have been laid down by Council Regulation (EEC) 1536/92, which is supplemented in Great Britain by the Preserved Tuna and Bonito (Marketing Standards) Regulations 1994, as amended. Requirements are prescribed as to the presentation, covering media and labelling of preserved tuna and bonito and the use of that description is reserved to defined products.

Fruit and vegetables

10.4.16 The classification, by reference to a set of standards, of products to be delivered fresh to the consumer has long been an element of the European Community fruit and vegetables regime. The enabling powers are now to be found in Council Regulation (EC) 1234/2007, with implementing rules being contained in Commission Regulation (EC) 1580/2007. These Regulations apply to all fruit and vegetables except potatoes, bananas, sweetcorn and olives. However, detailed marketing standards for individual types of fruit and vegetables are laid down by specific Commission Regulations. Although in an attempt to simplify the law, plans are under discussion to reduce their numbers[1], at the time of writing marketing standards still exist for 36 products including apples; pears, artichokes; asparagus; aubergines; avocados; beans; Brussels sprouts; cabbages; carrots; cauliflowers; ribbed celery; cherries; courgettes; cucumbers; lettuce; garlic; kiwifruit; leeks; lettuce; melons; onions; oranges; peaches and nectarines; peas for shelling; plums; spinach; strawberries; sweet peppers; table grapes; tomatoes; water melons; witloof chicory (endives); hazelnuts and walnuts.

Marketing within the Community of products covered by the quality standards otherwise than in conformity with the standards is prohibited[2]. However, there are exemptions for products, within a given production area, transported to preparation and packaging stations or storage facilities, or from storage facilities to preparation and packaging stations. Also exempt from compliance with the quality standards are: (a) products consigned to processing plants, unless quality criteria have been set for products for industrial processing; and (b) products transferred by the producer on his holding to consumers for their personal use.

The marketing standards for the various products are similar in that each set lays down criteria as to quality (such as colour, cleanliness, shape), size, packaging, presentation and marking.

The standards for each product generally specify three quality classifications. These are Extra Class, which must be of superior quality; Class I, which must be of good quality; and Class II, which must meet the prescribed minimum requirements.

Provision is made for the legible marking of packaging and, at the retail stage, of unpackaged products. Labelling requirements are also prescribed for sales packages of mixed fruit and vegetables. Commission Regulation (EC) 1580/2007, as amended, provides for quality inspection of fresh fruit and vegetables.

In Great Britain, the Grading of Horticultural Produce (Amendment) Regulations 1973, as amended, provide for the application, subject to modifications, of the Agriculture and Horticulture Act 1964 in relation to Community grading rules and standards.[3] Further provision is made by the Grading of Horticultural Produce (Forms of Labels) Regulations 1982 and the Horticultural Produce Act 1986. Enforcement of the Community standards in England and Wales is the responsibility of the Rural Payments Agency Inspectorate.

It should be noted that any description or mark applied in pursuance of the Agriculture and Horticulture Act 1964 or any Community grading rules within the meaning of Part III of that Act is deemed not to be a trade description.[4]

1　Mariann Fisher Boel, Commissioner for Agriculture and Rural Development, has made it clear that she would like to cut down to 10 the number of fruits and vegetables subject to marketing standards, 'We want more agriculture for our future' speech 19 June 2008 but so far all Member States are not in agreement..
2　Case C-253/00 *Antonio Muñoz Y Cia v Frumar Ltd* [2002] ECR I-7289, [2002] 3 CMLR 26.
3　See *DEFRA v ASDA* [2003] UKHL 71, [2004] 1 WLR 105, where the House of Lords made it clear that whenever Community grading rules change, the relevant sections of the 1964 Act apply automatically.
4　Trade Descriptions Act 1968, s 2(4)(d).

Bananas

10.4.17   Council Regulation (EC) 1234/2007, as amended, makes provision for common quality standards for bananas intended for consumption fresh, not including plantains. The standards are laid down by Commission Regulation (EEC) 2257/94, as amended.

Like most products subject to the fresh fruit and vegetables regime, bananas are classified into three classes. These are Extra Class, which must be of superior quality; Class I, which must be of good quality; and Class II, which must meet the specified minimum requirements. Criteria are also similarly prescribed as to size, packaging, presentation and marking with the identification of the packer and/or dispatcher; the nature of the produce; the origin of the produce; and the commercial specifications.

Commission Regulation (EEC) 2898/95, as amended, provides for verification of compliance with the standards.

The enforcement legislation and responsibilities in Great Britain for the Community grading rules and standards for bananas are the same as those described for fruit and vegetables in para **10.4.16**.

10.5   COMMUNITY REGULATIONS ON QUALITY MARKS AND LABELS

Introduction

10.5.1   Generally speaking the Commission has pursued a different quality promotion policy for agricultural products from that for products controlled within the internal market[1].

Within the framework of the common agricultural policy, we have already noted in section **10.4** above the provision made for origin marking of wine, spirit drinks and olive oil. Community quality marking provisions have also been made: (1) by Regulation (EC) 510/2006, for products that originate in areas known for their traditional production; (2) by Regulation (EC) 509/2006, for products that are subject to special production quality requirements; and (3) by Regulation (EC) 834/2007, for products produced using organic methods. These provisions are considered in paras **10.5.2–10.5.4** below.

The Commission regards the third item as but the main example of a wider class of foods that should have special status on account of their production methods. Thus, only eggs and poultrymeat complying with specified criteria have since 1991 been permitted to bear the term 'Free range' and similar expressions concerning the type of specialist farming employed in their production[2].

Although the provisions on the origin marking of beef and beef products are arguably concerned more with traceability than with laying down quality standards, it might usefully be noted here that they are mentioned in para **9.2.24** above and that the general traceability obligation imposed by Art 18 of Regulation (EC) 178/2002 is described in paras **3.2.40–3.2.43**.

The Commission's general approach to the quality of foodstuffs controlled within the internal market sector was formulated in 1985. Following the *Cassis de Dijon* judgment[3], the Commission decided normally to leave the question of quality standards and certification within the internal market to the initiative of operators. In establishing trade codes of practice, operators are encouraged to adhere to the standards recognised at international and European level, in particular the ISO 9000 and EN 29 000 series on quality management and quality assurance standards[4]. Rather than proceeding by way of legislation, the Commission has also mandated the European Committee for Standardisation (CEN) to devise a significant number of sampling and analysis methods for the purpose of enforcing of food law.[5]

Most recently, the European Community has set up a 'New European Legislative Framework' comprised of Regulation (EC) 764/2008 (which lays down procedures for the application of national rules to products lawfully marketed in another Member State), Regulation (EC) 765/2008 (which sets out requirements for accreditation and market surveillance by Member States) and Decision 768/2008 (which establishes a common framework for Community harmonisation legislation). Regulation (EC) 764/2008 is described in paras **1.3.3** and **1.4.1** above; food and feed are exempt from Regulation (EC) 765/2008; and, for reasons explained in para **1.5.1**, it seems unlikely that Decision 768/2008 will have much relevance to food and feed law.

1   Commission Green Paper COM (97) 176 on 'the General Principles of Food Law in the European Union' Part III.7.3.
2   See respectively paras **10.4.6** and **10.4.7** above.
3   See paras **1.3.1–1.3.3** above.
4   See further Council Resolution of 7 May 1985 on a new approach to technical harmonisation and standards (85/C 136/01), OJ C 136 4.6.85, and Council Resolution of 21 December 1989 on a global approach to conformity assessment (90/C 10/01) OJ C 10 16.1.90, p 1.
5   See COM (2001) 527 final: Commission Report on actions taken following the Resolutions on European Standardisation adopted by the Council and the European Parliament in 1999.

Protection of geographical indications and designations of origin

10.5.2   Provision for registration to protect geographical indications and designations of origin for agricultural products and foodstuffs is made by Council Regulation (EC) 510/2006, with the detailed rules to be found in Commission Regulation (EC) 1898/2006[1].

Regulation (EC) 510/2006 generally applies to agricultural products listed in the EC Treaty[2] and in the Regulation[3] and to foodstuffs listed in the Regulation. It covers meat and meat products, milk and dairy products, eggs, honey, fruit, vegetable and food plants, animal and vegetable fats, fish, shell fish and molluscs, spices, bread, pastries, cakes, beer and beverages made from plant extracts. However, wine products and spirits are excluded since provision is already made to protect their geographical descriptions[4].

Diversity in Member States' previous practices made it appropriate to allow for the protection of two different types of geographical description — namely, the designation of origin and the geographical indication. Each signifies the name of a region, a specific place or, exceptionally, a country, used to describe an agricultural product or a foodstuff originating in that region, place or country. In the case of a 'designation of origin', the quality or characteristics of the product must essentially or exclusively be due to a particular geographical environment with its inherent natural and human factors, and the production, processing and preparation of which take place in the defined geographical area. The term is thus used to describe foodstuffs that are produced, processed and prepared in a given geographical area using recognised know-how. By contrast, in the case of a 'geographical indication', the product must possess a specific quality, reputation or other characteristics attributable to that geographical origin and the production and/or processing and/or preparation of which takes place in the geographical area. In this case, therefore, the geographical link must occur in at least one of the stages of production, processing or preparation. In exceptional cases the definition of designation of origin is extended to certain traditional geographical or non-geographical names and to products the raw materials of which come from outside the processing area.

Subject to specified conditions, rights to register third country geographical indications and to object to registrations are conferred on third country citizens in implementation of the Agreement on Trade-Related Aspects of Intellectual Property Rights (TRIPS) 1994 .[5]

Geographical descriptions have been protected by the Community in respect of products such as meat, meat products, cheese, eggs, honey, milk products, olive oil, fruit, vegetables, cereals, natural mineral and spring waters, bread, pastry, cakes, confectionery, biscuits, baker's wares, natural gums and resins and shell fish. Among United Kingdom descriptions, 'Orkney beef', 'White Stilton cheese' and 'Jersey Royal potatoes' have been protected as designations of origin; and 'Exmoor blue cheese', 'Scotch beef', 'Herefordshire cider', 'Kentish Ale' and 'Whitstable oysters' as geographical indications.

The importance of the rights attached to registration should not be underestimated even within a Member State. Judicial review of the proposal that 'Melton Mowbray Pork Pie' should become a protected name was sought by a major producer on the ground that the specified geographical area was artificially large: their principal competitor was included but their own factories were not. The High Court rejected this challenge[6] and the excluded business is transferring production to the Melton Mowbray area.[7]

A name may not be registered if it has become generic (taking account of the existing situation in the originating and other Member States and national and Community law) or where it conflicts with the name of a plant variety or animal breed and is likely to mislead the public as to the true nature of the product.

A name may also not be registered if this is likely to mislead the consumer as to the true identity of the product due to the reputation, renown and long usage of an existing trade mark.

To be eligible to use a protected designation of origin (PDO) or a protected geographical indication (PGI) an agricultural product or foodstuff must comply with a specification, which must at least include:

(a)   the name of the agricultural product or foodstuff, including the designation of origin or geographical indication;
(b)   a description of the agricultural product or foodstuff including the raw materials, if appropriate, and principal physical, chemical, microbiological and/or organoleptic characteristics of the product or foodstuff;
(c)   the definition or the geographical area;
(d)   evidence that the agricultural product or foodstuff originates in the geographical area;
(e)   a description of the method of obtaining the agricultural product or foodstuff;
(f)   the details bearing out the link with the geographical environment or geographical origin;
(g)   details of the inspection structures;
(h)   the specific labelling details relating to the permitted designation of origin or permitted geographical indication or traditional national indication;

(i)   any requirement laid down by Community and/or national provisions. Requirements may include conditions that certain functions related to the product, such as the grating and packaging of Grana Padano cheese and the slicing and packaging of Parma ham, must take place in the region of production. [8]

Provision is made for applications for registration of designations of origin or geographical indications, for temporary protection by the Member State, for registering objections by other Member States and for registration and publication of entries in the 'Register of protected designations of origin and protected geographical indications'.

By Art 17 of the original Regulation (EEC) 2081/92 (which was repealed and replaced by Regulation (EC) 510/2006), following entry into force of the Regulation[9], Member States were allowed six months in which to forward to the Commission their legally protected names or, where there was no protection system, those of the names protected by usage that they wished to register. The prescribed objection procedure did not apply to these applications. The names registered as PDOs or PGIs as a result of this initial simplified procedure were published in Commission Regulation (EC) 1107/96, as amended. On 16 March 1999 in joined cases C-289/96, C-293/96 and C-299/96 *Denmark, Germany and France v Commission*[10], the European Court annulled Regulation (EEC) 1107/96 to the extent that it registered 'Feta' as a protected designation for cheese. As noted above, a name may not be registered if it has become generic and, in rejecting this possibility and making the registration, the Commission had failed to take account of the fact that it had been used for a considerable time for cheese produced and marketed in Member States other than Greece. Following this judgment, Commission Regulation (EC) 1070/99 deleted 'Feta' from the Register, declaring that, in accordance with Art 17(3) of Regulation 2081/92/EEC, the name 'Feta' remains protected at national level until such time as a decision was taken in this regard. Eventually feta was re-registered as a protected designation of origin by Regulation (EC) 1829/2002. Once again this was challenged in *Germany and Denmark v Commission*[11] and this time the ECJ declared that 'feta' had not become a generic name.

Names registered under the normal procedure are published in Commission Regulation (EC) 2400/96, as amended and supplemented.

A scientific expert group set up by Decision 2007/71/EC may be consulted by the Commission on any matter relating to the protection of PDOs, PGIs and Traditional Specialities Guaranteed (see para **10.5.3** below).

The indications PDO and PGI, equivalent traditional indications and the prescribed Community symbol may appear only on products that comply with Regulation (EC) 510/2006.

The registered name of the product is protected from any direct or indirect commercial use by an unregistered producer. This includes expressions such as 'style', 'type', 'method', 'as produced in', 'imitation' or similar words. False or misleading indications as to the provenance, origin, nature or essential qualities of the product on the packaging and any other practice liable to mislead the public as to the true origin of the product are also prohibited. In particular, applications for registration of a trade mark corresponding to one of these situations in relation to a registered PDO or PGI must be refused, although the use of such a trade mark registered in good faith before the application of the PDO or PGI may continue provided there are no grounds for invalidity or revocation under Council Directive 89/104/EEC to approximate the laws of Member States relating to trade marks[12]. The question of whether a constituent part of a 'compound' protected designation of origin is itself protected is a matter for determination by the national court on the basis of a detailed analysis of the facts[13].

Amendment of a PDO or PGI specification may be requested by the Member State concerned, in particular to take account of developments in scientific and technical knowledge to redefine the geographical area. A Member State may not, by adopting provisions of national law, alter a designation of origin for which it has requested registration.

Member States are obliged to have in place inspection structures to ensure that products bearing a protected name meet the requirements in the specifications. Compliance with each specification must be checked by a designated inspection authority or a private body approved for the purpose. They must offer adequate guarantees of objectivity and impartiality and must fulfil the requirements laid down in standard EN45011 of 26 June 1989 on general requirements for bodies operating product certification systems.

1   Defra has produced a guidance booklet on the EU legislation on protecting food names.
2   See EC Treaty, Annex I (ex-Annex II).
3   By Art 32 (ex-Art 38) EC, products of first-stage processing directly related to products of the soil, of stockfarming and of fisheries are themselves 'agricultural products'.
4   As to wine products, see paras **10.4.8–10.4.9**. As to spirits, see para **10.4.10**.
5   See para **1.9.1** above.
6   See *Regina* (*Northern Foods*) *v DEFRA* (2006) Times, 9 January. The application was accepted by the European Commission (see OJ C 85, 4.4.2008, p 17).
7   See '*The Melton pie is coming home'The Melton Times,* 19 July 2007.
8   See respectively case C-469/00 *Ravil Sarl v Bellon Import Sarl* [2003] ECR I-5053; and case C-108/01 *Consorzio del Prosciutto di Parma v Asda Stores Ltd* [2003] ECR I-5121.
9   Regulation 2081/92/EEC entered into force 12 months after its date of publication in the Official Journal that was 24 July 1992.
10 Joined cases C-289/96, C-293/96 and C-299/96 *Denmark, Germany and France v EC Commission* [1999] ECR I–1541.
11 Joined cases C-465/02 and C-466/02 [2005] ECR 1–9115. See C MacMaoláin, 'Eligiblity Criteria for Protected Geographical Food Names' (2006) 31 European Law Review 576.
12 See case C-87/97 *Consorzio per la tutela del formaggio Gorgonzola v Käserei Champignon Hofmeister GmbH & Co KG and Eduard Bracharz GmbH* [1999] ECR I-1301, [1999] 1 CMLR 1203 (legality of 'Cambozola' trade mark). As to Directive 89/104/EEC and the registration of geographical names as trade marks, see joined cases C-108/97 and C-109/97 *Windsurfing Chiemsee Produktions- und Vertriebs GmbH v Boots und-Segelzubehör Walter Huber* [1999] ECR I-2779.
13 See joined cases C-129/97 and C-130/97 *Chiciak and Fol* [1998] ECR I–3315; and case T-291/03 *Consorzio per la tutela del Formaggio Grana Padano v Officer for Harmonisation in the Internal Market* (*Trade marks and Design*) (*OHIM*) *sub nom. Biraghi's Community Trade Mark application* [2008] ETMR 3.

Traditional Specialities Guaranteed

10.5.3   Rules under which 'Traditional Specialities Guaranteed' may be registered are laid down by Council Regulation (EC) 509/2006 with detailed rules in Commission Regulation (EC) 1216/2007. The Community has abandoned the concept of 'certificates of specific character', formerly used to convey its recognition by registration of the special character of such specialities.[1]

Regulation (EC) 509/2006 applies to agricultural products listed in the EC Treaty[2] and to foodstuffs listed in the Regulation. More products are included than is the case for geographical indications and designations of origin. In addition to covering meat and meat products, milk and dairy products, eggs, honey, fruit, vegetable and food plants, animal and vegetable fats, fish, shell fish and molluscs, spices, bread, pastries, cakes, beer and beverages made from plant extracts, the Regulation (EC) 509/2006 list extends to chocolate, pasta, prepared dishes, sauces and seasoning, soups, ice cream and sorbets, wine and vinegar. However, the Regulation applies without prejudice to other specific Community provisions.

As defined in Regulation (EC) 509/2006:

- 'traditional speciality guaranteed' means a traditional agricultural product or foodstuff recognised by the Community for its specific character through its registration under this Regulation;
- 'traditional' means proven usage on the Community market for a time period showing transmission between generations; this time period should be the one generally ascribed to one human generation, at least 25 years; and
- 'specific character' means the characteristic or set of characteristics which distinguishes an agricultural product or foodstuff clearly from other similar products or foodstuffs of the same category.

By contrast with protected geographical indications and designations of origin, the designation 'Traditional Speciality Guaranteed' (TSG) does not refer to the origin, but emphasises traditional character, either in composition or in means of production. A product bearing it can thus be produced anywhere in the European Community. Examples of products in respect of which the TSG designation are appropriate are Belgian-style beers and mozzarella cheese. The first British TSG product was 'traditional farm fresh turkeys'.

The Commission is required to administer the 'Register of Traditional Specialities Guaranteed' which has two lists according to whether or not use of the name of the product or foodstuff is reserved to producers who comply with the specification.

As indicated, to appear in the Register, a product must either be produced using traditional raw materials or be characterised by a traditional composition or a mode of production and/or processing reflecting a traditional type of production and/or processing.

To be registered, the name must:

- be specific in itself (e g pumpernickel, haggis), traditional and comply with national provisions or be established by custom; or
- express the specific character of the product (e g corn-fed chicken) and not be misleading.

In order to qualify as a TSG, a product must comply with a product specification that must include:

(a) the name of the product in one or more languages;
(b) a description of the agricultural product or foodstuff;
(c) a description of the production method;
(d) the key elements that define the product's specific character;
(e) the key elements that prove the product's traditional character;
(f) the minimum requirements and procedures to check the specific character.

Only groups of producers, including third country groups, may apply for registration of TSGs, provision being made for objections to registrations and for amendment of product specifications. Names entered in the Register are published in Commission Regulation (EC) 2301/97, as amended.

Reference on labelling to a TSG is reserved to products complying with the relevant specification. However, the registered name is not reserved to such products, unless on application the group so requested and the name was not found to be used in a lawful, renowned and significant manner for similar products. Registered names must be protected against any practice liable to mislead the public including false suggestions that a product is a TSG.

Member States are required to designate competent authorities responsible for controls in conformity with Regulation (EC) 882/2004. Compliance with the relevant specifications must be checked before TSG products and foodstuffs are placed on the market.

1   Defra has produced a guidance booklet on the EU legislation on protecting food names.
2   See EC Treaty, Annex I (ex-Annex II).

Organic products

10.5.4   Council Regulation (EC) 834/2007 applies from 1 January 2009 and establishes criteria for the organic production and labelling of organic products. It is wider than the original Council Regulation (EEC) 2029/91 that only established criteria for the organic production of agricultural products. Regulation (EC) 834/2007 applies to plant, livestock and acquaculture production, including rules for collection of wild plants and seaweed, rules on conversion and rules on the production of processed food, including wine and feed and organic yeast. As GMOs and ionising radiation are considered incompatible with organic production they cannot be used in organic farming or in the processing of organic products.

The objectives and principles for organic production are set out in Title II and the production and labelling rules in Titles III and IV respectively. Subject to limited exceptions, the term 'organic' and other indications referring to organic production methods are reserved to products that comply with relevant provisions of Regulation (EC) 834/2007. Products must have been produced in accordance with prescribed rules, or imported from a third country under prescribed arrangements, in each case, by an operator who is subject to the specified inspection system. Processed foods must in particular be at least 95% comprised of ingredients of agricultural origin that are organic.

For the implementation of Regulation (EC) 834/2007, detailed rules are laid down by Commission Regulation (EC) 889/2008, as well as by Commission Regulation (EC) 345/2008 (in respect of imports from third countries) and Commission Regulation (EC) 605/2008 (in respect of the inspection certificate for imports from third countries).

In the United Kingdom the Community Regulations are supplemented by the Organic Products Regulations 2004 and, in respect of inspection certificate for imports, the Organic Products (Imports from Third Countries) Regulations 2003. These national provisions will require further amendment to take account of Regulation (EC) 834/2007, Regulation (EC) 605/2008 and the other Commission Regulations.

In the United Kingdom, the inspection system under Regulation (EC) 834/2007 is administered by the Advisory Committee on Organic Standards (ACOS), the successor to the Register of Organic Food Standards (UKROFS), and nine approved organic sector bodies. ACOS sets standards for organic food in accordance with the EC Regulations and certifies conformity with these standards of schemes operated by the sector bodies and of production by independent operators. Operators producing, preparing or importing organic products for the market are required to notify the competent authority and submit to the inspection system. Most fulfil these obligations by registering with a sector body or with ACOS direct.[1]

Labelling is required to include a reference to the code number of the relevant inspection body and, for pre-packed food as from 1 July 2010, the Community logo with an indication that the agricultural raw materials are EU, non-EU or both.

Imports from third countries are restricted to products produced and inspected under rules equivalent to those applying in the Community.

1   It is an infringement of the freedom to provide services under Art 49 EC for a Member State to require a private inspection body to maintain an establishment in the country in order to provide inspection services there, when that body is already approved in another Member State. See case C-393/05 *Commission v Austria* [2007] ECR I-10195, [2008] CMLR 42; and case 404/05 *Commission v Germany* [2007] ECR I-10239, [2008] 1CMLR 43.

10.6   NATIONAL REGULATIONS ON SPECIFIC FOODS

10.6.1   We have already seen how the scope to enact national food standards has been limited through the occupation of the field by Community provisions[1], the obligation to notify draft technical legislation to the Commission[2] and the European Court's *Cassis de Dijon* doctrine[3]. The exemption from national standards that this doctrine confers on many imports, coupled with the Government's inclination during the 1990s to deregulate business, led it greatly to reduce their numbers[4]. Nevertheless, even in areas that are densely controlled by Community legislation, gaps remain that it is sometimes thought right to fill. As noted in para **10.4.5** above, the Spreadable Fats (Marketing Standards) and Milk and Milk Products (Protection of Designations) (England) Regulations 2008 not only supplement the Community standards, but also continue to lay down national compulsory vitamin content requirements for margarine sold by retail[5]. The remaining national food standards are summarised below. It is interesting to observe that the margarine example above and the obligation to fortify wheat flour described in para **10.6.2** below exceptionally promote consumers' health by requiring the incorporation of particular ingredients in staple foods. Consideration is currently being given to the FSA's recommendation in May 2007 that folic acid should be compulsorily added to bread or flour to reduce the incidence of pregnancies affected by neural tube defects.

1   See para **1.1.3** above.
2   See para **1.4.1** above.
3   See paras **1.3.1** and **1.3.2** above.
4   See in particular the Food (Miscellaneous Revocations and Amendments) Regulations 1995.
5   See also para **10.2.9** on the national provisions for fruit curds and mincemeat made by the Jam and Similar Products (England) Regulations 2003.

Bread and flour

10.6.2   The Bread and Flour Regulations 1998 require, subject to exceptions, that wheat flour be fortified with specified minimum proportions of calcium carbonate, iron, thiamin (vitamin B1) and nicotinic acid or nicotinamide. The use of flour bleaching agents in flour and bread is prohibited and, in labelling bread the indication must be given of the presence of any flour improving agent. The names 'wholemeal' and 'wheat germ' are reserved to bread complying with specified requirements.

Meat products

10.6.3 In the labelling and advertising of meat products, the Meat Products (England) Regulations 2003,[1] as amended, restrict the use of specified names to products complying with prescribed meat content requirements. Meat has the definition assigned by the Food Labelling Directive 2001/101/EC, which has created a generic definition of meat for labelling purposes.

Requirements are specified for meat products that might be taken to consist purely of meat. The ingredients must, subject to exceptions, be indicated as part of the name. Products must bear a declaration of the meat or cured meat content.

1   The FSA has issued Guidance Notes, 'Labelling and Composition of Meat Products'.

Scotch whisky

10.6.4   The Scotch Whisky Order 1990 defines this product and specifies its minimum alcoholic strength. The enabling statute, the Scotch Whisky Act 1988, makes it unlawful to sell as Scotch whisky any spirits not conforming to these requirements and provides for injunctive action to restrain contraventions.[1]

As to Community legislation on Scotch whisky and other spirit drinks, see para **10.4.10** above.

1   At the time of writing Defra was consulting on draft Scotch Whisky Regulations to replace the current legislation and to enhance and safeguard the geographical indication of Scotch whisky.

10.7   REGULATIONS TO PREVENT MISLEADING DESCRIPTIONS

10.7.1   As indicated in section **8.3** above, any description of a food product that is misleading may contravene the FSA 1990[1]. In each case the court has to decide on the deceptiveness or otherwise of the description in question. In addition to this general restriction, the Food Labelling Regulations 1996 prohibit the use of specified words and descriptions[2] in the labelling or advertising of a food unless certain conditions are satisfied.

The difference between, on the one hand, reserving descriptions (summarised below) to prevent consumers from being misled about the food in question and, on the other hand, reserving descriptions (see para **10.1.2** above) so as to assure consumers of a reliable food standard, is not one of kind. In both cases, low quality food is being denied unfair use of the name that consumers expect. Indeed, the descriptions of 'ice cream', 'dairy ice cream', 'indian tonic water', 'quinine tonic water' and the various types of 'cheese' and 'cream' now protected by the Food Labelling Regulations 1996 were separately reserved to prescribed standards for these respective foods until the relevant sets of Regulations were revoked in the Government's 1995 deregulation exercise[3].

Moreover, the provisions, considered in section **11.3** below, restricting the making of claims in respect of food are likewise akin to those restricting descriptions. Whether or not the legislator aims the restriction at preventing a misleading description or a misleading claim will, it is submitted, depend on the terms in which unscrupulous traders are perceived to practice their deception. Certainly, as explained below, some descriptions considered in this section are understood to fall within the scope of Regulation (EC) 1924/2006 explained in section **11.3** concerning nutrition and health claims made on food.

Descriptions subject to conditions imposed by the Food Labelling Regulations 1996 are considered below.

By virtue of reg 3(4) and (5) of the Food Labelling Regulations 1996, the provisions described below, other than that explained in para **10.6.2**, do not apply to natural mineral water unless it has been artificially carbonated.

1   FSA 1990, s 15.
2   Food Labelling Regulations 1996, reg 42, Sch 8.
3   See the former Ice Cream Regulations 1967, SI 1967/1866; Soft Drinks Regulations 1964, SI 1964/760; Cheese Regulations 1970, SI 1970/94; and Cream Regulations 1970, SI 1970/752.

Dietary or dietetic

10.7.2   In implementation of Art 2 of Council Directive 89/398/EEC (on the approximation of the laws of the Member States relating to foodstuffs intended for particular nutritional uses)[1], the descriptions 'dietary' or 'dietetic' must not be applied to any food unless it is a food for a particular nutritional use (excluding such foods formulated for infants and young children in good health) which (a) has been specially made for a class of persons whose digestive process or metabolism is disturbed or who, by reason of their special physiological condition, obtain special benefit from a controlled consumption of certain substances and (b) is suitable for fulfilling the particular nutritional requirements of that class of persons.

1   See further para **11.7.1** below.

Flavours

10.7.3   Any description incorporating the name of a food in such a way as to imply that the food, or the part of the food, being described has the flavour of the food named in the description may not be applied to any food unless the flavour of the food is derived wholly or mainly from the food named in the description. However, any description incorporating the word 'chocolate' which is such as to imply that the food has a chocolate flavour (e g 'chocolate cake') may be applied to a food that has a chocolate flavour derived wholly or mainly from non-fat cocoa solids where the purchaser would not be misled by the description. The Food Standards Agency's 2006 revision of Guidance Notes on the Cocoa and Chocolate Products Regulations 2003 confirms that the Agency intends to examine whether this chocolate dispensation is still appropriate in the modern marketplace.

The foregoing does not prevent the use of the word 'flavour' preceded by the name of a food when the flavour of the food is not derived wholly or mainly from the food named in the description. This is to allow the use of artificial flavours and to distinguish them from flavours derived from natural foods.

A pictorial representation of a food that is such as to imply that the food to which the representation is applied has the flavour of the food depicted in the representation must not be applied to any food unless the flavour of the food to which the representation is applied is derived wholly or mainly from the depicted food.

Thus, a flavour of a soft drink may be communicated by a picture of a fruit on the label, if that flavour is derived wholly or mainly from that fruit.

Ice cream

10.7.4   The description 'ice cream' is reserved to a defined frozen product. It must contain not less than 5% fat and not less than 2.5% milk proteins, not necessarily in natural proportions. It must be obtained by subjecting an emulsion of fat, milk solids and sugar (including any sweetener permitted in ice cream by the Sweeteners in Food Regulations 1995[1]), with or without the addition of other substances, to heat treatment and either to subsequent freezing or evaporation, addition of water and subsequent freezing.

The description 'dairy ice cream' is reserved to food that fulfils these conditions and other requirements. The minimum 5% fat content must consist exclusively of milk fat and the food must contain no fat other than milk fat or any fat present by reason of the use as an ingredient of any egg, any flavouring, or any emulsifier or stabiliser.

1   See para **12.2.4** below.

Milk of animals other than cows

10.7.5   The word 'milk' or any other word or description that implies that the food being described contains milk must not be used as part of the name of a food that contains the milk of an animal other than a cow unless:

(a)   (i)   such milk has all the normal constituents in their natural proportions, and
         (ii)   the word or description is accompanied by the name of that animal; or
(b)   (i)   such milk has been subjected to a process or treatment, and
         (ii)   the word or description is accompanied by the name of that animal and an indication of that process or treatment; or
(c)   the word or description is used in accordance with any regulations or order made or continued in force under the Food Safety Act 1990.

The word 'milk' must not be used as the name of an ingredient where the ingredient is the milk of an animal other than a cow unless the word or description is accompanied by the name of that animal and its use complies in all other respects with the Food Labelling Regulations 1996.

Starch-reduced

10.7.6   This description is understood to be subject to Regulation (EC) 1924/2006 but is not listed in its Annex of permitted nutrition claims. If on the market before 1 January 2006, it has the benefit of the transitional provision in Art 28(3) and may continue to be used until 19 January 2010 subject to the conditions prescribed by the Food Labelling Regulations 1996.

These provide that the description must not be applied to any food unless less than 50% of the food consists of anhydrous carbohydrate calculated by weight on the dry matter of the food, and the starch content of a given quantity of the food is substantially less than that of the same quantity of similar foods to which the description is not applied.

Vitamins

10.7.7   The word 'vitamin' or any other word or description that implies that the food to which the word or description relates is a vitamin must not be used in labelling or advertising unless the food is one of the vitamins specified in column 1 of Table A in Sch 6 to the 1996 Regulations[1] or is vitamin K.

1   See para **11.3.12** below.

Alcohol-free

10.7.8   The description 'alcohol-free' must not be applied to any alcoholic drink from which the alcohol has been extracted, unless the drink has a strength by volume of not more than 0.05%, and it is marked or labelled with an indication of its maximum alcoholic strength immediately preceded by the words 'not more than' or, in an appropriate case, with an indication that it contains no alcohol.

Continued application of this provision is understood to be authorised by Art 4(3) of Regulation (EC) 1924/2006 on nutrition and health claims.

Dealcoholised

10.7.9   The description 'dealcoholised' must not be applied to any drink unless the drink, being an alcoholic drink from which the alcohol has been extracted, has an alcoholic strength by volume of not more than 0.5%, and is marked or labelled with an indication of its maximum alcoholic strength immediately preceded by words 'not more than' or, in an appropriate case, with an indication that it contains no alcohol. (See para **10.7.8** on the effect of Regulation (EC) 1924/2006.)

Low alcohol

10.7.10   The description 'low alcohol' or any other word or description that implies that the drink being described is low in alcohol must not be applied to an alcoholic drink unless the drink has an alcoholic strength of not more than 1.2%, and the drink is marked or labelled with an indication of its maximum alcoholic strength immediately preceded by the words 'not more than'. (See para **10.7.8** on the effect of Regulation (EC) 1924/2006.)

Low calorie

10.7.11   According to the Food Labelling Regulations 1996, the description 'low calorie' or any other word or description that implies that the drink being described is low in calories must not be applied to a soft drink unless the soft drink (where applicable, after subsequent preparation – which may include dilution – in accordance with accompanying instructions) contains not more than 10 kcal per 100 ml and 42 kJ per 100 ml of the drink. However, it is understood that this provision has now been overridden by Regulation (EC) 1924/2006 on nutrition and health claims and that the description is no longer authorised.

Non-alcoholic

10.7.12 The description 'non-alcoholic' must not be used in conjunction with a name commonly associated with an alcoholic drink, except in the composite name 'non-alcoholic wine' when that composite is used as in para **10.7.18** below. (See para **10.7.8** on the effect of Regulation (EC) 1924/2006.)

Liqueur

10.7.13 The name 'liqueur' may be applied only to a drink qualifying under the definition of that term in Regulation (EC) 110/2008[1].

1   Replacing Regulation (EEC) 1576/89. See para **10.4.10** above.

Indian tonic water or quinine tonic water

10.7.14 The name 'Indian tonic water' or 'quinine tonic water' must not be applied to any drink unless it contains not less than 57 mg of quinine (calculated as quinine sulphate BP) per litre of the drink.

Tonic wine

10.7.15 The name 'tonic wine' must not be applied to any drink unless there appears in immediate proximity to the words 'tonic wine' the clear statement: 'the name "tonic wine" does not imply health giving or medicinal properties'. No recommendation as to consumption or dosage may appear in the labelling or advertising of the drink.

Cheese

10.7.16 In the labelling or advertising of cheese, the names Cheddar, Blue Stilton, Derby, Leicester, Cheshire, Dunlop, Gloucester, Double Gloucester, Caerphilly, Wensleydale, White Stilton and Lancashire, whether or not qualified by any other words, are reserved to products that comply with maximum percentages of water respectively prescribed and contain not less than 48% milk fat.

Cream

10.7.17 In the labelling or advertising of cream, the names 'clotted cream', 'double cream', 'whipping cream', 'whipped cream', 'sterilised cream', 'cream' or 'single cream', 'sterilised half-cream' and 'half cream', whether or not qualified by any other words, are reserved to products that comply with minimum percentages of milk fat and other requirements respectively prescribed. The requirements as to milk fat content need not be complied with if the name contains qualifying words that indicate that the milk fat content is greater or less than prescribed.

The word 'wine' in composite names for other foods or drinks

10.7.18 On the authority of Art 25(2) of Regulation (EC) 479/2008, reg 43 of the Food Labelling Regulations 1996 provides that the word 'wine' may be used in a composite name that is not wine as defined in that Regulation[1], unless the composite name is likely to cause confusion with wine or table wine.

Each word in a composite name must appear in lettering of the same type and colour and of such a height that the composite name is clearly distinguishable from other products. The composite name 'non-alcoholic wine' must not be used except for a drink derived from unfermented grape juice that is intended exclusively for sacramental use and is labelled as such.

When the word 'wine' is used in a composite name for a drink that is derived from fruit other than grapes, that drink shall be obtained by an alcoholic fermentation of that fruit.

1   See Regulation 479/2008, Annex IV point 1.

Chapter 11

Food claims and nutrition

11.1 INTRODUCTION

11.1.1 This chapter deals with the related topics of food claims and nutrition. They overlap but are not co-extensive. Claims are made about matters other than nutrition. Nutritional legislation includes rules about the composition of food irrespective of how it is labelled.

In recent years Community legislation to protect consumers from misleading claims and unsafe health foods has developed considerably to supplement the long-established national safeguards in the Food Labelling Regulations 1996 and the Food Safety Act 1990. The original Council Directive 77/94/EEC which established a framework for the approximation of Member States' laws in relation to food claimed to be suitable for particular nutritional uses was replaced by Council Directive 89/398/EEC, which has been amended many times. As a result the Commission has begun the process of recasting Directive 89/398/EC to codify the text.[1] Directive 2002/46/EC has set down rules governing the production and marketing of food supplements and Regulation (EC) 1925/2006 has laid down rules on the addition of vitamins and minerals. The most important development has been Regulation (EC) 1924/2006 on nutrition and health claims. This has made provision for long awaited[2] rules to complement not only the prohibition in Art 2(1) of labelling Directive 2000/13/EC (on the use of information that could mislead the purchaser or attribute medicinal properties to food), but also now the more general prohibition in Art 16 of Regulation (EC) 178/2002 on labelling or other presentation that may mislead consumers).[3] Moreover, the Regulation has applied to health claims the requirement in Council Directive 90/496/EEC that makes nutritional labelling compulsory where nutrition claims appear on food.

The White Paper on a Strategy for Europe on Nutrition, Overweight and Obesity related health issues [4] stressed the importance of consumers having access to clear, consistent and evidence-based information. It was agreed that the effectiveness of nutrition labelling could be strengthened as a means to support the ability of consumers to choose a balanced diet, as it is an effective means of providing information to support health conscious food choices. The Commission is therefore proposing a Regulation of the European Parliament and of the Council on the provision of food information to consumers. The intention is to modernise, simplify and clarify the existing food labelling legislation. If it becomes law, the legislation will combine into one instrument Directive 2000/13/EC (described in ch 9) and Directive 90/496/EC (described in sections **11.4** and **11.5**) and result in major changes in this area.[5]

This chapter considers:

(a)   nutrition and health claims, in section **11.2**;
(b)   claims controlled by the Food Labelling Regulations, in section **11.3**;
(c)   prescribed nutrition labelling, in section **11.4**;
(d)   requirements for nutrition labelling given voluntarily, in section **11.5**;
(e)   other claims, in section **11.6**;
(f)   foodstuffs for particular nutritional uses, in section **11.7**;
(g)   food supplements, in section **11.8**; and
(h)   addition of vitamins and minerals, in section **11.9**.

1   Proposal for a Directive of the European Parliament and of the Council on foodstuffs intended
     for particular nutritional uses (Recast), COM (2008) 3 final.
2   See, in particular, Directive 2000/13/EC, Art 2(2), which in fact dates back to its predecessor,
     Directive 79/112/EEC.
3   With regard to the implementation of these provisions in domestic law, see paras **8.3.1** and
     11.3.2 as to Directive 2000/13/EC, Art 2(1)(a) and (b); and paras **3.2.36- 3.2.37** as to
     Regulation (EC) 178/2002, Art 16.
4   COM (2007) 279 final.
5   Proposal for a Regulation of the European Parliament and of the Council on the provision of
     food information to consumers, COM (2008) 40 final.

11.2   NUTRITION AND HEALTH CLAIMS

11.2.1   Food producers are often keen to make claims about the health and
nutritional benefits of the food they produce. The difficulty for the consumers is
to know what claims to believe. Directive 2000/13/EC prohibits any health
claim relating to human diseases (see below at para **11.3.1**) but this still leaves
room for a variety of claims. Countries within the EU took different approaches
to the consequent need to regulate health claims. In the United Kingdom, an
exhortatory approach was adopted, with advice being given on good practice in
complying with existing legislation in the FSA 1990, s 15 (see section **8.3**
above) and the Food Labelling Regulations 1996, reg 40 and Sch 6 (see section
11.3 below). On the basis of a 1990 Food Advisory Committee report, guidelines
on the most common nutritional claims were issued in 1999 by the Food
Standards Agency. In addition, a group representing the interests of consumers,
industry and enforcement officers[1] established a code of practice and agreed
standards for a number of generic health claims about specific foods and blood
cholesterol or heart health.

Recognising that existing discrepancies can 'act as a barrier to guaranteeing a
high level of consumer public health protection, and can constitute obstacles to
the free movement of foods and the proper functioning of the internal market'
the Commission proposed a Regulation on Nutrition and Health Claims Made
on Food.[2] There was also a desire to bring EC law in line with Codex
Alimentarius guidance on claims[3] and ease trade outside the Union. As a result,
Regulation (EC) 1924/2006, as amended, now regulates this area.[4] The
Regulations came into force on 1 July 2007 but the transitional measures mean
that there is a considerable lead in time for compliance by a number of
pre-existing foods, products and claims.

Regulation (EC) 1924/2006 does not affect Directive 89/398/EC on foodstuffs
for particular nutritional uses that remains in force (see below at para **11.7.1**).
The Regulation is executed and enforced by the Nutrition and Health Claims
(England) Regulations 2007.

1   The Joint Health Claims Initiative set up in 1997.
2   Proposal for a Regulation of the European Parliament and the Council on nutrition and health
     claims made on foods, COM (2003) 424.

3   Codex Guidelines for Use of Nutrition and Health Claims, Codex Guidelines 23/1997, revised
     2004. See also *Nutrition labels and health claims: the global regulatory environment* (WHO,
     2004).
4   The Food Standards Agency has prepared guidance, European Regulation (EC) 1924/2006 on
     nutrition and health claims made on foods: Food Standards Agency Guidance on Compliance,
     Version 1, April 2008. This is expected to be revised and updated prior to the expected adoption
     by 31 January 2010 of a list of authorised EC health claims.

11.2.2   A 'claim' is defined as 'any message or representation that is not
mandatory under Community or national legislation, including pictorial,
graphic or symbolic representation, in any form, which states, suggests or
implies that food has a particular characteristic.' A 'nutrition claim' is 'any
claim which states, suggest or implies that a food has particular beneficial
nutritional properties due to: (a) the energy (calorific value) it (i) provides; (ii)
provides at a reduced or increased rate; or (iii) does not provide; and/or (b) the
nutrients or other substances it (i) contains; (ii) contains in reduced or increased
proportions; or (iii) does not contain. As examples, the FSA Guidance, offers
'source of calcium', 'low fat', 'high fibre' and 'reduced salt'. A 'health claim' is
defined as 'any claim that states, suggests or implies that a relationship exists
between a food category, a food or one of its constituents and health.' The FSA
Guidance suggests that this would include 'calcium helps build strong bones'
and that more general claims such as 'good for you' may also be health claims.

11.2.3   Title II of Regulation (EC) 1924/2004 prescribes general principles
and conditions for the use of nutrition and health claims. Claims must not be
false, ambiguous or misleading and must not encourage or condone excess
consumption of a food. Suggestions that imply that a balanced diet cannot
provide the necessary nutrients are not permitted. Where a health claim is made,
nutrition labelling is obligatory as it is, under Directive 90/496, when a nutrition
claim is made (see para **11.3.1** and section **11.4** below).

Subject to exemptions, food must also in particular comply with specific
nutrient profiles in order to bear nutrition or health claims. The Commission is
required to establish these profiles and related conditions by 19 January 2009.

11.2.4   The nutrition claims that can be made are restricted to those set out in
the Annex in respect of which the product meets with the specific conditions of
use. For example, 'sugars-free' can only be made where the product contains no
more than 0.5g of sugars per 100g or 100 ml. The full list of authorised claims is
Low Energy; Energy-reduced; Energy-Free; Low Fat, Fat-Free; Low Saturated
Fat; Saturated Fat-Free; Low Sugars; Sugars-Free; With no added sugars; Low
Sodium/Salt; Very Low Sodium/Salt; Sodium-Free or Salt-Free; Source of
Fibre; High Fibre; Source of Protein; High Protein; Source of [Name of
Vitamin/s] and/or [Name of Mineral/s]; High [Name of Vitamin/s] and/or
[Name of Mineral/s]; Contains [Name of the Nutrient or other substance];
Increased [Name of the Nutrient]; Reduced [Name of the Nutrient]; Light/Lite;
Naturally/Natural.

11.2.5   Health claims cannot be made that: (a) suggest that health could be
affected by not consuming the food; (b) refer to the rate or amount of weight
loss; or (c) make reference to recommendations of individual doctors or health
professionals. Any health claim must be authorised and included in the list of
authorised health claims. By 31 January 2008, a list of claims, with the relevant
scientific justifications and conditions applying to them, had to be submitted by
each Member State to the European Commission who, on the advice of the
European Food Safety Authority (EFSA), must, by 31 January 2010 at the
latest, adopt the Community list of permitted claims and conditions for their
use.[1] A procedure for changes to the list is prescribed. Special provision is made

in respect of applications for the listing of claims that refer to the reduction in the risk of disease[2] or to children's development and health and of claims based on new or emerging science.

1 The Food Standards Agency website explains the UK list of potential health claims that it submitted to the EFSA on 30 January 2008.
2 Notwithstanding Directive 2000/13, Art 2(1)(b), as to which see para **11.3.2** below.

11.2.6 The Commission is obliged to establish a publicly available Community Register of nutrition and health claims showing details of rejected claims, as well as the conditions and restrictions applying to authorised ones.

11.3 CLAIMS CONTROLLED BY THE FOOD LABELLING REGULATIONS

11.3.1 Until the enactment of Regulation (EC) 1924/2006, the core provisions of British law on claims in respect of food were in the Food Labelling Regulations 1996, regs 40 and 41, read with Schs 6 and 7. It is vital to bear in mind that, since 1 July 2007, any product put on the market must comply with the requirements of Regulation (EC) 1924/2006 unless it has the benefit of a transitional measure in Art 28. In particular, nutrition claims used before 1 January 2006 may, although not listed in the Annex of authorised claims, continue in use until 19 January 2010, subject to the provisions of the Food Labelling Regulations 1996 and the Food Safety Act 1990. The FSA Guidance on Regulation (EC) 1924/2006 provides comprehensive assistance on the transitional periods and their relationship with the 1996 Regulations.

Given that during the transitional periods the national legislation will remain in place, this section continues to explain the restrictions that they impose on the making of specific claims, while endeavouring, where appropriate, to direct the reader to Directive 1924/2006. As will be observed, of particular importance to these national provisions are the conditions imposed in respect of each 'nutrition claim'. This term is defined in the Regulations as meaning 'any statement, suggestion or implication in any labelling, presentation or advertising of a food that that food has particular nutritional properties, but does not include a reference to any quality or quantity of any nutrient where such reference is required by law'. In implementation of Art 2(2) of Council Directive 90/496/EEC (on the nutrition labelling of food), the Regulations require nutrition labelling to be given when a nutrition claim is made. As will be seen below, this is achieved in relation to the various nutrition claims, by requiring the food in question to be marked or labelled with the 'prescribed nutrition labelling'. The detailed provisions imported by the use of this term are explained later in section **11.4**.

It should be noted that the requirements summarised in section **11.3** are subject to qualifications set out in reg 41(1)–(3) of the Food Labelling Regulations 1996. Thus, nothing in the provisions as to claims should be taken to prevent the dissemination of useful information or recommendations intended exclusively for persons having qualifications in dentistry, medicine, nutrition, dietetics or pharmacy[1]. In implementation of Art 6(2) of Directive 89/398/EEC, this provision is an exception to the prohibition on claims that a food has the property of preventing, treating or curing a human disease noted in para **11.3.2** below. Moreover, a reference to a substance in a list of ingredients or in any nutrition labelling does not of itself constitute a claim of a type considered below[2].

Finally, any condition that a food shall be labelled with the prescribed nutrition labelling shall not apply in the case of:

(a)   a food (other than sold from a vending machine) which is not prepacked and that is sold to the ultimate consumer at a catering establishment, or

(b)   a claim contained within generic advertising.

For food described at (a), elements of the prescribed nutrition labelling may nevertheless be given subject, *mutatis mutandis*, to compliance with relevant provisions described in section **11.4**[3].

Also, reg 41(5) makes it clear that the regulations cannot prohibit or restrict a claim made in accordance with the conditions of Regulation (EC) 1924/2006 on nutrition and health claims made on foods (see above and para **11.2**).

By virtue of reg 3(4) and (5) of the Food Labelling Regulations 1996, of the claims provisions described in sections **11.3** and **11.4**, only those described in para **11.3.4** apply to natural mineral water (other than such water that has been artificially carbonated).

1   Food Labelling Regulations 1996, reg 41(1).
2   Food Labelling Regulations 1996, reg 41(2).
3   Food Labelling Regulations 1996, reg 41(3).

Prohibited claims[1]

11.3.2   The Regulations wholly forbid the making, either expressly or by implication, of two kinds of claims in the labelling or advertising of food. The first of these is any claim that a food has tonic properties. However, the use of the word 'tonic' in the description 'Indian tonic water' or 'quinine tonic water' does not of itself constitute such a claim.

Secondly, in implementation of Art 2(1)(b) of the general food labelling Directive 2000/13/EC and Art 6(1) of the particular nutritional uses Directive 89/398/EEC, a claim that a food has the property of preventing, treating or curing a human disease or any reference to such a property is prohibited[2]. An exception is noted in para **11.3.1** above and the provision is subject to Directive 1924/2006 which, as explained in para **11.2.5** above, allows for the possibility of listing claims which refer to the reduction in the risk of disease.

1   Food Labelling Regulations 1996, reg 40(1) and Pt I of Sch 6.
2   See case C-221/2000 *Commission v Austria* [2003] ECR I–1007.

Restricted claims: generally[1]

11.3.3   A claim of a type described in paras **11.3.4–11.3.11** below shall not be made, either expressly or by implication, in the labelling or advertising of a food except in accordance with the stated appropriate conditions. Where a claim of two or more of these types is made, the conditions appropriate to each must be observed.

1   Food Labelling Regulations 1996, reg 40(2) and (3) and Pt II of Sch 6.

Claims relating to foods for particular nutritional uses

11.3.4   In implementation of Council Directive 89/398/EEC[1], claims that a food is suitable, or has been specially made for a particular nutritional purpose are subject to the conditions set out below. 'Particular nutritional purpose' is defined as the fulfilment of the particular nutritional requirements of:

(a)   a person whose digestive processes are, or whose metabolism is disturbed, or

(b)   a person whose physiological condition renders him able to obtain a special benefit from the controlled consumption of any substance in food, or

(c)   infants or young children[2] in good health.

Conditions

1. The food must be capable of fulfilling the claim.

2. The food must be marked or labelled with an indication of the particular aspects of its composition or manufacturing process that give the food its particular nutritional characteristics.

3. The food:

(a)   must be marked or labelled with the prescribed nutrition labelling[3] and may be marked or labelled with further information in respect of either or both of:
>   (i) any nutrient or component of a nutrient (whether or not a claim is made in respect of such nutrient or component), or
>   (ii) any other component or characteristic which is essential to the food's suitability for its particular nutritional use, and

(b)   when sold to the ultimate consumer, must be prepacked and completely enclosed by its packaging.

1   See further para **11.7.1** below.
2   By the Food Labelling Regulations 1996, reg 2(1), 'infants' is defined as children under the age of 12 months and 'young children' as children between one and three years.
3   See para **11.3.1** and section **11.4**.

Reduced or low energy value claims

11.3.5   Although the Food Labelling Regulations 1996 still contain the provisions described here, it appears that the conditions prescribed by Regulation (EC) 1924/2006 in respect of 'Low energy' and 'Energy- reduced' claims now apply.

Claims that a food has a reduced or low energy value are, under the Food Labelling Regulations 1996, subject to the conditions set out below. There are two qualifications to this. First, the appearance of the words 'low calorie' on a container of soft drink in accordance with the conditions in Sch 11 to the Food Labelling Regulations 1996[1] does not of itself constitute a claim. Secondly, where a food is in concentrated or dehydrated form and is intended to be reconstituted by the addition of water or other substances, condition 2 below applies to the food when reconstituted as directed.

Conditions

1. If the claim is that the food has a reduced energy value, the energy value of a given weight of the food, or of a given volume in the case of a liquid food, must not be more than three quarters of that of the equivalent weight, or volume, of a similar food in relation to which no such claim is made, unless the food is:

(a)   an intense sweetener, or
(b)   a product which consists of a mixture of an intense sweetener with other

substances and which, when compared on a weight for weight basis, is significantly sweeter than sucrose.

2. If the claim is that the food has a low energy value:

(a)   the energy value of the food must not be more than 167 kJ (40 kcal) per 100 g or 100 ml, as appropriate, unless the food is:

    (i) an intense sweetener, or

    (ii) a product which consists of a mixture of an intense sweetener with other substances and which, when compared on a weight for weight basis, is significantly sweeter than sucrose,

(b)   the energy value of a normal serving of the food must not be more than 167 kJ (40 kcal), and

(c)   in the case of an uncooked food which naturally has a low energy value, the claim must be in the form 'a low energy food' or 'a low calorie food' or 'a low joule food'.

3. The food must be marked or labelled with the prescribed nutritional labelling[2].

1   See para **10.7.11** above.
2   See para **11.3.1** and section **11.4**.

Protein claims

11.3.6   Although the Food Labelling Regulations 1996 still contain the provisions described here, it appears that the conditions prescribed by Regulation (EC) 1924/2006 in respect of 'Source of protein' and 'High protein' claims now apply.

  Under the Food Labelling Regulations 1996, claims that a food, other than a food intended for babies or young children[1] which satisfy the conditions of the item described in para **11.3.4** above, is a source of protein are subject to the conditions set out below.

Conditions

1. The quantity of the food that can reasonably be expected to be consumed in one day must contribute at least 12 g of protein.

2.

(1)   If the claim is that the food is a rich or excellent source of protein, at least 20% of the energy value of the food must be provided by protein.

(2)   In any other case at least 12% of the energy value of the food must be provided by protein.

3. The food must be marked or labelled with the prescribed nutritional labelling[2].

1   By the Food Labelling Regulations 1996, reg 2(1), 'young children' is defined as children between one and three years.
2   See para **11.3.1** and section **11.4**.

Vitamin claims

11.3.7   It appears that the conditions prescribed by Regulation (EC) 1924/2006 in respect of 'Source of vitamins' and 'High in vitamins' claims now apply, except as regards a generic claim 'contains vitamins'. In that case, if the claim was in use before 1 January 2006 it may, by virtue of the transitional provision in Art 28(3), continue to be used until 19 January 2010 subject to the conditions prescribed by the Food Labelling Regulations 1996.

Under the Food Labelling Regulations 1996, claims that a food other than a food intended for babies or young children[1] which satisfies the conditions of the item described in para **11.3.4** above, is a source of vitamins are subject to the conditions set out below. Table A referred to in this paragraph is in para **11.3.12**.

A reference to a vitamin in the name of a food does not of itself constitute a claim of a type to which this item applies if the food consists solely of:

(i)   vitamins, or
(ii)   a mixture of vitamins and minerals, or
(iii) a mixture of vitamins, or vitamins and minerals, and a carrying agent, or
(iv)   a mixture of vitamins, or of vitamins and minerals, and other substances sold in tablet, capsule or elixir form.

Conditions

1.

(1)   If the claim is not confined to named vitamins, every vitamin named in the claim must be a vitamin specified in column 1 of Table A below, and:
    (a) where the claim is that the food is a rich or excellent source of vitamins, the quantity of the food that can reasonably be expected to be consumed in one day must contain at least one half of the recommended daily allowance of two or more of the vitamins specified in column 1 of Table A below, and
    (b) in any other case, the quantity of the food that can reasonably be expected to be consumed in one day must contain at least one sixth of the recommended daily allowance of two or more of the vitamins specified in column 1 of Table A below.

(2)   If the claim is confined to named vitamins, every vitamin named in the claim must be a vitamin specified in column 1 of Table A below, and:
    (a) where the claim is that the food is a rich or excellent source of vitamins, the quantity of the food that can reasonably be expected to be consumed in one day must contain at least one half of the recommended daily allowance of every vitamin named in the claim, and
    (b) in any other case, the quantity of the food that can reasonably be expected to be consumed in one day must contain at least one sixth of the recommended daily allowance of every vitamin named in the claim.

2. The food must be marked or labelled:
    (a) in the case of a food to which nutrition labelling[2] relates:

        (i) where the claim is in respect of unnamed vitamins (whether alone or together with named vitamins), then in respect of any of those unnamed vitamins that are listed in Table A, with the prescribed nutrition labelling[3] and, in addition, with a statement of the percentage of the recommended daily allowance for such vitamins as are contained in either a quantified serving of the food or, provided that the total number of portions contained in the sales unit of the food is stated, in one such portion of the food, and

(ii) where the claim is in respect of a named vitamin or of named vitamins (whether alone or together with unnamed vitamins), then in respect of that named vitamin or those named vitamins, with the prescribed nutrition labelling[3] and, in addition, with a statement of the percentage of the recommended daily allowance for such vitamins as are contained in either a quantified serving of the food or, provided that the total number of portions contained in the sales unit of the food is stated, in one such portion of the food, and

(b) in the case of food supplements or waters other than natural mineral waters, in respect of any vitamins, whether unnamed, named or both:

(i) with a statement of the percentage of the recommended daily allowance of those vitamins contained in either a quantified serving of the food or (provided that the food is prepacked) a portion of the food, and

(ii) where the food is prepacked, of the number of portions contained in the package,

and the name used in any such marking or labelling for any such vitamin shall be the name specified for that vitamin in column 1 of Table A in para **11.3.12**.

1   By the Food Labelling Regulations 1996, reg 2(1), 'young children' is defined as children between one and three years.
2   As to the meaning of 'nutrition labelling', see para **11.5.1** below.
3   See para **11.3.1** and section **11.4**.

Mineral claims

11.3.8   It appears that the conditions prescribed by Regulation (EC) 1924/2006 in respect of 'Source of minerals' and 'High in minerals' claims now apply, except as regards a generic claim 'contains minerals'. In that case, if the claim was in use before 1 January 2006 it may, by virtue of the transitional provision in Art 28(3), continue to be used until 19 January 2010 subject to the conditions prescribed by the Food Labelling Regulations 1996.

Under the Food Labelling Regulations 1996, claims that a food other than a food intended for babies or young children[1] which satisfies the conditions of the item described in para **11.3.4** above, is a source of minerals are subject to the conditions specified below.

A claim that a food has a low or reduced level of minerals shall not be regarded as a claim of a type described in this item.

The note on the item summarised in para **11.3.7** above applies equally to this item with the substitution of the word 'mineral(s)' for 'vitamin(s)' and vice versa as appropriate. Table B referred to in this paragraph is in para **11.3.12**.

Conditions

The conditions are the same as those set out in the item described in para **11.3.7** above with appropriate substitution of the word 'mineral' for 'vitamin' and 'Table B' for 'Table A'.

1   By the Food Labelling Regulations 1996, reg 2(1), 'young children' is defined as children between one and three years.

Cholesterol claims

11.3.9 It appears that Regulation (EC) 1924/2006 now applies so that use of this claim on the market before 1 January 2006 has the benefit of the transitional provision in Art 28(3) and may continue until 19 January 2010 subject to the conditions prescribed by the Food Labelling Regulations 1996.

Under the Food Labelling Regulations 1996, claims relating to the presence or absence of cholesterol[1] in a food are subject to the conditions set out below.

Conditions

1. Subject to condition 3, the food must contain no more than 0.005% of cholesterol.

2. The claim must not be accompanied by a suggestion, whether express or implied, that the food is beneficial to human health because of its level of cholesterol.

3. If the claim relates to the removal of cholesterol from, or its reduction in, the food and condition 1 is not met, such claims shall only be made:

(a)   as part of an indication of the true nature of the food,
(b)   as part of an indication of the treatment of the food,
(c)   within the list of ingredients, or
(d)   as a footnote in respect of a prescribed nutrition labelling[2].

4. The food must be marked or labelled with the prescribed nutritional labelling[2].

1   Cheshire County County Council Fair Trading and Advice Service v Mornflakes Oats Ltd (1993) 157 JP 1011.
2   See para **11.3.1** and section **11.4**.

Other nutrition claims

11.3.10 Nutrition claims not dealt with under any of the items described in paras **11.3.4–11.3.9** above are subject to the conditions specified below.

Conditions

1. The food must be capable of fulfilling the claim.

2. The food must be marked or labelled with the prescribed nutritional labelling[1].

1   See para **11.3.1** and section **11.4**.

Claims that depend on another food

11.3.11 By Art 5(3) of Regulation (EC) 1924/2006, nutrition and health claims must refer to the food ready for consumption in accordance with the manufacturer's instructions. This takes precedence over the Food Labelling Regulations 1996, but a claim of this kind used on the market before 1 January 2006 has the benefit of the transitional provision in Art 28(3) and may continue in use until 19 January 2010 subject to the conditions prescribed by the Food Labelling Regulations 1996.

These provide that, in the case of claims that a food has a particular value or conveys a particular benefit, the value or benefit must not be derived wholly or partly from another food that is intended to be consumed with the food in relation to which the claim is made.

Vitamins and minerals

11.3.12 The tables referred to in paras **11.3.7** and **11.3.8** above in relation to vitamins and minerals respectively are as follows:

Table A – Vitamins in respect of which claims may be made

Vitamin	Recommended daily allowance
Vitamin A	1100 micro g
Vitamin D	5 micro g
Vitamin E	10 mg
Vitamin C	60 mg
Thiamin	1.4 mg
Riboflavin	0.16 mg
Niacin	111 mg
Vitamin B6	2 mg
Folacin	200 micro g
Vitamin B12	1 micro g
Biotin	0.15 mg
Pantothenic acid	6 mg

Table B – Minerals in respect of which claims may be made

Mineral	Recommended daily allowance
Calcium	1100 mg
Phosphorus	1100 mg
Iron	14 mg
Magnesium	300 mg
Zinc	15 mg
Iodine	150 micro g

Note: As a rule, a significant amount means 15% of the recommended daily allowance listed in respect of each vitamin and mineral specified in Table A and B above that is supplied by 100 g or 100 ml of a food, or per package of a food if the package contains only a single portion.

11.4 PRESCRIBED NUTRITION LABELLING

11.4.1 As noted in section **11.3**, the Community requirement that nutrition labelling must be given where a nutrition claim appears is imposed by the condition that the food must be marked or labelled with the 'prescribed nutritional labelling'. Parts I and II of Sch 7 to the Food Labelling Regulations 1996 respectively set out the requirements for the presentation and the contents of prescribed nutritional labelling[1]. These provisions are summarised below.

It should be noted that Art 2(2) of nutrition labelling Directive 90/496, which these provisions implement, is applied directly by Art 7 of Regulation (EC) 1924/2006 so that nutrition labelling is required where a health claim is made, as well as where a nutrition claim is made (see para **11.2.3**).

1   In relation to the requirements of the 1996 Regulations that implement nutrition labelling Directive 90/496/EEC, Guidance Notes on Nutrition Labelling were issued by the Ministry of Agriculture, Fisheries and Food in May 1999. These notes precede the establishment of the Food Standards Agency but remain valid.

Contents of prescribed nutrition labelling

11.4.2 For the purposes of explanation, it will be clearer to deal first with the contents of prescribed nutritional labelling.

Subject to exceptions mentioned below for non-prepacked foods, prescribed nutrition labelling must consist of one of the two following groups of information:

(a)   by the first alternative called 'group 1' by Directive 90/496/EEC, the information given must be the energy and the amounts of protein, carbohydrate and fat;

(b)   by the second alternative called 'group 2' by Directive 90/496/EEC, the information given must be the energy and the amounts of protein, carbohydrate, sugars, fat, saturates, fibre and sodium.

Where a nutrition claim is made for sugars, saturates, fibre or sodium, the information given must be in accordance with (b).

The amounts of any polyols, starch, mono-unsaturates, polyunsaturates, cholesterol and, if present in significant amounts, minerals or vitamins may also be included in the nutrition labelling and must be included where such is the subject of a nutrition claim. As a rule, 'a significant amount', in relation to vitamins or minerals, means 15% of the recommended daily allowance listed in respect of each vitamin or mineral specified in Table A or B in para **11.3.12** that is supplied by 100 g or 100 ml of a food, or per package of a food if the package contains only a single portion.

Where the amount of any mono-unsaturates, polyunsaturates or cholesterol is given with labelling in accordance with (a) above, the amount of saturates must also be included.

Where such is the subject of a nutrition claim, the prescribed nutrition labelling must also include the name and amount of any substance that belongs to, or is a component of, one of the nutrients already required or permitted to be included. As examples of components, the MAFF Guidance notes give fructose as a component of sugars and trans fatty acids as a component of fat.

In exercise of the derogation in Art 11 of Directive 90/496/EEC, the prescribed nutritional labelling that must be borne by non-prepacked food sold to ultimate consumers, other than at catering establishments, from vending machines and to catering establishments, is restricted to information about any nutrition claim, but information may be given voluntarily for any or all of the energy or nutrients listed in the Regulations.

Presentation of prescribed nutrition labelling

11.4.3   The rules on the presentation of prescribed nutrition labelling are in Part I of Sch 7 to the Food Labelling Regulations 1996. Subject to the further provisions below, the order and manner of prescribed nutrition labelling must, where appropriate, be as follows:

energy value			[x] kJ and [x] kcal
protein			[x] g
carbohydrate			[x] g
	of which:		
		—sugars	[x] g
		—polyols	[x] g
		—starch	[x] g
fat			[x] g
	of which:		
		—saturates	[x] g
		—mono-unsaturates	[x] g
		—polyunsaturates	[x] g
		—cholesterol	[x] mg
fibre			[x] g
sodium			[x] g
[vitamins]			[x units]
[minerals]			[x units].

If there is also an obligation to give the name and amount of any substance that belongs to, or is a component of, an item already given, the substance or component must be listed immediately after the item to which it relates, thus:

[item]		[x] g or mg
	of which:	
	— [substance or component]	[x] g or mg.

For [vitamins] and [minerals] there shall be substituted, as appropriate, the names of any vitamin or mineral listed in Table A or B listed in para **11.3.12** above.

For [item] there shall be substituted the name of the relevant item [from the above list].

For [substance or component] there shall be substituted the name of the substance or component.

For [x] there shall be substituted the appropriate amount in each case and, in respect of vitamins and minerals, such amounts:

(i)   shall be expressed in the units of measurement specified in relation to the respective vitamins and minerals given in Table A or B listed in para **11.3.12** above, and

(ii)   shall also be expressed as a percentage of the recommended daily allowance specified for such vitamins and minerals in those Tables.

In implementation of Art 6 of Directive 90/496/EEC, all amounts are required to be given per 100 g or 100 ml, as appropriate. In addition, this information may be given per serving as quantified on the label or per portion, provided that the number of portions contained in the package is stated. The amounts shall be as contained in the food sold to the ultimate consumer or to a catering establishment, or they may (if expressly said to be so) be such amounts as are contained in the food after the completion of such preparation in accordance with detailed instructions given for the preparation for consumption of the food.

The amounts shall be averages based, either alone or in any combination, on:

(i)   the manufacturer's analysis of the food;

(ii)   a calculation from the known or actual values of the ingredients used;

(iii)   a calculation from generally established and accepted data,

and 'averages' means the figures which best represent the respective amounts of the nutrients that a given food contains, there having been taken into account seasonal variability, patterns of consumption and any other factor which may cause the actual amount to vary.

In implementation of Art 5 of Directive 90/496/EEC, the following conversion factors are required to be used for the purposes of calculating the energy value:

*   1 g of carbohydrate (excluding polyols) shall be deemed to contribute 17 kJ (4 kcal)
*   1 g of polyols shall be deemed to contribute 10 kJ (2.4 kcal)
*   1 g of protein shall be deemed to contribute 17 kJ (4 kcal)
*   1 g of fat shall be deemed to contribute 37 kJ (9 kcal)
*   1 g of ethanol shall be deemed to contribute 29 kJ (7 kcal)
*   1 g of organic acid shall be deemed to contribute 13 kJ (3 kcal)
*   1 gram of salatrims shall be deemed to contribute to 25kJ (6 kcal).

In implementation of Art 7 of Directive 90/496/EEC, any prescribed nutrition labelling is required to be printed together in one conspicuous place:

(a)   in tabular form, with any numbers aligned, or

(b)   if there is insufficient space to permit tabular listing, in linear form.

11.5   REQUIREMENTS FOR NUTRITION LABELLING GIVEN VOLUNTARILY

11.5.1   Paragraph **11.1.2** referred to the Community requirement that nutrition labelling, if given, must be given in accordance with specified rules. This requirement is to be found in Arts 2(1) and 4 of the nutrition labelling Directive 90/496/EEC and is implemented in Great Britain by reg 41(4) of and Sch 7 to the Food Labelling Regulations 1996.

As defined by the Food Labelling Regulations 1996, 'nutrition labelling', in relation to a food (other than a natural mineral water or other water intended for human consumption or any food supplement), means any information appearing on labelling (other than where it appears solely as part of a list of ingredients) and relating to energy value or any nutrient or to energy value and any nutrient, including any information relating to any substance which belongs to, or is a component of, a nutrient.

Where food is labelled voluntarily with nutrition labelling, the requirements for prescribed nutrition labelling[1] apply except in two express particulars. These are the requirements that[2]:

(a)   the Group 2 information must be given where a nutrition claim is made for sugars, saturates, fibre or sodium; and
(b)   the labelling must include the name and amount of any substance that belongs to, or is a component of, one of the nutrients required or permitted to be included, where such is the subject of a nutrition claim.

1   See section **11.3**.
2   See para **11.3.2**.

11.6   OTHER CLAIMS

11.6.1   In addition to legislative requirements regarding claims in Regulation (EC) 1924/2006 and the Food Labelling Regulations 1996, mention should be made of certain non-statutory material that can constitute a guide to good practice and might be relevant in proceedings, for example, under s 15 of the FSA 1990[1].

Useful sources are to be found in guidance notes prepared by the Food Standards Agency and standards drawn up by the Codex Alimentarius Commission[2]. The work of the Codex Alimentarius Commission continues to contribute to the development of international food standards, not least in relation to labelling and nutrition claims.

This section considers non-statutory material on:

(a)   claims that food is 'fresh', 'pure', natural' etc;
(b)   claims about 'vegetarian' and 'vegan' food;
(c)   claims concerning food assurance schemes.

1   See section **8.3**.
2   See para **1.9.2**.

'Fresh', 'Pure', 'Natural' etc claims

11.6.2   The Food Standards Agency, following research, issued revised guidance in July 2008 on the 'Criteria for the use of the terms fresh, pure, natural, etc in food labelling.' The guidelines do not have the force of law .

The guidance gives revised definitions for the following marketing terms: 'original', 'traditional', 'authentic', 'real', 'fresh', 'pure', 'natural'[1] and 'farm-house'. The original recommendations for the term 'homemade' have been maintained and guidance has also been added for the following terms: 'farm-house (pâté)', 'hand-made', 'selected', 'quality', 'premium', 'finest', 'best', 'seasonal' 'style', 'wild' and 'type'.

The aim of the guidance is to help manufacturers, producers, retailers and caterers decide when to use such descriptions; to assist enforcement authorities to provide consistent advice about labelling; and to help consumers. The Food

Standards Agency believes that by encouraging consistent and transparent labelling practices, consumers are better able to make an informed choice about the products they purchase.

In terms of general best practice, the guidance recommends that before any term is used the following points should be considered and applied where possible:

(a)   foods should be sold without deceit and therefore should be labelled and advertised so as to enable a prospective purchaser to make a fair and informed choice, based on clear and informative labelling;

(b)   a food must be able to fulfil the claim being made for it and therefore adequate information must be available to show that the claim is justified;

(c)   where the use of the marketing term is potentially ambiguous or imprecise, the likely understanding of the 'average' consumer is a good benchmark; and

(d)   claims should allow fair comparison and competition between products, sectors and traders.

As pictures etc have at least the same potential as words to mislead, the guidance stresses that it is important that as much attention is paid to background illustrations and pictures, as is to the written word. The labelling and presentation of food as a whole should be used in assessing whether a particular label or description is likely to be considered misleading. The guidance considers that it is not appropriate to use any marketing term unless its meaning is clear. Where any qualification or explanation is necessary to understand the meaning of the marketing term this should accompany the term and associated imagery.

1   As to the meaning of the word 'natural' used in relation to orange juice and strawberry jam, see respectively *Amos v Britvic* (1984) 149 JP 13; and case C-465/98 *Darbo* [2000] ECR I-2297. As to the use of the term 'natural' in relation to flavouring ingredients, see para **9.2.9** above.

'Vegetarian' and 'Vegan'

11.6.3   There is no legal definition of 'vegetarian or 'vegan' but the Food Standards Agency has produced guidance on the use of these terms in food labelling. The Agency suggests that the term 'vegetarian' should not be applied to foods that are, or are made from, or with, the aid of products derived from animals that have died, have been slaughtered or animals that die as a result of being eaten. The term 'vegan' should not be applied to foods that are, or are made from or with the aid of animals or animal products. Products that use additives such as milk and eggs would be suitable to be labelled 'vegetarian' but not 'vegan'. It is important that the risk of contamination is avoided if the food is to be labelled appropriately.

Food assurance schemes

11.6.4   Food assurance schemes are voluntary systems (with the exception of organic schemes that are regulated by Regulation (EC) 2092/91) which aim to verify that farmers and growers meet certain standards of production. Members of a scheme can use the scheme's logo on their produce and/or use a specific claim to advertise to consumers that the product has been produced to this standard. The Food Standards Agency has produced guidance on these schemes to try and ensure that the standards behind the schemes are communicated to the consumers as transparently as possible. The Agency recommends that minimum standards applied to the participating producers by an assurance scheme should be set by a board with a strong independent element, that producers should be regularly inspected and that clear procedures for dealing with non-compliance should be introduced and effectively implemented. It is considered to be important that consumers are made aware in what ways, if any, the scheme standards exceed the legal minimum.

11.7 FOODSTUFFS FOR PARTICULAR NUTRITIONAL USES

11.7.1 Council Directive 89/398/EEC, as amended, provides a Community framework for provisions relating to foodstuffs intended for particular nutritional uses, often colloquially designated 'PARNUTS'. These products are foodstuffs which, owing to their special composition or manufacturing process, are clearly distinguishable from foodstuffs for normal consumption, which are suitable for their claimed nutritional purposes and which are marketed in such a way as to indicate such suitability[1]. As indicated in para **11.3.4**[2], a particular nutritional use must fulfil the particular nutritional requirements of persons falling within one of three defined categories. Subject to any changes necessary to meet these criteria, the products must comply with mandatory provisions applicable to foodstuffs for normal consumption[3] as well as bearing the prescribed nutrition labelling.

A few substantive provisions in Directive 89/398/EEC have called for implementation by the Food Labelling Regulations 1996[4]. A key element is Art 4 that confers on the Commission power to draw up specific implementing provisions for six groups of foods for particular nutritional uses[5]. Specific Directives have been enacted for the following groups:

(a)   infant formulae and follow-on formulae,
(b)   processed cereal-based foods and baby foods for infants and young children,
(c)   foods intended for use in energy-restricted diets for weight reduction, and
(d)   dietary foods for special medical purposes.

In the context of the implementing Regulations, the requirements of these Directives are respectively summarised in paras **11.7.2–11.7.5** below.

Article 4(2) of Directive 89/398/EEC provides for the establishment of a list of substances that may be used in the manufacture of foods for particular nutritional uses. Lists were included in the specific Directives on infant formulae and follow-on formulae and on processed cereal-based foods and baby foods for infants and young children. The substances authorised for addition to other 'parnuts' foods are listed in Directive 2001/15/EC explained in para **11.7.6**.

Additionally, Art 4a of Directive 89/398/EEC provides for the adoption of rules governing the use of terms concerning low-sodium foods and gluten-free foods[6].

For foodstuffs for particular nutritional uses which do not belong to one of the specified groups, Art 9 of Directive 89/398/EEC requires the national competent authority to be notified when a product is first placed on the market. The Notification of Food for Particular Nutritional Uses (England)

Regulations 2007 confirm the Food Standards Agency as the competent authority and prohibit the sale of such products if the correct notification has not been given. The 2007 Regulations also enable the FSA, by written declaration, to suspend or restrict trade in specified products intended for a particular nutritional use where it has detailed grounds for establishing that the product does not comply with Art 1(2) of the Directive or endangers human life.

1   See case C-107/97 *Ministère Public v Max Rombi* [2000] ECR I-3367.
2   The term considered in para **11.3.4** is 'particular nutritional purpose' used in the Food Labelling Regulations 1996, Sch 6, Pt II item 1. However that provision implements the definition of 'foodstuffs for particular nutritional uses' in Directive 89/398/EEC and the three categories of persons are in substance the same.
3   See C-101/98 *Union Deutsche Lebensmittelwerke GmbH v Schutzverband gegen Unwesen* [1999] ECR I-8841.
4   See paras **10.7.2**, **11.3.2** and **11.3.4**.
5   Regulation of additives permitted in foodstuffs intended for particular nutritional uses is reserved to the Council.
6   The Commission is currently consulting on a draft Regulation concerning the composition and labelling of foodstuffs suitable for people intolerant to gluten based on a Codex Alimentarius standard.

Infant formula and follow-on formula

11.7.2   The Infant Formula and Follow-on Formula (England) Regulations 2007, as amended,[1] implement Commission Directive 2006/141/EC (on infant formulae and follow-on formulae), as amended, and Council Directive 92/52/EEC (on infant formulae and follow-on formulae intended for export to third countries) and are intended to ensure stricter controls on the promotion, labelling and compostion of infant formula and follow-on formula.[2]

For the purposes of the Regulations, 'infant formulae' are defined as foodstuffs intended for particular nutritional use by infants during the first few months of life, and satisfying by themselves the nutritional requirements of such infants until the introduction of appropriate complementary feeding and 'follow-on formulae' are defined as foodstuffs intended for particular nutritional use by infants when appropriate complementary feeding is introduced, and constituting the principal liquid element in a progressively diversified diet of such infants.

The marketing of infant formula or follow-on formula is prohibited unless it complies with specified requirements as to composition, labelling, appearance and packaging. There are strict limits on the maximum levels of pesticides that may be present. Similar compositional restrictions are imposed on exports to third countries. Advertising of infant formula and follow-on formula is restricted and specified promotion of infant formula prohibited, so as not to discourage breastfeeding. Requirements are also laid down about the provision of information and education regarding infant and child feeding.

1   The FSA has issued Guidance Notes on the Infant Formula and Follow-On Formula Regulations 2007, Revision 1, May 2008.
2   In *R (on the application of the Infant & Dietetic Food Association Ltd) v Secretary of State for Health, the Welsh Ministers* [2008] EWHC 575 (Admin) the lack of transitional arrangements for bringing the Regulations into force with regard to labelling and packaging was successfully challenged. As a result the Regulations were amended to take account of this ruling and there is now a transitional period until 1 January 2010 as regards the labelling of infant formula and follow-on formula; and with regard to presentation in so far as it relates to the shape, appearance and packaging of infant formula and follow-on formula.

Processed cereal-based foods and baby foods for infants and young children

11.7.3   The Processed Cereal-based Foods and Baby Foods for Infants and Young Children Regulations 2003, as amended, implement Commission Directive 2006/125/EC (on processed cereal-based foods and baby foods for infants and young children), as amended.

For the purposes of the Regulations, 'processed cereal-based foods' are foods for particular nutritional use within specified categories of cereal products fulfilling the particular requirements of infants and young children in good health and intended for use by infants while they are being weaned, and by young children as a supplement to their diet and/or for their progressive adaptation to ordinary food and 'baby foods' are other foods for particular nutritional use fulfilling the same particular requirements. The Regulations do not, however, apply to baby food that is milk intended for young children.

The sale of processed cereal-based food and baby food is prohibited unless it is labelled and complies with specified requirements as to manufacture and composition, including restrictions on the addition of nutritional substances and nutrients and maximum limits for pesticide residues.

Foods intended for use in energy-restricted diets for weight reduction

11.7.4   The Foods Intended for Use in Energy Restricted Diets for Weight Reduction Regulations 1997, as amended, implement Commission Directive 96/8/EEC, as amended (on foods intended for use in energy-restricted diets for weight reduction).

The Regulations control specially formulated food intended for use in energy restricted diets for weight reduction, being food that complies with specified compositional requirements and which, when used as instructed by the manufacturer, replaces:

(a)   the whole of the total diet; or
(b)   one or more meals of the daily diet.

The controlled food must be sold under the name 'total diet replacement for weight control' or 'meal replacement for weight control', as appropriate, the use of those names being reserved to such food. The sale of the food is prohibited if it is not labelled with specified particulars, if reference is made to the rate or amount of weight loss that may result from its use and, in the case of food intended as a replacement for the whole daily diet, if all the components are not contained in the same package.

Dietary foods for special medical purposes

11.7.5   The Medical Food (England) Regulations 2000, as amended, implement Commission Directive 1999/21/EC, as amended (on foods for special medical purposes).

'Dietary foods for special medical purposes' are defined as a category of foods for particular nutritional uses specially processed or formulated and intended for dietary management of patients and intended to be used under medical supervision. They are intended for the exclusive or partial feeding of patients with a limited, impaired or disturbed capacity to take, digest, absorb, metabolise or excrete ordinary foodstuffs or certain nutrients contained therein or metabolites, or with other medically-determined nutrient requirements, whose dietary management cannot be achieved only by modification of the normal diet, by other foods for particular nutritional uses, or by a combination of the two. Foods for special medical purposes are classified as (i) nutritionally complete foods with a standard formulation, (ii) nutritionally complete foods specific for a disease, disorder or medical condition or (iii) nutritionally incomplete foods. The Commission has confirmed that the definition is not intended to catch freely available products that are not aimed at patients with specific problems, other foods for particular nutritional uses and low birth weight formulae.

The implementing Regulations prohibit the marketing of dietary foods for special medical purposes unless they comply with specified compositional criteria, are sold under the prescribed name 'Food(s) for special medical purposes' and are labelled with mandatory particulars.

Substances added to foods for particular nutritional uses

11.7.6   Directive 2001/15/EC (on substances that may be added for specific nutritional purposes in foods for particular nutritional uses) is implemented by the Food for Particular Nutritional Uses (Addition of Substances for Specific Nutritional Purposes) (England) Regulations 2002. The Regulations prohibit the sale of Parnuts foods (other than infant formulae, follow-on formulae, processed cereal-based foods and baby foods intended for infants and young children) in the manufacture of which specified substances, failing to meet particular conditions, have been used for specific nutritional purposes.

11.8   FOOD SUPPLEMENTS

11.8.1   The Food Supplements (England) Regulations 2003, as amended, implement Directive 2002/46/EC, as amended, on food supplements.[1] The Regulations define the term 'food supplement' as 'any food the purpose of which is to supplement the normal diet and which: (a) is a concentrated source of a vitamin or mineral or other substance with a nutritional or physiological effect, alone or in combination; and (b) is sold in dose form.' The Regulations do not apply to medicinal products as defined by Directive 2001/83/EC. Regulation 2 prohibits the sale of a food supplement to the ultimate consumer unless it is prepacked. Food supplements may contain only vitamins and minerals listed in Sch 1, which are in the forms listed in Sch 2 and meet the relevant purity criteria (reg 5).

Labelling requirements, in addition to those prescribed by the Food Labelling Regulations 1996, are set out in regs 6 and 7. In particular, a food supplement must be labelled with the term 'food supplement', although this may be qualified by other required particulars. The FSA's guidance gives the example of 'Food Supplement – containing vitamins and minerals.'

In October 2003 the validity of the Regulations was challenged in the High Court on the basis that Directive 2002/46/EC was invalid. The High Court sought a preliminary ruling from the ECJ on this point and in 2005 the Directive was declared valid. The Regulations, therefore, remain good law.[2]

1   The Food Standards Agency has issued Guidance Notes on Legislation implementing Directive 2002/46/EC on Food Supplements.

2   Case C-154/04 *R (on the application of Alliance for Natural Health) v Secretary of State for Health* [2005] ECR I-6451, [2005] 2 CMLR 61.

11.9   ADDITION OF VITAMINS AND MINERALS

11.9.1   Regulation (EC) 1925/2006, on the addition of vitamins and minerals and certain other substances, lists the vitamins and minerals and the vitamin formulations and mineral substances that may be added to food.[1] Restrictions are imposed that prohibit the addition of vitamins and minerals to non-processed foods and beverages containing more than 1.2% by volume of alcohol. If a vitamin or mineral is added to food it is obligatory to provide nutrition labelling. The Regulations do not apply to mandatory addition of vitamins or minerals or where the addition is required by law. They also do not apply to vitamin and mineral food supplements or the use of substances for additive purposes, which continue to be controlled by separate legislation.

Additionally, Regulation (EC) 1925/2006 includes a procedure for the prohibition or restriction and for the listing of other substances having a nutritional or physiological effect, such as fibre and essential fatty acids, that may be added to foods or used in their manufacture under conditions that result in the ingestion of excessive amounts, or otherwise represent a risk to consumers.

The Commission is required to maintain a publicly available register of information listed under the Regulation.

Provision for the execution and enforcement of Regulation (EC) 1925/2006 is made by the Addition of Vitamins, Mineral and Other Substances (England) Regulations 2007.

1   The Food Standards Agency has produced 'Guidance to Compliance', April 2008.

Chapter 12

Food safety: additives, contaminants, flavourings, contact materials, residues and other substances in food

12.1 INTRODUCTION

12.1.1 The general food safety requirements laid down by the Food Safety Act 1990 (FSA 1990) are described in ch 5. Article 14 of general Regulation (EC) 178/2002, which prohibits the marketing of unsafe food and has superseded s 8 of the 1990 Act, is described in paras **3.2.20–3.2.30**. We deal here with the Regulations that make provision for the chemical safety of food by controlling the presence in or on food of specific classes of substances. These classes are summarised below as follows:

(a)   additives, in section **12.2**;
(b)   flavourings, in section **12.3**;
(c)   other added substances, in section **12.4**;
(d)   contaminants, in section **12.5**;
(e)   food contact materials, in section **12.6**;
(f)   pesticide residues, in section **12.7**; and
(g)   veterinary residues, in section **12.8**.

12.2 ADDITIVES

The food additive framework Directive

12.2.1 Council Directive 89/107/EEC, as amended, established the framework for food additives authorised for use in foodstuffs for human consumption.

The Directive applies to food additives the various categories of which are set out in Annex I and which are used or intended to be used as ingredients during the manufacture or preparation of a foodstuff and are still present in the final product, even if in altered form.

The categories of food additives are:

*   colour
*   preservative
*   antioxidant
*   emulsifier

- emulsifying salt
- thickener
- gelling agent
- stabiliser (including foam stabilisers)
- flavour enhancer
- acid
- acidity regulator (can act as two-way acidity regulators)
- anti-caking agent
- modified starch
- sweetener
- raising agent
- anti-foaming agent
- glazing agent (including lubricants)
- flour treatment agent
- firming agent
- humectant
- sequestrant (without prejudice to any further decision or mention thereof in the labelling of foodstuffs)
- enzyme (without prejudice to any further decision or mention thereof in the labelling of foodstuffs; only those used as additives)
- bulking agent
- propellant gas and packaging gas.

For the purposes of the Directive, 'food additive' is defined as any substance not normally consumed as a food in itself and not normally used as a characteristic ingredient of food whether or not it has nutritive value, the intentional addition of which to food for a technological purpose in the manufacture, processing, preparation, treatment, packaging, transport or storage of such food results, or may be reasonably expected to result, in it or its by-products becoming directly or indirectly a component of such foods.

The Directive does not apply to:

(a)   processing aids;
(b)   substances used in the protection of plants and plant products in conformity with plant health;
(c)   flavourings for use in foodstuffs, falling within the scope of Council Directive 88/388/EEC[1];
(d)   substances added to foodstuffs as nutrients (for example minerals, trace elements or vitamins).

By way of derogation from the general rules on additives permitted under Directive 89/107/EEC, the maintenance of certain national restrictions on the use of additives in particular traditional foodstuffs is authorised by Decision of the European Parliament and Council 292/97/EC.

The Commission announced in the White Paper on Food Safety that it would update and simplify Community legislation on food additives. Amended proposals for a Regulation establishing a common authorisation procedure for food additives, food enzymes and food flavouring (COM (2007) 672 final); a Regulation on food enzymes (COM (2007) 670 final); and a Regulation on food additives (COM (2007) 673 final), have all been drawn up by the Commission but not yet passed.

1   See para **12.3.1**.

Food additives labelling

12.2.2   Articles 7 and 8 of the food additive framework Directive 89/107/EEC lay down requirements for the labelling of food additives respectively not intended and intended for sale to the ultimate consumer. These requirements are implemented in Great Britain by the Food Additives Labelling Regulations 1992, as amended.

The specific food additive Directives

12.2.3   On the basis of general criteria laid down in Annex II to the food additive framework Directive (which, in particular, limit approved food additives to those that perform a useful purpose, are safe and do not mislead the consumer), specific Directives 94/35/EC, 94/36/EC and 95/2/EC have prescribed lists of sweeteners, colours and other additives respectively[1]. Like the previous national provisions, the Community food additive framework Directive operates on the 'positive list principle': only those food additives included in the lists may be used in the manufacture or preparation of foodstuffs and only under the conditions of use specified therein. The inclusion of a food additive in a category is on the basis of the principal function normally associated with it. However, by contrast with previous British additive legislation, the allocation of an additive to a particular category does not exclude the possibility of its authorisation for other functions. For example, although when sorbitol is used for its commonly known sweetening properties it is subject to the sweeteners Directives 94/35/EC and implementing Regulations[2], it may also be used as a humectant within the scope of the miscellaneous additives Directive 95/2/EC and the Regulations that implement it[3].

The specific Directives manifest further common features:

(a)   foodstuffs to which permitted additives may be added are specified, together with the conditions that apply;

(b)   for this purpose, each specific Directive lists a number of food categories. These were left undefined to accommodate food product differences between Member States. In cases of difficulty, some assistance may be obtained from Guidance Notes on food additives legislation produced by the Food Standards Agency or from food authority enforcement officers. Ultimately, decisions on the appropriate category for a food are taken by the Standing Committee on the Food Chain and Animal Health[4];

(c)   for many additives in food, a 'maximum level' or, in the case of sweeteners Directive 94/35/EC, 'maximum usable dose' is prescribed by the Directives. This refers, in the sweeteners and colours Directives 94/35/EC and 94/36/EC, to ready-to-eat foodstuffs prepared according to the instructions, and, in the other additives Directive 95/2/EC, except where otherwise stated, to foodstuffs as marketed;

(d)   where there is no need on safety grounds to set a maximum level for particular additive use, a *quantum satis* level is specified. In these cases, the additive is to be used in accordance with good manufacturing practice, at a level no higher than is necessary to achieve the intended purpose and provided such use does not mislead the purchaser;

(e)   additives are permitted in most compound foods to the extent permitted in an ingredient, and in foods intended as such ingredients, to the extent permitted for their destined compound foods.

Under powers in the food additive framework Directive, the Commission has also laid down specific purity criteria for sweeteners, colours and other additives in Directives 2008/60/EC, 95/45/EC and 2008/84/EC respectively[5].

1   As to these Directives and their implementation, see further paras **12.2.4**, **12.2.5** and **12.2.6** respectively. The Food Standards Agency has produced *Food Additives Legislation: Guidance Notes*, 2002.
2   See para **12.2.4**.
3   See para **12.2.6**.
4   See Directives 94/35/EC, Art 4, 94/36/EC, Art 4 and 95/2/EC, Art 6 and, generally as the Committee, para **3.4.2** above.
5   See n 1 above.

Sweeteners

12.2.4   European Parliament and Council Directive 94/35/EC, as amended (on sweeteners for use in foodstuffs), is implemented in Great Britain by the Sweeteners in Food Regulations 1995[1], as amended. The Regulations also implement the specific purity criteria concerning sweeteners for use in foodstuffs. These were laid down by Commission Directive 95/31/EC which has been repealed and replaced by Directive 2008/60/EC. At the time of writing, the implementing Regulations have yet to be consequentially amended.

The main provisions of the Regulations:

(a)   define permitted sweetener in terms of a list of sweeteners which satisfy the specific purity criteria for those sweeteners;

(b)   prohibit the sale of any sweetener intended either for sale to the ultimate consumer or for use in or on any food, other than a permitted sweetener;

(c)   prohibit the use of any sweetener in or on any food, other than for certain foods in which only specified permitted sweeteners may be used in accordance with conditions contained in the Regulations;

(d)   prohibit the use of any sweetener in or on foods for infants and young children specified in Council Directive 89/398/EEC (on the approximation of the laws of the Member States relating to foodstuffs intended for particular nutritional uses)[2];

(e)   prohibit the sale of table top sweeteners unless they contain no sweetener other than a permitted sweetener and are labelled in accordance with the Regulations;

(f)   prohibit the sale of any food containing added sweetener other than a permitted sweetener used in or on it in accordance with the Regulations;

(g)   make provision in relation to compound foods.

1   Guidance Notes on the Regulations have been provided by the Food Standards Agency, *Food Additives Legislation: Guidance Notes* (2002).
2   As to Directive 89/398/EEC, see para **11.7.1** above.

Colours

12.2.5   European Parliament and Council Directive 94/36/EC (on colours for use in foodstuffs) and Commission Directive 95/45/EC (laying down specific purity criteria concerning colours for use in foodstuffs), as amended, are implemented in Great Britain by the Colours in Food Regulations 1995, as amended[1].

The main provisions of the Regulations:

(a)   define permitted colour in terms of a list of colours which satisfy the specific purity criteria for those colours in Directive 95/45/EC;

(b)   prohibit the use in or on any food of any colour other than a permitted colour;

(c)   prohibit the use of any permitted colour in or on food, otherwise than in accordance with the Regulations;

(d)   prohibit the use of any colour other than certain permitted colours for the health marking etc of certain meat and meat products;

(e)   prohibit the use of any colour on eggshells other than a permitted colour[2];

(f)   make provision in relation to compound foods;

(g)   prohibit the sale for use in or on any food of any colour other than a permitted colour, of which only some may be sold directly to consumers;

(h)   prohibit the sale of any food containing any added colour other than a permitted colour used in or on it in accordance with the Regulations.

In recent years there has been some concern that there may be a link between the use of colours in food and hyperactivity in children. As the result of research, the Food Standards Agency has issued advice to parents that if children do show signs of hyperactivity eliminating some named colours from their diet might have some beneficial effect on their behaviour.[3] As part of the European Commission's moves to update the law in the general area of additives (see para **12.2.1**) the Commission has also asked the European Food Safety Authority (EFSA) to carry out a systematic re-evaluation of all authorised additives, starting with colours, which it expects to complete around the end of 2008.

1   Guidance Notes on the Regulations have been produced by the Food Standards Agency, Food Additives Legislation: Guidance Notes (2002).
2   See Regulations (EC) 1234/2007 Annex XIV Part AIII and 589/2008 considered at para **10.4.6** above.
3   See Food Standards Agency communication on food additives and children's behaviour, Annex 5, April 2008 (FSA 08/04/04).

Miscellaneous additives

12.2.6   European Parliament and Council Directive 95/2/EC (on food additives other than colours and sweeteners) are implemented in Great Britain by the Miscellaneous Food Additives Regulations 1995[1], as amended. The Regulations also implement the specific purity criteria concerning additives other than colours and sweeteners for use in foodstuffs. These were laid down by Commission Directive 96/77/EC which has been repealed and replaced by Directive 2008/84/EC. At the time of writing, the implementing Regulations have yet to be consequentially amended.

The Regulations define 'miscellaneous additive' as any food additive which is used or intended to be used primarily as an acid, acidity regulator, anti-caking agent, anti-foaming agent, antioxidant, bulking agent, carrier, carrier solvent, emulsifier, emulsifying salt, firming agent, flavour enhancer, flour treatment agent, foaming agent, gelling agent, glazing agent, humectant, modified starch, packaging gas, preservative, propellant, raising agent, sequestrant, stabiliser or thickener, but does not include any processing aid or any enzyme except invertase or lysozyme.

The Regulations define 'carrier' and 'carrier solvent' as any substance, other than a substance generally considered as food, used to dissolve, dilute, disperse or otherwise physically modify a miscellaneous additive, flavouring, colour or sweetener, or an enzyme which is not acting as a processing aid, without its technological function (and without exerting any technological effect itself) in order to facilitate its handling, application or use.

A 'processing aid' means any substance not consumed as a food by itself, intentionally used in the processing of raw materials, foods or their ingredients to fulfil a certain technological purpose during treatment or processing, and which may result in the unintentional but technically unavoidable presence of residues of the substance or its derivatives in the final product, provided that these residues do not present any health risk and do not have any technological effect on the finished product.

The main provisions of the Regulations:

(a)   define permitted miscellaneous additive in terms of lists of miscellane-
       ous additives which satisfy any purity criteria for those miscellaneous
       additives;
(b)   prohibit the use in or on any food of any miscellaneous additive other
       than a permitted miscellaneous additive;
(c)   prohibit the use of any permitted miscellaneous additive in or on food,
       otherwise than in accordance with the Regulations;
(d)   restrict the use of miscellaneous additives primarily as a carrier or
       carrier solvent and the presence of such additives in certain foods;
(e)   make provision in relation to compound foods;
(f)   make provisions in relation to flavourings;
(g)   prohibit the sale for use in or on food, or the sale direct to the consumer,
       of any miscellaneous additive other than a permitted miscellaneous
       additive;
(h)   restrict the sale of miscellaneous additives primarily as a carrier or
       carrier solvent and the sale of food additives in combination with
       miscellaneous additives that have been so used;
(i)   prohibit the sale of food containing any added miscellaneous additive
       other than a permitted miscellaneous additive used or present in
       accordance with (b) and (c) above.

1   Guidance Notes on the Regulations have been produced by the Food Standards Agency, *Food
    Additives Legislation: Guidance Notes* (2002).

12.3   FLAVOURINGS

Flavourings framework Directive

12.3.1   Council Directive 88/388/EEC, as amended ('the flavourings framework Directive'), established a framework for Community control of flavourings used or intended for use in or on foodstuffs to impart odour and/or taste, and of source materials used in the production of flavourings. Given the complexity of the subject, the flavourings framework Directive mainly sets up the mechanisms by which appropriate provisions will be prescribed:

•   for individual categories of flavourings and source materials and for
       their use and production methods (see further para **12.3.2**); and
•   for specified detailed Commission rules (see further para **12.3.3**).

But substantive provisions were prescribed by the flavourings framework Directive on definitions, general purity criteria and labelling (see further paras **12.3.4** and **12.3.5**).

Flavouring sources and substances

12.3.2 For seven specified classes of flavouring sources and substances used in the preparation of flavourings:

(a) Council Decision 88/389/EEC requires the Commission to draw up an inventory of those sources and substances; and

(b) Article 5 of the flavourings framework Directive requires the Council to adopt appropriate provisions, as well as any provisions generally necessary for the production of flavourings, the use of additives and the maximum limits for contaminants and undesirable substances.

The seven specified classes of flavouring sources and substances are:

(1) flavouring sources composed of foodstuffs, and of herbs and spices normally considered as foods;

(2) flavouring sources composed of vegetable or animal raw materials not normally considered as foods;

(3) flavouring substances obtained by appropriate physical processes or by enzymatic or microbiological processes from vegetable or animal raw materials;

(4) chemically synthesised or chemically isolated flavouring substances chemically identical to flavouring substances naturally present in foodstuffs or in herbs and spices normally considered as foods;

(5) chemically synthesised or chemically isolated flavouring substances chemically identical to flavouring substances naturally present in vegetable or animal raw materials not normally considered as foods;

(6) chemically synthesised or chemically isolated flavouring substances other than those referred to above;

(7) source materials used for the production of smoke flavourings or process flavourings, and the reaction conditions under which they are prepared.

For flavouring substances (ie classes (3), (4), (5) and (6)), Council Regulation (EC) 2232/96 has prescribed general use criteria (as to safety and not misleading the consumer) and laid down a Community procedure for the establishment of a positive list (ie a list of substances the use of which is to be permitted to the exclusion of all others). A register has been adopted of flavouring substances the use of which in one Member State must be recognised by the others[1]. The substances are now to be evaluated and the positive list drawn up. Until the list is enacted, the use at national level of substances not included on the register is not prohibited.

1   See Commission Decision 1999/217/EC.

Detailed flavouring rules

12.3.3 Article 6 of the flavourings framework Directive provides for the adoption, by a management procedure, of lists of additives, diluents and processing aids, analysis and sampling methods, purity and microbiological criteria and, for flavourings intended for sale to the final consumer, labelling rules. By amendment to the flavourings framework Directive, Commission Directive 91/71/EEC prescribed these labelling rules.

Directive 2003/114/EC amended Directive 95/2/EC to prescribe rules on the use of additives in flavourings.[1]

1   See para **12.2.6**.

'Flavouring'

12.3.4 The complexity of flavouring control is further demonstrated by the definition of the term in the flavourings framework Directive. 'Flavouring' is defined as:

'flavouring substances, flavouring preparations, process flavourings, smoke flavourings or mixtures thereof.'

These subsidiary concepts are themselves defined as follows:

- 'flavouring substance' means a defined chemical substance with flavouring properties which is obtained:
  (i) by appropriate physical process (including distillation and solvent extraction) or enzymatic or microbiological processes from material of vegetable or animal origin either in the raw state or after processing for human consumption by traditional food preparation processes (including drying, torrefaction and fermentation);
  (ii) by chemical synthesis or isolated by chemical processes and which is chemically identical to a substance naturally present in material of vegetable or animal origin as described in (i) above;
  (iii) by chemical synthesis but which is not chemically identical to a substance naturally present in material of vegetable or animal origin as described in (i) above;
- 'flavouring preparation' means a product, other than the substances defined in sub-paragraph (i) of the definition of 'flavouring substance', whether concentrated or not, with flavouring properties, which is obtained by appropriate physical processes (including distillation and solvent extraction) or by enzymatic or microbiological processes from material of animal or vegetable origin, either in the raw state or after processing for human consumption by traditional food preparation processes (including drying, torrefaction and fermentation);
- 'process flavouring' means a product which is obtained according to good manufacturing practices by heating to a temperature not exceeding 180°C for a period not exceeding 15 minutes a mixture of ingredients, not necessarily themselves having flavouring properties, of which at least one contains nitrogen (amino) and another is a reducing sugar;
- 'smoke flavouring' means a smoke extract used in traditional foodstuffs smoking processes.

The flavourings framework Directive does not apply to:

- edible substances and products intended to be consumed as such, with or without reconstitution;
- substances which have exclusively a sweet, sour or salt taste;
- material of vegetable or animal origin, having inherent flavouring properties, where they are not used as flavouring sources.

Flavourings in Food Regulations

12.3.5 The substantive provisions of the flavourings framework Directive are implemented by the Flavourings in Food Regulations 1992, as amended. The Regulations:

(a)   restrict, to flavourings complying with general purity criteria, the added flavourings permitted in or on food;
(b)   set a maximum limit for 3,4 benzopyrene in food by virtue of the presence of a flavouring as an ingredient;

(c)   define agaric acid, aloin, beta asarone, berberine, coumarin, hydrocyanic acid, hypericine, pulegone, quassine, safrole and isosafrole, santonin or thuyone (alpha and beta) as 'specified substances';

(d)   prohibit the presence in food containing flavourings, of specified substances added as such;

(e)   prohibit the presence in food containing flavourings, of specified substances other than substances present naturally or as a result of flavourings prepared from natural raw materials;

(f)   prohibit the presence, in food generally and in particular specified foods containing flavourings, of more than permitted proportions of specified substances;

(g)   prohibit the sale of food which does not comply with these provisions.

The sale and advertisement for sale of flavourings for use as ingredients in the preparation of food is restricted to flavourings complying with general purity criteria.

The Regulations also prescribe labelling requirements for business and consumer sales of flavourings. Restrictions are imposed on the use of the word 'natural' and similar expressions.

Smoke flavourings

12.3.6   The Smoke Flavourings (England) Regulations 2005 provide for enforcement of Regulation (EC) 2065/2003[1]. This sets up Community procedures for the authorisation and listing of primary products from which smoke flavourings may be made and prescribes conditions for the production of primary products. Authorisation is restricted to smoke flavourings that do not present a risk to human health or mislead consumers. The Regulation prohibits marketing of any smoke flavouring or food in which it is present, unless the flavouring is an authorised primary product for which the use conditions have been met. Further provision is, in particular, also made for 10-yearly renewal of authorisations, for the traceability of authorised products and for the continued marketing temporarily of products and flavourings already on the market.

1   As to the legality of Regulation (EC) 2065/2003, see case C-66/04 *United Kingdom v European Parliament and Council* [2005] ECR I-10553.

12.4   OTHER ADDED SUBSTANCES

12.4.1   Besides additives and flavourings as defined by Community law, there are various other substances for which the quantity added to food is controlled by Community or national legislation. The relevant provisions are summarised in paras **12.4.2–12.4.7** below.

12.4.2   *Mineral hydrocarbons* in the composition or preparation of food are generally prohibited by the Mineral Hydrocarbons in Food Regulations 1966, as amended. Limited exceptions are prescribed for lubricants, chewing compounds, the rind of cheese and permitted miscellaneous additives[1].

1   See para **12.2.6**.

12.4.3   *Erucic acid* is a normal constituent of colza oil and other edible oils and fats. Due to undesirable effects that it was found to cause in experimental animals, a maximum level was fixed for it by Council Directive 76/621/EEC, as amended, in oils and fats and in foodstuffs containing added oils and fats sold for human consumption. The Directive is implemented for England and Wales by the Erucic Acid in Food Regulations 1977, as amended. The Regulations also implement Commission Directive 80/891/EEC which prescribes the method of analysis for determining erucic acid content.

12.4.4 *Chloroform* added to food sold in or imported into England and Wales is prohibited by the Chloroform in Food Regulations 1980, as amended, except in medicinal products to which the Medicines (Chloroform Prohibition) Regulations 1979, SI 1979/382, apply.

12.4.5 *Tryptophan* is an amino acid, used in certain food supplements. It was perceived in 1990 to be the cause of unusual but serious clinical symptoms known as eosinophilia myalgia syndrome. The addition of tryptophan to food and the exposure for sale of food containing it was consequently prohibited by the Tryptophan in Food Regulations 1990, as amended, except for persons needing the food on medical grounds. However, following a review by the Committee on Toxicity the 1990 Regulations were replaced by the Tryptophan in Food (England) Regulations 2005. The new Regulations continue to prohibit the sale of food containing tryptophan, subject to some exceptions. L-tryptophan can now be added to food supplements if certain criteria regarding purity and recommended daily doses are met.

12.4.6 *Extraction solvents* are used for the extraction from food of ingredients or components, including contaminants, or for the extraction of food from other articles or substances. The Extraction Solvents in Food Regulations 1993, as amended, implement Council Directive 88/344/EEC, as amended, to prohibit the sale or importation into Great Britain of extraction solvents other than permitted extraction solvents and, subject to specified conditions, of food having in it or on it any extraction solvent other than a permitted extraction solvent. Labelling requirements for permitted extraction solvents are also prescribed.

12.4.7 *Kava-kava* derives from a plant of the pepper family native to many Pacific Ocean islands. In Europe products containing Kava-kava were in recent years increasingly consumed to reduce anxiety, tension and restlessness, but evidence grew that in a number of cases its use had been associated with severe liver damage. The Kava-kava in Food (England) Regulations 2002 were therefore made to prohibit the sale, possession for sale, offer, exposure or advertisement for sale, and the importation into England from outside the United Kingdom, of any food consisting of, or containing, Kava-kava.

A challenge to the legality of the Regulations on the ground that the Secretary of State had overlooked an important adverse opinion was rejected by the Court of Appeal in *R* (*on the application of National Association of Health Stores*) *v Secretary of State for Health*[1]. However, having undertaken during the proceedings to reconsider whether the Regulations should have exempted goods in transit between one EEA State and another, the Secretary of State amended them by SI 2004/255 so as to introduce a mutual recognition clause such as is described in para **1.3.2** above and to exempt EEA imports.

1   See [2005] EWCA Civ 154, (2005) Times, 9 March, [2005] All ER (D) 324 (Feb).

12.5 CONTAMINANTS

Introduction

12.5.1   Community procedures for contaminants in food have been laid down by Council Regulation (EEC) 315/93, as amended. This defines 'contaminant' as any substance not intentionally added to food which is present in such food as a result of the production (including operations carried out in crop husbandry, animal husbandry and veterinary medicine), manufacture, processing, preparation, treatment, packing, packaging, transport or holding of such food, or as a result of environmental contamination. Extraneous matter, such as, for example, insect fragments, animal hair, etc, is not covered by this definition.

The Regulation does not apply to contaminants that are the subject of more specific Community rules. The Community provisions on contact materials and pesticide and veterinary residues are explained in sections **12.6–12.8** below and various other specific Community provisions have prescribed contaminant levels. For example, maximum levels for various contaminants have been specified as purity criteria for sweeteners (by Commission Directive 2008/60/EC), for colours (by Commission Directive 95/45/EC), for other additives (by Commission Directive 2008/84/EC) and for flavourings (by Art 4 of Council Directive 88/388/EEC).

Council Regulation (EEC) 315/93 prohibits the placing on the market of food containing contaminants in amounts unacceptable from the public health viewpoint. No specific offence has been created to enforce this prohibition in England and Wales, but contravention might reasonably be expected to be a breach of Art 14 of the general food Regulation (EC) 178/2002 or s 14 of the FSA 1990[1].

1   See paras **3.2.20** ff and **8.2.1** ff above respectively.

Maximum Community contaminant levels

12.5.2   In exercise of powers in Council Regulation (EEC) 315/93, Commission Regulation (EC) 1881/2006, as amended, sets maximum levels for certain contaminants in food. This Regulation lays down the maximum quantities for certain contaminants: nitrates, mycotoxins, metals, monochloropropane-1, 2- diol (3-MCPD), dioxins and PCBs and polycyclic aromatic hydrocarbons (PAH).

Food with levels of contaminants higher than those specified in the Annex to the Regulation may not be placed on the market. These maximum limits cover the edible part of food and also apply to compound or processed, dried or diluted foods, whereby a concentration or dilution factor may be applied or the relative proportions of the ingredients in the compound product may be taken into account.

The Regulation also lays down the lowest maximum levels for contaminants that are reasonably achievable with good manufacturing practices or good agricultural practices (ALARA – As Low As Reasonably Achievable). It reduces the maximum levels of contaminants for infants and young children.

The sampling and analysis methods are laid down in a number of Regulations: Regulation (EC) 333/2007 for the levels of lead, cadmium, mercury, inorganic tin, 3-MCPD and benzo(a)pyrene in foodstuffs; Commission Regulation (EC) 1883/2006 for the official control of levels of dioxins and dioxin-type PCBs in certain foodstuffs; Commission Regulation (EC) 1882/2006 for the official control of the levels of nitrates in certain foodstuffs; Commission Regulation (EC) 401/2006 for the official control of the levels of mycotoxins in food.

The Contaminants in Food (England) Regulations 2007, as amended, enforce these Community provisions.

Maximum national contaminant levels

12.5.3   Where Community provisions concerning maximum tolerances have not been adopted, Council Regulation (EEC) 315/93 provides that, subject to compliance with the EC Treaty, the relevant national provisions shall be applicable. Only arsenic is now subject to domestic provisions. *Arsenic* in food is, subject to certain exceptions, generally limited to 1.0 milligram per kilogram. Lower limits are prescribed for drinks; and higher ones for certain other foods including onions, hops, liquorice, gelatine, yeast, chicory, herbs, spices, finings and clearing agents and specified chemicals[1].

1   Arsenic in Food Regulations 1959, as amended.

12.6   FOOD CONTACT MATERIALS

Materials and articles in contact with food

12.6.1   Control of food contact materials and articles is another dynamic area of Community law. Its foundation is now European Parliament and Council Regulation (EC) 1935/2004. Covering or coating materials forming part of the food and possibly being consumed with it are not within the scope of the Regulation. However, it does apply to covering or coating materials that cover cheese rinds, prepared meat products or fruit but that do not form part of the food.

Like its predecessors, this Regulation is a framework measure that requires that any material or article intended to come into contact directly or indirectly with food must be manufactured so as, under normal or foreseeable conditions of use, to preclude substances from being transferred to food in quantities large enough (a) to endanger human health or (b) to bring about an unacceptable change in the composition of the food or (c) to bring about a deterioration in its organoleptic properties.

New types of materials and articles designed to actively maintain or improve the condition of the food (active food contact materials and articles) are not inert by their design, unlike traditional materials and articles intended to come into contact with food. Other types of new materials and articles are designed to monitor the condition of the food (intelligent food contact materials and articles). Both these types of materials and articles may be brought into contact with food. The Regulation therefore specifically provides that, in the application of (b) and (c) above, active food contact materials and articles may change the composition or the organoleptic properties of the food only if the changes comply with the Community provisions applicable to food, such as the provisions of Directive 89/107/EEC on food additives. Pending the adoption of additional rules on active and intelligent materials and articles, substances deliberately incorporated into them to be released into food or the environment must also be authorised and used in accordance with relevant Community provisions and comply with the requirements of Regulation (EC) 1935/2004. In addition, adequate labelling or information should support users in the safe and correct use of active materials and articles in compliance with the food legislation, including the provisions on food labelling. Regulation (EC) 1935/2004 therefore further provides that active and intelligent food contact materials and articles should not change the composition or the organoleptic properties of food or give information about the condition of the food that could mislead consumers.

The Regulation also in particular:

- confers power on the Commission, in respect of prescribed groups of materials and articles (including active and intelligent materials and articles), to adopt specific measures, including provision for the authorisation and listing of substances used in their manufacture;
- requires business operators using authorised substances to comply with attached conditions and to inform the Commission of any new scientific or technical information; and
- prescribes labelling requirements for materials and articles placed on the market.

Commission Regulation (EC) 2023/2006 on good manufacturing practice for materials and articles intended to come into contact with food lays down the rules on good manufacturing practice (GMP) for materials intended to come into contact with foodstuffs, so that these are safe for the consumer and do not change either the composition or the organoleptic characteristics of the food. This good practice applies to active and intelligent materials and articles, and to adhesives, ceramics, cork, rubbers, glass, ion-exchange resins, metals and alloys, paper and board, plastics, printing inks, regenerated cellulose, silicones, textiles, varnishing and coatings, waxes and wood (in accordance with Annex 1 to Regulation (EC) 1935/2004). In carrying out manufacturing operations in accordance with the rules on GMP, each business operator is required to establish a quality assurance system, a quality control system and appropriate documentation with regard to specifications, manufacturing formulae and processing relevant to compliance and safety of the finished material or article.

The Materials and Articles in Contact with Food (England) Regulations 2007, as amended, provide for the enforcement of Regulation (EC) 1935/2004 and Regulation (EC) 2023/2006 within England. The Regulations make it an offence to contravene specified provisions of Regulations 1935/2004 and 2023/2006. In implementation of Council Directive 78/142/EEC and Commission Directives 80/766/EEC and 81/432/EEC, for materials and articles manufactured with vinyl chloride polymers or co-polymers, limits are prescribed for the quantity of vinyl chloride monomer that they may contain and to the quantity of vinyl chloride that they may transfer to the food. Likewise, in implementation of Commission Directive 2007/42/EC for materials and articles made of regenerated cellulose film, the substances from which they may be manufactured are prescribed together with conditions and restrictions on use. At marketing stages other than retail, these materials and articles must be accompanied by a written declaration of compliance with the applicable legislation.

Commission Directive 2002/72/EC, as amended, on plastic materials and articles intended to come in contact with food, is an important specific Directive. Together with the related EC legislation mentioned below, it is implemented in England by the Plastic Materials and Articles in Contact with Food (England) Regulations 2008. Directive 2002/72/EC applies to materials and articles made exclusively of plastic, which in their finished state, are intended for use in contact with food. Such materials, and parts thereof, may be composed either of plastic material only or of several layers of plastic material or of different types of materials. 'Plastics' are, broadly, organic polymers. However, regenerated cellulose film, elastomers and rubber, paper and board, surface coatings containing paraffin or micro-crystalline waxes, ion-exchange resins and silicones, are excluded. Also excluded are materials and articles composed of two or more layers, of which at least one does not consist of plastics. An example would be plastic coatings on paper or metal cans, which must meet the general requirements of the framework Directive.

The 2008 Regulations:

- prohibit the use, sale and import of plastic materials and articles which fail to meet the prescribed standards;
- impose requirements for approved monomers and additives;
- specify the standard for products obtained by bacterial fermentation;
- specify overall migration limits on the quantities of constituents of plastic materials and articles permitted to transfer into food;
- specify the standards relating to the migration of primary aromatic amines;
- specify the standard relating to plastic multi-layer materials and articles;
- provide for the enforcement of Commission Regulation (EC) 1895/2005 on the restriction of use of certain epoxy derivatives in materials and articles intended to come into contact with food;
- in implementation of Council Directives 82/711/EEC and 85/572/EEC, specify methods for determining the capability of a plastic materials or article to transfer its constituents to food, and for detecting the presence of any such constituents in food;
- at marketing stages other than retail, require plastic materials and articles to be accompanied by a written declaration of compliance with the applicable legislation.

Two materials and articles Directives are implemented by Regulations made in whole or in part under the Consumer Protection Act 1987. Council Directive 84/500/EEC, as amended, is implemented by the Ceramic Articles in Contact with Food (England) Regulations 2006 to set limits for the migration of lead and cadmium from ceramic articles and to require them, prior to the retail stage, to be accompanied by a compliance declaration. Commission Directive 93/11/EEC is implemented by the N-nitrosamines and N-nitrosatable Substances in Elastomer or Rubber Teats and Dummies (Safety) Regulations 1995 to restrict the amount of release of those substances in the rubber of babies' teats and dummies.

Other food contact materials and food imitations

12.6.2 The Community has yet to make specific legislation for food contact metals, but the Cooking Utensils (Safety) Regulations 1972, having effect under the Consumer Protection Act 1987, restrict the lead content of tin or other metallic coatings for kitchen utensils.

The Food Imitations (Safety) Regulations 1989 have also been made under the 1987 Act to implement Council Directive 87/357/EEC concerning products that, appearing to be other than they are, endanger the health or safety of consumers.

12.7 PESTICIDE RESIDUES

12.7.1 Approval and use of pesticides in Great Britain is controlled under Part III of the Food and Environment Protection Act 1985 (F&EPA 1985) and the Control of Pesticides Regulations 1986, as amended, and, in implementation of Council Directive 91/414/EEC (concerning the placing of plant protection products on the market), as amended, under the Plant Protection Products Regulations 2005[1], as amended, and the Plant Protection Products (Basic Conditions) Regulations 1997. The Biocidal Products Regulations 2001, as amended, implement European Parliament and Council Directive 98/8/EC, for the approval and placing on the market of biocidal products that are not controlled as veterinary medicinal products, food additives, food flavourings, food contact materials and articles, plant protection products or other specified products.

By way of additional measures to protect consumers from harmful effects, maximum pesticide residue levels for particular pesticides in specified foods were prescribed by Directive 86/362 (for cereals), Directive 86/363 (for food of animal origin) and Directive 90/642 (for certain products of plant origin, including fruit and vegetables). From 1 September 2008, Regulation (EC) 396/2005, as amended, repealed and replaced these provisions with a comprehensive regime on the maximum residue levels (MRLs) of pesticides in or on food and feed of plant and animal origin that is co-ordinated with the plant protection product rules in Directive 91/414.

The foods protected by Regulation (EC) 396/2005 are listed in Annex I. All products intended for human or animal consumption are covered, including in particular those dealt with by Directives 86/362, 86/363 and 90/642. Annex II lists the MRLs that had been defined by those Directives while, for those that had not, Annex III lists temporary MRLs in respect of the plant protection active substances concerned. Annex IV lists active substances evaluated under Directive 91/414 for which no MRLs are required.

Subject as mentioned below, from the time that products covered by Annex I are placed on the market as food or feed, they must not contain any pesticide residue exceeding:

(a)   the MRLs set out for them in Annexes II and III;

(b)   0.01 mg/kg, for those products for which no specific MRLis set out in Annexes II and III, or for active substance not listed in Annex IV unless different default values have been fixed while taking account of the routine analytical methods available.

Limited derogations are provided that permit Member States to authorise sales on their own territories of products that have been treated with post-harvest fumigants or otherwise.

Other important provisions of Regulation (EC) 396/2005 lay down the application procedure for further MRLs and the special provisions relating to the incorporation of existing MRLs.

Commission Directive 2002/63/EC establishes Community methods of sampling for the official control of pesticide residues in and on products of plant and animal origin.

Regulation (EC) 396/2005 is executed and enforced by the Pesticides (Maximum Residue Levels) (England and Wales) Regulations 2008. The Health and Safety Executive, to which the Pesticides Safety Directorate now reports[2], is the designated body for the purposes of coordinating cooperation with the Commission, the European Food Safety Authority, other Member States, manufacturers, producers and growers and it is also the enforcement body in England. In Wales the Regulations are enforced by Welsh Ministers[3].

As to maximum levels for pesticide residues in foods for babies and young children, see paras **11.7.2** and **11.7.3** above.

1   See also the Plant Protection Products (Fees) Regulations 2007.
2   See para **2.2.6** above.
3   See para **2.1.2** above.

12.8 VETERINARY RESIDUES

12.8.1   The British rules on veterinary residues in food are wholly derived from Community law. Council Regulation (EEC) 2377/90, as amended, establishes, under a Community procedure, maximum residue limits for veterinary medicinal products authorised in foodstuffs of animal origin and prohibits the administration to animals of specified hazardous and unlicensed substances[1]. Council Directive 96/22/EC,as amended, prohibits the use in stockfarming of certain substances having a hormonal or thyrostatic action and of beta-agonists and Council Directive 96/23/EC, as amended, lays down measures to monitor certain substances and residues thereof in live animals and animal products. In compliance with the WTO Appellate Body's 1998 finding that the EU ban on growth promoting hormones was unjustified, a thorough scientific appraisal was undertaken and Directive 96/22 was amended by Directive 2003/74.

In Great Britain, Regulation (EEC) 2377/90 and Directives 96/22/EC and 96/23/EC are implemented by the Animals and Animal Products (Examination for Residues and Maximum Residue Limits) Regulations 1997, as amended.

The Regulations:

(a)   prohibit the sale for administration to animals (i) of thyrostatic substances, stilbenes, stilbene derivatives their salts and esters; and (ii) where the animals or products from them are intended for human consumption, of oestradiol 17β and its ester-like derivatives and beta-agonistes;

(b)   prohibit the possession of oestradiol 17β and its ester-like derivatives and beta-agonistes;

(c)   prohibit the administration to animals of unlicensed[2] or hazardous substances[3] in contravention of Council Regulation 2377/90;

(d)   prohibit the possession, slaughter, or processing of meat of animals intended for human consumption which contain, or to which have been administered prohibited substances;

(e)   prohibit:
     (i) the sale or supply for slaughter of animals if the appropriate withdrawal period has not expired; and
     (ii) the sale or supply for slaughter of animals, or sale for human consumption of animal products which contain unauthorised products or an excess of authorised substances;

(f)   prohibit, subject to an exception, the disposal for human or animal consumption of slaughtered animals containing specified unauthorised substances.

The Regulations also provide for sampling and analysis, offences, penalties and defences and record keeping.

Charges to cover the cost of residue surveillance under Directive 96/23/EC are made by the Charges for Residues Surveillance 2006, as amended, and give effect in part to official controls Regulation (EC) 9882/2004, Art 27.

1   See case C-248/99P *France v Monsanto* [2002] ECR I-1; and case C-32/00 *Commission v Boehringer* [2002] ECR I-1917.
2   The prohibition on administration of 'unlicensed products', gives effect to the judgment in case C-297/94 *Dominique Bruyère v Belgium* [1996] ECR I-1551, in so far as the judgment relates to the administration of veterinary medicinal products to animals within the meaning of 96/22/EC and 96/23/EC.
3   See joined cases C-129/05 and C-130/05 *NV Raverco and Coxon & Chatterton Ltd v Minister van Landbouw, Natuur en Voedselkwaliteit* [2006] ECR I-9297.

Chapter 13

Food hygiene: general

13.1 INTRODUCTION

13.1.1 In the last few years there have been enormous changes to the law on food hygiene. Directive 93/43/EEC on the hygiene of foodstuffs had laid down the general rules on hygiene of foodstuffs and the procedures to be followed to ensure that the rules were complied with. In addition, there were numerous other pieces of European legislation relating to hygiene of products of animal origin. The Commission's White Paper on Food Safety noted that as a consequence there was 'a series of different hygiene regimes according to whether the food is of animal or plant origin, which can only be justified for historical reasons.'[1] The Commission, therefore, proposed 'recasting the existing legal requirements to introduce consistency and clarity throughout the food production chain.'[2] Food operators were to bear full responsibility for the safety of the food they produced and a hazard analysis critical control point (HACCP) system was proposed to be at the centre of the legislation.[3] Following much debate a package of legislation was brought forward that was to modernise, consolidate and simplify the previous mass of legislation. A 'farm to fork' approach has been taken by including, for the first time, primary production in the food hygiene legislation. Primary production is specifically considered in section **13.9** below. Directive 2004/41/EC repealed the previous mass of hygiene legislation and in its place came three central regulations: Regulation (EC) 852/2004 on the hygiene of foodstuffs, Regulation 853/2004 laying down specific hygiene rules for food of animal origin and Regulation (EC) 854/2004 laying down specific rules for the organisation of official controls on products of animal origin intended for human consumption. The legislation came into force on 1 January 2006 and the Food Hygiene (England) Regulations 2006 provides the framework for the EU legislation to be enforced in England. The provisions of the 2006 Regulations as to hygiene improvement notices, hygiene prohibition orders, hygiene emergency prohibition notices and orders and remedial action notices and detention orders are considered in chapter 6.

Regulations (EC) 853/2004 and 854/2004 are explained in ch 14, while ch 15 describes certain miscellaneous food preparation and temperature control provisions. Regulation (EC) 882/2004, which sets out the general official controls including those on feed and food of non-animal origin, is considered in ch 18.

1   COM (1999) 719, final at para 72.
2   *Ibid.*
3   See below at section **13.6**.

13.2 REGISTRATION AND APPROVAL OF FOOD BUSINESSES

13.2.1 Article 6(2) of Regulation (EC) 852/2004 requires food businesses to be registered with the competent authority. The definition in Art 3(2) of Regulation (EC) 178/2002 of food business is wide and the FSA Guidance indicates that this means each separate unit of a food business, including game centres and collection centres must be registered.[1] Certain activities like primary production for private domestic use and domestic preparation, handling or storage of food for private domestic consumption are exempt from the registration requirement by virtue of the general exclusion from the scope of Regulation (EC) 852/2004, explained in section **13.4** below. Also excepted are activities such as the occasional preparation of food by individual or groups for gathering or for sale at charitable events.[2] The purpose of registration is to ensure that competent authorities know where the food businesses are situated and what their activities are, so as to ensure that they can be inspected when required. Article 31(1)(a) of Regulation (EC) 882/2004 requires the competent authorities to establish a procedure for food business operators to follow when applying for registration.

Registration is simple. A standard application form for the registration of a food business establishment is available and the operator must provide full details of the activities to be undertaken. An operator must register the establishment and should do so at least 28 days before food operations commence. If subsequently there are any changes to the details supplied, the competent authority must be notified as soon as possible and certainly no later than 28 days after the change has happened. The Food Law Code of Practice indicates that in two tier food authority areas District Councils receiving registration information under Art 6(2) of Regulation (EC) 852/2004 should supply this information to the County Council within 28 days of receipt.[3] Under reg 17 of the Food Hygiene (England) Regulations 2006 it is an offence to fail to register a food business or to supply up to date information. Certificates of registration are not given to a food business 'because of their potential to mislead consumers into believing that a food business establishment has "official approval" '.[4]

Competent authorities are required to keep and maintain a list of registered food business under Art 31(1)(b) of Regulation (EC) 882/2004. A separate list should also be maintained for inspection by the general public at all reasonable times. This list should contain the name and address of the food business establishment and the particulars and nature of the food business.[5]

If a food business is involved in the handling of food of animal origin then it will normally need to be approved, rather than registered, before it can put products on the market (see below at section **14.4**). This is required under Art 4 of Regulation (EC) 853/2004 because foodstuffs of animal origin present specific microbiological, and even sometimes chemical, hazards to human health.[6]

It is apparent from a consideration of these rules that while registration allows competent authorities to perform official controls efficiently, approval constitutes an expeditious and stringent way of penalising serious deficiencies or other contraventions of a kind specified in Regulation (EC) 882/2004, Art 31(1)(e). Rather than having to await the outcome of criminal proceedings, the enforcement authority takes direct action to withdraw the establishment's approval. In consequence, reg 12 of the Official Feed and Food Controls (England) Regulations 2007 provides aggrieved persons with a right of appeal to the magistrates' court and onward to the Crown Court.

1 FSA Guidance on the requirements of food hygiene legislation. The Food Law Code of
   Practice illustrates this by using the example of a supermarket that has a coffee shop on the site
   run by a different food operator, such as a coffee shop chain. In these circumstances the coffee
   shop is not covered by the supermarket's registration and it must be registered in its own right
   by its operator.
2 Recital 9 to Regulation (EC) 852/2004 states that Community rules 'should only apply to
   undertakings the concept of which implies a certain continuity of activities and a certain degree
   of organisation.'
3 Food Law Code of Practice, section 1.1.5.
4 Food Law Code of Practice, ch 1.5.6.
5 Food Law Code of Practice, ch 1.5.4.2.
6 See generally ch 14.

13.3 ENFORCEMENT

13.3.1 Regulation 5 of the Food Hygiene (England) Regulations 2006
provides for the enforcement of Regulations (EC) 852/2004 and 853/2004 (see
below at section **14.3** for a detailed consideration of enforcement of Regulation
(EC) 853/2004). Depending on the nature of the food business operator, the
Food Standards Agency or the food authority in whose area the food business
operator carries out the business is responsible for enforcement. In line with the
general official controls obligations described at para **18.2.2** below, inspections
should be carried out at all stages of production, processing and distribution to
establish whether the requirements of the law are being met. Chapter 4.1.10 of
the Food Law Code of Practice reminds food authorities to 'document, maintain
and implement a food hygiene inspection programmes that includes all
businesses in which the food authority has food hygiene law enforcement
responsibility.' Annex 5 of the Code provides an inspection rating scheme to
determine the food hygiene inspection frequencies of food business so that the
food authority has a planned food hygiene inspection programme. A first visit to
'assist the operator in putting in place and implementing procedures based on
the HACCP principles' (see section **13.6** below) can be regarded as a formal
inspection.[1]

1 Food Law Code of Practice, ch 4.1.2.

13.4 EXCLUSIONS

13.4.1 Whilst the new hygiene legislation now covers all stages of
production, processing and distribution of food, and exports, there are still some
exclusions to be found in Art 1(2) of Regulation (EC) 852/2004. The most
obvious exemption is primary production for domestic use and the domestic
preparation, handling or storage of food for private domestic consumption. Also
exempt from the hygiene legislation is the direct supply, by the producer, of
small quantities of primary products to the final consumer or to local retail
establishments directly supplying the final consumer.[1] It seems to cover farmers
selling fruit and vegetables directly to shops for direct sale to the final consumer
and to local restaurants. It should be noted, however, that these activities are still
subject to the general requirements, described in paras **3.2.20–3.2.30** above,
relating to placing on to placing unsafe food on the market under Art 14 of
Regulation (EC) 178/2002, which is an offence under reg 4 of the General Food
Regulations 2004. The final exemption relates to collection centres and
tanneries that fall within the definition of food businesses only because they
handle raw material for the production of gelatine or collagen. Although such
businesses do not have to comply with hygiene legislation they are still required

to be authorised by the local food authority and meet requirements to prevent contamination.

1   There is no definition of 'small quantities' but some guidance can be found in *Guidance Document: Implementation of certain provisions of Regulation (EC) No 852/2004 on the hygiene of Foodstuffs*, para 3.3 and *FSA Guidance on the Requirements of Food Hygiene Legislation*, Annex H.

13.5   GENERAL FOOD HYGIENE REQUIREMENTS UNDER REGULATION (EC) 852/2004

13.5.1   In implementation of the principle established by Art 17 of general food Regulation (EC) 178/2002 and described in para **3.2.38** above, Art 1(a) of Regulation (EC) 852/2004 confirms that primary responsibility for food safety rests with food business operators while Art 3 obliges them to ensure that the requirements of the Regulation are met at all stages of production, processing and distribution of food under their control. The general hygiene requirements for all food business operators (except those involved in primary production, see below at section **13.9**) are contained in Annex II of Regulation (EC) 852/2004. Where a food business operator is also involved in producing products of animal origin further requirements apply under Regulation (EC) 853/23004 (see below at chapter 14).

Requirements applying to all stages of production, processing and distribution of food

13.5.2   Requirements applying to all stages of production, processing and distribution of food are contained in Annex II, Chapters V–XII of Regulation (EC) 852/2004. Chapter V deals with equipment requirements. This covers such issues as the need for all articles, fittings and equipment coming into contact with foodstuffs to be properly cleaned and kept in good order etc. Chapter VI makes provision for dealing with food waste and Chapter VII sets out the requirements for the water supply. The issue of personal hygiene, including diseases and wounds is addressed in Chapter VIII and 'every person working in a food-handling area is to maintain a high degree of personal cleanliness and is to wear suitable, clean and, where necessary, protective clothing.' In specifying provisions applicable to foodstuffs, Chapter IX prohibits food business operators from accepting raw materials or ingredients (other than live animals) if it is known that they are, or are reasonably likely to be, 'contaminated with parasites, pathogenic microorganisms or toxic, decomposed or foreign substances to such an extent that, even after the food business operator had hygienically applied normal sorting and/or preparatory or processing procedures, the final product would be unfit for human consumption.' This chapter also deals with prevention from contamination and lays down general temperature requirements for foodstuffs (see below at section **13.8** for detailed rules on temperature control). In Chapter X there are provisions on the wrapping and packaging of foodstuffs and Chapter XI deals with heat treatment. Finally, provisions as to the training of food handlers are set out in Chapter XII. As a general rule, food handlers do not themselves have to undergo training in food hygiene matters provided that they are supervised and instructed. Food authorities are empowered to provide training courses in food hygiene, whether within or outside their area, for persons who are or intend to become involved in food businesses whether as proprietors or otherwise.[1] A food authority may contribute towards the expenses incurred by any other food authority or towards expenses incurred by any other person in providing such courses.

1   FSA 1990, s 23.

General requirements for food premises[1]

13.5.3   Food premises are to be kept clean and maintained in good repair and condition. Provisions are made concerning the layout, design, construction, siting and size of such premises. Adequate numbers of flush lavatories and washbasins must be provided. Ventilation must be suitable and sufficient, as must be lighting.

1   Other than moveable and/or temporary premises, premises used primarily as a private dwelling but where foods are regularly prepared for placing on the market and vending machines: Annex II, Chapter I, Regulation (EC) 852/2004.

Specific requirements in rooms where foodstuffs are prepared, treated or processed[1]

13.5.4   Rooms where food is prepared, treated or processed must be designed and laid out in such a way as to permit good food hygiene practices, including protection against contamination between and during operations. Particular attention must be paid to floor and wall surfaces, ceilings, windows, doors and surfaces in areas where foods are handled. There must be adequate provision for washing food, where necessary. Again, as necessary, adequate provision must also be made for cleaning, disinfecting and storage of working utensils and equipment. By Art 7 of Regulation (EC) 2074/2005, Member States may grant specified derogations from this Chapter (and also from Chapter V) to establishments manufacturing 'foods with traditional characteristics' as defined in that Article.

1   Excluding dining areas and moveable and/or temporary premises, premises used primarily as a private dwelling but where foods are regularly prepared for placing on the market and vending machines: Annex II, Chapter II, Regulation (EC) 852/2004.

Requirements for moveable and/or temporary premises, premises used primarily as a private dwelling but where foods are regularly prepared for placing on the market and vending machines[1]

13.5.5   So far as is reasonably practicable to do so, premises and vending machines are to be sited, designed, constructed and kept clean and maintained in good repair and condition so as to avoid the risk of contamination, in particular by animals and pests. If necessary, facilities must be available to maintain adequate personal hygiene. Again, if necessary, surfaces coming into contact with food must be suitable, foodstuffs must be capable of being cleaned hygienically and there must be an adequate supply of hot and/or cold potable water. The arrangements and/or facilities for the hygienic storage and disposal of hazardous and/or inedible substances and waste must be adequate. So far as is reasonably practicable, foodstuffs need to be placed so as to avoid the risk of contamination.

1   Annex II, Chapter III, Regulation (EC) 852/2004.

Transport[1]

13.5.6 Conveyances and/or containers used for transporting foodstuffs are to be kept clean and maintained in good repair and condition to protect foodstuffs from contamination and are, where necessary, to be designed and constructed to permit adequate cleaning and/or disinfection. Receptacles in vehicles and/or containers should not be used to transport anything but foodstuffs where this might result in contamination. Bulk foodstuffs in liquid, granulates or powder form are to be transported in receptacles and/or container/tankers reserved for the transport of foodstuffs. As necessary, the conveyances and/or containers must be capable of maintaining the foodstuffs at an appropriate temperature and the temperature must be capable of being monitored.

In implementation of derogations in Directives 96/3/EC and 98/28/EC[2], Sch 3 to the Food Hygiene (England) Regulations 2006 continues to make specific provision for the bulk transport in sea-going vessels of liquid oils and fats and the bulk transport by sea of raw sugar.

1 Annex II, Chapter IV, Regulation (EC) 852/2004.
2 Saved by Regulation (EC) 852/2004, Art 17(3).

13.6 HAZARD ANALYSIS AND CRITICAL CONTROL POINTS

13.6.1 Hazard analysis critical control point (HACCP) systems were first developed in the United States, initially to provide hygiene assurance of space mission food. A hazard is a 'biological, chemical or physical agent in, or condition of, food or feed with the potential to cause an adverse health effect'.[1] A HACCP preventative control system can be used to manage any part of the food chain that might contribute to a hazardous situation. The system can be used to identify potential hazards, 'these critical points (CCPs) are then monitored *in situ* and specified remedial action is taken if any CCPs deviate from their safe limits.'[2] Under the system, the processes must first be defined, and any hazards identified. Next, there must be an assessment of the hazards and risks and any CCPs identified. Finally, the system must specify monitoring and control procedures.

Article 5(2) of Regulation (EC) 852/2004 states the HACCP principles, thus:

'(a) identifying any hazards that must be prevented, eliminated or reduced to acceptable levels;

(b) identifying the critical control points at the step or steps at which control is essential to prevent a hazard or to reduce it to acceptable levels;

(c) establishing critical limits at critical control points which separate acceptability from unacceptability for the prevention, elimination or reduction of identified hazards;

(d) establishing and implementing effective monitoring procedures at critical control points;

(e) establishing corrective actions when monitoring indicates that a critical control point is not under control;

(f) establishing procedures, which shall be carried out regularly, to verify that the measures outlined in subparagraphs (a) to (e) are working effectively; and

(g) establishing documents and records commensurate with the nature and size of the food business to demonstrate the effective application of the measures outlined in subparagraphs (a) to (f).'

Except in the case of activities at the level of primary production(see below at section **13.9**), food business operators must, under Art 5 of Regulation (EC) 852/2004, 'put in place, implement and maintain a permanent procedure or procedures based on the HACCP principles.' This requirement does give some flexibility 'in that it requires that the procedures be *based* on those principles. It does not necessarily constrain food business operators to implement a HACCP *system* if this is not appropriate.'[3] Regulation 17 of the Food Hygiene (England) Regulations makes it an offence not to comply with Art 5[4]. The law, therefore, firmly places primary responsibility for food safety on the food business operator but the 'HACCP system should not be regarded as a method of self-regulation and should not replace official controls.'[5]

Articles 7–9 provide for the development of both national and community guides to good practice for hygiene and the application of HACCP principles. Food business operators may use these guides on a voluntary basis, as an aid to compliance with the food hygiene requirements. The FSA has produced *Guidelines for the development of national voluntary guides to good hygiene practice and the application of HACCP principles in accordance with EC food hygiene regulations.*[6] The food industry has to take the initiative for developing a guide but if the industry wants official recognition for its guide it needs to work with the FSA. Importantly, guides that are officially recognised by the FSA have special legal status because where a food business is using a recognised guide the enforcement authority must take this into account when assessing compliance with hygiene requirements. Therefore, recognised guides may be used with confidence by food businesses as a practical guide to compliance with relevant hygiene legislation. Only guidance on compliance with the relevant legal requirements (and not any additional material included, for example, about quality standards) has this special status for enforcement purposes.'[7] At the time of writing mail order, wholesale distributors, flour milling and vending and dispensing guides have been published and guides on bottled water, retail, and dermesal, nephrops and pelagic fishing are near completion. The Commission has also prepared guidelines for the development of Community guides to good practice and it maintains register of national guides to good practice.

As many food business operators had not before been required to operate a food safety management system based on the HACCP principles some guides have been produced aimed at particular types of operator. For example, to help caterers comply the FSA has produced a guidance pack '*Safer food, better business*', which was developed in partnership with small catering businesses and more than 50 local authorities. The Commission has also produced *Guidance Document: Implementation of procedures based on the HACCP principles and facilitation of the implementation of the HACCP principles in certain food businesses.*

1   Regulation (EC) 852/2004, Art 3(14).
2   *Report of the Committee on the Microbiological Safety on Food, Part I*, HMSO, 1990, para A.4.1.
3   *FSA Guidance on the Requirements of Food Hygiene Legislation*, section 8.
4   As to the 2007 prosecution of Cadbury Schweppes for this offence, see para **3.2.30** above.
5   Recital 13, Regulation (EC) 852/2004.
6   FSA, 2nd edn, 2007.
7   *Guidelines for the development of national voluntary guides to good hygiene practice and the application of HACCP principles in accordance with EC food hygiene regulations* (FSA, 2nd

edn, 2007), para 21. See also Art 10(2)(d) of Regulation (EC) 882/2004 on the official controls performed to ensure the verification of compliance with feed and food Law, animal health and animal welfare rules.

13.7 MICROBIOLOGICAL CRITERIA FOR FOODSTUFFS

13.7.1 Microbiological hazards in foodstuffs form a major source of food-borne diseases in humans and, as such, foodstuffs 'should not contain micro-organisms or their toxins or metabolites in quantities that present an unacceptable risk for human health.[1] Article 4(3) of Regulation (EC) 852/2004 requires food business operators, as appropriate, to adopt specific hygiene measures including compliance with microbiological criteria for foodstuffs, sampling and testing and procedures to meet pathogen reduction or other targets. The microbiological criteria are set out in Annex I of Commission Regulation (EC) 2073/2005 which harmonised the old criteria contained in numerous directives.[2] There are two types of microbiological criterion: the 'food safety criterion' defined as 'a criterion defining the acceptability of a product or a batch of foodstuffs applicable to products placed on the market' and the 'process hygiene criterion' which is 'a criterion indicating the acceptable functions of the production process. Such a criterion is not applicable to products placed on the market. It sets an indicative contamination value about which corrective actions are required in order to maintain the hygiene of the process in compliance with food law'.[3]

The Regulation does not specify minimum requirements for testing, except for carcasses, minced meat, meat preparations and mechanically separated meat. In other cases, operators must consider in what circumstances it is appropriate to use microbiological testing to demonstrate compliance with the criteria. For small business in which food safety management procedures based on HACCP principles and good hygiene practice are in place, routine monitoring of matters such as time/temperature profiles, the pH level of preservative and water activity may provide adequate assurance that the criteria are being met.

Regulation 17 and Sch 2 of the Food Hygiene (England) Regulations 2006 make it an offence for a food business operator not to deal with unsatisfactory results in the manner required by Art 7 of Regulation (EC) 2073/2005.

1 Regulation (EC) 2073/2005 on microbiological criteria for foodstuffs, recital 2.
2 The FSA has prepared guidance, *General Guidance for Food Business Operators: EC Regulation No 2073/2005 on Microbiological Criteria for Foodstuffs.*
3 Regulation (EC) 2073/2005, Art 2.

13.8 TEMPERATURE CONTROLS

13.8.1 Article 4(3) of Regulation (EC) 852/2004 requires food business operators, as appropriate, to have hygiene measures in place to ensure compliance with temperature control requirements for foodstuffs and the maintenance of the cold chain. The Regulation contains a general requirement on temperature control: 'Raw materials, ingredients, intermediate products and finished products likely to support the reproduction of pathogenic micro-organisms or the formation of toxins are not be kept at temperatures that might result in a risk to health. The cold chain is not to be interrupted. However, limited periods outside temperature control are permitted, to accommodate the practicalities of handling during preparation, transport, storage, display and service of food, provided that it does not result in risk to health.'[1] Annex II

Chapter IX points 6 and 7 to the Regulation also contain requirements on the cooling and thawing of foodstuffs. Regulation 30 and Sch 4 of the Food Hygiene (England) Regulations 2006 set out the domestic requirements with regard to temperature control[2]. The FSA has prepared a guidance document on both sets of requirements[3] and the Food Law Code of Practice contains guidance on enforcement.[4]

Chill holding requirements are prescribed by Sch 4 for foods likely to support the growth of pathogenic micro-organisms or the formation of toxins. The FSA's guidance indicates that examples of foods likely to fall into this category are dairy products, cooked products, smoked and cured fish smoked or cured ready-to-eat meat that is not ambient shelf-stable, prepared ready-to-eat foods and uncooked or partly cooked pastry and dough products.[5] Foods of this kind with respect to which a commercial operation is being carried out at or in food premises must not be kept at a temperature above 8°C. Those supplied by mail order must not be kept at a temperature that has given rise to or is likely to give rise to a risk to health. Exemptions from the chill holding requirements are specified for foods such as those that, for the duration of their shelf-life, may be kept at ambient temperatures with no risk to health. A defence is provided where the food business manufacturing, preparing or processing the food has recommended that it be kept at a specified temperature between 8°C and ambient temperatures for a period not exceeding a specified shelf life. Such recommendations must be supported by a well-founded scientific assessment of the safety of the food at the specified temperature. Other defences allow tolerance periods for which food may be held at above the chill holding level of 8°C.

Schedule 4 additionally prescribes hot holding requirements for foods that need to be kept hot in order to control the growth of pathogenic micro-organisms or the formation of toxins. If, in the course of the activities of a food business, such food has been cooked or reheated and is for service or on display for sale, it must not be kept at a temperature below 63°C. Defences permit lesser temperatures on the basis that a well-founded scientific assessment of the safety of the food has concluded there is no risk and, in any case, for a period of less than two hours.

1   Annex II, Chapter IX, point 5.
2   Originally made under hygiene Directive 93/43, Art 7, these requirements are saved Regulation (EC) 852/2004, Art 17(3).
3   *Guidance on Temperature Control Legislation in the United Kingdom: Regulation (EC) 852/2004 The Food Hygiene Regulations 2006 (as amended)*, Food Standards Agency 2007.
4   Chapter 3.6.
5   *Guidance on Temperature Control Legislation in the United Kingdom: Regulation (EC) 852/2004 The Food Hygiene Regulations 2006 (as amended)*, Food Standards Agency 2007, para 9.

13.9   HYGIENE REQUIREMENTS FOR PRIMARY PRODUCTION

13.9.1   Annex I Part A to Regulation (EC) 852/2004 sets out the general hygiene provisions for food business operators carrying out primary production and associated operations listed in Annex I[1]. 'Primary production' is defined by Art 3(17) of Regulation (EC) 178/2002 as 'the production, rearing or growing of primary products including harvesting, milking and farmed animal production prior to slaughter. It also includes hunting and fishing and the harvesting of wild products.'

The hygiene rules applicable to primary production also apply to the following operations that are associated with primary production: the transport, storage and handling of primary products at the place of production, provided that this does not substantially alter their nature; the transport of live animals, where necessary to achieve the objectives of Regulation (EC) 852/2004; and in the case of products of animal origin, fishery products and wild game, transport operations to deliver primary products, the nature of which has not been substantially altered, from the place of production to an establishment.[2]

'Primary products' are defined by Art 2(1)(b) of Regulation (EC) 852/2004 as 'products of primary production including products of the soil, of stock farming, of hunting and fishing'. Primary products therefore include grains, fruits, vegetables, herbs, mushrooms, eggs, raw milk, honey, fishery products and live bivalve molluscs. Fresh meat is not a primary product because it is obtained after slaughter. Fish remains a primary product until it is filleted etc.[3]

The general duty to be complied with by primary producers is that 'as far as possible' the food business operator should 'ensure that primary products are protected against contamination, having regard to any processing that primary products will subsequently undergo.'[4] The food business operator must, moreover, take measures to control contamination arising from the air, soil, water, feed, fertilisers, veterinary medicinal products, plant protection products and biocides and the storage, handling and disposal of waste. Steps must also be taken to ensure animal health and welfare and plant health, to prevent implications for human health. This includes programmes for the monitoring and control of zoonoses and zoonotic agents.[5] More specific duties then apply depending in part on whether the primary production involves, on the one hand, the producing or harvesting of plant products, or, on the other, the rearing, harvesting or hunting animals or producing primary products of animal origin.

As regards cleanliness and staff health and training, different requirements are imposed by Annex 1, Part A, points (4) and (5) for production of animal and plant products respectively. In each case, the food business operator is obliged take appropriate remedial action when informed of problems identified during official controls[6].

All operators are required by Annex 1, Part A, point (7) to keep and produce records of their hazard control measures, separate provision being made by points (8) and (9) for the recording by animal and plant product producers of the use of chemicals, the occurrence of diseases and the results of analyses. Those rearing animals must also record the nature and origin of feed employed and relevant reports of checks on animals or products. In the keeping of records, all operators may be assisted by persons such as veterinarians, agronomists and farm technicians[7].

Regulation 4(1) of Regulation (EC) 852/2004 also requires food business operators carrying out primary production and associated operations to comply with any specific requirements provided for in Regulation (EC) 853/2004. As explained in the next chapter, this applies exclusively to products of animal origin.

Thus, if the business produces domestic bovine, porcine, ovine and caprine animals and domestic solipeds, there are further conditions laid down in Annex III, Section 1, Chapter I and Chapter VI of Regulation (EC) 853/2004 and relating to transport of live animals to the slaughterhouse and emergency slaughter hygiene (see below at para **14.5.2**). The same rules apply to the production of farmed even toed game animals (deer, pigs, boar and bison), together, in some cases, with additional requirements concerning on farm slaughter (see below at para **14.5.4**).[8]

If the food business produces 'poultry',[9] rabbits, hares or rodents, the further provisions of Regulation (EC) 853/2004 relating to transport of live animals to the slaughterhouse and slaughter hygiene apply (see below at para **14.5.3**).[10] If the business produces farmed ratites e.g. ostriches, the same requirements apply together, in some cases, with additional requirements concerning on farm slaughter (see below at para **14.5.4**).[11]

If the food business operator keeps farmed animals to produce milk with the intention of placing it on the market as food, Annex III, Section IX, Chapters I and II of Regulation (EC) 853/2004 set out detailed rules on the health requirements for raw milk and colostrums production, hygiene on milk and colostrums production holdings and requirements concerning dairy and colostrums-based products (see below at para **14.5.10**). Where the business keeps farmed birds to produce eggs for direct human consumption or for the preparation of egg products for food, the extra rules in Annex III, Section X, Chapter 1 of Regulation (EC) 853/2004 concern the storage and transportation of eggs (see below at para **14.5.11**). Similarly, if the business cultivates or gathers live bivalve molluscs and does not operate a dispatch centre or a purification centre[12] additional provisions in Annex III, Section VII, Chapter I (2)–(7), Chapter II, Chapter VIII(1) and Chapter IX, as appropriate of Regulation (EC) 853/2004 apply. These concern the placing on the market of live bivalve molluscs, hygiene requirements relating to production and harvesting, and specific requirements for pectinidae harvested outside classified protection areas (see below at para **14.5.8**).

1   Regulation (EC) 852/2004, reg 4(1).
2   Regulation (EC) 852/2004, Annex 1, Part A, point 1(1).
3   *Guidance Document: Implementation of certain provisions of Regulation (EC) 852/2004 on the hygiene of foodstuffs*, para 3.2.
4   Regulation (EC) 852/2004, Annex 1, Part A, point 2(2).
5   Regulation (EC) 852/2004, Annex 1, Part A, point 2(2).
6   Regulation (EC) 852/2004, Annex 1, Part A, point 6.
7   Regulation (EC) 852/2004, Annex 1, Part A, point 10.
8   Annex III, Section III, (3) and (4) of Regulation (EC) 853/2004.
9   Defined as farmed birds, including birds that are not considered as domestic but which are farmed as domestic animals, with the exception of rarities, Annex I, 1.3 of Regulation (EC) 854/2004.
10 Annex III, Section II, Chapter 1 and Chapter VI of Regulation (EC) 853/2004.
11 Annex III, Section III, (3) of Regulation (EC) 853/2004.
12 Operations that take place after live bivalve molluscs arrive at a dispatch or purification centre are not primary production, Annex III, Section VII (4)(b) of Regulation (EC) 853/2004.

Chapter 14

Food hygiene: production and importation of products of animal origin for human consumption

14.1 INTRODUCTION

14.1.1 Since the UK's accession to what is now the European Community and especially since the completion of the internal market, national law on the hygienic production and importation of food has progressively been replaced by rules of Community inspiration. The relevant Community legislation addresses animal as well as human health issues.

In respect of both intra-Community trade in and importation from third countries of animals and of products of animal origin (including those for human consumption), a harmonised Community regime of veterinary checks has long been in place to ensure that they comply with animal and public health conditions. Inspections are primarily at the place of dispatch for intra-Community trade and at entry into the Community for third country imports. For products of animal origin, the rules are to be found, as regards intra-community trade, in Directive 89/662 and, as regards EC imports, Directive 97/78 which are respectively implemented by the Products of Animal Origin (Import and Export) Regulations 1996 and by the Products of Animal Origin (Third Country Imports) (England) Regulations 2006. As explained in para **7.4.3** above, it is within the framework of the veterinary checks that the Community has enacted emergency measures to combat avian influenza and similar diseases. The import of products of animal origin from third countries is considered further in section **14.7** below.

As has already been noted Regulation (EC) 178/2002 lays down the general principles and requirements of food law and Regulation (EC) 852/2004 lays down general rules on the hygiene of foodstuffs. However, as food of animal origin has caused particular problems and presents specific hazards to human health it is the subject of additional legislation, Regulation (EC) 853/2004 laying down specific rules for food of animal origin. Its provisions supplement those laid down in Regulation (EC) 852/2004.[1] As with that Regulation, Regulation (EC) 853/2004 sets out to simplify and consolidate the legislation in the area, replacing numerous directives. The principal objective of the Regulation is 'to secure a high level of consumer protection with regard to food safety, in particular by making the food business operators throughout the Community subject to the same rules, and to ensure proper functioning of the internal market in products of animal origin, thus contributing to achievement of the objectives of the common agricultural policy.'[2]

It should further be noted that the Animal By-Products (Identification) Regulations 1995 continue to make provision to protect public health from animal by-products not intended for human consumption. The products, as defined in the Regulations, are required to be stained and sterilised and their movement is controlled. Exempt from these Regulations are animal by-products that are derived from products of animal origin regulated by Regulation (EC) 1774/2002 laying down detailed rules on the collection, transport, storage, handling, processing, use or disposal of animal by-products and on their placing on the market, export and transit. Provision for the administration and enforcement of Regulation (EC) 1774/2002 is made by the Animal By-Products Regulations 2005[3].

As briefly explained in para **14.6.1** below, the Transmissible Spongiform Encephalopathies (England) Regulations 2008, lay down rules for the prevention, control and eradication of certain transmissible encephalopathies in implementation of Regulation (EC) 999/2001 as amended.

1   It must be remembered that businesses that have to comply with Regulation (EC) 853/2004 must also comply with the general hygiene requirements for all food business operators set out in Annex II of Regulation (EC) 852/2004, see above at para **13.5**.
2   Recital 9, Regulation (EC) 853/2004.
3   The Zoonoses and Animal By-Products (Fees) (England) Regulations 2008 allow the Secretary of State to charge fees for carrying out activities required under the Animal By-Products Regulations 2005.

14.2   WHEN DO THE PROVISIONS OF REGULATION (EC) 853/2004 APPLY?

14.2.1   Regulation (EC) 853/2004 lays down specific rules for food business operators only on the hygiene of unprocessed and processed food of animal origin. The definitions of processed and unprocessed are to be found in Regulation (EC) 852/2004.[1] ' "Processing" means any action that substantially alters the initial products, including heating, smoking, curing, maturing, drying, marinating, extraction or a combination of those processes.' ' "Unprocessed products" means foodstuffs that have not undergone processing and includes products that have been divided, parted, severed, sliced, bonded, minced, skinned, ground, cut, cleaned, trimmed, husked, milled, chilled, frozen, deep-frozen or thawed.' ' "Processed products" means foodstuffs resulting from processing of unprocessed products. These products may contain ingredients that are necessary for their manufacture or to give them specific characteristics.' Further definitions of particular 'processed products' are then given in section 7 of Annex I of Regulation (EC) 853/2004 for the purpose of the Regulation.

Annex I of the European Commission's Guidance Document[2] gives a non-exhaustive list of unprocessed products of animal origin that includes: fresh meat; minced meat; mechanically separated meat; untreated intestines, stomach and bladders; meat preparations that have not been processed; blood; live bivalve molluscs, live echinoderms, live tunicates and live marine gastropods; raw milk; whole eggs and liquid egg; frogs' legs; snails; and honey. Annex I gives a non-exhaustive list of processed products of animal origin that includes: meat products (ham, salami etc); processed fishery products (smoked fish, marinated fish etc); dairy products (heat treated milk, cheese, yogurt etc); egg products (egg powder etc); rendered animal fat; greaves; gelatine; collagen; and treated intestines, stomachs and bladders etc. Therefore, some aspects of primary production are covered, i e live bivalve molluscs, fishery products, raw milk and eggs.

Regulation (EC) 853/2004 does not usually apply to production of food containing both products of plant origin and processed products of animal origin because it is considered that the risk posed by the ingredient of animal origin can be sufficiently dealt with by implementing the rules in Regulation (EC) 852/2004. However, the processed products of animal origin used in foods containing both products of plant origin and processed products of animal origin must have been obtained and handled in accordance with the requirements of Regulation (EC) 853/2004.[3] The Commission's Guidance explains, that for example, this means that meat products used to prepare a pizza must have been obtained in accordance with Regulation (EC) 853/2004 but the manufacture of the pizza falls under Regulation (EC) 852/2004.[4] Retail is not covered by Regulation (EC) 853/2004 unless the contrary is indicated.[5]

1 Article 2(1).
2 *EC Guidance Document: Implementation of certain provisions of Regulation (EC) 853/2004 on the hygiene of food of animal origin.*
3 Article 1(2), Regulation (EC) 853/2004.
4 *EC Guidance Document: Implementation of certain provisions of Regulation (EC) 853/2004 on the hygiene of food of animal origin* at para 3.4.
5 Article 1(5), Regulation (EC) 853/2004.

14.3 OFFICIAL CONTROLS AND ENFORCEMENT

Official controls on products of animal origin

14.3.1 Regulation (EC) 854/2004 contains detailed rules for the organisation of official controls on products of animal origin intended for human consumption[1], which apply, by virtue of Art 1(1a), in addition to the general feed and food official controls in Regulation (EC) 882/2004 described in ch 18. Article 4 of Regulation (EC) 854/2004 requires Member States to ensure that food business operators offer all assistance needed to ensure that official controls can be carried out effectively by competent authorities. The competent authorities have to carry out official controls to verify that food operators comply with their obligations. This requires audits of good hygiene practices and HACCP-based procedures.[2] Article 5 of Regulation (EC) 854/2004 on official controls for fresh meat is explained in para **14.3.2** and the provisions of Art 6 (live bivalve molluscs), Art 7 (fishery products) and Art 8 (raw milk and dairy products) are summarised below in paras **14.5.8**, **14.5.9** and **14.5.10** respectively.

1 Regulation (EC) 854/2004 must be read with implementing Regulation (EC) 2074/2005 and, in respect of transitional arrangements until 21 December 2009, Regulation (EC) 2076/2005.
2 See above at para **13.6** for what HACCP-based procedures involve.

Official controls for fresh meat[1]

14.3.2 Article 5 of Regulation (EC) 854/2004 provides for official controls on fresh meat to take place in accordance with Annex I. The official veterinarian[2] must carry out auditing and inspection tasks in slaughterhouses, game handling establishments and cutting plants placing meat in the market. The tasks involve checking and analysing the documentation that accompanies the animals intended for slaughter, carrying out ante-mortem inspections, checking compliance with animal welfare, conducting post-mortem inspections and checking that specified risk material and other animal by-products have been removed, separated and marked, as appropriate. It is also the veterinarian's task to ensure that samples are taken and sent to the appropriate laboratory for testing and that health marking is done correctly. Regulation (EC) 854/2004 sets out when the official veterinarian must be present to carry out the tasks and when the role can be undertaken by official auxiliaries.[3] In some circumstances it is also possible for slaughterhouse staff to take over the activities of official auxiliaries in controlling the production of poultry and rabbit meat.[4]

After the controls have been carried out the official veterinarian must take appropriate action. The inspection results must be communicated to specified persons; slaughter of animals must be prevented or meat declared unfit for human consumption unless relevant food chain information is provided; and the identity and condition of animals must be checked before slaughter is permitted. The official veterinarian must also ensure that animal welfare rules are respected at the time of slaughter. Meat is to be declared unfit for human consumption in a wide range of circumstances.[5]

Specific requirements are set concerning post-mortem inspections of bovine animals under six weeks old,[6] bovine animals over six weeks old,[7] domestic sheep and goats,[8] domestic solipeds[9] and wild game.[10] There are ante-mortem and post-mortem requirements for domestic swine,[11] poultry,[12] farmed lagomorphs[13] and farmed game.[14]

In view of the threat of serious disease in humans caused by consumption of meat infested with *Trichinella*, Regulation (EC) 2075/2005 makes provision for additional examinations of meat of domestic swine, wild boar, horses and other susceptible animal species.

1   'Fresh meat' is meat from domestic ungulates, poultry, lagomorphs, farmed game, small wild game and large wild game that has not undergone any preserving process other than chilling, freezing or quick chilling, including meat that is vacuum wrapped in a controlled atmosphere.
2   A veterinarian qualified, in accordance with the Regulation, to act in such a capacity and appointed by the competent authority, Art 2(1)(f), Regulation (EC) 854/2004. Annex I, Section III, Chapter IV (A), Regulation (EC) 854/2004 sets out the professional qualifications for an official veterinarian.
3   The qualifications for an official auxiliary are set out in Annex I, Section III, Chapter IV (B), Regulation (EC) 854/2004.
4   Annex I, Section III, Chapter IIIA, Regulation (EC) 854/2004.
5   Annex I, Section II, Regulation (EC) 854/2004.
6   Annex I, Section IV, Chapter I, Part A, Regulation (EC) 854/2004.
7   Annex I, Section IV, Chapter I, Part B, Regulation (EC) 854/2004.
8   Annex I, Section IV, Chapter II, Regulation (EC) 854/2004.
9   Annex I, Section IV, Chapter III, Regulation (EC) 854/2004.
10 Annex I, Section IV, Chapter VIII, Regulation (EC) 854/2004.
11 Annex I, Section IV, Chapter IV, Regulation (EC) 854/2004.
12 Annex I, Section IV, Chapter V, Regulation (EC) 854/2004.
13 Annex I, Section IV, Chapter VI, Regulation (EC) 854/2004.
14 Annex I, Section IV, Chapter VII, Regulation (EC) 854/2004.

Execution and enforcement of Regulations (EC) 853/2004 and 854/2004

14.3.3   As in the case of Regulation (EC) 852/2004[1], provision is made for the execution and enforcement of Regulations (EC) 853/2004 and 854/2004 by the Food Hygiene (Hygiene) Regulations 2006. The nature of the food business determines who the enforcement body is[2]. The Food Standards Agency's Meat Hygiene Service is responsible for enforcement in slaughterhouses, cutting plants and game handling establishments (i e where control falls to the official veterinarian). It is also responsible for enforcement regarding meat products, minced meat, meat preparations, mechanically separated meat plants, cold stores, or edible co-products establishments co-located within an approved slaughterhouse, cutting plant or game establishment. Food authorities are responsible for enforcement in approved stand alone cold stores, re-wrapping establishments and establishments that produce meat products, minced meat, meat preparations, mechanically recovered meat, edible co-products, live bivalve molluscs, fishery products, raw milk (other than raw cows' milk), dairy products, eggs (other than primary production), egg products and frogs' legs and snails. In the case of dairy production holdings, DEFRA's Animal Health Dairy Hygiene inspectors undertake enforcement work on behalf of the Food Standards Agency.

1   See para **13.1.1** above.
2   Food Hygiene (England) Regulations 2006, reg 5. See also *FSA Guidance on the Requirements of Food Hygiene Legislation*, section 10.

Charges for official controls

14.3.4   Articles 27 and 28 of Regulation (EC) 882/2004 authorise the collection of fees and charges to cover the cost of official controls and require the recovery of expenses due to non-compliance. In execution and enforcement of these provisions, charges for official controls on products of animal origin are collected, under the Meat (Official Controls Charges) (England) Regulations 2008, for meat of domestic ungulates, poultry, lagomorphs, farmed and wild game and, under the Fishery Products (Official Controls Charges) (England) Regulations 2007, for fishery products.

Also on the authority of Art 27, fees are collected under the Charges for Residues Surveillance Regulations 2006 in respect of surveillance of animals and animal products for residues of veterinary medicinal products and other substances.

14.4   APPROVAL AND IDENTIFICATION OF ESTABLISHMENTS

14.4.1   As explained in para **13.2.1** above, most food businesses concerned with food of animal origin must be approved rather than simply registered. By virtue of Art 4 of Regulation (EC) 853/2004, this applies to all establishments handling products for which Annex III lays down requirements, as described in section **14.5** below. Approval is thus, in particular, required for slaughterhouses, cutting plants, slaughter on the farm (with some exemptions), game handling establishments, establishments producing minced meat, meat preparations and mechanically separated meat, establishments manufacturing meat products, dispatch and purification centres for live bivalve molluscs, freezer vessels and factory vessels and establishments on land for fishery products, milk collection centres and establishments processing eggs. No approval is needed for establishments handling products like honey that are of animal origin, but for which no requirements are prescribed by Annex III. They must be registered and comply with import requirements of Article 6 and other general rules of Regulation (EC) 853/2004.[1]

Establishments subject to approval are further required by Art 5 of Regulation (EC) 853/2004 to ensure that all products of animal origin that they place on the market bear either a health mark or an identification mark, the same obligation being imposed by Art 6 on operators importing products of animal origin from third countries. As explained in para **3.2.40** above, the traceability of food is seen as an even more essential element of food safety since the crises of the 1990s.[2]

As part of their enforcement responsibilities explained in para **14.3.3**, approval of establishments is undertaken by either the Food Standards Agency or the food authority, depending on the nature of the business. The procedures to be followed in granting approval are set out in Art 3 of Regulation (EC) 854/2004 and Art 31(2) of Regulation (EC) 882/2004. An approval requires an onsite visit and it is an offence to operate the business without the requisite approval. Approval will not be granted unless the operator demonstrates that the business complies with the relevant requirements of the law. A conditional approval can be granted if 'it appears that the establishment meets all the infrastructure and equipment requirements' but conditional approval cannot exceed six months.[3] Once approval, or conditional approval, has been granted, the food authority should notify the food business operator in writing, indicating the nature and scope of the approval and any conditions or limitations that apply.[4]

Approvals can be suspended or withdrawn if the competent authority 'identifies serious deficiencies or has to stop production at an establishment repeatedly' and the operator is 'not able to provide adequate guarantees regarding future production.'[5] The Food Law Code of Practice sets out the minimum number of food hygiene inspections in 12 months for each type of approved establishment.[6]

If an application for approval is refused the applicant should be informed in writing of that decision, and the reasons for it, at the earliest opportunity. The applicant should also be made aware of the right of appeal to the magistrates' court against the decision.[7] The right to appeal must be exercised within one month on which the date of the decision was served. If the food business operator immediately before the refusal, or withdrawal, of approval was using the establishment, it can continue to be used, pending the result of the appeal, subject to any conditions that the authority has imposed for the protection of public health. If the Food Authority considers that any activities undertaken in an establishment may present a risk to public health, it should consider the use of other relevant enforcement powers (see in particular regs 6–9 of the Food Hygiene (England) Regulations 2006 considered in ch 6).

1   See the Commission's Guidance Document: Implementation of certain provisions of Regulation (EC) 853/2004 on the hygiene of food of animal origin. Annex E of the FSA Guidance on the Requirements of Food Hygiene Legislation contains a flow chart to help a business establish whether it needs approval.
2   See Regulation (EC) 853/2004, recital (15).
3   Chapter 5.1.8 of the Food Law Code of Practice gives guidance on when conditional approval should be granted and how it should be monitored.
4   Food Law Code of Practice, ch 5.1.15. A template for an approval form is provided at Annex II, A.11.2 of the Practice Guidance.
5   Article 31(2) (e), Regulation (EC) 882/2002. (See para **13.2.1** as to appeals.)
6   Chapter 4.3.4 and Annex 5 A 2ii.
7   Official Feed and Food Controls (England) Regulations 2007, reg 12.

14.5 HYGIENE RULES FOR FOOD OF ANIMAL ORIGIN UNDER REGULATION (EC) 853/2004

14.5.1   Article 3 of Regulation (EC) 853/2004 requires food businesses processing or handling food subject to the Regulation to comply with all relevant provisions of Annexes II and III.

Annex II specifies requirements that apply to several products. When an identification mark is required in accordance with Art 5 or 6 (see para **14.4.1** above), and subject to Annex III, the mark must be applied in accordance with the requirements prescribed by Section I of Annex II. Section II lays down specific requirements that must be met by the HACCP-based procedures put in place by slaughterhouse operators in response to Art 5 of Regulation (EC) 852/2004 described in para **13.6.1** above. Section III also applies to slaughterhouse operators. In respect of all animals other than wild game, it requires them to to receive, check and act on specified details – called 'food chain information' – relating to the animals' disease status and other matters that can inform decisions relating to their acceptance for human consumption.

A description of the specific hygiene requirements laid down by Annex III to Regulation (EC) 853/2004 for particular classes of products of animal origin is given below according to the headings adopted by the Annex.

Meat of domestic ungulates[1]

14.5.2   Under Regulation (EC) 853/2004 Annex III Section I Chapter I those responsible for transporting the live animals to the slaughterhouse have responsibilities to ensure that the animals are handled carefully and not subject to unnecessary stress and that diseased animals are only transported with the appropriate permission.

If the business is a slaughterhouse then the HACCP-based procedures that must be in place have to ensure that each animal (or lot of animals) is properly identified, accompanied by the relevant documentation, has not come from a holding or area where movement is not permitted (unless the competent authority has granted permission) and that it is clean, healthy and in a satisfactory state as regards welfare on arrival at the slaughterhouse.[2] The slaughterhouse, itself, must comply with requirements and there are provisions on slaughter hygiene.[3] The Commission's guidance document points out the principle of proportionality must be respected and so for small slaughterhouses 'there is no need to require sophisticated or extensive infrastructures' etc.[4] Provisions are made for the emergency slaughter of animals outside the slaughterhouse. It is still possible to use such meat for human consumption provided requirements are followed.[5]

As noted in para **14.6.1** below, the TSE (England) Regulations 2008, in enforcement of Regulation (EC) 999/2001 (as amended) make it an offence to consign to a slaughterhouse, or to slaughter for human consumption a bovine animal born or reared in the UK before 1 August 1996. It is also an offence for the occupier to use a slaughterhouse to slaughter for human consumption a bovine animal over 30 months unless the Secretary of State has approved both the required method of operation at the slaughter house and the occupier. The 2008 Regulations also contain requirements aimed at controlling and eradicating TSE in animals. With regard to bovine animals, suspected animals must be reported to the Secretary of State and the slaughter of such animals is closely controlled.[6] When it is confirmed that an animal was affected with TSE off spring must be killed. Similar provisions apply to control and eradicate TSE in sheep and goats.[7]

Cutting plants must be appropriately constructed and cutting and boning must take place under hygienic conditions, which are set out in Regulation (EC) 853/2004 Annex III, Section I, Chapter V. The storage and transport of the meat should be carefully controlled and particular attention must be paid to the temperature of the meat.

1   Domestic ungulates are defined as domestic bovine (including *Bubalus* and Bison species), porcine, ovine and caprine animals and domestic soliped, Annex I, Regulation (EC) 853/2004.
2   Annex II, Section II, Regulation (EC) 853/2004.
3   Annex III, Section I, Chapters II and IV, Regulation (EC) 853/2004.
4   *Guidance Document: Implementation of certain provisions of Regulation (EC) 853/2004 on the hygiene of food of animal origin* at para 5.2.
5   Annex III, Section I, Chapter VI, Regulation (EC) 853/2004.
6   Transmissible Spongiform Encephalopathies (England) Regulations 2008, Sch 3.
7   Transmissible Spongiform Encephalopathies (England) Regulations 2008, Sch 4.

Meat from poultry and lagomorphs[1]

14.5.3 The provisions for poultry and lagomorphs are similar to those for domestic ungulates but with specific requirements relating to the nature of the animals. For example, with regard to transport of live animals to the slaughterhouses, there are requirements concerning the crates for delivery of the animals.[2] The nature of the requirements within the slaughterhouse are different but similar.[3] In cutting plants there are additional requirements if geese or duck reared for foie gras are being dealt with. Again, there are slightly different rules on slaughter hygiene and hygiene during cutting and boning. It is possible for some poultry to be slaughtered on the farm and be used for human consumption if the correct requirements are complied with.[4]

Although exempt from Regulation (EC) 853/2004 by virtue of Art 1(3)(d) of that Regulation, the direct supply by the producer of small quantities of meat from poultry or lagomorphs slaughtered on farm is subject to Regulation (EC) 852/2004 and requirements specified by the Food Hygiene (England) Regulations 2006, reg 31 and Sch 5.

1   'Poultry' means farmed birds, including birds that are not considered as domestic but which are farmed as domestic, with the exception of ratites and 'Lagomorphs' means rabbits, hares and rodents, Annex I, Regulation (EC) 853/2004.
2   Annex III, Section II, Chapter I, Regulation (EC) 853/2004.
3   Annex III, Section II, Chapter II, Regulation (EC) 853/2004.
4   Annex III, Section II, Chapter VI, Regulation (EC) 853/2004.

Meat of farmed game[1]

14.5.4 The production and placing on the market of meat from even toed farmed game mammals follows the same rules as those for meat of domestic ungulates unless the competent authority considers them inappropriate. Meat from ratites follows the requirements for poultry and lagomorphs unless the competent authority considers it more appropriate to follow the rules applicable to domestic ungulates.[2] With the permission of the competent authority it is possible for farmed game to be slaughtered at the place of origin, provided certain requirements are complied with.

1   'Farmed game' means farmed ratites and farmed land mammals other than domestic ungulates.
2   Annex III, Section III, Regulation (EC) 853/2004.

Wild game meat[1]

14.5.5 Where wild game is hunted with a view to placing it on the market for human consumption, there is a requirement that at least one of the hunting team is trained in health and hygiene. The hunter needs to be able to indentify abnormal behaviour and pathological changes in wild game due to diseases etc.[2] It is also important that hygiene rules and proper technique for handling, transportation, evisceration etc of the animals are followed after killing. The requirements for handling the carcases of large wild game include the obligation to attach a numbered declaration by the trained person that there was no abnormal behaviour or suspicion of environmental contamination. There are similar, but less onerous requirements for the handling of small wild game.

1 'Wild game' means wild birds that are hunted for human consumption and wild ungulates and lagomorphs, as well as other land mammals that are hunted for human consumption and are considered to be wild game in the Member State concerned. This can include mammals living in enclosed territory under conditions of freedom similar to those of wild game.
2 Annex III, Section IV, Chapter I, Regulation (EC) 853/2004.

Minced meat, meat preparations and mechanically separated meat (MSM)[1]

14.5.6   As well as the general obligations, food business operators producing this type of meat have particular requirements to follow.[2] The raw meat used in minced meat must comply with the requirements for fresh meat. It can be formed from skeletal muscle, including adherent fatty tissues, but it must not be derived from scrap cuttings and scrap trimmings, MSM, meat containing fragments of bone or skin or most parts of the head. The raw materials that can be used to prepare meat preparations are fresh meat, meat suitable for minced meat and, if the meat preparation is not intended for consumption without first undergoing heat treatment, it can contain some meat derived from mincing or fragmentation of meat and some MSM. MSM must meet the requirements of fresh meat and it must not include the feet, neck skin or head from poultry, or the bones of the head, feet, tails, femur, tibia, fibula, humerus, radius or ulna of other animals. Requirements are set out for hygiene during and after production, which are most onerous when dealing with MSM.[3]

It is also an offence for a person to fail to comply with Community requirements that bones or bone-in cuts of bovine, ovine and caprine animals should not be used in the production of MSM.[4]

1 'Minced meat' is boned meat that has been minced into fragments and contains less than 1% sale. 'Meat preparations' is fresh meat including meat that has been reduced to fragments, which has had foodstuffs, seasonings or additives added to it or that has undergone processes insufficient to modify the internal muscle fibre structure of the meat and thus eliminate the characteristics of fresh meat. 'Mechanically separated meat' or 'MSM' is the product obtained by removing meat from flesh-bearing bones after boning of from poultry carcases, using mechanical means resulting in the loss or modification of the muscle fibre structure.
2 Annex III, Section V, Chapter II, Regulation (EC) 853/2004.
3 Annex III, Section V, Chapter III, Regulation (EC) 853/2004.
4 Regulation (EC) 999/2001, Annex V, para 5 and Transmissible Spongiform Encephalopathies (England) Regulations 2008, reg 5 and Sch 7.

Meat products[1]

14.5.7   All meat used to produce meat products must meet the requirements for fresh meat. Food business operators must ensure that the following items are not used in meat products: genital organs of either male or female animals, except testicles; urinary organs, except the kidneys and bladder; the cartilage of larynx, the trachea and the extra-lobular bronchi; eyes and eyelids; the external auditory meatus; horn tissues; and in the case of poultry, the head (except the comb and ears, the wattles and caruncles), the oesophagus, the crop, the intestines and the genital organs.[2]

1 'Meat products' are processed products resulting from the processing of meat or from the further processing of meat, so that the cut surface shows that the product no longer has the characteristics of fresh meat.
2 Annex III, Section VI, Regulation (EC) 853/2004.

Live bivalve molluscs[1]

14.5.8 Live bivalve molluscs must not be put on the market for retail sale unless they have come through a dispatch centre[2] and have had an identification mark attached. It is important that the correct documentation is in place. The hygiene requirements for the production, harvesting and subsequent handling of live bivalve molluscs must be followed. Structural and hygiene requirements are set for dispatch and purification centres[3] and there are hygiene standards for live bivalve molluscs. Finally, there are specific requirements for pecitinidae harvested outside classified production areas.

Member States have an obligation to ensure that the production and placing on the market of live bivalve molluscs, live echinoderms, live tunicates and live marine gastropods have undergone the official controls described in Regulation (EC) 854/2004, Art 6 and Annex II. This requires the classification and monitoring of production and laying areas, which is carried out by the Food Standards Agency and the relevant food authority.[4]

1 Annex III, Section VII, Regulation (EC) 853/2004. 'Bivalve molluscs' means filter-feeding lamellibranch molluscs. The law in this area also covers live echinoderms, tunicates and marine gastropods, except with regard to provisions on purification.
2 A 'dispatch centre' means any off-shore establishment for the reception, conditioning, washing, cleaning, grading, wrapping and packaging of live bivalve molluscs for human consumption.
3 A 'purification centre' is an establishment with tanks fed by clean seawater in which live bivalve molluscs are placed for the time necessary to reduce contamination to make them fit for human consumption.
4 See Food Law Code of Practice, ch 5.1.10–5.1.11 and ch 5.3.

Fishery products[1]

14.5.9 Food business operators must ensure that the vessels used comply with structural and equipment requirements, which differ depending on the type of vessel, and there are hygiene requirements to be followed.[2] Further hygiene and temperature control requirements apply during and after landing. If fishery products are kept alive they must be maintained at a temperature and in a manner that does not adversely affect food safety or their viability.

Member States have obligations under Regulation (EC) 854/2004, Art 7 and Annex III to carry out regular checks on hygienic conditions of landing and first sale, inspections of vessels and establishments on land, including auction houses and wholesale markets, and checks on storage and transport conditions.[3] Checks must also be made on freshness and safety of the fish.

1 'Fishery products' are all seawater or freshwater animals (except live bivalve molluscs, live echinoderms, live tunicates and live marine gastropods, and all mammals, reptiles and frogs) whether wild or farmed and including all edible forms, parts and products of such animals.
2 Annex III, Section VIII, Chapter I, Regulation (EC) 853/2004.
3 Inspections of vessels will normally be carried out whilst vessels are in port. If an inspection is to be undertaken whilst the vessel is at sea it should not normally be carried out by the officers of the food authority, Food Law Code of Practice, ch 4.1.11.

Raw milk,[1] colostrum[2], dairy products[3] and colostrum-based products

14.5.10 The production of raw milk and colostrum must comply with health requirements.[4] In particular, the products must come from animals that show no signs of infectious diseases communicable to humans through consumption and that are in a good general state of health. There are particular requirements to prevent the spread of brucellosis and tuberculosis. The premises and the equipment on the holdings on which milk and colostrum are produced must comply with hygiene requirements and hygiene must be respected during milking, collection and transport. There are strict criteria set for raw milk and colostrum and, on the authority of Regulation (EC) 853/2004, Art 10(8), reg 32 and Sch 6 of the Food Hygiene (England) Regulations 2006 impose restrictions on the sale of raw milk intended for direct human consumption. On behalf of the Food Standards Agency, DEFRA's Animal Health Dairy Hygiene inspectors carry out sampling, analysis and examination of the milk, as necessary, to ensure that the standards are complied with.

Where dairy and colostrum products are being made the food business operator must follow temperature requirements, requirements for heat treating, and particular attention is paid to the use of raw cow's milk.

Regulation (EC) 854/2004, Art 8 and Annex IV requires animals on milk or colostrum holdings to be subject to official controls to verify the health requirements for raw milk and colostrum production. The production holdings must also undergo official checks to verify that the hygiene requirements are being complied with

1 'Raw milk' is milk produced by the secretion of the mammary gland of farmed animals that has not been heated to more than 40°C or undergone any treatment that has an equivalent effect.
2 'Colostrum' is fluid secreted by the mammary glands of milk producing animals up to three to five days post parturition that is rich in antibodies and minerals, and precedes the production of raw milk.
3 'Dairy products' are processed products resulting from the processing of raw milk or from the further processing of such processed products.
4 Annex III, Section IX, Chapter I, Regulation (EC) 853/2004.

Eggs and egg products[1]

14.5.11 Eggs must be kept clean, dry, free from extraneous odour, effectively protected from shock and out of direct sunshine. They must be stored and transported at an appropriate temperature and have to be delivered to the consumer within a maximum time limit of 21 days of laying.[2] Requirements are set for establishments that manufacture egg products, for the raw materials used to manufacture egg products and for the manufacturing process.[3]

Although exempt from Regulations (EC) 852/2004 and 853/2004 by virtue of Arts 1(2)(c) and 1(3)(c) respectively of those Regulations, the direct supply by the producer of small quantities of eggs to consumers is subject to the ban on retail sales of cracked eggs enacted by the Ungraded Eggs (Hygiene) Regulations 1990.

1 'Eggs' means eggs in the shell (other than broken, incubated or cooked eggs) that are produced by farmed birds and are fit for direct human consumption or for the preparation of eggs products. 'Egg products' are processed products resulting from processing of eggs or of various components or mixtures of eggs, or from the further processing of such processed products.
2 Annex III, Section X, Chapter I, Regulation (EC) 853/2004.
3 Annex III, Section X, Chapter II, Regulation (EC) 853/2004.

Frogs' legs and snails[1]

14.5.12 Food business operators preparing frogs' legs and snails for human consumption must ensure compliance with requirements concerning the place where the frogs' legs and snails are killed and prepared. They must be examined for hazards, fully washed and kept at the correct temperature. Frogs' legs and snails that die otherwise than being killed in the establishment must not be prepared for human consumption.[2]

1   'Frog's legs' are the posterior part of the body divided by a transverse cut behind the front limbs, eviscerated and skinned, of the species RNA. 'Snails' are terrestrial gastropods of the species *Helix pomatiaLinné, Helix aspersaMuller, Helix lucorum* and species of the family Achatinidae.
2   Annex III, Section XI, Regulation (EC) 853/2004.

Rendered animal fats and greaves[1]

14.5.13 Requirements are set for establishments that collect or process the raw materials for the production of rendered animal fats and greaves.[2] Hygiene requirements must also be followed for the preparation of rendered animal fats and greaves.[3]

1   'Rendered animal fat' is fat derived from rendering meat, including bones, and intended for human consumption. 'Greaves' means the protein-containing residue of rendering, after partial separation of fat and water.
2   Annex III, Section XII, Chapter I, Regulation (EC) 853/2004.
3   Annex III, Section XII, Chapter II, Regulation (EC) 853/2004.

Treated stomachs, bladders and intestines[1]

14.5.14 Food business operators that treat stomach, bladders and intestines must comply with requirements as to the derivation of the animals, treatment and storage.[2]

1   'Treated stomachs, bladders and intestines' are stomachs, bladders and intestines that have been submitted to treatment such as salting, heating or drying after they have been obtained and after cleaning.
2   Annex III, Section XIII, Regulation (EC) 853/2004.

Gelatine[1]

14.5.15 Gelatine intended for use in food can be made from bones; hides and skins from farmed animals; pig skins; poultry skin; tendons and sinews; and fish skin and bone and these raw materials must comply with requirements as to where they have been sourced.[2] In place of the standard identification mark, the raw materials must be accompanied during transport by specified documentation. They must also be transported and stored as required.[3] The production process for gelatine must be adhered to and the finished product must comply with the set residue limits.[4]

1   'Gelatine' is natural, soluble protein, gelling or non-gelling, obtained by the partial hydrolysis of collagen producing bones, hides and skins, tendons and sinews of animals.
2   Annex III, Section XIV, Chapter I, Regulation (EC) 853/2004.
3   Annex III, Section XIV, Chapter II, Regulation (EC) 853/2004.
4   Annex III, Section XIV, Chapters III and IV, Regulation (EC) 853/2004.

Collagen[1]

14.5.16 Collagen intended for use in food can be made from hides and skins of farmed ruminant animals; pig skins and bones; poultry skin and bones; tendons; wild game hides and skins; and fish skin and bones and the raw materials must have been sourced in accordance with the requirements.[2] As with gelatine, the raw materials do not need the standard identification mark if suitable documentation accompanies the goods and they must be transported and stored correctly.[3] Suitable procedures must be followed for the manufacture of collagen and the finished products must comply with the set residue limits.[4]

1 'Collagen' is the protein-based product derived from animal bones, hides, skins and tendons manufactured in accordance with the relevant requirements of Regulation (EC) 853/2004.
2 Annex III, Section XV, Chapter I, Regulation (EC) 853/2004.
3 Annex III, Section XV, Chapter II, Regulation (EC) 853/2004.
4 Annex III, Section XV, Chapters III and IV, Regulation (EC) 853/2004.

14.6 TRANSMISSIBLE SPONGIFORM ENCEPHALOPATHIES

14.6.1 Transmissible Spongiform Encephalopathies (TSEs) are fatal brain diseases suffered by a variety of species. One of the most common forms is Bovine Spongiform Encephalopathy (BSE). Exposure to BSE through the consumption of infected meat products is thought to be the most likely cause of variant Creuzfeldt-Jakob Disease (vCJD) in humans. As at 4 July 2008, there have been 164 deaths from definite and probable vCJD in the United Kingdom.[1]

Comprehensive provision for the prevention, control and eradication of TSEs is now to be found in Regulation (EC) 999/2001, as amended. The rules include preventative measures requiring annual monitoring, regulation of animal feed and removal of specified risk material[2] and control and eradication measures providing for rapid detection, slaughter and destruction. The Regulation applies to the production, placing on the market and export of live animals and derived products.

For enforcement of Regulation 999/2001, the Transmissible Spongiform Encephalopathies (England) Regulations 2008 make provision for TSE monitoring; control and eradication of TSE in bovine animals; control and eradication of TSE in sheep and goats; control and eradication of TSE in animals that are not bovine, ovine or caprine; feeding stuffs;[3] specified risk material, mechanically separated meat and slaughtering techniques; and restrictions on export. It is not possible here to give a comprehensive explanation of these provisions. It may be noted, however, that the 2008 Regulations make it an offence in particular to:

- consign to a slaughterhouse, or to slaughter for human consumption a bovine animal born or reared in the United Kingdom before 1 August 1996 (Sch 2, Part 1, para 2 – see para **14.5.2** above);
- use a slaughterhouse to slaughter for human consumption a bovine animal over 30 months unless the Secretary of State has approved both the required method of operation at the slaughter house and the occupier (Sch 2, Part 1, para 5 – see para **14.5.2** above);
- slaughter for human consumption a TSE susceptible animal that has had access to potentially infected material (Sch 6, Part 1, para 7);
- use illegal mechanically separated meat in the preparation of any food for sale for human consumption or of any feeding stuff (Sch 7, para 3 – see para **14.5.6** above); and

- sell or supply for human consumption any specified risk material or any food containing specified risk material (Sch 7, para 18).

1   See Explanatory Memorandum to the TSE Regulations 2008, para 7.1.
2   Skulls and other organs of specified bovine, ovine and caprine animals as defined in Regulation (EC) 999/2001 Annex V
3   See section **17.7** below.

14.7   PRODUCTS OF ANIMAL ORIGIN FROM OUTSIDE THE EC

14.7.1   The framework for import of food and feed into the European Community is laid down by Regulation (EC) 178/2002, Art 11, which requires it to comply with relevant requirements of food law or equivalent conditions, and official controls Regulation (EC) 882/2004 Title VI Chapter II, which explains these import conditions. In implementation of the principles and conditions thus established, the procedures concerning imports of products of animal origin are spelled out by Regulation (EC) 854/2004, Chapter III.

If a food business operator is importing specified products of animal origin from outside the Community this can only be done if the country of dispatch appears on a list drawn up in accordance with Art 11 of Regulation (EC) 854/2004.[1] In determining whether a country should be put on the list the legislation of the third country needs to be taken into account in terms of products of animal origin, the use of veterinary medicinal products and the preparation and use of feedingstuffs. Consideration also needs to be given to hygiene conditions, zoonoses controls programme and the results of Community controls carried out in that country etc.

Further, by Art 12 of Regulation (EC) 854/2004, products of animal origin can only be imported into the Community if they have been dispatched from, and obtained or prepared in, establishments that appear in lists drawn up by the Commission. These lists are drawn up based on guarantees given by the competent authorities of the third countries. If the product is fresh meat, minced meat, meat preparations and MSM it must have been manufactured from meat obtained in slaughterhouses and cutting plants that are on approved lists. Similarly, in the case of live bivalve molluscs, echinoderms, tunicates and marine gastropods, Art 13 requires the production area to appear on an approved list. Further provision is made, by Art 14, for the documents to accompany imports of products of animal origin and, by Art 15, in respect of fishery products.

Any product imported must also satisfy the requirements of Regulation (EC) 853/2004, Regulation (EC) 852/2004 and any import conditions laid down in accordance with Community legislation governing imports of products of animal origin. Council Directive 97/78/EC lays down the principles governing the organisation of veterinary checks on products entering the Community from third countries, which are implemented in England by the Products of Animal Origin (Third Country Imports) (England) Regulations 2006, as amended.

Significant import conditions are prescribed by the Decisions noted in relation to the products of animal origin listed below.

Fresh meat, including minced meat

Decision 79/542 contains the list of third countries and lays down animal and public health and veterinary certification decisions for import of certain live animals and their meat. Since amendment by Decision 2004/212 it has also covered minced meat. Third country establishments from which Member States import farmed game and wild game are listed in Decisions 97/467 and 97/468 respectively.

Meat of poultry, ratites and wild game-birds, eggs and egg products

Chapter III of Decision 2006/696 lists the third countries from which meat, minced meat and mechanically separated meat of poultry, ratites and wild game-birds, eggs and egg products and specified pathogen-free eggs may be imported and transit through the Community (see now Regulation (EC) 798/2008).

Rabbit and certain game meat

The scope of Decision 2000/585 is now limited to the meat of wild rabbits and hares (leporidae), farmed rabbits and wild land mammals other than ungulates and leporidae. It sets out the list of third countries from which Member States authorise imports of this meat and lays down the animal and public health and veterinary certification conditions for such imports. The establishments from which Member States import rabbit meat and farmed game, other than ratite, meat are listed in Decision 97/467.

Meat preparations

Decision 2000/572 lays down animal and public health and veterinary certification conditions for import of meat preparations.

Meat products, stomachs, bladders and intestines

Decision 2007/777 sets out the animal and public health conditions and model certificates for imports from third countries for human consumption of meat products (referred to in para **14.5.7** above) and treated stomachs, bladders and intestines (see para **14.5.14**).

Milk and milk-based products

As regards the introduction into the Community of heat-treated milk, milk-based products and raw milk intended for human consumption, Decision 2004/438 specifies the animal, public health and veterinary certifications conditions and the third countries from which imports are authorised.

Fishery products and live bivalve molluscs

Decision 2006/766 lists the third countries and territories from which the import of bivalve molluscs, tunicates, marine gastropods and fishery products are permitted.

Snails and frogs' legs

In respect of products for human consumption subject to Directive 92/118, Decision 2003/812, specifies lists of third countries from which Member States authorise imports of snails and frogs' legs respectively. The lists include countries listed in Parts I and II of the Annex to Decision 97/296 (fishery products).

Animal casings

For animal casings, Decision 1999/120 and Decision 2003/779 respectively list the third country establishments from which products may be imported and specify the health certification requirements.

1   Article 6, Regulation (EC) 853/2004.

Chapter 15

Food preparation and temperature controls: miscellaneous provisions

15.1 INTRODUCTION

15.1.1 Related to but falling outside EC Regulations 852/2004, 853/2004 and 854/2004 considered in chs 13 and 14 are certain miscellaneous provisions. They are of two types: hygiene provisions of domestic inspiration and miscellaneous EC and international temperature controls.

Most items in the first of these groups have already been mentioned in chs 13 or 14 because they are expressly permitted or exempted by Regulation (EC) 852/2004, or Regulation (EC) 853/2004, or both. Of this kind are the national temperature controls described in para **13.8.1**, poultry and lagomorph meat direct supply requirements noted in para **14.5.3**, raw milk restrictions specified in para **14.5.10** and ungraded eggs rules recalled in para **14.5.11**. Still outstanding, however, is the concept of 'preparation' which has formed an important part of food hygiene controls in and under the Food Safety Act 1990, particularly in regulations on the processing or treatment of specific foods. This is described in section **15.2** below.

Turning to the second group, it should be noted that, in addition to the general temperature controls for hygiene purposes laid down by Regulation (EC) 852/2004 and referred to in para **13.8.1**, specific temperature requirements are prescribed by Annex III to Regulation (EC) 853/2004 for meat of domestic ungulates; meat from poultry and lagomorphs; wild game meat; minced meat; meat preparations and mechanically separated meat; live bivalve molluscs; fishery products; raw milk, colostrums, dairy products and colostrums-based products; eggs and egg products; frogs' legs and snails; rendered animal fats and greaves; treated stomachs, bladders and intestines; gelatine; and collagen.

But this is not all. Beyond these provisions, there are the marketing standards temperature controls summarised in section **15.3**. Moreover, in implementation of Directive 89/108/EEC, the Quick-frozen Foodstuffs Regulations 1990 sets out the food quality temperature controls summarised at section **15.4**. Finally, the provisions on the international carriage of perishable foodstuffs are briefly noted in section **15.5**.

15.2 FOOD PREPARATION

15.2.1 The concept of 'preparation' has been an important element in British food hygiene legislation. In relation to food, preparation 'includes manufacture and any form of processing or treatment', while preparation for sale 'includes packaging, and prepare for sale shall be construed accordingly': treatment is defined as including the subjecting of food to heat or cold[1].

Chapter 6 explains how the administrative controls[2] of which preparation for sale of food is an important element[3], have been largely superseded by the similar provision made in the Food Hygiene (England) Regulations 2006 for the purposes of executing and enforcing EC hygiene legislation. Nevertheless, defective preparation for sale of food may result in an offence of rendering food injurious to health[4]. Moreover, the concept is material to important presumptions that food is intended for human consumption[5] and to the standard of proof required to establish a 'due diligence' defence[6].

Particularly important in the control of harmful microorganisms in food have been the powers to regulate processing and treatment[7], as supplemented by powers in respect of novel foods and food sources and genetically modified food sources and foods derived from them[8]. Although use of these powers is no longer necessary for the purpose of implementing the EC products of animal origin legislation described in ch 14, the provisions on food irradiation are not of this kind and are summarised in para **15.2.2** below.

In relation to food, the terms 'preparation' and 'prepare' are also used in EC hygiene legislation[9]. They must, however, be construed in their own context, not in the light of the provisions in and under the FSA 1990.

1   As to these definitions, see FSA 1990, s 53(1). As to 'preparation', see also *Leeds City Council v J H Dewhurst Ltd* [1990] Crim LR 725.
2   That is, improvement notices, prohibition orders and emergency prohibition notices and orders.
3   Via the definitions of 'commercial operation' and 'food business', see FSA 1990, s 1(3) and para **4.8.1** above.
4   FSA 1990, s 7 and see section **5.2** above.
5   FSA 1990, s 3(3) and see section **4.3** above.
6   FSA 1990, s 21 and see section **20.3** below.
7   FSA 1990, s 16(1)(c).
8   FSA 1990, s 18(1)(a) and (b) invoked in the Novel Foods and Novel Food Ingredients Regulations 1997 and the Genetically Modified Food (England) Regulations 2004.
9   See, for example, Regulation (EC) 852/2004 Annex II and Regulation (EC) 853/2004, Art 4.

Irradiation

15.2.2 Ionising radiation produces an effect similar to pasteurisation, cooking or other forms of heat treatment and can be used to kill pathogenic organisms in a range of foods. It can also be used to reduce spoilage, to delay ripening in fruit and to prevent sprouting in vegetables such as potatoes and onions.

Directive 1999/2/EC of the European Parliament and of the Council as amended provides for the approximation of Member States' laws concerning foods and food ingredients treated with ionising radiation. Member States are required to ensure that irradiated foodstuffs placed on the market are restricted to those that comply with specified provisions. Conditions for authorising food irradiation, the sources of ionising radiation and the method of calculating the overall average absorbed dose are prescribed. Although the maximum radiation dose for a foodstuff may be given in partial doses, it must not be exceeded nor used in combination with any chemical treatment having the same purpose. Different labelling requirements are specified according to whether or not the irradiated food is intended for the ultimate consumer and mass caterers. Irradiation facilities must be approved and records must be kept of foodstuffs treated. Conditions are specified for the importation of irradiated foods from third countries.

The provisions laid down by this framework Directive are completed by Directive 1999/3/EC of the European Parliament and of the Council that will progressively list the irradiated foodstuffs and maximum radiation doses that are permitted in Community trade. Dried aromatic herbs, spices and vegetable seasonings remain the only foodstuffs to have been authorised for irradiation treatment, with a maximum radiation dose of 10 kGy.

The Food (Control of Irradiation) Regulations 1990 implement the Directives. A licence is required in order to treat food by ionising radiation. Schedule 2 permits the importation of food irradiated in other Member States provided that the irradiation has taken place in a plant subject to official authorisation. Storage, transport and sale of treated food are subject to prescribed conditions.

15.3 TEMPERATURE CONTROLS FOR CERTAIN SPECIFIC FOODS

The nature of the controls

15.3.1 As was seen in chs 13 and 14 the EC Hygiene Regulations now generally deal with temperature controls. This section summarises the remaining sundry temperature requirements in relation to certain other specific foods. Those relating to eggs and poultrymeat described in paras **15.3.2** and **15.3.3** are aimed at marketing standards rather than hygiene. Also in pursuit of food quality, the Quick-frozen Foodstuffs Regulations 1990 enact the temperature controls summarised at section **15.4** in implementation of Directive 89/108/EEC. The provisions on the international carriage of perishable food-stuffs are briefly noted in section **15.5**.

Eggs

15.3.2 Regulation (EC) 589/2008/EC (laying down detailed rules for implementing Regulation (EC) 1234/2007/EC on certain marketing standards for eggs) lays down temperature control requirements. This is because eggs can be infected by bacteria if, as a result of being left out cold at room temperature, condensation forms on their shells. Class A eggs are not to be treated for preservation or chilled in premises or plants where the temperature is artificially maintained at less than 5°C. However, if the eggs have been kept at a temperature below 5°C during transport for not more than 24 hours or on retail premises, or their annexes, for not more than 72 hours, then this is not considered to be chilled.[1]

1   Hygiene Regulations 852/2006/EC and 853/2006/EC described in chs 13 and 14 also apply to eggs, See, in particular paras **13.9.1**, and **14.5.11**.

Poultrymeat

15.3.3 Temperature control is integral to marketing standards for poultrymeat, now to be found in Regulation (EC) 1234/2007/EC. Poultrymeat may be marketed in one of four conditions: 'poultrymeat', which is poultrymeat suitable for human consumption which has not undergone any treatment other than cold treatment; 'fresh', which is poultrymeat not stiffened by the cooling process and (subject as explained below) kept at between –2°C and 4°C; 'frozen', which must be frozen as soon as possible and (subject as explained below) is kept at a temperature no higher than –12°C; and 'quick-frozen', which is to be kept at a temperature no higher than –18°C within tolerances provided for by the quick frozen food Directive 89/108/EEC[1]. With regard to fresh poultrymeat, Member States are allowed to fix different temperature requirements for the cutting and storage of fresh poultrymeat performed in retail shops or in premises adjacent to sales points, where the cutting and storage are performed solely for the purpose of supplying the ultimate consumer directly on the spot. By Article 6 of Regulation (EC) 543/2008, which lays down detailed rules for the application of Regulation (EC) 1234/2007 as regards the marketing standards for poultrymeat, brief upward fluctuations of no more than 3°C are permitted in the maximum temperature of frozen poultrymeat in accordance with good storage and distribution practice during local distribution and in retail display cabinets.

1   See section **15.4** below.

15.4   QUICK-FROZEN FOODS

Definition and description

15.4.1   The Quick-frozen Foodstuffs (England) Regulations 2007 implement Directive 89/108/EEC and subordinate Directive 92/2/EEC and provide for the execution and enforcement of Regulation (EC) 37/2005/EC on the monitoring of temperatures in the means of transport, warehousing and storage of quick-frozen foodstuffs intended for human consumption. They define a quick-frozen foodstuff as a product comprising food which has undergone a freezing process known as 'quick-freezing' whereby the zone of maximum crystallisation is crossed as rapidly as possible, depending on the type of product, and which is labelled for the purpose of sale to indicate that it has undergone that process, but does not include ice cream or any other edible ice. The Regulations do not, therefore, apply to a product, even though it may have undergone the quick-freezing process, unless it is labelled as such.

Labelling, packaging and temperature

15.4.2   The description 'quick frozen' and other descriptions listed in Directive 89/108/EEC are reserved to quick-frozen foodstuffs and food which by virtue of that labelling becomes a quick-frozen foodstuff. Where a quick-frozen foodstuff is marked with the description 'quick frozen' it must also be labelled with a sales name and:

(a)   an indication of the date of minimum durability[1];
(b)   an indication of the maximum period during which it is advisable to store it;
(c)   an indication of one or other, or both of:
    (i) the temperature at which, and
    (ii) the equipment in which it is advisable to store it;
(d)   a reference allowing identification of the batch to which it belongs[2];
(e)   a clear message of the type 'do not refreeze after defrosting'.

It is unlawful to sell to the ultimate consumer any quick-frozen foodstuff unless it has been packed by its manufacturer or packer in such prepackaging as is suitable to protect it from microbial and other forms of external contamination and against dehydration and it has remained in such prepackaging up to the time of sale.

Quick-freezing must result in the temperature of the food after thermal stabilisation being -18°C or colder and it must be maintained, subject to permitted exceptions, at that temperature or below. There are special requirements as to the equipment (including air temperature recording equipment in storage and transport) to be used by the manufacturer, storer, transporter, local distributor and retailer. Subject to transitional provisions, new air temperature recording instruments must now comply with CEN standards.

The sampling and method of measuring temperatures laid down by Directive 92/2/EEC must be applied by an authorised officer who has reasonable doubt that the prescribed temperature requirements are not being or have not been observed.

1   See paras **9.2.15** and **9.2.16** above.
2   See para **9.2.27** above.

15.5   INTERNATIONAL CARRIAGE OF PERISHABLE FOODSTUFFS

15.5.1   The International Carriage of Perishable Foodstuffs Act 1976 provided for the UK's accession to the Agreement on the International Carriage of Perishable Foodstuffs (ATP) which was concluded in Geneva on 1 September 1970[1]. The International Carriage of Perishable Foodstuffs Regulations 1985, as amended, implements the ATP by laying down maximum temperatures at which certain foods may be carried on loading, during carriage and on unloading.

Cmnd 6441.

Chapter 16

Quantity and price marking requirements

16.1.1 The regulatory powers conferred by the Food Safety Act 1990 (FSA 1990)[1] do not extend to the marking of food with statements of quantity by weight or other measurement by number[2]. For food, requirements have traditionally been imposed in respect of quantity marking by and under the Weights and Measures Act 1985 (W&MA1985). Through these provisions, relevant Community legislation has been implemented – in particular, the general food labelling Directive 2000/13/EC[3], the average quantity packaged goods Directives 75/106/EEC and 76/211/EEC and the units of measurement Directive 80/181/EEC. However, in response to Community developments and the need to simplify the law, major changes in the legislation are currently in train that have required additional recourse to the powers in the European Communities Act 1972. First, following consultation[4] Part V of the 1985 Act, the related Sch 8 to the Act, the Weights and Measures (Packaged Goods) Regulations 1986 and those parts of the Code of Practical Guidance for Packers and Importers given statutory effect by the 1986 Regulations have all been repealed by reg 1(2) of the Weights and Measures (Packaged Goods) Regulations 2006[5]. These 2006 Regulations now implement the provisions of the above European legislation relating in particular to the average quantity system described in section **16.4** below. Secondly, as explained in para **16.3.1**, Directive 2007/45/EC must shortly be implemented to enable most foods to be marketed in packs of any size.

Considered below is the British legislation on general offences relating to deficient quantity etc (section **16.2**), quantity requirements for certain foods (section **16.3**), the average quantity system (section **16.4**), manner of quantity marking and abbreviations of measurement units (section **16.5**) and other manner of marking provisions (section **16.6**).

The chapter concludes with a summary of the price marking rules. Section **16.7** deals with the prohibition by the new Consumer Protection from Unfair Trading Regulations 2008[6] of misleading price indications[7]: section **16.8** explains the implementation of Directive 98/6/EEC and other provisions in and under the Prices Act 1974 requiring selling and unit prices to be indicated.

1   FSA 1990, ss 16–18.
2   W&MA 1985, s 93.
3   As to the Food Labelling Directive 2000/13/EC, see in particular section **9.1** above.
4   See the most recent consultation, see DTI, URN 05/1372.
5   SI 2006/659
6   SI 2008/1277 (implementing Directive 2005/29/EC on Unfair Commercial Practices).
7   Formerly regulated by ss 20–26 of the Consumer Protection Act 1987

16.2 GENERAL OFFENCES RELATING TO DEFICIENT QUANTITY ETC

16.2.1 Sections 28–31 of the W&MA 1985 prescribe offences in respect of the delivery of short weight or measure in selling goods; quantities less than stated on sale containers and documents; and materially incorrect statements in documents that are required, by or under Part IV of the Act, to be associated with goods. It previously contained an offence on misrepresentation as to quantity; but this has been repealed by the Consumer Protection from Unfair Trading Regulations 2008 (Sch 2); and a misleading statement or omission as to quantity will be an offence under these 2008 Regulations (see regs 5 and 9 and see further below at **16.7**).

Offences are also prescribed by s 25 of the W&MA 1985 for non-compliance with specified requirements as to sales by quantity of non-pre-packed and pre-packed goods[1]. The requirements include those in the Orders described in section **16.3** below.

1 'Pre-packed' means made up in advance ready for retail sale in or on a container. See W&MA 1985, s 94(1).

16.3 QUANTITY REQUIREMENTS FOR CERTAIN FOODS

16.3.1 Detailed provision is made under Part IV of the W&MA 1985 for quantity indications on pre-packed food and sales by quantity of non-pre-packed food. For most pre-packed foodstuffs, requirements are laid down by Community Directives. Quantity indications are prescribed generally by food labelling Directive 2000/13/EC, as well as for some specific food categories such as additives (by Directive 89/107/EEC) and quick frozen foodstuffs (by Directive 89/108/EEC). Additionally, weights and measures provisions are laid down by directly applicable Community common agricultural policy Regulations in respect of poultrymeat[1] and fruit and vegetables[2]. Finally, to reduce so far as possible the confusion for consumers arising from the multiplicity of different amounts in which packaged products were made up, Directives 75/106/EEC and 80/232/EEC laid down the 'prescribed quantities' permitted for specific types of drink and food.

The British quantity requirements are thus (in part) of domestic inspiration and (in part) made in implementation of these Community obligations. At present, they are to be found in the Weights and Measures Act 1963 (Cheese, Fish, Fresh Fruits and Vegetables, Meat and Poultry) Order 1984 (see para **16.3.2**), the Weights and Measures (Miscellaneous Foods) Order 1988 (see paras **16.3.3–16.3.7**) and the Weights and Measures (Intoxicating Liquor) Order 1988 (see para **16.3.8**).

It should be noted, however, that radical changes to the domestic legislation may be expected soon. This is because, in response to developments in the European Court[3], as well as to changes in consumer preferences, pre-packing innovations and the existence now of other consumer protection legislation[4], the control of nominal quantities for pre-packaged products will be substantially deregulated by Directive 2007/45 on 11 April 2009. Directives 75/106/EEC and 80/232/EEC, which previously regulated this area, will then be repealed and, subject to limited exceptions, Member States will henceforth no longer be able, on grounds relating to nominal quantities of the package, to 'refuse, prohibit or restrict the placing on the market of pre-packed products'. Directive 76/211 will also be amended so as to include prepacked liquids and maintain metrological requirements formerly applied to them by Directive 75/106.

Member States were required by 11 October 2008 to adopt and publish the laws necessary to comply with Directive 2007/45/EC. Countries in which mandatory nominal quantities are prescribed for milk, butter, dried pasta and coffee may maintain their restrictive rules until 11 October 2012. Rules relating to white sugar may be maintained until 11 October 2013.

Proposals have now been published for amendment in April 2009 of the Weights and Measures (Miscellaneous Foods) Order 1988 and the Weights and Measures (Intoxicating Liquor) Order 1988 in part implementation of Directive 2007/45.[5] Besides removal of the mandatory quantities for most pre-packed foods, the main changes are:

- a reduction in the range of sizes of pre-packed spirits subject to specified quantities so that those outside the range 100 ml to 2000 ml will no longer be regulated;
- the addition of the 1750 ml size for pre-packaged spirits;
- a reduction in the ranges of pre-packages still wines subject to specified quantities so that those outside the range 100 ml to 1500 ml will no longer be regulated;
- the removal of the restriction on the use of the 187 ml size for pre-packaged still wines, which limited its use to duty free sales.

Views are also sought first on whether, in respect of milk, butter, dried pasta, coffee and white sugar, advantage should be taken of the temporal derogations referred to above and, secondly, whether the current specified quantities for non-pre-packed intoxicating liquor and unwrapped bread should be amended or revoked.

The proposal to bring existing food weights and measures legislation into line with food labelling Directive 2000/13 has been deferred in view of the EC proposal to update and consolidate the Directive into a Regulation on the provision of food information to consumers[6]. The consultation document points out that this will certainly replace parts of the Weights and Measures Act 1963 (Cheese, Fish, Fresh Fruits and Vegetables, Meat and Poultry) Order 1984. The Order is, in any event, at odds with Community law in so far as it reproduces directly applicable Community rules on poultry and fruit and vegetables. In such cases the United Kingdom should do no more than provide legislation to enforce the rules, as it has long done in relation to the Community egg weight grade-marking requirements[7].

For the moment, however, British law remains as described below.

1   See Commission Regulation (EC) 543/2008; see para **10.4.7** above.
2   See Commission Regulation (EC) 1580/2007; see para **10.4.16**above.
3   See case C-3/99 *Cidrerie Ruwet SA v Cidre Stassen SA and HP Bulmer Ltd* [2000] ECR I-8749 described in para **16.3.4** below.
4   Notably Directive 98/6/EC explained in section **16.8** below.
5   See NWML Consultation of 23 October 2008 on weights and measures legislation dealing with specified quantities and quantity labelling of food.
6   See further para **9.1.3** above.
7   See para **10.4.6** above.

Cheese, fish, fresh fruits and vegetables, meat and poultry

16.3.2   Products controlled by the Weights and Measures Act 1963 (Cheese, Fish, Fresh Fruits and Vegetables, Meat and Poultry) Order 1984 must, generally speaking, be sold by net weight or, subject to maximum container weights, by gross weight when not pre-packed. When pre-packed, the container must usually be marked with an indication of net weight.

Subject to maximum container weights, certain pre-packed cheeses sold by gross weight and soft fruit and mushrooms sold by retail need not be marked with a statement of weight, but the weight must be made known to the buyer before he pays for or takes possession of the food.

There are exemptions in particular for specified meat and fish products, and certain fruits and vegetables may be sold by number or by the bunch.

Quantities of less than 5 g (25 g in the case of cheese) are exempt, as are quantities of more than 5 kg of fresh fruits or vegetables and 10 kg of cheese.

The Order makes special provision for quantity marking in respect of multipacks that contain two or more packs of goods. Different requirements, in particular, apply according to whether the enclosed packs contain different goods, or the same or different quantities of identical goods.

Miscellaneous foods: generally

16.3.3   The Weights and Measures (Miscellaneous Foods) Order 1988 ('the Miscellaneous Foods Order') requires named foods to be sold only in prescribed quantities. It also generally requires pre-packed food (unless exempted) to be marked with an indication of net weight or volume or (in some cases) number and non-pre-packed food to be sold by net weight or (in some cases) by number. Paragraphs **16.3.4–16.3.7** below summarise the provisions respectively on prescribed quantities, quantity marking for prescribed quantity foods, quantity marking for non-prescribed quantity foods and exempted foods and multi-packs.

Miscellaneous foods: prescribed quantities

16.3.4   By provisions that also in part implement Council Directives 75/106/EEC and 80/232/EEC[1], the Miscellaneous Foods Order specifies foods that are, subject to exemptions, required to be pre-packed only in prescribed quantities (reg 3). For the foods in question and the exemptions see Sch 1 (column 1 and columns 3–5 respectively). In 2005 the Order was amended to comply with Community law and reduce the scope of its requirement to pack only in prescribed quantities. The provisions needed to be brought into line with the interpretation of Directives 75/106 and 80/232 following the ECJ judgment in case C-3/99 *Cidrerie Ruwet SA v Cidre Stassen SA and HP Bulmer Ltd*[2]. In application of the *Cassis de Dijon* doctrine[3], this held that Member States are precluded from prohibiting the marketing of pre-packages lawfully manufactured in other Member States and having nominal values not included in the optional Community range, unless the prohibition meets an overriding consumer protection requirement. In consequence, a mutual recognition clause[4] was introduced into the Miscellaneous Foods Order so as to exempt, from the prescribed quantities requirement, UK imports from EC or other EEA Member States. The amending Order also removed the requirement that chocolate and cocoa be packaged only in prescribed quantities since the EC provision that had previously necessitated this was repealed in 2000[5].

1   See para **16.3.1** above.
2   [2000] ECR I-8749.
3   See para **1.3.1** above.
4   See para **1.3.2** above.
5   See Directive 73/241/EEC, Art 6 repealed by Directive 2000/36/EC, Art 7. See further para **10.2.4** above.

Miscellaneous foods: quantity marking for prescribed quantity foods

16.3.5   The Miscellaneous Foods Order (reg 3 and Sch 1) also makes provision for the quantity marking of foods mentioned in para **16.3.4** above.

When pre-packed[1], the foods (other than milk) must be marked with an indication of quantity. Packs of less than 5 g or 5 ml are generally exempt. For biscuits, sugar, chocolate and cocoa products the exemption is for 50 g or less. Bread is exempt where the net weight of each loaf is less than 300 g and the number of items if more than one in the container is marked on the container or is clearly visible and capable of being easily counted through the container. Packs of potatoes are exempt where the net weight of each potato is not less than 175 g and there is an indication of the number of potatoes in the pack and the container is marked with a statement of the minimum net weight of each potato.

When not pre-packed, the foods (other than bread, chunk honey, comb honey and milk) if sold by retail must be sold by net weight. Exemptions are provided for eight or less biscuits and for less than 50 g of cocoa products.

1   Or, in specified cases, 'when made up in a container for sale'.

Miscellaneous foods: quantity marking for non-prescribed quantity foods and exempted foods

16.3.6   Most pre-packed foods that are not subject to the prescribed quantity requirements are nevertheless required by the Miscellaneous Foods Order to be marked with an indication of quantity by weight, capacity, volume or number. There are special requirements for certain biscuits, shortbreads, bread, caseins and caseinates, cocoa and chocolate products (not in bar or tablet form), liquid coffee and chicory products, liquid edible oil, milk (when not pre-packed, in small quantities or sold from vending machines), preserved milk and potatoes.

Miscellaneous foods: multipacks

16.3.7   There is special provision for quantity marking in respect of containers holding two or more packs of goods. Different requirements, in particular, apply according to whether the enclosed packs contain different goods, or the same or different quantities of identical goods.

Intoxicating liquor

16.3.8   By provisions that also in part implement Council Directive 75/106/EEC[1], the Weights and Measures (Intoxicating Liquor) Order 1988 requires pre-packed wines and spirits to be sold only in prescribed quantities.

Provision is also made for the sale only in prescribed quantities, of draught beer and cider and spirits, wines and made wines for consumption on the premises at which they are sold.

The Order requires pre-packed intoxicating liquors to be marked with an indication of volume.

1 See para **16.3.1** above.

16.4 THE AVERAGE QUANTITY SYSTEM

The system

16.4.1 Any legislation on the quantity of goods has to make allowance for inherent errors in weighing and measuring equipment. In Great Britain controls were traditionally based on the 'minimum system' by which the buyer is expected to receive the stated weight or measure, defences being provided to protect diligent manufacturers and sellers[1]. A different approach was adopted in Directives 75/106/EEC and 76/211/EEC which harmonised rules for intra-Community trade in specified products. This is known as the 'average quantity system' whereby the contents of packages are required to be no less, on average, than their nominal quantity[2]. Compliant goods may bear the prescribed 'e' mark and have free access to all Member States[3]. As indicated (at para **16.1.1** above) these Community rules were previously implemented by Part V of the W&MA 1985; but are now regulated in a simplified manner under the Weights and Measures (Packaged Goods) Regulations 2006.

1 W&MA 1985, ss 33–37. See further paras **20.3.1** and **20.6.1** and *Bibby-Cheshire v Golden Wonder Ltd* [1972] 3 All ER 738, [1972] 1 WLR 1487 noted at para **20.3.13** below.
2 See further para **16.4.2** below.
3 See para **16.6.2** below. See also case 96/84 *Vereniging Slachtpluimvee-Export v REWE-Zentral-Aktiengesellschaft* [1985] ECR 1157.

The duties of packers and importers

16.4.2 Regulation 4 lays down three rules to ensure compliance with the European Directive. These are that:

(a)   the contents of the packages shall be not less on average than the nominal quantity;

(b)   the proportion of packages having a negative error greater than the tolerable negative error shall be sufficiently small for batches of packages to satisfy the requirements specified in Sch 2;

(c)   no package shall have a negative error greater than twice the tolerable negative error.

Compliance with rules (a) and (b) is determined by the reference test set out in Sch 2.

Packers and importers are also obliged (by regs 5 and 6) to comply with marking requirements in the Regulations and (by reg 9) to comply with the equipment, checks and documentation requirements.

16.5 MANNER OF QUANTITY MARKING AND ABBREVIATIONS OF MEASUREMENT UNITS

16.5.1   The Weights and Measures (Quantity Marking and Abbreviations of Units) Regulations 1987, as amended ('the Quantity Marking Regulations'), prescribe the manner in which quantity information is to be marked on containers and abbreviations and symbols of units of measurement to be used as required in and under Part IV of the W&MA 1985 and for the purposes of the average quantity system[1].

The Regulations implement Community obligations in Directives 75/106/EEC and 76/211/EEC, the general food labelling Directive 2000/13/EC and Directive 80/181/EEC, as amended, on units of measurement.

Detailed requirements of the Quantity Marking Regulations are summarised in paras **16.5.2–16.5.7** below.

1   See the Weights and Measures (Packaged Goods) Regulations 2006.

Marking with quantity by measurement

16.5.2   The marking of any container with information as to quantity by measurement (weight, capacity or volume) must comprise the numerical value of the unit of measurement expressed in words or by means of the relevant symbol or abbreviation which may be lawfully used for trade in relation to that unit. Where the numerical value of the unit of measurement is expressed in words, the reference to that unit must be expressed in words and not by means of a symbol or abbreviation.

If the goods are packed by gross weight, the information as to quantity must include the word 'gross' or the words 'including container' or other words which indicate that the marked weight includes the weight of the container. No abbreviation of the word 'gross' is permitted.

It is unnecessary to use the word 'net' where goods are packed by net weight but, if used, the word must not be abbreviated.

Any metric quantity used in the marking may not be expressed as a vulgar fraction.

Legibility and position of marking

16.5.3   Any marking of a container with information as to quantity must be easy to understand, clearly legible and indelible. It must be easily visible to an intending purchaser under normal conditions of purchase and must not in any way be hidden, obscured or interrupted by any other written or pictorial matter. If the information is not on the actual container or on a label securely attached to the container, it must be so placed that it cannot be removed without opening the container.

Size of marking

16.5.4   Except in the case of catchweight products (i e any product that is not pre-packed according to a pre-determined fixed weight pattern, but is packed in varying quantities), where in any marking of any container the quantity by number or the numerical value of a unit of measurement is expressed in figures, all the relevant figures must be at least of the height specified[1] according to whether the marking is of weight, capacity, volume or number.

1   Weights and Measures (Quantity Marking and Abbreviations of Units) Regulations 1987, Sch 1

Metric and imperial units

16.5.5   The marking of containers with information as to quantity must be in metric units. However, information as to quantity by measurement may additionally be marked on returnable containers used for milk, by reference to the pint. Moreover, the Quantity Marking Regulations enable any container marked in metric units of measurement to be marked with a supplementary indication.

These provisions must be read with the W&MA 1985 and the Units of Measurement Regulations 1986. Section 8 of the W&MA 1985 prohibits the use in trade of units of measure other than listed metric units, subject to exceptions:

- for the use of the pint in the sale of draught beer or cider and in the sale of milk in returnable containers[1]; and
- for the use of supplementary indications in imperial measure until 31 December 2009[2].

The exceptions implement units of measurement Directive 80/181/EEC and both are under apparent threat because the authority to use the pint currently subsists only until a date to be fixed by the United Kingdom and Ireland. However, with the 2009 deadline approaching fast and a need for continued use of imperial measure in trade with the United States, the Community is currently considering further amendments to Directive 80/181[3] which, if passed, will indefinitely permit use of the exceptions.

Generally, things have not been encouraging for those who have continued to oppose UK metrication legislation. In appeals challenging judgments against them for non-compliance with metrication provisions in proceedings under W&MA 1985, s 8 and other legislation, the appellants failed in their contention that the European Communities Act 1972, s 2(2) had been repealed by the W&MA 1985. The 1972 Act is by common law a constitutional statute and cannot be impliedly repealed[4]. However, no doubt in the light of the evident EC change of heart, on 22 October 2008 the National Weights and Measures Laboratory (NWML) and Department for Innovation, Universities and Skills expressed themselves keen to encourage enforcement action on the part of Trading Standards Officers (TSOs) that is proportionate, consistent and in the public and consumer's interest. Accordingly they are in discussion with the Local Authorities Coordinators of Regulatory Services[5] with a view to updating their guidance for TSOs. They are also reviewing the current legislative framework with the object of making it easier for everyone to understand, for business to comply with and for TSOs to enforce.

1   W&MA 1985, s 8(1)(d). See also the Units of Measurement Regulations 1986, s 14 and Sch 3B.
2   W&MA 1985, s 8(5A). See also the Units of Measurement Regulations 1986, s 7.
3   See COM(2007) 510 final. See also *Government saves the Pint and Mile*: Department for Innovation, Universities & Skills press notice of 16 December 2008.
4   *Thorburn v Sunderland City Council;Hunt v Hackney London Borough Council; Harman v Cornwall County Council; Collins v Sutton London Borough Council* [2002] EWHC 195 Admin, (2002) Times, 22 February.
5   See para **18.3.2** below.

Units of measurement

16.5.6 Subject to the special provision for milk mentioned in para **16.5.5** above, metric units of measurement to be used in marking any container with information as to quantity by measurement are specified. For volume, the units are cubic metre, cubic centimetre, litre, centilitre and millilitre. For capacity the units are litre, centilitre and millilitre. And for mass or weight, the units are kilogram and gram.

Symbols and abbreviations

16.5.7 The following symbols for and abbreviations of relevant units of measurement are permitted by the Quantity Marking Regulations:

Unit of Measurement	Symbol
cubic metre	m^3
cubic centimetre	cm^3
litre	l or L
decilitre	dl or dL
centilitre	cl or cL
millilitre	ml or mL
tonne	t
kilogram	kg
hectogram	hg
gram	g
milligram	mg

Where the pint is used in connection with returnable containers for milk or the dispensing of draught beer or cider, the abbreviation 'pt' may be used and the letter 's' may be added, where appropriate, to indicate the plural.

16.6 OTHER MANNER OF MARKING PROVISIONS

16.6.1 Other relevant manner of marking provisions are noted in the following two paragraphs.

The 'e' mark

16.6.2 The Weights and Measures (Packaged Goods) Regulations 1986 previously prescribed the form of the average quantity system 'e' mark referred to in para **16.4.1** above; but this is now dealt with by the Weights and Measures (Packaged Goods) Regulations 2006, regs 2, 5 and 6 and Sch 4. When applied to a container it must be at least 3 mm high; be placed in the same field of vision as that of the statement of quantity marked on the package; and be indelible, clearly legible and visible under normal conditions of purchase.

Field of vision

16.6.3 The indication of net quantity on packages of food is required by the

Food Labelling Regulations 1996 to appear in the same field of vision (i e to be simultaneously visible) as the name of the food, the indication of minimum durability or 'use by' date, the alcoholic strength and specified cautionary words, as appropriate (see para **9.2.26** above).

16.7   MISLEADING PRICE INDICATIONS

16.7.1   The former offence of misleading pricing (under Part III of the Consumer Protection Act 1987[1]) has now been replaced by the new general misleading practice offence under the Consumer Protection from Unfair Trading Regulations 2008[2]. This offence is committed where there is a misleading action and where there is a misleading omission. There is a misleading action where there is false information or information that deceives or is likely to deceive the average consumer (in relation to a huge list of matters, including price) and causes or is likely to cause the average consumer to take a transactional decision that he would not have taken otherwise. A commercial practice is a misleading omission if, in its factual context, taking into account all its features and circumstances, and the limitations of the communication medium, it omits material information that the average consumer needs, according to the context, to take an informed transactional decision and thereby causes him, or is likely to cause him to take a transactional decision that he would not have taken otherwise.

1   CPA 1987, s 20.
2   SI 2008/1277, regs 5, 6, 9 and 10 (implementing Directive 2005/29/EC on Unfair Commercial Practices See also para **8.1.1**.

16.8   PRICE MARKING INDICATIONS

16.8.1   The law requiring the price marking of food was changed as a result of European Parliament and Council Directive 98/6/EC on consumer protection in the indication of the prices of products offered to consumers. This in particular repealed and replaced Directive 79/581/EEC on the indication of the prices of foodstuffs. The newer Directive aims at simplifying the comparison of products by abandoning the link with prescribed quantities[1] in favour of straightforward indications of the selling price and unit price.

In the United Kingdom, the Directive was originally implemented by the Price Marking Order 1999[2], which was made under the Prices Act 1974; but this has now been replaced by the Price Marking Order 2004[3]. A related Order (the Price Marking (Food and Drink on Premises) Order 1979[4]) was originally replaced by the Price Marking (Food and Drink) Services Order 2003; but this has now been repealed by the Consumer Protection from Unfair Trading Regulations 2008[5].

1   See section **16.3** above.
2   SI 1999/3042.
3   SI 2004/102.
4   SI 1979/361.
5   Regulation 30 (1) and Sch 2

Obligations to indicate the selling price and the unit price

16.8.2   Where a trader indicates that a product is or may be for sale to a consumer, art 4 of the Price Marking Order 2004 requires that he indicate the selling price except in the case of products offered in the provision of a service, those sold by auction and works of art or antiques (see art 3(1)). The requirement also does not apply to products sold from bulk or to advertisements and products sold from bulk (see art 4(2)). Article 1 defines the selling price as the final price including VAT and other taxes.

Article 5 of the 2004 Order requires, subject to specified exceptions, that the unit price must be indicated for all products sold from bulk or for pre-packaged products required (by or under Part IV of the W&MA 1985 or the Weights and Measures (Packaged Goods) Regulations 2006) to be marked with an indication of quantity or to be made up in a quantity prescribed under the relevant legislation. The exceptions, first are, as above, where services, auctions and works of art or antiques are concerned. Second, there are specific exceptions related to:

(a)   products offered by particular aural advertisements, products offered at prices reduced on account of damaged condition or the danger of their deterioration, and products that comprise an assortment of different items sold in single packages (see art 5(3)(a) and Sch 2);

(b)   products of which the unit prices are identical to the selling prices (art 5(3)(b));

(c)   bread made up in a prescribed quantity and sold in small shops, by itinerant traders or from vending machines (art 5(2)(c);

(d)   products that are pre-packaged in constant quantities and sold in small shops, by itinerant traders or from vending machines (art 5(2)(d)); and

(e)   advertisements in which the selling price of the product is not indicated (art 5(4)).

Manner of indication of prices and unit price roundings

16.8.3   Article 6 of the Price Marking Order 2004 requires that the selling and unit prices be displayed in sterling, but, subject to specified conditions, permits additional indications of price in foreign currency.

Article 7 requires that prices and other required indications be given in a clear and unambiguous manner.

Chapter 17

Feeding stuffs

17.1 INTRODUCTION

17.1.1 Contamination of fertilisers and feeding stuffs can lead to the contamination of the final link in the food chain – the human consumer. The use of artificial manures and concentrated feeding stuff did not begin until the nineteenth century and towards the end of that century questions started to be asked about the purity of the products being used. The first piece of legislation passed to combat adulteration and fraud in this area was the Fertilisers and Feeding Stuffs Act 1893, similar provision to which are now found in Part IV of the Agriculture Act 1970 (AA 1970). Since UK accession to the European Community, feeding stuffs legislation has essentially been made in implementation of Community Directives and Regulations, mostly by domestic regulations under the AA 1970 powers as fortified by the European Communities Act 1972 (ECA 1972).

When the link was made between BSE and animal feed important controls were put in place under the Animal Health Act 1981. The need to control animal feeding stuffs in the context of food safety resulted in the Food Standards Agency being given the same general functions in relation to matters connected to feeding stuffs as it was for food safety matters in general.[1] The use of genetically modified feed ingredients also emerged as an issue of public concern. In addition, therefore, the Advisory Committee on Animal Feedingstuffs (ACAF) was established in June 1999, with particular emphasis on protecting human health and with reference to new technical developments and new feed materials and products.[2]

The European Community has also taken important new initiatives to control animal feed. Paramount amongst these are the provisions in general food Regulation (EC) 178/2002, Art 12 (on export or re-export to third countries), Art 15(1) (prohibiting unsafe feed), Art 16 (prohibiting misleading labelling, advertising or presentation), Art 18(2) and (3) (on traceability) and Art 20 (on the responsibilities of business operators). These provisions and the domestic Regulations enforcing them are explained in ch 3.

'Feed' is excluded from the definition of 'food' in Art 1 of Regulation (EC) 178/2002[3] but, it is accepted that 'within the context of food law it is appropriate to include requirements for feed, including its production and use where that feed is intended for food-producing animals.'[4] Therefore, the Regulation's definition of 'food law' covers the production, processing and distribution of feed for food-producing animals.[5]

Feeding stuffs law is no longer confined to basic composition and labelling provisions. In response to modern developments, this chapter now extends to feed hygiene, feeding stuffs containing veterinary medicinal products and related feed additives, as well as to measures to combat transmissible spongiform encephalopathies and control of genetically modified feed. Feed is subject to Regulation (EC) 834/2007 on the production and labelling of organic products explained in para **10.5.4** above and, from 1 September 2008, maximum pesticide residues in feed, as well as food, are controlled by Regulation (EC) 396/2005 described in para **12.7.1** above.

Part 4 of the Feed (Hygiene and Enforcement) (England) Regulations 2005 makes additional provision for the administration and enforcement of specified feed legislation, including that covered by sections **17.2, 17.3** and **17.5** of this chapter, official controls Regulation (EC) 882/2004 (under which the sampling and analysis rules considered in section **17.4** are now made) and Regulation (EC) 178/2002 (in so far as it relates to feed). By provisions analogous to those for unhygienic food businesses made by ss 10–12 of the Food Safety Act 1990 and considered in ch 6 above, improvement notices, prohibition orders, emergency prohibition notices and emergency prohibition orders may now be applied to feed businesses that fail to comply with the law. Additionally, Part 4 confers further powers of entry, seizure, sampling and analysis.

Under reg 6 of the Official Feed and Food Controls (England) Regulations 2007 and equivalent powers for Scotland and Wales, a Feed Law Code of Practice has been issued for Great Britain to which local authorities must have regard in carrying out their enforcement functions. Reference to specific guidance in the Code about Incidents and Hazards and UK food alerts is to be found in ch 7 above.

1   Food Standards Act 1999, s 9. See also para **2.3.4** above.
2   *The Food Standards Agency: A Force for Change* (Cm 3830, 1998), paras 4.14–4.22. As to the ACAF, see para **2.4.6** above.
3   This definition has been inserted into s 1 FSA 1990. See paras **4.3.1** and **3.2.2–3.2.3** above.
4   Recital (7) to Regulation (EC) 178/2002.
5   Article 3.

17.2   AGRICULTURE ACT 1970, PART IV

17.2.1 Part IV of the AA 1970 regulates the preparation and sale of animal feeding stuffs. Over the years it has been progressively adapted for the purpose of implementing Community law[1], but recourse to the ECA 1972 has been necessary for the control of hygiene, BSE and genetically modified feed to which its powers do not extend.

Principal requirements of the AA 1970 are that feeding stuffs should be fit for their intended purpose and free from harmful ingredients. The seller must give particulars of specified attributes claimed to be present, a warranty being implied that these particulars are correct. A warranty by the seller is also in particular implied as to the suitability of the feeding stuff for use as such. The sale of feeding stuffs containing deleterious ingredients or of dangerous or unwholesome material for use as feeding stuffs is prohibited.

Moreover, the AA 1970 requires a written statutory statement of prescribed compositional information to be given to the purchaser of feeding stuffs and makes provision for the marking of material prepared for sale. Where a feeding stuff is sold under a name or description for which a meaning has been assigned by Regulations, there is an implied warranty that it accords with that meaning and failure of a sample to accord with that meaning renders the seller liable to a fine.

Detailed provisions for the operation of these compositional requirements are laid down by Regulations as noted in para **17.3.1** below.

Enforcement is the responsibility, in England, of county, metropolitan district and London borough councils and the Common Council of the City of London and, in Wales, of county and county borough councils. These authorities are required to appoint inspectors and agricultural analysts. In practice, enforcement is mainly undertaken by the local authority trading standards officers.

It should also be noted that any statement made in respect of, or mark applied to, any material in pursuance of Part IV of the AA 1970 or any name or expression to which a meaning has been assigned under s 70 of that Act when applied to any material in the circumstances specified in that section are deemed not to be trade descriptions and thus not caught by the Trade Descriptions Act 1968 (TDA 1968).[2]

1   See for example, ECA 1972, Sch 4, para 6; the Agriculture Act 1970 Amendment Regulations 1982; the Feeding Stuffs (Safety Requirements for feed for Food-Producing Animals) Regulations 2004, regs 9–11; and the Feeding Stuffs (England) Regulations 2005, regs 3 and 4.
2   TDA 1968, s 2(4).

17.2.2   Part IV of the AA 1970 also provides for purchasers to have samples taken and analysed, for inspectors to enter premises and take samples, for the division of samples and analysis by agricultural analysts, for further analysis by the Government Chemist and for regulations prescribing sampling and analysis methods.

The current Regulations prescribing sampling and analysis methods for feeding stuffs are noted in para **17.4.1** below.

17.3   COMPOSITIONAL REGULATIONS

17.3.1   The Feeding Stuffs (England) Regulations 2005[1], as amended, currently lay down the detailed compositional requirements for the operation of Part IV of the AA 1970. In particular they cover aspects of the composition, labelling and marketing of animal feeding stuffs and contain provisions intended to safeguard animal and human health.

The Regulations are the main means by which the substantial body of European Community legislation on the composition of feeding stuffs is implemented. Principal rules enacted by the Council are to be found in Directive 79/373/EEC (on the marketing of compound feeding stuffs), Directive 82/471/EEC (concerning certain protein sources used in animal nutrition), Directive 93/74/EC (on feeding stuffs intended for particular nutritional purposes), Directive 96/25/EC (on the circulation of feed materials), Directive 2002/32/EC (on undesirable substances in feed materials), Directive 2004/116/EC (inclusion of *Canidida guilliermondi*), Decision 2004/217/EC (prohibited ingredients in animal nutrition) and Regulation (EC) 1831/2003 (feed additives).

The Regulations specify the material that is 'prescribed material' for the purposes of the AA 1970 as any material useable as a feeding stuff. The presentation and composition of feeding stuffs are dealt with in Part 2 of the Regulations that:

(a)   prescribes the limits of inaccuracy permitted in the declaration of ingredients;

(b)   attributes meanings to the names of certain materials for the purposes of the AA 1970;

(c)   prescribes the way in which compound feeds may be sealed and packaged;

(d)   regulates the putting into circulation and use of feed materials;

(e)   restricts the putting into circulation or use of feeding stuffs containing specified undesirable substances;

(f)   prohibits the putting into circulation or use of any feeding stuff containing certain prescribed substances;

(g)   controls the marketing and use of certain protein sources and non-protein nitrogenous compounds in feed;

(h)   regulates the iron content of milk replacer feeds;

(i)   prohibits the putting into circulation of compound feeding stuffs in which the amount of ash insoluble in hydrochloric acid exceeds specified levels; and

(j)   controls the marketing of feeds intended for particular nutritional purposes.

1   SI 2005/3281.

17.3.2   As regards the control of additives in feeding stuffs, Regulation (EC) 1831/2003 is executed and enforced by the Regulations by making it an offence not to comply with certain specified requirements in the EC Regulation. The Regulations also contain a duty of confidentiality on anyone, who may in the course of processing an application for authorisation, have acquired commercially sensitive information. Part 3 of the Regulations deal with enforcement.

Provision for enforcement of Regulation (EC) 1831/2003 in respect of medicated feedingstuffs and specified feed additives is made by the Veterinary Medicines Regulations 2008, reg 14 and Sch 5, para 3.

17.4   SAMPLING AND ANALYSIS REGULATIONS

17.4.1   The European Community soon found it necessary to provide for the introduction of common sampling and analysis methods for the official control of feeding stuffs. There have now been a number of Directives establishing Community methods of analysis for animal feeding stuffs. Only the methods specified in the Directives (as amended) may be used.

Under the powers of AA 1970, these provisions are generally implemented by the Feeding Stuffs (Sampling and Analysis) Regulations 1999 (as amended).

Sampling and analysis is now regulated within the framework of official control Regulation (EC) 882/2004 described in ch 18. Pending replacement by new provisions, the existing sampling and analysis Directives, which are listed in Annex C attached, are saved by Art 61 of the Regulation so far as they are not in conflict with it.

17.5   FEED HYGIENE

17.5.1   Regulation (EC) 183/2005 lays down general rules on feed hygiene and conditions and arrangements both for ensuring traceability of feed and for registration and approval of establishments. 'Feed hygiene' in this context evidently has a rather wider meaning than might be expected. It extends to the control of all hazards – not just biological ones.[1]

Since primary responsibility for feed safety rests with feed business operators, Chapter II of Regulation (EC) 183/2005 imposes on them a series of new obligations. A 'feed business' is defined as 'any undertaking whether for profit or not and whether public or private, carrying out any operation of production, manufacture, processing, storage or transport or distribution of feed, including any producer producing, processing or storing feed for feeding to animals on his own holding.' This, therefore, covers the whole of the feed chain, including manufacturers, transporters, storers and relevant farmers.[2] There are exemptions, in particular, for private domestic production of feed for food producing animals kept for private domestic production and for animals not kept for food production.[3]

A feed business operator's obligations depend to some extent on the type of business conducted. Annex 1 contains requirements for businesses involved in primary production concerning general hygiene and record keeping. Annex II specifies requirements for businesses other than primary production and relates mainly to facilities, personnel, quality control, storage, transport and record keeping. Finally, Annex III contains a code on good animal feeding practice for food-producing animals that must be complied with by livestock farmers.

Further, the Regulation requires feed business operators, other than at the level of primary production, to put in place and operate a hazard analysis and critical control point (HACCP) system based on specified principles.

Conditions and arrangements for approving and registering businesses in the animal feed sector were originally laid down by Council Directive 95/69/EC, which have since been replaced by provisions of Regulation (EC) 183/2005.

Food business operators must register their establishments with the national competent authorities and keep up to date the information they provide. Manufacture and marketing of higher risk feed additives and products specified in Art 10 are conditional on prior approval of the operator's establishment. Approval is granted only where inspection by the authority shows that the establishment meets the Regulation's requirements.

Regulation (EC) 183/2005 also provides for the development of guides to good practice and lays down conditions for import of feed from third countries.

Regulation (EC) 183/2005/EC is enforced within England by Part 2 of the Feed (Hygiene and Enforcement) (England) Regulations 2005 and, in respect of medicated feedingstuffs and specified feed additives, by the Veterinary Medicines Regulations 2008, reg 14 and Sch 5, para 5. Offences for breach of specified provisions of Regulation (EC) 183/2005 are prescribed and provision made for registration and approval of feed business establishments and for approval of manufacturers and distributors of feedingstuffs containing veterinary products.

1   See Regulation (EC) 183/2005, Arts 3(a) and 4(2).
2   As to 'feed business' and the primary responsibility of food business operators, see Regulation (EC) 178/2002, Arts 3(5) and 17 described at para **3.2.38** above.
3   Regulation (EC) 183/2005, Art 2(2).

17.6 MEDICATED FEEDINGSTUFFS AND SPECIFIED FEED ADDITIVES

17.6.1 The Veterinary Medicine Regulations 2008, reg 14 and Sch 5 implement the EC rules on medicated feedingstuffs in Directive 90/167/EC (so far as not superseded by Regulation (EC) 183/2005) and those on specified feed additives controlled by Regulation (EC) 1831/ 2003.[1] 'Specified feed additives' are coccidiostats, histomonostats and all other zootechnical additives, except gut flora stabilisers, digestibility enhancers, substances incorporated with the intention of favourably affecting the environment. Medicated feedingstuffs are feedingstuffs containing a veterinary medicinal product.

Schedule 5 imposes requirements as to the incorporation of veterinary medicinal products within feedingstuffs and premixtures, the manner of labelling such products and their supply. Record keeping is required. The requirements concerning the supply and labelling of specified feed additives are also set out. Prescriptions for feedingstuffs containing a veterinary medicinal product are required and must contain all of the stated information. It is an offence to be in possession of any specified feed additive, veterinary medicinal products, or premixture containing such products or feedingstuff containing a veterinary medicinal product, without the appropriate approval. If enforcement action is to take place the specified sampling and analysis procedures must be followed.

Veterinary medicinal products, feedingstuffs or premixtures containing them must be securely stored and the packages or containers of veterinary medicinal products must be suitably sealed. Where feedingstuffs containing veterinary medicinal products are to be transported this must be in accordance with the regulations.

1   See Arts 1(2)(b), 6(1)(d) and Annex I para 4.

17.7 TRANSMISSIBLE SPONGIFORM ENCEPHALOPATHIES

17.7.1   Section **14.6** above summarised the legislation to prevent any danger to humans from BSE or other transmissible spongiform encephalopathies through the consumption of food. This section describes measures taken in respect of feeding stuffs.

Very soon after the appearance of BSE, scientists in Britain suspected that the consumption of meat and bone meal by cattle was responsible for the disease. In 1988 a ban was imposed on the feeding to ruminants of rations containing ruminant protein. In 1994, Commission Decision 94/381/EC required Community Member States to prohibit the feeding of protein derived from mammalian tissues to ruminant species. The British provisions were amended in implementation of this requirement.

British measures were further strengthened to prevent contamination of cattle feed with material intended for monogastric animals following the advice of the Government's Spongiform Encephalopathy Advisory Committee in 1996. The sale or supply of mammalian meat and bone meal for the purpose of feeding to all farm animals was banned. Since then the European Community, taking account of further evidence on TSEs, has developed a comprehensive set of controls on feed.

The relevant provisions are now to be found in Sch 6 of the Transmissible Spongiform Encephalopathies (England) Regulations 2008, which implement Art 7 and Annex IV of EC Regulation (EC) 999/2001 as regard animal nutrition, as amended.[1] Other notable provisions of the 2008 Regulations make it an offence to use mechanically recovered meat produced from bovine, ovine or caprine bones (Sch 7, para 3(2)) and enable inspectors to seize and dispose of feedingstuffs that may contain animal protein and to serve notices prohibiting or requiring their movement and requiring their disposal or recall (regs 14 and 15.)

1 The 2008 Regulations do not implement the provisions of Regulation (EC) 727/2007 suspended by interim order of 28 September 2007 in case T-257/07R *France v Commission* [2007] ECR II-4253.

Restrictions on feeding animal proteins to animals

17.7.2   Ruminant and non-ruminant farmed animals are not to be fed directly, or in feedingstuffs, processed animal protein or gelatine from ruminants. The only permitted animal proteins are milk, milk-based products, colostrums, eggs and egg products, gelatine from non-ruminants and hydrolysed proteins derived from non-ruminants or from ruminant hides and skins. Such permitted proteins must have been sourced and processed in accordance with the Animal By-Product Regulations 2005. Non-ruminant-farmed animals can be fed fishmeal, blood products, blood meal (only where fed to farmed fish) and dicalcium phosphate and tricalcium phosphate of animal origin. Any farm animal feed production using such proteins must have authorisation to do so. Such feedingstuffs must be clearly labelled 'contains [name of restricted protein] – shall not be fed to ruminants'. There are rules on the transport of proteins, including procedures on cleansing of the vehicles.

17.8   ANIMAL WASTE

17.8.1   The protection of feeding stuffs from biological contamination by BSE and other spongiform encephalopathy agents is an aspect of the wider problem of preventing pathogens in feeding stuffs of animal or fish origin. Further Community rules about this are laid down by and under EC Regulation (EC) 1774/2002, as amended, on health rules concerning animal by-products not intended for human consumption and related measures. This Regulation is administered and enforced within England by the Animal By-Products Regulations 2005. The Regulation divides animal by-products into three risk categories and specifies the permitted treatment or disposal method for each category of material and the standards of operation of the permitted outlets. The feeding of catering waste or feed materials containing or derived from catering waste to farmed animals, other ruminant animals, pigs or birds is prohibited. It is an offence to feed to the animals of the same species processed animal protein derived from the bodies or parts of bodies of that species. However, it is permitted to feed fish with processed animal protein from the bodies or parts of bodies of fish, if done in accordance with correct procedures. Catering waste or other animal by-products must not be brought onto premises where any livestock are kept (with exceptions) and livestock must not have access to this material.

17.9 GENETICALLY MODIFIED ANIMAL FEED

17.9.1   As explained in section **10.3** above, genetic modification is now the subject of two EC Regulations. They are Regulation (EC) 1829/2003 on genetically modified food and feed; and Regulation (EC) 1830/2003 concerning the traceability and labelling of genetically modified organisms (GMOs) and the traceability of food and feed products produced from GMOs.[1]

Genetically modified feed is regulated by Chapter III of Regulation (EC) 1829/2003 which applies to GMOs for feed use, feed containing or consisting of GMOs and feed produced from GMOs.

GM feed must not:

- have adverse effects on human life, animal health or the environment;
- mislead the user;
- harm or mislead the consumer by impairing the distinctive features of the animal products;
- differ from feed which it is intended to replace to such an extent that its normal consumption would be nutritionally disadvantageous for animals or humans.

Marketing or processing of GM feed is prohibited unless authorised in accordance with the Regulation, which makes thorough provision for the grant, supervision, revocation and renewal of authorisations.

GM feed must also be labelled, as specified in Regulation (EC) 1829/2003, with the name of the GM organism and, as specified in the authorisation, with any characteristic or property that distinguishes it from its conventional counterpart, or that may give rise to ethical or religious concerns.

The European Commission maintains a publicly available Community register of GM food and feed.

The Genetically Modified Animal Feed (England) Regulations 2004 provide for the execution and enforcement of the provisions of Regulation (EC) 1829/2003 relating to feed.

Regulation (EC) 1830/2003 applies at all marketing stages to products (including feed) containing or consisting of GMOs. As indicated in para **10.3.3** and **10.3.4**, it requires operators:

- at each marketing stage, to transmit in writing an indication that products contain or consist of GMOs, together with the GMOs' unique identifiers;
- to label products that are pre-packaged, or display products that are not, with a statement that they contain GMOs.

The Genetically Modified Organisms (Traceability and Labelling) (England) Regulations 2004 provide for the execution and enforcement of Regulation (EC) 1830/2003.

---

1   Guidance notes on the Regulations have been issued by the Food Standards Agency and DEFRA.

Chapter 18

Enforcement: official controls on food and feed

18.1 INTRODUCTION

18.1.1 No matter how good substantive food laws are, they will be ineffective without sound enforcement. Dating back essentially to 1875[1], British provisions for enforcement by local authority officers have been adapted to serve the purposes of Community official food control. Administrative penalties were considered earlier in this book (see section **5.4** on the inspection, detention and seizure of suspected food; ch 6 on improvement notices, prohibition orders and emergency prohibition notices and orders etc; and section **14.4** on registration and approval of food businesses).

This chapter describes the general powers of inspection; ch 19 deals with prosecutions and evidence, including Code C under the Police and Criminal Evidence Act 1984[2] and the provisions of the Criminal Procedure and Investigations Act 1996. General food inspection is considered below under the following headings:

(a)   Community requirements (section **18.2**);
(b)   official controls in England and Wales (section **18.3**);
(c)   food: sampling and analysis etc (section **18.4**);
(d)   food: powers of entry, obstruction etc (section **18.5**);
(e)   feed: enforcement powers (section **18.6**);
(f)   weights and measures enforcement powers (section **18.7**);
(g)   other legislation (section **18.8**).

1   See para **1.1.1** above.
2   Police and Criminal Evidence Act 1984 (Codes of Practice) Order 2008.

18.2   COMMUNITY REQUIREMENTS

Official food and feed control Regulation

18.2.1   Regulation (EC) 882/2004 lays down the general rules for the performance of official controls to verify compliance with rules aimed at preventing, eliminating or reducing to acceptable levels risks to humans and animals and guaranteeing fair practices in feed and food trade and protecting consumer interests.[1] 'Official control' means 'any form of control that the competent authority or the Community performs for the verification of compliance with feed and food law, animal health and animal welfare rules.' The Regulation does not apply to official controls for the verification of compliance with rules on common market organisations of agricultural products[2] but is otherwise of very wide scope. Although this book is not generally concerned with animal health and welfare, Regulation (EC) 882/2004 applies, in respect of food and feed, for the enforcement not only of general Regulation (EC) 178/2002, but also of more specific rules for areas such as animal nutrition including medicated feedingstuffs, feed and food hygiene, zoonoses, animal by-products, residues and contaminants, feed and food labelling, pesticides, feed and food additives, vitamins, mineral salts, trace elements and other additives, materials in contact with food, quality and compositional requirements, drinking water, ionisation, novel foods and genetically modified organisms (GMOs).[3]

1 Regulation (EC) 882/2004, Art 1. The FSA has prepared guidance: *Regulation (EC) 882/2004 on official controls performed to ensure the verification of compliance with feed and food law, animal health and animal welfare rules – Q&A Notes for enforcement authorities on the feed and food elements*, Revision 2, February 2008.
2 See section **10.4** above.
3 See Regulation (EC) 882/2004 recitals (2) and (3).

Official controls by Member States: General obligations

18.2.2   Article 3 of Regulation (EC) 882/2004/EC imposes general obligations on Member States to ensure that official controls are carried out on a regular basis and with appropriate frequency so as to achieve the objectives of the Regulation. The controls must be proportionate to the end to be observed and must cover all stages of production, manufacture, import into the Community, processing, storage, transport, distribution and trade. It should be carried out at the stage most appropriate to achieve the objective. As a general rule, controls should be carried out without prior warning.

Official controls by Member States: Role of competent authorities

18.2.3   The 'competent authority' is the central authority of the Member State competent for the organisation of official controls and any other authority to which that competence has been conferred. The competent authority is responsible for ensuring the effectiveness and appropriateness of official controls on live animals, feed and food at all stages of production, processing and distribution and on the use of feed and that there are a sufficient number of suitably qualified and experienced staff to carry out the duties and that they are free from any conflict of interest. There must be contingency plans prepared for an emergency, legal powers to carry out official controls and suitable facilities and equipment to ensure that staff can carry out official controls efficiently and effectively. The competent authority is required to carry out internal audits or have external audits carried out. Specific tasks can be delegated to a 'control body'[1]. The training of staff performing official controls is the responsibility of the competent authority. All activities must be carried out in a transparent manner and information made public unless covered by professional secrecy. Official controls should be carried out in accordance with documented procedures, which contain information and instructions for staff. Reports on controls that have been carried out must be prepared and copies of these must be given to the business operators concerned, at least in the case of non-compliance.

1 An independent third party to which the competent authority has delegated certain control tasks (see Art 2.5). This could, for example, be a privately owned laboratory used to undertake

chemical analysis or microbiological examination. Under Art 5 action concerning non-compliance cannot be delegated.

Official controls by Member States: further provisions

18.2.4   Article 10 of Regulation (EC) 882/2004 requires tasks related to official controls to be carried out using appropriate control methods and techniques such as monitoring, surveillance, verification, audit, inspection, sampling and analysis. The following are subject to inspection:

(a)   primary producers' installations, feed and food businesses, including their surroundings, premises, offices, equipment, installations and transport and machinery, as well as feed and food;

(b)   raw materials, ingredients, processing aids and other products used for the preparation and production of feed and food;

(c)   semi-finished products;

(d)   materials and articles intended to come into contact with foodstuffs;

(e)   cleaning and maintenance products and processes and pesticides;

(f)   labelling, presentation and advertising.

There must be examination of any control systems that feed or food operators have put in place, checks on hygiene conditions, assessment of good manufacturing practices (GMP), good hygiene practices (GHP) and HACCP and interviews with businesses and their staff etc. Regulation (EC) 882/2004, Arts 11 and 12 also provide for the taking of samples and their analysis by official laboratories. To be authorised, laboratories must comply with the quality standards and use the validated methods prescribed by Art 12.[1]

The Regulation's provisions on official controls by Member States additionally include chapters on:

• crisis management (explained in ch 7 above);

• controls on feed and food from third countries that, in requiring controls on feed and food of non-animal origin, supplement veterinary checks on products of animal origin under Directive 97/78 (see section **14.7** above);

• financing of official controls that, besides continuing mandatory charging arrangements for matters such as meat and fish hygiene inspections (see section **14.3**), require competent authorities to charge for additional controls following detection of non-compliance[2].

1   The FSA maintains a list of designated official laboratories.
2   The FSA has issued guidance: *Official Feed and Food Controls (England) Regulations 2007 – regulation 41 on expenses arising from 'additional official controls'*.

Other official control provisions

18.2.5   Further, Regulation (EC) 882/204 makes provision for:

• Community and national reference laboratories;

• administrative assistance and cooperation between Member States;

• the national control plans described in the next paragraph;

• Community checking etc of official controls in Member States and third countries;

• national action, under Art 54, where non-compliance is identified and under Art 55, to prescribe effective, proportionate and dissuasive sanctions applicable to infringements of feed and food law.

National control plan

18.2.6   All Member States are required to have a multi-annual national control plan, to ensure that national monitoring and enforcement arrangements are in place. It must describe the roles and responsibilities of the various competent authorities and provide details of how the various Regulations are being met. In the United Kingdom the responsibility for preparing the plan lies with the Food Standards Agency, Defra and its agencies and the devolved Agriculture and Rural Affairs Departments.

18.3   OFFICIAL CONTROLS IN ENGLAND AND WALES

Implementation of official controls Regulation (EC) 882/2004

18.3.1   As elsewhere in this book, references in this paragraph to English subordinate legislation, Codes of Practice and Practice Guidance are, in respect of Wales, to be read as references to the Welsh equivalents.

Regulation (EC) 882/2004 is implemented principally by the Official Feed and Food Controls (England) Regulations 2007. Additionally, the Official Controls (Animals, Feed and Food) (England) Regulations 2006 provide for enforcement of the following feed and food law topics that are the responsibility of DEFRA rather than the FSA:

- veterinary medicines residues;
- pesticides residues;
- protected name food products and specific character food products;
- organic products, including imported organic food products;
- beef labelling;
- the import from third countries of, and intra-Community trade in, products of animal origin; and
- TSEs in relation to BSE testing, including sampling controls on bovine, ovine and caprine animals slaughtered for human consumption;
- animal by-products.

Except in relation to most of the DEFRA topics mentioned above[1], official controls on food under Regulation (EC) 882/2004 are further implemented by the Food Safety Act 1990[2] in conjunction with the Food Law Code of Practice (England)[3] and Food Law Practice Guidance (England). Official controls on feed under Regulation (EC) 882/2004 are further implemented by Part IV of the Agriculture Act 1970[4] in conjunction with the Feed Law Code of Practice[5]. Under these statutes, the competent authorities undertaking the inspections are the enforcement authorities specified in FSA 1990, s 6 and AA 1970, s 67. Their activities are co-ordinated as described in para **18.3.2** below. The detailed statutory enforcement provisions for food are considered in sections **18.4** and **18.5** and, for feed, in section **18.6** below.

Also of relevance is the Food Standards Agency's Framework Agreement on Local Authority Enforcement, updated in July 2004. As further explained in para **2.3.6** above, this sets out the Agency's expectations on the planning and delivery of food and feed law enforcement.

In accordance with the requirement in Art 3 of Regulation (EC) 882/2004 that official controls be carried out on a risk basis, enforcement authorities are required to draw up inspection programmes in respect of food establishments based on an inspection rating system set out in Annex 5 of the Food Law Code of Practice. In carrying out their duties, however, enforcement authorities should not confine themselves to official controls. Chapter 4.1 of the Code requires them also to support food businesses in achieving compliance with food law by providing targeted education and advice[6]. A food business operator may thus be assisted in putting in place and implementing procedures based on HACCP principles as required by Art 5 of Regulation (EC) 852/2004/EC on the hygiene of foodstuffs.

The enforcement provisions of the Weights and Measures Act 1985 (W&MA 1985) and other legislation are briefly noted in sections **18.7** and **18.8** respectively.

1   But see the Animals and Animal Products (Examination for Residues and Maximum Residue Limits) Regulations 1997 made in part under the 1990 Act.
2   See in particular FSA 1990, Pt III and ss 40, 41, and 42; Food Safety (Enforcement Authority) (England and Wales) Order 1990 and Food Safety (Sampling and Qualifications) Regulations 1990. See also the Food Hygiene (England) Regulations 2006 Part 3.
3   See in particular sections 1.2 (Qualifications and experience); 1.5 (Registration of Food Business establishments); 2.5 (Liaison with other Member States); 4.1 (Interventions); and 5.1 (Product-specific establishments subject to approval).
4   See in particular AA 1970, ss 75–83.
5   See in particular sections 1.2 (Qualifications and training); 1.5 (Registration of Feed Business establishments); 2.5 (Liaison with other Member States); 3.6 (Enforcement options with regard feed materials imported from third countries); and 4.1 (Inspections).
6   See also Feed Law Code of Practice, ch 4.2

Co-ordination of local authority enforcement

18.3.2   As indicated in para **8.2.11** above, with the removal of war-time controls, it was no longer seen as appropriate for central government to issue extra statutory food rules. For the purpose of assisting with trade codes of practice, local enforcement authorities were instead encouraged to establish a joint committee. This evolved into a means of reconciling conflicts in advice on compliance with food law given by individual local authorities to companies trading nationally. As consumer protection legislation developed in the 1960s, the committee was replaced by the Local Authorities Co-ordinating Body on Food and Trading Standards (LACOTS) with a wider mandate of promoting good law and best practice in trading standards and food safety. In 2002 LACOTS changed its name to LACORS (Local Authorities Co-ordinators of Regulatory Services) to reflect the body's extended remit to include a wider range of regulatory services.

LACORS has devised the 'home authority principle' as the key method of food and feed enforcement co-ordination. In summary, this:

- encourages authorities to place special emphasis on goods and services originating within their area;
- provides businesses with a home authority source of guidance and advice;
- supports efficient liaison between local authorities;
- provides a system for the resolution of problems and disputes.

Generally, advice on compliance should be sought by a manufacturer from the enforcement authority where its decision-making base is located (that is, its 'home authority') and any other authority undertaking inspections, sampling or investigations or dealing with complaints (that is, an 'enforcing authority') should consider liaising with the home authority before pursuing detailed investigation or legal action. Where the manufacturer produces or packs products in an area other than where its decision-making base is located, the authority for that area (an 'originating authority') has particular responsibilities for ensuring that those products conform to legal requirements. In co-operation with the home authority, it will determine those aspects on which it should exercise the home authority functions and advise the manufacturer and enforcing authorities. The home authority principle is intended to help businesses to comply with the law in a spirit of consultation rather than confrontation. It removes neither their obligation to comply with the law, nor the responsibility of the enforcement authority for an area in which a particular contravention is perceived to have taken place[1].

Some formal status has been given to the LACORS home authority principle by the requirement in the statutory Codes of Practice that enforcement authorities should, where possible, adopt and implement its provisions[2]. It remains to be seen how far the home authority principle will change as a result of the primary authority partnership scheme introduced by Part 2 of the Regulatory Enforcement and Sanctions Act 2008 briefly mentioned in para **18.3.3** below.

The Food Standards Agency has a central role in relation to enforcement of feeding stuffs as well as food legislation. It is the UK body responsible, under Art 35 of Regulation (EC) 882/2004, for liaison with competent authorities in other Member States and, as explained in para **2.3.6** above, s 12 of the Food Standards Act 1999 (FSA 1999) empowers the Agency to monitor, set standards for and audit performance of enforcement authorities. Moreover, in fulfilment of its general role under FSA 1999, s 9, the FSA chairs the Animal Feed Law Enforcement Liaison Group that includes not only representatives of LACORS, but also those from DEFRA's Veterinary Medicines Directorate and Animal Health executive agencies given their respective responsibilities as regards TSEs and medicated feeding stuffs.[3]

In the context of food law enforcement co-ordination it is also right to have in mind the Secretary of State's powers, in s 6(3) of the FSA 1990, to direct that a duty imposed by the FSA 1990 on a food authority shall be discharged by the Secretary of State, the Minister of Agriculture, Fisheries and Food or the Food Standards Agency and, in s 6(5) and (5A), to take over, or direct that the Agency takes over, the conduct of proceedings instituted by some other person.[4]

1   *Walker's Snack Foods Ltd v Coventry City Council* [1998] 3 All ER 163.
2   See ch 1.1.7 Food Law Code of Practice and ch 1.1.5 Feed Law Code of Practice.
3   See paras **2.2.4** and **2.2.5** above.
4   See para **2.5.2** above.

Better Regulation initiatives

18.3.3   A summary of the basis on which food and feed enforcement authorities proceed in England and Wales would be incomplete without brief reference to the Government's Better Regulation initiatives.

Since 1998 most enforcement authorities have adopted the Enforcement Concordat[1] thereby committing themselves in their activities to clear standards, openness, helpfulness, proportionality and consistency and to a published complaints procedure.

For England, the Concordat is now to be revised in the light of provision on exercise of regulatory functions in the Legislative and Regulatory Reform Act 2006[2]. This imposes duties on persons exercising specified regulatory functions to have regard:

- to the five principles of good regulation, which require regulatory activities to be carried out in a way that is transparent, accountable, proportionate and consistent and targeted only at cases in which action is needed; and

- to the Regulators' Compliance Code issued under the Act, when determining general policies or principles by reference to which those functions are exercised.

Based on the seven Hampton principles[3], the Code exhorts those involved in the imposing and enforcing of regulations to consider supporting economic progress; using risk assessment; giving information and advice; targeting inspections; minimising data requirements; seeking proportionate sanctions; and being accountable, yet independent, in their decisions.

The functions to which these duties apply are specified by the Legislative and Regulatory Reform (Regulatory Functions) Order 2007. They include (1) all regulatory functions of the Food Standards Agency; (2) Ministerial regulatory functions in and under a series of Department of Health and DEFRA statutes, Regulations and CAP instruments relating to food and feed and the Weights and Measures Act 1985; (3) regulatory functions of local authorities in and under a series of statutes and Regulations relating to food and feed, including the FSA 1990, the AA 1970 and the Weights and Measures Act 1985; and (4) all local authority regulatory functions conferred by secondary legislation made under the European Communities Act 1972, s 2(2) in relation to food hygiene, food standards and animal feed.

Most recently, the Regulatory Enforcement and Sanctions Act 2008 has introduced:

- a Local Better Regulation Office (LBRO) that will co-ordinate local authority regulatory enforcement (including that in relation to food and feed legislation[4]) and be able to register 'primary authorities' having responsibility for particular businesses or organisations; and

- on the basis of the Macrory Review[5], powers to give regulators access to four new civil sanctions (ie fixed money penalties; variable money penalties and other discretionary requirements; stop notices; and enforcement undertakings).

It is understood that LBRO will work closely with the Food Standards Agency and LACORS. The Act will allow the new civil sanction powers to be granted by order, amongst others, to the Food Standards Agency and those who enforce specified food, feed and weights and measures enactments[6]. They may also be granted to those who enforce offences in statutory instruments made, in particular, under the Food Safety Act 1990 Part 2, the Food Standards Act 1999, s 27 and the Weights and Measures Act 1985, s 22[7]. Guidance on the Act was issued in July 2008 by the Department for Business, Enterprise and Regulatory Reform.

1 See *Enforcement Concordat: Good Practice Guide for England and Wales.*
2 Legislative and Regulatory Reform Act 2006, ss 21–24.
3 *Reducing administrative burdens: effective inspection and enforcement* (Philip Hampton, March 2005).
4 Regulatory Enforcement and Sanctions Act 2008, s 4 and Sch 3.
5 *Regulatory Justice: Making Sanctions Effective. Final Report* (November 2006).
6 Regulatory Enforcement and Sanctions Act 2008, Part 3 and Schs 5 and 6.
7 Regulatory Enforcement and Sanctions Act 2008, s 62 and Sch 7.

18.4 FOOD: SAMPLING AND ANALYSIS ETC

18.4.1 Sampling and analysis are important control techniques specified by Art 10 of Regulation (EC) 882/2004. Provision for the methods to be used is made by Art 11, with Annex III prescribing the criteria that must characterise the methods of analysis. Article 12 requires competent authorities to designate official laboratories to carry out the analysis of samples taken during official controls.

In Great Britain these Community provisions are implemented by ss 29–31 of the FSA 1990 and the Food Safety (Sampling and Qualifications) Regulations 1990 considered in the following paragraphs of this section. Regulations 12 and 13 of the Food Hygiene (England) Regulations 2006 must also be considered. Guidance on sampling for analysis or examination is given in section 6 of the Code of Practice and section 6 of the Food Law Practice Guidance.

It will be recalled that the FSA 1990 continues in part to treat chemical and biological contamination separately[1]. As noted in para **2.8.1** above, 'analysis' is defined as including microbiological assay and any technique for establishing the composition of food[2], while 'examination' means microbiological examination[3]. The distinct methods of dealing with samples for analysis and examination respectively are described in paras **18.4.3** and **18.4.4** below. Both concepts are, however, embraced by the term 'analysis' as used in Community law. Although the provisions of the FSA 1990 and the 2006 Hygiene Regulations both apply to analysis and examination, the Food Law Code of Practice advocates that samples for analysis should be procured under section 29, while those for examination should be procured under reg 12 (see chs 6.1.5 and 6.1.10 respectively).

1   See in particular paras **1.1.1** and **2.5.2** above.
2   FSA 1990, s 28(2).
3   FSA 1990, s 53(1).

Procurement of samples

18.4.2 Under s 29 of the FSA 1990 and reg 12 of the Food Hygiene (England) Regulations 2006, an authorised officer of an enforcement authority may:

(a)   purchase a sample of any food, or any substance capable of being used in the preparation of food;

(b)   take a sample of any food which:
   (i) appears to him to be intended for sale, or to have been sold, for human consumption; or
   (ii) is found by him on or in any premises which he is authorised to enter[1],

(c)   take a sample from any food source, or a sample of any contact material, which is found by him on or in any such premises;

(d)   take a sample of any article or substance which is found by him on or in any such premises and which he has reason to believe may be required as evidence in proceedings under any of the provisions of the FSA 1990, of regulations or orders made under the Act or of the 2006 Regulations.

The following points might usefully be noted about s 29 and reg 12.

(1)   Samples considered here are to be distinguished from those taken for other purposes (for example, for surveillance under s 11(4) of the FSA 1999[2]). This chapter concerns the powers of sampling for the purposes

of enforcement of provisions in and under the FSA 1990 and the Hygiene Regulations 2006.

(2)   Although very wide, these sampling powers are not without limit. The words 'take' and 'purchase' are mutually exclusive[3] with the result that, for example, a sample of a food source or contact material cannot be purchased. The term 'procure' is used in the Act to embrace both concepts.

(3)   The whole of the food or other material procured will often form the subject of subsequent proceedings: a 'sample' is not confined to a small quantity from which conclusions about the bulk may be inferred. If such conclusions are to be drawn, the sample must certainly be fair, that is, representative of the whole[4].

(4)   An item of food handed by a complainant purchaser to an authorised officer has by definition not been procured in accordance with s 29 or reg 12 is neither a sample[5], nor subject to the procedures prescribed by the Food Safety (Sampling and Qualifications) Regulations 1990[6]. This does not, of course, prevent the food from being submitted by the food authority for analysis or examination, as the purchaser himself might have chosen to do[7].

1   See section **18.5** below.
2   See para **2.3.5** above.
3   *Marston v Wrington Vale Dairies Ltd* (1963) 61 LGR 202.
4   See, for example, *Crawford v Harding* 1907 SC(J) 11; *Heatlie v Reid* 1961 JC 70, 1961 SLT 317.
5   *Arun District Council v Argyle Stores Ltd* (1986) 150 JP 552; *Love v Strickland and Holt Ltd* (3 February 1981, unreported); and *Leach v United Dairies Ltd* [1949] 1 All ER 1023.
6   See paras **18.4.3** and **18.4.4** below.
7   See FSA 1990, s 30(2) and para **18.4.5** below.

Procedure where sample is to be analysed

18.4.3   The Food Hygiene (England) Regulations 2006 not only adopt the provisions of ss 29 and 30 of the FSA 1990 on the procurement, analysis and examination of samples. By reg 13(10) they also apply the provisions of the Food Safety (Sampling and Qualifications) Regulations 1990 described in paras **18.4.3**, **18.4.4** and **18.4.8**.

An authorised officer who has procured a sample under s 29 of the FSA 1990 or reg 12 of the Hygiene Regulations 2006 and who considers that it should be analysed, is required by reg 6(1) of the Food Safety (Sampling and Qualifications) Regulations 1990, forthwith[1] to divide it into three parts.

In the majority of cases the procedure stated in reg 6(3) must then be followed. The authorised officer must:

(a)   if necessary, place each part in a suitable container and seal each container;
(b)   mark each part or container;
(c)   as soon as it is reasonably practicable to do so, give one part to the owner and give him notice[2] that the sample will be analysed;
(d)   submit one for analysis; and
(e)   retain one part for future submission for 'checking analysis' as described in para **18.4.8** below.

As to (c), the definition of 'owner' in reg 1(2) of Food Safety (Sampling and Qualifications) Regulations 1990 does not make clear whether a part given to, for example, a store manager of a corporate body is sufficient compliance.

Different provision is made for two exceptional sets of circumstances. The first relates to certain products in sealed containers. By reg 6(2), if the sample consists of sealed containers and opening them would, in the opinion of the authorised officer, impede a proper analysis, the authorised officer must divide the sample into parts by putting the containers into three lots, and each lot must be treated as being a part. When considering whether this procedure should be used, it must be borne in mind that analysis of the retained part, noted at (e) above, may be made some considerable time after sampling. Examples where analysis may be affected are foods containing evanescent ingredients (eg vitamins that disappear quickly after opening); foods containing volatile substances such as alcohol; foods packaged in modified atmospheres that require gas analysis or that, if lost, could alter preservative levels; foods packed in aerosols; 'aerated' foods (eg carbonated soft drinks); and products for which an unopened container is necessary for a particular test (eg condensed milk claiming contents equivalent to a specified quantity of whole milk).

Secondly, special provision is made for samples that cannot be divided into parts. By reg 6(4), if the authorised officer is of the opinion that division of the sample into parts is either not reasonably practicable or is likely to impede a proper analysis, he must, as soon as is reasonably practicable to do so, give to the owner notice that it will be analysed and submit it for analysis.

The 1998 Report on the Review of Public Analyst Arrangements in England and Wales recommended that, although not required by product safety legislation, the three-part sampling requirement under the FSA 1990 should be retained[3].

In the normal way, if a prosecution follows the exercise by a sampling officer of the statutory powers, due compliance with reg 6(1) of the Food Safety (Sampling and Qualifications) Regulations 1990 is a condition precedent to a valid conviction for an offence in or under the Act or the Hygiene Regulations[4]. *Skeate v Moore* (a case considered under previous legislation) shows the problems in dealing with discrete items like meat pies and sausages. Because of the great difficulties of dividing such products equally, the sampling officer in that case divided six Cornish pasties he had purchased into three lots of two each. Of the two pasties submitted for analysis, the public analyst found that the aggregate of meat was less than was required for one pasty by the relevant Regulations[5]. The shopkeeper's conviction was reversed on appeal. The purpose of the three-way division is to give the defendant and the court in due course as good an opportunity as the public analyst had, when he made his analysis, of ascertaining and establishing whether the offence charged has been committed. If the offence charged related exclusively to the part that the public analyst alone had the opportunity to examine, the object of the statutory procedure would be seriously impeded. The sample must be coextensive with the subject of the charge or representative of some larger entity. The Divisional Court took the view that if, as the justices thought, it was possible only to sample in the manner adopted, then the Regulations should be modified.

It is for consideration whether, in the case of any particular class of discrete items, the problems of dividing a sample are so severe that division is 'either not reasonably practicable or likely to impede proper analysis' within the meaning of reg 6(4). Since the reg 6(4) procedure denies the trader his part of the sample and the possibility of a future checking analysis, it should evidently be adopted only in exceptional circumstances. One such case is said to be where insufficient product is available. Although not compulsory for this exceptional procedure, it is essential that the sample should be sealed and marked before submission for analysis.

1   Compare *A-G's Reference (No 2 of 1994)* [1995] 2 All ER 1000.
2   The notice must be in writing. See FSA 1990, s 49(1)(b).
3   See para **2.7.1** above.
4   *Skeate v Moore* [1971] 3 All ER 1306, [1972] 1 WLR 110; and compare *National Rivers Authority v Harcros Timber and Building Supplies Ltd* [1993] Crim LR 221.
5   See now Meat Products (England) Regulations 2003.

Procedure where sample is to be examined

18.4.4   By reg 8 of the Food Safety (Sampling and Qualifications) Regulations 1990, an authorised officer who has procured a sample under s 29 of the FSA 1990 or reg 12 of the Hygiene Regulations 2006 and who considers that it should be examined must:

(a)   if necessary place the sample in a suitable container and seal the container;
(b)   mark the sample or container;
(c)   as soon as it is reasonably practicable to do so, give notice[1] to the owner that the sample will be examined; and
(d)   submit it for examination.

Unlike most samples for analysis, those for examination are not required to be divided into three parts because bacterial contamination is not heterogeneously distributed in food and, in a retained part, might be expected to change over time.

1   The notice must be in writing. See FSA 1990, s 49(1)(b).

Submission of samples to public analysts and food examiners

18.4.5   Under s 30(1) of the FSA 1990 and reg 13 of the Hygiene Regulations 2006, an authorised officer who has procured a sample must, if he considers that it should be analysed, submit it for analysis by a public analyst or, if he considers that it should be examined, submit it to a food examiner[1]. In s 30, 'sample', in relation to an authorised officer of an enforcement authority, includes any part of a sample retained by him in pursuance of the procedure considered in para **18.4.3** above[2].

The public analyst to whom the sample is submitted can be either one appointed by the food authority for the area where the sample was procured or one appointed for the area of the food authority concerned. The first alternative allows for the submission of a sample procured by an authorised officer outside his own area to the public analyst for the area where the sample was procured.

By s 30(2) or reg 13(2), a person, other than an authorised officer, who has purchased any food or substance capable of being used in the preparation of food may submit a sample of it to the public analyst for the area where the purchase was made or to a food examiner.

If the office of public analyst for an area is vacant, s 30(3) or reg 13(3) provides for the sample to be submitted to the public analyst for some other area.

Evidence of analysis or examination is not an essential prerequisite for a prosecution. For example, the presence of a foreign body in food[3] might be proved without analysis or the misdescription of a type of fruit or a cut of meat[4] might perhaps be established by expert testimony from a person other than a public analyst. However, in cases concerning the composition of food, it would seem prudent in all but exceptional cases to refer to the public analyst who is the food authority's scientific adviser for such matters.

The sample must be referred for analysis or examination to one of the laboratories listed as complying with the quality standards and using the validated methods prescribed by Art 11 of Regulation (EC) 882/2004[5].

Where Community methods of analysis have not been prescribed, Art 11 of Regulation (EC) 882/2004 requires methods used to comply with internationally recognised rules and protocols, to be fit for the intended purpose, or to have been developed in accordance with scientific protocols. In any other case, validation of methods of analysis may take place within a single laboratory according to an internationally accepted protocol. Analyses must, wherever possible take into account the criteria set out in Annex III.

1 As to public analysts and food examiners, see sections **2.7** and **2.8** above.
2 See FSA 1990, s 30(9).
3 See para **3.2.23** above.
4 See for example para **8.2.6** above.
5 See para **18.2.4** above.

Analysis and examination of samples

18.4.6 Where a food analyst[1] or examiner is for any reason unable to perform the analysis or examination, the sample must be submitted or, as the case may be, sent by him to another food analyst or examiner[2]. This might evidently arise through lack of specialist equipment, conflict of interest or simply pressure of work. Certainly, the food analyst or food examiner is required to analyse or examine the sample as soon as practicable[3]. This is particularly important in the case of samples of short life foods that should obviously be submitted for analysis or examination without delay.

After an analysis or examination, the food analyst or examiner must give a certificate in the prescribed form[4] to the person by whom the sample was submitted, specifying the result. The certificate must be signed by the food analyst or examiner, but the analysis or examination may be made by a person acting under his direction[5].

1 That is, a public analyst or other person having the requisite qualifications, see section **2.8** above.
2 FSA 1990, s 30(4); Food Hygiene (England) Regulations 2006, reg 13(4).
3 FSA 1990, s 30(5); Food Hygiene (England) Regulations 2006, reg 13(5).
4 See Food Safety (Sampling and Qualifications) Regulations 1990, reg 9(2) and Sch 3.
5 FSA 1990, s 30(6) and (7); Food Hygiene (England) Regulations 2006, reg 13(6) and (7).

Evidential status of certificates of analysis and examination

18.4.7 In any proceedings under the Food Safety Act 1990 or the Food Hygiene (England) Regulations 2006, the production by one of the parties:

(a) of a document purporting to be a certificate given by a food analyst or examiner under the Act; or

(b) of a document supplied to him by the other party as being a copy of such a certificate,

is sufficient evidence of the facts stated in it unless, in a case falling within (a), the other party requires that the food analyst or examiner shall be called as a witness[1]. The evidence of a food analyst or examiner may be rebutted. Where there is doubt in any proceedings about the correctness of the analysis or examination or as to any opinion offered in the certificate relied on by the other party, notice should always be given that the food analyst or examiner is required to give evidence.

1   FSA 1990, s 30(8); Food Hygiene (England) Regulations 2006, reg 13(8).

Reference to the Government Chemist

18.4.8   Where an authorised officer and the owner of the sample at the time of its procurement agree, or where a court so orders, the authorised officer must submit it for analysis to the Government Chemist or to such other food analyst as the Government Chemist may direct[1]. This 'checking analysis' is used if there is a difference between the public analyst's evidence and that from the defendant's food analyst.

1   Food Safety (Sampling and Qualifications) Regulations 1990, reg 7.

Supply to owners of copies of certificates of analysis or examination

18.4.9   Where a sample procured under s 29 of the FSA 1990 or reg 12 of the Hygiene Regulations has been analysed or examined, the owner of food is entitled on request to be supplied with a copy of the certificate of analysis or examination by the enforcement authority[1]. In addition, the defendant charged with an offence triable either way[2] is entitled to advance information of the prosecution case and the rules on disclosure of expert evidence must be complied with[3].

1   Food Safety (Sampling and Qualifications) Regulations 1990, reg 9. See also para 6.1.13 of the Food Law Code of Practice.
2   See para **19.3.8** below.
3   See para **19.5.6** below.

18.5   FOOD: POWERS OF ENTRY, OBSTRUCTION ETC

18.5.1   By Art 8(2) of Regulation (EC) 882/2004, Member States are required to 'ensure that they have legal procedures in place in order to ensure that staff of the competent authorities have access to premises of and documentation kept by feed and food business operators so as to be able to accomplish their tasks properly'. In respect of food, this obligation is implemented by numerous Regulations, most of which are made in implementation of substantive European Community legislation. Examples of bespoke powers of entry are to be found in the Products of Animal Origin (Import and Export) Regulations 1996, reg 6, the Products of Animal Origin (Third Country Imports) (England) Regulations 2006, reg 8 and the Transmissible Spongiform Encephalopathies Regulations 2008, reg 13. However, by far the majority of powers of entry in food Regulations rely on or derive from the general provisions in ss 32 and 33 of the Food Safety Act 1990 (FSA 1990) that are described in this section. Even amongst these there is a diversity of forms. Regulations made under the Act have sometimes needed to adapt its powers of entry [1] in order to extend them to an EC Regulation for which enforcement provision is being made[2], while food Regulations, made under the European Communities Act 1972 because the FSA 1990 does wholly cover the topic in question, have generally needed to modify the powers still further in order to meet the specific EC obligation[3].

In this latter category, the Food Hygiene (England) Regulations 2006 are the most prominent by virtue of the special provision that is made for execution and enforcement of the three important food hygiene Regulations (EC) 852/2004, 853/2004 and 854/2004 described in chs 13 and 14. The Food Law Code of Practice advocates that food hygiene matters – and in particular samples procured for examination – should be dealt with under the 2006 Regulations rather than under the Act[4], while the provisions of the Regulations on unhygienic food businesses have largely superseded those of the FSA 1990[5]. Consistent with this approach, the Food Law Code of Practice envisages that the provisions of the 2006 Regulations, rather than those of FSA 1990, will apply in respect of powers of entry and attendant obstruction offence[6]. These are to be found in regs 14 and 15 of the Food Hygiene (England) Regulations 2006. In providing for contraventions of and performance of functions under the Regulations, their terms are virtually identical with those of ss 32 and 33 of the Act, save that reg 14(2) confers specific powers of entry on the Food Standards Agency that has enforcement responsibilities with regard to matters such as primary production, slaughterhouses and raw cows' milk.

Guidance on powers of entry is given in the Food Law Code of Practice and the Practice Guidance. In particular, the Code of Practice, ch 3.1.8 contains a reminder that right to privacy and respect for personal property are key principles under the European Convention on Human Rights and the Human Rights Act 1998. This means that the powers of entry, search and seizure 'should be fully and clearly justified before use because they may significantly interfere with the occupier's privacy. Officers should consider if the necessary objectives could be met by less intrusive means.'

1   Under the power in FSA 1990, s 48(1)(a) described in para **4.1.4** above.
2   See, for example , the General Food Regulations 2004, reg 7(2) implementing general food Regulation (EC) 178/2002.
3   See, for example , the Organic Products Regulations 2004, reg 13.
4   See chs 3.1.7 and 6.1.10 of the Food Law Code of Practice and, as to samples for examination, para **18.4.1** above.
5   See para **6.1.1** above.
6   See the Food Law Code of Practice chs 1.1.8 and 1.6.2.

Power to enter premises

18.5.2   By s 32(1) of the FSA 1990, an authorised officer of an enforcement authority shall, on producing, if so required, some duly authenticated document[1] showing his authority, have a right at all reasonable hours[2]:

(a)   to enter any premises within the authority's area for the purpose of ascertaining whether there is or has been on the premises any contravention of the provisions of the Act, or regulations or orders made under it, or the hygiene regulations; and

(b)   to enter any business premises, whether within or outside the authority's area, for the purpose of ascertaining whether there is on the premises any evidence of any contravention within that area of any of such provisions; and

(c)   in the case of an authorised officer of a food authority, to enter any premises for the purpose of the performance by the authority of their functions under the Act[3].

An authorised officer may thus enter both domestic and business premises within his own authority's area, but outside that area may enter only business premises for the purpose of ascertaining whether there is on the premises any evidence of a contravention within that area. The power to enter business premises in the area of another food authority allows for visits, for example, to a manufacturer as part of an investigation into an offence concerning one of his products found in the area of the visiting officer[4]. However, it is recommended that such visits should be co-ordinated with the home authority.

Entry to premises used only as a private dwelling-house may not be demanded as of right unless 24 hours' notice of the intended entry has been given to the occupier.

1   See FSA 1990, s 49.
2   As to 'reasonable hours', see para **5.4.2** above.
3   As to 'premises' and 'business', see para **4.8.1** above.
4   *Walker's Snack Foods Ltd v Coventry City Council* [1998] 3 All ER 163.

Refusal of admission

18.5.3   Where admission to premises has been refused, or refusal is apprehended, an authorised officer may, on sworn information in writing and having given notice to the occupier of the premises, apply to a justice of the peace for a warrant, under s 32(2) of the FSA 1990, authorising the officer to enter the premises, if need be by reasonable force. If an application for admission, or the giving of notice, would defeat the object of entry, or in a case of urgency, or where the premises are unoccupied or the occupier is temporarily absent, the justice may nevertheless issue the warrant. Section 32(3) provides for the warrant to continue in force for one month.

Other persons and co-ordination

18.5.4   Authorised officers entering premises may take with them such other persons as they consider necessary and must leave unoccupied premises as effectively secured as they found them[1]. When an enforcing officer enters premises for the purposes of executing and enforcing official controls he can also take a Commission expert to allow that expert to carry out audit functions under Art 45 of Regulation (EC) 882/2004[2].

The Food Law Practice Guidance recommend co-ordination of inspection visits and inclusion in inspection teams of all expertise necessary to inspect the premises in question[3].

1   FSA 1990, s 32(4).
2   Regulation (EC) 15, Official Feed and Food Control (England) Regulations 2007.
3   Practice Guidance, ch 4.2.3.

Inspection of records and computers

18.5.6   On entering premises in accordance with the Act, an authorised officer may inspect any records (in whatever form they are held) relating to a food business and, where such records are kept by means of a computer:

(a)   may have access to, and inspect and check the operation of, any computer and any associated apparatus or material which is or has been in use in connection with the records; and

(b)   may require any person having charge of, or otherwise concerned with the operation of, the computer, apparatus or material to afford him such assistance as he may reasonably require[1].

The officer may seize and detain any records which may be required as evidence and, where the records are kept by means of a computer, may require the records to be produced in a form in which they may be taken away[2].

1   FSA 1990, s 32(5).
2   FSA 1990, s 32(6).

Confidentiality

18.5.7   Section 32(7) of the FSA 1990 makes it an offence, except in the performance of duty, for anyone exercising the FSA 1990 powers of entry to disclose information obtained in the premises with regard to any trade secret[1], including, it would appear, any secret manufacturing process.

1   See also reg 16, Official Feed and Food Controls (England) Regulations 2007 and Art 7(2) and (3) of Regulation (EC) 882/2004.

Limitations on powers of entry

18.5.8   Two express limitations on the s 32 powers should be noted. First, nothing in the section authorises any person, except with the permission of the local authority under the Animal Health Act 1981, to enter any premises:

(a)   in which an animal or bird affected with any disease to which that Act applies is kept; and
(b)   which is situated in a place declared under that Act to be infected with such a disease[1].

Secondly, by virtue of s 54(4) the powers are not exercisable in relation to any Crown premises[2] which the Secretary of State has certified accordingly in the interests of national security. This limitation does not expressly apply to the Hygiene Regulations but the Code of Practice states that in practice food authorities should apply the same approach to the enforcement of the hygiene regulations in respect of Crown premises as they do in respect of the Food Safety Act 1990[3].

1   FSA 1990, s 32(8).
2   As to application to the Crown, see para **4.1.6** above.
3   Food Law Code of Practice, ch 1.6.2.

Obstruction etc of officers

18.5.9   It is an offence for any person intentionally[1] to obstruct any person acting in the execution of the Act, or, without reasonable cause, to fail to give to any such person any assistance or information which he may reasonably require for the performance of his functions under the Act. It is also an offence for any person responding to a request for information to furnish information that he knows to be false or misleading in a material particular; or recklessly to furnish information that is false or misleading in a material particular[2]. Obstruction need not involve physical violence[3]. Anything that might make the task of the authorised officer more difficult may amount to obstruction[4].

A false statement made to an authorised officer during an interview under caution is a statement to which the criminal sanction applies[5].

The offence of failing, without reasonable cause, to give an authorised officer reasonable assistance or information does not require any person to answer any questions or give any information if to do so might incriminate him[6]. The privilege against self-incrimination does not extend to an employee not authorised to speak for the company in respect of questions asked by authorised officers the answers to which might tend to incriminate the employer[7]. An authorised officer must not be prevented from exercising the statutory power of inspection. On the other hand, it would not be an offence, by virtue of this provision, for a person to refuse to answer questions about his or her alleged failure to comply with company instructions.

1   As to 'intentionally' obstructing, see para **20.1.1** below.
2   FSA 1990, s 33(1) and (2). See also Food Hygiene (England) Regulations 2006, reg 15(1) and (2) and Official Feed and Food Controls (England) Regulations 2007, reg 19(1) and (2).
3   *Borrow v Howland* (1896) 74 LT 787; *Betts v Stevens* [1910] 1 KB 1.
4   *Hinchcliffe v Sheldon* [1955] 3 All ER 406, [1955] 1 WLR 1207; but see *Rice v Connolly* [1966] 2 QB 414, [1966] 2 All ER 649.
5   *R v Page* (1995) 94 LGR 467. As to an interview under caution, see para **19.5.9** below.
6   FSA 1990, s 33(3). See also Food Hygiene (England) Regulations 2006, reg 15(3) and Official Feed and Food Controls (England) Regulations 2007, regs 19(3).
7   *Walker's Snack Foods Ltd v Coventry City Council* [1998] 3 All ER 163.

Reports on inspections

18.5.10   Although there is no statutory requirement for authorised officers to report back to the owner of the food business in writing, the Food Law Code of Practice at para 4.5.2 states that the outcome of a primary inspection should always be reported in writing to the food business operator either at the conclusion of the inspection or as soon as practicable, even if the outcome of the inspection is satisfactory.

18.6   FEED: ENFORCEMENT POWERS

18.6.1   Close parallels with the FSA 1990 are to be found for feeding stuffs in the enforcement provisions of Part IV of the Agriculture Act 1970. Already summarised in chs **17.2.2** and **17.4.1** above, the provisions include in particular a requirement to appoint agricultural analysts and powers of entry, taking, dividing and analysis of samples, and further analysis by the Government Chemist, together with the special rules on sampling and analysis methods.

For the purpose of implementing Regulation (EC) 882/2004, these provisions have now been substantially fortified by Part 4 of the Feed (Hygiene and Enforcement) (England) Regulations 2005, which provides for the administration and enforcement of feed law not only in Part IV of the 1970 Act, but also in additives Regulation (EC) 1831/2003, the Feeding Stuffs (England) Regulations 2005, hygiene Regulation (EC) 183/2005, the Feed (Hygiene and Enforcement) (England) Regulations 2005 and, in so far as they relate to feed, general Regulation (EC) 178/2002, official controls Regulation (EC) 882/2004 and the Official Feed and Food Controls (England) Regulations 2007. The Regulations in particular make provision for feed business improvement notices, prohibition orders, emergency prohibition notices and emergency prohibition orders[1] and powers of entry, inspection seizure and detention of non-compliant feed[2]. In so far as Regulations (EC) 178/2002, 1831/2003, 882/2004 and 183/2005 apply to veterinary medicinal products used in feedingstuffs, and to some specified feed additives used in feedingstuffs, they are enforced by the Veterinary Medicines Regulations 2008, Sch 5[3].

The Feed Law Code of Practice, ch 3.1.7 repeats the reminder that exercise of the powers of entry and seizure must have regard to the right to privacy and personal property under the European Convention on Human Rights (see, as to food, para **18.5.1** above). It also notes that, by virtue of the Feed (Hygiene and Enforcement) Regulations 2005, reg 24, authorised officers may take other persons with them (see, as to food para **18.5.4** above). Section 5 of the Code gives guidance on sampling and analysis.

1   Compare the provisions for food described in ch 6.
2   Compare the provisions for food described in section **5.4** above.
3   See also para **17.6.1** above.

18.7   WEIGHTS AND MEASURES ENFORCEMENT POWERS

Quantity marking and metrological controls

18.7.1   Since the enactment of Regulation (EC) 882/2004 official control has evidently applied to quantity labelling of pre-packaged food. The substantive requirement is to be found in Arts 3.1(4) and 8 of food labelling Directive 2000/13/EC. Prepackaged foodstuffs must be labelled with the net quantity in units of volume, in the case of liquids, and in units of mass, in the case of other products, using the litre, centilitre, millilitre, kilogram or gram, as appropriate. By Art 10.2(b)(vi) of Regulation (EC) 882/2004 official controls on food must include inspection of labelling, presentation and advertising.

The requirements in respect of quantity marking (explained in ch 16) are enforced through the W&MA 1985, ss 79–85. Enforcement is the responsibility of local weights and measures authorities[1]. In England, they are the non-metropolitan county councils, metropolitan district and London borough councils, the Common Council of the City of London, the Inner and Middle Temples and the Council of the Isles of Scilly. In Wales, they are the county and county borough councils. The officers responsible for enforcement are inspectors of weights and measures under the direction of chief inspectors of weights and measures who may have deputies[2]. They are generally known as trading standards officers and also enforce those functions under the FSA 1990 that are allocated to county councils[3].

1   W&MA 1985, s 69, as amended.
2   W&MA 1985, s 72.
3   See in particular para **2.5.2** above.

Enforcement powers

18.7.2   The powers of inspection, entry and seizure and the provisions in respect of obstruction are similar to those in the FSA 1990[1].

1   W&MA 1985, ss 79–81.

18.8   OTHER LEGISLATION

18.8.1   Enforcement provision like that in the FSA 1990 is also to be found elsewhere in consumer protection legislation relevant to food. Only a brief comparison can be made here of the similarities. Those who exercise or are subject to the respective powers should study them carefully in order to see precisely how they differ.

Orders made under the Prices Act 1974[1] are enforced by local weights and measures authorities who have powers of entry backed by provision in respect of obstruction and are subject to restrictions on disclosure of information.

The safety provisions of Part II of the Consumer Protection Act 1987 have limited application in the food context. However, regulations have been made under those powers to control goods such as cooking utensils[2]. Once again enforcement rests with local weights and measures authorities and provision is made for test purchases, powers of search, detention of goods and in respect of obstruction. In addition, there are extensive powers to serve prohibition notices, notices to warn and suspension notices, to forfeit goods and to obtain information. The General Product Safety Regulations 2005[3], unlike the 1994 Regulations, do not rely on these powers for the purpose of enforcement.

More specialised is the Agriculture and Horticulture Act 1964[4] which, in addition to conferring powers of entry to premises and making provision in respect of obstruction, is enforced by the Rural Payments Agency Inspectorate and includes power to regrade produce.

Even less familiar to those accustomed to the FSA 1990 are the extensive enforcement powers to enter and require information provided by s 19 of the Food and Environment Protection Act 1985 in respect of Regulations, made under s 16 of that Act, on pesticide residues in crops, food and feeding stuffs. Recently, however, these powers have been disregarded. Regulations to enforce Regulation (EC) 396/2005 on maximum residue levels of pesticides in or on food of plant or animal origin were made under the European Communities Act 1972.[5]

Reference should also be made to regulations providing enforcement mechanisms for food standards specified in Community common agricultural policy Regulations. As explained in para **10.4.1** above, even where it has been found necessary to make these under the European Communities Act 1972, the concepts and enforcement methods of the FSA 1990 have been applied to the food standards aspects. For example, the Common Agricultural Policy (Wine) (England and Northern Ireland) Regulations 2001, as amended,[6] provide for enforcement by food authorities at the retail stage and powers of entry akin to those in the FSA 1990, as well as for analysis and examination within the meaning of that Act.

1   See section **16.8** above.
2   See paras **12.6.1** and **12.6.2** above.
3   See para **5.1.2** above.
4   See para **10.4.16** above.
5   See the Pesticides (Maximum Residue Levels) (England and Wales) Regulations 2008 considered in para **12.7.1** above.
6   See para **10.4.8** above.

Chapter 19

Enforcement: prosecutions and evidence

19.1 INTRODUCTION

19.1.1 Articles 54 and 55 of official controls Regulation (EC) 882/2004 require action to be taken and sanctions applied in respect of non-compliance with food and feed law. Of the responses available in England and Wales, section **5.4**, ch 6 and para **13.2.1** have already explained the administrative powers to destroy food, to issue improvement and hygiene improvement notices, prohibition and hygiene prohibition orders, emergency and hygiene emergency prohibition notices and orders and remedial action and detention notices, and to withdraw approvals from food businesses. However, the most obvious penalties are to be found in criminal law. If, in respect of a particular breach, advice or a warning is not enough, some kind of penalty or formal caution may be called for.

This chapter briefly comments first on prosecutions (and the possibility of issuing a simple caution), before summarising relevant statutory provisions regarding criminal evidence.

Section 20 of the FSA 1990 on offences due to the fault of another person is considered in the next chapter. However, the provisions made by the Interpretation Act 1978 (IA 1978) in respect of duplicated offences might usefully be noted here. Where an act or omission constitutes an offence under two or more Acts, or both under an Act and at common law, the offender is, unless the contrary intention appears, liable to be prosecuted and punished under either or any of those Acts or at common law, but is not liable to be punished more than once for the same offence. An example of this duplication is to be found in the overlap, mentioned in para **8.1.1** above, between ss 14 and 15 of the Food Safety Act 1990 (FSA 1990) and the Consumer Protection from Unfair Trading Regulations 2008.

19.2 ENFORCEMENT ACTION

19.2.1 Chapters 3.1.3 of the Food Law Codes of Practice for England and Wales confirm that enforcement action taken by food authorities should be reasonable, proportionate and consistent with good practice. Authorised officers should take account of the full range of enforcement options that 'includes educating food business operators, giving advice, informal action, sampling, detaining and seizing food, serving hygiene improvement notices/ improvement notices, hygiene improvement procedures/prohibition procedures and prosecution procedures'. Except where circumstances indicate a significant risk, officers are advised to 'operate a graduated and educative approach starting at the bottom of the pyramid ie advice/education and informal action and only move to more formal action where the informal does not achieve the desired effect'. Moreover, in considering whether to initiate enforcement action, an authority should take account of the Code for Crown Prosecutors[1], the Enforcement Concordat, the Regulators' Compliance Code[2] and its own Enforcement Policy[3]. Para **18.3.3** describes the Concordat and Compliance Code and explains how the options open to food authorities are expected in due course also to include civil sanctions provided for by the Regulatory Enforcement and Sanctions Act 2008.

1 See para **19.3.2** below.
2 The Statutory Code of Practice for Regulators made under the Legislative and Regulatory Reform Act 2006, which repealed and replaced the Regulatory Reform Act 2001.
3 See *R v Adaway* (2004) 168 JP 645; (2004) Times, 22 November. Failure by a local authority to observe its prosecution policy when proceeding in relation to strict liability offences under the Trade Descriptions Act 1968 may be an abuse of process.

19.3   PROSECUTIONS

The power to prosecute

19.3.1   Paragraph **2.5.2** above explained the responsibilities for enforcement of provisions in and under the FSA 1990. Subject to what is said there, the key provision to be recalled in relation to prosecutions is section 6(5) whereby in England and Wales an enforcement authority may institute proceedings under any provisions of the Act or any regulations or orders made under it[1].

Although persons other than an enforcement authority have the common law right to institute prosecutions under the FSA 1990, this would be a rare occurrence. A private citizen does not have the statutory powers to secure evidence and, if injured or damaged through a food product, would no doubt do better to consider civil proceedings as explained in ch 21.

1 In Scotland the decision on whether to prosecute lies with the Procurator Fiscal.

The decision to prosecute: the Code for Crown Prosecutors

19.3.2   Paragraphs 3.1.10 of the Food Law Codes of Practice for England and Wales give advice on the decision as to whether to prosecute there. They advocate recourse to the Code for Crown Prosecutors[1], which is explained in this paragraph, and set out certain criteria of their own, which are explained in para **19.3.3**. Relevant judicial comment is noted in para **19.3.4**.

Although the Code for Crown Prosecutors (the latest edition of which was published in November 2004) is directed at the Crown Prosecution Service, the full code test that it explains should be applied by those responsible for deciding on prosecution of offences described in this book[2]. The test consists of the following two stages:

(a)   *the evidential stage*, which requires that there be enough admissible and reliable evidence to 'offer a realistic prospect of conviction' against the defendant on each charge; and
(b)   *the public interest stage*, which requires that public interest factors for and against prosecution be balanced carefully and fairly.

If the case passes the evidential stage, prosecutors must proceed to the second stage and decide if a prosecution is needed in the public interest. If the case does not pass the evidential stage it must not go ahead no matter how important or serious it may be.

In considering the 'realistic prospect of conviction' called for by the evidential stage, it will be helpful first to recall the standard of proof required in court. In criminal proceedings, the prosecution must prove its case 'beyond reasonable doubt'[3]. As will be seen in the next chapter, with 'strict liability' offences such as most of those under the FSA 1990 and other consumer protection legislation, the prosecutor is absolved from having to prove the defendant's criminal intention. On the other hand, regard must be had as to whether the defendant is likely to be able to establish a due diligence or other statutory defence, having in mind that, where the defence bears the legal burden of proof, the standard required is the civil one of the balance of probabilities[4]. However, for proof beyond reasonable doubt to be required for prosecution decisions would be excessive and tend to usurp the function of the court. 'A realistic prospect of conviction', according to the Code for Crown Prosecutors, 'means that a jury or bench of magistrates or judge hearing a case alone, properly directed in accordance with the law is more likely than not to convict the defendant of the charge alleged'.

As regards whether there is enough evidence to justify prosecution, the Code requires prosecutors to consider whether the evidence can be used and is reliable, specifying questions that they should ask themselves for the purpose. Understandably the Code does not explain the law of evidence, but a summary of important aspects is to be found in section **19.5** below.

Moving on to the public interest stage of the Test, the Code emphasises that 'it has never been the rule of this country ... that suspected offences must automatically be the subject of prosecution' [5]. It lists some public interest factors both for and against prosecution. They are not exhaustive and, of course, are aimed at the work of the Crown Prosecution Service. For food authorities, the main importance of the Code is no doubt the analytical method that the full code test advocates.

1   The Code can be obtained from the Crown Prosecution Service or from its website.
2   The Code also prescribes the threshold test, as to which see para **19.3.10** below.
3   *Miller v Minister of Pensions* [1947] 2 All ER 372 at 373–374. As to the standard of proof, see also para **21.1.1**.
4   See para **20.3.4** below.
5   Attorney-General Lord Shawcross (HC Debs, vol 483, col 681, 29 January 1951). See also para **19.3.4** below.

The decision to prosecute: Food Law Codes of Practice

19.3.3   Chapters 3.1.10 of the Food Law Codes of Practice for England and Wales give further guidance on the decision to initiate a prosecution. They emphasise that the Food Authority should take the decision at the earliest opportunity after the consideration of a number of factors.

First of all, the Codes reiterate factors already noted in this section: the hierarchy of enforcement structure should indicate that a prosecution – as opposed to, say, informal action or an enforcement notice – is appropriate; the Enforcement Policy must have been adhered to; there must be a sufficiency of evidence in accordance with the Test in the Code for Crown Prosecutors; and, if there is such a sufficiency, the public interest Test set out in that Code must have been satisfied.

As to the sufficiency of evidence, factors identified as of particular note are:

- the likely cogency of any important witness, and their willingness to cooperate;
- the alleged person or persons responsible have been identified;
- any explanation offered by the suspect;
- the likelihood of the suspect being able to establish a defence – in particular a due diligence defence.

As to the public interest, factors noted as included among those favouring prosecution are:

- the seriousness of the offence;
- the prevalence of that type of offence in the area in which it was committed (if the offence is not serious in itself);
- the suspect's previous convictions or cautions.

Conversely, factors cited as included among those against prosecution are:

- the likelihood of a nominal penalty;
- the offence was committed as a result of a genuine mistake or misunderstanding;
- whether other action, such as issuing a formal caution in accordance with Home Office circular 30/2005[1] would be more appropriate.

Two final pieces of advice are directed to authorised officers. First, they are exhorted to 'brief their legal advisers fully on the public health aspects of the case in hand, including the public health basis for the legal requirements that have been breached, so that they can, in turn, impress upon the Court the seriousness of the charges'. No doubt, in cases of false description or presentation, briefing is of equal importance on the seriousness of the deception and the point of the statutory requirement. Secondly, 'officers should explain, where possible, the reason for bringing a prosecution and record that reason, which may later be referred to in open Court'.

1   Home Office circular 30/2005 on *The Cautioning of Adult Offenders*. See para **19.3.10** below.

The decision to prosecute: judicial comment

19.3.4   The courts have frowned on the prosecution of trivial cases[1]. In *Smedleys Ltd v Breed*, which was an appeal against conviction, under what is now s 14 of the FSA 1990, for selling a tin of peas containing a caterpillar, the House of Lords was critical of the enforcement authority for bringing proceedings in what it regarded as a trivial case. Pointing out that the authority had no duty to prosecute every case automatically, Viscount Dilhorne stated: 'where it is apparent that a prosecution does not serve the general interests of consumers the justices may think fit, if they find that the Act has been contravened, to grant an absolute discharge'.

Had the case arisen under the present Act, the appellants would probably have been able to establish the due diligence defence[2] that it introduced.

1   *Smedleys Ltd v Breed* [1974] AC 839, [1974] 2 All ER 21, at 33, HL; *Sunblest Bakeries Ltd v Andrews* (1985, unreported).
2   FSA 1990, s 21, see section **20.3**.

Responsibility for the decision to prosecute and conduct of proceedings

19.3.5   Prosecutions are conducted for the police by the Crown Prosecution Service (CPS) set up for the purpose by the Prosecution of Offences Act 1985 following the recommendation in the 1981 *Report of the Royal Commission on Criminal Procedure* that the roles of the investigator and lawyer should be separated. The perceived need for legal input into prosecutions was one reason for this recommendation, but it was also seen as unsatisfactory that the person responsible for the decision to prosecute should be one who had carried out or been concerned in the investigation. Officers carrying out investigations inevitably and properly form views about the guilt of suspects. Having done so, they may, without any kind of improper motive, be inclined to shut their minds to other evidence telling against the guilt of suspects, or to overestimate the strength of the evidence they have assembled. Although the Royal Commission did not advocate that the CPS should take on central and local government prosecutions, it acknowledged that there were similar arguments of principle for their doing so[1]. It would therefore be imprudent for those concerned with such prosecutions not to have regard for the spirit of the Royal Commission proposals.

As to the prosecution decision, delegation by the authority to a senior council officer should generally be capable of meeting this objective. However, acting by committee in open session is an unacceptable way of making the decision, since it may well prejudice the food business and its right to a fair trial.

As to the conduct of proceedings, any authorised member or officer of a local authority may appear for them although not a qualified lawyer[2]. Such officers have played a long and honourable part in prosecuting offences under food legislation that is specialised and unfamiliar to many lawyers. It would appear that the separation of functions advocated by the Royal Commission can be honoured by arrangements under which the prosecutor is a senior officer who has played no part in the investigation.

Prosecuting, however, is itself an increasingly specialist task that, for example, demands a knowledge of evidence[3] and procedure beyond the confines of the FSA 1990. As a result, there is evidently an increasing trend by enforcement authorities to the use of legally qualified prosecutors.

1   Cmnd 8092, in particular, at paras 6.23, 6.24 and 7.41.
2   Local Government Act 1972, s 223.
3   See section **19.5** below.

Time limits for prosecutions

19.3.6   Prosecutions for offences triable either way under the FSA 1990 (including regulations and orders) cannot be begun after the expiry of three years from the commission of the offence, or one year from its discovery by the prosecutor, whichever is the earlier[1]. 'Discovery' in this context means a time when all the facts material to the charge are disclosed to the appropriate officer[2]. In respect of prosecutions for offences triable only summarily, such as those under s 33(1) of the FSA 1990 and those under reg 44 of the Food Labelling Regulations 1996, the time limit is six months as specified by s 127 of the Magistrates' Courts Act 1980 (MCA 1980)[3].

It should also be noted that offences under previous food hygiene Regulations have been held to be continuing offences, committed afresh each day that the Regulations are not complied with[4].

Unreasonable delay in bringing proceedings may be an abuse of process notwithstanding the fact that they have been commenced within the statutory time limits[5]. The relevant considerations for a court when considering whether to stay proceedings for an abuse of process are the degree of delay and whether the alleged abuse directly affected the fairness of the trial[6].

1   FSA 1990, s 34.
2   *Tesco Stores Ltd v London Borough of Harrow* [2003] EWHC 2919, (2003) 167 JP 657.
3   As to offences triable either way and summarily, see para **19.3.8** below.
4   *R v Thames Metropolitan Stipendiary Magistrate, ex p Hackney London Borough Council* (1993) 92 LGR 392.
5   See, for example, *Daventry District Council v Olins* (1990) 154 JP 478, DC, in which the information was not laid and the complainant's identity was not disclosed until nine and ten months respectively after the sale of an unfit pie.
6   *Wei Hai Restaurant Ltd v Kingston upon Hull City Council* [2001] EWHC Admin 490, (2002) 166 JP 185 in which convictions for offences in contravention of the FSA 1990 and the Food Safety (General Food Hygiene) Regulations 1995 were upheld on appeal notwithstanding that the informations had not been laid until the last day of the 12-month limitation period.

Commencement of proceedings

19.3.7   Legal proceedings are commenced by laying an information at the offices of the clerk to the justices for the relevant area[1] and the issue of a summons in accordance with the Criminal Procedure Rules 2005. It is essential that charges are laid correctly. For example, to charge an offence as to misleading labelling of food without stating whether the offence was under s 15(1) of the FSA 1990 or – for contravention of Art 16 of Regulation (EC) 178/2002 – reg 4(c) of the General Food Regulations 2004 would be bad for uncertainty because the defendant would not know which enactment he was alleged to have contravened[2]. Moreover, an information must not charge more than one offence[3]. An information that charged the defendant under what is now s 14 of the FSA 1990 with selling food 'not of the nature or of the substance or of the quality demanded' was held to be for more than one offence and bad for duplicity[4].

Section 222 of the Local Government Act 1972 is not intended to preclude a local authority from issuing a summons in respect of breaches of the FSA 1990 in its own name rather than in the name of a particular official[5].

1   *R v Manchester Stipendiary Magistrate, ex p Hill* [1983] 1 AC 328, sub nom *Hill v Anderton* [1982] 2 All ER 963.
2   As to FSA 1990, s 15(1), Regulation (EC) 178/2002 and the General Food Regulations 2004, see further paras **3.2.36–3.2.37** above.
3   Criminal Procedure Rules 2005, r 7.3.
4   *Bastin v Davies* [1950] 2 KB 579, [1950] 1 All ER 1095. See further para **8.2.5** above.
5   *Monks v East Northamptonshire District Council sub nom Monks v Northamptonshire District Council* [2002] EWHC 473, (2002) 166 JP 592.

Mode of trial

19.3.8   In relation to the provision for punishment of offences made by s 35 of the FSA 1990, it is desirable first to consider the mode of trial. All but one of the offences against the FSA 1990 itself are triable either way; that is, they are triable either on indictment (by jury in the Crown Court) or summarily (by magistrates)[1]. Obstruction offences under s 33(1) alone are triable summarily only.

Provision for trial either way is also to be found in regulations dealing with food hygiene, food contact materials and pesticide residues, and has recently been adopted in regulations concerning GM food, added vitamins and minerals and nutrition and health claims[2].

The procedure for offences triable either way is laid down by ss 17A–28 of the MCA 1980. If the defendant does not plead guilty, the magistrates' court hears the parties and considers whether the case should be dealt with summarily or in the Crown Court. In deciding which mode of trial is appropriate, the court must, in particular, have regard to the nature of the case, whether the circumstances make the offence one of a serious character and whether summary powers, including the prescribed maximum penalties, would be adequate. It must not, however, be informed of any previous conviction of the defendant[3]. A decision by the magistrates in favour of summary trial is subject to the consent of the defendant who, by not consenting, elects to be tried in the Crown Court.

It should also be noted that a defendant charged with an offence triable either way has a right to advance information of the prosecution case[4].

1   See IA 1978, Sch 1.
2   For regulations made under the FSA 1990, the enabling power is in s 26(3).
3   *R v Colchester Justices, ex p North Essex Building Co Ltd* [1977] 3 All ER 567, [1977] 1 WLR 1109.
4   See Criminal Procedure Rules 2005, r 21.

Maximum penalties

19.3.9   Section 35 of the FSA 1990 also specifies maximum penalties. On conviction on indictment, they are an unlimited fine or imprisonment for up to two years or both.

The maximum penalties on summary conviction are more complex. Subject to separate provision for obstruction offences explained below, the penalties are a fine of specified maximum amount or imprisonment for a term not exceeding six months or both. In the case of offences under s 7 or 14[1] food safety may be at issue and the maximum fine is £20,000. In any other case, the maximum fine is the 'statutory maximum', which (by virtue of Sch 1 to the IA 1978 and s 32 of the MCA 1980[2]), in relation to England and Wales, is currently £5,000. As noted in the previous paragraph, obstruction offences under s 33(1) are triable summarily only. The penalties that may be imposed are a fine not exceeding a specified maximum or imprisonment for a term of three months or both. The specified maximum for a fine is level 5 on the 'standard scale' which (by virtue of Sch 1 to the IA 1978 and s 37 of the Criminal Justice Act 1982[3]), is currently £5,000.

The previous paragraph also referred to food regulations that provide for trial either way. When made under the FSA 1990, in compliance with s 26(3) of that Act, they normally specify the maximum penalties, on conviction on indictment, of a fine or imprisonment for a term not exceeding two years or both and, on summary conviction, of a fine not exceeding the statutory maximum or imprisonment for a term not exceeding six months or both[4]. On the other hand, when the regulations are made under the ECA 1972, the maximum term of imprisonment on summary conviction is restricted to three months in accordance with Sch 2, para 1(d) to that Act[5].

In other regulations under the FSA 1990, contraventions generally render defendants liable on summary conviction to a fine not exceeding level 5 on the standard scale.[6]

1 See sections **5.2** and **8.2** respectively above.
2 As amended by s 17(2) of the Criminal Justice Act 1991 (CJA 1991).
3 As amended by s 17(1) of the CJA 1991.
4 See, for example, the Genetically Modified Food (England) Regulations 2004, reg 5. See also the General Food Regulations 2004, reg 5 which exceptionally prescribe a maximum fine of £20,000 on summary conviction for a contravention of Regulation (EC) 178/2002, Art 14 (food safety requirements), as did FSA 1990, s 8 that it replaced.
5 See, for example, the Transmissible Spongiform Encephalopathies (England) Regulations 2008, reg 18.
6 See, for example, the Food Labelling Regulations 1996, reg 44(1); the Honey (England) Regulations 2003, reg 7(1); and the Contaminants in Food (England) Regulations 2007, reg 3(4).

Informal warnings and cautions

19.3.10 For many years enforcement authorities have been accustomed to give offenders written warnings in cases where the food law contravention was not felt to warrant prosecution. Such informal letters identify the provision contravened, advise on compliance and warn against future failures. They can be a useful means of preventing recurrence, but they have no status in law.

Since 1985 a more formal system has been available providing for a warning that can be cited in any subsequent proceedings. Originally called a 'Formal Caution', it is redesignated a 'Simple Caution' by the current guidance set out in Home Office circular 30/2005 so as to distinguish it from the 'Conditional Caution' initiated by the Criminal Justice Act 2003 to provide for the imposition of rehabilative or reparative conditions. At present, the Conditional Cautioning Scheme is confined to the police and the CPS but LACORS has been consulted by the Attorney-General's Office on how conditional cautions and other forms of diversions from criminal proceedings might be implemented by prosecutors other than the CPS.

The guidance given by circular 30/2005 on 'Simple Cautioning' is extensive. A reading of the full text is essential. The following brief summary attempts to highlight only the principal features.

The simple caution is a non-statutory disposal for adult offenders. There are no definitive rules on the circumstances in which it should be employed. In each case the officer having the discretion should consider whether a simple caution is appropriate to the offence and the offender and whether it is likely to be effective in the circumstances. The aims are to deal quickly and simply with less serious offences, to divert offenders where appropriate from appearing in criminal courts and to reduce the likelihood of re-offending. In assessing whether a simple caution is appropriate, circular 30/2005 states that the following should be considered:

- Is there sufficient evidence of the suspect's guilt to meet the threshold test (as outlined in the Director's Guidance[1])?
- Is the offence indictable only (and the available evidence meets the threshold test)? If the answer is 'yes', this disposal option must be referred to a Crown Prosecutor.
- Has the suspect made a clear and reliable admission of the offence (either verbally or in writing)?[2] An admission of the offence, corroborated by some other material and significant evidential fact will be sufficient evidence to provide a realistic prospect of conviction. This corroboration could be obtained from information in the crime report or obtained during the course of the investigation. A simple caution will not be appropriate where a person has not made a clear and reliable

admission of the offence (for example if intent is denied or there are doubts about their mental health or intellectual capacity, or where a statutory defence is offered).

- Is it in the public interest to use a simple caution as the appropriate means of disposal? Officers should take into account the public interest principles set out in the Code for Crown Prosecutors[3].
- Is the suspect 18 years or over? Where a suspect is under 18, a reprimand or final warning would be the equivalent disposal.

If all the above requirements are met, the officer must consider whether the seriousness of the offence makes it appropriate for disposal by a simple caution.

Some comment on these criteria may be of assistance. It will be appreciated that they are directed primarily at police officers and extend to cases way beyond the ambit of food law. The second and fifth of the criteria area are either of no, or of very little, concern to food law. It embraces none, such as murder, rape and robbery, that are tried on indictment only, nor are many suspected of contravening it likely to be less than 18 years old. Enforcement officers might therefore expect to direct their minds to the first, third and fourth criteria, dealing respectively with sufficient evidence, the suspect's admission and the public interest.

As to the evidential requirement, the threshold test is prescribed by the Code for Crown Prosecutors and is not itself relevant to regulatory offences considered by this book. It is applied 'to those cases in which it is proposed to keep the suspect in custody after charge, but the evidence required to apply the Full Code Test is not yet available'[4]. However, the Director's Guidance on the Threshold Test is applicable, *mutatis mutandis*, in the present context. The Guidance states:

'Application of the Threshold Test will require an overall assessment of whether in all the circumstances of the case there is at least a reasonable suspicion against the person of having committed an offence[5] (in accordance with Article 5 of the European Convention on Human Rights[6]) and that at that stage it is in the public interest to proceed.

The evidential decision in each case will require consideration of a number of factors including:

- the evidence available at the time and the likelihood and nature of further evidence being obtained;
- the reasonableness for believing that evidence will become available; the time that will take and
- the steps being taken to gather it; the impact of the expected evidence on the case, and the charges the totality of the evidence will support.

The public interest means the same as under the Full Code Test, but will be based on the information available at the time of charge, which will often be limited.'

Circular 30/2005 continues with guidance in particular on aggravating or mitigating factors, recording the admission, the victim, making the decision, administering a simple caution, consequences of receiving a simple caution and other considerations. Before making a decision it is important to check whether the suspect has any other cautions for similar offences and that he or she has been made aware of the significance of a simple caution and has given informed consent to being cautioned. Suspects who do not agree to receive a caution may be charged instead. Once a simple caution has been administered, the offender should sign a form accepting its terms and be given a copy. The accurate recording of all simple cautions is essential in order to avoid multiple cautioning and to ensure consistency. As noted above, the fact of the simple caution may also be cited in court in any subsequent court proceedings.

For local authority enforcement officers a useful supplement to circular 30/2005 is to be found in LACORS Revised Guidance on Cautioning Offenders[7]. In particular this points out that simple cautions must be recorded not only by the local authority, but also, where appropriate, on any national information databases. In December 2007, the National Policing Improvement Agency stated that, at the present time, the police service would not record on the National Police Computer details of cautions delivered by non-police prosecution agencies. LACORS has separately agreed to establish a list of databases that local authorities can use to view and record convictions and cautions for various regulatory agencies. Offences relating to the composition and labelling of food may be registered on the Office of Fair Trading (OFT) online Criminal Register of Convictions. However, there is currently no central recording system for most food hygiene offences and LACORS has advised the Food Standards Agency and OFT of this unsatisfactory situation.

1   *The Director's Guidance on Charging: Guidance to Police Officers issued by the Director of Public Prosecutions under section 37A of the Police and Criminal Evidence Act 1984* (3rd edn, February 2007).
2   See *R* (*on the application of Stoddart*) *v Oxfordshire Magistrates' Court* [2005] All ER (D) 97. A defendant charged with an offence but who later accepted a caution was entitled to his costs when the case was dismissed notwithstanding that he had admitted the offence.
3   As to the Code and the public interest stage of the Full Code Test, see para **19.3.2** above.
4   As to the Code and the Full Code Test generally, see again para **19.3.2** above.
5   Contrast the evidential stage of the Full Code Test in the Code for Crown Prosecutors described in para **19.3.2** above.
6   The right to liberty and security, in particular, from unlawful arrest.
7   Issue 2 – January 2008.

Offences by bodies corporate

19.3.11 Section 36 of the FSA 1990 makes special provision in respect of offences by bodies corporate. A body corporate or 'corporation' is a legal entity distinct from the individuals who constitute it from time to time. A company formed and registered under the Companies Act 1985 (CA 1985)[1] is the main but by no means the only sort. Another example, that is, 'a body corporate established by or under any enactment for the purpose of carrying on under national ownership any industry or part of an industry or undertaking', is the subject of s 36(2).

A body corporate can be prosecuted and punished in its own name. Offences are customarily applied to persons and a 'person' includes a body of persons corporate or unincorporate[2]. However, where its offence is proved to have been committed with the consent or connivance of, or to be attributable to, any neglect on the part of any director, manager, secretary or other similar officer, or any person who was purporting to act in any such capacity, that person as well as the body corporate must be deemed to be guilty of the offence, and is liable to be prosecuted and punished accordingly[3].

1   CA 1985, ss 1 and 735(1).
2   IA 1978, Sch 1.
3   FSA 1990, s 36(1).

19.4 OTHER LEGISLATION

19.4.1   For the most part, consumer protection and other statutes relevant to food make provision parallel to the FSA 1990 for punishment of offences, time limits[1] and bodies corporate.

The main penalty specified by the legislation is a fine on summary conviction not exceeding level 5 on the standard scale[2]. Additionally, Part II of the Consumer Protection Act 1987 (CPA 1987) provides for a maximum of six months' imprisonment.

Either way offences allowing for a fine on conviction on indictment are provided by the Prices Act 1974 (PA 1974), s 20 of the CPA 1987 and – in respect of pesticides – the Food and Environment Protection Act 1985 (F&EPA 1985), while the Consumer Protection from Unfair Trading Regulations 2008, the Trade Descriptions Act 1968 (TDA 1968) and – in respect of emergency orders – the F&EPA 1985 add the possibility of imprisonment for a maximum term of two years.

Regulations made under the European Communities Act 1972 (ECA 1972) to enforce food standards specified in Community common agricultural policy Regulations generally contain provisions similar to regulations under the FSA 1990. The criminal penalties prescribed cannot exceed the limits specified in para 1(1)(d) of Sch 2 to the ECA 1972.

Prosecution under the Consumer Protection from Unfair Trading Regulations 2008 or the TDA 1968 is not restricted by the FSA 1990 protection in respect of samples procured for analysis. Until repeal by the 2008 Regulations, s 22(2) of the TDA 1968 provided that, where an act or omission constituted an offence under both statutes, evidence on behalf of the prosecution concerning any such sample was not admissible in proceedings under the TDA 1968 unless s 31 of the FSA 1990 and regulations made under it had been complied with.

It should further be noted that proceedings may be instituted under the PA 1974[3] and the W&MA 1985 only by or on behalf of a local weights and measures authority or, in the latter case, the chief officer of police for a police area[4]. Proceedings under Part III of the Agriculture and Horticulture Act 1964 (A&HA 1964) may be instituted only by or with the consent of the Secretary of State (or Welsh Ministers, in Wales) or with the consent of the Attorney-General[5].

Those who enforce the CPA 1987, s 12, the PA 1974, the F&EPA 1985, the TDA 1968 and the A&HA 1964 may also in due course be able to impose the civil sanctions provided for in the Regulatory Enforcement and Sanctions Act 2008 described in para **18.3.3** above.

1   As to time limits, see further MCA 1980, s 127.
2   See, for example, W&MA 1985, s 84(6); and, as amended by the Criminal Justice Act 1982, the Agriculture and Horticulture Act 1964, s 20(2) and the Agriculture Act 1970, ss 68(4), 69(4), 70(2), 71(2) and 73(4).
3   PA 1974, Sch, para 8(1).
4   W&MA 1985, s 83.
5   A&HA 1964, s 20(3).

19.5 EVIDENCE

Introduction

19.5.1   Paragraph **19.3.5** above considered responsibility for the decision to prosecute. Sound decisions depend on good reports from investigating officers. These should include the identity of the person alleged to have committed the offence, any previous convictions and other relevant facts, followed by the admissible evidence set out in logical and chronological sequence. Opinions and recommendations as to appropriate action may be helpful but should be separate from the main body of the report.

Although many food law cases are simple, others are very complex. A food product may have to be traced from source, through a chain of distribution to the point where the primary offence has been committed and, at each stage, the necessary evidence established and the culpability assessed of every company, director and manager involved.

Authorised officers thus need a variety of qualities. In addition to investigative and reporting skills, a knowledge of food law and a grasp of the scientific and technical issues, they require some understanding of the relevant law relating to evidence. Food cases may be lost through failure to adduce the necessary evidence or to follow correct procedures.

Prosecution evidence may be excluded by the court either at common law or under s 78 of PACE[1]. In general, it must be admissible and be obtained fairly and impartially.

A full consideration of the law of evidence must be sought elsewhere[2]. This section summarises some important statutory rules on witness statements, other documentary evidence, questioning suspects and disclosure of unused material.

1   See further para **19.5.7** below.
2   See *Cross and Tapper on Evidence* (Oxford, 11th edn, 2007).

Hearsay evidence in criminal proceedings: general principle

19.5.2   Until recently there has been a common law rule against hearsay in criminal proceedings. This rule meant that:

> 'any assertion other than one made by a person while giving oral evidence in the proceedings was inadmissible if tendered as evidence of the facts asserted'[1].

Common law and statutory exceptions had developed over the years and this area of law is now governed by the Criminal Justice Act 2003 (CJA 2003), Part II, Chapter 2. As a general rule hearsay evidence is now admissible provided that certain conditions are met. Under s 114(1) a statement not made in oral evidence in the criminal proceedings is admissible if, and only if:

- any provision of the CJA 2003, Part 11, Chapter 2 or any other statutory provision makes it admissible,
- any rule of law preserved by s 118 makes it admissible;
- all parties to the proceedings agree to it being admissible, or
- the court is satisfied that it is in the interests of justice for it to be admissible.

In deciding whether or not to admit such evidence the court must have regard to a number of factors outlined in s 114(2). Safeguards against prejudice that might be caused by the admissibility of hearsay evidence are contained in ss 123–126.

1 See Keane *The Modern Law of Evidence* (Oxford, 7th edn, 2007), p 568.

Criminal Justice Act 2003: hearsay evidence where a witness is unavailable

19.5.3   Section 116 CJA 2003, subject to specified provisions[1], allows hearsay evidence, both oral and documentary, to be admitted to court where a witness is unavailable, in two categories of cases[2]. The first category is where:

(a)   the person who made the statement in the document is dead, or by reason of his bodily or mental condition unfit to be a witness; or

(b)   the person who made the statement is outside the United Kingdom and it is not reasonably practicable to secure his attendance; or

(c)   all reasonable steps have been taken to find the person who made the statement, but he cannot be found.

The second category is where the witness does not give evidence through fear. ' "Fear" is to be widely construed and (for example) includes fear of the death or injury of another person or of financial loss.'[2] A statement in these circumstances will not be admitted unless it is in the interests of justice to do so, having regard in particular to the statement's contents and 'any risk that its admission or exclusion will result in unfairness to any party to the proceedings'.[3]

1 CJA 2003, ss 114 and 116(1)
2 CJA 2003, s 116(3).
3 CJA 2003, s 116(4).

Criminal Justice Act 2003: business etc documents

19.5.4   The CJA 2003 also enables business and similar documents to be put in evidence. Subject to specified provisions[1], s 117 allows for a statement in a document to be admissible in criminal proceedings as evidence of any fact of which direct oral evidence would be admissible if:

'(a)   the document or the part containing the statement was created or received by a person in the course of a trade, business, profession or other occupation, or as the holder of a paid or unpaid office;

(b)   the person who supplied the information contained in the statement (the relevant person) had or may reasonably be supposed to have had personal knowledge of the matters dealt with, and

(c)   each person (if any) through whom the information was supplied from the relevant person to the person mentioned in paragraph (a) received the information in the course of a trade, business, profession or other occupation, or as the holder of a paid or unpaid office.'

Section 117 applies whether the information contained in the document was supplied directly or indirectly, in other words, it may include 'multiple hearsay'. However, if the information was supplied indirectly, the section applies only if each person through whom it was supplied received it:

(a)   in the course of trade, business, profession or other occupation; or

(b)   as the holder of a paid or unpaid office.

1   CJA 2003, ss 114 and 117(1).

Proof by written statement

19.5.5   Section 9 of the Criminal Justice Act 1967 provides a very useful procedure whereby agreed written statements of facts may be received in evidence with the same effect as oral evidence[1] if specified conditions are met. In particular, the statement must be signed by the witness, must contain a declaration of his knowledge that it is subject to penalties if false, must be served on the other party and must not have been objected to within seven days.

It is common practice in food cases to take advantage of this procedure. A written witness statement is, for example, useful to set out a consumer's complaint about a food product.

1   *Ellis v Jones* [1973] 2 All ER 893.

Criminal Justice Act 1988: expert reports

19.5.6   We have already observed, in para **18.4.7** above, the circumstances in which the production of a certificate of analysis or examination is sufficient evidence of the facts stated in it. Paragraph **18.4.5** noted that prosecutors in food cases might wish to put in to the court expert evidence other than that which is provided by public analysts and food examiners. Similarly, a food company may wish to use reports from experts on food science or technology in defence of proceedings. Section 30 of the CJA 1988 provides that an expert report is admissible whether or not the person making it attends to give oral evidence, but only with the leave of the court. For the purpose of determining whether to give leave, the court is required to have regard to the contents of the report, to the reason why the person making the report shall not give oral evidence, to any risk of unfairness to the accused and to any other relevant circumstances. An expert report when admitted is evidence of any fact or opinion of which the person making it could have given oral evidence.

For these purposes, an 'expert report' means a written report by a person dealing wholly or mainly with matters of which he is (or would if living be) qualified to give expert evidence.

Under r 24 of the Criminal Procedure Rules 2005 if a party to a criminal trial proposes to put an expert report in evidence, that party needs to disclose the report to the other party or parties as soon as it is practicable to do so.

Police and Criminal Evidence Act 1984: exclusion of unfair evidence

19.5.7   Part VII of PACE makes general provision in respect of evidence in criminal proceedings. In particular, section 78 enables a court to refuse to allow evidence on which the prosecution proposes to rely if it appears that, having regard to all the circumstances, including circumstances in which the evidence was obtained, the admission of the evidence would have such an adverse effect on the fairness of the proceedings that the court ought not to admit it.

In food cases, care must be taken that documents, such as recipes, production records, staff instructions, invoices and correspondence, which are often necessary as evidence, have been obtained and used fairly[1].

1   *Walker's Snack Foods Ltd v Coventry City Council* [1998] 3 All ER 163.

Police and Criminal Evidence Act 1984: codes of practice

19.5.8   Part VI of PACE provides for the issue of codes of practice in relation to statutory powers of search and seizure and detention, treatment and questioning. Although these provisions are directed primarily at police officers, other persons who are charged with the duty of investigating offences or charging offenders must, in the discharge of that duty, have regard to any relevant provisions of a PACE code of practice[1]. Thus, a routine inspection by a trading standards officer has been held to be a search within the ordinary meaning of the word so that the provisions of PACE Code B (search of premises and seizure of property) applied[2]. On the other hand, a request for information from environmental health officers carrying out their statutory duty under s 32(1)(b) of the FSA 1990[3] was held to be governed neither by PACE Code C (detention, treatment and questioning of persons), nor, since the officers were relying on their statutory powers rather than on consent to enter premises, by PACE Code B[4]. Similarly, it was held that the obligation under Code C to inform an interviewee as to the availability of legal aid does not apply to trading standards officers conducting interviews under caution.[5]

Failure to comply with the provisions of any relevant code of practice does not render the officer liable to civil or criminal proceedings[6] but any evidence so obtained may be inadmissible[7].

For authorised officers investigating offences against food law PACE Code C will be the most important. PACE Codes C and E (tape recording of interviews with suspects) are addressed further in paras **19.5.9** and **19.5.10** respectively below.

The latest editions of the PACE Codes B, C, D and E were issued by the Police and Criminal Evidence Act 1984 (Codes of Practice) Order 2008.

1   PACE, s 67(9).
2   *Dudley Metropolitan Borough Council v Debenhams plc* (1995) 159 JP 18.
3   See para **18.5.2** above.
4   *Walker's Snack Foods Ltd v Coventry City Council* [1998] 3 All ER 163.
5   *R (on the application of Beale) v South East Wiltshire Magistrates* [2002] EWHC 2961 (Admin).
6   PACE, s 67(10).
7   See *Dudley Metropolitan Borough Council v Debenhams plc* (1995) 159 JP 18.

Police and Criminal Evidence Act 1984 Code C: questioning of suspected persons

19.5.9   The modern rules to secure the fair questioning of suspected persons are to be found in PACE and PACE Code C made under it. The parts most relevant to questioning for the purposes of food law are noted below. In application they must, of course, be adapted to the particular circumstances. For example, the need to search in exercise of powers of stop and search are not relevant to food cases.

Cautions

1. A person of whom there are grounds to suspect of an offence must be cautioned before any questions about it (or further questions if it is his answers to previous questions that provide the grounds for suspicion) are put to him regarding his involvement or suspected involvement in that offence if his answers or silence (ie failure or refusal to answer a question or to answer satisfactorily) may be given in evidence to a court in a prosecution. He therefore need not be cautioned if questions are put to him for other purposes, for example solely to establish his identity or his ownership of any vehicle or to obtain information in accordance with any relevant statutory requirement or in furtherance of the proper and effective conduct of a search (for example to determine the need to search in exercise of powers of stop and search or to seek co-operation while carrying out a search) or to seek verification of a written record.

2. The caution shall be in the following terms: 'You do not have to say anything. But it may harm your defence if you do not mention when questioned something which you later rely on in court. Anything you do say may be given in evidence.'

   Minor deviations do not constitute a breach of this requirement provided that the sense of the caution is preserved.

3. Where there is a break in questioning under caution the interviewing officer must ensure that the person being questioned is aware that he remains under caution. If there is any doubt, the caution shall be given again in full when the interview resumes.

Interviews

4. As soon as a police officer who is making enquiries of any person about an offence believes that a prosecution should be brought against him and that there is sufficient evidence for it to succeed, he shall ask the person if he has anything further to say. If the person indicates that he has nothing more to say the officer shall without delay cease to question him about that offence.

5. (a) An accurate record must be made of each interview with a person suspected of an offence, whether or not the interview takes place at a police station.

   (b) The record must state the place of the interview, the time it begins and ends, the time the record is made (if different), any breaks in the interview and the names of those present; and must be made on the forms provided for this purpose or in the officer's pocket book or in accordance with the code of practice for tape recording police interviews with suspects (Code E)[1].

   (c) Any written record must be made and completed during the interview, unless in the investigating officer's view it would not be practicable or would interfere with conduct of the interview, and must constitute either a verbatim record of what has been said or, failing this, an account of the interview that adequately and accurately summarises it.

6. If a written record is not made during the course of the interview it must be made as soon as practicable after its completion.

7. Written interview records must be timed and signed by the maker.

8. If a written record is not completed in the course of the interview the reason must be recorded in the interview record.

9. Unless it is impracticable the person interviewed shall be given the

opportunity to read the interview record and to sign it as correct or to indicate the respects in which he considers it inaccurate. If the interview is tape-recorded the arrangements set out in Code E apply. If the person concerned cannot read or refuses to read the record or to sign it, the senior interviewer present shall read it to him and ask him whether he would like to sign it as correct (or make his mark) or to indicate the respects in which he considers it inaccurate. The interviewer shall then certify on the interview record itself what has occurred.

10. If the appropriate adult or the person's solicitor is present during the interview, he shall also be given an opportunity to read and sign the interview record (or any written statement taken down by the police officer).

11. Any refusal by a person to sign an interview record when asked to do so in accordance with the provisions of the Code must itself be recorded.

12. A written record shall also be made of any comments made by a suspected person, including unsolicited comments, which are outside the context of an interview but that might be relevant to the offence. Any such record must be timed and signed by the maker. Where practicable the person shall be given the opportunity to read that record and to sign it as correct or to indicate the respects in which he considers it inaccurate. Any refusal to sign shall be recorded.

The caution set out in PACE Code C relates to s 34 of the Criminal Justice and Public Order Act 1994. This enables a court to draw such inferences 'as appear proper' from the accused's failure, at specified times, to mention any fact relied on in his defence that in the circumstances existing at the time he could reasonably have been expected to mention. The specified times are any time before being charged on being questioned under caution, or on being charged with the offence or officially informed he might be prosecuted for it.

1   See para **19.5.10** below.

Police and Criminal Evidence Act 1984 Code E: audio recording interviews with suspects

19.5.10 PACE Code E relates to the audio recording of interviews with suspects. Authorised officers must have regard to the Code and the practice direction on it[1], if tape recording is used for this purpose.

1   *Practice Note* (*Criminal Evidence*) (*Tape Recording of Police Interviews*) [1989] 2 All ER 415, [1989] 1 WLR 631.

Criminal Procedure and Investigations Act 1996 (CP&IA 1996): disclosure

19.5.11 The law requiring disclosure of unused material by the prosecution[1] was strengthened by the CP&IA 1996. Part I of the CP&IA 1996[2] makes provision in relation to disclosure of information, by the prosecutor and the accused, in criminal proceedings relating to alleged offences that have not hitherto been subject to criminal investigation. Part I covers investigations that police officers or other persons have a duty to conduct, with a view to it being ascertained whether a person should be charged with an offence, or whether a person charged with an offence is guilty of it. Criminal investigations by authorised officers investigating contraventions of food law are thus included.

The prosecutor has a duty either to disclose to the accused any material that has not previously been disclosed and that in the prosecutor's opinion might reasonably be considered capable of undermining the case for the prosecution, or to give to the accused a written statement that there is no such material. Where material does not consist of information (for instance, a food sample) the prosecutor discloses it by allowing the accused to inspect it at a reasonable time and a reasonable place.

Part I of the CP&IA 1996 also provides for compulsory disclosure by the accused in relation to indictable offences (and voluntary disclosure in relation to summary ones) of a written 'defence statement' to the court and the prosecutor. The statement must set out in general terms the nature of the defence (including any particular defence he intended to rely on), indicate the matters on which issue is taken with the prosecution case and set out, in the case of each such matter, the reason why this is. The prosecution has a continuing duty to keep under review and disclose to the accused any material that has not previously been disclosed and that might be reasonably expected to assist the accused's defence.

Further provisions of Part I, in particular, enable the accused, in specified circumstances, to make application for disclosure.

The accused in criminal proceedings also has a right to know who has made the accusation.

1   See, for example, *R v Leyland Justices, ex p Hawthorn* [1979] QB 283, [1979] 1 All ER 209; *R v Maguire* [1992] QB 936, [1992] 2 All ER 433; *R v Ward* [1993] 2 All ER 577, [1993] 1 WLR 619.
2   As amended by the Criminal Justice Act 2003.

Criminal Procedure and Investigations Act 1996: criminal investigations

19.5.12   Part II of the CP&IA 1996 provides for a code of practice designed to secure that:

(a)   the police take all reasonable steps in criminal investigations;
(b)   unused material is revealed to the prosecutor;
(c)   where the prosecutor so requests, unused material is disclosed to the accused; and
(d)   the prosecutor is given a statement that the activities required by the code have been carried out.

Like Part I of the CP&IA 1996, authorised officers investigating contraventions of food law are bound by the code since it applies to persons, other than police officers, who are charged with the duty of conducting criminal investigations. By s 26 of the CP&IA 1996, they must, in discharging the duty, have regard to any relevant provisions of the code that would apply if the investigation were conducted by police officers. Failure to comply with this obligation does not, however, in itself render the officer liable to criminal or civil proceedings.

Criminal Procedure and Investigations Act 1996: code of practice[1]

19.5.13   Those responsible for investigating food law offences should consult the full code, but a summary of relevant provisions is set out below. Of the definitions in the code it might, in particular, be noted here that 'disclosure officer' is defined as the person responsible for examining material retained by the police during the investigation; revealing material to the prosecutor during the investigation and any criminal proceedings resulting from it, and certifying that he has done this; and disclosing material to the accused at the request of the prosecutor.

General responsibilities

Separate functions are specified for investigators, officers in charge of investigations and disclosure officers. In conducting an investigation, the investigator should pursue all reasonable lines of inquiry, whether these point towards or away from the suspect. What is reasonable in each case will depend on the particular circumstances. If the officer in charge of an investigation believes that other persons may be in possession of material that may be relevant to the investigation, and if this has not already been obtained he should ask the disclosure officer to inform them of the existence of the investigation and to invite them to retain the material in case they receive a request for disclosure.

Recording of information

If material that may be relevant to the investigation consists of information that is not recorded in any form, the officer in charge of an investigation must ensure that it is recorded in a durable or retrievable form. Negative information is often relevant to an investigation. If it may be relevant it must be recorded.

Retention of material

The investigator must retain material obtained in a criminal investigation that may be relevant to the investigation. This includes not only material coming into the possession of the investigator but also material generated by him.

Where material has been seized in exercise of the powers, the duty to retain it under this code is subject to the provisions on retention of seized material in s 22 of PACE.

The following are categories of material that may be relevant to the investigation and must be retained:

- crime reports (including crime report forms, relevant parts of incident record books or the police officer's notebook);
- custody records;
- records that are derived from tapes of telephone messages (for example 999 calls) containing descriptions of an alleged offence or offenders:
- final versions of witness statements and draft versions where their content differs from the final version (including any exhibits mentioned), interview records (written records, or audio or video tapes, of interviews with actual or potential witnesses or suspects);
- communications between the police and experts such as forensic scientists, reports of work carried out by experts, and schedules of scientific material prepared by the expert for the investigator, for the purposes of criminal proceedings;
- records of the first description of a suspect by each potential witness who purports to identify or describe the suspect, whether or not the description differs from that of subsequent descriptions by that or other witnesses;

- any material casting doubt on the reliability of a confession;
- information provided by the accused that indicates an explanation for the offence with which he has been changed;
- any material casting doubt on the reliability of a prosecution witness.

All material which may be relevant to the investigation must be retained until a decision is taken whether to institute proceedings against a person for an offence.

Preparation of material for prosecutor

The Code sets out in detail how material should be prepared.

Revelation of material to prosecutor

The disclosure officer must give the schedules to the prosecutor. Wherever practicable this should be at the same time as he gives him the file containing the material for the prosecution case. He should also draw the attention of the prosecutor to any material an investigator has retained.

Certification by disclosure officer

The disclosure officer must certify to the prosecutor that to the best of his knowledge and belief, all material that has been retained and made available to him has been revealed in accordance with the code.

Disclosure of material to the accused

If material has not already been copied to the prosecutor, and he requests its disclosure to the accused, on the ground that:

- it satisfies the test for prosecution disclosure, or
- the court has ordered its disclosure after considering an application from the accused,

the disclosure officer *must* disclose it to the accused.

1   Brought into operation by the Criminal Procedure and Investigations Act 1996 (Code of Practice) Order 2005, SI 2005/985.

Chapter 20

Strict liability, defences etc

20.1 STRICT LIABILITY

20.1.1   The normal rule of English criminal law is that 'a man's deed does not make him guilty unless his mind be guilty': he must have a criminal intention (*mens rea*) in order to be guilty of the offence in question. There are, however, exceptions to this rule where the legislature has thought it so important to prevent a particular act from being committed that it forbids it absolutely to be done in any case. In such circumstances if the act is done, the offender is liable to the prescribed penalty whether or not he has any *mens rea*[1]. Modern food legislation has since its inception generally been of this kind[2]. Although a few offences in the Food Safety Act 1990 (FSA 1990) contain the word 'knowingly'[3] or depend on the intention of the defendant[4], liability under most of them do not require proof of criminal intent. Since the mere commission of the unlawful act or failure to do something required by law is sufficient for conviction in these cases, they are known as offences of 'strict liability'.

To relieve the harshness of strict liability offences, Parliament has customarily added provisions that enable liability to be passed on to the person truly responsible for a contravention and afford honest traders statutory defences. These provisions in the FSA 1990 are considered in sections **20.2–20.5** below.

1   See *Pearks, Gunston & Tee v Ward* [1902] 2 KB 1.
2   *Betts v Armstead* (1888) 20 QBD 771.
3   See FSA 1990, ss 9(3), 11 (5), 12(5), 12(6) and 13(2) considered respectively in paras **5.4.2, 6.3.8, 6.4.2, 6.4.3** and **7.4.8** above.
4   See FSA 1990, ss 7(1) and 33(1)(a) considered respectively in paras **5.2.1** and **18.5.9** above.

20.2 OFFENCES DUE TO FAULT OF ANOTHER PERSON

20.2.1   Section 20 of the FSA 1990 provides that where the commission by any person of an offence is due to the act or default of some other person, that other person is guilty of the offence; and a person may be charged with and convicted of the offence whether or not proceedings are taken against the first-mentioned person. This is what is known as the 'by-pass procedure' through which a food authority may bring proceedings against a manufacturer[1], importer, supplier, agent or employee[2] in addition to or instead of the principal offender who may well be the retailer seller. So that the food authority are in a position, if necessary, to bring proceedings under this procedure against whoever was essentially responsibility for the breach of food law, it is important that investigating officers should in each case identify and interview all potential 'other persons'. Proceedings against the other person alone would be appropriate where it appears that, unlike the principal offender, the other person cannot establish a statutory defence[3].

1   See, for example, *Birds Eye Wall's Ltd v Shropshire County Council* (1994) 158 JP 961.
2   *Tesco Supermarkets Ltd v Nattrass* [1972] AC 153, [1971] 2 All ER 127, HL.
3   See sections **20.3–20.5** below.

20.3   DEFENCE OF DUE DILIGENCE

The statutory provision

20.3.1   At the time that the FSA 1990 was in preparation, the main defences in the then food legislation were manifestly either too impractical for defendants or too generous to importers[1]. They were outmoded by comparison with the defence of 'all reasonable precautions and all due diligence' that, for some 30 years, had been developing in parallel consumer protection legislation[2]. The opportunity was therefore seized in 1990 to replace unsatisfactory specific provisions[3] with a comprehensive due diligence defence tailored to modern food manufacturing and distribution practice. Section 21(1) of the FSA 1990 states the basic defence thus:

> '... it shall ... be a defence for the person charged to prove that he took all reasonable precautions and exercised all due diligence to avoid the commission of the offence by himself or by a person under his control.'

Special provision was, however, made by s 21(2) for persons who are charged with offences under s 14 (food not of the nature or substance or quality demanded) or s 15 (false or misleading labelling or advertising of food)[4] and who neither prepared the food in respect of which the offence is alleged to have been committed, nor imported it into Great Britain. They are 'taken to have established the defence if they satisfy the requirements' of either s 21(3) or s 21(4).

A person satisfies the requirements of s 21(3) if he proves:

'(a)   that the commission of the offence was due to an act or default of another person who was not under his control, or to reliance on information supplied by such a person;

(b)   that he carried out all such checks of the food in question as were reasonable in all the circumstances, or that it was reasonable in all the circumstances for him to rely on checks carried out by the person who supplied the food to him; and

(c)   that he did not know and had no reason to suspect at the time of the commission of the alleged offence that his act or omission would amount to an offence under the relevant provision.'

A person satisfies the requirements of s 21(4) if he proves:

'(a)   that the commission of the offence was due to an act or default of another person who was not under his control, or to reliance on information supplied by such a person;

(b)   that the sale or intended sale of which the alleged offence consisted was not a sale or intended sale under his name or mark; and

(c)   that he did not know, and could not reasonably have been expected to know, at the time of the commission of the alleged offence that his act or omission would amount to an offence under the relevant provision.'

Before moving on in the next paragraph to consider these due diligence provisions, it should be noted that conditions are imposed if the defence involves the allegation that the commission of the offence was due to the act or default of another person. The person charged will not, without leave of the court, be entitled to rely on the defence unless, in accordance with s 21(5), he gives the prosecution such information identifying or assisting in the identification of that other person as is in his possession.

1   See Food Act 1984 (FA 1984), ss 100 and 102 respectively.
2   See further section **20.6** below.
3   For example, the now repealed FA 1984, s 3 which, in particular, allowed a defence where the presence of extraneous matter 'was an unavoidable consequence of the process of collection or preparation'. The defendant failed to prove this in the notorious case of *Smedleys Ltd v Breed* [1974] AC 839, [1974] 2 All ER 21, noted at paras **8.2.7** and **19.3.4** above.
4   See sections **8.2** and **8.3** above.

The philosophy of the defence

20.3.2   The qualifications to the simple due diligence defence respectively laid down by s 21(3) and s 21(4) impose a lesser burden of proof on persons who neither prepared the food nor imported it. The aim is that those who are at the head of the British marketing chain and have the greatest influence over the final product should bear the greatest responsibility.

Persons who prepare food are subject to the full rigour of the due diligence defence. It will be recalled from section **15.2** above that 'preparation' includes the manufacture and any form of processing or treatment; and that 'treatment' includes subjecting food to heat or cold[1]. These wide definitions would appear to catch manufacturers, processors, caterers and retailers who, for example, bake bread and flour products themselves; who heat pies or other products, or who chill or freeze products. On the other hand, they do not extend to the secondary activity of slicing meat that does nothing to change its physical condition[2].

Importers were considered at para **4.7.1** above. Like those preparing food, they are responsible for placing food on the British market[3] and are allowed no special dispensation in pleading the due diligence defence.

Persons other than those described above can take advantage of the provisions of s 21(3) or (4) in respect of offences against s 14 or 15 of the Act. The conditions with which they must comply depend on whether or not they were marketing the food product under their own name or mark. Where the food is an 'own-label' product of the kind often manufactured for and sold by major supermarket chains, there is a higher level of responsibility because all three limbs of s 21(3) must be proved. Where, however, the food is a manufacturer's branded product, the seller will by definition satisfy s 21(4)(b) and have only to prove (a) and (c). This, as explained below, is an easier task.

As to application of these provisions by Regulations under the FSA 1990, see section **20.5** below.

1   FSA 1990, s 53(1).
2   *Leeds City Council v J H Dewhurst Ltd* [1990] Crim LR 725.
3   See case 25/88 *Ministère Public v Esther Renée Bouchara, née Wurmser and Norlaine* [1989] ECR 1105, [1991] 1 CMLR 173; and see, more recently case C-315/05 *Lidl Italia Srl v Comune di Arcole* [2006] ECR I-11181.

Case law on due diligence

20.3.3   Although there have as yet been few judicial decisions on s 21 of the

FSA 1990, a substantial body of case law in relation to the concept of 'all reasonable precautions and all due diligence' has built up over the years under the kindred provisions in trade descriptions, weights and measures and consumer protection legislation. From the decisions it is possible to identify principles that food traders should take into account in establishing systems for the purpose of providing a due diligence defence if, despite their best endeavours, an offence is committed.

Paragraphs **20.3.4–20.3.8** below consider the principles deriving from the case law.

The defendant's burden of proof

20.3.4   Whether all reasonable precautions have been taken and all due diligence exercised are essentially questions of fact that in each case must be proved by the defendant on whom the burden rests[1]. As noted in para **4.3.3** above, he must meet the civil law standard of proof and satisfy the court 'on the balance of probabilities'[2]. These general observations must now be seen in the light of the Human Rights Act 1988; the presumption of innocence in relation to a criminal offence under Art 6 of the Convention on Human Rights; and the decision of the House of Lords in *R v Lambert*[3]. The suggestion in *Lambert* (possibly applicable to the due diligence defence) is that a full burden of proof on a defendant may be incompatible with Art 6 and should be viewed only as an evidential burden of proof. This would mean the need for the defence to establish simply that there is some evidence that is capable, if believed, of establishing the defence; it then being for the prosecution to disprove the defence, beyond reasonable doubt, ie to show that it is beyond reasonable doubt that there is either no evidence, or insufficient evidence, to show that there was the requisite due diligence.

1   *Amos v Melcon (Frozen Foods) Ltd* (1985) 149 JP 712, DC.
2   *R v Carr-Briant* [1943] KB 607, [1943] 2 All ER 156, CCA; *Robertson v Watson* 1949 JC 73; *R v Jenkins* (1923) 39 TLR 458, CCA; *Cant v Harley & Sons Ltd* [1938] 2 All ER 768.
3   [2001] 3 All ER 577.

All reasonable precautions and all due diligence

20.3.5   In considering the scope of the concept of 'all reasonable precautions and all due diligence', it is instructive to compare, with s 21(1) of the FSA 1990, the duty of care that citizens owe to their fellows if the tort of negligence is to be avoided[1]. In his famous judgment in *Donaghue v Stevenson*[2], Lord Atkin expressed this duty in the following terms: 'you must take reasonable care to avoid acts or omissions that you can reasonably foresee would be likely to injure your neighbour'. In a civil law context, an obligation to exercise due diligence has been construed as indistinguishable from this obligation to exercise reasonable care[3].

Nevertheless, although the duty of care in negligence indicates the extent of the s 21 due diligence duty, the parallel with civil law cannot be carried too far. Thus, the presence of a small piece of bone in a jar of baby food, which created an offence under s 14 of the FSA 1990, could not of itself also be sufficient to negative the statutory defence. The maxim *res ipsa loquitur* (the thing speaks for itself) relates to the burden of proof in civil cases, not criminal cases[4].

The case law certainly emphasises that sitting back and doing nothing would be most unwise for a trader hoping to maintain that he has been duly diligent.

Courts have regularly rejected the defence where they have identified reasonable precautions that defendants have failed to take. It has been held, for example, that samples of defective 'waterproof' watches could have been checked by a simple immersion test[5] and that a detector at the end of the production line would have prevented metal in chocolate[6]. Moreover, in a further case[7] concerning the sale of goods falsely described as complying with a BS standard, Lloyd LJ stated that:

> 'reasonable diligence required the appellants to establish some kind of system, whether by random sampling of the goods or whatever, to ascertain whether the goods conformed to the description. That does not mean that the system had to be foolproof – no system could be that. Nor did the appellants have to examine every article. But they did have to do something.'

In practice, then, the prudent food business should establish and keep up a system to ensure that all reasonable precautions are taken and all due diligence exercised.

What such action entails in any particular case will depend on the facts including the size and resources of the defendant's business. Precautions that might be reasonable for a large retailer might not be reasonable for the village shop[8].

That a system does not have to be foolproof to establish the defence is confirmed by a recent case[9]. The fact that the prosecutor could suggest something else that a defendant supermarket might have done to have avoided mistaken sales by its staff of food after expiry of the 'use by' date did not mean that it had failed to take all reasonable precautions and to exercise all due diligence.

1   See section **21.3** below.
2   [1932] AC 562 at 580.
3   *Riverstone Meat Co v Lancashire Shipping Co* [1960] 1 All ER 193 at 219. See also *Tesco Supermarkets Ltd v Nattrass* [1972] AC 153 at 199.
4   *Cow and Gate Ltd v Westminster City Council* (1995) Independent, 27 April.
5   *Sherratt v Geralds the American Jewellers Ltd* (1970) 68 LGR 256, 114 Sol Jo 147.
6   *R v F & M Dobson Ltd* (1995) 16 Cr App 957.
7   *Texas Homecare Ltd v Stockport Metropolitan Borough Council* (1987) 152 JP 83.
8   *Garrett v Boots Chemists Ltd* (16 July 1980, unreported).
9   *Lincolnshire County Council v Safeway Stores plc* (1999, unreported). See further para **20.3.12** below.

Testing and supplier's assurances

20.3.6   Much of the case law on due diligence systems has been concerned with the adequacy or otherwise of testing and supplier's assurances.

In 1977 the Divisional Court decided that it would have been possible for a wholesaler to have had toys analysed for excess lead in paint: it was not enough to get a written assurance from the manufacturers and invite Trading Standards Officers to sample for analysis[1]. But in a more recent case concerning pencils containing unsafe amounts of hexavalent chromium, other wholesalers, who dealt in about 10,000 lines, satisfied the magistrates that it would not have been reasonable for them to have carried out random sampling. In the event, the due diligence defence was still denied them because, although they had dealt with reliable suppliers for 15 years, they had failed to get from them a positive assurance of compliance with the specific Regulations that were contravened[2].

Importation has posed particular problems for defendants. A foreign agent's verbal assurance and past satisfactory record has been held to be insufficient to meet the requirements of the defence[3] and, even where analyses and random sampling were arranged, the defendants had to show that tests abroad were actually being carried out[4] and that tests within the jurisdiction were adequate and (preferably in the form of independent statistical evidence) sufficient in number[5].

1   *Taylor v Lawrence Fraser (Bristol) Ltd* [1978] Crim LR 43, 121 Sol Jo 757.
2   *Riley v Webb* (1987) 151 JP 372.
3   *Hicks v SD Sullam Ltd* (1983) 147 JP 493, 3 Tr L 129.
4   *Rotherham Metropolitan Borough Council v Raysun (UK) Ltd* (1988) 153 JP 37, [1989] CCLR 1.
5   *P & M Supplies (Essex) Ltd v Devon County Council* (1991) 156 JP 328; *Dudley Metropolitan Council v Firman* (15 October 1992, unreported).

Official testing of products

20.3.7   The decision in *Taylor v Lawrence Fraser (Bristol) Ltd* referred to in the previous paragraph made clear that defendants cannot simply transfer to the enforcement authority the responsibility for taking precautions. However, two more recent decisions indicate that defendants, who carried out no specific checks of their own, may nevertheless sometimes be able to establish the due diligence defence through their reliance on official testing.

In the first[1], the Divisional Court upheld the justices' decision that the defence was made out by retailers of Piesporter wine that had been incorrectly labelled as to alcoholic strength by the German producer. The retailers had two shops only but sold some 1,200 different types of wine. In view of the tight German control regime, it was held to be reasonable for them to have relied on the assurances of their suppliers.

The second case[2] was more controversial. The Divisional Court confirmed that a meat trader, charged with consigning beef that was unfit for human consumption contrary to s 8(1)(b) of the FSA 1990[3], was not prevented from relying on a Government meat hygiene inspector's certificate, if it was otherwise reasonable to do so, to show he had taken all reasonable precautions and exercised all due diligence.

In each of these cases the food was an agricultural product for the purposes of the common agricultural policy for which official testing was undertaken before it was put into circulation on the market. The decisions are, it is submitted, of limited application and, even in relation to agricultural products, traders would generally be acting at their peril if they were to assume that official tests will absolve them from the need to consider and take positive precautions.

1   *Hurley v Martinez & Co Ltd* (1990) 154 JP 821.
2   *Carrick District Council v Taunton Vale Meat Traders Ltd* (1994) 158 JP 347.
3   Section 8 (1) (b) has now been replaced by Art 14 of Regulation (EC) 178/2002, the offence being provided by reg 4(b) of the General Food Regulations 2004.

Directing mind or will of the company

20.3.8   It was noted, in para **20.2.1** above, that an employee may be 'another person' for the purposes of proceedings under the by-pass procedure in s 20 of the FSA 1990 and, in para **20.3.1**, that s 21 specifically contemplates circumstances in which the due diligence defence involves the allegation that the commission of the offence was due to the act or default of 'another person'. In the leading case of *Tesco Supermarkets Ltd v Nattrass*[1], employers established a due diligence defence on the ground that the offence was actually the fault their employee. The House of Lords decided that in instituting, by means of a chain of command, an effective system of control to avoid the commission of offences under the Trade Descriptions Act 1968 (TDA 1968), the supermarket company had taken all reasonable precautions and exercised all due diligence. This was not a delegation of the duty to exercise due diligence but the performance of that duty. The store manager, whose default had led to the commission of the offence, could not be identified with the company: he was 'another person' for the purposes of the Act.

However, the due diligence defence was not made out by another company that failed to carry out regular checks and undertake adequate supervision or to give shop managers sufficient training and instructions[2].

1   [1972] AC 153, [1971] 2 All ER 127, HL.
2   *Baxters (Butchers) Ltd v Manley* (1985) 4 Tr L 219.

Control systems

20.3.9   In the light of the case law each proprietor needs to devise a control system suitable to his business.

Following the enactment of the FSA 1990, some simple guidance was issued that outlined for farmers, growers, food processors, wholesalers, importers, distributors and retailers what systems might satisfy a court that all steps have been taken to avoid committing an offence. These *Guidelines on the Statutory Defence of Due Diligence* were published jointly in 1991 by the National Consumer Council, LACOTS, the Institution of Environmental Health Officers, the National Farmers Union, the Retail Consortium and the Food and Drink Federation, with the support of the then Parliamentary Secretary to the Ministry of Agriculture, Fisheries and Food. This publication is referred to below as the 'Due Diligence Guidelines'. The following notes on control systems draw on the guidance that it contains, taking account of subsequent case law. Readers are recommended to consult other detailed sources[1].

In general, the following points should be considered in establishing a control system:

(a)   Subject to what was said in para **20.3.7**, positive steps to set up a system are essential to satisfy the defence.

(b)   To prove that all reasonable precautions have been taken and all due diligence exercised, it must be shown not only that the control system has been set up, but also that it is working.

(c)   If there is a precaution that can be reasonably taken, then it must be taken.

(d)   The control system must be capable of dealing with perceived risks, but does not have to be foolproof.

(e)   The extent of the control system depends on the size and resources of the business. What is required for a large corporate body may not be appropriate for a small private business.

(f)   The control system must cover every aspect of the company's business. Because the defence in the FSA 1990 is similar to those in other relevant statutes, a common control system can be established to deal with all matters subject to that Act, plus quantity controls, price checks and general product descriptions.

A non-exhaustive list of subjects that might be covered is :

 (i) hygiene of premises, equipment and staff;
 (ii) bought-in stock, raw materials, food sources and packaging;
 (iii) production, processing, handling and storage;
 (iv) recipes, product specifications;
 (v) labelling and advertising;
 (vi) quantity marking, weighing and measuring;
 (vii) price marking, misleading indications of price;
 (viii) staff training;
 (ix) monitoring of customer complaints.

(g)   All staff participating in the system must be given written instructions and be asked to acknowledge them in writing. If possible, their duties should be identified in their job specifications.

(h)   The system must be pro-active and re-active. It must be capable of identifying and preventing risks and of correcting them if they occur.

(i)   The system must be kept under review and updated as necessary.

(j)   The adequacy of the control system will be judged by the nature of the products, the manufacturing, processing or retailing techniques involved, and all other relevant factors. Although there are many common matters in due diligence defences, there is no such thing as a standard due diligence system. Every system must be fitted to the business that operates it.

Further matters of concern are addressed in the remainder of this section including, in para **20.3.13**, some points (supplemental to what is said in the 'Due Diligence Guidelines') on specific food trade sectors.

1   See, in particular, *A Guide to Good Manufacturing Practice: A Guide to its Responsible Management* (Institute of Food Science and Technology, 5th edn).

Hazard analysis, quality control and codes of practice

20.3.10   The 'Due Diligence Guidelines' note particular elements that need to be covered by a control system.

The first is the Hazard Analysis and Critical Control Points ('HACCP') approach to food control that, as explained in para **13.6.1** above, is required by Art 5 of directly applicable Regulation (EC) 852/2004 that is now enforced here by the Food Hygiene (England) Regulations 2006. As indicated, the HACCP approach involves identifying and weighting each risk that the business will fail to meet any safety or other imperative, and then devising and implementing appropriate control measures. Although perhaps best suited to food manufacturing, HACCP is applicable for all stages in the food supply chain[1].

As well as HACCP, the business might usefully consider the adoption of a Quality Assurance scheme, the most obvious instance of which is provided by the ISO 9000 series. It should be noted, however, that the statutory defence will not be established solely by observance of quality assurance techniques, which are not as such directed at securing the legality of products.

Additionally, the prudent proprietor will wish to take account of trade and government codes of good practice for and guidance on the preparation of food and for its labelling, storage, handling and distribution[2].

1   The European Commission's 2005 guidance document on *Implementation of procedures based on HACCP principles, and facilitation of the HACCP principles in certain food businesses*, is available at http://ec.europa.eu/food/food/biosafety/hygienelegislation/guidance_doc_haccp_en.pdf

2   For information on current publications, see the guidance for food industries available on the
Food Standards Agency website at www.food.gov.uk/.

Assuring test standards

20.3.11 The 'Due Diligence Guidelines' also point out that sample testing
should be undertaken by accredited laboratories and that, where in-house
facilities are used, steps should be taken to verify the methodology and
accuracy of results by obtaining independent accreditation (eg under the UK
Accreditation Service scheme), by conducting paired audit tests with other
laboratories or by some other appropriate method. It would, for example, be
possible to arrange an audit by a company offering quality systems and due
diligence control services. The contractor should have the necessary
professional qualifications, accreditation and operate quality systems to ISO
9000, as well as being covered by professional indemnity insurance.

It should also be borne in mind that agents involved in the operation of due
diligence systems by whose act or default an offence is committed may be
subject to prosecution[1].

1   See para **20.2.1** above.

Records and written assurances from suppliers

20.3.12 Written records of the control system will be required if the due
diligence system has to be proved in court. The text laying down the basic
procedures should be adopted by those having the directing mind or will of the
business, and checks and other actions carried out within this framework should
be recorded and signed by the staff involved. Ideally, defect reports and
remedial action should be recorded in writing, but oral reporting may be
sufficient, for example within a supermarket, if errors are traceable to the
person concerned and are followed by warnings, additional training and extra
checks[1].

For bought-in products, the system must manifestly be able to confirm by way
of suppliers' written assurances, test data or otherwise that every reasonable
effort has been taken to secure compliance with legal requirements.

Evidence of a carefully devised and run system that stands scrutiny by
enforcement officers may, if a contravention does occur, persuade the
prosecution that there will be a sound defence if the matter is taken to court.

1   *Lincolnshire County Council v Safeway Stores plc* (1999, unreported).

Specific food trade sectors

20.3.13 It will be apparent from what has already been said, that some
indication can be gathered from the case law as to the sorts of control systems
that might be adequate for particular sectors of the food trade.

Subject to the special circumstances noted in para 20.**3.7** above, s 21 of the FSA
1990 imposes a heavy burden on those, like manufacturers and importers, who
do not get the benefit of s 21(3) or (4). Paragraph **20.3.6** cited examples of
failures to meet the strict obligations in respect of imports. However, in
Bibby-Cheshire v Golden Wonder Ltd[1], a manufacturer managed to meet the
onerous requirements of the due diligence defence. The case concerned an
under-weight packet of crisps. The magistrates found that the best available

machines had been used; that it was economically impossible to weigh individually the 20 million packets produced every week; and that there was an efficient system of random checking that ensured that no machine consistently produced under-weight bags. Although demanding, the requirements of the defence can be met. Paragraph **21.6.1**(a) below also notes the need for manufacturers to ensure that their food control and management systems take account of the possibility of civil as well as criminal liability.

Subject to what is said below, further examples in para **20.3.6** show that the burden on wholesalers is scarcely less heavy. They too will normally be in a large way of business and will seldom be able to rely simply on written assurances from their suppliers.

Judicial interpretation of the bespoke provisions of s 21(3) and (4) of the FSA 1990 is for the moment still awaited. As noted above, the provisions in s 21(3) for own-labellers include specific requirements that they should have carried out all such checks of the food in question as were reasonable in all the circumstances, or that it was reasonable in all the circumstances to rely on checks by their suppliers. This requirement is a halfway-house between the full due diligence obligation required of manufacturers and importers and lesser one required of sellers of branded goods. The ratio of self-checking to reliance on a supplier's checks must depend on the confidence the retailer has in the checking system operated by the supplier. This confidence can be achieved by regular checks on the supplier's due diligence system by the retailer's staff or agents. In effect, the supplier and retailer must in combination have implemented a full due diligence system.

Sellers of other products (also generally speaking retailers) have the advantage of s 21(4). It should be noted that the threshold imposed by this provision is lower than that in s 21(3) not only because it will be self evident that the sale was not 'under his own name or mark', but also because s 21(4)(c) is less taxing in practice than s 21(3)(c). The seller of a manufacturer's branded product has to prove that he 'could not reasonably have been expected to know' that his act or omission would amount to an offence. The obligation of the own-labelling business to prove that it 'had no reason to suspect' this will be no easy task if, as will normally be the case, it has imposed precise product requirements on the manufacturer.

The size and resources of the seller's business will determine what s 21(4) demands of him. Large retailers must organise and operate effective systems throughout their stores[2], as well as taking steps to assure themselves as to the reliability of their purchases. Apart from himself complying with relevant legislation, the small retailer could in general be expected to do no more than buy from reputable suppliers, to obtain from them positive assurances as to the legality of the products and to check that the supplies conform with what was ordered. Exceptionally, butchers, bakers and other small businesses 'preparing' food, are subject to the full rigour of the due diligence defence[3].

1   [1972] 3 All ER 738, [1972] 1 WLR 1487.
2   See, for example, *Tesco Supermarkets Ltd v Nattrass* [1972] AC 153, [1971] 2 All ER 127, HL and *Lincolnshire County Council v Safeway Stores plc* (1999, unreported).
3   See para **20.3.2** above.

20.4   DEFENCE OF PUBLICATION IN THE COURSE OF BUSINESS

20.4.1   The FSA 1990 repeats the now common defence for persons who innocently publish advertisements. It provides that it is a defence for the defendant to prove that he is a person whose business it is to publish or arrange for the publication of advertisements and that he received the offending advertisement in the ordinary course of his business and did not know, and had no reason to suspect, that its publication would amount to an offence[1].

An advertising agency that designed an offending advertisement, is unlikely be able to sustain this defence and would have to consider the possibilities of recourse to s 21.

1   FSA 1990, s 22.

20.5   DEFENCES IN REGULATIONS

Due diligence and publishing defence

20.5.1   The defences of due diligence and publication in the course of business are customarily applied to Regulations under the FSA 1990 as they apply for the purpose of s 14 or 15. Persons other than those who prepared or imported the food in question are therefore eligible to claim the benefit of s 21(3) and (4) in respect of offences enacted by the Regulations.

Special defences

20.5.2   As explained in para **4.7.2** above, a special defence for exports is provided in respect of proceedings for offences of contravening or failing to comply with food law; and Regulations under the FSA 1990 often make transitional provision by means of defences[1].

Special defences are, moreover, sometimes provided by Regulations to meet particular circumstances. So, see, for example, the provisions of the Food Hygiene (England) Regulations 2006[2]; and the Plastic Materials and Articles in Contact with Food Regulations 2008[3].

Food businesses whose products are affected by any special defence, will need to ensure that their control systems are adapted to take advantage of it.

1   See, for example, Food Labelling Regulations 1996, reg 50.
2   SI 2006/14 (Sch 4, paras 4, 5 and 7).
3   SI 2008/916 (regs 4, 5 and 9).

20.6   OTHER LEGISLATION

20.6.1   Provision of the kind described in this chapter is not exclusive to the FSA 1990, since other relevant legislation operates through strict liability offences.

Provision in respect of offences due to the fault of another person (the by-pass procedure described in para **20.2.1** above) is also included, for example, in the Weights and Measures Act 1985 (W&MA 1985), the Agriculture and Horticulture Act 1964 (A&HA 1964) and the Agriculture Act 1970.

Likewise, as illustrated in the case law cited above, the due diligence defence appears in Part IV of the W&MA 1985. There was previously a due diligence defence in relation the Part V quantity system. However, (as seen at para **16.4.1** above) there is now a new system on average quantity, in the Weights and Measures (Packaged Goods) Regulations 2006; and the relevant due diligence defence is in reg 19(4) of these regulations. Forms of it are also to be found in the A&HA 1964, the Agriculture Act 1970, the Food and Environment Protection Act 1985 and subordinate legislation like the Common Agricultural Policy (Wine) (England and Northern Ireland) Regulations 2001. It used to feature in the Trade Descriptions Act (on false statements as to goods and services) and the Consumer Protection Act, Part III (on misleading pricing); but has now been transferred across to the new Consumer Protection from Unfair Trading Regulations 2008, SI 2008/1277, which replace this previous legislation with new offences of misleading actions and omissions in relation to food and other products and services; these offences being applicable right through from the stage of advertising to enforcement of a contract. In particular, these offences can be committed by the default of another person (reg 16), the due diligence defence being in reg 17.

The Prices Act 1974 applies the by-pass and due diligence provisions of the Trade Descriptions Act 1968.

The A&HA 1964 and Part IV of the W&MA 1985 include defences, of the kind in s 102 of the now repealed FA 1984, where the defendant bought with a warranty that the produce complied with relevant legislation.

Other defences relating to special circumstances are to be found in s 35–37 of the W&MA 1985.

Traders subject to any such other legislation will need to ensure that their control systems are sufficiently comprehensive in scope.

Chapter 21

Civil remedies

21.1 INTRODUCTION

21.1.1 In laying the foundations of modern consumer protection legislation, Victorian statutes took account of existing contractual relations between buyer and seller. Even today, an offence under what is now s 14 of the Food Safety Act 1990 (FSA 1990) depends on the nature, substance or quality demanded by the purchaser[1]. Moreover, for the purpose of providing protection for purchasers of feeding stuffs, Part IV of the Agriculture Act 1970 still relies in part on implying warranties into the contract for sale[2].

The requirements enforced by criminal law that have progressively been imposed have not reduced the need for civil remedies available to consumers. In fact those remedies have themselves been augmented over the years. In addition to improvements to the contractual route, tortious and Community-law-based avenues are also now open to aggrieved consumers. Most will no doubt decide to report defective food to a food authority for investigation and possible prosecution. A court by or before which a person is convicted of an offence may make an order requiring him to pay compensation for any personal injury, loss or damage resulting from the offence[3]. However, the consumer who has suffered significant loss may wish to bring an action against the retailer or producer for damages instead of or in addition to seeking to initiate criminal proceedings.

It might usefully be noted here that the standard of proof in criminal proceedings is higher than that in civil proceedings[4]. In the former, the prosecution's case must be proved 'beyond reasonable doubt'[5]. In the latter, the plaintiff has simply to satisfy the court 'on the balance of probabilities', even where in the civil proceedings commission of a crime is alleged[6].

To avoid prejudicing a fair trial, civil proceedings will normally[7] be deferred until a prosecution arising from the same facts is completed. There is, in any event, practical advantage to the plaintiff in waiting because, by s 11(1) of the Civil Evidence Act 1968, the fact that a person has been convicted of an offence by or before any court in the United Kingdom is admissible in evidence where relevant in civil proceedings to prove that the offence was committed.

Sections **21.2**, **21.3** and **21.4** below respectively summarise the remedies that may be pursued by the consumer for breach of contract, tort or strict product liability in respect of a defective food product. In contemplation of civil proceedings, sections **21.5** and **21.6** note some elementary precautions for consumers and producers. These are merely indicators and should in no way be

355

treated as a substitute for full legal advice on the specific circumstances of a particular trade or incident.

It should also be borne in mind that civil actions relating to food may be brought by others besides consumers and business purchasers. Three sorts warrant brief mention here. The first is an action against the food authority. In *Welton v North Cornwall District Council*[8] an environmental health officer negligently required the owner of food premises to undertake works that were unnecessary to secure compliance with the FSA 1990 and food hygiene regulations. The owner incurred substantial and unnecessary expenditure in executing the works and sued the local food authority. The authority was held by the Court of Appeal to be under a common duty of care to the owner and liable in damages for the economic loss sustained.

Secondly, there are civil actions pursued by food manufacturers to protect their products against misrepresentation. The scope of the present work does not admit more than a brief reference to this subject. It might usefully be noted, however, that the tort of passing off, the main kind of injurious falsehood, provides an important safeguard where it can be established that the public are being deceived into believing that another trader's food products are those of the plaintiff. Recent conspicuous cases concerning champagne[9], whisky[10], chocolate[11] and chocolate biscuits[12] have also involved interpretation of Community Regulations or trade mark disputes.

Thirdly, it has recently been made clear, certainly as regards common agricultural policy quality standards, that directly effective EC provisions are capable of enforcement, not only by criminal prosecution, but also by means of civil proceedings instituted by a trader against a competitor[13].

1   See section **8.2** above.
2   See section **17.2** above.
3   Powers of Criminal Courts Act 1973, s 35, as amended; Magistrates' Courts Act 1980, s 40.
4   *Miller v Minister of Pensions* [1947] 2 All ER 372 at 373–374.
5   See further para **19.3.2** above.
6   *Hornal v Neuberger Products Ltd* [1957] 1 QB 247, [1956] 3 All ER 970.
7   *Harris v Crisp* [1992] 33 LS Gaz R 36, CA.
8   [1997] 1 WLR 570.
9   *Taittinger v Allbev* [1994] 4 All ER 75, [1993] 2 CMLR 741 (the Elderflower champagne case).
10 See *Scotch Whisky Association v Glen Kella Distillers* [1997] 16 LS Gaz R 29, [1997] Sol Jo LB 91 ('Manx whiskey'); *Matthew Gloag and Son Ltd v Welsh Distillers Ltd* [1998] FSR 718, [1998] 2 CMLR 203 (1998) Times, 27 February, ('Welsh whisky').
11 *Chocosuisse Union des Fabricants Suisses de Chocolat v Cadbury Ltd* [1998] RPC 117.
12 *United Biscuits (UK) Ltd v Asda Stores Ltd* [1997] PRC 513.
13 Case C-253/00 *Antonio Muñoz Y Cia v Frumar Ltd* [2002] ECR I-7289, [2002] 3 CMLR 26.

21.2   SELLER'S LIABILITY FOR BREACH OF CONTRACT

21.2.1   A shopper seeking to sue a shopkeeper in contract for supply of defective food clearly first needs to show the existence of that contract. The extended meaning of 'sale' in s 2 of the FSA 1990[1] does not apply to the law of contract. In English law a bare promise is not legally binding. Besides an intention to create legal relations, an enforceable contract requires that there be an offer by one party and acceptance of the offer by the other, and, in addition, 'valuable consideration', that is to say a benefit to the defendant or detriment to the plaintiff by which the defendant's promise was obtained.

For the contract for sale of food to fall within the ambit of the Sale of Goods Act 1979 (SGA 1979)[2], it must be one by which the seller transfers or agrees to transfer the property in goods to the buyer for a money consideration called the price[3].

The normal contract for sale of food in a supermarket will be formed when the offer to purchase the food is accepted at the check-out[4]. The purchase price paid to the shop assistant constitutes the consideration passing from the shopper.

1   See para **4.6.1** above.
2   See para **21.2.3** below.
3   SGA 1979, s 2(1).
4   *Pharmaceutical Society of Great Britain v Boots Cash Chemists (Southern) Ltd* [1952] 2 QB 795, [1952] 2 All ER 456.

21.2.2   At common law, a contract generally confers rights and imposes obligations only on persons who are parties to it, this relationship between them being known as 'privity of contract'. An action by the purchaser of a defective food product claiming damages for breach of contract may be brought only against the immediate vendor (ie normally the retailer where the buyer is a consumer). Unless buying direct, such a consumer purchaser has no action against the manufacturer or processor of a defective food product for breach of contract. However, each seller in the supply chain may in turn be liable to his buyer for breach of the contract by which he sold the defective food until the party responsible for the defect is reached[1].

The privity of contract relationship also means that a stranger to the contract cannot sue on it: the vendor is liable only to the purchaser of the food. However, in some cases, although only one party has actually paid for the food, it may be possible to show that others are actually party to the contract; and therefore able to sue under it. This sort of analysis is most likely where the other parties are present at the time of purchase, eg in the situation where there is a family or other form of group outing to a restaurant.[2]

Another possibility would be to establish that the party physically making the purchase is actually acting as an agent for another (who may or may not be physically present at the time of purchase). Such an analysis would obviously be possible if it was expressly indicated that the party in question was acting as an agent; and might be possible also where the background (including perhaps a previous course of dealing) would suggest to the seller that the party paying is actually an agent. This analysis does not seem possible where the food is obviously being bought as a present or for some form of party for friends or family. One possibility (in cases where food is bought for consumption by third parties, but there is no agency) is for the buyer himself to claim. Now, it is clear that such a buyer cannot, as such, claim on behalf of the affected third parties[3]. However, if the actual buyer can be said to have suffered additional losses (eg disappointment at seeing his wedding guests suffer poor quality service or food poisoning[4] or perhaps even if the buyer pays medical expenses for injured parties), this buyer may be able to recover for such losses.

Now, however, in addition to these common law routes to recovery of losses suffered by those who do not physically buy the goods, there is also the possibility of a claim on the basis of the Contracts (Rights of Third Parties) Act 1999.

This will be helpful to the extent that the contracting buyer would have no common law right to claim for the loss in question and in cases where the contracting buyer does have such a right, but refuses to exercise it.

The Act allows enforcement by a third party to a contract in two situations:

(1) Section 1(1)(a), (2) and (3) read together allow a third party to enforce a term of a contract if the contract expressly provides for this and if the third party is expressly identified by name, class or description. Section 1(5) provides that such a third party is entitled to the same remedies as would have been available of he had been a party to the contract. So if a retailer and a consumer agree that a particular person will have the right to enforce an express or implied term of the contract then these provisions should enable this person to recover damages for breach of the term[5].

One difficult question is what it means to say that a third party has been *expressly* identified by *class or description*. What if it is clear that *a* non-buyer is to have the right to enforce but *the* non-buyer has not been named? For example, what if a consumer tells a retailer that the goods are a present for a friend and asks whether the friend will be able to enforce the terms of the contract? Has the unnamed friend been identified as a member of a class or answering a description, or are they only so identified if the buyer narrows down the identification – 'wife', 'husband', 'brother', 'sister', 'son', 'work colleague', 'classmate' etc? The question is open[6].

(2) The second situation in which a non-buying user will be entitled to enforce a term of a contract is where the contract does not say expressly that this is to be possible; but nevertheless there is a term in the contract which on its true construction purports to confer such a benefit. This is provided for by s 1(1)(b). Again (by virtue of s 1(3)) the party must have been identified by name, class or description. Presumably s 1(1)(b) will cover a case where the buyer says that the food is a gift or where this is clear (e g because he asks the seller to gift wrap the product). Again, of course, if the non-buyer is not actually named, it is an open question as to the degree of identification required for the non-buyer to be treated as having been identified by class or description.

Even if a contract does purport to confer a benefit on a non-buying user who is sufficiently well identified for the purposes of the legislation the right to enforce only arises as a rebuttable presumption. There is no right to enforce if it appears that the parties did not intend the term to be enforceable by the third party. This is provided by s 1(2).

If a party who is a stranger to the contract cannot bring himself within any of these common law or statutory 'exceptions' he would have to proceed for damages in tort as described in section **21.3** below.

1   *Kasler and Cohen v Slavouski* [1928] 1 KB 78; *Dodd and Dodd v Wilson and McWilliam* [1946] 2 All ER 691.
2   *Lockett v A & M Charles* [1938] 4 All ER 170.
3   *Woodar Investment Development Ltd v Wimpey Construction UK Ltd* [1980] 1 WLR 277.
4   *Jackson v Horizon Holidays Ltd* [1975] 1 WLR 1468, and *Woodar Investment Development Ltd v Wimpey Construction (UK) Ltd*, ibid; and for a detailed discussion see *Butterworths Product Liability (2nd edn, 2007), 2.130*.
5   For a fuller discussion see *Butterworths Product Liability*, 2.131
6   See the discussion in Miller and Goldberg *Product Liability* (2nd edn, 2004), 2.24–5.

21.2.3   Terms are implied into contracts of sale of goods by the SGA 1979, as amended by the Sale and Supply of Goods Act 1994 (S&SGA 1994).

The most important of these are:

(a)   where there is a contract for sale of goods by description, that the goods will correspond with the description[1];

(b)   where the seller sells goods in the course of a business, that the goods are of satisfactory quality[2]; and

(c)   where the seller sells goods in the course of a business and the buyer makes known the particular purpose for which the goods are being bought, that the goods supplied under the contract are reasonably fit for that purpose[3].

A retail sale of food may give rise to an action for breach of the condition as to compliance with description ((a) above) so long as it is sold not merely as the specific thing but as a thing corresponding to a description[4], or for breach of the condition as to the fitness for purpose ((c) above), [5] except where there was no reliance on the skill and judgment of the seller or such reliance would have been unreasonable. However, most relevant today is likely to be the condition noted at (b) above, that goods be of satisfactory quality. As modernised by the S&SGA 1994, goods are of satisfactory quality for the purposes of the 1979 Act if they meet a standard that a reasonable person would regard as satisfactory, taking account of any description of the goods, the price (if relevant) and all other relevant circumstances[6]. The quality of goods includes their state and condition and, among other aspects, their fitness for all the purposes for which goods of the kind in question are commonly supplied, their freedom from minor defects and their safety[7]. The implied quality condition is excluded in the case of defects specifically drawn to the buyer's attention or defects that ought to have been revealed by examination by the buyer[8]. In order to implement the European Parliament and Council Directive 1999/44/EC on certain aspects of the sale of consumer goods and associated guarantees[9], where the buyer is a consumer it is also relevant to take into account:

> 'any public statements on the specific characteristics of the goods made about them by the seller, the producer or his representative, particularly in advertising or on labelling'[10].

However, such statements will not be taken into account if the seller shows that:

(a)   at the time the contract was made, he (ie the seller) was not, and could not reasonably have been, aware of the statement,

(b)   before the contract was made, the statement had been withdrawn in public or, to the extent that it contained anything that was incorrect or misleading, it had been corrected in public, or

(c)   the decision to buy the goods could not have been influenced by the statement[11].

Even though these public statements rules are aimed at consumer buyers, it is expressly stated that these provisions do not prevent any public statement from being a relevant circumstance where the buyer is not a consumer if the statement would have been such a circumstance apart from those subsections[12].

Damages can, of course, be claimed for breach of these implied terms; covering such matters as basic diminution in value caused by poor quality and any injury caused by the breach. Where the buyer is a business, there may also be a claim for lost profits caused by the breach. There is also a right to reject the food and recover the price as the implied terms in question are conditions of the contract. Further, a new layer of remedies (applicable only to consumer sales) was introduced in 2002 (implementing Art 3 of Directive 1999/44/EC on certain aspects of the sale of consumer goods and associated guarantees). These are remedies of repair, replacement, price reduction and rescission[13]. Of course, rejection of the goods and these new remedies will only be applicable in practice to food products in limited circumstances[14].

1   SGA 1979, s 13.
2   SGA 1979, s 14(2).
3   SGA 1979, s 14(3).
4   *Grant v Australian Knitting Mills Ltd* [1936] AC 85, 100 per Lord Wright. See also SGA 1979, s 13(3).
5   See, for example, *Wallis v Russell* [1902] 2 IR 585, CA (unfit crabs); *Chaproniére v Mason* (1905) 21 TLR 633 (stone in a bun).
6   SGA 1979, s 14(2A).
7   SGA 1979, s 14(2B).
8   SGA 1979, s 14(2C)(a) and (b).
9   See Art 2(2)(d).
10 S 14(2D)
11 S 14(2E)
12 S 14(2F)
13 SGA, Part 5A (ss 48B and 48C).
14 For a full discussion of all possible remedies see *Butterworths Product Liability* (2nd edn, 2007), 2.67–2.93.

21.2.4   By virtue of s 6(2) of the Unfair Contract Terms Act 1977, liability for breach of the obligations arising from the implied terms summarised in para **21.2.3** above cannot be excluded or restricted by contract as against a person dealing as a consumer[1]. Where the buyer is not a consumer, exclusion or limitation of these implied terms is subject to a test of reasonableness[2].

In parallel with these provisions are the Unfair Terms in Consumer Contracts Regulations 1999 that implement Council Directive 93/13/EEC. The Regulations apply, with certain exceptions, to unfair terms in contracts concluded between consumers and sellers or suppliers[3]. An unfair term is one that has not been individually negotiated and that contrary to the requirement of good faith, causes a significant imbalance in the parties' rights and obligations under the contract to the detriment of the consumer[4]. More specifically, it appears that a provision excluding the legal rights of the consumer described in para **21.2.3** would be unfair. Of course, such terms are wholly void in any case under the Unfair Contract Terms Act; but the Regulations also contain powers for preventive (injunctive) action to be taken by local authorities and the Office of Fair Trading against the use of such terms[5].

1   See Unfair Contract Terms Act, s 12 for a definition of 'dealing as a consumer'.
2   Unfair Contract Terms Act, s 6 (3) and see s 11 of the same Act for the reasonableness test and *Butterworths Product Liability* (2nd edn, 2007), 2.104–2.116 for a full discussion. For application of the test in the context of food, see *Bacardi-Martini Ltd v Thomas Hardy Packings Ltd* [2002] 2 Lloyds Rep 378.
3   Unfair Terms in Consumer Contracts Regulations 1999, reg 4. See the decision in Case C-541/99, *Cape and Idealserve* [2001] I-9049, to the effect that a 'consumer' can only be a natural person.
4   Unfair Terms in Consumer Contracts Regulations 1999, reg 5.
5   Unfair Terms in Consumer Contracts Regulations 1999, regs 10–15.

21.2.5   With the growth of food purchasing otherwise than by face-to-face contact, brief mention should also be made of the Consumer Protection (Distance Selling) Regulations 2000 that implement Directive 96/7/EC. Distance selling occurs where the contract is made by any means without the simultaneous physical presence of the consumer and the supplier. The Regulations apply to contracts for the sale of food except where (as with milk deliveries) it is intended for everyday consumption supplied to the consumer's residence or workplace by regular roundsmen. The Regulations lay down important requirements as to the information that the consumer must receive before the sale, as to the consumer's right to cancel the contract and, on cancellation, as to the recovery of sums paid and the restoration of the goods. The Food Safety Agency has produced distance-selling guidance for food businesses.

21.3 MANUFACTURERS' LIABILITY FOR THE TORT OF NEGLIGENCE

21.3.1   Until 1932 a consumer damaged by a defective product generally had no civil remedy other than in contract as a buyer. That year it was established that a manufacturer of products owes the consumer a duty of care which, if breached with resulting damage to the consumer, will render him liable for the tort of negligence. This major change was brought about by the landmark House of Lords' decision in *Donoghue v Stevenson*[1]. In this case, a young woman claimed to have suffered gastro-enteritis as a result of drinking a bottle of ginger beer contaminated by the remains of a decomposed snail. The bottle had been bought from the retailer by her companion thus depriving her of action in contract. In his judgment, Lord Atkin said:

> 'A manufacturer of products, which he sells in such a form as to show that he intends them to reach the ultimate consumer in the form in which they left him with no reasonable possibility of intermediate examination, and with the knowledge that the absence of reasonable care in the preparation or putting up of the products will result in an injury to the consumer's life or property, owes a duty to the consumer to take reasonable care.'

1   *Donoghue v Stevenson* [1932] AC 562, HL.

21.3.2   Negligence soon became one of the most important torts, actionable duties of care having been recognised by the courts in a whole range of human activities beyond the manufacture of foodstuffs[1]. In 1977 the customer's position was further strengthened in respect of contracts or notices excluding or restricting liability for negligence. Henceforth, such provisions were absolutely prohibited when in respect of liability for death or personal injury and, in the case of other loss or damage, acceptable only if reasonable[2]. Yet there remained a demand for a regime of strict product liability (i e a regime under which there is no need to establish negligence).

1   For a particular example relating to food hygiene enforcement, see *Welton v North Cornwall District Council* noted at para **21.1.1** above.
2   Unfair Contract Terms Act 1977, s 2.

21.4 STRICT LIABILITY

21.4.1   In 1978 the Royal Commission on Civil Liability and Compensation for Personal Injury (the Pearson Commission)[1] recommended that producers should be strictly liable for death or personal injury caused by a defect in their products. But it was not until 1985 that Council Directive 85/374/EEC (on the approximation of the laws, regulations and administrative provisions of the Member States concerning liability for defective products) finally introduced a strict product liability regime. The purpose of the Directive is to reduce distortions in competition between Member States by giving similar protection to consumers throughout the Community against defective products.

1   Cmnd 7054 (1978).

Liability for defective products

21.4.2   Council Directive 85/374/EEC is implemented by Part I of the Consumer Protection Act 1987 (CPA 1987). Subject to what is said below, s 2 provides that producers, those holding themselves out as producers[1] and those importing into a Member State from outside the Community are liable for damage caused wholly or partly by defects in their products. It is for the injured person to prove the damage, the defect and the causal relationship between defect and damage[2]. Where two or more persons are liable for the same damage, their liability is joint and several[3]. Section 2 is without prejudice to any liability otherwise arising[4], so actions in contract and negligence remain available in appropriate cases.

'Product' is defined as including a product that is comprised in another product whether by virtue of being a component part or raw material or otherwise[5]. As originally enacted, s 2 did not apply to persons in respect of defects in game or agricultural produce which they supplied before it had undergone an industrial process[6]. However, in order to implement Directive 1999/34/EC, this exemption for unprocessed primary agricultural products has been removed by the Consumer Protection Act 1987 (Product Liability) (Modification) Order 2000. The amendment is aimed at helping to restore consumer confidence in the safety of unprocessed primary agricultural products, in particular following the BSE scare[7].

1　Ie suppliers who market the products of others as their 'own-brand' or who fail to identify the producer, importer or own brander when asked to do so by an injured person.
2　Directive 85/374/EEC, Art 4.
3　CPA 1987, s 2(5).
4　CPA 1987, s 2(6).
5　CPA 1987, s 1(2).
6　CPA 1987, s 2(4).
7　See in particular the Commission Green Paper COM (97) 176 on 'the General Principles of Food Law in the European Union' Pt IV.8.

Meaning of 'defect'

21.4.3　For the purposes of the legislation, there is a defect in a product where the safety of that product is not such as persons generally are entitled to expect. In order to decide what persons generally are entitled to expect, regard must be had to all relevant circumstances, including the manner in which the product is marketed, any instructions or warnings given with it, what might reasonably be expected to be done with it and the time when the product was supplied by the producer[1].

On this basis it appears, for example, that the failure of a food, in some unsafe way, to meet the expectations of a particular nutritional use[2] for which it had been marketed, would constitute a defect. On the other hand, scrupulous compliance with statutory requirements as to warnings and use instructions is important as a means of limiting liability under the CPA 1987 as is advocated at para **21.6.1** below.

Further comment on this definition is to be found in Miller's *Product Liability and Safety* (Butterworths), Vol III, at paras 118–121 and 256.

1　CPA 1987, s 3.
2　See section **11.7.1** above.

Damage giving rise to liability

21.4.4　'Damage' is defined in s 5 of the CPA 1987. It means death, personal injury or specified loss or damage to property. Liability for property under s 2 is excluded in respect of:

(a)　damage to the defective product itself;

(b)   property not of a description ordinarily intended for private use or consumption;

(c)   property not intended by the injured person for his or her own private use or consumption; and

(d)   damage valued at no more than £275.

No limit is set to the damages that may be awarded by a court.

According to the Commission's 1999 Green Paper on liability for defective products[1], 'non-material damage (any damage not affecting property, moral damage, mental suffering etc) is not at present covered' by Directive 85/374/EEC. Assuming that the European Court would embrace this limited interpretation, it is apparent that Part I of the CPA 1987 extends beyond the Directive in this particular, notwithstanding that it generally purports to have 'effect for the purpose of making such provision as is necessary in order to comply with the product liability Directive and shall be construed accordingly'[2]. Miller notes that 'personal injury' is defined in s 45(1) of the Act to include 'any disease and any other impairment of a person's physical or mental condition' and concludes that 'nervous shock in the form of recognised psychiatric illness is within the range of compensation'[3].

However, what is clear is that the exclusion of a claim in respect of damage to the defective product itself (see above) means that there is no claim for simple diminution in value, ie food that is simply of poor quality. Such a claim can only be made in contract law, ie where there has been a breach of the implied terms discussed above. Of course, the difficulty is that such a claim will not be available to a consumer who has bought from a retailer that has since become insolvent.

1   Commission Green Paper COM (1999) 396 final on 'liability for defective products', p 31.
2   See CPA 1987, s 1(1).
3   *Product Liability and Safety* (Butterworths), Vol III, para 81.

Defences

21.4.5   Section 4 of the CPA 1987 prescribes six defences to civil proceedings by virtue of Part I of the Act in respect of a defect in a product. They are that:

(a)   the defect is attributable to compliance with a Community or national law requirement. The defendant must show that the defect was the result of compliance. In an action by a consumer for injury caused by food containing a damaging additive, the manufacturer would be unable to sustain the defence unless he had been required by law to incorporate it[1];

(b)   the defendant did not supply[2] the product. This is important in cases where counterfeit or out-of-date foods are sold by unauthorised retailers;

(c)   the defendant did not supply the product in the course of a business and would be caught by the Act only by virtue of things done otherwise than with a view to profit. This, for example, excludes private individuals making food at home;

(d)   the defect was not in the product at the time it was supplied. This may be important in cases of bad storage of food by a retailer or where a consumer fails to observe storage instructions on a label or simply keeps the food too long before eating it;

(e)   the state of scientific and technical knowledge at the time the product was supplied was not such that a producer of products of the same description as the product in question might be expected to have discovered the defect if it had existed in his products while they were under his control[3]. This so-called 'development risks' defence may be of value in regard to novel foods[4];

(f)   in the case of an ingredient of a food, the defect constituted a defect in that food and was wholly due to its design (ie recipe) or to compliance by the ingredient producer with instructions given by the producer of the food.

1   For examples of regulations that require the incorporation of ingredients, see para **10.6.1** above.
2   See CPA 1987, s 46.
3   See case C-300/95 *EC Commission v United Kingdom* [1997] ECR I-2649.
4   See para **10.3.2** below.

Prohibition on exclusions from liability

21.4.6   Liability under Part I of the CPA 1987 to a person who has suffered damage caused wholly or partly by a defect in a product, or to a dependant or relative of such a person, may not be limited or excluded by a contract term, notice or any other provision[1].

1   CPA 1987, s 7.

Limitation of actions

21.4.7   An action must be commenced not later than three years from the date of injury to the plaintiff by the defective product or, if later, the date when the plaintiff knew he had a claim against the defendant. The right of action is extinguished upon expiry of a period of 10 years from the date on which the defective product was supplied by the producer unless the injured person has in the meantime instituted proceedings against the producer[1].

1   Limitation Act 1980, s 11A, inserted by CPA 1987, Sch 1. On the question as to when a product is to be treated as having been 'supplied' ('put into circulation' in the words of the actual Directive) see C-127/04, *O'Byrne v Sanofi Pasteur MSD Ltd* [2006] ECR I-1313.

21.5 SOME ELEMENTARY PRECAUTIONS FOR CONSUMERS

21.5.1   Where injury to a person or death or damage to property has resulted from a defective food product, procedural mistakes at an early stage can have an adverse effect on any proceedings that may follow. The following points might be borne in mind:

(a)   ensure that any remains of the food and its container are retained and kept safely;

(b)   in the event of illness, seek advice from your doctor, ensure that stool and/or other samples are obtained as soon as possible and keep the results;

(c)   report the matter to the environmental health department of the local food authority (see section **2.5** above). This is most important in cases where contaminated or defective food may still be on sale. Make it clear to the officer that civil proceedings may follow and that the evidence may be required in court;

(d)   if the environmental health officer wishes to take remnants of the food and/or its container away, ask for a written receipt giving details of the food and other evidence taken;

(e) in cases of injury to a person or death, ask the doctor attending the injured person to certify in writing the nature and extent of the injury or the cause of death;

(f) unless the injury to a person or damage to property is trivial, and in all cases of death, seek early advice from a solicitor;

(g) with the assistance of the solicitor, where instructed, prepare a written statement as soon as possible of the time, date and place of purchase of the food and the events leading up to and immediately following the injury, death or damage;

(h) through the solicitor, where instructed, notify the retailer and the producer (where his identity is known) in writing of the incident, its seriousness, and the intention to seek damages;

(i) do not risk prejudicing the proceedings by statements to the press, radio or television about the incident.

21.6 SOME ELEMENTARY PRECAUTIONS FOR PRODUCERS

21.6.1   Although Regulation (EC) 178/2002 is not specifically intended to have the effect of introducing a Community regime regulating the allocation of liability among the different links of the food chain[1], food and feed business operators should now keep in mind the potential civil liability that might flow from breach of their statutory duties under Articles 17, 19 and 20 of that Regulation[2].

In general, to minimise the risk from actions for damages, the following elementary precautions might be considered by food producers:

(a) ensure that the food control and management systems[3] take account of the possibility of civil as well as criminal liability;

(b) ensure full compliance with statutory requirements as to warnings and use instructions[4] that may also serve to limit liability under the CPA 1987[5];

(c) make appropriate arrangements for product liability insurance;

(d) ensure that staff responsible for handling consumer complaints are properly trained in dealing sensitively with the public and in the basic principles of criminal and civil liability;

(e) on receipt of a complaint, seek full details, preferably in writing, with the object in particular of establishing:
   (i) whether or not there has been any death, personal injury or damage to property and of determining the nature and extent of injury or damage;
   (ii) the name, pack size and code number of the product alleged to have caused the problem;
   (iii) the name and address of the retailer (if any) who sold the product;

(f) obtain from the retailer:
   (i) in appropriate cases, a full report on the incident; and
   (ii) if possible, samples for testing of the batch from which the product was drawn;

(g) if the injured person claims to have been medically examined, request a copy of the doctor's report;

(h)   if the complaint is of a serious nature and suggests that other products may be defective, implement the product recall procedures;

(i)   comply with the notification obligations etc under the product liability insurance;

(j)   if at any stage there appears to be substance to the complaint, refer the matter to the producer's lawyers;

(k)   except on the advice of lawyers, make no admission of any kind or offer of compensation. A chance remark such as 'Oh, we have had several complaints about that', might seriously affect liability.

1   See para I.3.2 of the Commission Guidance on implementation of Arts 11, 12 and 17–20 of Regulation (EC) 178/2002 on general food law (20 January 2005).

2   As to Regulation (EC) 178/2002, Arts 17, 19 and 20, see paras **3.2.38** and **3.2.44–3.2.53** above.

3   See para **20.3.9** above.

4   See, for example, paras **9.2.17** and **9.2.19** above.

5   CPA 1987, s 3(2).

Digest of food and feeding stuffs legislation relating to England

Notes

1. Measures concerning the presence in food and feeding stuffs of substances such as pesticides and veterinary medicines and genetically modified organisms are included in this Appendix, but those concerning their approval are outside the scope of this book.
2. Since they are normally of short duration, emergency instruments under s 1 of the Food and Environment Protection Act 1985, s 13 of the Food Safety Act 1990 and s 2(2) of the European Communities Act 1972 are not included.
3. Amendments to the legislation listed in this Appendix are not shown.

PART I: STATUTES APPLICABLE IN WHOLE OR IN PART TO FOOD OR FEEDING STUFFS

Agriculture Act 1970 (c 40), Pt IV, fertilisers and feeding stuffs.

Agriculture and Horticulture Act 1964 (c 28), Pt III, grading of horticultural produce.

Agricultural Produce (Grading and Marking) Act 1928 (18 & 19 Geo 5, c 19), grading and marking of agricultural produce.

Animal Health Act 1981 (c 22) consolidated various enactments relating to diseases of animals and in particular, in section 29, provided for the control of zoonoses.

Consumer Protection Act 1987 (c 43), Pt I, product liability; Pt II, consumer safety (Pt III – misleading indications of price – was repealed by the Consumer Protection from Unfair Trading Regulations 2008.)

European Communities Act 1972 (c 68) made provision in connection with the enlargement of the European Communities to include the United Kingdom.

European Economic Area Act 1993 (c 51) made provision in relation to the European Economic Area established under the Agreement signed at Oporto on 2 May 1992 as adjusted by the Protocol signed at Brussels on 17 March 1993.

Food and Environment Protection Act 1985 (c 48), Pt I, contamination of food; Pt III, pesticides etc.

Food Safety Act 1990 (c 16), Pt I, Preliminary; Pt II, main provisions – food safety, consumer protection, regulations, defences etc, miscellaneous and supplemental; Pt III, administration and enforcement – administration, sampling and analysis etc, powers of entry and obstruction etc, offences, appeals; Pt IV, miscellaneous and supplemental—powers of ministers, protective provisions, financial provisions, instruments and documents, amendments of other Acts, supplemental.

Food Standards Act 1999 (c 28) established the Food Standards Agency and made provisions as to its functions; amended the law relating to food safety and other interests of consumers in relation to food; enabled provision to be made in relation to the notification of tests for food-borne diseases; and enabled provision to be made in relation to animal feeding stuffs.

Government of Wales Act 1998 (c 38) in particular established and made provision for the transfer of functions to the National Assembly for Wales.

Government of Wales Act 2006 (c 32) made further provision about the government of Wales.

Horticultural Produce Act 1986 (c 20) conferred on authorised officers (within the meaning of Pt III of the Agriculture and Horticulture Act 1964) powers in relation to the movement of horticultural produce.

International Carriage of Perishable Foodstuffs Act 1976 (c 58) made provision to enable the United Kingdom to accede to the Agreement on the International Carriage of Perishable Foodstuffs.

Prices Act 1974 (c 24) in particular made provision for requiring prices to be indicated on or in relation to goods offered or exposed for sale by retail.

Sale of Goods Act 1979 (c 54) consolidated the law of sale of goods in the amended Sale of Goods Act 1893.

Scotch Whisky Act 1988 (c 22) made provision as to the definition of Scotch whisky and as to the production and sale of whisky. (*At the time of writing, the Scotch Whisky Regulations 2008 have been proposed to repeal and replace the 1988 Act and enhance and safeguard, in respect of the United Kingdom, the geographical indication of Scotch Whisky.*)

Scotland Act 1998 (c 46) in particular provided for the establishment and legislative competence of a Scottish Parliament and for the establishment of and transfer of functions to a Scottish Administration.

Trade Descriptions Act 1968 (c 29), in particular, replaced the Merchandise Marks Acts 1887 to 1953 by fresh provisions prohibiting misdescriptions of goods, services, accommodation and facilities provided in the course of trade. (*The Act was mostly repealed by the Consumer Protection from Unfair Trading Regulations 2008.*)

Unfair Contract Terms Act 1977 (c 50) imposed further limits on the extent to which civil liability for breach of contract, or for negligence or other breach of duty, can be avoided by means of contract terms or otherwise.

Weights and Measures Act 1985 (c 72) consolidated enactments relating to weights and measures.

PART IIA: SUBORDINATE LEGISLATION APPLICABLE IN WHOLE OR IN PART TO FOOD AND FEEDING STUFFS

Animal by-products

(*See also Part IIB of this Appendix 'Animal by-products'.*)
Animal By-Products Regulations 2005 [SI 2005/2347] (*The Regulations apply to England for the purpose of implementing Regulation (EC) 1774/2002 (animal products not intended for human consumption)*)

Consumer protection etc

Unfair Terms in Consumer Contracts Regulations 1999 [SI 1999/2083] (*These Regulations apply to the United Kingdom for the purpose of implementing Directive 93/13/EEC*)

Consumer Protection (Distance Selling) Regulations 2000 [SI 2000/2334] (*These Regulations apply to the United Kingdom for the purpose of implementing Directive 97/7/EC*)

Sale and Supply of Goods to Consumers Regulations 2002 [SI 2002/3045] (*These Regulations apply to the United Kingdom for the purpose of implementing Directive 1999/44/EC*)

Business Protection from Misleading Marketing Regulations 2008 [SI 2008/1276] (*These Regulations apply to the United Kingdom for the purpose of implementing Directive 2006/114/EC*)

Consumer Protection from Unfair Trading Regulations 2008 [SI 2008/1277] (*These Regulations apply to the United Kingdom for the purpose of implementing Directive 2005/29/EC and Art 6.2 of Directive 1999/44/EC*)

Official controls

Official Feed and Food Controls (England) Regulations 2007 [SI 2007/3185] (*The Regulations implement Regulation (EC) 882/2004 and Regulation (EC) 178/2002 Art 11*)

Official Controls (Animals, Feed and Food) (England) Regulations 2006 [SI 2006/3472] (*The Regulations implement Regulation (EC) 882/2004*)

Organic products

Organic Products Regulations 2004 [SI 2004/1604] (*The Regulations apply to the United Kingdom for the purpose of implementing Regulation (EEC) 2092/91 – now replaced by Regulation (EC) 834/2007*)

Organic Products (Imports from Third Countries) Regulations 2003 [SI 2003/2821] (*The Regulations apply to the United Kingdom for the purpose of implementing Regulation (EC) 1788/2001 – now replaced by Regulation (EC) 605/2008*)

Pesticide residues

Pesticides (Maximum Residue Levels) (England and Wales) Regulations 2008 [SI 2008/2570] (*The Regulations apply to England and Wales for the purpose of implementing Regulation (EC) 396/2005*)

Transmissible spongiform encephalopathies

Transmissible Spongiform Encephalopathies Regulations 2008 [SI 2008/1881] (*The Regulations apply to England for the purpose of implementing Regulation (EC) 999/2001*)

PART IIB: SUBORDINATE LEGISLATION APPLICABLE IN WHOLE OR IN PART TO FOOD

(*See further Part IIA of this Appendix.*)

Animal by-products

(*See also Part IIA of this Appendix 'Animal by-products'.*)
Animal By-Products (Identification) Regulations 1995 [SI 1995/614]. (*The Regulations apply to Great Britain but, commencing with SI 2002/1619, have been amended separately for England*)

Food additives, contaminants, residues and other substances

Additives

Colours in Food Regulations 1995 [SI 1995/3124] (*The Regulations apply to England and Wales for the purpose of implementing Directives 94/36/EC and 95/45/EC but, commencing with SI 2000/481, have been amended separately for England*)
Miscellaneous Food Additives Regulations 1995 [SI 1995/3187] (*The Regulations apply to England and Wales for the purpose of implementing Directives 95/2/EC and 96/77/EC (see now Directive 2008/84/EC) but, commencing with SI 2001/60, have been amended separately for England*)
Sweeteners in Food Regulations 1995 [SI 1995/3123] (*The Regulations apply to England and Wales for the purpose of implementing Directives 94/35/EC and 95/31/EC (see now Directive 2008/60/EC) but, commencing with SI 2001/2294, have been amended separately for England*)

Additives: Labelling

Food Additives Labelling Regulations 1992 [SI 1992/1978]. (*The Regulations apply to Great Britain for the purpose of implementing in part Directive 89/107/EEC but, commencing with SI 2001/2294, have been amended separately for England*)

Flavourings

Flavourings in Food Regulations 1992 [SI 1992/1971]. (*The Regulations apply to England and Wales for the purpose of implementing Directive 88/388/EEC but, commencing with SI 2002/890, have been amended separately for England*)
Smoke Flavourings (England) Regulations 2005 [SI 2005/464]. (*The Regulations implement Regulation (EC) 2065/2003*)

Other added substances

Chloroform in Food Regulations 1980 [SI 1980/36] (*The Regulations apply to England and Wales but, by SI 2005/2626, have been amended separately for England*)

Erucic Acid in Food Regulations 1977 [SI 1977/691] (*The Regulations apply to England and Wales for the purpose of implementing Directive 76/621/EEC but, by SI 2005/2626, have been amended separately for England*)

Extraction Solvents in Food Regulations 1993 [SI 1993/1658] (*The Regulations apply to England and Wales for the purpose of implementing Directive 88/344/EEC but, by SI 2005/2626, have been amended separately for England*)

Mineral Hydrocarbons in Food Regulations 1966 [SI 1966/1073] (*The Regulations apply to England and Wales but, commencing with SI 2001/3775, have been amended separately for England*)

Tryptophan in Food (England) Regulations 2005 [SI 2005/2630]

Kava-kava in Food (England) Regulations 2002 [SI 2002/3169]

Contaminants

Arsenic in Food Regulations 1959 [SI 1959/831] (*The Regulations apply to England and Wales but, by SI 2005/2626, have been amended separately for England*)

Contaminants in Food (England) Regulations 2007 [SI 2007/210] (*The Regulations implement Regulation (EC) 1881/2006*)

Food contact materials

Materials and Articles in Contact with Food (England) Regulations 2007 [SI 2007/2790] (*The Regulations implement Regulation (EC) 1935/2004*)

Plastic Materials and Articles in Contact with Food (England) Regulations 2008 [SI 2008/916] (*The Regulations implement Directives 82/711/EEC, 85/572/EEC and 2002/72/EC and Regulation (EC) 1895/2005*)

Ceramic Articles in Contact with Food (England) Regulations 2006 [SI 2006/1179] (*The Regulations implement Directive 84/500/EEC*)

Cooking Utensils (Safety) Regulations 1972 [SI 1972/1957] (*The Regulations apply to the United Kingdom*)

N-nitrosamines and N-nitrosatable Substances in Elastomer or Rubber Teats and Dummies (Safety) Regulations 1995 [SI 1995/1012] (*The Regulations apply to the United Kingdom for the purpose of implementing Directive 93/11/EEC*)

Veterinary residues

Animals and Animal Products (Examination for Residues and Maximum Residue Limits) Regulations 1997 [SI 1997/1729] (*The Regulations apply to Great Britain for the purposes of implementing Regulation (EEC) 2377/90 and Directives 96/22/EC and 96/23/EC*)

(*See also Part IIA of this Appendix 'Pesticide residues'*)

Food enforcement

Food authorities

Food Safety (Enforcement Authority) (England and Wales) Order 1990 [SI 1990/2462]

Forms

Detention of Food (Prescribed Forms) Regulations 1990 [SI 1990/2614]
Food Safety (Improvement and Prohibition—Prescribed Forms) Regulations 1991 [SI 1991/100]

Premises

Food Safety (Ships and Aircraft) (England and Scotland) Order 2003 [SI 2003/1895]

Revision of penalties

Food (Revision of Penalties) Regulations 1982 [SI 1982/1727]
Food (Revision of Penalties) Regulations 1985 [SI 1985/67]

Sampling and qualifications

Authorised Officers (Meat Inspection) Regulations 1987 [SI 1987/133]
Food Safety (Sampling and Qualifications) Regulations 1990 [SI 1990/2463]

Food: fees and charges

Meat (Official Controls Charges) (England) Regulations 2008 [SI 2008/447] (*The Regulations implement Regulation (EC) 882/2004, Arts 26 and 27*)
Fishery Products (Official Controls Charges) (England) Regulations 2007 [SI 2007/3392] (*The Regulations implement Regulation (EC) 882/2004, Arts 26 and 27*)
Charges for Residues Surveillance Regulations 2006 [SI 2006/2285] (*The Regulations apply to Great Britain for the purposes of implementing Regulation (EC) 882/2004, Art 27*)
Novel Foods and Novel Food Ingredients (Fees) Regulations 1997 [SI 1997/1336] (*The Regulations apply to Great Britain for the purposes of implementing Regulation (EC) 258/97, but SI 1999/1756 and SI 2000/253 provide for the appropriate fee to be accompany applications in Scotland and Wales respectively*)

Food: general

General Food Regulations 2004 [SI 2004/3279] (*The Regulations apply to Great Britain for the purpose of implementing Regulation (EC) 178/2002 Arts 14, 16, 18 and 19*)

Food hygiene and preparation

Food irradiation

Food (Control of Irradiation) Regulations 1990 [SI 1990/2490] (*The Regulations apply to Great Britain but, commencing with SI 2000/2254,*

have been amended separately for England for the purpose of
implementing Directive 1999/2/EC)

Hygiene of foodstuffs

Eggs

Ungraded Eggs (Hygiene) Regulations 1990 [SI 1990/1323] (*The Regulations
apply to England and Wales*)

General

Food Hygiene (England) Regulations 2006 [SI 2006/14] (*The Regulations
implement in particular Regulation (EC) 852/2004 (food hygiene),
Regulation (EC) 853/2004 (hygiene of food of animal origin) and
Regulation (EC) 854/2004 (official controls on products of animal origin)*

Imports: general

Products of Animal Origin (Import and Export) Regulations 1996
[SI 1996/3124] (*The Regulations apply to Great Britain for the purpose of
implementing Directive 89/662/EEC but, commencing with SI 2000/225,
have been amended separately for England*)
Products of Animal Origin (Third Country Imports) (England)
Regulations 2006 [SI 2006/2841] (*The Regulations implement Directive
97/78/EC*)
Animals and Animal Products (Import and Export) (England) Regulations 2006
[SI 2006/1471] (*The Regulations implement Directives 90/425/EEC and
91/496/EEC*)

Temperature control

International Carriage of Perishable Foodstuffs Regulations 1985
[SI 1985/1071] (*The Regulations apply to the United Kingdom*)

Food labelling etc

Beef labelling

Beef Labelling (Enforcement) (England) Regulations 2000 [SI 2000/3047]
(*The Regulations implement Regulation (EC) 1760/2000. At the time of
writing, the Beef and Veal Labelling (England) Regulations 2008 have
been proposed to revoke and replace the 2000 Regulations and, in
particular, implement for England Regulations (EC) 1760/2000, 566/2008
and 1234/2007, Art 113b and Annex XIa, para II*)

Fish labelling

Fish Labelling (England) Regulations 2003 [SI 2003/461] (*The Regulations
implement provisions of Regulation (EC) 104/2000*)

General labelling

Food Labelling Regulations 1996 [SI 1996/1499] (*For the purpose in particular of implementing Directive 79/112/EEC (now Directive 2000/13/EC) and Directives 87/250/EEC, 89/398/EEC, 90/496/EEC and 94/54/EC, the Regulations apply to Great Britain but, commencing with SI 2000/768, have been amended separately for England*)

Labelling of food with added phytosterols or phytostanols

Food with Added Phytosterols or Phytostanols (Labelling) (England) Regulations 2004 [SI 2004/3344] (*The Regulations implement Regulation (EC) 608/2004*)

Lot marking

Food (Lot Marking) Regulations 1996 [SI 1996/1502] (*The Regulations apply to Great Britain for the purpose of implementing Directive 89/396/EEC*)

Nutrition and health claims

Nutrition and Health Claims (England) Regulations 2007 [SI 2007/2080] (*The Regulations implement Regulation (EC) 1924/2006*)

Food standards

Food quality standards: general

Bananas

(*See under 'Fruit and Vegetables'*)

Bread and flour

Bread and Flour Regulations 1998 [SI 1998/141] (*The Regulations apply to England and Wales but, by SI 2005/2626, have been amended separately for England*)

Caseins and caseinates

Caseins and Caseinates Regulations 1985 [SI 1985/2026] (*The Regulations apply to England and Wales for the purpose of implementing Directive 83/417/EEC but, by SI 2005/2626, have been amended separately for England*)

Cocoa and chocolate products

Cocoa and Chocolate Products (England) Regulations 2003 [SI 2003/1659] (*The Regulations implement Directive 2000/36/EC*)

Part IIB: Subordinate legislation applicable in whole or in part to food

Coffee extracts and chicory extracts

Coffee Extracts and Chicory Extracts (England) Regulations 2000 [SI 2000/3323] (*The Regulations implement Directive 1999/4/EC*)

Condensed milk and dried milk

Condensed Milk and Dried Milk (England) Regulations 2003 [SI 2003/1596] (*The Regulations implement Directive 2001/114/EC*)

Eggs

Eggs and Chicks (England) Regulations 2008 [SI 2008/1718] (*The Regulations implement Regulations (EC) 1234/2007, 589/2008 and 617/2008*)

Eggs (Marking and Storage) Regulations 1965 [SI 1965/1000] (*The Regulations apply to England and Wales*)

Fishery and aquaculture products

Sea Fish (Marketing Standards) Regulations 1986 [SI 1986/1272] (*The Regulations apply to the United Kingdom for the purpose of implementing Regulations (EEC) 103/76 and (EEC) 104/76. The Community Regulations have been replaced by Regulation (EC) 2406/96 but SI 1986/1272 has yet to be updated for England*)

Preserved Sardines (Marketing Standards) Regulations 1990 [SI 1990/1084] (*The Regulations apply to England and Wales for the purpose of implementing Regulation (EEC) 2136/89*)

Preserved Tuna and Bonito (Marketing Standards) Regulations 1994 [SI 1994/2127] (*The Regulations apply to Great Britain for the purpose of implementing Regulation (EEC) 1536/92*)

Fruit and vegetables

Grading of Horticulture Produce (Amendment) Regulations 1973 [SI 1973/22] (*These Regulations amended Part III of the Agriculture and Horticulture Act 1964, which applies to Great Britain, to enable European Community grading rules to be implemented under it*)

Grading of Horticultural Produce (Forms of Labels) Regulations 1982 [SI 1982/387]

Fruit juices and fruit nectars

Fruit Juices and Fruit Nectars (England) Regulations 2003 [SI 2003/1564] (*The Regulations implement Directive 2001/112/EC*)

Honey

Honey (England) Regulations 2003 [SI 2003/2243] (*The Regulations implement Directive 2001/110/EC*)

Jam and similar products

Jam and Similar Products (England) Regulations 2003 [SI 2003/3120] (*The Regulations implement Directive 2001/113/EC*)

Meat products

Meat Products (England) Regulations 2003 [SI 2003/2075]

Milk and milk products and spreadable fats

Spreadable Fats (Marketing Standards) and Milk and Milk Products (Protection of Designations) (England) Regulations 2008 [SI 2008/1287] (*The Regulations implement Regulation (EC) 1234/2007, Art 114(1) and Annex XII; and Art 115 and Annex XV*)

Drinking Milk (England) Regulations 2008 [SI 2008/1317] (*The Regulations implement Regulation (EC) 1234/2007, Art 114(2) and Annex XIII*)

Olive oil

Olive Oil (Marketing Standards) Regulations 2003 [SI 2003/2577] (*The Regulations apply to Great Britain in particular for the purpose of implementing Regulation (EC) 1019/2002*)

Poultry Meat

Poultry Meat (Water Content) Regulations 1984 [SI 1984/1145] (*The Regulations applied to England and Wales for the purpose of implementing Regulation (EEC) 2967/76 but have been obsolete since this was repealed and replaced by Regulation (EC) 2891/93 amending Regulation (EC) 1538/91*)

Quick-frozen foodstuffs

Quick-Frozen Foodstuffs (England) Regulations 2007 [SI 2007/191] (*The Regulations implement Directives 89/108/EEC and 92/2/EEC and Regulation (EC) 37/2005*)

Spirit drinks

Spirit Drinks Regulations 1990 [SI 1990/1179] (*The Regulations apply to England and Wales for the purpose of implementing Regulation (EEC) 1576/89. At the time of writing, the Spirit Drinks Regulations 2008 have been proposed to revoke and replace the 1990 Regulations and to implement, in respect of the United Kingdom, Regulation (EC) 110/2008*)

Scotch Whisky Order 1990 [SI 1990/998] (*The Regulations apply to Great Britain. At the time of writing, the Scotch Whisky Regulations 2008 have been proposed to revoke and replace the 1990 Order and enhance and safeguard, in respect of the United Kingdom, the geographical indication of Scotch Whisky*)

Sugar products

Specified Sugar Products (England) Regulations 2003 [SI 2003/1563] (*The Regulations implement Directive 2001/111/EC*)

Water

Natural Mineral Water, Spring Water and Bottled Drinking Water (England) Regulations 2007 [SI 2007/2785] (*The Regulations implement Directives 80/777/EEC, 2003/40/EC and 98/83/EC*)

Whisky

(*See under 'Spirit drinks'*)

Wine

Common Agricultural Policy (Wine) (England and Northern Ireland) Regulations 2001 [SI 2001/686] (*The Regulations implement EC Regulations concerned with the production and marketing of wine and related products. At the time of writing, the Wine Regulations 2008 have been proposed to revoke and replace for England the 2001 Regulations and implement changes in the EC wine regime coming into force on 1 August 2008, in particular, by virtue of Regulations (EC) 479/2008 and 423/2008*)

Foodstuffs for particular nutritional uses

Infant Formula and Follow-on Formula (England) Regulations 2007 [SI 2007/3521] (*The Regulations implement Directives 2006/141/EC and 92/52/EEC*)
Processed Cereal-based Foods and Baby Foods for Infants and Young Children (England) Regulations 2003 [SI 2003/3207] (*The Regulations implement Directive 96/5/EC – now Directive 2006/125/EC*)
Foods Intended for Use in Energy Restricted Diets for Weight Reduction Regulations 1997 [SI 1997/2182] (*The Regulations apply to Great Britain for the purpose of implementing Directive 96/8/EC but, commencing with SI 2005/2626, have been amended separately for England*).
Medical Food (England) Regulations 2000 [SI 2000/845] (*The Regulations implement Directive 1999/21/EC*)
Food for Particular Nutritional Uses (Addition of Substances for Specific Nutritional Purposes) (England) Regulations 2002 [SI 2002/1817] (*The Regulations implement Directive 2001/15/EC*)
Notification of Marketing of Food for Particular Nutritional Uses (England) Regulations 2007 [SI 2007/181] (*The Regulations implement Directive 89/398/EEC*)

Genetically modified and novel foods

Genetically modified foods

Genetically Modified Food (England) Regulations 2004 [SI 2004/2335] (*The Regulations implement provisions of Regulation (EC) 1829/2003*)

Genetically Modified Organisms (Traceability and Labelling) (England) Regulations 2004 [SI 2004/2412] (*The Regulations implement Regulation (EC) 1830/2003*)

Novel foods

Novel Foods and Novel Food Ingredients Regulations 1997 [SI 1997/1335] (*The Regulations apply to Great Britain for the purpose of implementing Regulation (EC) 258/97, but, commencing with SI 1999/3182, have been amended separately for England*)

Vitamins and minerals etc in food

Food Supplements (England) Regulations 2003 [SI 2003/1387] (*The Regulations implement Directive 2002/46/EC*)
Addition of Vitamins, Minerals and Other Substances (England) Regulations 2007 [SI 2007/1631] (*The Regulations implement Regulation (EC) 1925/2006*)
(*See also under 'Food Labelling etc.'*)

Food: revocations and amendments

Those of particular importance include:
Food (Miscellaneous Revocations) Regulations 1991 [SI 1991/1231]
Food (Miscellaneous Revocations and Amendments) Regulations 1995 [SI 1995/3267]

General safety

General product safety

General Product Safety Regulations 2005 [SI 2005/1803] (*These Regulations apply to the United Kingdom for the purpose of implementing Directive 2001/95/EC*)

Food imitations

Food Imitations (Safety) Regulations 1989 [SI 1989/1291] (*These Regulations apply to the United Kingdom for the purpose of implementing Directive 87/357/EC*)

Quantity and price marking of food

Quantity marking

Weights and Measures Act 1963 (Cheese, Fish, Fresh Fruits and Vegetables, Meat and Poultry) Order 1984 [SI 1984/1315] (*These Regulations apply to Great Britain for the purpose of implementing in particular Directive 2000/13/EC.*)

Weights and Measures (Intoxicating Liquor) Order 1988 [SI 1988/2039] (*These Regulations apply to Great Britain for the purpose of implementing in particular Directive 2000/13/EC. At the time of writing, consultation is in progress on proposals for amendment of the 1988 Order to implement Directive 2007/45/EC*)

Weights and Measures (Miscellaneous Foods) Order 1988 [SI 1988/2040] (*These Regulations apply to Great Britain for the purpose of implementing in particular Directive 2000/13/EC. At the time of writing, consultation is in progress on proposals for amendment of the 1988 Order to implement Directive 2007/45/EC*)

Weights and Measures (Quantity Marking and Abbreviations of Units) Regulations 1987 [SI 1987/1538] (*These Regulations apply to Great Britain for the purpose of implementing in particular Directives 2000/13/EC and 2007/45/EC*)

Weights and Measures (Packaged Goods) Regulations 2006 [SI 2006/659] (*These Regulations apply to the Great Britain for the purpose of implementing Directives 2007/45/EC, 76/211/EEC and 80/181/EEC*)

Units of Measurement Regulations 1986 [SI 1986/1082] (*These Regulations apply to the United Kingdom for the purpose of implementing Directive 80/181/EEC*)

Price marking

Price Marking Order 2004 [SI 2004/102] (*These Regulations apply to the Great Britain for the purpose of implementing Directive 98/6/EC*)

Product liability

Consumer Protection Act 1987 (Product Liability) (Modification) Order 2000 [SI 2000/2771] (*These Regulations apply to England and Wales for the purpose of implementing Directive 1999/34/EC amending Directive 85/374/EEC*)

PART IIC: SUBORDINATE LEGISLATION APPLICABLE TO FEEDING STUFFS

(*See further Part IIA of this Appendix.*)

Composition

Feeding Stuffs (England) Regulations 2005 [SI 2005/3281] (*The Regulations implement Directives 70/524/EEC, 79/373/EEC, 82/471/EEC, 93/74/EEC, 96/25/EC, 2002/32/EC and 2008/38/EC; Decision 2004/217/EC; and Regulation (EC) 1831/2003*)

(*See also Part IIA of this Appendix 'Pesticide residues'*)

Hygiene and enforcement

Feed Hygiene and Enforcement (England) Regulations 2005 [SI 2005/3280] (*The Regulations implement Regulations (EC) 183/2005 and 178/2002*)

Sampling and analysis

Feeding Stuffs (Sampling and Analysis) Regulations 1999 [SI 1999/1663] (*The Regulations apply to Great Britain for the purpose of implementing Directives 71/250/EEC, 71/393/EEC, 73/46/EEC, 73/47/EEC, 76/372/EEC, 98/88/EC, 72/199/EC, 74/203/EEC, 76/371/EEC and 78/633/EEC, but, commencing with SI 2001/541, have been amended separately for England*)

Veterinary medicinal products

Veterinary Medicines Regulations 2008 [SI 2008/2297] (*The Regulations apply to the United Kingdom for the purpose of implementing Directive 2001/82/EC, Regulations (EC) 178/2002, 1831/2003, 882/2004, and 183/2005, in so far as they apply to veterinary medicinal products used in feedingstuffs and to some specified feed additives used in feedingstuffs; and medicated feedingstuffs Directive 90/167 so far it is not superseded by Regulation (EC) 183/2005*)

Genetically modified animal feed

Genetically Modified Animal Feed (England) Regulations 2004 [SI 2004/2334] (*The Regulations implement provisions of Regulation (EC)1829/2003*)

Appendix B

Digest of food and feeding stuffs legislation relating to Wales

Notes

1.   Measures concerning the presence in food and feeding stuffs of substances such as pesticides and veterinary medicines and genetically modified organisms are included in this Appendix, but those concerning their approval are outside the scope of this book.
2.   Since they are normally of short duration, emergency instruments under s 1 of the Food and Environment Protection Act 1985, s 13 of the Food Safety Act 1990 and s 2(2) of the European Communities Act 1972 are not included.
3.   Amendments to the legislation listed in this Appendix are not shown.

PART I: STATUTES APPLICABLE IN WHOLE OR IN PART TO FOOD OR FEEDING STUFFS

See the statutes listed in Part I of Appendix A and in particular:

Government of Wales Act 1998 (c 38) which in particular established and made provision for the transfer of functions to the National Assembly for Wales; and

Government of Wales Act 2006 (c 32) which made further provision about the government of Wales.

PART IIA: SUBORDINATE LEGISLATION APPLICABLE IN WHOLE OR IN PART TO FOOD AND FEEDING STUFFS

Animal by-products

(*See also Part IIB of this Appendix 'Animal by-products'.*)
Animal By-Products (Wales) Regulations 2006 [SI 2006/1293] (W.127) (*The Regulations apply to Wales for the purpose of implementing Regulation (EC) 1774/2002 (animal products not intended for human consumption)*)

Consumer protection etc

Unfair Terms in Consumer Contracts Regulations 1999 [SI 1999/2083] (*These Regulations apply to the United Kingdom for the purpose of implementing Directive 93/13/EEC*)

Consumer Protection (Distance Selling) Regulations 2000 [SI 2000/2334] (*These Regulations apply to the United Kingdom for the purpose of implementing Directive 97/7/EC*)

Sale and Supply of Goods to Consumers Regulations 2002 [SI 2002/3045] (*These Regulations apply to the United Kingdom for the purpose of implementing Directive 1999/44/EC*)

Business Protection from Misleading Marketing Regulations 2008 [SI 2008/1276] (*These Regulations apply to the United Kingdom for the purpose of implementing Directive 2006/114/EC*)

Consumer Protection from Unfair Trading Regulations 2008 [SI 2008/1277] (*These Regulations apply to the United Kingdom for the purpose of implementing Directive 2005/29/EC and Art 6.2 of Directive 1999/44/EC*)

Official controls

Official Feed and Food Controls (Wales) Regulations 2007 [SI 2007/3294] (W.290)] (*The Regulations implement Regulation (EC) 882/2004 and Regulation (EC) 178/2002, Art 11*)

Official Controls (Animals, Feed and Food) (Wales) Regulations 2007 [SI 2007/196] (W.15] (*The Regulations implement Regulation (EC) 882/2004*)

Organic products

Organic Products Regulations 2004 [SI 2004/1604] (*The Regulations apply to the United Kingdom for the purpose of implementing Regulation (EEC) 2092/91 – now replaced by Regulation (EC) 834/2007*)

Organic Products (Imports from Third Countries) Regulations 2003 [SI 2003/2821] (*The Regulations apply to the United Kingdom for the purpose of implementing Regulation (EC) 1788/2001 – now replaced by Regulation (EC) 605/2008*)

Pesticide residues

Pesticides (Maximum Residue Levels) (England and Wales) Regulations 2008 [SI 2008/2570] (*The Regulations apply to England and Wales for the purpose of implementing Regulation (EC) 396/2005*)

Transmissible spongiform encephalopathies

Transmissible Spongiform Encephalopathies (Wales) Regulations 2006 [SI 2006/1226] (W.117) (*The Regulations implement Regulation (EC) 999/2001. At the time of writing, the Transmissible Spongiform Encephalopathies (Wales) Regulations 2008 have been proposed to revoke and replace the 2006 Regulations and the Bovine Products (Restrictions on Placing on the Market) (Wales) (No 2) Regulations 2005 noted below*)

Bovine Products (Restrictions on Placing on the Market) (Wales) (No 2) Regulations 2005 [SI 2005/3296] (W.254) (*The Regulations implement Decision 2007/411/EC replacing Decision 2005/598/EC. At the time of writing, revocation and replacement of the 2005 Regulations is proposed by the Transmissible Spongiform Encephalopathies (Wales) Regulations 2008 noted above*)

PART IIB: SUBORDINATE LEGISLATION APPLICABLE IN WHOLE OR IN PART TO FOOD

(See further Part IIA of this Appendix.)

Animal by-products

(See also Part IIA of this Appendix 'Animal by-products'.)
Animal By-Products (Identification) Regulations 1995 [SI 1995/614] *(The Regulations apply to Great Britain but, commencing with SI 2002/1472 (W.146), have been amended separately for Wales)*

Food additives, contaminants, residues and other substances

Additives

Colours in Food Regulations 1995 [SI 1995/3124] *(The Regulations apply to England and Wales for the purpose of implementing Directives 94/36/EC and 95/45/EC but, commencing with SI 2000/1799 (W.124), have been amended separately for Wales)*
Miscellaneous Food Additives Regulations 1995 [SI 1995/3187] *(The Regulations apply to England and Wales for the purpose of implementing Directives 95/2/EC and 96/77/EC (see now Directive 2008/84/EC) but, commencing with SI 2001/1787 (W.126). have been amended separately for Wales)*
Sweeteners in Food Regulations 1995 [SI 1995/3123] *(The Regulations apply to England and Wales for the purpose of implementing Directives 94/35/EC and 95/31/EC (see now Directive 2008/60/EC) but, commencing with SI 2001/2679 (W.220), have been amended separately for Wales)*

Additives: Labelling

Food Additives Labelling Regulations 1992 [SI 1992/1978]. *(The Regulations apply to Great Britain for the purpose of implementing Directive 89/107/EEC but, commencing with SI 2002/330 (W.43), have been amended separately for Wales)*

Flavourings

Flavourings in Food Regulations 1992 [SI 1992/1971]. *(The Regulations apply to England and Wales for the purpose of implementing Directive 88/388/EEC but, commencing with SI 2002/1886 (W.195), have been amended separately for Wales)*
Smoke Flavourings (Wales) Regulations 2005 [SI 2005/1350] (W.98). *(The Regulations implement Regulation (EC) 2065/2003)*

Other added substances

Chloroform in Food Regulations 1980 [SI 1980/36] *(The Regulations apply to England and Wales but, by SI 2005/3254 (W.247), have been amended separately for Wales)*

Erucic Acid in Food Regulations 1977 [SI 1977/691] (*The Regulations apply to England and Wales for the purpose of implementing Directive 76/621/EEC but, by SI 2005/3254 (W.247), have been amended separately for Wales*)

Extraction Solvents in Food Regulations 1993 [SI 1993/1658] (*The Regulations apply to England and Wales for the purpose of implementing Directive 88/344/EEC but, by SI 2005/3254 (W.247), have been amended separately for Wales*)

Mineral Hydrocarbons in Food Regulations 1966 [SI 1966/1073] (*The Regulations apply to England and Wales but, commencing with SI 2002/329 (W.42), have been amended separately for Wales*)

Tryptophan in Food (Wales) Regulations 2005 [SI 2005/3111] (W.231)

Kava-kava in Food (Wales) Regulations 2006 [SI 2006/1851] (W.194)

Contaminants

Arsenic in Food Regulations 1959 [SI 1959/831] (*The Regulations apply to England and Wales but, by SI 2005/3254 (W.247), have been amended separately for Wales*)

Contaminants in Food (Wales) Regulations 2007 [SI 2007/840] (W.73) (*The Regulations implement Regulation (EC) 1881/2006*)

Food contact materials

Materials and Articles in Contact with Food (Wales) Regulations 2007 [SI 2007/3252] (W.287) (*The Regulations implement Regulation (EC) 1935/2004*)

Plastic Materials and Articles in Contact with Food (Wales) (No 2) Regulations 2008 [SI 2008/1682] (W.162) The Regulations implement Directives 82/711/EEC, 85/572/EEC and 2002/72/EC and Regulation (EC) 1895/2005)

Ceramic Articles in Contact with Food (Wales) Regulations 2006 [SI 2006/1704] (W.166) (*The Regulations implement Directive 84/500/EEC*)

Cooking Utensils (Safety) Regulations 1972 [SI 1972/1957] (*The Regulations apply to the United Kingdom*)

N-nitrosamines and N-nitrosatable Substances in Elastomer or Rubber Teats and Dummies (Safety) Regulations 1995 [SI 1995/1012] (*The Regulations apply to the United Kingdom for the purpose of implementing Directive 93/11/EEC*)

Veterinary residues

Animals and Animal Products (Examination for Residues and Maximum Residue Limits) Regulations 1997 [SI 1997/1729] (*The Regulations apply to Great Britain for the purposes of implementing Regulation (EEC) 2377/90 and Directives 96/22/EC and 96/23/EC*)

(*See also Part IIA of this Appendix 'Pesticide residues'*)

Food enforcement

Food authorities

Food Safety (Enforcement Authority) (England and Wales) Order 1990 [SI 1990/2462]

Forms

Detention of Food (Prescribed Forms) Regulations 1990 [SI 1990/ 2614]
Food Safety (Improvement and Prohibition—Prescribed Forms) Regulations 1991 [SI 1991/100]

Premises

Food Safety (Ships and Aircraft) (Wales) Order 2003 [SI 2003/1774] (W.191)

Revision of penalties

Food (Revision of Penalties) Regulations 1982 [SI 1982/1727]
Food (Revision of Penalties) Regulations 1985 [SI 1985/67]

Sampling and qualifications

Authorised Officers (Meat Inspection) Regulations 1987 [SI 1987/133]
Food Safety (Sampling and Qualifications) Regulations 1990 [SI 1990/2463]

Food: fees and charges

Meat (Official Controls Charges) (Wales) Regulations 2008 [SI 2008/601] (W.63) (*The Regulations implement Regulation (EC) 882/2004, Arts 26 and 27*)
Fishery Products (Official Controls Charges) (Wales) Regulations 2007 [SI 2007/3462] (W.307) (*The Regulations implement Regulation (EC) 882/2004, Arts 26 and 27*)
Charges for Residues Surveillance Regulations 2006 [SI 2006/2285] (*The Regulations apply to Great Britain for the purposes of implementing Regulation (EC) 882/2004, Art 27*)
Novel Foods and Novel Food Ingredients (Fees) Regulations 1997 [SI 1997/1336] (*The Regulations apply to Great Britain for the purposes of implementing Regulation (EC) 258/97, but SI 1999/1756 and SI 2000/253 provide for the appropriate fee to accompany applications in Scotland and Wales respectively*)

Food: general

General Food Regulations 2004 [SI 2004/3279] (*The Regulations apply to Great Britain for the purpose of implementing Regulation (EC) 178/2002, Arts 14, 16, 18 and 19*)

Food hygiene and preparation

Food irradiation

Food (Control of Irradiation) Regulations 1990 [SI 1990/2490] *(The Regulations apply to Great Britain but, commencing with SI 2001/1232 (W.66), have been amended separately for Wales for the purpose of implementing Directive 1999/2/EC)*

Hygiene of foodstuffs

Eggs

Ungraded Eggs (Hygiene) Regulations 1990 [SI 1990/1323] *(The Regulations apply to England and Wales)*

General

Food Hygiene (Wales) Regulations 2006 [SI 2006/31] (W.5) *(The Regulations implement in particular Regulation (EC) 852/2004 (food hygiene), Regulation (EC) 853/2004 (hygiene of food of animal origin) and Regulation (EC) 854/2004 (official controls on products of animal origin)*

Imports: general

Products of Animal Origin (Import and Export) Regulations 1996 [SI 1996/3124] *(The Regulations apply to Great Britain for the purpose of implementing Directive 89/662/EEC but, commencing with SI 2001/1660 (W.119), have been amended separately for Wales)*
Products of Animal Origin (Third Country Imports) (Wales) Regulations 2007 [SI 2007/376] (W.36) *(The Regulations implement Directive 97/78/EC)*
Animals and Animal Products (Import and Export) (Wales) Regulations 2006 [SI 2006/1536] (W.153) *(The Regulations implement Directives 90/425/EEC and 91/496/EEC)*

Temperature control

International Carriage of Perishable Foodstuffs Regulations 1985 [SI 1985/1071] *(The Regulations apply to the United Kingdom)*

Food labelling etc

Beef labelling

Beef Labelling (Enforcement) (Wales) Regulations 2001 [SI 2001/1360] *(The Regulations implement Regulation (EC) 1760/2000. At the time of writing, the Beef and Veal Labelling (England) Regulations 2008 have been proposed to revoke and replace the 2000 Regulations and, in particular, implement for England Regulations (EC) 1760/2000, 566/2008 and 1234/2007, Art 113b and Annex XIa, para II. Regulations for Wales are expected to be made in due course)*

Fish labelling

Fish Labelling (Wales) Regulations 2003 [SI 2003/1635] (W.177) (The Regulations implement provisions of Regulation (EC) 104/2000)

General labelling

Food Labelling Regulations 1996 [SI 1996/1499] (*For the purpose in particular of implementing Directive 79/112/EEC (now Directive 2000/13/EC) and Directives 87/250/EEC, 89/398/EEC, 90/496/EEC and 94/54/EC, the Regulations apply to Great Britain but, commencing with 2000/1925 (W.134), have been amended separately for Wales*)

Labelling of food with added phytosterols or phytostanols

Food with Added Phytosterols or Phytostanols (Labelling) (Wales) Regulations 2005 [SI 2005/1224] (W.82) (*The Regulations implement Regulation (EC) 608/2004*)

Lot marking

Food (Lot Marking) Regulations 1996 [SI 1996/1502] (*The Regulations apply to Great Britain for the purpose of implementing Directive 89/396/EEC*)

Nutrition and health claims

Nutrition and Health Claims (Wales) Regulations 2007 [SI 2007/2611] (W.222) (*The Regulations implement Regulation (EC) 1924/2006*)

Food standards

Food quality standards: general

Bananas

(*See under' Fruit and Vegetables'*)

Bread and flour

Bread and Flour Regulations 1998 [SI 1998/141] (*The Regulations apply to England and Wales but, by SI 2005/3254 (W.247), have been amended separately for Wales*)

Caseins and caseinates

Caseins and Caseinates Regulations 1985 [SI 1985/2026] (*The Regulations apply to England and Wales for the purpose of implementing Directive 83/417/EEC but, by SI 2005/3254 (W.247), have been amended separately for Wales*)

Digest of food and feeding stuffs legislation relating to Wales

Cocoa and chocolate products

Cocoa and Chocolate Products (Wales) Regulations 2003 [SI 2003/3037] (W.285) (*The Regulations implement Directive 2000/36/EC*)

Coffee extracts and chicory extracts

Coffee Extracts and Chicory Extracts (Wales) Regulations 2001 [SI 2001/1440] (W.120) (*The Regulations implement Directive 1999/4/EC*)

Condensed milk and dried milk

Condensed Milk and Dried Milk (Wales) Regulations 2003 [SI 2003/3053] (W.291) (*The Regulations implement Directive 2001/114/EC*)

Eggs

Eggs (Marketing Standards) Regulations 1995 [SI 1995/1544] (*At the time of writing, the Eggs and Chicks (Wales) Regulations 2008 have been proposed, in respect of Wales, to revoke and replace the 1995 Regulations and implement Regulations (EC) 1234/2007, 557/2007 and 617/2008*)

Eggs (Marking and Storage) Regulations 1965 [SI 1965/1000] (T*he Regulations apply to England and Wales*)

Fishery and aquaculture products

Sea Fish (Marketing Standards) Regulations 1986 [SI 1986/1272] (*The Regulations apply to the United Kingdom for the purpose of implementing Regulations (EEC) 103/76 and (EEC) 104/76. The Community Regulations have been replaced by Regulation (EC) 2406/96 but SI 1986/1272 has yet to be updated for Wales*)

Preserved Sardines (Marketing Standards) Regulations 1990 [SI 1990/1084] (*The Regulations apply to England and Wales for the purpose of implementing Regulation (EEC) 2136/89*)

Preserved Tuna and Bonito (Marketing Standards) Regulations 1994 [SI 1994/2127] (*The Regulations apply to Great Britain for the purpose of implementing Regulation (EEC) 1536/92*)

Fruit and vegetables

Grading of Horticulture Produce (Amendment) Regulations 1973 [SI 1973/22] (*These Regulations amended Part III of the Agriculture and Horticulture Act 1964, which applies to Great Britain, to enable European Community grading rules to be implemented under it*)

Grading of Horticultural Produce (Forms of Labels) Regulations 1982 [SI 1982/387]

Fruit juices and fruit nectars

Fruit Juices and Fruit Nectars (Wales) Regulations 2003 [SI 2003/3041] (W.286) (*The Regulations implement Directive 2001/112/EC*)

Part IIB: Subordinate legislation applicable in whole or in part to food

Honey

Honey (Wales) Regulations 2003 [SI 2003/3044] (W.288) (*The Regulations implement Directive 2001/110/EC*)

Jam and similar products

Jam and Similar Products (Wales) Regulations 2004 [SI 2004/553] (W.56) (*The Regulations implement Directive 2001/113/EC*)

Meat products

Meat Products (Wales) Regulations 2004 [SI 2004/1396] (W.141)

Milk and milk products and spreadable fats

Spreadable Fats (Marketing Standards) and Milk and Milk Products (Protection of Designations) (Wales) Regulations 2008 [SI 2008/1341] (W.141) (*The Regulations implement Regulation (EC) 1234/2007, Art 114(1) and Annex XII; and Art 115 and Annex XV*)

Drinking Milk Regulations 1998 [SI 1998/2424] (*The Regulations applied to Great Britain for the purposes of implementing Regulation (EEC) 2597/79. Since this has been replaced by Regulation (EC) 1234/2007, Art 114(2) and Annex XIII, the 1998 Regulations are expected to be revoked and replaced for Wales by legislation similar to the Drinking Milk (England) Regulations 2008 [SI 2008/1317] – see Appendix A*)

Olive oil

Olive Oil (Marketing Standards) Regulations 2003 [SI 2003/2577] (*The Regulations apply to Great Britain in particular for the purpose of implementing Regulation (EC) 1019/2002*)

Poultry Meat

Poultry Meat (Water Content) Regulations 1984 [SI 1984/1145] (*The Regulations applied to England and Wales for the purpose of implementing Regulation (EEC) 2967/76, but have been obsolete since this was repealed and replaced by Regulation (EC) 2891/93 amending Regulation (EC) 1538/91*)

Quick-frozen foodstuffs

Quick-Frozen Foodstuffs (Wales) Regulations 2007 [SI 2007/389] (W.40) (*The Regulations implement Directives 89/108/EEC and 92/2/EEC and Regulation (EC) 37/2005*)

Spirit drinks

Spirit Drinks Regulations 1990 [SI 1990/1179] (*The Regulations apply to England and Wales for the purpose of implementing Regulation (EEC)*)

1576/89. At the time of writing, the Spirit Drinks Regulations 2008 have been proposed to revoke and replace the 1990 Regulations and to implement, in respect of the Unitied Kingdom, Regulation (EC) 110/2008)

Scotch Whisky Order 1990 [SI 1990/998] *(The Regulations apply to Great Britain. At the time of writing, the Scotch Whisky Regulations 2008 have been proposed to revoke and replace the 1990 Order and enhance and safeguard, in respect of the United Kingdom, the geographical indication of Scotch Whisky)*

Sugar products

Specified Sugar Products (Wales) Regulations 2003 [SI 2003/3047] (W.290) *(The Regulations implement Directive 2001/111/EC)*

Water

Natural Mineral Water, Spring Water and Bottled Drinking Water (Wales) Regulations 2007 [SI 2007/3165] (W.276) *(The Regulations implement Directives 80/777/EEC, 2003/40/EC and 98/83/EC)*

Whisky

(See under 'Spirit drinks')

Wine

Common Agricultural Policy (Wine) (Wales) Regulations 2001 [SI 2001/2193] (W.155) *(The Regulations implement EC Regulations concerned with the production and marketing of wine and related products. At the time of writing, the Wine Regulations 2008 have been proposed to revoke and replace for England the 2001 Regulations and implement changes in the EC wine regime coming into force on 1 August 2008, in particular, by virtue of Regulations (EC) 479/2008 and 423/2008. Regulations for Wales are expected to be made in due course)*

Foodstuffs for particular nutritional uses

Infant Formula and Follow-on Formula (Wales) Regulations 2007 [SI 2007/3573] (W.316) *(The Regulations implement Directives 2006/141/EC and 92/52/EC)*

Processed Cereal-based Foods and Baby Foods for Infants and Young Children (Wales) Regulations 2004 [SI 2004/314] (W.32) *(The Regulations implement Directive 96/5/EC – now Directive 2006/125/EC)*

Foods Intended for Use in Energy Restricted Diets for Weight Reduction Regulations 1997 [SI 1997/2182] *(The Regulations apply to Great Britain for the purpose of implementing Directive 96/8/EC but, commencing with SI 2005/3254 (W.247), have been amended separately for Wales)*

Medical Food (Wales) Regulations 2000 [SI 2000/1866] (W.125) *(The Regulations implement Directive 1999/21/EC)*

Food for Particular Nutritional Uses (Addition of Substances for Specific Nutritional Purposes) (Wales) Regulations 2002 [SI 2002/2939] (W.280) *(The Regulations implement Directive 2001/15/EC)*

Notification of Marketing of Food for Particular Nutritional Uses (Wales) Regulations 2007 [SI 2007/1040] (W.100) (*The Regulations implement Directive 89/398/EEC*)

Genetically modified and novel foods

Genetically modified foods

Genetically Modified Food (Wales) Regulations 2004 [SI 2004/3220] (W. 276) (*The Regulations implement provisions of Regulation (EC) 1829/2003*)
Genetically Modified Organisms (Traceability and Labelling) (Wales) Regulations 2005 [SI 2005/1914] (W.157) (*The Regulations implement Regulation (EC) 1830/2003*)

Novel foods

Novel Foods and Novel Food Ingredients Regulations 1997 [SI 1997/1335] (*The Regulations apply to Great Britain for the purpose of implementing Regulation (EC) 258/97, but, commencing with SI 2000/1925 (W.134), have been amended separately for Wales*)

Vitamins and minerals etc in food

Food Supplements (Wales) Regulations 2003 [SI 2003/1719] (W.186) (*The Regulations implement Directive 2002/46/EC*)
Addition of Vitamins, Minerals and Other Substances (Wales) Regulations 2007 [SI 2007/1984] (W.165) (*The Regulations implement Regulation (EC) 1925/2006*)
(*See also under 'Food Labelling etc'*)

Food: revocations and amendments

Those of particular importance include:
Food (Miscellaneous Revocations) Regulations 1991 [SI 1991/1231]
Food (Miscellaneous Revocations and Amendments) Regulations 1995 [SI 1995/3267]

General safety

General product safety

General Product Safety Regulations 2005 [SI 2005/1803] (*These Regulations apply to the United Kingdom for the purpose of implementing Directive 2001/95/EC*)

Food imitations

Food Imitations (Safety) Regulations 1989 [SI 1989/1291] (*These Regulations apply to the United Kingdom for the purpose of implementing Directive 87/357/EC*)

Quantity and price marking of food

Quantity marking

Weights and Measures Act 1963 (Cheese, Fish, Fresh Fruits and Vegetables, Meat and Poultry) Order 1984 [SI 1984/1315] (*These Regulations apply to Great Britain for the purpose of implementing in particular Directive 2000/13/EC*)

Weights and Measures (Intoxicating Liquor) Order 1988 [SI 1988/2039] (*These Regulations apply to Great Britain for the purpose of implementing in particular Directive 2000/13/EC. At the time of writing, consultation is in progress on proposals for amendment of the 1988 Order to implement Directive 2007/45/EC*)

Weights and Measures (Miscellaneous Foods) Order 1988 [SI 1988/2040] (*These Regulations apply to Great Britain for the purpose of implementing in particular Directive 2000/13/EC. At the time of writing, consultation is in progress on proposals for amendment of the 1988 Order to implement Directive 2007/45/EC*)

Weights and Measures (Quantity Marking and Abbreviations of Units) Regulations 1987 [SI 1987/1538] (*These Regulations apply to Great Britain for the purpose of implementing in particular Directives 2000/13/EC and 2007/45/EC*)

Weights and Measures (Packaged Goods) Regulations 2006 [SI 2006/659] (*These Regulations apply to Great Britain for the purpose of implementing Directives 2007/45/EC, 76/211/EEC and 80/181/EEC*)

Units of Measurement Regulations 1986 [SI 1986/1082] (*These Regulations apply to the United Kingdom for the purpose of implementing Directive 80/181/EEC*)

Price marking

Price Marking Order 2004 [SI 2004/102] (*These Regulations apply to Great Britain for the purpose of implementing Directive 98/6/EC*)

Product liability

Consumer Protection Act 1987 (Product Liability) (Modification) Order 2000 [SI 2000/2771] (*These Regulations apply to England and Wales for the purpose of implementing Directive 1999/34/EC amending Directive 85/374/EEC*)

PART IIC: SUBORDINATE LEGISLATION APPLICABLE TO FEEDING STUFFS

(*See further Part IIA of this Appendix.*)

Composition

Feeding Stuffs (Wales) Regulations 2006 [SI 2006/116] (W.14) (*The Regulations implement Directives 70/524/EEC, 79/373/EEC,*

82/471/EEC, 93/74/EEC, 96/25/EC, 2002/32/EC and 2008/38; Decision 2004/217/EC; and Regulation (EC) 1831/2003)
(See also Part IIA of this Appendix 'Pesticide residues')

Hygiene and enforcement

Feed Hygiene and Enforcement (Wales) Regulations 2005 [SI 2005/3368] (W.265) (*The Regulations implement Regulations (EC) 183/2005 and 178/2002*)

Sampling and analysis

Feeding Stuffs (Sampling and Analysis) Regulations 1999 [SI 1999/1663] (*The Regulations apply to Great Britain for the purpose of implementing Directives 71/250/EEC, 71/393/EEC, 73/46/EEC, 73/47/EEC, 76/372/EEC, 98/88/EC, 72/199/EC, 74/203/EEC, 76/371/EEC and 78/633/EEC, but, commencing with SI 2001/2253 (W.163), have been amended separately for Wales*)

Veterinary medicinal products

Veterinary Medicines Regulations 2008 [SI 2008/2297] (*The Regulations apply to the United Kingdom for the purpose of implementing Directive 2001/82/EC, Regulations (EC) 178/2002, 1831/2003, 882/2004, and 183/2005, in so far as they apply to veterinary medicinal products used in feedingstuffs and to some specified feed additives used in feedingstuffs; and medicated feedingstuffs Directive 90/167 so far it is not superseded by Regulation (EC) 183/2005*)

Genetically modified animal feed

Genetically Modified Animal Feed (Wales) Regulations 2004 [SI 2004/3221] (W.277) (*The Regulations implement provisions of Regulation (EC)1829/2003*)

Appendix C

Digest of European Community food and feeding stuffs legislation

Notes

1. Of EC Regulations regarding agricultural and fishery products subject to market organisation, only those concerned with marketing standards and consumer information are included.
2. Measures concerning the presence in food and feeding stuffs of substances such as pesticides and veterinary medicines and genetically modified organisms are included in this Appendix, but those concerning their approval are outside the scope of this book.
3. Since they are normally of short duration, emergency instruments are not included.
4. Amendments to the legislation listed in this Appendix are not shown.
5. National implementing legislation is listed in Appendices A and B for England and Wales respectively.

PART I: COMMUNITY LEGISLATION APPLICABLE IN WHOLE OR IN PART TO FOOD AND FEEDING STUFFS

Animal waste

Regulation (EC) 1774/2002 (health rules concerning animal by-products not intended for human consumption)

Consumer protection etc: general

Directive 2001/95/EC (general product safety)
Directive 87/357/EEC (products which, appearing to be other than they are, endanger the health or safety of consumers)
Directive 85/374/EEC (liability for defective products)
Directive 2006/114/EC (misleading and comparative advertising)
Directive 93/13/EEC (unfair terms in consumer contracts)
Directive 97/7/EC (protection of consumers in relation to distance contracts)
Directive 98/27/EC (injunctions for the protection of consumers' interests)

Directive 1999/44/EC (certain aspects of the sale of consumer goods and associated guarantees)

Directive 2005/29/EC (unfair business to consumer practices)

General food and feed safety

Regulation (EC) 178/2002 (laying down general principles and requirements of food law, establishing the European Food Safety Authority and laying down procedures in matters of food safety)

Genetically modified food and feed

Regulation (EC) 1829/2003 (genetically modified food and feed)

Regulation (EC) 641/2004 (detailed rules for the implementation of Regulation 1829/2003 as regards the application for the authorisation of new genetically modified food and feed, the notification of existing products and adventitious or technically unavoidable presence of genetically modified material which has benefited from a favourable risk evaluation)

Regulation (EC) 1981/2006 (detailed rules for the implementation of Art 32 of Regulation (EC) 1829/2003 as regards the Community reference laboratory for genetically modified organisms)

Regulation (EC) 1830/2003 (traceability and labelling of genetically modified organisms and the traceability of food and feed products produced from genetically modified organisms)

Regulation (EC) 1946/2003 (transboundary movements of genetically modified organisms)

Official controls

Regulation (EC) 882/2004 (official controls performed to ensure the verification of compliance with feed and food law animal health and animal welfare rules)

Directive 98/68/EC (standard document referred to in Art 9(1) of Directive 95/53 and certain checks at the introduction into the Community of feeding stuffs from third countries)

Organic products

Regulation (EC) 834/2007 (organic production and labelling of organic products)

Regulation (EC) 889/2008 (detailed rules for implementation of Regulation 834/2007)

Regulation (EEC) 345/2008 (detailed rules for implementing the arrangements for imports from third countries)

Regulation (EC) 605/2008 (detailed rules for implementing the provisions concerning the certificate of inspection for imports from third countries)

Pesticide residues

Regulation (EC) 396/2005 (maximum residue levels of pesticides in products of plant and animal origin)

Directive 2002/63/EC (Community methods of sampling for the official control of pesticide residues in and on products of plant and animal origin)

Radioactive contamination of foodstuffs and feeding stuffs

Export conditions

Regulation (EEC) 2219/89 (special conditions for exporting foodstuffs and feeding stuffs following a nuclear accident or any other case of radiological emergency)

Import conditions for agricultural products from third countries

Regulation (EC) 733/2008 (conditions governing imports of agricultural products originating in third countries following the accident at the Chernobyl nuclear power station). (*The Regulation has repealed and replaced Regulation (EEC) 737/90.*)

Regulation (EC) 1635/2006 (detailed rules for the application of Regulation (EEC) 737/90 on the conditions governing imports of agricultural products originating in third countries following the accident at the Chernobyl nuclear power station)

Regulation (EC) 1609/2000 (list of products excluded from the application of Regulation (EEC) 737/90 on the conditions governing imports of agricultural products originating in third countries following the accident at the Chernobyl nuclear power station)

Maximum permitted levels of contamination

Regulation (Euratom) 3954/87 (maximum permitted levels of radioactive contamination of foodstuffs and feeding stuffs following a nuclear accident or any other case of radiological emergency)

Regulation (Euratom) 944/89 (maximum permitted levels of radioactive contamination in minor foodstuffs following a nuclear accident or any other case of radiological emergency)

Regulation (Euratom) 770/90 (maximum permitted levels of radioactive contamination of feeding stuffs following a nuclear accident or any other case of radiological emergency)

Transmissible spongiform encephalopathies

Regulation (EC) 999/2001 (prevention, control and eradication of certain transmissible spongiform encephalopathies)

Regulation (EC) 1326/2001 (transitional measures to permit the changeover to Regulation (EC) 999/2001)

Decision 96/385/EC (approving the plan for the control and eradication of bovine spongiform encephalopathy in the United Kingdom)

PART II: COMMUNITY LEGISLATION APPLICABLE IN WHOLE OR IN PART TO FOOD

Food additives, contaminants, residues and other substances

Food additives

Additives framework Directive

Directive 89/107/EEC (food additives for use in foodstuffs intended for human consumption)

Additives other than colours and sweeteners

Directive 95/2/EC (food additives other than colours and sweeteners)
Directive 2008/84/EC (specific criteria of purity on food additives other than colours and sweeteners)

Colours

Directive 94/36/EC (colours for use in foodstuffs)
Directive 95/45/EC (specific criteria of purity concerning colours for use in food stuffs)

Sweeteners

Directive 94/35/EC (sweeteners for use in foodstuffs)
Directive 2008/60//EC (specific criteria of purity concerning sweeteners for use in food stuffs)

Restrictions on additives in traditional foodstuffs

Decision 292/97/EC (maintenance of national laws prohibiting the use of certain additives in the production of certain specified foodstuffs)

Verification of purity criteria for additives

Directive 81/712/EC (Community methods of analysis for verifying that certain additives used in foodstuffs satisfy purity criteria)

Food contaminants

Regulation (EEC) 315/93 (Community procedures for contaminants in food)
Regulation (EC) 1881/2006 (maximum levels for certain contaminants in foodstuffs)
Regulation (EC) 333/2007 (methods of sampling and analysis for the official control of the levels of lead, cadmium, mercury, inorganic tin, 3-MCPD and benzo(a)pyrene in foodstuffs)

Regulation (EC) 401/2006 (methods of sampling and analysis for the official control of the levels of mycotoxins in foodstuffs)

Regulation (EC) 1882/2006 (methods of sampling and analysis for the official control of levels of nitrates in certain foodstuffs)

Regulation (EC) 1883/2006 (methods of sampling and analysis for the official control of levels of dioxins and dioxin-like PCBs in certain foodstuffs)

Food flavourings

Directive 88/388/EEC (flavourings for use in foodstuffs and source materials for their production)

Decision 88/389/EEC (establishment of an inventory of the source materials and substances used in the preparation of flavourings)

Regulation (EC) 2232/96 (laying down a Community procedure for flavouring substances used or intended for use in or on foodstuffs)

Decision 1999/217/EC (adopting a register of flavouring substances used in or on foodstuffs drawn up in application of Regulation (EC) 2232/96)

Regulation (EC) 2065/2003 (smoke flavourings used or intended for use in or on foods)

Materials and articles in contact with food

General material and articles

Regulation (EC) 1935/2004 (materials and articles intended to come into contact with food)

Regulation (EC) 2023/2006 (good manufacturing practice for materials and articles intended to come into contact with food)

Plastics materials and articles

Directive 2002/72/EC (plastics materials and articles intended to come into contact with foodstuffs)

Directive 82/711EEC (basic rules necessary for testing migration of the constituents of plastics materials and articles)

Directive 85/572/EEC (list of simulants to be used for testing migration of the constituents of plastics materials and articles)

Vinyl chloride

Directive 78/142/EEC (materials and articles which contain vinyl chloride monomer and are intended to come into contact with foodstuffs)

Directive 80/766/EEC (Community method of analysis for the official control of the vinyl chloride monomer in materials and articles)

Directive 81/432/EEC (Community method of analysis for the official control of vinyl chloride released by materials and articles)

Epoxy derivatives

Regulation (EC) 1895/2005 (restriction of use of certain epoxy derivatives in materials and articles intended to come into contact with food)

Ceramic articles

Directive 84/500/EEC (ceramic articles intended to come into contact with foodstuffs)

Regenerated cellulose film

Directive 2007/42/EC (materials and articles made of regenerated cellulose film intended to come into contact with foodstuffs)

Elastomer or rubber teats and soothers

Directive 93/11/EEC (concerning the release of the N-Nitrosamines and N-Nitrosatable substances from elastomer or rubber teats and soothers)

Other substances added to food

Erucic acid

Directive 76/621/EEC (maximum level of erucic acid in oils and fats intended as such for human consumption and in foodstuffs containing added oils and fats)
Directive 80/891/EEC (Community method of analysis for determining the erucic acid content of oils and fats intended to be used as such for human consumption and foodstuffs containing added oils and fats)

Extraction solvents

Directive 88/344/EEC (on extraction solvents used in the production of foodstuffs and food ingredients)

Veterinary residues

Regulation (EEC) 2377/90 (maximum residue limits of veterinary medicinal products in foodstuffs of animal origin)
Directive 96/22/EC (prohibition on the use in stockfarming of certain substances having a hormonal or thyrostatic action and of beta-agonistes)
Directive 96/23/EC (on measures to monitor certain substances and residues thereof in live animals and animal products)
(*See also Part I of this Appendix 'Pesticide residues'*)

Food hygiene

Food hygiene: general

Regulation (EC) 852/2004 (the hygiene of foodstuffs)
Directive 96/3/EC (derogation for transport by sea of bulk liquid oils and fats)
Directive 98/28/EC (derogation for transport by sea of bulk raw sugar)
Regulation (EC) 2073/2005 (microbiological criteria for foodstuffs)

Food hygiene: products of animal origin

Provisions common to several categories

Regulation (EC) 853/2004 (specific hygiene rules for food of animal origin)
Regulation (EC) 854/2004 (specific rules for the organisation of official controls on products of animal origin intended for human consumption)
Regulation (EC) 2073/2005 (microbiological criteria for foodstuffs)
Regulation (EC) 2074/2005 (implementing measures for certain products under Regulation (EC) 853/2004 and for the organisation of official controls under Regulation (EC) 854/2004 and Regulation (EC) 882/2004, derogating from Regulation (EC) 852/2004 and amending Regulations (EC) No 853/2004 and (EC) 854/2004)
Regulation (EC) 2075/2005 (specific rules on official controls for Trichinella in meat)
Regulation (EC) 2076/2005 (transitional arrangements for the implementation of Regulations 853/2004, 854/2004 and 882/2004)

Fresh meat, including minced meat

Decision 79/542/EEC (drawing up a list of third countries or parts of third countries, and laying down animal and public health and veterinary certification conditions, for importation into the Community of certain live animals and their fresh meat)

Meat of poultry, ratites and wild game-birds, eggs and egg products

Decision 2006/696/EEC (laying down a list of third countries from which meat of poultry, ratites and wild game-birds, eggs and egg products may be imported into and transit through the Community and the applicable veterinary certification conditions). (*The Decision has now been repealed and replaced by Regulation (EC) 798/2008.*)

Rabbit and certain game meat

Decision 2000/585/EC (animal and public health conditions and veterinary certifications for import of wild and farmed game meat and rabbit meat from third countries and repealing Decisions 97/217/EC, 97/218/EC, 97/219/EC and 97/220/EC)

Meat preparations

Decision 2000/572/EC (animal and public health conditions and veterinary certification for imports of meat preparations into the Community from third countries)

Meat products, stomachs, bladders and intestines

Decision 2007/777/EC (animal and public health conditions and model certificates for imports of certain meat products and treated stomachs, bladders and intestines for human consumption from third countries)

Milk and dairy products

Decision 2004/438/EC (animal and public health and veterinary certifications conditions for introduction in the Community of heat-treated milk, milk-based products and raw milk intended for human consumption)

Fishery products and bivalve molluscs etc.

Decision 2006/766/EC (establishing the lists of third countries and territories from which imports of bivalve molluscs, echinoderms, tunicates, marine gastropods and fishery products are permitted)

Animal casings

Decision 1999/120/EC (drawing up provisional lists of third country establishments from which the Member States authorise imports of animal casings)
Decision 2003/779/EC (animal health requirements and the veterinary certification for the import of animal casings from third countries)

Miscellaneous products

Decision 2003/812/EC (drawing up lists of third countries from which Member States are to authorise imports of certain products for human consumption subject to Directive 92/118/EEC)

Veterinary checks on products of animal origin

Directive 89/662/EEC (veterinary checks in intra-Community trade)
Directive 97/78/EC (principles governing the organisation of veterinary checks on products entering the Community from third countries)
Regulation (EC) 745/2004 (measures with regard to imports of products of animal origin for personal consumption)

Food irradiation

Directive 1999/2/EC (foods and food ingredients treated with ionising radiation)
Directive 1999/3/EC (establishment of a Community list of foods and food ingredients treated with ionising radiation)
Decision 2002/840/EC (list of approved facilities in third countries for the irradiation of foods)

Food labelling

Alcoholic beverages

Directive 87/250/EEC (indication of alcoholic strength by volume in the labelling of alcoholic beverages for sale to the ultimate consumer)

Beef and beef products

Regulation (EC) 1234/2007 (common organisation of agricultural products) Art 113b and Annex IXa)

Regulation (EC) 1760/2000 (system for the identification and registration of bovine animals and regarding the labelling of beef and beef products and repealing Council Regulation (EC) 820/97)

Regulation (EC) 1825/2000 (detailed rules for the application of Regulation (EC) 1760/2000)

Regulation (EC) 911/2004 (implementing Regulation (EC) 1760/2000 as regards eartags, passports and holding registers)

Regulation (EC) 1082/2003 (detailed rules for the implementation of Regulation (EC) 1760/2000 as regards the minimum level of controls to be carried out in the framework of the system for the identification and registration of bovine animals)

Regulation (EC) 494/98 (detailed rules for the implementation of Council Regulation (EC) 820/97 as regards the application of minimum administrative sanctions in the framework of the system for the identification and registration of bovine animals)

Fish labelling

Regulation (EC) 104/2000 (common organisation of the markets in fishery and aquaculture products) Title I Chapter II

Regulation (EC) 2065/2001 (detailed rules for the application of Regulation 104/2000 as regards informing consumers about fishery and aquaculture products)

General labelling

Directive 2000/13/EC (labelling, presentation and advertising of foodstuffs)

Directive 1999/10/EC (derogations from Art 7 of Directive 79/112/EEC – now Directive 2000/13/EC)

Directive 2002/67/EC (labelling of foodstuffs containing quinine and foodstuffs containing caffeine)

Regulation (EC) 608/2004 (labelling of food and food ingredients with added phytosterols and phytostanols)

Directive 2008/5/EC (compulsory indication of particulars other than those provided for in Directive 2000/13/EC

Lot marking

Directive 89/396/EEC (indications or marks identifying the lot to which a foodstuff belongs)

Nutrition labelling and claims

Directive 90/496/EEC (nutrition labelling for foodstuffs)

Regulation (EC) 1924/2006 (nutrition and health claims made on foods)

Food standards

Common agricultural policy marketing standards

Bananas

Regulation (EC) 1234/2007 (common organisation of agricultural products), in
 particular, Art 113
Regulation (EC) 2257/94 (quality standards for bananas)

Eggs

Regulation (EC) 1234/2007 (common organisation of agricultural products), in
 particular, Art 116 and Annex XIV
Regulation (EC) 589/2008 (detailed rules for implementing Regulation (EC)
 1234/2007 as regards maketing standards for eggs)

Fruit and vegetables

Regulation (EC) 1234/2007 (common organisation of agricultural products), in
 particular, Art 113

Note: Under the power now in Art 113 of Regulation (EC) 1234/2007,
marketing standards exist for apples, citrus fruit, kiwi fruit, lettuces, peaches/
nectarines, pears, strawberries, sweet peppers, table grapes and tomatoes
although, at the time of writing, proposals are under consideration for the repeal
of standards for 26 other categories.

Regulation (EC) 1580/2007 (implementing rules for Council
 Regulations 2200/96, 2201/96 and 1182/2007 in the fruit and vegetable
 sector)

Milk and milk products

Regulation (EC) 1234/2007 (common organisation of agricultural products, in
 particular, Art 114 and Annexes XII and XIII)
Regulation (EC) 445/2007 (detailed rules for the application of Regulation
 (EC) 2991/94 laying down standards for spreadable fats and of Regulation
 (EEC) No 1898/87 on the protection of designations used in the marketing
 of milk and milk products – now Regulation (EC) 1234/2007 Annexes XII
 and XIII)

Olive oil

Regulation (EC) 1234/2007 (common organisation of agricultural products, in
 particular, Arts 113 and 118 and Annex XVI)
Regulation (EEC) 2568/91 (characteristics of olive oil and olive-residue oil and
 relevant methods of analysis)
Regulation (EC) 1019/2002 (marketing standards for olive oil)

Poultrymeat

Regulation (EC) 1234/2007 (common organisation of agricultural products, in
 particular, Arts 116 and Annex XIV)

Regulation (EC) 543/2008 (detailed rules for the application of Regulation (EC) 1234/2007 as regards the marketing standards for poultry meat)

Spirit drinks

Regulation (EC) 110/2008 (general rules on the definition, description, presentation, labelling and protection of geographical indications of spirit drinks)

Regulation (EEC) 1014/90 (detailed implementing rules on the definition, description and presentation of spirit drinks)

Regulation (EC) 1267/94 (applying the agreements between the European Union and third countries on the mutual recognition of certain spirit drinks)

Spreadable fats

Regulation (EC) 1234/2007 (common organisation of agricultural products, in particular, Arts 115 and Annex XV)

Regulation (EC) 445/2007 (detailed rules for the application of Regulation (EC) 2991/94 laying down standards for spreadable fats and of Regulation (EEC) No 1898/87 on the protection of designations used in the marketing of milk and milk products – now Regulation (EC) 1234/2007 Annexes XII and XIII)

Wine

Regulation (EC) 479/2008 (common organisation of the market in wine replacing Regulation (EC) 1493/1999)

Regulation (EC) 423/2008 (implementing former Regulation (EC) 1493/1999)

Regulation (EC) 753/2002 (certain rules for applying former Regulation (EC) 1493/1999 as regards the description, designation, presentation and protection of certain wine sector products)

Regulation (EEC) 1601/91 (general rules on the definition, description and presentation of aromatised wines, aromatised wine-based drinks and aromatised wine product cocktails)

Common fishery and aquaculture products marketing standards

Regulation (EC) 104/2000 (common organisation of the market in fishery and aquaculture products) in particular, Title I Chapter I

Regulation (EC) 2406/96 (common marketing standards for certain fishery products)

Regulation (EC) 3703/85 (detailed rules for applying the common marketing standards for certain fresh or chilled fish)

Regulation (EC) 3863/91 (determining a minimum marketing size for crabs applicable to certain coastal areas of the United Kingdom)

Regulation (EC) 2136/89 (marketing standards for preserved sardines)

Regulation (EC) 1536/92 (marketing standards for preserved tuna and bonito)

Foodstuffs intended for particular nutritional uses

Directive 89/398/EEC (foodstuffs intended for particular nutritional uses)

Directive 2006/141/EC (infant formulae and follow-on formulae)

Directive 92/52/EC (infant formulae and follow-on formulae intended for export to third countries)

Directive 2006/125/EC (processed cereal-based foods and baby foods for infants and young children)

Directive 96/8/EC (foods intended for use in energy-restricted diets for weight reduction)

Directive 1999/21/EC (dietary foods for special medical purposes)

Directive 2001/15/EC (substances that may be added for specific nutritional purposes in foods for particular nutritional uses)

Internal market and environmental standards

Caseins and caseinates

Directive 83/417/EEC (certain lactoproteins (caseins and caseinates) intended for human consumption)

Cocoa and chocolate products

Directive 2000/36/EC (cocoa and chocolate intended for human consumption)

Coffee and coffee extracts

Directive 1999/4/EC (coffee extracts and chicory extracts)

Dehydrated preserved milk

Directive 2001/114/EC (certain partly or wholly dehydrated preserved milk for human consumption)

Fruit juices and similar products

Directive 2001/112/EC (fruit juices and certain similar products intended for human consumption)

Honey

Directive 2001/110/EC (honey)

Jams, jellies, marmalades and chestnut puree

Directive 2001/113/EC (fruit jams, jellies and marmalade and chestnut purée)

Natural mineral waters and spring and other bottled water

Directive 80/777/EEC (exploitation and marketing of natural mineral waters)

Directive 2003/40/EC (establishing the list, concentration limits and labelling requirements for the constituents of natural mineral waters and the conditions for using ozone-enriched air for the treatment of natural mineral waters and spring waters)

Directive 98/83/EC (quality of water intended for human consumption)

Quick frozen foodstuffs

Directive 89/108/EEC (quick frozen foodstuffs for human consumption)
Directive 92/2/EEC (sampling procedure and the Community method of analysis for the control of the temperatures of quick-frozen foods intended for human consumption)
Regulation (EC) 37/2005 (monitoring of temperatures in the means of transport, warehousing and storage of quick-frozen foodstuffs intended for human consumption)

Sugars

Directive 2001/111/EC (certain sugars intended for human consumption)

Novel foods and novel food ingredients

(*See also Part I of this Appendix 'Genetically modified food and feed'*)
Regulation (EC) 258/97 (novel foods and novel food ingredients)
Recommendation 97/618/EC (scientific aspects and presentation of information necessary to support applications for the placing on the market of novel foods and novel food ingredients and the preparation of initial assessment reports under Regulation (EC) 258/97)

Protected food names

Geographical indications and designations of origin

Regulation (EC) 510/2006 (protection of geographical indications and designations of origin for agricultural products and foodstuffs)
Regulation (EC) 1898/2006 (detailed rules of implementation of Regulation (EC) 510/2006)
Regulation (EEC) 1107/96 (registration of geographical indications and designations of origin under the procedure in Art 17 of former Regulation 2081/92)
Regulation (EC) 2400/96 (entry of certain names in the 'Register of protected designation of origin and protected geographical indications' provided for in former Regulation 2081/92)
Decision 2007/71/EC (scientific group of experts for designations of origin, geographical indications and traditional specialities guaranteed)

Agricultural products and foodstuffs as traditional products guaranteed

Regulation (EC) 509/2006 (agricultural products and foodstuffs as traditional specialities guaranteed)
Regulation (EC) 1216/2007 (detailed rules for the implementation of Regulation (EC) 509/2006)
Regulation (EC) 2301/97 (entry of certain names in the 'Register of certificates of specific character' provided for in former Regulation 2082/92 on certificates of specific character for agricultural products and foodstuffs)

(See also Decision 2007/71/EC under 'Geographical indications and designations of origin'.)

Vitamins and minerals etc. in food

Directive 2002/46/EC (food supplements)
Regulation (EC) 1925/2006 (addition of vitamins and minerals and of certain other substances to foods)

Notification procedures

Directive 98/34/EC (procedure for the provision of information in the field of technical standards and regulations and of rules on information society services)
Regulation (EC) 764/2008 (procedures relating to the application of certain national technical rules to products lawfully marketed in another Member State and repealing Decision 3052/95/EC)

Quantity and price marking of food

Quantity marking

Nominal quantities

Directive 2007/45/EC (nominal quantities for prepacked products)

Metrological requirements

Directive 76/211/EEC (making up by volume of certain prepackaged products)

Units of measurement

Directive 80/181/EEC (units of measurement)

Price marking

Directive 98/6/EC (consumer protection in the indication of the prices of products offered to consumers)

PART III: COMMUNITY LEGISLATION APPLICABLE TO FEEDING STUFFS

(See further Part I of this Appendix.)

Additives in feeding stuffs

Regulation (EC) 1831/2003 (additives for use in animal nutrition). The Regulation repealed Directives 70/524/EEC (concerning additives in feedingstuffs) and 87/153/EEC (guidelines for the assessment of additives in animal nutrition), although some of their provisions remain temporarily in force.

In accordance with Art 17 of Regulation (EC) 1831/2003, the Commission has established a Community Register of Feed Additives. It was published for the first time in November 2005 and revision 22 was released in December 2007. The Community acts authorising the additives are noted in the Register and constitute the legal basis for their placing on the market and use.

The 'List of authorised additives in feedingstuffs published in application of Art 9t(b) of Council Directive 70/524/EEC concerning additives in feedingstuffs' (OJ C 50, 25.2.2004, p.1) notes the additives authorised before 15 July 2003 under that Directive together with references to the respective legal acts which authorised them.

Circulation of feed materials

Directive 96/25/EC (circulation of feed materials)
Decision 2004/217/EC (list of materials whose circulation or use for animal nutrition purposes is prohibited)

Compound feeding stuffs

Directive 79/373/EEC (marketing of compound feeding stuffs)
Directive 80/511/EEC (compound feeding stuffs in unsealed packages)
Directive 82/475/EEC (categories of ingredients which may be used for the purposes of labelling compound feeding stuffs for pet animals)

Enzymes, micro-organisms and their preparations

Directive 93/113/EC (use and marketing of enzymes, micro-organisms and their preparations in animal nutrition)

Feed hygiene

Regulation (EC) 183/2005 (feed hygiene)

Medicated feedingstuffs

Directive 90/167/EEC (preparation placing on the market and used of medicated feedingstuffs in the Community)

Particular nutritional purposes

Directive 93/74/EEC (feeding stuffs intended for particular nutritional purposes)
Directive 2008/38/EC (establishing a list of intended uses of animal feedingstuffs for particular nutritional purposes)

Protein sources

Directive 82/471/EEC (certain products used in animal nutrition)
Directive 83/228/EEC (guidelines for assessment of certain products used in
   animal nutrition)
Decision 85/382/EEC (prohibiting the use in feedingstuffs of protein products
   obtained from Candida yeasts cultivated on n-alkanes)

Sampling and analysis

Determination of constituents of animal origin for the official control of feedingstuffs

(*See Regulation (EC) 882/2004, Art 61 and Annex VIII*)
Directive 2003/126/EC (analytical method for the determination of constituents
   of animal origin for the official control of feedingstuffs)

Specific analysis methods for feeding stuffs

(*See Regulation (EC) 882/2004, Art 61 and Annex VIII*)
First Directive 71/250 (on analysis methods)
Second Directive 71/393 (on analysis methods)
Third Directive 72/199 (on analysis methods) (with derogation specified by
   Regulation (EC) 121/2008)
Fourth Directive 73/46 (on analysis methods)
Seventh Directive 76/372 (on analysis methods)
Eighth Directive 78/633 (on analysis methods)
Ninth Directive 81/715 (on analysis methods)
Tenth Directive 84/425 (on analysis methods)
Eleventh Directive 93/70 (on analysis methods)
Twelfth Directive 93/117 (on analysis methods)
Directive 98/64/EC (on analysis methods for amino-acids, crude oils and fats,
   and olaquindox)
Directive 1999/27 (on analysis methods for amprolium, diclazuril and
   carbadox)
Directive 1999/76 (on analysis methods for lasalocid sodium)
Directive 2000/45/EC (Community methods of analysis for the determination
   of vitamin A, vitamin E and tryptophan in feedingstuffs)
Directive 2002/70/EC (requirements for the determination of levels of dioxins
   and dioxin-like PCBs in feedingstuffs)

Specific sampling methods for feeding stuffs

(*See Regulation (EC) 882/2004, Art 61 and Annex VIII*)
First Directive 76/371 (on sampling methods)

Undesirable substances and products

Directive 2002/32/EC (undesirable substances in animal feed)
(*See also Part I of this Appendix 'Pesticide residues'*)

Veterinary medicinal products

Directive 2001/82/EC (Community code relating to veterinary medicinal products)

Appendix D

Some Useful Addresses

Note: Websites identified † below give free access to legislation, legislative analysis or case law.

Advertising Standards Authority
Mid City Place
71 High Holborn
London
WC1V 6QT
Telephone 020 7492 2222
Textphone 020 7242 8159
Fax 020 7242 3696
Email enquiries@asa.org.uk
Website www.asa.org.uk

Association of Port Health Authorities
2.02 Suffolk Enterprise Centre
Felaw Maltings
44 Felaw Street
Ipswich
IP2 8SJ
Telephone 01473 407040
Email apha@porthealth.co.uk
Website www.porthealth.co.uk

Association of Public Analysts
Honorary Secretary
c/o Edinburgh Scientific Services
4 Marine Esplanade
Edinburgh
EH6 7LU
Website www.the-apa.co.uk

British and Irish Legal Information Institute (BAILII)
Institute of Advanced Legal Studies
University of London
Charles Clore House
17 Russell Square
London
WC1B 5DR
Email, for user support, feedback@bailii.org
Telephone Joseph Ury 020 7862 5806
Fax 020 7862 5770
† Website www.bailii.org

British Meat Processors Association
12 Cock Lane
London
EC1A 9BU
Telephone 020 7329 0776
Fax 020 7329 0653
Email info@bmpa.uk.com

British Nutrition Foundation
High Holborn House
52–54 High Holborn
London
WC1V 6RQ
Telephone 020 7404 6504
Fax 020 7404 6747
Email postbox@nutrition.org.uk
Website www.nutrition.org.uk

British Retail Consortium
21 Dartmouth Street
London
SW1H 9BP
Telephone 020 7854 8900
Fax 020 7854 8901
Website www.brc.org.uk

BSI British Standards
389 Chiswick High Road
London
W4 4AL
Telephone 020 8996 9001
Fax 020 8996 7001
Email cservices@bsigroup.com
Website www.bsi-global.com

Campden and Chorleywood Food Research Association
Chipping Campden
Gloucestershire
GL55 6LD;
Telephone 01386 842000
Fax 01386 842100
Email info@camden.co.uk
Website www.camden.co.uk

Centre for Environment, Fisheries and Aquaculture Science (Cefas)
Business Development Unit
Pakefield Road
Lowestoft
Suffolk,
NR33 0HT
Telephone 01502 524430
Fax 01502 524569
Email s.f.rollo@cefas.co.uk
Website http://www.cefas.co.uk

Chartered Institute of Environmental Health
Chadwick Cour
15 Hatfields
London
SE1 8DJ
Telephone 020 7928 6006
Fax 020 7827 5862
Website www.cieh.org

Codex Alimentarius
Viale delle Terme di Caracalla
00153 Rome
Italy
Telephone +39(06)5705.1
Telefax +39(06)5705.4593
Telex: 610181 FAOI
E-mail: Codex@fao.org
Website www.codexalimentarius.net

Communicable Disease Surveillance Centre (CDSC)
National Public Health Service for Wales
The Temple of Peace and Health
Cathays Park
Cardiff
CF10 3NW
Telephone (Consultants and General Enquiries) 029 2040 2471
(Surveillance Team) 029 2040 2472
(WHAIP Team): 029 2040 2473
Fax 029 2040 2506
Website www.wales.nhs.uk

Crown Prosecution Service Headquarters,
50 Ludgate Hill
London
EC4M 7EX
Telephone 020 7796 8000
Email enquiries@cps.gsi.gov.uk
Website www.cps.gov.uk

Dairy Hygiene Inspections
(Contact information for Dairy Hygiene Inspectors is given on the DEFRA website)

Department for Business, Enterprise & Regulatory Reform (BERR)
Ministerial Correspondence Unit
1 Victoria Street
London
SW1H 0ET
Telephone 020 7215 5000
(Minicom) 020 7215 6740
Fax 020 7215 0105
Email enquiries@berr.gsi.gov.uk
Website www.berr.gov.uk

Department for Environment, Food and Rural Affairs (DEFRA)
Nobel House
17 Smith Square
London
SW1P 3JR
Telephone 020 7238 6000 (switchboard)
Website www.defra.gov.uk
Defra Helpline: Telephone 08459 33 55 77
Email helpline@defra.gsi.gov.uk
(See also 'Dairy Hygiene Inspections', 'Egg Marketing Inspections', 'Horticultural Marketing Inspectorate', 'Veterinary Medicines Directorate')

Department of Health
Richmond House
79 Whitehall
London
SW1A 2NS
Telephone 020 7210 4850
Email dhmail@dh.gsi.gov.uk
Website www.dh.gov.uk
(See also 'Communicable Disease Surveillance Centre (CDSC) National Public Health Service for Wales', 'Health Protection Agency', 'Health Protection Agency Centre for Infections', 'Medicines and Healthcare Products Regulatory Agency')

Egg Marketing Inspections
(Contact information for Egg Marketing Inspectors is given on the DEFRA website)

Europa – Gateway to the European Union
† Website http://europa.eu.int/ provides information on the activities, institutions, documents (including legislation and case law) and services of the European Union. It includes the Europe Direct service whereby questions are answered by telephone (00800 6 7 8 9 10 11) or Email and more specific contact information given.

European Commission
DG Health and Consumer Protection (DG SANCO)
B-1049 Brussels
Telephone 00800 6 7 8 9 10 11
Email via Europe Direct
Website http://ec.europa.eu/comm/dgs/health_consumer/index.htm
DG SANCO administers the Rapid Alert System for Food and Feed (RASSF)
the purpose of which is to provide control authorities with a fast method for
exchange of information on measures taken to ensure food safety
Website http://ec.europa.eu/food/food/rapidalert

European Commission Representation in the UK
8 Storey's Gate
London
SW1P 3AT
Acting Head of Representation: Sarah Lambert
Telephone 020 7973 1992
Fax 020 7973 1900/1910
Email Sarah.Lambert@ec.europa.eu
Website http://ec.europa.eu/unitedkingdom/index.htm

European Commission Office in Wales/Swyddfa'r Comisiwn Ewropeaidd yng Nghymru
2 Caspian Point/2 Pentir Caspian
Caspian Way/Ffordd Caspian
Cardiff/Caerdydd
CF10 4QQ
Telephone 029 20895020
Fax 029 20895035
Head of Office/ Pennaeth Gweithredol y Swyddfa: Andy Klom
Email Andy.Klom@ec.europa.eu
Website http://ec.europa.eu/unitedkingdom/index.htm

European Food Safety Authority
Largo N. Palli 5/A (on the Viale Mentana)
I-43100 Parma
Italy
Telephone +39 0521 036111
Fax +39 0521 036110
Telephone +39 0521 036911 (for urgent enquiries outside of office hours)
Website www.efsa.europa.eu

European Free Trade Area (EFTA) Headquarters Secretariat
9–11, rue de Varembé
CH-1211 Geneva 20
Switzerland
Telephone (+41 22) 332 2626
Fax (+41 22) 332 2677
Email: mail.gva@efta.int
Website http://secretariat.efta.int

Food and Agriculture Organization of the United Nations
Viale delle Terme di Caracalla
00153 Rome
Italy
Telephone (+39) 06 57051
Fax:(+39) 06 570 53152
Email FAO-HQ@fao.org
Website www.fao.org
† The International Portal on Food Safety, Animal & Plant Health has been developed by FAO to facilitate trade in food and agriculture products and support the implementation of the Sanitary and Phytosanitary (SPS) Agreement by providing a single access point for authorized official international and national information across the sectors of food safety, animal and plant health.
Telephone +39 06 570 54439
Fax +39 06 570 56347
Email IPFSAPH@fao.org
Website www.ipfsaph.org
(See also 'Codex Alimentarius')

Foodaware
Co-ordinator (Lucy Harris)
36 Leyland Avenue
St Albans
Herts
AL1 2BE
Telephone 020 8789 8278
Email: info@foodaware.org.uk
Website www.foodaware.org.uk

Food and Drink Federation
6 Catherine Street
London
WC2B 5JJ
Telephone 020 7836 2460
Fax 020 7836 0580
Email (general enquiries) generalenquiries@fdf.org.uk
Website www.fdf.org.uk
The FDF organises the Foodlink food safety programme
Telephone 020 7836 2460
Fax 020 7379 0481
Email foodlink@fdf.org.uk
Website www.foodlink.org.uk

Food and Veterinary Office (FVO)
Grange
Dunsany
County Meath
Ireland
Telephone +353-46-90 61 789
Fax +353-46-90 61 706
Email jennifer.egan@ec.europa.eu
Website http://ec.europa.eu/comm/food/fvo/index_en.htm

Food From Britain

4th Floor Manning House
22 Carlisle Place
London
SW1P 1JA
Telephone 020 7233 5111
Fax 020 7233 9515
Email ibocchetta@foodfrombritain.co.uk
Website www.foodfrombritain.com

FFB is responsible for handling for DEFRA applications under the European Community protected food name scheme within England.

Food Standards Agency UK Headquarters

Aviation House
125 Kingsway
London
WC2B 6NH
Switchboard 020 7276 8000
Emergencies only 020 7270 8960
FSA Helpline 020 7276 8829
Email helpline@foodstandards.gsi.gov.uk
FSA Information Centre Email InfoCentre@foodstandards.gsi.gov.uk
(Information Centre helpdesk number for outside callers 020 7276 8181)
Website www.food.gov.uk (also provides contact details for staff concerned with specific topics)
(See also 'Meat Hygiene Service', 'Wine Standards')

Food Standards Agency Wales,

11th Floor South Gate House
Wood Street
Cardiff
CF10 1EW
Telephone 02920 678999
Email wales@foodstandards.gsi.gov.uk

Government Chemist

LGC
Queens Road
Teddington
Middlesex
TW11 0LY
Telephone 020 8943 7000
Fax 020 8943 2767
Email info@lgc.co.uk
Website www.lgc.co.uk

Some Useful Addresses

Health and Safety Executive
London Headquarters
Rose Court
2 Southwark Bridge
London
SE1 9HS
Liverpool Headquarters
Redgrave Court
Merton Road
Bootle
Merseyside
L20 7HS.
HSE Infoline
Caerphilly Business Park
Caerphilly
CF83 3GG
Telephone Infoline 0845 345 0055
Fax 0845 408 9566
Minicom 0845 408 9577
Email hse.infoline@natbrit.com
Website www.hse.gov.uk/index.htm
(See also 'Pesticides Safety Directorate')

Health Protection Agency Central Office
7th Floor
Holborn Gate
330 High Holborn
London
WC1V 7PP
Telephone 020 7759 2700 / 2701
Fax 020 7759 2733
Email webteam@hpa.org.uk
Website www.hpa.org.uk

Health Protection Agency Centre for Infections
61 Colindale Avenue
London
NW9 5EQ
Telephone 020 8200 4400
Fax 020 8200 7868
Email infections@hpa.org.uk
Website www.hpa.org.uk

Her Majesty's Revenue and Customs (HMRC)
International Trade Written Enquiries Team
Crownhill Court
Tailyour Road
Plymouth
PL6 5BZ
(National Advice Service) Telephone 0845 010 9000
(International Trade) Fax 01752 765807
Email: intenquiries@hmrc.gsi.gov.uk
(See also www.uktradeinfo.com a web based alert service developed by HMRC
with DEFRA for UK importers and exporters.)

Home Office
Direct Communications Unit
2 Marsham Street
London
SW1P 4DF
Telephone 020 7035 4848
Fax 020 7035 4745
Minicom 020 7035 4742
Email public.enquiries@homeoffice.gsi.gov.uk
Website www.homeoffice.gov.uk

Horticultural Marketing Inspectorate
Tony Crouch
Service Manager for Horticultural Inspections
DEFRA Rural Payments Agency
Branch C Horticultural Inspections
Room D10
Olantigh Road
Wye
Ashford
TN25 5EL
Telephone 01233 812321
Fax 01233 813069
Enquiries Telephone 01483 403340
Email HMI-TDC@rpa.gsi.gov.uk
Website www.rpa.gov.uk

Institute of Food Science & Technology
5 Cambridge Court
210 Shepherds Bush Road
London
W6 7NJ
Telephone 020 7603 6316
Fax 020 7602 9936
Email info@ifst.org
Website www.ifst.org

Leatherhead Food International
Randalls Road
Leatherhead
Surrey
KT22 7RY
Telephone 01372 376761
Fax: +44(0)1372 386228
E-mail: help@leatherheadfood.com
Website www.leatherheadfood.com

Local Authorities Coordinators of Regulatory Services (LACORS)
Local Government House
Smith Square
London
SW1P 3HZ
General Enquiries: Telephone 020 7665 3888
Fax 020 7665 3887
Email info@lacors.gov.uk
Website www.lacors.gov.uk

Local Government Association
Local Government House
Smith Square
London SW1P 3HZ
Telephone 020 7664 3131
Fax 020 7664 3030
Email info@lga.gov.uk
Website www.lga.gov.uk

Meat Hygiene Service
Kings Pool
Peasholme Green
York
YO1 7PR
Telephone 01904 455501
(General enquiries) telephone 01904 455501
Email mhs.enquiries@mhs.gov.uk

Medicines and Healthcare Products Regulatory Agency
Market Towers
1 Nine Elms Lane
London
SW8 5NQ
Telephone (weekdays 0900 -1700) 020 7084 2000; (other times) 020 7210 3000
Fax 020 7084 2353
Email info@mhra
Website www.mhra.gov.uk

Ministry of Justice
Selborne House
54 Victoria Street
London
SW1E 6QW
Telephone 020 7210 8500
Fax 020 7210 0647
Email general.queries@justice.gsi.gov.uk
Website www.justice.gov.uk
(*See also 'Office of Public Sector Information'*)
† The Ministry of Justice is responsible for the UK Statute Law Database website www.statutelaw.gov.uk which, although still in course of completion, gives on-line access to revised UK primary legislation. It contains primary legislation that was in force at 1 February 1991 and primary and secondary legislation produced since that date. Contact for all user enquiries: spohelpdesk@justice.gsi.gov.uk

National Assembly for Wales

Cardiff Bay
Cardiff
CF99 1NA
Telephone 0845 010 5500
Website www.assemblywales.org

National Consumer Council

20 Grosvenor Gardens
London
SW1W 0DH
Telephone 020 7730 3469
Fax 020 7730 0191
Minicom 020 7730 3469
Email (General enquiries) info@ncc.org.uk
(Press enquiries) press@ncc.org.uk
(Publications enquiries) pubs@ncc.org.uk

National Consumer Federation

180 High Street
West Molesey
KT8 2LX
Telephone 020 8941 2513
Email secretary@ncf.info
Website www.nfcg.org.uk

National Weights and Measures Laboratory (NWML)

Stanton Avenue
Teddington
TW11 0JZ
Telephone 020 8943 7272
Fax 0 20 8943 7270
Email info@nwml.gov.uk
Website www.nwml.gov.uk

Office of Fair Trading

Enquiries Unit
Fleetbank House
2–6 Salisbury Square
London
EC4Y 8JX
Telephone (switchboard) 020 7211 8000
Consumer Direct (helpline) 08454 04 05 06
(Welsh-speaking) 08454 04 05 05
(Minicom users) 08451 28 13 84
Website www.oft.gov.uk

Office of Public Sector Information*
Statutory Instruments Registrar and Publishing Services Team
Admiralty Arch
Room 1.35
North Entrance
The Mall
London
SW1A 2WH
Telephone 020 7276 5210
Email Siregistrar@opsi.x.gsi.gov.uk
Publishing Contracts team
St Clements House
2 – 16 Colegate
Norwich
NR3 1BQ
Telephone 01603 72302
Email hmsopublishing@opsi.x.gsi.gov.uk
* The OPSI is part of the National Archives which is itself a government department and an executive agency of the Ministry of Justice.
† The OPSI is responsible for the United Kingdom Legislation website www.opsi.gov.uk/legislation/uk which gives on-line access is available in particular Public General Acts 1988 onwards, UK Statutory Instruments 1987 onwards and Statutory Instruments made by the National Assembly of Wales 1999 onwards.

Pesticides Safety Directorate
Mallard House
Kings Pool
3 Peasholme Green
York
YO1 7PX
(General Enquiries) Telephone 01904 455775
Fax 01904 455763
Email information@psd.defra.gsi.gov.uk
Website www.pesticides.gov.uk

Royal Pharmaceutical Society of Great Britain
1 Lambeth High Street
London
SE1 7JN
Telephone 020 7735 9141
Fax 020 7735 7629
e-mail: enquiries@rpsgb.org
Website www.rpsgb.org.uk
RPSGB Welsh Office
Unit 2
Ashtree Court
Woodsy Close
Cardiff Gate Business Park
Cardiff
CF23 8RW
Telephone 029 2073 0310
Fax 029 2073 0311
e-mail: wales@rpsgb.org

Sustain – the alliance for better food and farming
94 White Lion Street,
London
N1 9PF
Telephone 020 7837 1228
Email sustain@sustainweb.org
Website www.sustainweb.org

Tottel Publishing Ltd (Head Office
41–43 Boltro Road
Haywards Heath
West Sussex
RH16 1BJ
Telephone 01444 416119
Fax 01444 440426
Email customerservices@tottelpublishing.com
Website www.tottelpublishing.com

Trading Standards Institute
1 Sylvan Court
Sylvan Way
Southfields Business Park
Basildon
Essex
SS15 6TH
Telephone 0845 608 9400
Email institute@tsi.org.uk
Website www.tsi.org.uk
(See also Trading Standards Central www.tradingstandards.gov.uk – a one-stop website supported and maintained by TSI supplying consumer protection information in the United Kingdom for consumers, businesses and others.)

TSO (The Stationery Office) Ltd
Head Office
St Crispins
Duke Street
Norwich
NR3 1PD
Telelephone 01603 622211
(information and publishing solutions) 0870 600 5522
Email tsoservices@tso.co.uk Website www.tso.co.uk

Veterinary Medicines Directorate
Woodham Lane
New Haw
Addlestone
Surrey
KT15 3NB
Telephone 01932 336911
Fax 01932 336618
Email postmaster@vmd.defra.gsi.gov.uk
Website www.vmd.gov.uk

† Wales Legislation
(See 'Office of Public Sector Information: United Kingdom Legislation')

† **Wales Legislation Online**

Cardiff Law School
Law Building
Museum Ave
Cardiff
CF10 3AT
Telephone 029 208 74644
Fax 029 208 74479
Email enquiries@waleslegislation.org.uk
Website www.wales-legislation.org.uk

Created by Cardiff University Law School supported by the House Committee and Welsh Assembly Government of the National Assembly of Wales, Wales Legislation Online is a detailed database of the functions of the National Assembly of Wales and of the statutory instruments which it has made. Consideration is still being given as to how best to reflect the radical changes brought about by the Government of Wales Act 2006.

Welsh Assembly Government

Cathays Park
Cardiff
CF10 3NQ
Telephone 0845 010 3300 (English) or 0845 010 4400 (Welsh)
Website http://new.wales.gov.uk

Welsh Consumer Council

5th Floor
Longcross Court
Newport Road
Cardiff
CF24 0WL
Telephone 029 2025 5454
Fax 029 2025 5464
Email info@wales-consumer.org.uk
Website www.wales-consumer.org.uk

Welsh Local Government Association

Local Government House
Drake Walk
Cardiff CF10 4LG
Telephone 029 2046 8600
Fax 029 2046 8601
Website www.wlga.gov.uk

Wine Standards Branch,

Imported Food Division
Food Standards Agency
125 Kingsway
London
WC2B 6NH
Telephone 0207 276 8351
Fax 0207 276 8463
Email John.Boodle@foodstandards.gsi.gov.uk

World Organisation for Animal Health (OIE)
12, rue de Prony
75017 Paris,
France
Telephone 33 – (0)1 44 15 18 88
Fax: 33 – (0)1 42 67 09 87
Email oie@oie.int
Website www.oie.int

Index